D1523181

THE COURT AND CULTURAL DIVERSITY

Cultural differences in medieval European literary practice are reflected in many different ways, as this volume illustrates. The essays cover a range of courtly topics, in particular questions of context, genre and poetic voice. The five sections explore contexts for courtliness, especially the position of the vernacular poet at or near the court; the ways in which courtly values and political aspirations are reflected in the work of medieval chronicle and romance writers; questions of register, convention, gender, and narrative technique; problems of literary production and reception, particularly the transmission of courtly and quasi-courtly texts among widely differing medieval audiences; and broader issues such as the clues to the courtly mentality provided by peripheral narrative details, the blurring of conventional courtly boundaries, and the perennial fascination of tales with strong folklore or fabliau elements.

Dr EVELYN MULLALLY and Dr JOHN THOMPSON are Senior Lecturers at The Queen's University of Belfast.

THE COURT AND
CULTURAL DIVERSITY

SELECTED PAPERS FROM
THE EIGHTH TRIENNIAL CONGRESS
OF THE
INTERNATIONAL COURTLY LITERATURE SOCIETY

THE QUEEN'S UNIVERSITY OF BELFAST
26 JULY – 1 AUGUST 1995

edited by

EVELYN MULLALLY
The Queen's University of Belfast

JOHN THOMPSON
The Queen's University of Belfast

D. S. BREWER

© Contributors 1997

All Rights Reserved. Except as permitted under current legislation
no part of this work may be photocopied, stored in a retrieval system,
published, performed in public, adapted, broadcast,
transmitted, recorded or reproduced in any form or by any means,
without the prior permission of the copyright owner

First published 1997
D. S. Brewer, Cambridge

ISBN 0 85991 517 4

D. S. Brewer is an imprint of Boydell & Brewer Ltd
PO Box 9, Woodbridge, Suffolk IP12 3DF, UK
and of Boydell & Brewer Inc.
PO Box 41026, Rochester, NY 14604–4126, USA

A catalogue record for this book is available
from the British Library

Library of Congress Cataloging-in-Publication Data
International Courtly Literature Society. Congress (8th : 1995 :
  Belfast, Northern Ireland)
    The court and cultural diversity : selected papers from the Eighth
  triennial Congress of the International Courtly Literature Society,
  the Queen's University of Belfast, 26 July–1 August 1995 / edited by
  Evelyn Mullally, John Thompson.
      p.   cm.
    Includes bibliographical references.
    ISBN 0–85991–517–4
    1. Literature, Medieval – History and criticism – Congresses.
  2. Courtly love in literature – Congresses.   3. Culture and society –
  Congresses.   I. Mullally, Evelyn.   II. Thompson, John, 1955–
  III. Title.
  PN682.C6I58   1995
  809'.93353–dc21   97–14205

This publication is printed on acid-free paper

Printed in Great Britain by
St Edmundsbury Press Ltd, Bury St Edmunds, Suffolk

CONTENTS

Preface   ix

I. Contexts for Courtliness

Poet and Prince in Medieval Ireland   3
  Gearóid Mac Eoin (University College, Galway)

Court Poets and Historians in Late Medieval Connacht   17
  Nollaig Ó Muraíle (The Queen's University of Belfast)

Courtly Acculturation in the *Lais* and *Fables* of Marie de France   27
  Rupert T. Pickens (University of Kentucky)

Locating the Court: Socio-Cultural Exchange in Jean Renart's *L'Escoufle*   37
  Françoise Le Saux (University of Reading)

Negative Self-Promotion: the Troubadour "Sirventes Joglaresc"   47
  Catherine Léglu (The Queen's University of Belfast)

Odd Man Out: Villon at Court   57
  Barbara N. Sargent-Baur (University of Pittsburgh)

Animating Medieval Court Satire   67
  Ad Putter (University of Bristol)

II. Fashioning History and Romance

La Fin des *Chroniques* de Froissart et le tragique de la cour   79
  Michel Zink (Collège de France)

Domesticating Diversity: Female Founders in Medieval Genealogical   97
Literature and *La Fille du comte de Pontieu*
  Donald Maddox (University of Massachusetts)

"Dame Custance la gentil": Gaimar's Portrait of a Lady and her Books   109
  Jean Blacker (Kenyon College)

Alterity and Subjectivity in the *Roman de Mélusine*   121
  Sara Sturm-Maddox (University of Massachusetts)

Passelion, Marc l'Essilié et l'idéal courtois   131
  Michelle Szkilnik (Université de Nantes)

The Political Songs in the *Chronicles* of Pierre de Langtoft and Robert   139
Mannying
  Thea Summerfield (Universiteit Utrecht)

Romance after Bosworth   149
    Helen Cooper   (University College, Oxford)

III. Negotiating a Courtly Voice

Courtliness in Some Fourteenth-Century English Pastourelles   161
    John Scattergood   (University of Dublin, Trinity College)

Amor in Marie de France's *Equitan* and *Fresne*: the Failure of the Courtly   179
Ideal
    June Hall McCash   (Middle Tennessee State University)

Secondary Characters in *Equitan* and *Eliduc*   189
    Joan Brumlik   (University of Alberta)

The Optimistic Love-Poet: Philippe de Beaumanoir   197
    Leslie C. Brook   (University of Birmingham)

The Lady Speaks: The Transformation of French Courtly Poetry in the   207
Fourteenth and Fifteenth Centuries
    Maureen Boulton   (University of Notre Dame)

Nice Young Girls and Wicked Old Witches: The "Rightful Age" of Women   219
in Middle English Verse
    Jessica Cooke   (West Suffolk College, Bury St Edmunds)

Readers, Writers, and Lovers in *Grimalte y Gradissa*   229
    Diane M. Wright   (Grand Valley State University)

Shota Rustaveli and the Structure of Courtly Love   239
    G. Koolemans Beynen   (Des Moines Area Community College)

IV. Texts and Readers

The Tournai *Rose* as a Secular and a Sacred Epithalamium   251
    Lori J. Walters   (Florida State University)

The *Gesta Henrici Quinti* and the Bedford Psalter-Hours   267
    Sylvia Wright

Medieval Equivalents of "quote-unquote": the Presentation of Spoken   287
Words in Courtly Romance
    Frank Brandsma   (Universiteit Utrecht)

Courtly Romances in the Privy Wardrobe   297
    Carter Revard   (Washington University in St Louis)

John Shirley and the Emulation of Courtly Culture   309
    A.S.G. Edwards   (University of Victoria)

Richard Hill – a London Compiler   319
    Heather Collier   (The Queen's University of Belfast)

V. The Limits of Courtliness

Our Food, Foreign Foods: Food as a Cultural Delimiter in the Middle Ages   333
Terence Scully   (Wilfred Laurier University)

Courtly Cooking *all'italiana*: Gastronomical Approaches to Medieval Italian   343
Literature
Christopher Kleinhenz   (University of Wisconsin-Madison)

The Outsider at Court, or What is so Strange about the Stranger?   357
William MacBain   (University of Maryland)

"Pseudo"-Courtly Elements in a Canonical Epic   367
Sara I. James   (University of Virginia)

The Prodigal Knight, the Hungry Mother and the Triple Murder: Mirrors and   375
Marvels in the *Dolopathos* Dog Story
Mary B. Speer   (State University of New Jersey)

Une recluse fort (peu) courtoise: destin d'une anecdote dans le *Roman des*   385
Sept Sages
Yasmina Foehr-Janssens

Courtly Discourse and Folklore in *La Manekine*   395
Carol J. Harvey   (University of Winnipeg)

The First-Person Narrator in Middle Dutch Fabliaux   405
Bart Besamusca   (Universiteit Utrecht)

The Diabolic Hero in Medieval French Narrative: *Trubert* and *Wistasse le*   415
Moine
Keith Busby   (University of Oklahoma)

PREFACE

Scholars who work with courtly literature have long been aware that their chosen field covers an enormous range of topics and preoccupations, reaching into many different European and other cultures. The topic of The Court and Cultural Diversity therefore presented itself quite naturally as the overall theme of the Eighth Triennial Congress of the International Courtly Literature Society, held at The Queen's University of Belfast, 26 July – 1 August 1995.

One hundred and twenty five papers were given at the congress. The present volume contains thirty-seven of these, selected from later revised versions. Such work seems to us to illustrate well the diversity of approach which has marked recent scholarship on courtly literature. Following the example of the previous volume in this series – *Literary Aspects of Courtly Culture*, ed. Donald Maddox and Sara Sturm-Maddox (Cambridge: D.S. Brewer, 1994) – we have grouped the selected papers into five sections, three of which are organized around the themes and approaches introduced by three plenary speakers: Gearóid Mac Eoin, Michel Zink and John Scattergood. We have also borne in mind the drawbacks of over-rigid categorization of such diverse material and our five sections have been organized to avoid the risk of ghettoizing minority interests. Readers will naturally find that consideration of such major courtly topics as love, women, chivalry, questions of context, genre and poetic voice occurs in more than one section of this volume.

The opening section, CONTEXTS FOR COURTLINESS, first explores the Irish context and then the wider interplay of courtly cultures, poets at court, and the satire so frequently provoked by court life and manners. FASHIONING HISTORY AND ROMANCE deals with the literary skills of diverse chronicle writers and the use of the romance genre to reflect courtly values and political aspirations. NEGOTIATING A COURTLY VOICE investigates questions of register, convention and narrative technique in courtly dialogues and other works. TEXTS AND READERS focusses on illuminated and other manuscripts, including the business of circulating courtly and quasi-courtly literature among different audiences. The last section, THE LIMITS OF COURTLINESS, takes us to the far reaches of courtly literature: the clues to the courtly mentality provided by the literary treatment of food, outsiders, the generic limits of courtliness, tales with strong elements of folklore or fabliau, and heroes so removed from the courtly ideal as to approach the diabolical.

It was unfortunately not possible to include all the interesting papers given at the conference, but we are glad to note that several are to be published elsewhere, including a number of specialist short studies on Arthurian and other topics, a presentation of the Medieval Woman Multimedia Project, and a plenary session on Cross-Cultural Exchange in Late Medieval England.

Finally, in these difficult times of shrinking university budgets, we are grateful to the Academic Council Office of The Queen's University of Belfast for a grant towards the the publication of this volume.

Evelyn Mullally
John Thompson
The Queen's University of Belfast   August, 1996

I. CONTEXTS FOR COURTLINESS

POET AND PRINCE IN MEDIEVAL IRELAND

Gearóid Mac Eoin

In 1607 there took place an event which is generally interpreted by Irish historians and by popular perception as the final episode in the struggle between the traditional Irish political system and the Tudor/Stuart power in Britain. This was the so-called "Flight of the Earls," the departure from Ireland of the last important members of the hereditary Irish nobility after they had been beaten on the fields of battle and diplomacy by the more powerful and more wily English. Hugh O'Neill and Hugh O'Donnell, Earls of Tyrone and Tyrconnell respectively, and over ninety other nobles of Ulster took ship from Rathmullan on Lough Swilly on 3 September 1607 and went into exile on the continent. Therewith ended the last strong resistance of Irish politics and Irish culture against the encroachments of the English. Politically, of course, it was a disastrous, if inevitable, act but what concerns us here is its effect on the literary culture of Ireland. Thereafter there remained in Ireland very few families who could afford to act as patrons to poets, as the nobles whose last remnants left Lough Swilly on that day had done. The economic and social structure which had supported the poetic class from time immemorial was thrown down and the poets were left with no demand for their poems and no means of livelihood. They were immediately conscious of the effects of this disaster on their art and on their economic position, and their concern is clear in the verse of many of them. In the early seventeenth century, Mathghamhain Ó Hifearnáin asks:

> Tell me, who will buy a poem
> containing the true knowledge of the wise?
> Who would like or who will accept
> a noble poem that will perpetuate his fame?
>
> A trade like this brings no profit,
> though a pity it is that it should pass,
> making combs were a nobler trade,
> what's the point in following art?
>
> I am a merchant ship that has lost its cargo
> after the Fitzgeralds who merited praise,
> I do not hear – it sears my heart –
> an answer to the point I raised.[1]

---

[1]   Osborn Bergin, *Irish Bardic Poetry, Texts and Translations, together with an Introductory Lecture* (Dublin Institute for Advanced Studies, 1970), 145–6, translation 279–80. The translations here and in the following are my own.

This poem seems to have been addressed to the Fitzgeralds of Munster and a very similar one was addressed about the same time by Seán mac Ruaidhri Uí Uiginn to one of the O'Byrnes of Wicklow:

> Will anyone buy a poem of nine verses,
> even if he should get it for a bargain?[2]

The point was that a poem of only nine stanzas was a very short and really unworthy composition – bargain basement stuff – and though he hawked it round in Leinster and Munster he could still find no one to buy it except Aodh mac Seáin Uí Bhroin, the O'Byrne chief whom he was addressing.

Another well-known poet from the North, Fear Flatha Ó Gnímh, whose patrons were the O'Neills of Clandeboy and the Magennises of Iveagh, Co. Down, laments:

> Alas for him who follows his father's trade . . .

and goes on to refer to the inventor of poetry:

> A pity that that wise teacher
> did not teach horse-riding or boatmanship
> or the hitching of the plough behind the ox
> to the men who make the verses.[3]

Carpentery and cooperage are suggested as other trades which would be more profitable than composing verse.

These wry sentiments are all expressed by poets who were active in the early seventeenth century. How much the situation had changed within a single generation may be judged from the fact that a prominent poet who died in 1591, Tadhg Dall Ó hUiginn, held an estate from his patrons, the O'Conors of Sligo.[4] This, while it may seem exceedingly generous, was not unique, and we find another contemporary poet in the 1590s, Eochaidh Ó hEodhusa, asking his patron, Hugh Maguire, that he be given another farm instead of the one already granted him because of attacks on him by his neighbours.[5] In fact, in those good old days under the native Irish nobility it was usual that the chief's poet was granted land to support him while he produced verse for the chief and his family. In the case of a hereditary office the grant was made to the poetic family.[6]

The poets referred to in the foregoing were the last representatives of a class which had played an important role in the political and social life of Ireland for a documented period of a thousand years, since the beginning of written records about the year 600, and for an incalculable length of time before that. In the course of the

2   Seán Mac Airt, *Leabhar Branach: The Book of the O'Byrnes* (Dublin Institute for Advanced Studies, 1944), 31–2.
3   Bergin, 120–3, translation 266–8.
4   Eleanor Knott, ed., *The Bardic Poems of Tadhg Dall Ó hUiginn (1550–1591)*, 2 vols. (Irish Texts Society 22, 23, 1922, 1926, repr. 1983), vol. I, p. xxix.
5   Bergin, 136–8, translation 274–5.
6   Pádraig Breatnach, "The Chief's Poet," *Proceedings of the Royal Irish Academy*, 83, C, 3 (1983), esp. 61–6.

millennium in question the order of poets had undergone many changes, which I shall refer to in the course of this paper, but what did not change was the essential relationship of the poet with his patron. The poet provided the patron with encomiastic verse which helped to preserve his honour in a society in which the concept of honour had been formalised and evaluated, so that a man's economic standing as well as his social position was affected by his honour. The patron not only rewarded the poet with rich gifts, as we have already seen, but he provided the poet with social rank, as the poet was equal in standing to his patron. This symbiosis of the wielders of political and of verbal power is one which is found in many other societies, in Europe and beyond, so that it was not anything peculiar to Ireland. What is interesting in the Irish context, however, is the continuity of the class and of their tradition over such a long period of time. The families who held almost a monopoly of the poetic trade in the sixteenth century had their origin in the eleventh and twelfth centuries, but some of them traced their ancestry, with what authenticity it is hard to say, back as far as the seventh century.

Since the eleventh century, at the latest, this poetic caste was structured in such a way as to preserve its identity and its tradition from generation to generation. The senior members, the fully-qualified poets, who, though attached to the retinue of one ruler, could move around and visit the residences of other friendly chiefs, were legally entitled to be accompanied by a group of anything from eight to twenty-four persons who had to be provided for by their host. This retinue was called *dám* "household" and would have included apprentice poets who were learning the craft from their senior. According to a detailed curriculum of such a course of training which survives in an eleventh-century metrical tract, it lasted a minimum of seven years, as the learner progressed from one grade to another in his qualifications.[7] Only when he had completed his course and achieved the full status of senior poet could he aspire to become a royal poet, attached to the household of a king.

In the later Middle Ages, say from the thirteenth to the sixteenth century, the professional training of the poet may have taken place in a more institutional form, in a school of poetry. The great poetic families all ran such schools and there may have been many more in existence than are specifically mentioned in our sources. There are two well-known descriptions in English of schools of poetry, both of the early eighteenth century but probably representing the reality of poetic training for centuries before. The first of these is in the Introduction to the *Memoirs of the Marquis of Clanricarde* by Thomas O'Sullevane (1722) and I give merely a short extract:

> The structure was a snug, low hut, and beds in it at convenient distances, each within a small apartment without much furniture of any kind, save only a table, some seats, and a conveniency for cloaths to hang upon. No windows to let in the day, nor any light at all used but that of candles, and these brought in at a proper season only. The students upon thorough examination being first divided into classes, wherein a regard was had to every one's age, genius, and the schooling had before, if any at all, or otherwise. The Professors (one or more as there was occasion) gave a subject suitable to the capacity of

---

7 For a discussion of the metrical tracts see Donncha Ó hAodha, "The First Middle Irish Metrical Tract," in *Metrik und Medienwechsel: Metrics and Media*, ed. Hildegard L.C. Tristram (Tübingen: Gunter Narr, 1991), 207–44, esp. 207–22, with the literature there cited.

each class, determining the number of rhimes, and clearing what was to be chiefly observed therein as to syllables, quartans, concord, correspondence, termination, and union, each of which were restrained by peculiar rules. The said subject, . . . having been given overnight, they worked it apart each by himself upon his own bed, the whole next day in the dark, till at a certain hour in the night, lights being brought in, they committed it to writing. Being afterwards dressed and come together into a large room, where the masters waited, each scholar gave in his performance, which being corrected and approved of (according as it required) either the same or fresh subjects were given against the next day. This part being over the students went to their meal which was then served up; and so after some time spent in conversation and other diversions, each retired to his rest, to be ready for the business of the next morning.[8]

The second extract is from Martin's *Description of the Western Isles of Scotland* (London 1703). Having spoken of the poets, their duties and privileges, he goes on:

I must not omit to relate their way of study, which is very singular. They shut their doors and windows for a day's time, and lie on their backs with a stone on their belly, and plaids about their heads, and their eyes being covered they pump their brains for rhetorical encomium or panegyric; and indeed they furnish such a style from this dark cell as is understood by very few.[9]

These fairly detailed descriptions of schools of poetry from Ireland and Scotland at the end of the period of their existence provide the key to the understanding of certain fleeting references in the work of some of the poets to composition in darkness and in bed, like the eleventh-century onomastic poem which begins

Though it be dark for me in my bed[10]

contrasting the darkness of the poet's surroundings with the light of knowledge which he is about to cast on his subject. At the end of the sixteenth century Fearghal Óg Mac an Bhaird was castigated by Fear Flatha Ó Gnímh, whom we have mentioned above, for allegedly composing verse out of doors and even on horseback.[11] The practice of the older poets (enumerated by Ó Gnímh) was to compose their verse in a prone position and in the dark, making no use of the artificial aid of writing until the process had been completed. This is surely a throwback to the preliterate days of versemaking, before the introduction of writing through contact with the Romans in perhaps the third or fourth century, when all the lore and craft of the poet was mental and oral. But we shall return to this topic later.

First let us look at the function of the court poets in the period between 1200 and 1600. This is well summarised in the Preface to the *Memoirs of the Marquis of Clanricarde*, from which we have already taken an extract:

As every professor or chief poet depended on some prince or great lord that had endowed his tribe, he was under strict ties to him and family, as to record in good metre

---

[8] For the full text see Bergin, 5–8, from which the above extract is taken.
[9] For the full text see Bergin, 8–9, from which the above extract is taken.
[10] Edward Gwynn, *The Metrical Dindshenchas, Text, Translation, and Commentary*, I–V (Dublin: Royal Irish Academy: 1903–35, repr. Dublin Institute for Advanced Studies, 1991), III, 110–11.
[11] Bergin, 118–19, translation 265–6.

his marriages, births, deaths, acquisitions made in war and peace, exploits, and other remarkable things relating to the same. He was likewise bound to offer an elegy on the decease of the said lord, his consort, or any of their children, and a marriage song when there should be occasion. But as to any epick, or heroic verse to be made for any other lord or stranger, it was required that at least a paroemion or metre therein, should be upon the patron, or the name in general.[12]

This list gives the principal functions of the poets in the Early Modern or Classical Modern Irish period. It omits any mention of religious verse of which the poets of the period composed a great deal, so much that one must conclude that it was expected of them, though it did not occur in the formal job-description in the passage I have just cited. Another side-line of the poets was political comment, which arose out of the poet's position as confidant and adviser to the lord. It is difficult sometimes to see where praise of the lord's exploits in war ends and encouragement to adopt or continue a particular policy begins. As early as the first quarter of the thirteenth century, when the Normans were only forty or fifty years in Ireland, we find in the middle of a conventionally laudatory poem to Cathal Crobhdhearg (†1224), King of Connacht, by Muireadhach Albanach Ó Dálaigh, a stanza which borders on incitement to war against the Normans:

> It is the Redhand (*Crobhdhearg*) who will drive eastwards
> the foreigners who have captured Tara.
> We would not be disappointed
> if he drove them all from Ireland.[13]

A fifteenth-century example is a poem by Seithfín Mór celebrating the military successes of An Calbhach O'Connor of Offaly from which I cite a few lines:

> The Leinster troop has words of war
> a troop who reddens foreign castles,
> the troop from the land of Almhain
> is on a march that cannot be resisted . . .
>
> He reddened Cashel, he reddened Thurles,
> an expedition of exceeding fury,
> He will yet give a day to Limerick
> when the market is at its fullest . . .[14]

That such fiery words could also be a mere literary flourish is evident from similar poems written at a time when military action of the kind proposed was no longer practicable: a late sixteenth-century poem by an unknown author inviting Séamas mac Aonghuis Mhic Domhnaill of Islay in Scotland to come and unite the people of Ireland under his leadership cannot have been meant as a serious political initiative at a time when English power was dominant in Ireland. The flowery, archaic language of the poem also suggests that the poet was merely flattering the Scottish lord by pretending that he would be the saviour of the Irish race from

---

12 Bergin, 7.
13 Bergin, 106, translation 260.
14 Bergin, 154–5, translation 284.

English conquest.[15] Roughly contemporary with this is an ode composed by Fearghal Óg Mac an Bhaird for the inauguration of Aodh Ruadh Ó Domhnaill as chief of Cinéal gConaill (Donegal) on 3 May 1592.[16] This too has the flowery language and the profusion of literary and historical allusion of the other poem as well as a very complicated metrical structure. It styles Ó Domhnaill *rí* "king" and forecasts that he will take possession of Tara and unite Ireland under his leadership. However, the contemporary Annals of the Four Masters make it clear that on that day he could not even unite his own people and that many Donegal septs had boycotted his inauguration.[17] That such flattering invitations had a long history in Irish verse is shown by a similar invitation issued by an unknown poet (possibly Muireadhach Albanach Ó Dálaigh) to Raghnall, King of Man, 1187–1229, to take the kingship of Tara and assume the kingship of Dublin – which at that time, of course, was firmly in the hands of the Normans.[18]

This too is the context in which we have to read the poem by Fearghal Óg mac an Bhaird on the coronation of James I of England in 1603 in which he asserts James's title to the kingdom of Ireland as well as those of Scotland and England and applies to James the ancient mythic concept that the King was the spouse of the land:

> You are her spouse by all signs.[19]

The role played by the poets in Ireland between 1200 and 1600 was probably little different from that of court poets elsewhere. That the centuries in which they flourished corresponded to those which saw the Norman conquest, the absorption and gaelicisation of the Normans, and the final conquest of Ireland under the Tudors and Stuarts is probably not accidental. It is noteworthy how many of the poets in this period are said to have been attached to the great families who descended from the twelfth-century Norman invaders, the Fitzgeralds, the Butlers, the Burkes, the Nugents, the Fitzmaurices, the Roches, and the Barrys. That this attachment began very shortly after the coming of the Normans is evident from the poem *Crét agaibh aoidhigh a gcéin?* "Whence comes it that ye have guests from afar?," composed by Muireadhach Albanach Ó Dálaigh in 1215 for Richard Fitz William de Burgh, Earl of Clanrickard, when the poet had a serious dispute with his own patron, Aodh Ó Domhnaill, and took refuge in the house of the Earl. The fact that the Earl's mother was a daughter of the head of the O'Brien family probably meant that the Earl would have been able to understand Irish, whether or not he understood the literary lan-

---

15 Bergin, 161–6, translation 287–90.

16 Text without translation in L. Mac Cionnaith, S.J., ed., *Dioghluim Dána* (Dublin: Stationery Office, 1938, repr. 1969).

17 John O'Donovan, ed., *Annala Rioghachta Eireann: Annals of the Kingdom of Ireland by the Four Masters from the Earliest Period to the Year 1616*, I–VII (Dublin: Hodges, Smith and Co., 1854, repr. New York: AMS Press, 1966), VI, 1928–9.

18 Brian Ó Cuív, ed., "A Poem in Praise of Raghnall, King of Man," *Éigse: A Journal of Irish Studies* 8 (1957), part 4, pp. 283–301.

19 Lambert McKenna, S.J., ed., *Aithdioghluim Dána: A Miscellany of Irish Bardic Poetry, Historical and Religious, including the historical poems of the Duanaire in the Yellow Book of Lecan*, I–II (London: Irish Texts Society, vols. 37 and 40, 1939, 1940), I, 177–80, translation II, 104–6, esp. stanza 23.

guage in which the poem was composed. He was clearly more favourably disposed towards Irish poets than his father, William de Burgh, who expelled the Ó Cléirigh family of poets and scholars from the lands they held in Co. Galway and forced them to migrate to North Mayo. However, in the troubled conditions of the time, with a war of succession going on in Connacht, this expulsion may have been for political reasons rather than out of any aversion to Irish literature.[20]

Many of the descendants of the Normans lived a double life, putting up a show of loyalty to the English king while conforming to Irish language, law, and culture at home. The third Earl of Desmond, Gerald Fitz Gerald, was Justiciar of Ireland under Edward III in 1367–69 and held many other positions in government between his succession to the title in 1358 and his death in 1398. But in his other *persona* he was an accomplished poet in Irish and about forty of his compositions have survived. In one of these, entitled *Anois tráth an charadraidh/ do chomhall do na cairdibh* "Now is the time for friends to fulfill their friendship," he addresses his Irish friends and begs for understanding of his position:

> The English are faulting me
> for the closeness of our friendship,
> so that to save myself
> I opposed the troops of the Irish.
>
> The English would accuse me
> in secret places
> that I had not more frequently condemned
> the Irish than the English.
>
> I support the land of the Irish
> and I would not oppose the Gaels
> were there not the force majeure
> of the English king driving me.
>
> I made a decision,
> but from it came my destruction,
> to oppose my true friends
> for fear of the anger of the English king.
>
> I would rather be with my brothers,
> whatever their mind towards me,
> than be held captive
> by the king of England in London.[21]

Such men, educated in both Irish and English ways, could very well have been the channel through which a renewed consciousness of their position *vis-à-vis* their patrons arose among the poets after the political and literary collapse of the twelfth century.

It has long been recognised that an important change occurred in Irish poetry about the year 1200 and that the verse of the early thirteenth century differs much

---

[20] Paul Walsh, *The Ó Cléirigh Family of Tír Chonaill. An essay* (Dublin, 1938).
[21] Gearóid Mac Niocaill, ed., "Duanaire Ghearóid Iarla," *Studia Hibernica* 3 (1963), 7–59, esp. 17–19; text without translation.

from that which survives from the later twelfth. First of all the older verse was produced exclusively in monasteries which adhered to the old Irish monastic way of life, whereas that of the thirteenth century and later was written either by lay poets who had no monastic attachments but worked as court poets for lay lords or by members of the new religious orders which had been introduced from the continent and Britain in the twelfth century. Secondly, a new strictness was applied to the metrical rules. This was of gradual growth from about the tenth century, but from the early thirteenth the convention prevailed that first-class verse had to conform to extremely strict and complex rules of structure and ornament. Thirdly, the language of the poets became standardised at this time and remained almost unchanged until the seventeenth century, so that it is often difficult to tell from the language of a poem whether it was written at the beginning or at the end of the period. This standard language, which was based on the usage of Ireland and Scotland in the late twelfth century, was systematically taught to the aspiring poets in the following centuries and the textbooks of this instruction survive in the so-called *Grammatical Tracts* and *Syntactical Tracts*, which represent a native Irish analysis of the language on a basis independent of Latin grammar.[22]

The mechanics of these changes are obscure. Robin Flower, in his excellent little book *The Irish Tradition*,[23] adverts to the fact that the annals of the first half of the twelfth century already record the deaths of members of the families which were later to produce poets, scribes, and historians and suggests that the rise of the poetic order may have been due to a policy initiated by the "culture-king," Brian Bóroma, in the early eleventh century. David Greene[24] and Proinsias Mac Cana[25] are of the opinion that these changes were the result of a deliberate, concerted effort on the part of the poets during the twelfth century to improve and standardise their art. Following a hint of Robin Flower's, Proinsias Mac Cana goes on to make a very strong case for continuity between the monastic scholars of the twelfth century, by then largely laicised, and the learned families who began to emerge in that same century. While there is no way of proving how the changes in Irish poetic organisation and conventions occurred, it is at least possible to say that they must have gone hand in hand with the great social and political changes which followed the ecclesiastical reform of the twelfth century and the Norman invasion of 1170 and the banishment of Irish verse and learning from the monasteries.

It is worth noting, though its relevance may be doubtful, that in Wales at the end of the eleventh century there arose the class of court poets called the *Gogynfeirdd* who sang the praises of the Welsh princes who fought the Normans in the twelfth

---

[22] Osborn Bergin, "Irish Grammatical Tracts," *Ériu* 8–10 (1915–28), Supplement. Lambert McKenna, S.J., *Bardic Syntactical Tracts* (Dublin Institute for Advanced Studies, 1944). For a discussion of the standard language see Brian Ó Cuív, "The Linguistic Training of the Mediaeval Irish Poet," *Celtica* 10 (1973), 114–40.

[23] Robin Flower, *The Irish Tradition* (Oxford: Clarendon Press, 1947), p. 94.

[24] David Greene, "Irish as a Vernacular before the Norman Invasion," in Brian Ó Cuív, ed., *A View of the Irish Language* (Dublin: Stationery Office, 1969), p. 20.

[25] Proinsias Mac Cana, "The Rise of the Later Schools of *Filidheacht*," *Ériu* 25 (1974), 126–46.

century. This revival of literature, which includes the composition of the *Mabinogi* and other tales, is attributed by some Welsh scholars[26] to the influence of the King of Gwynedd, Gruffudd ap Cynan, who was born about 1075 of a Welsh father and a Norse-Irish mother and was reared in Ireland, whence he also drew the mercenaries needed for his military campaigns. There exists a later tradition that he interested himself in literature and that he drew up rules for the regulation of the bards. However, Professor Caerwyn Williams,[27] who is familiar with the Irish as well as the Welsh evidence, doubts if anything of the kind ever happened: "... there is no proof that any changes were made or were called for to produce the bardic organisation and practice found in Wales at the beginning of the period of the Gogynfeirdd." Proinsias Mac Cana, too, emphasises the differences between the Welsh and Irish experience in the development of verse culture in the twelfth and thirteenth centuries, particularly in the participation of the new religious orders in the intellectual life of the two countries.[28]

The close relationship between the poet and the lord which we have seen in the period 1200–1600 is also evident in earlier centuries. There were some well-known poets associated with named kings:

Mac Liag († 1016) with Brian Bóroma († 1014), King of Munster and of Ireland
Airard mac Coise († 990) with Tadhg ua Cellaig, King of Uí Maine († 1014) and
    with Maelshechlainn mac Domnaill († 1022), King of Ireland
Flann mac Mael M'Aedóc († 979) with Donnchadh mac Flainn († 944), King of
    Ireland
Cinaed ua Artacáin († 975) with Congalach mac Maíle Mithig († 956), King of
    Ireland
Dallán mac Móre with Cerball mac Muirecáin († 909), King of Leinster
Flann mac Lonáin († 896) with Flann Sinna mac Maelshechnaill († 916), King of
    Ireland.

These associations and dates are reliable because they are well attested in annals or similar documents and the characters involved are close enough to the age from which manuscripts survive to be regarded as historical. Other pairings take us back as far as the seventh century and beyond:

Senchán Torpéist and Guaire, King of Uí Fhiachrach in Connacht († 660)
Eochu Rígéices and Fiachna mac Baetán, King of Ulster († 626)
Dubthach moccu Lugair and Loegaire mac Néill, King of Tara.

The last-named pair were both traditionally associated with the coming of St. Patrick, traditionally dated to AD 432. In the seventh-century Latin life of Patrick by Muirchú moccu Machtheni we find the King of Tara, Loegaire, accompanied by retainers who are described as *magi, incantatores, auruspices, et omnis artis omnis-*

[26] Thomas Parry, *A History of Welsh Literature*, translated from the Welsh by H. Idris Bell (Oxford: Clarendon Press, 1955), 44–6.
[27] J.E. Caerwyn Williams, *The Poets of the Welsh Princes* (Cardiff: University of Wales Press, 1978), pp. 5–10.
[28] Mac Cana, 144–6.

que doni inventores doctoresque "druids, enchanters, soothsayers, and the inventors and teachers of every craft and every skill."[29] In the corresponding episode in the other seventh-century life of Patrick by Tírechán Loegaire is accompanied only by *magi* "druids."[30] *Magus* in Latin texts corresponds generally to *druí* "druid" in texts written in Irish. This, in turn, frequently alternates with *fili* "seer" which is usually rendered in Latin by *poeta*. We shall see in the following that the functions of the retainers mentioned in Muirchú's text correspond to some of those of the early Irish poets, so that we may understand him to be saying that Loegaire was accompanied by his poets. But all of these early instances, even those from the Lives of Patrick, belong rather to the realm of traditional storytelling than to history. They do, however, show that the authors of the tales in question in the seventh, eighth, or ninth centuries accepted as appropriate the pairing of poet and lord in the same way as we find it in the period 1200–1600.

A large amount of verse of all kinds survives from the period 600–1200. A catalogue of pre-1150 verse in Irish currently being compiled by Gisbert Hemprich at the University of Freiburg already runs to 1500 items and is not yet complete.[31] However, the amount of court poetry surviving from the period is relatively small. Apart from some poems addressed to kings in the Book of Leinster (later twelfth-century) and one remarkable poem fortuitously preserved in a ninth-century manuscript (which has the appearance of a student's notebook) in the monastery of St. Paul in Unterdrauberg in Austria, the majority of praise-poems known from the period are fragments quoted in the annals in commemoration of the death of kings or cited as illustration in one of the four metrical tracts from the tenth or eleventh century already referred to above. It is possible that the reason for this scarcity of court poetry lies in the way in which the poetic class in those centuries was centred on the monasteries. In the six hundred years in question there is scarcely a poet known to us who was not either a member of a monastic community or closely attached to such a community. All the manuscripts surviving or otherwise known from the period were produced in monasteries. The monasteries were centres of political influence as well as of learning and piety, but they would not have had the same incentive to preserve the eulogistic verse addressed by lay poets to kings as would the kings themselves. And in this early period the practice, common from the fourteenth century on, of compiling *duanairí* "poembooks" in which noble families preserved the poems composed in their honour had not yet grown up.[32]

---

29 Ludwig Bieler, *The Patrician Texts in the Book of Armagh* (Dublin Institute for Advanced Studies, 1979), 84–5.

30 Bieler, 130–1.

31 Reported by Hildegard L.C. Tristram in *Ulidia: Proceedings of the First International Conference on the Ulster Cycle of Tales, Belfast and Emain Macha, 8–12 April 1994*, ed. J.P. Mallory and Gerard Stockman (Belfast: December Publications, 1994), 14.

32 Such as the *duanaire* of the O'Byrnes referred to in note 2 above. Other collections are: *Poems on the Butlers*, ed. James Carney (Dublin Institute for Advanced Studies, 1945); *The Book of Magauran*, ed. Lambert McKenna, S.J. (Dublin Institute for Advanced Studies, 1947); *Poems on the O'Reillys*, ed. James Carney (Dublin Institute for Advanced Studies, 1950); *The Book of O'Hara: Leabhar Í Eadhra*, ed. Lambert McKenna, S.J. (Dublin Institute for Advanced Studies, 1951); *Duanaire Mhéig Uidhir: The Poembook of Cú Chonnacht Mág*

In order to explain how the art of poetry, as well as the whole range of legal, genealogical and historical studies which were the intellectual underpinning of early Irish society, came to be located in the monasteries it is necessary to go back to the twilight period following the introduction of Christianity in the fourth and fifth centuries. At that time, when Ireland was just beginning to achieve literacy through contact with Roman Britain and particularly through the influence of the infant Christian Church, the basis of government and social organisation was the customary law which was not written down but was retained in their memory by a hereditary learned class specially deputed for this purpose.[33] In this Ireland had adopted a solution to the problem of government without literacy which had been resorted to by many other peoples, including the Greeks, who had their μνήμονες charged with the same task,[34] and the Maori, who had their School of Learning.[35] In Ireland the law and its attendant wisdom had been handed down orally for an unknown length of time. The attendant wisdom included all the information needed to administer the law, legal precedents, genealogies, and knowledge of such facts as how particular people came into possession of the land they occupied – title, one might say. In addition the expertise of the learned classes extended to arcane knowledge of such matters as divination and foretelling the future and the manipulation of natural and supernatural forces for their own ends.[36] As custodians of customary law they functioned also as society's watchdogs over the behaviour of the King, praising him in their verse when he showed the qualities of justice, courage, and generosity which were expected of him and (in theory at least) satirising him when he failed to behave in a proper kingly manner, especially when he failed to show generosity to the poets, for the *duan* "poem" presented by the poet to his lord had to be reciprocated with the *duas* "reward" to which the poet was entitled. The theory was that a king who was deservedly satirised could not continue to reign. Whether this ever occurred in practice is very doubtful, since the poets depended on their lord for reward and were unlikely to satirise him unless relations between them had broken down completely. It is notable that all the accounts of such satires relate to kings and poets of a remote past or to mythological figures. However, in the middle of a very sober eleventh-century metrical tract we are told that the metre *laíd* is appropriate for the satirising

Uidhir, Lord of Fermanagh 1566–1589, ed. David Greene (Dublin Institute for Advanced Studies, 1972).

[33] The best introduction to early Irish law is Fergus Kelly, *A Guide to Early Irish Law* (Dublin Institute for Advanced Studies, 1988).

[34] *Paulys Real-Encyclopädie der classischen Altertumswissenschaft*, Neue Bearbeitung, ed. Wilhelm Kroll, 30. Halbband, Met-Molaris lapis (Stuttgart: J.B. Metzler, 1932), cols. 2261–4.

[35] Elsdon Best, *The Maori School of Learning: Its Objects, Methods, and Ceremonial*, Museum Monograph no. 6 (Wellington: Dominion, 1974). I owe this reference to my colleague, Professor Anders Ahlqvist, whom I also have to thank for lending me a copy of the pamphlet.

[36] See Liam Mac Mathúna, "The Designation, Functions and Knowledge of the Irish Poet: A Preliminary Semantic Study," *Anzeiger der phil.-hist. Klasse der Österreichischen Akademie der Wissenschaften* 119 (1982), So 11, 225–38. Idem, "An Introductory Survey of the Word-field 'Knowledge' in Old and Middle Irish," in the *Akten der 10. Österreichischen Linguisten-Tagung, Innsbruck, 23.-26. Oktober 1982*, ed. Wolfgang Meid and Hans Schmeja, Innsbrucker Beiträge zur Sprachwissenschaft (Innsbruck, 1983), 149–57.

of a king and we are provided with a description of the elaborate ritual proper for such an occasion. The term for "satire" used in this passage is *glám dicinn*, literally "extreme satire," but the usual term is *aer*, literally perhaps "cutting":

> This is how it used to be done: A fast was carried out on the land of the King for whom the satire was to be composed and thereafter a council of thirty laymen, thirty bishops, and thirty poets was held about the composition of the satire. And it was not permitted for them to prevent the composition of the satire after the King had refused the reward. Then the poet himself went with six others, including the six [other] poetic grades . . . before daybreak to the top of a hill at which seven landholdings met. Each of them turned his face towards one of the parcels of land and the chief poet turned his face towards the land of the King whom he wished to satirise. And they turned their backs towards the thorn bush growing on the top of the hill. And the wind should be from the north. And each man held a cursing stone and a thorn from the bush in his hand. And each of them recited a stanza in this metre for the King: first the chief poet recited his stanza and then the rest of them together theirs. Thereupon each of them threw the stone and the thorn at the base of the bush. And if there was guilt on their part in doing this, then the ground of the hill would swallow them, and if there was guilt on the king's side the ground would swallow him and his wife, and his son, and his horse, and his weapons, and his clothes, and his dog . . .[37]

Whatever one may think of the details of this description, it certainly shows a general understanding of *glám dicinn* as a responsible utterance in which the *fili*, having consulted prominent members of society, declares public dissatisfaction with the ruler. That such satires, in Ireland as in medieval Iceland,[38] were believed to have the intended effects can be judged from some late annalistic entries. The Annals of Connacht, the manuscript of which was most probably written before 1506, record the following event which took place in 1414:

> John Stanley, lieutenant of the King of England, came to Ireland this year to destroy the Gaels of Ireland. He was a man who granted no protection to cleric or laymen or to the poets of Ireland, for he plundered every one of its clerics and men of skill in every part on whom he laid hands and exposed them to cold and beggary. He plundered Niall son of Aed Ó hUicinn in Usnagh of Meath, and Henry Dalton attacked the son of James Diuit and the King's followers and took from them a cow for each cow and a horse for each horse and a pig for each pig [which Niall had lost] and gave them to the Uí Uicinn. They were then conveyed into Connacht. After this the Uí Uicinn made lampoons [the word used in the text is *aerad* "to satirise"] on John Stanley and he lived only five weeks till he died from the venom of the lampoons. Now this was one of two poet's miracles [*firt filed*] which were worked for Niall Ó hUicinn: the freezing to death of the Clannconway on the night after he was plundered in Clada [in 1400], and the death of John Stanley from the venom of the lampoons.[39]

---

[37] Text in Rudolf Thurneysen, "Mittelirische Verslehren," in Whitley Stokes and Ernst Windisch, eds., *Irische Texte mit Übersetzungen und Wörterbuch*, Series 3 (1891), 1–182, esp. 96–7.

[38] Howard Meroney, "Studies in Early Irish Satire," *Journal of Celtic Studies* 1 (1950), 199–226. Dáithí Ó hÓgáin, *An File: Staidéar ar Ósnádúrthacht na Filíochta sa Traidisiún Gaelach* (Dublin: Stationery Office, 1982). Bo Almqvist, *Norrön Niddiktning. Traditionshistoriska studier i versmagi*, 2 vols. (Uppsala: Almqvist & Wiksell, 1965, 1974).

[39] A. Martin Freeman, ed., *Annála Connacht: The Annals of Connacht (AD 1224–1544)* (Dublin Institute for Advanced Studies, 1944), 422–3.

Another fatality attributed to satire concerns Cian son of Eoghan Ó Gadhra, who is said to have died suddenly in 1495 and his death is also described as a "poet's miracle." This is in the Annals of Ulster, the manuscript of which was being compiled at that time or very shortly thereafter, so that it is a contemporary account. These and other later accounts of poetic satire show that down to the end of the period of their existence the poets were viewed as practitioners in magic.

In the fifth and sixth centuries, when Christianity was still in the process of establishing itself, there existed two intellectual classes in Ireland: on the one hand the native poets, lawyers, historians, diviners and the like whose language was Irish, whose professions were carried on exclusively in an oral medium, and whose frame of reference was the pagan past of Ireland, and, on the other hand, the Christian clerics, whose language was Latin, whose work and teaching were book-based, and whose focus was on the foreign traditions associated with Christianity. It was only to be expected that these two groups would be rivals for the domination of the intellectual life of Ireland and indeed this is the picture presented by the earliest saints' lives. Here the *magi* "druids" at the King's side are portrayed as fearing the missionaries and opposing them. The seventh-century life of Patrick by Muirchú quotes the druids of the court of Loegaire, King of Tara, as prophesying that a foreign way of life was about to come to them, "a kingdom, as it were, with unheard-of and burdensome teaching, brought from afar over the seas, enjoined by a few, received by many; it would be honoured by all, would overthrow kingdoms, kill the kings who offered resistance, seduce the crowds, destroy all their gods, banish all the works of their craft, and reign forever." On Patrick's arrival in the presence of the King the druids again opposed him and challenged him to a contest in miracle-working, which Patrick easily won with God's help.[40] Again, in the life of Columba by Adamnán, who was a contemporary of Muirchú's, we read that Columba was opposed by the *magus* Broichan, the druid of Brude, King of the Picts, and that Columba overcame the druid's magic by the power of God.[41] This pattern repeats itself in many of the saints' lives of later centuries, in Latin and Irish, and clearly owes much to biblical sources, e.g. Exod. 7–11, Dn. 14.

However, there are other strands of tradition which show the contacts between the Christians and the men of native learning in a more conciliatory light. In his own writings, which are our only contemporary source for the story of the Christianisation of Ireland, Patrick makes no mention of opposition from druids or poets, though he does admit to having paid up to the value of fifteen men to those *qui iudicabant per omnes regiones* "who had jurisdiction in all districts" so that he might visit the Christians in their areas.[42] In his seventh-century life of Patrick Muirchú identifies the only man who rose to his feet out of respect when Patrick entered Tara as Dubthach moccu Lugair, *poeta optimus* "an excellent poet," which term is trans-

---

[40] Bieler, *Patrician Texts*, 74–77, 88–97.

[41] Alan Orr Anderson and Marjorie Ogilvie Anderson, eds., *Adomnán's Life of Columba* (Edinburgh: Nelson, 1961), revised ed. by Marjorie Ogilvie Anderson (Oxford: Clarendon Press 1991), 140–7.

[42] Ludwig Bieler, *Libri Epistolarum S. Patricii Episcopi*, 2 vols. (Dublin: Stationery Office, 1952), ch. 53.

lated into Irish in the Middle-Irish tripartite life of Patrick as *rígfhile* "royal poet."[43]
Dubthach had with him on that occasion an apprentice poet (*adolescens poeta*) called
Fiacc, whom Patrick is said to have subsequently consecrated bishop in Sléibte. The
story of Dubthach and Fiacc is told at greater length and with a lot of humour in Irish
in the Book of Armagh (c. AD 800)[44] and later in the tripartite life of Patrick.[45] In the
life of St. Brigit the same Dubthach recurs in the role of suitor for Brigit's hand, but
he is not titled poet in the text. It is worth recalling too that Brigit's fosterfather was a
druid, to whom the author of the ninth-century Irish life shows no animosity.[46]

This varying treatment of poets and druids in texts of the seventh to the ninth
centuries reflects, perhaps, the varying attitudes of the learned classes, native and
Christian, in the preceding centuries. It would appear that some of these accepted
Christianity while others did not, while some of the Christian missionaries and saints
took a more lenient view of native institutions and practices than others. In any
event, the struggle between poets and clerics was over by the early seventh century,
when contemporary documentation begins to become available. A *modus vivendi*
had been arrived at by which the poets practised their art in association with the
monasteries and the monks took an interest in the traditions of the poets. Some
monks had even been trained as poets before entering the religious life. The figure of
Colmán mac Lénéni may be taken as paradigmatic for the situation which emerged.[47]
Colmán was a professional lay poet who was active about the year 600, and some
fragments of his compositions in that capacity survive. He became a monk and
continued to compose verse, but now of a religious type, and some of this also
survives. This must have been the pattern for the emergence of the alliance between
the poets and the monks which persisted until the twelfth century.

This paper has not attempted to give a full account of the court poet in medieval
Ireland. Much has of necessity been omitted, such as the different grades or ranks of
poet, the part played by the poet in the election and inauguration of the King, the role
of the poet as storyteller, the whole subject of the metrical systems practised by the
poets at different times, and the complicated historical and mythological references
which decorate their poetry. Its aim has been to show the continuity of the learned
caste from pre-Christian times down to the seventeenth century and to demonstrate
that the court poets of late medieval Ireland were the inheritors of the office and
function of those who for a thousand years bore the ancient titles *fili*, *druí*, or *éices*.

[43] Kathleen Mulchrone, ed., *Bethu Phátraic: The Tripartite Life of Patrick, I. Text and
Sources* (Dublin: Royal Irish Academy, 1939), line 532.
[44] Whitley Stokes and John Strachan, eds., *Thesaurus Palaeohibernicus*, 2 vols. (Cambridge
University Press, 1901, 1903; repr. Dublin Institute for Advanced Studies, 1975), 241.
[45] Mulchrone, lines 2219–38.
[46] Donncha Ó hAodha, ed., *Bethu Brigte* (Dublin Institute for Advanced Studies, 1978), 1–5,
20–3.
[47] See Rudolf Thurneysen, "Colmán mac Lénéni und Senchán Torpéist," *Zeitschrift für
celtische Philologie* 19 (1932), 193–207.

COURT POETS AND HISTORIANS IN LATE MEDIEVAL CONNACHT

Nollaig Ó Muraíle

My aim in this paper is to look, necessarily rather sketchily, at some aspects of the role of official – or, as we may call them, court – poets and historians in Ireland in the later medieval period (roughly the fourteenth to, and including, the sixteenth century). I have decided to restrict myself somewhat further by looking not at the whole island but simply at the western province of Connacht (that is, most of the area west of the river Shannon) during the relevant period. I should perhaps emphasise that Connacht – although now considered the most remote of the Irish provinces – was in the later Middle Ages a veritable hive of literary activity. ("Remoteness", of course, is rather a problematical concept; many inhabitants of Connacht over the last century and a half would consider Dublin more remote from them than, say, Boston or other towns and cities in New England and elsewhere in the US. The reason for this is closely linked to the history of emigration from the west of Ireland, mainly since the Great Famine of the 1840s, and therefore lies outside the purview of this paper.) Why, one may ask, do I deal with both poets and historians? The reason, briefly, is that the two roles were often combined or interchangeable.

As Professor Gearóid Mac Eoin has already touched on the origins of Irish (that is, Gaelic) poetry in the dim mists of prehistory and made interesting observations on the achievements of the poets (or *filid*) down through subsequent ages,[1] I am relieved of the duty of going into much detail on the literary and political history of Ireland from the early period down to the later Middle Ages. Nevertheless, I feel that I should begin by mentioning a couple of crucial developments in the history of twelfth-century Ireland which were to give rise to a number of the things I will be discussing presently. One of these episodes or developments was ecclesiastical and the other political. The first was the attempted "reform" along continental lines of the Irish church, and the second was the arrival in 1169, not long after the church-reform had got under way, of French-speaking Cambro-Norman knights who were to have a very significant impact on subsequent Irish history.[2]

---

[1] Among the works which may be consulted on this topic are J.E. Caerwyn Williams, *The Court Poet in Medieval Ireland* (Oxford: Oxford University Press, 1972), Brian Ó Cuív, *The Linguistic Training of the Mediaeval Irish Poet* (Dublin: Dublin Institute for Advanced Studies, 1973), Eleanor Knott, *Irish Classical Poetry* (Dublin: Cultural Relations Committee, 1960), and eadem, *The Bardic Poems of Tadhg Dall Ó Huiginn (1550–1591)* (London: Irish Texts Society, 1922), pp. xxxiii–li.

[2] For an account of twelfth-century developments, see *A New History of Ireland II: Medi-*

The first half or so of the twelfth century was one of the richest and most productive periods in the history of Gaelic literature: from that era we have significant and substantial works of creative literature, both prose and poetry, together with impressive works of historical and quasi-historical literature (comprising several collections of annals, voluminous genealogical collections, toponymical lore, hagiographical works written with a political purpose, and so on), and also very important and sophisticated works of dynastic propaganda, often disguised as pseudo-historical narrative.[3]

This same period saw the beginning of a series of translations from other languages – starting with Latin and later also from French and English – of adventure-tales, religious texts and various other works: the list includes such items as an account of the destruction of Troy derived from Darius Phrygius's *De Excidio Troyae Historia*, Statius's *Thebaid*, The Civil War of the Romans from Lucan's *Pharsalia*, the Story of Hercules, the *chanson de geste* known to the Irish as the Story of Fierabras (or Fortibras), the Quest for the Holy Grail and various other Arthurian works, as well as Orlando Furioso, the Story of William of Palerne, the Book of Sir John Mandeville, the Book of Marco Polo, the Lives of Bevis of Hampton and of Sir Guy of Warwick, as well as numerous saints' lives from the work known as the *Legenda Aurea*. The purpose of this list,[4] which is by no means comprehensive, is to give some indication of how Ireland and literature in Irish in the later medieval period – despite the country's apparently isolated location – were in touch with what was going on in the wider world outside. All of the works I have listed in this and the preceding paragraph were written in the rich and supple forms of the Irish language known as Middle Irish and Early Modern Irish.

All of this literary activity had commenced by the year 1100 (and would continue for more than four centuries thereafter). And then, into this vigorously creative milieu in the early twelfth century came the continental religious orders, most notably the Cistercians and the Augustinian canons; these represented the spearhead of a reform-movement which aimed at bringing the Irish church into conformity in matters of organisation and discipline with the papally-dominated church in England and western Europe generally. Fired with puritanical zeal, the reformers set about purging the Irish church of those elements they considered unchristian. Among the first casualties was the cultivation of what we might term profane literature – indeed, of virtually all literature in the vernacular. Such cultivation had hitherto taken place almost entirely in monastic seats of learning – monasteries which the reformers considered scandalously lax and worldly. We hear an echo, I think, of the arrival of

eval Ireland, 1169–1534, ed. A. Cosgrove (Oxford: Oxford University Press, 1987), especially chapters 1 and 2.
[3] For some details of this period, written in English, see J.E. Caerwyn Williams and P.K. Ford, *The Irish Literary Tradition* (Cardiff: University of Wales Press; Belmont, Massachusetts: Ford and Bailie, 1992), pp. 96, 104–7, 116–17, 126–28, 148; also B. Ó Cuív, ed., *Seven Centuries of Irish Learning, 1000–1700* (Cork, 1971), pp. 11–13, 22–37, 56–58, 106–7.
[4] Williams and Ford, *Tradition*, pp. 134–45 and 149–52; also Robin Flower, *The Irish Tradition* (Oxford: Oxford University Press, 1947), pp. 121–38, and B. Ó Cuív, *Seven Centuries*, pp. 19, 29–30, 107.

the new "political correctness" in the rather nervous note of apology – in Latin – which the scribe of the twelfth-century manuscript known as the Book of Leinster appended to his copy of the celebrated medieval Irish saga *Táin Bó Cúalnge* (The Cattle-Raid of Cooley):

> But I who have written this story, or rather this fable, give no credence to the various incidents related in it. For some things in it are the deceptions of demons, others poetic figments; some are probable, other improbable; while still others are intended for the delectation of foolish men.

The reformers were not long in banishing from the monasteries the learned men who had produced literary works like the *Táin*, and some of the other vernacular works listed above.[5] Many such learned men, although formally monks, had carried on the old traditions from their fathers and grandfathers – who likewise were often formally monks – and intended to transmit them to their children in turn. (As may be gathered from this, celibacy was then the exception rather than the norm in the Irish church. It may also be noted that there appear to have been few, if any, female authors at this period.)

Then there was the other, political, development I alluded to earlier, the so-called Norman "invasion" and the subsequent efforts over many centuries by the English crown first to control the stubbornly independent and headstrong Normans and later also to subdue those Gaelic lords who gradually won back some of the land and power they had lost to the Normans. These events, as might be expected, caused a great deal of disruption on the Irish political scene from the late twelfth century onwards, and this was matched by something of a desert-period in the story of Irish literature, running from about the end of the twelfth to the middle of the fourteenth century. It is from after this "desert-period" that many of the translations listed above date.

I will, I hope, be pardoned for this apparent digression into the fields of ecclesiastical and political history when I ask (and try to answer) the question: "What became of the often hereditary practitioners of Irish literature and learning when they were banished from the monasteries?" The answer, albeit in slightly telescoped and simplified form, is that the scribes, the poets, the annalists, the genealogists, the practitioners of native law and medicine, and so on, sought shelter under the auspices of the various local lords. At first these lords were the Gaelic chieftains who had managed to hold on to some part of their ancestral territories, but after a while the new Norman lords were also willing to furnish similar patronage. For it was the case that many of these lords had intermarried with their Gaelic neighbours and, in many cases, become gaelicised to a considerable degree. The most celebrated example of such gaelicisation was no doubt that of Gerald Fitz Gerald (1338–98), third earl of Desmond, who – as mentioned by Professor Mac Eoin – although he served as the English king's justiciar from 1367 to 1369, was immersed in Gaelic culture; known

5 An up-to-date account of some of the issues relating to the *Táin* will be found in J.P. Mallory and G. Stockman, eds., *Ulidia: Proceedings of the First International Conference on the Ulster Cycle of Tales* (Belfast: December Publications, 1994); see also J.P. Mallory, ed., *Aspects of the Táin* (Belfast: December Publications, 1992).

in Irish simply as Gearóid Iarla ("Gerald the Earl"), he was an accomplished Gaelic poet who is credited with some forty surviving poems, many of them on the theme of courtly love.[6]

From the ranks of the aforementioned banished practitioners came one of the most characteristic features of the Gaelic literary "scene" in the later Middle Ages, the hereditary learned family. (A certain proportion of such learned families, however, originated as discard segments of ruling dynasties; having been squeezed out of the political game, they turned to learning.) These hereditary families operated in a variety of fields: in Connacht alone O Mulconry and O Duigenan served as annalists and historians (and sometimes also as poets), O Higgins as poets, MacEgan as lawyers, O Fergus and Mac Alea (Mac an Leagha) as medical men, and so on.[7] Probably the most farflung of these learned families was that of O Daly which was to be found in virtually all parts of Ireland from the beginning of the thirteenth right down to the seventeenth century,[8] and also in the other part of the Gaelic world, Gaelic Scotland[9] – which in that period may have comprised up to two-thirds of the area which the name Scotland now designates.

In Connacht one of the most versatile of the hereditary learned families was that of Mac Fir Bhisigh (later anglicised to MacFirbis and Forbes). They were based in north Connacht, in the vicinity of Killala Bay – first on the western, or Mayo, side and later on the eastern, or Sligo, side. In view of the restrictions on the permitted length of this paper, I propose to look briefly at some of the activities of Clann Fhir Bhisigh who first appear in the annalistic records early in the twelfth century.[10] While the early evidence connects them with the famous Connacht monastery of Cong – at which time they were already professors of poetry to the ruling north Connacht dynasty of Uí Fhiachrach – from the thirteenth century onwards they appear as practitioners of history and poetry, and of other aspects of native Irish learning (including prose literature, annals and genealogy), under the patronage of the O Dowd lords of north Connacht, and also for a time in the employ of the MacDonnells. (These latter were a branch, settled in Connacht, of the celebrated Scottish family from the Western Isles; they had come in as mercenary soldiers in the service of Irish lords in Connacht from the later fourteenth century onwards. In return for their services they gradually acquired land and became lords themselves –

6 The poems have been edited by Gearóid Mac Niocaill, "Duanaire Ghearóid Iarla," *Studia Hibernica* 3 (1963), pp. 7–59.
7 For some details of the learned families see Brian Ó Cuív, "The Irish language in the early modern period," in *New History of Ireland III: Early Modern Ireland, 1534–1691*, ed. T.W. Moody et al. (1976), pp. 509–45; also Paul Walsh, *Irish Men of Learning* (Dublin: Three Candles Press, 1947). For a summary of research to date on the origins of the learned families see my book, *The Celebrated Antiquary, Dubhaltach Mac Fhirbhisigh (c. 1600–71): His Lineage, Life and Learning* (Maynooth: An Sagart, 1996), chapter 1, appendix 2.
8 Proinsias Mac Cana, "The rise of the later schools of *filidheacht*," *Ériu* 25 (1974), pp. 128, n. 8, and 134–35.
9 Derick S. Thomson, "Gaelic learned orders and literati in medieval Scotland," *Scottish Studies* 11 (1967), pp. 57–78.
10 The most detailed account to date will be found in my *Celebrated Antiquary*, especally chapters 1–3.

just one further element in the mix.[11]) But – returning to Clann Fhir Bhisigh – it is as scribes that they are best known, having produced some of the most important of the great manuscript codices which were penned – in Connacht especially – in the later fourteenth and fifteenth centuries.

The head of the family from c. 1390 to c. 1420 was named Giolla Íosa – an Irish personal name meaning "Servant of Jesus," from which we get the well-known Scottish and Irish surnames Gilleese/Gillies and McAleese (Mac Giolla Íosa). Under his direction, a team of scribes compiled two of the most important extant Irish manuscripts, the Yellow Book of Lecan and the Great Book of Lecan. These volumes have been justly characterised as "mini-libraries" of early and medieval Gaelic learning and literature. As one indication of its importance, the Yellow Book, compiled in or about the year 1392, contains the only virtually complete copy of the earliest version of *Táin Bó Cúalnge*. The Great Book of Lecan was compiled between the years 1397 and 1418 and runs to some 600 pages, densely written, of historical, quasi-historical, genealogical and topographical material.[12]

In a paper of this length, I can only look at one of the items in the last-mentioned volume. This is an immensely valuable poem of 224 quatrains which Giolla Íosa composed as an inauguration-ode for his chieftain and patron, Tadhg Riabhach O'Dowd, who succeeded to the lordship (or, as Mac Fir Bhisigh still grandly termed it, the "kingship") of Tireragh in north Connacht in the spring of 1417.[13] A detailed and fascinating work, it belongs to a genre of Irish poetry with its own conventions and conceits, and therefore – to one not accustomed to these – some of its language (particularly in English translation) may seem rather strange. Two motifs which merit some attention are the way the land was supposedly made fruitful by the just rule of a good king and the way that a poet's words of praise or eulogy (which to us may seem the most shamelessly selfserving flattery) can likewise bring health and prosperity to the recipient – just as, conversely, a harsh or satirical word from the poet could bring disaster to the one on whom his wrath was turned.

It was firmly believed that a poetic satire could literally raise blisters on the person satirised, and even in extreme cases cause death.[14] This arguably goes back to the shamanistic and quasi-priestly roots of Celtic poet-craft. (Professor Mac Eoin in his paper has given a vivid account of the use of satire by Gaelic poets – particularly in the late medieval period.) This belief in the power of the poet persisted among the

---

[11] G.A. Hayes-McCoy, "The MacDonalds of Mayo," *Journal of Galway Archaeological and Historical Society* [hereafter *JGAHS*] 17 (1936), pp. 65–82.

[12] The most detailed accounts of these two manuscripts are William O'Sullivan, "Ciothruadh's Yellow Book of Lecan," *Éigse* 18 (1981), pp. 177–81, and Tomás Ó Concheanainn, "A note on the scribes of the Book of Lecan," *Ériu* 24 (1973), pp. 76–79; idem, "Gilla Ísa Mac Fir Bhisigh and a scribe of his school," *Ériu* 25 (1974), pp. 157–71.

[13] The poem (which was transcribed into the Book of Lecan under the author's supervision in or about the year 1418) was first edited by the pioneering nineteenth-century Irish scholar John O'Donovan in his *Genealogies, Tribes and Customs of Hy-Fiachrach* (Dublin: Irish Archaeological Society, 1844), pp. 176–99. The poem has recently been re-edited by Tomás Ó Concheanainn, emeritus professor of Classical Irish at University College, Dublin – see n. 16, below.

[14] E. Knott, *Classical Poetry*, pp. 73–8.

Irish-speaking population (especially in Connacht) down at least to the middle of the nineteenth century.[15] Of course, it suited the poets that such a belief should be held. But, selfserving though it might well be, there is no evidence that the poets used it cynically; they would appear to have believed in it as strongly as everybody else.

In order to give a flavour of the work of a fairly representative member of the poetic order which is the subject of this paper, I propose to quote some extracts from a new edition of that poem of Giolla Íosa Mac Fir Bhisigh's from 1417 which has recently been prepared for publication.[16] Since a detailed analysis of this fascinating work would require far more space than I have at my disposal here, I must confine myself to a few general observations. (The poem, I believe, richly merits such close and careful study.[17])

In reading Giolla Íosa's poem one notices the bombastic conferring of high-flown titles which appear to claim for the new king vast territories to which his family may have laid claim in the distant past, but which – in the circumstances of early fifteenth-century Ireland – he could have little or no hope of ever controlling. The poet's intention is obviously to seek to increase his patron's fortune or luck by an abundance of praise and wide-ranging claims – possibly in the hope that, even if his work does not bear fruit in the desired abundance, it will have at least some positive results. It is also interesting to note the conceit whereby the poet speaks of the positive and beneficent effects of Tadhg Riabhach's rule, even though his reign is just about to begin – after all, the poem is supposedly an inauguration ode! The idea is presumably that because the poet declares it, it is already a fact – perhaps a reflection of the ancient prophetic role of the *file* or poet, as illustrated in some of the earliest Irish literary texts. (Here I must acknowledge the demurral of Dr John Carey who made some characteristically thoughtful remarks in response to this paper. He stressed that continuity with the past was more important than the prophetic role in such poems as this. While emphasising the need for further detailed study of the matter, Dr Carey made the interesting observation that there appears to be very little praise poetry extant from before the early modern period.[18])

Very many of the following extracts draw attention to one overriding characteristic imputed to a great number of the families listed, namely, their hospitality and

---

[15] This is mentioned in relation to the early nineteenth-century Connacht poet Anthony Raftery (d. 1835) – see Douglas Hyde, Songs ascribed to *Raftery/Abhráin atá leagtha ar an Reachtúire* (Dublin, 1903; reprint, Shannon, Irish University Press, 1973).

[16] A characteristically meticulous edition has been prepared by Tomás Ó Concheanainn; it is to be hoped that it will appear without delay. (It should be noted that Giolla Íosa was also the author of two other substantial poems preserved in his great manuscript, the Book of Lecan, as well as of a very important prose account of his native territory of Uí Fhiachrach.)

[17] Such a synopsis, in Irish, has recently been furnished by Professor Ó Concheanainn, "Dán Ghiolla Íosa Mhic Fhir Bhisigh ar Uí Fhiachrach," *Léachtaí Cholm Cille* 24 (1994), pp. 136–51; see also my *Celebrated Antiquary* (1996), chap. 2, for a brief summary in English.

[18] Dr Carey drew attention to one early example – an unedited poem by Mael Mura of Othain in which long lists of battles are cited in praise of the recipient's family. Professor Mac Eoin in his paper also cites some examples of the genre from the twelfth-century Book of Leinster and one poem preserved in a ninth-century manuscript, as well as fragments quoted in the medieval Irish annals and metrical tracts.

generosity – particularly to the poetic profession.[19] One can hardly imagine that this emphasis is wholly disinterested! (It should be noted that some of the phrases which here appear identical are not quite thus in the original Irish – the word translated "refuse", for example, is rendered by three distinct Irish words. Nevertheless, there is a good deal of rather tiresome repetition.)

(71) Méig Fhionnáin, who gave refusal to no man . . .

(74) Ó hAodha, who did not give a poet refusal . . . branches eminent for hospitality.

(76) Uí Mhaoil Chonaire . . ., Uí Fhlannabhra . . ., Uí Shéaghdha . . ., people who did not give a poet refusal.

(79) Ui Mhaoil Fhaghmhair who provided feasts . . .

(92) . . . Ó hÉimheacháin, . . . a prosperous hospitaller . . .

(93) Ó Laochaille, a warrior without misfortune, a hospitaller who was wont to feed the raven, chief of Magh Fuara of the banquets; . . .

(94) Uí Laochaille . . . hospitallers who did not betray any class . . .

(97) Clann Fhir Bhisigh who mentioned no fault, poets of the province of Connacht . . .

(108) Uí Ghealagáin, men of the banquets . . .

(110) Uí Mhongáin, who were not miserly towards poets . . .

(112) . . . Ó Móráin goes triumphantly to Ard na Riagh – hospitable the man – to serve poets and guests.

(124) Ó hÍomhair, who was not miserly towards poets . . .

(143) Ó Beólláin, who refused no man . . .

(146) Ó Díscín, who refused not poets . . .

(162) Mic Giolla Mhir, who did not refuse poets, . . . a hospitaller who overcame hundreds, . . .

(164) The highminded Ó Liatháin of Muine na Feide of the banquets, a man who was brave in face of plunders, his house an abode of poets.

(168) Tón re Gó about which the wave is fruitful, district of sloes and apples, belongs to Ó hAodha, who did not give poets a refusal, . . .

(171) Ó Dúnchadha of the poetic companies . . .

(192) In the time of Tadhg, who refused no man, Ó Dubhda has received recognition: no smaller are the kernels of the fragrant nuts than the crop of the apple-trees.

(193) In your time flooding has decreased, . . . every person beside you is very prosperous, under your stewardship over the land of Uí Fhiachrach.

(194) Produce has come in the land during your time, . . . as you have brought every shower of rain you have given milk to our milch-cows.

(198) Every band of poets that comes from the north . . . you invite westwards across old Muaidh . . .

(204) To have a small company is not natural for you, O Ó Dubhda of Dún Cormaic; your mead-festivities are decked with satin by your tribe, the people most inclined towards poets.

(215) The poets of the world will say of the heir of the land of saints that he rightly spends his wealth; every goodness is magnified by its being extolled.

(217) Which is nobler that the poets of the race of Conn should praise the good son of Domhnall than that the produce of the land of the west should praise the (same) hero . . .?

---

[19] This aspect is also heavily emphasised in annalistic obituaries of famous people, particularly poets. See also E. Knott, *Tadhg Dall*, p. xli.

(218)   Had not Fear Feasa related it, I would relate a pedigree for Ó Dubhda (whose house is Tara) and his fair stem of genealogy.

(219)   I have composed for . . . the just-judging heir of Domhnall . . .

Finally, I would like to refer very briefly to an interesting text from late sixteenth-century Connacht which reflects the gaelicisation of the Norman families who had settled there in the early thirteenth century and who were among the very first of the Hiberno-Normans to intermarry with their Gaelic neighbours and adopt Gaelic surnames. They may not quite, as the old adage has it, have become *ipsis Hibernis Hiberniores*,[20] but they certainly came very near. The work in question is a dual-language – part Irish, part Latin – historical and genealogical tract compiled by (partly-) anonymous Gaelic authors in the year 1578 for the premier north Connacht Hiberno-Norman family of Burke. Originally de Burgo, the family became de Búrca or Búrc and later in English Burke and Bourke. The tract – now preserved among the manuscripts in the library of Trinity College, Dublin – is entitled in Irish *Senchas Búrcach* ("history of [the] Burkes").[21] It is an interesting illustration of a confluence of cultures – reflected in the intermixing of the two languages, Irish and Latin, in the manuscript – in relation to a family of Norman origin, albeit the recipients of a considerable infusion of Gaelic blood. (We may note that the most illustrious current member of this family is Mary Bourke – who is better known by her married name of Mary Robinson, president of Ireland.)

The manuscript contains: an Irish prose text (of which I will speak in more detail presently), a purported history, in Latin, of the de Burgos in the thirteenth and fourteenth centuries, and two lengthy praise-poems composed by members of the poetic family of Ó hUiginn (O Higgins). The work, however, is perhaps most celebrated for a feature which is most unusual in an Irish manuscript from this or any other period: a series of full-colour portraits of nine de Burgo lords, beginning with Riocard Mór who died in 1243. (Obviously most if not all of these "portraits" are conjectural.)

Before concluding, I propose to look briefly at one or two aspects of the opening text in the book; this takes the form of a rental (in Irish) in which are listed in great detail all the lands in late sixteenth-century County Mayo on which Mac Uilliam Íochtair (The Lower MacWilliam) – as the local Burke lord was styled – claimed rent. In all, more than 130 placenames occur in this very interesting, and much neglected, tract. Having studied them in some detail, I have discovered that up to 90% of these names are fairly readily identifiable: they are located mainly in the north Mayo barony of Tirawley, in the southern barony of Kilmaine and, to a lesser extent, in the western barony of Burrishoole. On the third folio of the manuscript there is a suggestive note: following a statement to the effect that Mac William was

[20] See A. Cosgrove, "Hiberniores ipsis Hibernis," in idem and D. McCartney, *Studies in Irish History presented to R. Dudley Edwards* (Dublin: University College Dublin, 1979), pp. 1–14.

[21] It occurs in TCD, MS F.4.13 and has been twice edited (neither time altogether satisfactorily) – by Standish Hayes O'Grady, *Caithréim Thoirdhealbhaigh* (London: Irish Texts Society, 1929), appendix, pp. 149–61, and by Tomás Ó Raghallaigh, "Seanchus na mBúrcach," *Journal of the Galway Archaeological and Historical Society* 13 (1926–27), pp. 50–60, 101–37; 14 (1928–29), pp. 30–51, 142–67.

entitled to a "defence rent" of five marks from the territory of O Dowd, the signature of "O Dowd, that is Cathal Dubh" appears – this individual was the "chief of his name" or "captain of his nation," to use designations found in English documents of the period. The signature is witnessed by "An Cosnaidhe Óg Mac an Bhreitheamhnaigh, judge ('brehon') to Mac Muiris." The appearance here of the heir to that Tadhg Riabhach O Dowd for whom the great inauguration poem of 1417 was composed 161 years earlier is interesting: it reflects his family's decline in status *vis-à-vis* the all-powerful Burkes. But even more interesting are the other two names. The first belongs to a Gaelic legal family (and is now generally anglicised Judge in County Mayo and Brehony in County Sligo) while the second – now anglicised Morris and Fitzmaurice – belongs to a Norman family (apparently a branch of the Prendergasts) who gave name to the south-east Mayo town of Claremorris. (Incidentally, the family of Mac an Bhreitheamhnaigh was almost certainly based at a townland just outside Claremorris known officially as Ballynabrehon, but called locally Ballybrehony.) Here again, then, in this brief, matter-of-fact note, penned at the very close of the Irish Middle Ages, we have further telling evidence of the utter gaelicisation of the Norman families who settled in late medieval Connacht, as well as a unique shaft of light thrown on the origin of the Connacht surname Mac an Bhreitheamhnaigh and an intriguing piece of circumstantial evidence linking them with the townland of Ballynabrehon or Ballybrehony.

COURTLY ACCULTURATION IN THE *LAIS* AND *FABLES* OF MARIE DE FRANCE

Rupert T. Pickens

Anthropologists define acculturation as both the process of exchanging information between cultures and the result of that process, which is the transformation of one or both of the cultures. The cultures are brought into contact directly through invasion and conquest or indirectly thanks to mediatory agents such as explorers, missionaries, and merchants. In general, according to Robert H. Winthrop, acculturation "occurs under conditions of significant inequality in the scale, power, and technological complexity" – we might add the prestige – "of the societies involved."[1]

In the French-speaking world of the twelfth century, cultural exchange took place on many fronts – between France and Occitania, for example. In England, varying degrees of acculturation were in progress between the Anglo-Norman superstratum, whose culture was centered in the noble court and most especially the royal court, and the English-speaking underclass, on the one hand, and, on the other, between the cultures of England and those of Celtic-speaking peoples at the kingdom's periphery, in Cornwall, already within the pale, in Wales and in Scotland. Elsewhere, Henry II's Angevin empire came into contact with Celtic cultures in Ireland and in Continental Brittany.

The present study examines how acculturation informs works attributed to Marie de France, who wrote in Anglo-Norman England in the 1170s and 1180s. She drew on Celtic sources in writing her *Lais* and, ostensibly, on an Anglo-Saxon text in translating her *Fables*, and she destined both collections for an aristocratic and courtly French-speaking audience. Both works turned out to be remarkably popular in their time.[2] Marie de France was thus a powerful agent of transcultural exchange.

Two of the three great narrative *matieres* of Old French literature – the *matiere de Rome* and the *matiere de Bretagne* – imply acculturation through the mediatory agency of author-translators who adapt foreign texts for French-speaking audiences.

---

[1]   Robert H. Winthrop, *Dictionary of Concepts in Cultural Anthropology* (New York/Westport, Connecticut/London: Greenwood Press, 1991), p. 3.
[2]   Denis Piramus attests to the popularity of the *Lais* in *La Vie Seint Edmund le Rei*, ed. Hilding Kjellman (Göteborg, 1935), lines 35–65. The *Fables* survive in an extraordinary number of manuscripts for a twelfth-century vernacular work (23); Marie is also a source for several other medieval collections (see Karl Warnke, ed., *Die Fabeln der Marie de France* [1898; repr. Geneva: Slatkine, 1974], pp. xlviii–lxxx).

As the foreign is assimilated with the familiar, acculturation is a function of *translatio*. In Chrétien de Troyes's *Cligés*, Greece, Arthurian Britain, and the German Empire are appealing not because they are exotic, but because their "otherness" is diluted in references to the familiar. Even Thessala's magic is "domesticated" thanks to overt associations with the already-assimilated Tristan matter.

Acculturation can also function thematically, that is, the process of acculturation itself is often depicted in the plot. In Chrétien's *Conte del Graal*, Perceval is a foreigner in the Arthurian kingdom, where he is set apart by his culture which is identified as Welsh – his language, behavior, outlook, clothing, weapons, style of fighting, etc. One of the plot's driving forces is the conflict between cultures as Chrétien portrays Perceval's assimilation into the Arthurian world.

Acculturation in *translatio* and thematic acculturation subtend both the *Lais* and the *Fables*. Marie's mediatory agency involves appropriating ancient texts pertaining to marginal or marginalized cultures – the Celtic which lies at the edge of the French-speaking world, the English which belongs to an underclass – and she reshapes those texts according to the tastes and needs of the Anglo-Norman court. In making foreign material her own, Marie of course ennobles it, as she makes explicit in the General Prologue to the *Lais* where she rejects the exalted *matiere de Rome* and adopts the *matiere de Bretagne* as more rewarding; in the *Fables* she names King Alfred as the author of her English source, a sainted authority in line with Æsop and the emperor Romulus. Marie shows reverence for her predecessors as authors, transmitters and translators of text, but her own achievements are equally praiseworthy; indeed, the courtly transformations she works in her French texts are superior thanks to their modernity.

Like the General Prologue to the *Lais*, the *Fables'* Prologue and Epilogue deal topically with the moral purpose of literature and more particularly with translation. In the Epilogue's famous opening lines,

> Al finement de cest escrit
> que en romanz ai treité e dit,
> me numerai pur remembrance:
> Marie ai nun, si sui de France.   (Epilogue 1–4)[3]

> (At the end of this written work which I have translated into French, I shall give my name for remembrance: my name is Marie, and I am from France)

Marie names herself and, by drawing attention to her native country, involves herself in translation in the physical sense of the word: she has literally been "brought over" to England. Extending the topic of literary translation, she next evokes the theme of textual appropriation:

---

3   The edition used is Marie de France, *Les Fables*, ed. Charles Brucker (Louvain: Peeters, 1991); English translations are my own. Warnke's text is reproduced in Marie de France, *Äsop*, trans. Hans U. Gumbrecht (Munich: Wilhelm Fink, 1973), and in *The Fables of Marie de France*, trans. Mary Lou Martin (Birmingham, Alabama: Summa, 1984). MS *A* (London, British Library, Harley 978), Warnke's and Brucker's base, is edited in Marie de France, *Fables*, ed. and trans. Harriet Spiegel (1982; repr. Toronto: University of Toronto Press, 1994).

Put cel estre que clerc plusur
prendreient sur eus mun labur,
ne voil que nul sur li le die . . .   (lines 5–7)

(Perhaps many clerks will take on the burden of my labor, but I want none to
claim it as his own . . .)

Specifically, Marie acknowledges that scribes are certain to be engaged in copying
and transmitting her fables,[4] but she wishes no one to appropriate her work without
giving her the credit she accords her own sources. She would be a fool not to be
concerned about her reputation: "cil fet que fol ki sei ublie" (Epilogue 8) ("he acts
the fool who is forgetful of himself"), an exordial topos which recurs in the *Lais*.[5]

The *Fables*' Epilogue continues with an abbreviation of the Prologue's expression
of indebtedness to her patron (cf. Prologue 27–37), that "flower of knighthood, of
learning, of courtesy" (Prologue 31–32) whom, having revealed her own name, she
now identifies as Count William (Epilogue 9).[6] It was for love of him – it was at his
command which it would have been discourteous of her to refuse (Prologue 30–36) –
that she undertook to write her book. In the Epilogue, Marie gives full expression to
the *translatio studii* topos which, in the Prologue, occurs in a more fragmentary
form. She translates from English into Romance a book called *Esopë* (or *Yspoet*)
because Æsop was the authority who first translated the work from Greek into Latin
(Epilogue 13–15, cf. Prologue 17–20). King Alfred next translated the book into
English. As for herself: ". . . jeo l'ai rimee en franceis" (Epilogue 18) ("I have
rhymed it in French").[7] Each stage in this history of *translatio* is marked by an
author's – an authority's – appropriation of a foreign text; Marie's Romance versification re-initiates a process of acculturation in conformity with new standards.

Scholars doubt that Alfred the Great, translator of Bede and Boethius, is the true
author of Marie's source, which is not extant and has never been identified. Edward
Mall argued on phonological grounds that English words which, according to some
manuscripts, Marie apparently left untranslated come from a Midlands dialect of the
early twelfth-century, not ninth-century Anglo-Saxon;[8] thus Marie may have been
confused about the identity of her source's author. Mary Lou Martin (p. 24) takes the
argument further and doubts that an English version of the *Fables* ever existed at all:
Marie could have translated directly from the so-called *Romulus Nilantinus*,[9] which

---

[4] Warnke (p. 411a) translates *prendre sur eus* in line 6 as "auf sich nehmen" ("to undertake
as a responsibility"). Brucker (p. 367), Gumbrecht (p. 275), Martin (p. 253), and Spiegel (p.
257) all take *prendre sur eus* – wrongly, I believe – to be synonymous with *sur li le dire* (line
7) ("to claim as one's own") (Warnke, p. 418a: "für sich beanspruchen").
[5] *Guigemar* prologue 3–4. The edition used is *Les Lais de Marie de France*, ed. Jean
Rychner (Paris: Champion, 1968); English translations are my own.
[6] See Madeleine Soudée, "Le Dédicataire des *Ysopets* de Marie de France," *Les Lettres
Romanes* 35 (1981), pp. 183–98, who makes a strong case for William Marshal.
[7] Cf. the *Lais*: "Rimé en ai e fait ditié . . ." (General Prologue 41) ("I have rhymed them
and made poems out of them"), ". . . M'entremis des lais assembler, / Par rime faire e
reconter" (lines 47–48) ("I set about assembling the *lais*, putting them into rhymed verse and
narrating them").
[8] See Warnke's Introduction, pp. xliv–xlv.
[9] Or the *Romulus Nilantii*, named in honor of the collection's first modern editor, J. Nilant

is the Latin collection closest to hers.[10] Hans R. Runte concludes that Marie must have known an English version of the *Romulus*, but he agrees, as do I, that she worked directly from the Latin text.[11] Whether or not Marie invented King Alfred as her source authority, the reference's overriding significance is that she, as translator in a court near the center of Anglo-Norman power, has made the work of an English monarch her own and has refashioned it to suit the now-dominant culture.

"De vespertilione" ("The Bat," no. 23) exemplifies the processes of translation as acculturation. Its source in the *Romulus Nilantinus* (pp. 532–33) is slightly longer than the average of those forty fables, but, with 66 lines, "The Bat" is the sixth longest of all Marie's fables and the third longest of her forty deriving from the *Romulus Nilantinus*. Thus Marie's text manifests an extraordinary degree of amplification as the product of translation.

In the Latin fable, war breaks out between the four-legged beasts and the birds, and neither side can gain the upper hand. The bat cannot decide which side to join, so she waits to foresee the outcome before going with the winners. The beasts appear to be ahead, so she joins them. But Mars brings in the eagle, who leads the birds to victory, whereupon the bat goes over to them. After peace is made, however, the birds punish the bat, condemning her to flee the light and, stripped of her feathers, to fly only at night.

Like all fables in the *Romulus Nilantinus*, this one is framed with moral commentary. The prologue announces, "The following fable advises us that no two-tongued, deceitful man can long have honor before he is found out by a wise person, for whoever would commit himself to two parties will not be thanked by either one and will be judged to be guilty rather than honorable."[12] The epilogue is more specific: "So it is just and fitting that whoever abandons his own master and his own comrades in the day of their need and offers his help to strangers must suffer being mistreated and held in contempt by all."[13]

The epilogue holds the seed of Marie's translation, for it explicitly provides a means for developing the theme of treason that is only implicit in the fable proper

(Nilantius) (Leyden, 1709). The edition used is *Romuli Nilantii Fabulae, ex Bodleianae Bibliothecae manuscripto codice lat. digbeiano 172 extractae*, in *Les Fabulistes latins depuis le siècle d'Auguste jusqu'à la fin du moyen âge*, ed. Léopold Hervieux, 5 vols. (2nd edn. 1883–1899; repr. New York: Burt Franklin, n.d.), vol. 2 (1894), pp. 513–48, cited as *Romulus*; English translations are my own. The collection is attributed to a legendary Roman emperor, confused with the twin founder.

10 That is, in nos. 1–40; the sources for the remaining sixty or so fables in Marie's collection are quite varied, and many are unknown.

11 Hans R. Runte, "Marie de France dans ses fables," in *In Quest of Marie de France: A Twelfth-Century Poet*, ed. Chantal A. Maréchal (Lewiston, Maine/Queenston, Ontario/Lampeter: Edwin Mellen, 1992), pp. 28–44, esp. pp. 36–41.

12 "Admonet subsequens fabula, quod nullus bilinguis et fallax homo habeat honorem longius, quoniam sit probatus ab aliquo sapiente, quia qui se duabus partibus obnoxius commiserit, ingratus ab vtraque viuit et reus pocius iudicandus est quam honorabilis" (*Romulus*, pp. 532–33).

13 "Sic itaque oportet iuste vt insidias et despeccionem paciatur ab omnibus, qui suum proprium seniorem et socios proprios in die necessitatis eorum derelinquit, alienis prebens adiutorium" (*Romulus*, p. 533).

where the bat is indecisive rather than devious, where the birds the bat finally joins condemn her, not the beasts she has deserted. In other versions in the *Romulus* tradition, the wrong the bat and humans like her do is to abandon their own kind.[14] Only Marie's contemporary Walter of England has a moral similar to hers: "he is not a good citizen who prefers the enemy to his fellow-citizens: no one can usefully serve two masters."[15] Walter abbreviates the *Romulus Nilantinus* text, but remains generally faithful to it. Marie considerably amplifies her source, turning the bat's indecision into treason and the judgment of the birds into a model of feudal jurisprudence.

Marie sets the stage by creating overlords for the warring parties, a king for each genus as in the bestiary tradition. Whereas, in the *Romulus*, the eagle comes late in the battle, in Marie's translation he assumes his traditional role as king of the birds, and the lion is introduced as king of the beasts. In fact, the lion is privileged as the apparent subject of the fable:

> De un lïun dit que assembla
> tutes les bestes e manda,
> ki aloënt sur quatre piez ... (lines 1–3)
>
> (This is about a lion who summoned and brought together all the beasts that walked on four feet . . .)

The eagle is likewise accorded high honors:

> e li egles ad purchaciez
> tuz les oisels quë eles unt
> e que volent en l'eir lamunt:
> bataille deivent od li tenir. (lines 4–7)
>
> (and the eagle has sought out all the winged birds that fly up into the air: they are to do battle with him [the lion].)

The bat is not mentioned until line 9. Implicitly, she has grounds for claiming allegiance to both sides, as a feathered, winged creature and as a quadruped, a "bald" mouse (*chalve suriz*). But she wants to be on the winning side. She watches the fighting and awaits the outcome. When it seems that the lion will win, she joins "the other mice" (line 20). But she deserts the four-legged creatures when the eagle brings in even stronger forces. After joining the birds, she tries to keep her feet hidden, but exposes them when she opens her wings:

> ... par devant tuz les descovri.
> Dunc est sa felunie overte
> e sa traïsun *tut* [sic] descuverte ... (lines 30–32)
>
> (she uncovered them before one and all. Thus her crime is out in the open and her betrayal fully revealed . . .)

[14] Hervieux, vol. 2, pp. 215, 437, 471, 495, 736, 762.
[15] "Non bonus est ciuis, qui prefert ciuibus hostem; / Vtiliter seruit nemo duobus heris" (Hervieux vol. 2, p. 338).

The birds drive her back to the quadrupeds' camp with cries of derision (line 33). Then all the creatures appeal to their god,[16] accusing the bat of breaking faith and committing treason: "e mustrent li sa felunie / e cum ele ad sa fei mentie" (lines 37–38) ("and they show him her crime, how she has broken her oath"). The god agrees with both sides, banishes the bat from their company (lines 43–44) and deprives her of flesh and feathers, thus forever exposing her body in reflection of her own self-revelation in uncovering her feet.

"It is thus with the traitor who wrongs his overlord . . ."[17] – so begins Marie's concluding commentary, a highly original amplification of the *Romulus Nilantinus* moral. To summarize: the forthright vassal should bear his lord honor, be loyal, and keep faith with him, but if he betrays his lord in his hour of need, he cannot expect to undo his evil when his lord prevails against the enemy the traitor has chosen; and so it is just that the traitor is stripped of his possessions and his heirs are shamed forever. In promoting her ethics of courtly rectitude, Marie saves the worst punishment for the last line: just as the bat can no longer fly by day, so the traitor loses his right to be heard in court (line 66).

Elizabeth A. Francis has observed that Marie's fables tend to deal with legal issues; she concludes that Marie wrote for a class of powerful barons and knights with aristocratic tastes for whom faithfulness to their overlord was a primary value.[18] Madeleine Soudée ("Le Dédicataire") perceives a strong concern for royal authority. Similarly, Karen K. Jambeck, in a persuasive study of Marie's *Fables* as a "mirror of princes," shows that more than half of the fables, in the narrative proper or in Marie's moral commentary, refer explicitly to the rank and duties of noble dignitaries.[19] Indeed, in fifty of the 103 fables in Brucker's edition,[20] the epimythia alone are concerned with such social, political, and juridical issues as justice (nos. 2, 4, 8, 23, 41, 47, 88, 95, 98, 101), the noble court (nos. 14, 23, 36, 88), loyalty (nos. 23, 29, 34, 78, 89, 98), honor and feudal honors (nos. 1, 3, 11, 18, 23, 27, 28, 29, 34, 67, 72, 84), the common good (no. 1), the duties of overlords towards those under their dominion (nos. 2, 6, 7, 10, 11, 16, 22, 27, 35, 65, 101), the duties of servants towards their lord (no. 84), respect for authority (no. 14), entrusting power to worthy people (nos. 29, 46, 49, 56, 62), social order (reaching higher than one should: nos. 5, 15, 67, 73, 74, 85; being content with one's own station: nos. 9, 18, 19, 22, 29, 31, 46, 95), treason (nos. 3, 12, 20, 23, 27, 34, 42, 49, 71, 89), bearing false witness (nos. 2, 4, 93), and giving evil counsel (nos. 12, 13, 20, 72, 89). Some fables touch on more than one of these themes, and "The Bat" is foremost among them. Other fables have common-sense morals that are less specifically political, but support feudal ideals. Eleven caution fools to heed the wise or warn the credulous against

---

[16] Warnke adopts *sepande* ("goddess"), a word derived from English, in lines 34 and 39, while Brucker's text has *criere* ("creator"), found in *A* and related manuscripts.

[17] "Autresi est del traïtur / que meseire vers sun seignur . . ." (lines 49–50).

[18] E.A. Francis, "Marie de France et son temps," *Romania* 72 (1951), pp. 78–99.

[19] "The *Fables* of Marie de France: A Mirror of Princes," in *In Quest of Marie de France*, pp. 59–106, esp. pp. 91–95.

[20] Nos. 1–16, 18–20, 22–23, 27–29, 31, 34–36, 41–42, 46–47, 49, 56, 62, 65, 67, 71–74, 78, 84–85, 88–89, 93, 95, 98, 101.

believing lies, which relates to the crimes of bearing false witness and offering evil counsel (nos. 17, 37, 57, 60, 64, 70, 83, 86, 91, 94, 100). Four also mention specific feudal values (nos. 41–42, 72, 98), while two others observe that evil acts can turn against the perpetrator (nos. 68, 77) and one explicitly links the evil deed to treason (no. 71). Five chastise the proud and the ambitious for praying for what they do not need (nos. 54–55, 58, 63, 99), which pertains to the question of social order, and three warn that people cannot change what they are born to (nos. 79–80, 102). These examples account for well over 75% of the formal epimythia – 76 of 98;[21] many of the others prescribe a practical morality that also has applications in the life of the court.

One characteristic of the bat that leads to her indecision is the fact that, in a world inhabited only by birds and quadrupeds, she shares features of both genera. She is a mouse, but she is endowed with wings and feathers. Caught between two societies, she cannot be acculturated or assimilated with either; she somehow seems unnatural, monstrous. So it does not come as a surprise that she commits the crime of treason, that most unnatural assault on the social order, and her exile and banishment from the light are a fitting retribution. It is in fact Marie who "acculturates" the bat by translating her story into courtly French.

Just as the fable about a monstrous bat exemplifies Marie's appropriation of foreign matter to extol Anglo-Norman values, so monstrous beasts in Marie's *Lais* serve as models of her appropriation of the *matiere de Bretagne* to entertain and edify the Anglo-Norman court. Marie's interest in birds and beasts constitutes an important link between the *Fables* and the *Lais*. Animals are prominent in several *lais*, but have particular significance in six, all of which are set in Celtic territory in Continental Brittany or Wales. In *Laüstic*, *Milun*, and *Eliduc*, a nightingale, a swan, and a pair of weasels behave naturalistically, according to the standards of medieval science; but in *Bisclavret*, *Guigemar*, and *Yonec*, beasts which are central to the plot are "unnatural": a werewolf, an androgynous deer, and a shape-shifting hawk-knight. Gerald of Wales authenticates the first two, the werewolf and the deer, as Celtic monsters;[22] the hawk-knight is monstrous by association: in Classical Latin the word for "shape-shifter," *versipellis* ("skin-changer"), also means "were-wolf."

In the *Lais*, Marie's monsters are her most compelling animals, and of these her werewolf has attracted the most attention.[23] Bisclavret is interesting for the ways he does and does not behave like other werewolves – particularly as they appear in the

[21] Four fables do not have formal epimythia: nos. 26, 30, 32, 65b.

[22] See Manfred Bambeck, "Das Werwolfmotiv im *Bisclavret*," *Zeitschrift für romanische Philologie* 89 (1973), pp. 123–47, and Urban T. Holmes, Jr., "A Welsh Motif in Marie's *Guigemar*," *Studies in Philology* 39 (1942), pp. 11–14.

[23] For example, Michelle A. Freeman, "Dual Natures and Subverted Glosses: Marie de France's *Bisclavret*," *Romance Notes* 25 (1984–1985), pp. 288–301; Dolores Warwick Frese, "The Marriage of Woman and Werewolf: Poetics of Estrangement in Marie de France's 'Bisclavret,' " in *Vox intexta: Orality and Textuality in the Middle Ages*, ed. A.N. Doane and Carol Braun Pasternack (Madison and London: University of Wisconsin Press, 1991), pp. 183–203; Kathryn I. Holten, "Metamorphosis and Language in the Lay of *Bisclavret*," in *In Quest of Marie de France*, pp. 193–211.

matiere de Bretagne.[24] Marie says that when werewolves are in their lupine state, they are wild, ferocious creatures that live in forests and go about devouring human beings (lines 5–14); similarly, Bisclavret runs through the thickest parts of woods, which he ravages as he hunts food (lines 63–66). When Bisclavret's wife connives with her suitor to steal her husband's clothing, she commits a number of specific crimes. One is that she imprisons her husband in perpetual savagery by depriving him of the means to regain his humanity.

Gerald of Wales also has a werewolf story.[25] A priest in Ireland encounters a pair of werewolves in a forest. The male tells him that he and his companion have been condemned to seven years in the wild; the female is at the point of death. The priest is moved by these creatures' profession of Catholic faith, and he administers last rites to the female. The sign of these werewolves' essential humanity is that they have the power of speech. In fact speech is characteristic of werewolves generally, according to the *matiere de Bretagne*: as Gerald's Irish werewolves speak, so the Breton, or pseudo-Breton, term for werewolf Marie uses as a common noun and as her hero's proper name – *Bisclavret, li bisclavrez* – means "talking wolf."[26] Like Gerald, Marie identifies her werewolf's power of speech not with his savagery, but indeed with his humanity.

So, in *Bisclavret*, another of the lady's crimes is that she deprives her husband of his voice. He is reduced to using gesture in order to communicate: embracing the king's foot as a sign of humility and allegiance, biting the man who stole his clothing, tearing off his wife's nose (see esp. Frese, p. 191). This is not the only time in her *Lais* when Marie portrays a process of silencing: it is the jealous husband's sin in *Laüstic*. Bisclavret's wife is punished by losing her nose, and she produces a line of disfigured females.[27]

Yet another of the lady's crimes is that she appropriates her husband's words. Kathryn Holten observes how she takes on his identity as werewolf in a process of "animalization,"[28] while Michelle Freeman ("Dual Natures") emphasizes how she

---

[24] See esp. M[arcel] Faure, "Le *Bisclavret* de Marie de France: une histoire suspecte de loup-garou," *Revue des Langues Romanes* 83 (1978), pp. 345–56, and François Suard, "*Bisclavret* et les contes du loup-garou: essai d'interprétation," *Marche Romane* (Mediaevalia 80) 30 (1980), pp. 267–76.

[25] *Topographica hibernica*, pt. 2, ch. 19: "De mirabilibus nostri temporis. Et primo, de lupo cum sacerdote loquente," in *Giraldi Cambrensis Opera*, ed. James F. Dimock, vol. 5 (1867; repr. London: Kraus Reprint, 1964), pp. 101–07.

[26] Breton *bleiz*, "wolf," combined with *lavaret*, "to say, speak"; cf. Gerald's subtitle (n. 25 above) "*de lupo* cum sacerdote *loquente*" ("about a *wolf talking* with a priest"). See Ferdinand Lot, "Etudes sur la provenance du cycle arthurien I," *Romania* 24 (1895), pp. 497–528, esp. p. 515 and n.; Ernst Brugger, "Eingennamen in den *Lais* der Marie de France," *Zeitschrift für französische Sprache und Literatur* 49 (1926–1927), pp. 201–52, 381–484, esp. pp. 248–51, 453–59; and H.W. Bailey, "*Bisclavret* in Marie de France," *Cambridge Medieval Celtic Studies* 1 (1981), pp. 95–97. Th.-M. Chotzen, "*Bisclavret*," *Etudes Celtiques* 2 (1937), pp. 33–44, proposes the Welsh cognate *bleidd llafar* ("talking wolf").

[27] As Bisclavret becomes less monstrous, his wife grows more wolf-like: Pliny the Elder writes that wolves can deprive humans of the power of speech (VIII, xxiv, 1); *Histoire naturelle de Pline*, ed. M.-E. Littré, 2 vols. (Paris: Firmin-Didot, 1883), vol. 2, p. 331.

[28] Kathryn Isabelle Holten, "Metamorphosis as Metaphor: The Animal Images in Six Lays

takes over his speech – his confession of lycanthropy – and turns it to her own advantage. These are two ways of saying the same thing: the lady uses Bisclavret's story to betray him. Eventually, when the king subjects her to juridical torture in order to find the truth, she learns how to formulate the werewolf's story in its first public "textual" performance in the service of truth and justice; her confession provides the prototype of Marie's own *Bisclavret*.

Meanwhile, Bisclavret himself undergoes transformations that also go beyond possibilities inherent in conventional werewolf stories. Before the king adopts him, Bisclavret "naturally" runs wild and hunts for prey. But after the king recognizes his uncommon intelligence, he domesticates him at court. Bisclavret sleeps indoors with the knights, right beside the king himself, and he becomes a pet beloved by everyone. His courtly acculturation is so complete, in fact, that reversions to wild behavior, when he bites his wife and her new husband, are regarded as meaningful aberrations that signal concealed injustices. In the course of his domestication, moreover, Bisclavret is also strangely feminized. When the king finds him transformed back into a man and asleep, he runs to embrace him: "Plus de cent feiz l'acole e baise" (line 301) ("more than a hundred times he puts his arms around him and kisses him"). Such language is suitable for medieval lovers, not for a king greeting his vassal. As Michelle Freeman and Judith Rothschild have both remarked, the king gives Bisclavret, as wolf and as man restored, the love and comfort denied him by his wife.[29] Such is the last – and lasting – image we have of Bisclavret: a monster domesticated, an epicene knight sleeping, ever silent, in a royal bed.

Marie's bat and her werewolf are both monstrous. In Classical and Christian traditions monsters are signs, demonstrations (*monstra*) of God's will, whether it is a question of species (giants, pygmies, Amazons, Cyclops, Androgynes, etc.) or accidental monstronsities such as the Minotaur and two-headed calves. Pliny the Elder remarks that monstrous births are sinister omens (VII, iii, 2; *Histoire naturelle*, vol. 1, p. 285). Isidore of Seville (XI, iii, 1–5),[30] adapting Cicero's discussion in *De divinitatione* (I, xlii, 93), explains how monsters function as portents. Isidore compares monsters with oracles and with *somnia*, true dreams sent by God to signify future events; moreover, the "meaning" of monsters, like that of oracles and *somnia*, is obscure and subject to interpretation.[31] He cites St. Augustine (*City of God*, XVI, 8 and XVIII, 17–18) as proof that, although Varro says monsters are unnatural, they go "against Nature" only as humans ordinarily perceive Nature to be; on the contrary, monsters are "natural" in the higher sense that God wills them to be created.

---

of Marie de France" (Ph.D. diss. Tulane University, 1988), pp. 91–108; "Metamorphosis and Language," p. 196.

[29] Judith Rice Rothschild, *Narrative Technique in the Lais of Marie de France: Themes and Variations*, vol. 1 (Chapel Hill: University of North Carolina Press, 1974), p. 134; cf. Freeman, "Dual Natures," p. 300 and n. 12.

[30] *Isidori hispalensis episcopi Etymologiarum, sive Originum libri XX*, ed. W.M. Lindsay, 2 vols. (Oxford: Clarendon Press, n.d.).

[31] Macrobius, *Commentarii in Somnium Scipionis*, ed. Jacobus Willis (Leipzig: Teubner, 1963) I, iii, 1–11.

The monster, as a means of discovery, is meant to be read as an emblematic text, which is how birds and beasts, their physiology and their habits, are interpreted in the medieval bestiary tradition. Monsters in Marie's *Lais* likewise function emblematically. But the *matiere de Bretagne* also ascribes to monsters more dynamic roles by empowering them to speak. Gerald's werewolves reveal their humanity by their speech. He also draws St. Augustine into his commentary and quotes the same passages from *The City of God* as Isidore uses. Linking the *matiere de Bretagne* with Christian tradition, Gerald lifts his werewolves above the realm of the emblematic and endows them with the power to prophesy – not unlike Merlin Sylvester, who, he says elsewhere, was driven into prophetic frenzy at the sight of a monster.[32] Indeed, the point of Gerald's werewolf story is that the male predicts the Plantagenet conquest of Ireland. Marie's werewolf foretells what will happen to him if his clothes are stolen, then he is reduced to silence by his increasingly monstrous wife, who makes his story her own. Marie de France, like the monstrous Breton lady whose descendant she is, drains her Celtic monster of his life and then, making his story her own, enshrines him in her own courtly narrative. The taming of the werewolf is a profound, multi-valent reflection of both Marie's artistry and the process of acculturation in which she is engaged.

Bonnie Leonard, citing Jeanette Beer,[33] quotes Isidore of Seville's distinction between history and fable:[34]

> Now histories consist of true things which have really happened. Arguments are things which, even if they have not really happened, could nevertheless take place. But fables consist of things which have not happened, nor could they ever take place, because they go *against Nature*.[35]

Characteristic of the fable as genre is the paradoxical fact that the moralist perceives truth in matter that is essentially false. The key to the paradox lies in Isidore's observation that the things which happen in fables are "against Nature." In other words, fables are a monstrous literary genre whose truthfulness transcends ordinary human experience. What is true of Marie's Celtic monsters in particular *lais* is true of her *Fables* generally. In both collections monstrous texts are appropriated by a monstrous woman whom we call Marie de France; she makes foreign matter her own and reshapes it for the pleasure, the benefit, and the edification of the dominant Anglo-Norman court. Such a program of acculturation implies a will to conquer through cultural assimilation and syncretism. Today the fact that we recognize Marie as a preeminent literary genius, while yet we can write about her in English, attests to the ways in which that program both succeeded and failed.

[32] *Itinerarium Kambriae*, II, viii, in *Giraldi Cambrensis Opera*, ed. James F. Dimock, vol. 4 (1868; repr. London: Kraus Reprint, 1964), p. 133.
[33] Jeanette M.A. Beer, *Narrative Conventions of Truth in the Middle Ages* (Geneva: Droz, 1981), p. 53, n. 18.
[34] Bonnie Herrmann Leonard, "Marie de France and the Poetics of Translation" (Ph.D. diss. University of Pennsylvania, 1993), pp. 94–95 and n. 19.
[35] "Nam historiae sunt res verae quae factae sunt; argumenta sunt quae etsi non sunt, fieri tamen possunt; fabulae vero sunt quae nec factae sunt nec fieri possunt, quia *contra natura* sunt" (I, xliv, 5, my emphasis) (my translation).

LOCATING THE COURT: SOCIO-CULTURAL EXCHANGE IN JEAN RENART'S *L'ESCOUFLE*

Françoise Le Saux

> What the court is, God knows, I know not. I do know however that the court is not time; but temporal it is, changeable and various, space-bound and wandering, never continuing in one state. When I leave it I know it perfectly: when I come back to it I find nothing or but little of what I left there [. . .] We courtiers are assuredly a number, and an infinite one, and all striving to please one individual. But to-day we are one number, to-morrow we shall be a different one: yet the court is not changed; it remains always the same.
>
> (Walter Map, *De nugis curialium*, Preface)[1]

Walter Map's jocular description of 'the court' as the locus of paradox is one that is well-known, and which touches directly on the nature of socio-political power as expressed in that institution. The court is defined as a state of permanent flux, devoid of the more obvious markers of permanence, yet despite this, possessed of an inherent identity which appears to transcend the accidents of geographical location or personal individuality. The reason for this, Map hints, is that whatever the changes which take place in 'the court,' there always remains one stable element, in the person of its lord; the 'character' of a court, and thus its stability, may therefore be said to be a direct function of the quality of the holder of authority at its heart. Map shrewdly avoids going into detail, but he has in effect drawn a thumbnail sketch of a functional court, where the holder of political power also has the required personal authority to ensure that he always retains the control of a group that is ever-changing in its composition.

A comparable analysis may be found some years later in Jean Renart's romance *L'Escoufle*.[2] But contrary to Map, who does not venture into discussing the dangers to 'the court,' Renart depicts a range of disfunctional courts, sometimes spelling out the causes of a given situation, but more often leaving the reader to draw his or her own conclusions.

The first court to appear in *L'Escoufle* is that surrounding Count Richart of Montivilliers (Moustierviler in the text). His household is described at some length

---

1 *Walter Map. De nugis curialium. Courtiers' trifles*, ed. and trans. M.R. James, revised by C.N.L. Brooke and R.A.B. Mynors (Oxford: Clarendon Press, 1983), p. 3.
2 *L'Escoufle* was probably composed between 1200 and 1202; see the introduction to Jean Renart, *L'Escoufle, roman d'aventure*, ed. Franklin Sweetser (Geneva, Paris: Droz, 1974). All quotations of the poem are made from this edition.

(lines 51–121): 100 men serve him every day, his lands furnish him with plentiful fish and game, he has 300 good knights as vassals and is successful in defending (and indeed increasing) his lands. His generosity secures the unswerving loyalty of his men, while his personal qualities are extolled by the poet, particularly his love of good and his rejection from birth of 'vilenie.' The extent and quality of the bond between Richart and his vassals are expressed by the massive response to his appeal to take the Cross; and the affection with which he is regarded by the common people is shown by the fact that, we are told, all the lanes and roads are full of well-wishers come to see their lord off.

That the *personal* qualities of Richart, more than his status of living seat of temporal authority, are of the essence in Renart's outlook is suggested by the repeated scenes displaying his generosity and his piety. The account of his donations to the abbey prior to his departure to the Holy Land covers some 70 lines (lines 192–265), whilst his gift of an ornate cup to the Holy Sepulchre is described in detail (lines 566–639).[3] Richart also ensures that food remains plentiful for his followers even during their travels, and it is noteworthy that as soon as he arrives in Jerusalem, a 'court' spontaneously gathers around him, giving Renart yet another opportunity to describe the count's lavish hospitality, his generosity and his winsome manners. Such a worthy lord could only bring victory: and indeed, Richart's Crusade is a success, securing a three-year truce for the beleaguered King of Jerusalem. The valiant count then goes on to the rescue of another monarch: the Emperor himself.

The Emperor's difficulties are not immediately perceptible, masked as they are by his extravagant display of hospitality to the returning crusaders, but they touch the very core of his court. He confides in Richart how

> Comme il vint primes a l'empire,
> Comme il mist ses sers de desus,
> Comme il ot maté et confus
> Contes, haus barons et chasés,[4]

with the result that he is no longer the master in his own lands: "Mi serf m'ont destruit et fait las, Por ce qu'il n'est qui me seceure." ("My serfs have ruined and destroyed me, because there is nobody to help me," lines 1502–3). Richart agrees to help him, punishes the overbearing villains, is given a noble wife in reward, and his

---

[3] This cup, depicting scenes from the story of Tristan, has been the object of considerable critical attention. See Daniel Poirion, "Fonction de l'imaginaire dans *L'Escoufle*," in *Mélanges de langue et littérature françaises du Moyen Age et de la Renaissance offerts à Monsieur Charles Foulon*, vol. 1 (Rennes: Institut de français, Université de Haute Bretagne, 1980), pp. 287–93; Rita Lejeune, "La coupe de la légende de Tristan dans *L'Escoufle* de Jean Renart," in *The Medieval Alexander Legend and Romance Epic. Essays in Honour of David J.A. Ross*, ed. Peter Noble, Lucie Polak and Claire Isoz (Millwood NY, London, Nendeln, Lichtenstein: Kraus International Publications, 1982), pp. 119–24; and Linda Cooper, "L'ironie iconographique de la coupe de Tristan dans *L'Escoufle*," *Romania* 104 (1983), pp. 157–76.

[4] "When he first came to the imperial throne, he had exalted his serfs, and subdued and humiliated the counts, great barons and fief holders," lines 1484–87.

son Guillaume is eventually proclaimed heir to the Emperor's throne and betrothed to the Emperor's only child, Aélis.

This negative attitude towards upwardly mobile 'vilains' has been read as a political statement on Renart's part, evidencing a pro-aristocratic stance. Anthime Fourrier, for example, stresses the importance of the theme in twelfth-century romances such as *Partonopeus de Blois*, and links it with the policy of the French monarchy to entrust the running of the realm to relatively low-born 'civil servants' in order to limit the power of the feudal grandees.[5] However, even though this policy was still very much in practice when Jean Renart wrote his romance, one suspects that something else might be at stake here, for the only distinguishing feature given these faceless 'vilains' is their moral inadequacy. The Emperor attributes the crisis to a youthful error of judgement when he first came to power; but after Richart's untimely death, he hastens to repeat the same error:

> Et l'emperere i a ja mis
> Entor lui noviax conseilliers,
> Les traïtors, les losengiers
> Qui jadis li fisent tans maus.[6]

The Emperor is well-placed to know that he cannot depend on his new councillors, both by personal experience and as a result of Richart's stern teaching. Yet he reinstates them with a swiftness that suggests a deep-rooted affinity between himself and these *losengiers*. This comes into the open when he himself decides to commit perjury, by allowing the "traïtor fel de putaire / Cui dyable ont douné honor" ("evil, ill-bred traitors, who honour the devil," lines 2698–9) to convince him to cancel the marriage plans between his daughter Aélis and Richart's son Guillaume, and to renege on his formal undertaking to make Guillaume heir to the throne. That the Emperor has disgraced himself in so doing is made obvious by the narrator:

> Di[e]x, quel dolor! Diex, quel damage!
> Com est l'emperere honis![7]

Aélis even uses the verb 'parjurer' (3244) in connection with her father's plans, and it is to save him from such a shame that she claims to herself that she must elope with her young lover.

At the outcome of this first part of the romance, it has become apparent that the three courts which are depicted may be said to represent three basic situations. Count Richart's court in Normandy is harmonious, stable and well-ruled by a strong yet judicious leader. The court of the King of Jerusalem, by contrast, has its stability endangered by external threat. Alone, the King could not overcome the Saracens, but he is not an unsatisfactory ruler for all that: he knows how to welcome his helpers,

[5] Anthime Fourrier, *Le courant réaliste dans le roman courtois en France au Moyen Age. Tome 1, Les débuts. XIIe siècle* (Paris: Nizet, 1960), pp. 315–446.
[6] "And the Emperor once again surrounded himself with new councillors, the traitors and false flatterers who had once harmed him so," lines 2660–63.
[7] "God, how sad! God, how dreadful! How dishonoured is now the Emperor!," lines 2908–9.

does not take umbrage at Richart's lavish entertaining, rewards everyone with the utmost generosity, and appears to be well-prepared to face the future.[8] The Emperor's court, on the other hand, suffers from an internal weakness which makes it liable to collapse for lack of an inner core. The enemy comes from within, and is seemingly to be identified to some extent with the Emperor himself.

It is striking that the apparently secure court of the Emperor does not seem to offer any space for difference, whereas both Count Richart and the King of Jerusalem consciously move in a culturally diverse world. The relations between the Christian rulers and their Turkish neighbours are of course hostile, but we are given indications that beyond the Turks' alien religious beliefs lie areas of similarity, and therefore the possibility of discussion and exchange. This is made particularly clear in the description of the young warrior killed in battle by Richart (lines 1133–71). His weapons, his coat of arms, his clothes are in impeccable taste, and he himself is described as a lover as courtly as any of his Christian counterparts, carrying his lady's favour to battle. This lady is the daughter of the King of Persia, but she has all the characteristics of the courtly heroine: golden hair, physical beauty, skilled in the art of embroidery, sincere in her feelings. The heathen enemies of the King of Jerusalem are thus shown to be compatible with their aristocratic Christian counterparts, because they share a certain world-view. Consequently, it is possible to negotiate with them and come to an agreement: Richart's Crusade culminates in a treaty which he can trust the Turks will respect.

There is no such common ground with the 'vilains' who manipulate the Emperor. Though nominally Christians, they do not baulk at perjury; they apparently have no sense of duty or loyalty, and are never connected with the finer feelings evidenced by the unfortunate young Turk. The cultural divide is such that no peaceful interaction is possible: Richart has to evict them from their ill-gotten strongholds *manu militari*, and their first concern after his death will be to destroy all that he achieved at the Emperor's court. The clash, as depicted in the first half of the romance, is between soulless, faceless administrators and the upholders of a social order based on moral principles. The arguments put to the Emperor in order to convince him to break his word towards Guillaume are eminently reasonable. They are also totally dishonourable. The adventures of Aélis and Guillaume thus take their starting-point in the breakdown of the values that held together the world in which they have been brought up.

The elopement of Aélis and Guillaume deals a final blow to the Emperor's court, in that it now has lost all hope of continuity in the legitimate transmission of power. As soon as the disappearance of both heirs to the throne is known, the 'vilains' who caused the problems in the first place abandon the court and secure elsewhere whatever financial interests they had in it:

> Cascuns des sers fuit et aloigne
> Son avoir et soi de la cort.[9]

---

[8]   The reading of the character of the King of Jerusalem will of course vary depending on how closely one wishes to connect this episode with the history of the Crusades.

[9]   "Each of the serfs flees and takes his possessions and his person far from the court," lines 4180–1.

The crisis is therefore one that touches the very heart of the social texture; the 'sers' are anticipating civil and political instability, and fear the economic upheaval that this implies. In marked contrast, the 'barons' come up with practical suggestions to find the missing children, and the Emperor in exchange learns the virtue of generosity advocated by Richart earlier in the work. However, the apparent regeneration of the ruler cannot disguise the fact that the imperial court is now impotent, and it disappears from the narrative. When it is next mentioned, it is as a thing of the past: the Emperor does not long survive the loss of his heirs, and it is a Roman Empire in the throes of anarchy that eventually begs Aélis and her husband to rebuild the imperial authority.

Renart's depiction of the young lovers' chequered existence before their eventual reunion and accession to power is celebrated for its realistic strain, but equally striking is the emblematic nature of their trials, which ultimately lead to the re-creation of a true court which will replace the debased one they had to flee. The focus for much of the second part of the romance is on Aélis, a fitting choice since it is through her that Guillaume is to become emperor. The heroine undergoes a gradual process of social ascension, starting off as a homeless (though not impecunious) waif, finding her first refuge under the roof of two poverty-stricken women, then establishing her own household before finding admittance into the court of the Count of St Gilles, whose position of authority is crucial not only for the reunion of the lovers, but also for their own rise to power, since it is he who supports Guillaume's claim to Richart's Norman lands.

Though this is not exactly a 'rags to riches' situation, inasmuch as Aélis is well provided with treasure from the outset, the upwardly-mobile pattern to the young heroes' adventures cannot be overlooked. The training of Aélis and Guillaume for leadership includes a first-hand experience of life at the lower levels of society – a situation not unlike that in *Havelock the Dane*.[10] In their different ways, the separated lovers prove the validity of the principles professed by Count Richart:

> Riches hom doit estre toustans
> Humles et dous, et ses consaus
> Li doit adés garder son miaus,
> Et faire droiture et justice
> A cascun. (. . .)
> Se grans avoirs vos vient as mains,
> S'en departés as gentix homes.
> Cil porteront por vos les sommes
> Es batailles et es estors.[11]

---

[10] Havelock worked as a kitchen scullion, Guillaume as a servant, and Aélis, if one accepts George Diller's reading of the Montpellier episode, performed services associated at the time with prostitutes. See George T. Diller, *"L'Escoufle. Une aventurière dans le roman courtois,"* *Le Moyen Age* 85 (1979), 33–43; also (less bluntly) Rita Lejeune, "Le personnage d'Aélis dans le *Roman de l'Escoufle* de Jean Renart," in *Mélanges de littérature du moyen-âge au xxe siècle offerts à Mademoiselle Jeanne Lods* (Paris: Ecole Normale Supérieure de Jeunes Filles, 1978), pp. 378–92.

[11] "A nobleman must always be humble and gentle, and must always follow his better judgment, and treat everyone with equity and justice . . . If a great fortune comes into your

Within the context of the second half of the poem, this speech becomes a moral as well as a political manifesto, which makes one look back upon the scathing remarks about the low-born 'vilains' with a fresh perspective. For most of the people who help Aélis are low-born; but in no way can they be called 'vilains.' When the girls first arrive in Montpellier, for example, they apparently have no problems finding kindly neighbours to lend them such household items as they require. Moreover, Isabel, Aélis's helpmeet, was rescued from dire poverty, and is undeniably of humble birth, yet is repeatedly referred to as *preus*, both by the narrator and by Aélis herself. The implication would appear to be that the term 'vilain' is closer to meaning 'not one of us,' or 'who does not share our fundamental cultural assumptions' than 'of humble parentage.' For it is clear that Aélis's meteoric rise from unknown embroiderer to member of the court at St Gilles is due directly to the fact that, in acting in the polite and generous manner advocated by Richart, she has secured the goodwill and loyalty of all those she has encountered; the seemingly universal recognition of the bonds she has thus created marks as 'gentix' *all* of the members of this society, irrespective of rank.

A similar observation may be made in connection with Guillaume, whose qualities of efficiency and politeness enable him to survive after having been robbed of his money. Like Aélis, Guillaume is acutely aware of the contractual nature of social bonding, and though he cannot express his generosity in monetary terms, he is ever ready to help those around him in a practical way – for example, by volunteering to help the hunt at St Gilles when they have been let down by one of their young men and need someone else to hold the last hawk. The hero's virtues are instrumental in his finding his lost lady: they earn him a good horse (bought at a bargain price from a pilgrim because it was lame), which enables him to join the hunt, which in turn secures the goodwill of the hunters, who introduce him to their lord's court, where Aélis is staying.

L'Escoufle has been termed an 'anti-Tristan,' and indeed, the Tristan story functions as a powerful counter-example in the account of Guillaume's socio-political education. Particularly at the beginning of his trials, the hero tends to think in terms of what Tristan would have done in his stead; and the decisions taken in this way are almost invariably errors, such as Guillaume's ill-fated choice to chase after the kite that had flown away with the purse containing Aélis's ring rather than stay beside his sleeping beloved. Moreover, after the young lovers have thus been separated, Guillaume's despair at falling short of his role model triggers bouts of horrific self-abuse, both physical and verbal: the socially destructive love affair of Tristan and Isolde is potentially destructive of Guillaume himself. The main thrust of the initiatory process he has to undergo is that he must cast aside this pernicious model, as his own father had done in a highly symbolical manner with his gift to the Holy Sepulchre (the precious cup was decorated with scenes from the Tristan: this could be read as a stylised sacrifice of what the story represented).

The episode where Guillaume tears out and eats the heart of the kite caught during the hunt at St Gilles therefore takes on particular prominence. This, needless to say,

possession, hand it out to the nobility. They will bear the burden for you in battles and fights," lines 1632–6, 1646–9.

is not a courtly gesture. The other hunters view it with astonishment and dismay. The function of the scene within the development of the narrative is obvious – without it, there would be no excuse to bring Guillaume to the court of the count. But there is more to it than meets the eye. The kite, a lowly bird despised by the aristocratic hunters, is an apt emblem of all that is alien to the culture which Aélis and Guillaume are called to uphold. The first kite in the story steals the most precious possession of Guillaume, though it is incapable of recognising its value; the second one is likewise a thief – it is caught eating a chicken. Guillaume's reaction may be read as a recognition of the fact that the contractual foundation of his society does not hold for this creature: and his response to this Other is to destroy it. He feeds on its heart, a political as well as a symbolical gesture, in that he thereby affirms himself as a predator to those who do not share his outlook on life. In so doing, he proves that he has attained the level of political insight that will enable him to succeed his father. He is prepared to destroy those who refuse to enter the socio-economic contract on which his culture is based: his initiation to power is completed.

It is fitting at this point that we consider the two aristocratic courts which appear in the second part of the poem, before Aélis and Guillaume found the third, their own court, which, one assumes, will reflect the perfection of that which gathered around Count Richart.

The first of these courts is that of the Lady of Montpellier. It appears to have very little impact on the life of the town proper, and the duty of hospitality and patronage connected with court life is conspicuously absent. Aélis has to gate-crash, hoping for the best, and relying on her gifts to find favour with the lady. The reason for this becomes clear only with reference to the Tristan story which underlies much of the romance: she is involved in a love affair. At no point does the narrator explicitly condemn this; however, Aélis shows some bemusement at the fact that a lady in love should be lacking in courtesy: "Et si m'a on dit qu'ele amot, Ki la deüst faire acointant." ("And yet I was told that she was in love, which should make her approachable," lines 5552–3).

The Lady of Montpellier, far from being ennobled by her passion, seems on the contrary to have become oblivious to her duties as châtelaine – as she freely admits to Aélis: "Ml't ai esté / Vers vos vilaine et desseüe / Ki prés de moi vos ai seüe / Et si ne vos ai acointie." ("I have been very rude and ignorant to have known you lived close to me without making your acquaintance," lines 5632–5). It has also obscured her judgement: she somewhat tactlessly gives to her lover the purse embroidered by Aélis, even though it bears the arms of her husband. Moreover, when her lover's wife – the Countess of St Gilles – betrays her sadness at this evidence of her misfortune, the sympathies of the reader are firmly diverted from the adulterous couple: the count allows himself (albeit briefly) to lapse far from the courtly behaviour which characterises him later in the narrative. Illicit love has deleterious effects on him too. In Aélis's initiation to power, the Lady of Montpellier thus figures as a counter-example, whilst the Countess of St Gilles, who remains dignified in the face of her husband's infidelity and strives to ignore it in order to maintain the honour of her court, provides a template for the younger woman.

The court at St Gilles is depicted as homely rather than impressive: a place where the lord has a post-prandial massage in front of the fire of an evening while he is waiting for his favourite dessert – cooked fruit – to be ready. There may be some irony in this image of domesticity, in that we know that the partnership on which it is founded is a flawed one; but it remains that this, the first really functional court for Aélis to have come across since she ran away, is also depicted as one where she experiences a form of family life. Even though she is initially called to St Gilles because of her skills, and technically speaking may be said to be an employee of the Count and Countess, she is treated by them with real affection, as may be seen by their concern when she bursts into tears at the thought of her lover (lines 7280–7357). Even her massaging of the Count in front of the fire, which has been regarded by some critics with suspicion, may be read as a quasi-filial gesture. When, at the end of the romance, she truly becomes a kinswoman to the Count and Countess, her new status merely strengthens pre-existing emotional bonds.

On a practical level, St Gilles is the place where Guillaume's maturity is revealed. There, he discovers that he has a family, a network of kinship that he can call upon to support his claims. The Count takes on the role of father-figure: his advice to Guillaume before leaving him to rule his Norman estates is strongly reminiscent of Richart's words in the first half of the narrative, enjoining him not to repeat the error of the Emperor who entrusted himself to his 'sers' rather than honouring his noblemen:

> Mors est li haus hom qui estruit
> Vilain, que quant il est deseure,
> Jamais n'ert a repos nule eure
> Qu'il ne pourquast anui et honte
> A celui qui en haut l'amonte.[12]

Yet, here, at the end of the story, these words take on a different resonance, because by this stage we know a little more about those 'vilains' forcibly put back into their place by Richart. The reader has heard Guillaume's account of his father's feats, told to the Count after the incident of the kite. In Guillaume's mouth, the tension does not appear to be social as much as political:

> Ce sachiés vous de verité
> Que ml't l'ont cremu et douté
> Li Genevois et li Pisen.
> Il destruit tous en mains d'un aen
> Cels a cui se sire avoit guerre.[13]

These 'vilains' were therefore prosperous Italian town-states attempting to break free from the authority of the Empire. This has nothing to do with low birth. Richart's marriage to the 'dame de Genvres' takes on a different colouring; it is revealed as a political union designed to secure the loyalty of rebellious Genoa. The early separa-

---

12 "The high-ranking man who elevates low-born men is as good as dead, for once they have the upper hand they will not cease to seek to hurt and shame he who exalted them," lines 8406–10.
13 "Know in truth that the people from Genoa and Pisa feared him greatly. In less than a year he destroyed all those with whom his lord was at war," lines 7478–83.

tion of Guillaume from his mother becomes sound policy to avoid his becoming a potential pawn in the hands of warring factions.

The 'retelling' of his father's history by Guillaume is pivotal to the understanding of the work. It proves that the once callow youth has cracked the code of courtesy, and is capable of distinguishing between facts and their conventional verbal representation, as expressed by Richart and echoed by St Gilles. It also shows that he has recognised the enemy of his world-view as a political rather than a cultural other. The warning of the Count of St Gilles is therefore likely to be heeded: Guillaume is indeed "de tel afaire / Com fu li quens Richars ses pere" ("Of the same mettle as was his father Count Richard," lines 8570–1, the ultimate reason given by the Romans to offer the Empire to him).[14] He speaks the same language.

This in turn presents Aélis's father in a different light. What had in the first half of the romance seemed close to moral inadequacy now has overtones of a tragic failure of communication between Richart and the Emperor. There was apparently every reason to trust a previous adversary when the heir to the Empire was one of their own (Guillaume was after all the son of the lady of Genoa); the hard political facts underlying Richart's courtly rhetoric remained ignored, because misunderstood. Beneath the sheer conventionality of his words lay the grim warning that at the root of the Emperor's problems with these Italian towns was an ideological incompatibility; that they should never be trusted entirely because the fundamental concepts underlying their political thought were alien to the feudal structure on which the Empire was based.

The implications of this situation for the new imperial court to be founded by Guillaume are not only political. We have seen from Guillaume's lucid account of his father's Italian campaign that he is capable of impartiality, and will therefore probably be able to avoid major frictions between the constitutive parts of his realm. His court, the ideal court, will thus be a meeting-point for differing world-views; a cultural and political centre of gravity which will keep in check the centrifugal forces at work in his world. But, just as Guillaume is shown to be the double of his father, to the virtual exclusion of the maternal element in him, it will be a place of exclusion as well as of exchange: only those cultures which recognise and reinforce the principles on which the court is founded will be allowed full access to it. Thus, the new imperial court should truly correspond to Walter Map's ideal description. The faces at court will be ever-changing, but the cultural complexion maintained by the Emperor will remain 'the same'.

[14] Beyond the conventionality of this, we may perhaps also detect some relief on the part of the Romans that Guillaume takes after his father rather than his Genoan mother.

NEGATIVE SELF-PROMOTION: THE TROUBADOUR "SIRVENTES JOGLARESC"

Catherine Léglu

In its broadest definition, the troubadour lyric is associated with love poetry, the addressing of praise to a desired object. This praise function, *laudatio*, carries with it its binary opposite in epideictic oratory, *vituperatio*. It is only logical, seen in this light, that troubadour *chansonniers* should anthologise pieces of crude invective and erotic praise side by side: without *vituperatio*, there can be no *laudatio*, and vice versa, since one mode of address defines the other.

Directions for invective are to be found in Classical rhetorical treatises, most notoriously in the *Rhetorica ad Herennium*'s list of devices to bring enemies of the speaker into contempt, through reduction, sarcasm and ridicule.[1] The devices listed for *vituperatio* accumulate dramatic and comical effects, and invite the speaker to use elaborate and exaggerated imagery in the creation of a negative, debased portrait of a given target. Medieval invective survives in a number of contexts, some of which imply a display of oratorical skill rather than biographical antagonism against a specific enemy.[2]

In the troubadour lyric, invective occurs most frequently in the *sirventes*, and satirical *vers*, which may be defined roughly as personal, political and critical poetry. Within this section, a significant number of songs address targets identified either by name or through insulting *senhals* (nicknames), in terms of violent or sharp personal criticism. This subgroup has most frequently been studied in terms of its political or historical significance, as akin to propaganda or journalism.[3]

Manuscripts cited: *A*: Rome, Bibl. Vat. Lat. 5232. *C*: Paris BN fr. 856. *D, Da*: Nodena: Bibl. Estense R4.4. *H*: Rome, Bibl. Vat. Lat. 3207. *I*: Paris BN fr. 854. *K*: Paris BN fr. 12473. *M*: Paris BN fr. 12474. *O*: Rome, Bibl. Vat. Lat. 3208. *R*: Paris BN fr. 22543. *a1*: Modena, Bibl. Estense, Campori γ N.8.4. 11, 12, 13. *Sg*: Barcelona, Bibl. Cat., 146.

[1] *Rhétorique à Hérennius*, edited and translated by Guy Achard (Paris: Les Belles Lettres, 1989), III.6.10–11, 7.13–14 and 8.15. See also Quintilian, *Institutio Oratoria*, Book III.7.10–18 (praise), 19–22 (blame), *Quintilien: Institut oratoire*, edited and translated by Jean Cousin, 7 volumes (Paris: Les Belles Lettres, 1976).

[2] For a collection of studies on Medieval uses of invective, see *L'Invective au Moyen Age: France, Espagne, Italie, Actes du Colloque "L'Invective au Moyen Age", Paris, 4–6 février, 1993*, edited by E. Beaumatin and M. Garcia, in *Atalaya: Revue Française d'Etudes Hispaniques* (Paris: Presses de la Sorbonne Nouvelle, 1994).

[3] See Karen Wilk Klein, *The Partisan Voice: A Study of the Political Lyric in France and Germany, 1180–1230* (The Hague: Mouton, 1971); Martin Aurell, *La Vielle et l'épée: trouba-*

An exception to this rule is a group of fifteen songs addressing insults to a named but unresponding figure identified as a *joglar*, in terms of his physique, character and skills; these were called *sirventes joglaresc* by Friedrich Witthoeft in his edition and study of 1891.[4] Witthoeft's edition includes Bertrand de Paris' *sirventes ensenhamen* to a *joglar* about his repertoire (Witthoeft, XXIII), but omits the preceding two songs by Guerau de Cabrera and Guiraut de Calanson; all three are edited and studied by François Pirot, who concludes that although this trio of songs sheds light on the *sirventes joglaresc*, it is independent of it (Pirot, pp. 46–49). For the purposes of this study, I have included all three in the table below; it is worth noting that the term *sirventes ensenhamen* is modern and disputed (Pirot, pp. 19–38, 66).

Both Witthoeft and Méjean omit the song by Lanfranc Cigala, which is all the more remarkable for having an answer by the *joglar*, addressing the poet as a judge rather than a troubadour. This answer has been added to the list as well.[5]

Table of *sirventes joglaresc*

Giraut de Bornelh	"Cardaillac, per un sirventes," Sharman XL	*ACDHIK*
Dalfin d'Alvernha	"Puois sai etz vengutz, Cardaillac," Brackney, III	*ADO*
Dalfin d'Alvernha	"Joglaretz, petitz Artus," Brackney, IV	*AD*
Bertran de Born	"Fulheta, vos mi preiatz," Paden, XL	*M*
Bertran de Born	"Fulheta, ges autres vergiers," Paden, XXVI	*M*

dours et politique en Provence au XIIIe siècle (Paris: Aubier, 1989). See also the discussion by Antonio Torres-Alcalà, "Del libelo politico al sirventés provenzal: una analogia," *Romance Quarterly* 38 (1991), 49–57.

[4] Friedrich Witthoeft, *Sirventes Joglaresc: Ein Blick auf das altfranzösische Spielmannsleben*, Ausgaben und Abhandlungen aus dem Gebiete der romanischen Philologie, volume 88 (Marburg: Elwert, 1891). See the discussion of the term and corpus by Suzanne Méjean, "Contribution à l'étude du *sirventes joglaresc*," in *Mélanges de philologie romane dédiés à la mémoire de Jean Boutière*, 2 volumes, edited by Irenée Cluzel and François Pirot (Liège: Solédi, 1971), vol. 1, pp. 377–95. This discussion is continued by François Pirot, *Recherches sur les connaissances littéraires des troubadours occitans et catalans des XIIe et XIIIe siècles: Les "sirventes ensenhamens" de Guerau de Cabrera, Guiraut de Calanson et Bertrand de Paris* (Barcelona: Real Academia de Buenas Letras, 1972), pp. 46–49.

[5] References are to Alfred Pillet and Henry Carstens, *Bibliographie der Troubadours* (Halle (Saale): Niemeyer, 1933). Manuscript *sigla* are from François Zufferey, *Recherches linguistiques sur les chansonniers provençaux* (Geneva: Droz, 1987). PC 242, 27, *The "Cansos" and "Sirventes" of Giraut de Bornelh: A Critical Edition*, edited by Ruth Verity Sharman (Cambridge: Cambridge University Press, 1989); PC 119, 7 and 119, 3, "A Critical Edition of the Poems of Dalfin d'Alvernhe," edited by Emmert M. Brackney (unpublished doctoral thesis, University of Minnesota, 1936); PC 80, 17, 80, 16 and 80, 24, *The Poems of the Troubadour Bertran de Born*, edited by William D. Paden, Tilde Sankovitch and Patricia H. Stäblein (Berkeley: University of California Press, 1986); PC 406, 1, 406, 11 and 406, 29, *Les Poésies du troubadour Raimon de Miraval*, edited by Leslie T. Topsfield (Paris: Nizet, 1971); PC 173, 4, *Les Poésies de Jausbert de Puycibot: troubadour du XIIIe siècle*, edited by William P. Shepard (Paris: Champion, 1924); PC 457, 21, *Les Poésies de Uc de Saint-Circ*, edited by Alfred Jeanroy and Jean-Jacques Salverda de Grave (Toulouse: Privat, 1913); PC 282, 13 and 283, 1, *Il Canzionere di Lanfranco Cigala*, edited by Francesco Branciforti (Florence: Olschki, 1954). PC 242a, 1, PC 243, 7a and PC 85, 1, all in Pirot, *Recherches*.

Bertran de Born	"Mailolis, joglars malastrucs," Paden, XXVII	*M*
Raimon de Miraval	"A Dieu me coman, Baiona," Topsfield, XXXIX	*CR*
Raimon de Miraval	"Baiona, per sirventes," Topsfield, XL	*CR*
Raimon de Miraval	"Forniers, per mos enseignamens," Topsfield, XLI	*AD*
Gausbert de Puycibot	"Gasc, pecs, laitz joglars e fers," Shepard, IV	*ACDIKR*
Uc de Saint-Circ	"Messonget, un sirventes," Jeanroy, XXII	*CR*
Lanfranc Cigala	"Lantelm, qui.us onra," Branciforti, XVII	*H*
Lantelm	"Senher Lanfrancs," Branciforti, XVIIb	*H*
Guerau de Cabrera	"Cabra juglar," Pirot, I	*Da*
Guiraut de Calanson	"Fadet juglar," Pirot, II	*Da R*
Bertrand de Paris	"Gordo, ieu fai," Pirot, III	*R al*

The songs are spread over a wide range of manuscripts, but tend to show very limited diffusion, with the exception of Giraut de Bornelh's and Gausbert de Puycibot's examples, both of which appear six times. By any criteria, these songs are a marginal phenomenon, which makes their similarity to each other all the more striking. Chronologically, they are spread between the later twelfth and the early thirteenth centuries, with the possible exception of Guerau de Cabrera's song, which may have been composed in Catalonia around 1165.[6]

Witthoeft's classification was based on an understanding of the term *joglaresc* as "in the interests of a *joglar*," a song addressing a *joglar*, rather than "in the style of a *joglar*," which would appear to be the meaning intended by the use of the term in the *vidas*. After rejecting other meanings, Suzanne Méjean suggests the songs were composed by established poets to promote a *joglar* to a prospective patron (Méjean, pp. 378–79, 381).[7] Why this should involve the postulant being called talentless, filthy and disreputable is explained in terms of a supposed comic intention, or a patron's privilege (Méjean, pp. 379, 388). If this literal reading is accurate, it begs the question of how – and why – such a self-promotion in the negative should have been cultivated.

One-sided invective is a powerful propaganda weapon. Songs addressing a social equal or superior in the context of a conflict of personal, diplomatic or territorial interests are largely self-explanatory, and aim to goad the addressee into action or riposte. The addressee of these songs, however, is neither a king nor a powerful political figure. He is described as a social inferior, a professional performer who begs poets for songs, and is not given a full name; his sobriquet reduces him further, moving him from the sphere of social hierarchies into a different, subordinate sphere of dependent performers and hired voices. The only answer by a *joglar* to his

---

[6] See Pirot, *Recherches*, pp. 17–73. Stefano Cingolani has argued that the song should be moved to Provence in the 1190s, "The *sirventes-ensenhamen* of Guerau de Cabrera: A proposal for a new interpretation," *Journal of Hispanic Research* 1 (1992–93), 191–200, but the evidence is not conclusive for either date.

[7] Dietmar Rieger, *Gattungen und Gattungsbezeichnungen der Trobadorlyrik* (Tübingen: Niemeyer, 1976), pp. 153–56, suggests the term means "of a jongleur," on the basis of Rudolph Zenker's definition, *Die Gedichte des Folquet von Romans* (Halle: Niemeyer, 1896), pp. 35–39.

attacker addresses Lanfranc in terms of his social status, as a powerful judge and diplomat rather than a troubadour. It is evident that issues of hierarchy are crucial to the dynamic of these songs.

One etymology of *sirventes* given in the treatises was that the word derived from *sirven*, and expressed the song's subordinate role, either composed by a servant, or serving an extant rhyme scheme, or a commissioned extra-textual purpose.[8] In the *vidas* of the *joglars* Guillem Ogier Novella, Folquet de Romans and the apocryphal "Peire Guillem de Tolosa," none of whom is attributed songs in the subgroup under study, the term *sirventes joglaresc* is used to describe songs that articulate praise and blame, *laus et vituperatio* (Boutière and Schutz, LXXIII, LXVI, LXXXI), "e fez sirventes joglarescs, que lausava l[os] uns e blasmava los autres" (and he composed *sirventes joglaresc* which praised some and criticised others).[9] Neither the treatises nor the biographies refer to a distinctive subgenre devoted exclusively to criticising a named but unresponding *joglar* through the mouth of a troubadour. On the contrary, it would seem that the *sirventes joglaresc* is associated with epideictic oratory "in the style of a *joglar*," in other words, of a commissioned performer. An attack on a person of a lower rank or status is not mentioned, nor perhaps envisaged, given the etymological positioning of the *sirventes* as a servant.[10]

Kastner rejected Witthoeft's interpretation of the term, and suggested this group of songs consisted of "an amusing parody of the recommendations one can imagine a jongleur carrying with him on his travels,"[11] an idea which may be adapted to oral "parades de jongleur" envisaged by Pirot (pp. 56–61). These suggestions, along with Méjean's mentioned earlier, depend on an assumption that the addressee was the intended performer of the song, and referred to himself in the second person throughout, speaking as the hostile troubadour. The result would have been a performer castigating himself in another's voice before the audience he intends to impress.

These songs may be read as recommendations turned upside-down in the structural as well as textual sense. In the mainstream troubadour lyric, the song ends with a *tornada* in which the troubadour dedicates and transmits the song, often into the safekeeping (the memory and mouth) of a named *joglar*:

> Joglars ab moz noveus
> De chantars porteras en cors
> A la bella cui nais ricors

8 See the *Doctrina de compondre dictatz*, lines 104–8, *Regles de trobar*, lines 33–37, both in John Marshall, *The "Razos de Trobar" of Raimon Vidal and Associated Texts* (London: Oxford University Press, 1972). For work on the etymology of sirventes, see Joachim Storost, *Ursprung und Entwicklung des altprovenzalischen Sirventes bis auf Bertran de Born* (Halle: Niemeyer, 1931), pp. 1–27; Pirot, *Recherches*, pp. 42–53; Suzanne Thiolier-Méjean, *Chansons satiriques et morales des troubadours du XIIe siècle à la fin du XIII siècle* (Paris: Nizet, 1978), pp. 26–33; and Rieger, *Gattungen*, pp. 47–184.
9 Jean Boutière and Alexander-H. Schutz, *Biographies des troubadours*, second edition with Irenée-Marcel Cluzel (Paris: Nizet, 1964).
10 It is worth noting that Bertran de Born's songs to Fulheta include praise of other figures.
11 L.E. Kastner, "Some notes on Bertran de Born," *Modern Language Review* 29 (1934), 142–49, p. 142. See also Brackney, "Critical edition," p. 70.

E digaz li q'eu sui plus sieus
Qe sos manteus.   (PC 242, 60, Sharman, XII, vv. 66–70, version *Sg, a*)[12]

(Joglar, carry a song with new words to the beautiful woman in whom
nobility is born, and tell her I'm more hers than her cloak is.)

The *sirventes joglaresc*'s concern with the transmitter as the focus of the text
rather than with the transmitted song breaks with this convention by turning it on its
head, placing the name of the appointed transmitter at the start rather than the end of
the song. The docile addressee is presented as an ambitious and demanding professional instead of a metaphorical vehicle for a poet's effusions.

The songs in the table play on a break with the scenario of the lyric, negating the
marginalised role of the troubadour's appointed mouthpiece and placing him centre-
stage. The distinction they make between troubadour and *joglar* constitutes another
source of controversy, given that these songs rehearse a construction of the *joglar* as
inherently negative and parasitical. Ruth Harvey has examined the possibility that
this hierarchy may be a false one up to the thirteenth century, when, as Aurell notes,
the professional *joglars* became a much more common figure (Aurell, pp. 119–29;
Harvey, p. 232).[13]

Trobador/trobaire derives from *trobar*, to find or compose, whereas *joglar* stems
from *ioculator*, an entertainer.[14] Harvey argues that court entertainers may have
combined such functions with employment as clerks or officials (Harvey, pp.
228–32), while the distinction between entertainers who compose and those who
only perform is less than secure (Harvey, pp. 222–23).[15] It is possible, therefore, to
be both a *trobador* and a *joglar*, and for the poet to work as a paid administrator. It is
noticeable that the majority of the troubadours to whom this group of songs is
attributed are noblemen, with the exception if Giraut de Bornelh (Gausbert de
Puycibot was a nobleman by birth, Boutière and Schutz, XXIX), who did not hold
such paid office. Could the *sirventes joglaresc* therefore articulate a perception of
social hierarchy between dilettante poets and their more needy colleagues?

In these songs, the speaker describes himself as a troubadour and patron, offering
advice and additions to the repertoire of a professional entertainer. The *vidas*, composed some fifty years later than the last datable song in the group, are markedly
ambivalent about terminology. Some poets are described as *joglars* who rise in fame

---

[12] Zufferey, *Recherches*, renames *Sg* manuscript *Z*, pp. 4–12. However, *Sg* continues to be
used for this *chansonnier*.

[13] Ruth Harvey, "*Joglars* and the professional status of the early troubadours," *Medium
Ævum* 62 (1993), 221–42. Linda Paterson suggests that the categories are interchangeable,
The World of the Troubadours: Medieval Occitan Society, c.1100–1300 (Cambridge: Cam-
bridge University Press, 1993), pp. 111–14, citing Edmond Faral, *Les Jongleurs en France au
Moyen Age* (Paris: Champion, 1910), p. 79.

[14] *Petit Dictionnaire Provençal-Français*, edited by Emil Levy, second edition (Heidelberg:
Carl Winter's Universitätsbuchhandlung, 1923), pp. 218, 373; *Provenzalisches Supplement-
Wörterbuch*, edited by Emil Levy, 8 volumes (Leipzig: Reisland, 1894–1924), IV, p. 260,
VIII, pp. 479–83. *Joglar* is derived from *joculari* in *Französisches Etymologisches Wörter-
buch*, edited by Walther von Wartburg, 24 volumes (Basel: Helbing und Lichtenhahn,
1925–83), V, pp. 41–2.

[15] See the discussion by Faral, *Jongleurs en France*, pp. 74–79.

and status through the quality of their *trobar* and become respected figures without losing the title, such as Peire de la Mula: "uns joglars q'estet e Monferrat en Peimont ab miser N'Ot del Carret . . . E fo trobaire de coblas e de sirventes" (a minstrel who stayed in Montferrat in Piedmont with my lord Ottone del Carretto . . . and he was a composer of *coblas* and *sirventes*) (Boutière and Schutz, XCVII).

The distinction between a fully-named poet and a figure known only through a sobriquet would seem to be crucial to the definition of a bad *joglar*-addressee and a good *joglar*-poet in the *vidas*. For example, Cadenet's career is said to start inauspiciously under the stage-name Baguas (the masculine form of *bagasa*, "whore").[16] Once he adopts that of Cadenet, which is not a sobriquet but the name of his lost fief, he is endowed with the ability to compose good songs (Boutière and Schutz, LXXX).[17] There is no sign that he did not compose in his earlier period.

Cadenet's biography promotes the idea that a *joglar*'s identity is inherently unstable, changing with every name he chooses to embody. Marcabru's *vida* in manuscript *A* (Boutière and Schutz, IIIb) may be viewed as the founding myth of this progression from *joglar* to troubadour: his apprenticeship is under the name Pan-Perdut ("Lost-bread/ land"), and working with Cercamon ("Search-the-world," Boutière and Schutz, II). His successful career and fame are under the aggressive name Marcabru, which could mean (as Mar-cabr[a]) "Damage the goat/ lecher";[18] the obsessive naming in the songs attributed to Marcabru emphasises how closely related are the name and the texts. As a foundling raised by a noble patron, this poet progresses from a passive apprenticeship to an aggressive and successful name and persona.

Such names as Perdigon ("Lost one"), Saill d'Escola ("Escape from School") and Albertet Cailla ("Little Albert the Quail") are presumed to indicate a successful *joglar* (Boutière and Schutz, LIX, X, LXVII), while troubadours use their full names, only adopting *senhals* when the pretence is transparent, such as Raimbaut d'Aurenga's use of Linhaure in his *tenso* with Giraut de Bornelh (PC, 242, 14/287, 1, Sharman, LIX). One group is defined by a sobriquet, while the other has a status defined by a name that is only masked, and never relinquished.

This distinction is unlikely to bear much relation to the biological figures outside the *chansonniers* and songs. The *vidas* are often constructed on the basis of texts, especially for the earlier generation of troubadours. It is possible that the exceptions among poets recruited from the lower nobility and bourgeoisie were those lords and barons such as Dalfin d'Alvernhe and Bertran de Born, who composed these *sirventes*.

To return to the group of songs edited by Witthoeft, the power relation between speaker and silent object is determined by the opposition between the full names of famous troubadours and the stage-names of *joglars* with whom no extant songs are connected. Certain sobriquets indicate geographical locations, such as Baiona and

---

[16] *P.Dict.*, p. 38 also notes *bagasier*, "ribaud, débauché". *FEW*, I, pp. 196–97 notes *bacassa* means a girl, but *bagasa* refers to a prostitute.
[17] See Boutière and Schutz, *Biographies*, p. 502, n.
[18] This suggestion was made by John Marshall in 1991 in discussion during the British Branch of the AIEO conference, Girton College, Cambridge.

Gasc (Bayonne, Gascon). Others are dehumanising epithets, such as those used by Bertran de Born to Fulhetas, "Little Leaves" and by Uc de Saint-Circ to Messonget, "Little Messenger/ Liar".[19]

The three longer *sirventes* about repertoire play on a more radical opposition. All three addressees, Cabra, Fadet and Gordo, are given insulting names, "Goat," "Madman" and "Fat," by fully named poets one of whom, Guerau de Cabrera, is a powerful lord (Pirot, pp. 109–32). They are encapsulated in a single image, which respectively animalises, dehumanises and reduces them to the physical level. The attack is structured from the first line as one by an individual upon a cypher, who is not necessarily present. The *joglar* is invoked and abused as a pretext for the *trobaire*'s self-display.

The scenario common to the songs edited by Witthoeft emerges as the following: the *joglar* has asked the speaker for a song to further his career (Topsfield, XXXIX, vv. 1–16, XL, vv. 1–6; Sharman, XL, vv. 1–2; Jeanroy, XXII, vv. 1–4; Paden, XXVII, vv. 1–4, XL, vv. 1–4) or for advice before training into the profession (Topsfield, XLI; Brackney, III). His career has comprised drifting from one profession to another. Cardaillac starts out as a mutilated soldier (Sharman, LX, vv. 10–23, 28–35), but appears at court as a pseudo-knight. Forniers is also described as a former mercenary given to robbing monks (Topsfield, XLI, vv. 11–16). The transition to *joglar* involves relinquishing swearing and gambling (ibid., vv. 21–30, without, however, becoming too controlled (ibid., vv. 51–56).

The addressee is constructed as an assemblage of negative skills and attributes, who can neither entertain nor sing (Brackney, II; Paden, XXVII), but whose apprenticeship involves a period as a mercenary. He embarks on a career as an entertainer out of pragmatic choice, not devotion to his craft or to *Amors*. However, the troubadour is also a performer by definition. Those who could not sing their own material, such as Giraut de Bornelh, were dependent on professional performers. Indeed, Giraut's *vida* notes he employed two *cantadors* (Boutière and Schutz, VIII). If the addressee is inadequate, the same may potentially be said of the speaker, who, after all, is the first-person voice of the song, and is equally dependent on the taste and judgement of his audience.

The songs focus on accidents of physique, such as an unattractive body, bad breath or hoarseness (Sharman, XL, vv. 3–6; Paden, X, vv. 8, 11–12), which may compromise the success of an oral performance; Bertran de Born's song to Mailolin emphasises the ugliness of his voice (translation from Paden): "canta plus clar li grailha./ Porc c'om regarda millargos/ fai meilhor escoutar que vos/ o nafrat qan hom lo tailha" (the grackle sings clearer. When they slaughter a pig that anyone can see is measled or wounded, it makes better listening than you do; Paden, XXVII, vv. 10–14).

In short, the physical shortcomings of their performers are used to figure the anxieties about their poetic success by troubadours whose social status makes them – theoretically – immune to such risks. This projection is typical of what Barbara A.

---

[19] See *PSW*, V, p. 201. Monica Calzolani comments that this is typical of the choice of names for minstrels, *Il Trovatore Guillem Augier Novella* (Modena: Mucchi, 1986), p. 41.

Babcock has named "symbolic inversion," the reversal of agreed norms and codes in order to reinforce those very codes.[20] In this case, the idea that a poet may lay claim to a mystique of natural inspiration and devotion to his craft is reasserted through mocking a figure depicted as mercenary, lacking in skill and physically inadequate. In so doing, the songs articulate the realities of performance and a poet's insecurities in the negative, by denying them and projecting them onto a silent, dehumanised addressee, constructed as the troubadour's hierarchical inferior.

In the case of Giraut de Bornelh, the portrait of Cardaillac is a reversed image of his own predicament, as a troubadour who was unable to sing, and who worked as a professional teacher in the winter months (Boutière and Schutz, VIII). A satirical portrait by Peire d'Alvernha mocks Giraut as a frail old woman with a weak voice, belittling him in the way he belittles Cardaillac (del Monte, XII, vv. 13–18).[21]

The *joglar* is the recipient of the poet's fears that his songs – and his appointed transmitters – will not be successful. He thereby becomes the troubadour's image in the negative, and his name occasionally appears to echo that of the speaker: Gausbert de Puycibot addresses Gasc, while Guerau de Cabrera mocks Cabra; the goat figured on the Cabrera family shield, and may be assumed to represent the family, or at least indicate that the *joglar* is part of the *familia* (Pirot, p. 555). By mocking their own debased mirror-image, the speakers assert that they, as troubadours, transcend their own transmission. The *tornada*'s message, that the song will transmit the subject's devotion to a lover or patron, is also demystified: the appointed mouthpiece will use it to further his own career.

In the long *sirventes* devoted to repertoire, reversal becomes the structuring principle, as the troubadour presents a display of erudition completely in the negative, as the literary baggage the addressee does not possess. The negative anaphora "Ni . . ./ ni . . ." in Guerau de Cabrera and Guiraut de Calanson's songs, as well as Dalfin d'Auvergne's to Cardaillac (Brackney, IV, vv. 21–25, 28–30, 42–44), lose their initial reference to the *joglar* and become a boasting harangue addressed to the audience.

The projection of ignorance or failure onto a low Other or "Not-me" figure constructed as a mirror-image of the speaker allows the articulation of failure to become a boast. The problem posed by this set of songs is that this boast depends on a hierarchical distinction between speaker and addressee that is fundamentally a matter of vocabulary, and rests on convention, the *tornada* structure turned on its head. As a result, the power relation established is markedly ambiguous.

This "Not-me" figure bears an uncomfortably close resemblance to the "I" addressing him. These songs set up an endless shifting of perspectives, as a formulaic *tornada* becomes a monologue to a delineated character, who in turn shifts from the poet's recipient to a potential performer. Instead of his putative *domna*, the poet's

---

[20] Barbara A. Babcock, *The Reversible World: Symbolic Inversion in Art and Society* (Ithaca: Cornell University Press, 1978), pp. 13–36, 14–15.

[21] *Peire d'Alvernha: Liriche*, edited by Alberto del Monte (Turin: Loescher-Chiantore, 1955), PC 323, 11. See also the Monk of Montaudon's *contrafactum*, PC 305, 16, *Les Poésies du Moine de Montaudon*, edited by Michael J. Routledge (Montpellier: Publications du Centre d'Etudes Occitanes de l'Université Paul Valéry, 1977), XVIII.

concern is exclusively with the messenger he appoints, as a reflection of himself. The whole is enclosed in a relentlessly negative frame, repeating "You do not know, you cannot sing" in order to state that the speaker does know and can sing.

These songs rest on an overt and acknowledged fiction that the lyric "I" and physical performer of the lyric song are not the same; they are personified as a noble speaker and a silent, cynical mercenary. Through an unverifiable hierarchical distinction (since a sobriquet may cover a fellow troubadour, a fully-named nobleman in other contexts),[22] these songs invoke the full engagement of the audience with the speaker against the created scapegoat. They depend on a collective agreement to deny that all oral performers are ultimately at the mercy of their audience, whatever their claimed status might be.

---

[22] Peire d'Alvernha mentions a Bertran de Cardalhac, PC 323, 11, del Monte, XII, vv. 53–54.

ODD MAN OUT: VILLON AT COURT

Barbara N. Sargent-Baur

Of all the lyricists writing in French in the late Middle Ages, François Villon is now the most celebrated among both scholars and the reading public. Most such encounters with him occur in the extended Francophone world, and specifically among lovers of poetry conversant with Middle French; but many readers possessing little French, Middle or Modern, are nevertheless familiar with versions of his works in many languages. Villon is a success in our day.

It was not always thus. The circle of his own contemporaries who knew of his literary abilities was a narrow one, although within it he was esteemed. Villon hints in his most substantial work, the *Testament*, at the reception of his other long poem, the *Lais*; this, by 1461, was already circulating, and being referred to by a title not of the author's choosing.[1] His limited fame during his lifetime is confirmed by the small number of surviving fifteenth-century copies; there are five sources of the *Lais*, four of the *Testament*; the independent poems are scattered in numerous manuscripts and incunabula.[2] These data suggest a modest primary readership; the work itself speaks mainly to, and of, a public very modest in socio-economic terms. By and large, Villon's contemporary readers or hearers were not to be found among the rich, the powerful, and the refined; far from it. Although some such personages do appear in his verses, it is most often in the context of appeals for money, of flattery, or of cautious and indirect allusion. He was clearly not very skillful at cultivating well-off potential patrons. And so Villon, except at rare intervals, remained an outsider; he sought for approbation and patronage, and sometimes in quest of them went to lengths that his modern readers may find regrettable, even embarrassing. Such efforts availed him little; the favor he craved eluded him, as consequently did financial security. There are excellent grounds for supposing that he aspired to a literary career, which would have meant a post as poet-in-residence at a court; and he exerted himself to catch the eye and ear of one or more highly-placed connoisseurs.

---

[1] About to flee from Paris, Villon made "Certains laiz, l'an cinquante six,/ Qu'aucuns, sans mon consentement,/ Voulurent nommer Testament;/ Leur plaisir fut, non pas le myen" ("Certain bequests, Year Fifty-Six, That some folk, without my consent, Saw fit to call a Testament; It was their pleasure and not mine"), *Testament*, 11.755–58. This and all subsequent Villon quotations come from *François Villon: Complete Poems Edited with English Translation and Commentary* by Barbara N. Sargent-Baur (Toronto: University of Toronto Press, 1994.)

[2] See Robert D. Peckham, *François Villon: A Bibliography* (New York: Garland, 1990), pp. 7–27, 41–45; and Jean Rychner and Albert Henry, eds., *Le Lais Villon et les Poèmes Variés* (Geneva: Droz, 1977), I, 33–39.

Nevertheless, for reasons that we can only conjecture, Villon seemingly gained no more than the occasional gift of money, and presumably bed and breakfast. His membership of a courtly-literature society, entered into on a trial basis, turned out to be of short duration, and was not renewed.

One person's loss can be the gain of many others. It is a paradox of literary history that for Villon greater success in his lifetime might well have spelled later obscurity and left us poorer. He did in fact compose for, and indeed at, at least one court: some verses in the elevated style and some decidedly not so, some developing a set theme or exploiting a rhetorical device and others designed to open a princely hand, all of them intended to curry favour and to obtain or retain support. These *poésies de circonstance*, always competent and sometimes clever, did not win him extended patronage. Hence rather than spend much of his no doubt short life in crafting calculatedly pleasing official verse, like dozens of his luckier contemporaries, he found himself driven by circumstance, or perhaps by a jarring personality, or by that goddess Fortune of whom he often complained, to other courses. He was unemployed, lived by expedients, knew misery and degradation, reflected on his reading and particularly on his experience, and wrote amateur poetry of a unique and memorable stamp.

This essay will focus not on the personal poetry (of which there is much, and much of it familiar) but on a smaller and somewhat neglected facet of Villon's activity: the compositions that may be labelled "courtly" because they were written in reality *at*, or in aspiration *for*, an aristocratic center. This requires identifying the court or courts involved, and the evidence of the poet's presence there. We must also single out the parts of his total *oeuvre* that owe their shape and theme and stylistic register to such a cultural locus: verses composed in the hope of gaining favor with some great personage, or to take advantage of opportunities encountered once their author was enjoying patronage, or more generally in response (positive or negative) to specific fashions and perceived tastes. All this will be preliminary to raising, and then attempting briefly to answer, the question: what kind of poetry did Villon offer his patrons?

First of all, the court or courts. Traditionally, two have been identified: that of Duke Charles d'Orléans at Blois, and that of the Duke of Bourbon at Moulins. The first identification is solid enough; the second has been shown to be very shaky indeed.[3] No other possible milieux have been seriously proposed. We are down to one court, and one securely-identifiable patron: Charles d'Orléans, himself a poet, an encourager of literary activities, and a collector of the results. (This does not of course rule out the possibility of Villon's sometimes hoping for other patrons, e.g., King Louis XI or the Provost of Paris; see below.) For Villon's being, if briefly, at Blois there is codicological evidence. Charles had his own early compositions professionally copied into a personal album,[4] now known as MS O^1; later he himself copied in, or had copied, many new poems of his own. The anthology was swelled

[3] For the arguments, see Rychner and Henry, ed. cit., II, 80–81.
[4] Paris, BN fr. 25458. For a description, see Pierre Champion, *Le Manuscrit autographe des poésies de Charles d'Orléans* (Paris: Champion, 1907; repr. Geneva: Slatkine, 1975).

by other contributors as well, for the duke had the pleasant custom of inviting his familiars, and even transient versifiers, to add their own poems. Some of these "guest authors" are identified by name, frequently in their hand and sometimes in the duke's.[5] Thus the inclusion in MS O[1] of someone's poem argues for a connection with the court at Blois; in many cases it suggests the writer's presence there, and on reasonably good terms with the duke. Among these contributions is the unique treatment of a noteworthy happening: the birth in December 1457 of a daughter to the duke, childless since 1432, and his third wife, Marie de Clèves. Here was a fine opening for an ambitious poet seeking employment, and who as a fugitive from justice dared not return to his native Paris. In MS O[1] figures a long poem celebrating the event and also, possibly, a later one: the *joyeuse entrée* into Orléans of Princess Marie in July 1460, when she was aged two years and seven months (*PV* I).[6] It effusively addresses the child, whose birth Villon seems to take as a personal favor, flatters her parents, and concludes with the author's name: "Vostre povre escolier Françoys." Further on in the album comes a series of ballades on a theme set by the duke and already treated by him: "Je meurs de soif auprés de la fontaine" ("I die of thirst right at the fountain's edge"). After three such ventures, anonymous and in various hands, comes one with "Villon" or, more likely, "Ballade Villon" as heading.[7] This is the piece traditionally known as the "Ballade des contradictions" (*PV* II). It is far superior to all the other treatments of the set topic, including the duke's; after the obligatory first line it abandons abstraction and conventional verbal posturings for concreteness, physical sensation, common experience, and an individual's direct knowledge of life's harshness. The ballade, begun on p. 163, continues to the facing page; the same hand filled the remaining space with the "Ballade franco-

---

[5] Duchess Marie also had an album of poems, now MS Carpentras, 375, containing works by the duke and other writers, but none by Villon.

[6] Internal references suggest a two-stage composition: first the "Dit" or "Louange" of ten stanzas, then the "Double Ballade" situated between stanzas VI and VII. André Burger categorically set the whole composition in July 1460; see "L'Epître à Marie d'Orléans," in *Mélanges de linguistique et de littérature romanes à la mémoire d'István Frank* (Saarbrucken: Universität des Saarlandes, 1959), pp. 91–99, especially p. 97. Daniel Poirion dated the whole as composed on or after Princess Marie's *joyeuse entrée* into Orléans in July 1460, and found no clear trace of Villon's presence at Blois before then; see "le Fol et le sage auprès de la fontaine," *Travaux de Linguistique et de Littérature* 6 (1968), pp. 53–68. Arguments for an earlier dating (late 1457 or early 1458) were advanced by Grace Frank in "Villon at the Court of Charles d'Orléans," *Modern Language Notes* 47 (1932), pp. 498–505; Sergio Cigada, "Studi su Charles d'Orléans e François Villon relativi al MS BN 25458," *Studi Francesi* 4 (1980), pp. 205–9; and by Rychner and Henry (*Lais* II, 64–65). These two editors have conjecturally termed the "Louange" or "Dit" a "lettre d'introduction à la cour de Blois" (op. cit., 51), proposing that the "Double ballade" was written once the poet was in residence. The arguments marshalled in favor of 1457/1458 carry much weight; and yet there remains the puzzling reference in stanza VIII to the child's unusual maturity of carriage and deportment . . .

[7] The eighteenth-century binder, trimming off the page, left only the lower extremities of the letters seemingly forming the name "Villon." In the copy of this manuscript (O[2]; Paris, BN fr. 1104, fol. 30), we read "Balade Villon," which presumably was once the heading in O[1], where the envoy begins "Prince." In the Carpentras manuscript the name "Fredet" leads off the envoy.

latine." Thematically this piece makes up the third in a set, in the first of which the duke himself counsels his newly-married friend Fredet while the second comprises Fredet's response of polite disagreement.[8] Both of them are in a mixture of French and Latin. As for the third poem, filling out p. 164, it was unquestionably written by someone who had read the other two; it has the same subject, bilingual treatment, stanzaic form, rhyme-scheme, and meter. Furthermore, the author specifically alludes in the second line to the "parfont conseil" on matrimonial matters contained in "ce saint livre," i.e., the book into which this third poem is at the moment being copied.[9]

It is entertaining to think of Villon, admitted we know not when or on what footing to the elegant court at Blois, producing for that "wise book" three new works. One thinks of him anxiously rummaging in the album to see what some other poets, including the duke, had done with the theme "je meurs de seuf," and in these explorations coming upon the duke's macaronic poem and Fredet's reply. It is noteworthy that as Villon prolongs that earlier debate he is tactfully at pains to side with the duke, as against Fredet.[10]

Here we have, then, a small body of work, its longest component internally signed by an "escollier Françoys," followed within a few pages by a "Balade Villon" and another ballade filling the remaining space. These poems are also linked paleographically, for they are all copied by the same hand, a highly distinctive one not suggesting a professional scribe, although it is clear enough to read.[11] Furthermore, and significantly, this handwriting appears nowhere else in the album. Everything points to these being autograph copies. There are additional signs that Villon had the album in his hands. A case could be made for reminiscence and even quotation from it figuring in other poems of his own. The second line of the *Testament* reads "Que toutes mes hontes j'euz beues" ("When I had drunk down all my shames"); it is very close to the first line, twice repeated, of the duke's Rondeau 201, "Qui a toutes ses hontes beues" (Cigada, 217–18). (Admittedly, the expression seems not to be original with Charles.) Even more likely, to my mind, is his finding, reading and digesting for future use a series of poems, again by the duke, on the subject of Fortune. It is in the album, after Charles's ballade on thirsting at the fountain (no.

---

[8]   See P. Champion, *Le Manuscrit autographe*, pp. 33–34; and Nancy Freeman Regalado, "*En ce saint livre*: mise en page et identité lyrique dans les poèmes autographes de Villon dans l'album de Blois (Bibl. Nat. MS fr. 25458)," in *L'Hostellerie de pensée (Etudes . . . Daniel Poirion)*, ed. M. Zink, D. Bohler, E. Hicks, M. Python (Paris: P.U.F., 1995), pp. 355–71.

[9]   This ballade was strangely omitted from the Villonian corpus until Rychner and Henry, 1977. As for its genesis, Gert Pinkernell imagines a whole drama of rivalry between Villon and Fredet in "Une nouvelle date dans la vie et dans l'oeuvre de François Villon: le 8 octobre 1458," *Romania* 104 (1983), pp. 377–91, especially 380–88.

[10]   *Pace* Pinkernell, ibid., who takes Villon's macaronic poem as a deliberate attack on the "insider" Fredet and as a serious blunder leading to Villon's loss of the duke's favour. Luciano Rossi, going further, sees in it a piece of deliberate insolence directed at the duke; see "François Villon et son prince redoubté," in *Romania ingeniosa: Festschrift für Prof. Dr. Gerold Hilty*, ed. G. Lüdi, H. Stricker and J. Wuest (Bern: Peter Lang, 1989), pp. 201–20, especially 217–18. Why Villon would intentionally offend his host remains unexplained.

[11]   There is a facsimile in Cigada, "Studi," between pp. 216 and 217.

100, p. 123, of which Villon follows the first line almost verbatim and re-works the second), and also after the macaronic pair of poems by the duke and Fredet (no. 104, 104a), but it comes before Villon's first contribution, the long "Louange" or "Dit" for little Princess Marie. The series forms a dialogue, the first and third ballades being placed in the mouth of the goddess and the second and the (unfinished) fourth spoken by the poet. Of course the theme of Fortune's power and caprice had been a literary commonplace since antiquity;[12] but here the verbal similarities go beyond the common fund of allusion and metaphor. Villon borrows the rhyme-words of the first and third lines (*nommee : renommee*), repeats Fortune's advice to take in stride (*prendre en gré*) whatever occurs, and picks up her claim that her license comes from God and that she always has acted, and will act, just as she pleases. The fact that Villon's far more powerful treatment of this theme does not appear in the ducal album stimulates conjecture. Perhaps the poem was composed at Blois but did not please the duke enough to gain entrée into his "guest book." Perhaps it was begun at Blois but finished elsewhere. Perhaps Villon later spun it out of his own hard experience, incorporating elements gleaned from his handling of his temporary patron's precious volume.

At any rate: three poems and the germ of a fourth, connected with an identifiable courtly milieu. And we can go further by turning to other fifteenth-century sources of Villon's works. In four of them[13] we find a begging poem giving the author's full name in the third line and saluting a "Prince": "Le mien seigneur et prince redoubté" ("My natural lord and most redoubted prince"). The former identification of this personage with the Duke of Bourbon, supposed feudal lord of Villon's shadowy father, is now generally rejected. The Duke of Orléans seems the most likely addressee; the place of composition is unknown but internal evidence suggests that it was elsewhere than Blois, and that it was presented or sent to Charles d'Orléans. Its absence from the album does not rule out the duke as addressee; there is no reason to suppose that all poetic composition accomplished at Blois, or created elsewhere and directed to the duke, was by the latter deemed worthy of being anthologized. The ballade under discussion, in fact, is somewhat curiously termed a "letter" in three of the four fifteenth-century sources, being so called in a quatrain added to the ballade. In the best source, MS H, this marginal and vertical quatrain is preceded by the words "Au doiz (= dos) de la lettre." Within the ballade itself Villon tries to cajole the addressee into "loaning" (= giving) him money, referring to an earlier "borrowing" of six *écus* from him. It rather looks as if the poet forwarded the request from a distance, perhaps following it up with a personal visit.

We may, if we are feeling venturesome, add three more poems to the catalogue of courtly production by Villon. Among his independent works are three exercises (*PV* V, VI, VII) of which the first two associate in the codicological tradition and the

---

[12] See Howard R. Patch, *The Goddess Fortuna in Mediaeval Literature* (Cambridge: Harvard University Press, 1927; repr. New York: Octagon, 1967), passim; and Italo Siciliano, *François Villon et les thèmes poétiques du moyen-âge* (Paris: Nizet, 1934), pp. 281–311.

[13] These are MSS H, P, R (H = Berlin, Kupferstichkabinett, Signatur 78 B 17; P = Paris, BN fr. 1719; R = Paris, BN fr. 12490); and I, the Imprimé (Paris: Levet, 1489).

1489 printing,[14] while the third appears in a single source (which also contains the other two poems). This isolated piece, traditionally known as the "Ballade des contre-vérités" and beginning "Il n'est soing que quant on a fain," is signed VILLON in acrostic. It parodies and immediately follows a serious and sententious ballade by Alain Chartier. The other two pieces in this group (called the "Ballade des proverbes" and the "Ballade des menus propos") include no authorial name, no dedicatee, no topical references, nothing to connect them with any specific poetic sensibility. Like the signed "Ballade des contradictions," these two poems are constructed of a series of examples offered in lines beginning with the same way. The use of *repetitio* and *frequentatio*, pervading all three of these ballades, creates a kinship among them. Yet aside from one acrostic, the codicological associations, and a few echoes of attitudes and verbal expressions showing up in other works unquestionably by Villon, there is little to connect this group of poems with any particular writer. They evoke, by their impersonality and rhetorical skill, a set of literary exercises of the sort that served as pastimes in noble circles. Such literary trifling was much in vogue. If Villon did indeed write these three ballades, but did not compose them for or at a court, one must wonder why he bothered with them at all.[15] They are then, if somewhat tentatively, to be added to the corpus of Villon's courtly output, if only because they conform to established and acceptable modes.

And then there is the controversial "Ballade contre les ennemis de la France" (*PV* VIII). Unsigned, lacking an addressee or any chronological peg, its manuscript tradition confused, its subject unparalleled in Villon's total *oeuvre*, the poem is certainly unusual. Its authenticity has been vigorously debated, although for the last century and a half editors (myself included) have published it with the rest of the poet's works. Its royalist sentiments and its imprecations against France's unspecified enemies might well have pleased King Louis XI.[16] It would also have been well

---

14 MSS F, J, P, R; and I (F = Stockholm, Kungl. Bibliotaket, V.u. 22; J = *Le Jardin de plaisance et fleur de rhetorique* [Paris: Vérard, c. 1501]). For MSS P and R, and for I, see note 13 above.

15 On slender evidence, Gert Pinkernell has proposed a specific date for these three ballades, and as their *raison d'être* Villon's hope of reconciliation with Charles d'Orléans, whom he is conjectured as having offended in attacking Fredet; see "Une nouvelle date."

16 Louis XI is fulsomely thanked and praised in *Testament*, 11.56–72, 81–88. It has recently been proposed again that in addition to these three octaves of Villon's major work, the "Ballade contre les ennemis de la France" too was directed to the new king; see Claude Thiry, "La Ballade contre les ennemis de la France," in *Etudes de philologie romane et d'histoire littéraire offertes à Jules Horrent*, ed. Jean-Marie d'Heur and Nicoletta Cherubini (Liège, 1980), 469–80; and also Gert Pinkernell, "La Ballade contre les ennemis de la France de François Villon. Un remerciement poétique à Louis XI (octobre 1461)," *Romanistische Zeitschrift für Literaturgeschichte* 14 (1990), 11–24. Both these scholars are convinced that this poem is by Villon, is addressed to Louis XI, post-dates the poet's liberation from the Meung prison (2 October 1461), and contains specific topical allusions intended to please the new king. I agree with Thiry and Pinkernell that there are excellent reasons to think that this ballade belongs in the Villonian corpus (as Grace Frank argued some sixty years ago in her review of *Deux Manuscrits de François Villon* in *Modern Language Notes* 47 [1932], p. 532). Much less persuasive is their contention that the addressee of the ballade was Louis XI and that the composition dates from the end of 1461. This would have it composed at the period when Villon was assembling and shaping his *Testament*; why did he not insert this ballade

received by many a French subject who, with reason, hated the English and the Burgundians: Charles d'Orléans, for instance, whose anti-English ballade (no. 101, p. 124) was in his album for all, including visiting poets, to see. Whoever was the addressee and whether he ever saw it, the author is, I think, very probably Villon; it has the energy, the erudition, the headlong rush, the accumulatory rhetoric that stamp much of his work. The immediate inspiration, if not gratitude toward the King, was perhaps the hope of gaining favour from someone.

I propose even more possible additions to this corpus. It is generally acknowledged that Villon's major work, the *Testament*, is among other things an anthology containing some fixed-form pieces conceived independently and then integrated into the thread of the mock-testamentary structure. As a rule these ballades and rondeaux, introduced with care, form a lyrical expansion of the theme explored in the preceding octaves; but on occasion the fixed-form poem comes in abruptly and/or provides a contrast in linguistic register. The so-called "Ballade a s'amye" (*T* 942–69) exemplifies this: after four introductory stanzas of pretty plain language we encounter a ballade presenting the writer as love's martyr and expressing his pains in elevated style. Villon's name and that of one "Marthe" appear in acrostic, a superfluous touch if the ballade was *ab initio* meant to be part of the *Testament*; and in the envoy the writer abandons his apostrophe to the false beauty, to make an appeal for succour to a *Prince amoureux* posited as capable of sympathy. The poem has all the air of having been composed for another occasion and another (unknown) audience. Similarly dissonant with their surroundings are the rondeaux "Mort, j'appelle de ta rigueur" (*T* 978–89) and "Au retour de dure prison" (*T* 1784–95), both conventional in subject and aristocratic in tone, both forcibly intruded into the sequence of octaves. Can we include, as well, the "Ballade pour Robert d'Estouteville" (*T* 1378–1405), a dramatic monologue placed into the mouth of this personage as an expression of love for his wife? It is as impersonal as anything Villon wrote, and was quite possibly composed to please and/or placate the powerful chief of Parisian law-enforcement against the day when the poet might need a friend in high places.[17]

---

among the others, thus reinforcing the three grateful octaves toward the beginning of the work? If he had intended to keep it as an independent poem, hoping that somehow it would be conveyed into the royal hands and be appreciated, one would have expected him to sign it in some way, as he did with many other pieces.

[17] For refutals of a proposed personal connection between the poet and Robert d'Estouteville, see Siciliano, *Thèmes*, pp. 52–58 and 452, n. 1; and Jean Dufournet, *Nouvelles Recherches sur Villon* (Paris: Champion, 1980), pp. 200–05. Dufournet dated this ballade late in 1461 or early in 1462, when the poet was putting the *Testament* together; see "A propos d'un article récent sur Villon et Robert d'Estouteville," *Romania* 85 (1964), pp. 342–54. Jean Frappier agreed in "Contribution au commentaire de Villon" in *Studi in Onore di Italo Siciliano* (Florence: Olschki, 1966), pp. 445–49. It should be mentioned that from the first of September of 1461 Robert d'Estouteville was in disgrace with the new king, Louis XI; and one may well wonder why Villon would take the trouble to compose a poem for a man out of office. In a long and informative article Sergio Cigada turns over the problem and some proposed solutions, and settles on 1452–55 as the most likely period for its composition; as to its later incorporation into the *Testament* he points to "una giustificazione estetica di tipo strutturale: l'emblema dell'amore coniugale come un altre segmento di un panorama completo delle vicende d'amore"; see "La Ballata per Robert d'Estouteville," in "Due Studi su Villon," in *Con-*

If all these poems qualify for the designation courtly, in style or in reason for being or both, they form a fair-sized body of composition. The three pieces in the ducal album comprise 192 lines; count in the "Requeste au prince" and we have 227; add to this the three ballades accumulating proverbs, trifles, and contradictions, and we are at 321. If we admit the "Ballade contre les ennemis de la France" it brings in another 38; the two ballades "A s'amye" and "Pour Robert d'Estouteville," inserted into the *Testament*, raise the sub-total to 415; the two rondeaux in that work count for some 40 more. Beyond this there is a gray area; for in addition to imitating courtly themes and language Villon sometimes mocked them, as in his send-up of modish pastoral poetry, the "Contreditz franc Gontier." And in both the *Lais* and the *Testament* he off and on strikes the pose of love's martyr, victim of a *belle cruelle*, as court writers had long done and were still doing.

Depending, then, on the criteria employed, the "courtly" portion of Villon's oeuvre (some 3,300 lines in all) comprises at the least nearly one-tenth and perhaps as much as one-seventh of the total. So much for quantity; what of its character?

Briefly, this verse is skillful, technically irreproachable, sometimes witty, often still interesting, at times illumined with a personal note or a touch of creatural realism that reaches beyond the usual fare provided for polite circles. To Villon's work as a whole some of this facet of it contributes both range and depth. The "Ballade a s'amye" and the "Ballade pour Robert d'Estouteville" represent two poles of sexual love, the one extramarital, venal, and heartless, its aftertaste metallic, its afterlife one of imagined vengeance; the other conjugal yet chivalrous, loyal, fruitful, a source of enduring joy, a refuge from raging Fortune. As for the "Ballade de Fortune," immediately inspired though it apparently was by compositions of another, and courtly, writer, it compresses into 41 lines a settled attitude frequently revealed, but dispersed and never elsewhere developed, in the personal poetry.[18]

Yet these are exceptional achievements. Except for the times when Villon is seeking patronage along lines coinciding with his own preoccupations, his courtly poetry is largely impersonal, its attitudes borrowed, its language conventional; it is scarcely distinguishable from the abundant production of other writers busy at the rhetoric of reward. Only the manuscript and early-print tradition, and here and there an authorial name, serve to identify these pieces as authentic. If the works in question constituted all of Villon's *oeuvre*, or were representative of it, it is doubtful that he would be much read today. And if he had achieved his goal of becoming a court poet, he would perforce have written copiously, if not exclusively, in that vein.

But, unlike Jean Meschinot, Georges Chastellain, and a whole population of other versifiers, Villon was no prince-pleaser. Even his attempts to ingratiate himself with a patron of writers and himself a poet, Charles d'Orléans, produced only temporary support. Villon remained the talented outsider. His courtly poetry was composed in

---

tributi dell'Istituto di Filologia Moderna (Serie francese, Volume settimo) (Milan: Editrice Vita e Pensiero, 1972), pp. 15–49; the quotation is from p. 49.
18 See my "Fortune versus François," in press.

and for a milieu foreign to him, a culture within the larger late-medieval culture, into which he could ultimately not be assimilated. The bulk of his work comprises the poetry of failure; failure was in fact what permitted and indeed inspired him to write for himself, for his marginalized companions, for his ideal reader – and for all of humanity that has known rejection, or that can at least sympathize with one who knew it all too well.

ANIMATING MEDIEVAL COURT SATIRE

Ad Putter

In this essay I want to look at some later medieval court satires in order to set a context for Skelton's *Bowge of Court*. My overall argument will be that Skelton's radical fictionalization of himself as a naive allegorical character enabled him to get around an embarrassing contradiction that debilitates earlier court satires, namely the position of moral and ontological security which the satirist of the court occupies within the slippery world that he exposes. I hope to show *en passant* that Skelton's innovative use of personification allegory in the *Bowge* has an interesting analogue in an earlier French court satire: *L'Abuzé en court.*

Let me begin simply by observing one of the curious facts about the genre of curial satire. From the twelfth century onwards, court satires denounced the rampant ambition, the backbiting and depravity of life at court, but almost without exception they were both composed and avidly read by courtiers themselves.[1] Like the tantalizingly similar spoofs on university life – with their scenes of graduates licking the boots of professors, of ambitious upstarts jockeying for positions of power – actually written for academics by academics, the most rancorous criticism of the court tends to reduce itself on closer inspection to an amusing insiders' game.

In the medieval and early Tudor period, that game became something of an art form, produced only by the most committed courtiers, whose belief in the social superiority of the court, or in the ultimate advantageousness of attending it, was strong enough to survive any awful truth about it. The goliardic poet of the thirteenth-century *Song of the Times* frankly admits as much when he concludes his poem about the hollowness of court existence with this last stanza:

> Rimatus omnes curias
> magnas, parvas, et medias,
> episcopales, regias,
> curiarum incurias
> multiformes et varias
> dum video, irrideo
> nec ideo
> a curiis abstineo
> sed ipsas semper adeo
> rimatus omnes curias.   (21–30)[2]

---

[1] Claus Uhlig's *Hofkritik im England des Mittelalters und der Renaissance* (Berlin: Walter de Gruyter, 1973) discusses the evolution of court satire from the reign of Henry II onwards.
[2] Thomas Wright, ed., *Anecdota Literaria* (London, 1844).

> (I have inspected all courts – big, small, and medium, episcopal and royal –
> and when I see the neglectfulness of courts in its many forms and variety I
> ridicule courts. I do not therefore stay away from them, but I am always in
> attendance, though I have inspected all the courts.)

The court and the court satirist may not always be happy bedfellows, but the mutual
satisfaction they derive from their relationship precludes an easy separation: the
satirist abides at court because he knows that he is fed by the hand he bites, and the
court goes on feeding the court satirist because the latter's ill will is perhaps the
greatest tribute to the court's power of attraction, a power so great that it can keep the
satirist in place despite his expressed desire to be somewhere else.

As the *Song of the Times* suggests, the satirist belongs to the court, and rather than
imagining his attacks to come from outside the cultural environment of the court, we
should see the genre of curial satire as a discursive possibility within it – as one of
many games that courtiers play. One poet who with wonderful honesty lays bare his
complicity with the courtiers he derides is William Dunbar. As a poet making a
living for himself at the court of James IV of Scotland, Dunbar might be expected to
know all about the court satirist's complicity with his fellow courtiers; but Dunbar's
frankness about being no better than anyone else at court is refreshing.[3] The poem *Be
divers wyis and operatiounes* belongs to the period of Dunbar's service at court
(1500–1513), and begins, conventionally enough, with a description of various
courtiers vying for the king's attention:

> Be divers wyis and operatiounes
> Men makis in court thair solistatiounes:
> Sum be service and diligence,
> Sum be continuall residence;
> Sum one his substance dois abyd
> Quhill fortoune do for him provyd;
> Sum singis, sum dances, sum tellis storyis,
> Sum lait at evin bringis in the moryis.
> Sum flirdis, sum fenʒeis and sum flatteris,
> Sum playis the fuill and all owt clatteris.   (1–10)[4]

At the end of the poem Dunbar himself takes up the familiar stance of the naive
courtier who cannot play along with such wicked games:

> My sempillnes among the laiff
> Wait off na way, so God me sayff,
> Bot with ane humble cheir and face
> Refferris me to the kyngis grace.   (21–24)

This avowal of "sempillnes" enables Dunbar to state his purpose with sufficient
clarity:

---

[3] On Dunbar's involvement "in the society he criticizes" see Priscilla Bawcutt, *Dunbar the
Maker* (Oxford: Clarendon Press, 1992), p. 114.
[4] *The Poems of William Dunbar*, ed. James Kinsley (Oxford: Clarendon Press, 1979), no. 20.

> Me think his graciows countenance
> In ryches is my sufficiance. (25–26)

As in many other lyrics, however, Dunbar's self-presentation, in this case as a paragon of innocence and "sempillnes", has a knowing and self-exposing reflexivity[5] – especially in this poem, where, among the "solisitaris" of the court, Dunbar's gaze falls on one courtier who shows an uncanny resemblance to the poet himself. He is, like Dunbar, the only suitor whose stance is defined negatively, by his apparent inability to imitate the impostors around him:

> Sum man musand be the waw
> Luikis as he mycht nocht do with aw. (12–13)

Visibly distanced from the flatterers and the wheedlers, this man, like Dunbar himself, appears "simple" in comparison with the others. His is in fact the stereotypical stance of the court satirist. He stands, as Dunbar does in some of his lyrics, on the court's periphery,[6] distanced from the corruption around him, but all the better placed to observe it. He is in the court, but only just: clearly dissociated from it by his apparent incapacity to "do with aw," to participate in the posturing which the court demands from its members.

But Dunbar's "luikis as" gives the game away. And by revealing that "certain man," his double, to be a posturer along with the other courtiers, he cannot fail to draw attention to the role-playing involved in his own pose of "sempillnes." In staging the courtly performance of good faith, the court satirist is always himself a leading actor, his honesty merely one of the possible roles which courtiers adopt as they labour "for premocione" (18).[7] Sycophants and moralists; loudmouths and loners; and last but not least the "plain-speaking" satirist himself – everyone is implicated in power politics; for how can one be an "outsider" to power at court, when not playing along is one way of playing the game?

Dunbar's insight into the poet's inevitable collusion with the collective false self he satirizes seems to me singularly perceptive about the practice of court satire in general; though, obviously, the cost of his witty self-exposure is that his satire loses all credibility as a moral indictment of court life. Unless the satirist conceals his collaboration with the enemy (a feat which, as we shall see, *L'Abuzé en court* and Skelton's *Bowge of Court* manage most successfully), the "doubleness" of his voice

---

[5] On Dunbar's self-conscious poses see Anthony J. Hasler, "William Dunbar: The Elusive Subject," in *Bryght Lanternes: Essays on the Language and Literature of Medieval Scotland*, ed. J. Derrick McClure and Michael R.G. Spiller (Aberdeen: Aberdeen University Press, 1989), pp. 194–208.

[6] For example, in *Schir, at this feist of benefice* (K 40), Dunbar stands at the margin: "Sum swelleis swan, sum swelleis duke,/ And I stand fastand in a nuke" (6–7).

[7] It is worth quoting Stephen Greenblatt on Thomas Wyatt, another court satirist *cum* courtier who shows an awareness that the satirist's artless rectitude may itself be a duplicitous pose: "Power, with its distorting influence, was supposed to be 'out there', the object of high-minded contempt, but the satirist himself stands on morally uncertain ground – his position may be itself a kind of pose taken in response to the dictates of power": *Renaissance Self-Fashioning* (Chicago and London: University of Chicago Press, 1980), p. 135.

cannot but inhibit the persuasive force of his protests. Chartier's influential *Libellus curialis* is in this respect representative of the weakness of most medieval court satires. Like other contemporary writers of curial satire, Nicolas of Clamanges and Jean de Montreuil, Alain Chartier was in fact firmly ensconced in the court.[8] When he wrote his *Libellus curialis*, c. 1422, he was secretary to the Dauphin, the future Charles VII.[9] Chartier's satire purports to be a letter to his brother, warning him not to join him at court. As the extracts from Chartier below show, the catalogue of the mortal dangers of court life is conventional. Chartier pictures the court as a place of flattery and conspiracy, where the courtier spends his time warding off the plots of his fellows, only to be supplanted by a rival. I quote from the Middle English translation, the *Curial*, made by Caxton in 1484 at the request of Anthony Woodville, Lord Rivers:

> Another new one cometh to the court and shall supplante thy benedicion [office]/ And shall take it gylefully fro the . . .   (p. 12)[10]

What is more, everyone who joins the court must necessarily give up his own morals:

> Thenne oughtest thou to knowe/ that thou shalt haue habundaunce [read: abandoned] thy self/ whan thou shalt wylle to poursewe the court/ whych maketh a man to leue hys propre maners/ And to applye himself to the maners of other.   (p. 7)[11]

If any courtier does not arm himself with complicity, writes Chartier, he will not survive:

> Who is he thenne that may kepe hym that he be not corrupt or coromped/ or who is he that shall escape without hauyng harme . . .   (p. 5)

These passages show that the contradictory status of Chartier himself, as both courtier *par excellence* and courtier's critic, resurfaces as an internal contradiction in the *Curial* itself. On the subject of the court, we hear the earnest voice of someone who has an insider's knowledge of its distortions, but who has somehow managed to preserve the integrity that authenticates the truth of his propositions. The paradox is encapsulated in a single line from the *Curial*:

> And yf thou wylt vse my counseyl/ Take none example by me . . .   (p. 3)

---

8   See Ezio Ornato, *Jean Muret et ses amis Nicholas de Clamanges et Jean de Montreuil* (Geneva: Droz, 1969), pp. 57–66, and Pascale Bourgain-Hemeryck, ed., *Les oeuvres latines d'Alain Chartier* (Paris: Centre national de recherche scientifique, 1977), p. 73.

9   On Chartier's career at the royal court, see C.J.H. Walravens, *Alain Chartier* (Amsterdam: Meulenhoff-Didier, 1971), pp. 21–26.

10 *Caxton's Curial*, ed. Paul Meyer and F.J. Furnivall, EETS ES 54 (London: Oxford University Press, 1888).

11 The English "haue habundaunce" is a mistranslation of the French original, which reads: "adonc devras tu sçavoir que tu aras habandonné toy mesmez" ("and so you should know that you will have abandoned yourself"): *Les oeuvres latines d'Alain Chartier*, ed. Bourgain-Hemeryck, p. 355.

In his capacity as satirist, the narrator dispenses trustworthy advice, but as a courtier he cannot be relied on. How, then, are we supposed to take the "counseyl" of a courtier whose "example" must not be followed?[12]

In passing himself off as a sincere courtier, the court satirist must always pose as someone who has escaped the all-pervasive and "inescapable" artificiality of court life. One unfortunate consequence that follows from the satirist's double life as an insider and an outsider at court is that satires like Chartier's can never develop into a story, although they have all the potential elements of one. All narrative ingredients are present: we have a hero in the form of the narrator; his enemies in the shape of deceiving courtiers; and, finally, the promised ending: the inevitable demise or contamination of the innocent. But Chartier cannot set the story in motion, cannot fully realize the triumph of evil, without compromising the position of immunity from which he speaks. This is why the stasis of Chartier's plot renders his picture of court life curiously reassuring rather than unsettling. One needs, after all, only identify with Chartier's narrator to believe that at court flattery and deception can be recognized as such; that the courtier can remain untarnished by the curial experience; that it is possible to be *at* the court but not *of* it. To escape from the purportedly inescapable perversions of language and identity at court, we need do no more than follow the satirist through the prison door which he leaves wide open.

It is the absence of such an escape-route that makes two satires – the anonymous *L'Abuzé en court* (c. 1450) and Skelton's *Bowge of Court* (c. 1498) – so much more effective. *L'Abuzé en court* deserves wider recognition. Widely disseminated in the fifteenth century in manuscripts and in printed editions,[13] it is both the closest analogue to Skelton's *Bowge of Court* and a compelling work of fiction in its own right. Like Skelton's *Bowge*, it is a personification allegory, which describes the perils of court not from the perspective of a detached narrator, but from the point of view of a simpleton called L'Abuzé (The Deluded One) – comparable with Skelton's Dread – who is himself a personification trapped inside the allegorical representation of court life. By giving the role of the satirist to a naive persona, the poet of *L'Abuzé* succeeds in setting the potential plot of earlier satires in motion, and in telling the

---

12 Another court satire that throws up the same contradictions as Chartier's *Curial* is Sir Francis Brian's *Dispraise of the Life of a Courtier* (London, 1548), an English adaptation of a court satire by Guevara. The narrator of the *Dispraise* urges everyone to flee from the court because it turns people into liars, as witness the fate of the author: "I went hither true and meanyng truth, and returned a lyar" (ch. 18). As in Chartier's *Curial*, we are asked to disbelieve courtiers, but to believe the propositions of the satirist who is, or has been, a courtier himself. Like Chartier, Brian attempts to speak at once with the voice of experience (as courtier) and with the voice of innocence (as satirist), and consequently fails to convince as either. And like Chartier, too, Sir Francis Brian lived this self-contradiction: his "dispraise" of the life of a courtier did not prevent him from spending his notoriously riotous life as "one of the kynges most honorable preuy chamber," a position proudly announced in his preface to the *Dispraise*. On the historical Brian, see Greenblatt, *Renaissance Self-Fashioning*, pp. 133–35; and David Starkey, "The Court: Castiglione's Ideal and Tudor Reality," *Journal of the Warburg and Courtauld Institutes* 45 (1982), pp. 232–39.
13 The first three printed editions were published in Bruges (1480), Lyon (1484), and Vienna (1484). See the introduction to *L'Abuzé en court*, ed. Roger Dubuis, Textes Littéraires Français (Geneva: Droz, 1973). Quotations from *L'Abuzé* will be from this edition.

story of vice triumphant of which earlier satirists speak, but which their position of secure omniscience prevents them from delivering.

L'Abuzé en court is thus best described as an animation of the warnings of earlier court satires. The hero (or anti-hero) of the story, Abuzé, has just finished his schooling when he is waylaid by two treacherous courtiers – Abuz and Folcuider – who persuade the credulous hero to join them at their wonderful abode at court. Their weapon is flattery, and in this respect *L'Abuzé* toes the line of earlier satires, which present courtiers as "people deceyuing by faire language" (*Curial*, pp. 4–5). However, the personification of the vices at court allows *L'Abuzé en court* to show us flattery in action, and so to breathe life into the genre's conventional *topoi*. The following passage illustrates how Abuz and Folcuider set about luring Abuzé to court:

> Abuz: 'Et je ne sçay (se dist Abuz) si sa pensee est en cest estat demeurer et si jamais vouldroit soy enhardir a pouoir a cestuy bien parvenir, car il est bel enfant et jeune et d'assez gracieuse maniere et propre pour en tel lieu estre.'
> 'O, saincte Marie (dist Folcuider) comment madame nostre maistresse le trouveroit propre a son gré! Et comment luy feroit voluntiers des biens assez et largement!'
> A dit Abuz, 'Parler de cela est du moins. Car, en moins d'une seule annee, seroit tout plain de toute richesse.'   (pp. 33–34)

> (Deceit: 'I don't know (says Deceit) whether it is his intention to remain in this state, or whether he will ever find the courage to be able to arrive at this joy, for he is a beautiful young man and is gracious and fitting enough to be in this place.'
> 'O, saint Mary (says Vanity) how our lady would find him to her liking! Plenty are the gifts that she would freely and liberally bestow on him!'
> And Deceit added, 'That at the very least! For in less than one year, he would be full of riches!')

At this point Abuzé notices something rather unusual about Folcuider's and Abuz's physique. The first has excessively long ears, while the second is disfigured. Abuz obligingly explains: his own deformities are the result of years of toil in the service of Lady Court, while Folcuider's long ears are likewise diagnosed as a *déformation professionnelle*:

> Et ainsi le convient il avoir a celuy qui veust estre en grace de nostre maistresse la Court. Car certes, mon enfant, elle a, de sa propre condition et coustume, aymé fort les grandes oreilles, lesquelles a plusieurs peuent donner souvent logis. Et, a besoing, celuy qui attent d'elle a proauffiter doit avoir en soy troys choses qui sont telles qui pourras oïr. C'est assavoir:
>
> > Tout esgarder et faindre rien ne voir,
> > Tout escouter, monstrant rien ne sçavoir,
> > Mot ne sonner de cas qu'il scet et voit.
> > Qu'ainsi ne fait tart a son cas porvoit.   (p. 37)

> (To have ears like this is proper for anyone who wishes to be in the grace of our lady the Court. Because certainly, young man, it is her condition and custom to love long ears greatly, which can often secure an office for many. And, of necessity, he who intends to profit by her needs to have in himself three qualities, which are those you may now hear, namely:
>
> To watch all, and pretend to see nothing; to hear all, without showing any sign of knowledge; not to say a word about a thing that he knows and sees. Whoever fails to do this, reaches his goal too late.)

Both in their words and in their iconographic appearance, the vices at Court are totally transparent, but Abuzé, who also does his name justice, proves utterly incapable of decoding the allegory he is in. He lacks, as *L'Abuzé* puts it later, the assistance of Dame Cognaissance. For years he labours fruitlessly at court in the hope of gaining Lady Court's recognition. But when the promises of Lady Court come to nought, he is abandoned by his friends and finally replaced by another courtier. Destitute and broken, he leaves the court, and takes up residence at an almshouse for the poor. Here he tells his life's story to the author inside the text, L'Aucteur, who comes to the startling realization that Abuzé's history bears an uncanny resemblance to his own:

> Car je me suis tenu en court, ja peut avoir l'espace de xv. ans ou de vingt ans, en laquelle j'ay assez peu proffité. Et quant je vous ay oy de vous mesmes nommer le povre homme abusé en court, ung doubte m'est entré subitement au cueur, comme si en ce cas me touchoit en partie cestuy nom.   (pp. 9–10)

> (For I have been at court, perhaps for the space of fifteen or even twenty years, but it has given me little gain. And when I heard you call yourself the poor and deluded man at court, a doubt suddenly entered my heart, as if that name partly concerned me.)

Not unlike Skelton's *Bowge of Court*, *L'Abuzé en court* gestures towards a veiled truth behind the allegory by suggesting that the naive hero stylizes certain aspects of the author's reality.

It is not impossible that Skelton knew *L'Abuzé en court* – it had appeared on the continent in at least four printed editions before 1498, when Skelton came to write his *Bowge of Court*[14] – but there are no verbal echoes to prove it. Even so, the French text claims our attention for its pioneering use of personification allegory, in which the detached "I" of earlier court satires is pitched directly against the allegorized vices and ruined in his dealings with them. For this reason alone, *L'Abuzé en court* is worth comparing with Skelton's *Bowge of Court*, in which the satirist similarly abandons his position of omniscience and security, is reduced to the personification Dread, and is driven out by a number of allegorized vices that he cannot comprehend, let alone satirize.

One short episode from the *Bowge* may indicate the similarity in technique between Skelton and the poet of *L'Abuzé en court*. After Skelton has fallen asleep, he, or more precisely, his displaced self, "Dread," is approached by Favell on the ship of the Bowge of Court. As in *L'Abuzé en court*, the allegorical characters are instantly "readable" to anyone but Dread himself, who, always eager to please, tries hard to make friends among the seven vices at court:

> And oftentymes I wolde myselfe avaunce
> With them to make solace and pleasure;

---

14 Melvin J. Tucker has proposed an earlier date: "Setting in Skelton's *Bowge of Courte*: A Speculation," *English Language Notes* 7 (1970), pp. 168–75. In a detailed discussion of the evidence, Greg Walker restates the case for the conventional date of 1498 or 1499: *John Skelton and the Politics of the 1520s* (Cambridge: Cambridge University Press, 1988), pp. 10–15.

But my dysporte they could not well endure:
They sayde they hated for to dele with Drede.   (143–46)[15]

Already feeling himself to be out of place, he is addressed as follows by Favell:

Favell

'Noo thyng erthely that I wonder so sore
As of your connynge, that is so excellent;
Deynte to have with us suche one in store,
So vertuously that hath his dayes spente;
Fortune to you gyftes of grace hath lente;
Loo, what it is a man to have connynge!
All erthely tresoure it is surmountynge.

Ye be an apte man, as ony can be founde
To dwell with us and serve my ladyes grace.
Ye be to her, yea, worth a thousande pounde.
I herde her speke of you within shorte space,
Whan there were dyverse that sore dyde you manace.
And, though I say it, I was myselfe your frende,
For here be dyverse that to you be unkynde'. . .

Drede

Than thanked I hym for his grete gentylnes.
But, as me thoughte, he ware on hym a cloke
That lyned was with doubtfull doublenes.
Me thoughte, of wordes that he hade full a poke;
His stomak stuffed ofte tymes did reboke.   (148–80)

One thing which the allegorized characters in the *Bowge of Court* are upfront about is the vices which they stand for. Like Folcuider with the long ears, Favell wears his heart on his sleeve: his compliments are excessive; his own disclaimers – "though I say it" – transparently rhetorical; and the mantle "lyned . . . with doubtful doubleness" makes a grotesque exhibition of his moral status.

However, by descending to the same level as these abstractions, Skelton is able to make his horror-story of court life come true at the expense of Dread, who, for all his naivety, retains a recognizable likeness to Skelton, the poet with "connynge", as Favell flatteringly refers to him. Half-taken in by Favell's "gentylnes" and alarmed by his suggestion (whether true or untrue, we never discover) that some unnamed entities are scheming against him, Skelton's persona is reduced to paralysis and paranoia, so that his name "Dread" increasingly turns into his fate. The nightmare ends, like *L'Abuzé en court*, with the disturbing triumph of evil and the downfall of the hero. When the words of the other vices at court have almost literally scared Dread to death, he rushes to the shipboard to throw himself overboard – at which point Skelton wakes up and returns to himself.

It might well be argued that Skelton's general picture of the court is conventional

---

[15] Quotations from the *Bowge of Court* are from the edition by John Scattergood, *John Skelton: The Complete Poems* (Harmondsworth: Penguin, 1983).

and, if anything, even more unreal and stylized than that of earlier court satires, such as Chartier's *Curial*.[16] Thus, the case for Skelton's literary achievement cannot rest primarily on the greater verisimilitude of his picture of court life, as Stanley Fish would argue:

> Skelton takes the literary man out of an isolation that is a bit unreal and brings him back to the moment of contact when the press of his antagonists is physical . . . It is something like what happens when Wordsworth decides to walk through his landscape rather than imagining it; the genre ceases to be a way of thinking and becomes a way of experiencing.[17]

In one way this observation gets to the heart of the matter. In earlier court satires (with the exception of *L'Abuzé*), the satirist appears immune from danger and corruption; and his warnings about a dangerous "moment of contact" cannot but lose force when that moment has plainly been survived by the satirist himself. The *Bowge of Court*, by contrast, actualizes this disastrous moment, as Skelton transports himself, in the figure of Dread, into the midst of satiric abstractions and commonplaces (the vices at court, the ship of fools, etc.) that have horribly taken on life.

The effect is chilling, but it is clearly not through realism that Skelton has achieved it. On the contrary, what Fish calls the "unreal" situation of the literary man isolated in his study surely represents the historical reality of Skelton far more closely than his nightmare. Literary men in princely libraries is largely what most court satirists (Skelton included) were; and their power to unsettle the reader thus depends on their ability to conceal their historical situation rather than on their ability to describe it realistically. Skelton possessed that talent, and his *Bowge of Court* bears out the paradoxical truth that the court satirist achieves credibility only by drastically reinventing himself, by fully entering into the fiction of court satire, as Skelton does when he becomes an allegorical personification called "Dread".

Skelton's actual circumstances at the time of writing the *Bowge* – when he was employed as tutor to the future king, Henry VIII – do not exempt him from the charge that could be levelled at most other court satirists: that these self-styled enemies of the court are in fact its closest allies.[18] But Skelton's self-displacement as a personification in an allegory, perhaps inspired by *L'Abuzé en court*, ensures that this contradiction does not appear in his fiction. Chartier, like so many court satirists before him, did not filter out his historical position so successfully, for by continuing to speak about the court as an insider he cannot but offer the reassurance that the

---

[16] A.R. Heiserman traces many themes and motifs of Skelton's *Bowge* back to earlier satires: *Skelton and Satire* (Chicago: University of Chicago Press, 1961), 14–65.

[17] Stanley Fish, *John Skelton's Poetry* (New Haven and London: Yale University Press, 1965), p. 78.

[18] The fact that Skelton entered the priesthood in 1498 has led to speculation that he momentarily had "genuine scruples" about his life at court: Alistair Fox, *Politics and Literature in the Reigns of Henry VII and Henry VIII* (Oxford: Blackwell, 1989), pp. 26–27. More likely, Skelton took holy orders in order to qualify for any ecclesiastical benefice that might come his way in time of need. It was, at any rate, not for another four or five years that Skelton took the jump which Dread makes in the *Bowge of Court*, leaving Prince Henry's court for a benefice in the country.

supposedly inescapable dangers of the court are in fact surmountable, that one can know the court's darkest secrets and still retain one's integrity. Only Skelton and *L'Abuzé en court* take the propositions of earlier court satires to their logical conclusion: that those who are truly innocent of the insidious intrigues at court cannot have the power to detect and resist them; that if the only way to survive at court is to become an accomplice, then the honest soul, be it Dread or Abuzé, must necessarily perish. In their downfall, Dread and Abuzé dramatize the inevitable fall of the "nice guy" at court. And so, in the *Bowge of Court*, bafflement and naivety, rather than the ability to strip and expose, establish the satirist's honesty, which is why the pretence of innocence continues after Skelton in the poem wakes up, writes down the story, and, still unsure about its import, passes the interpretative burden to the reader:

> Now constrewe ye what is the resydewe.   (539)

To this the gifted courtier responds by feigning innocence in turn: "Me? Others at court know better."

II. FASHIONING HISTORY AND ROMANCE

LA FIN DES *CHRONIQUES* DE FROISSART ET LE TRAGIQUE DE LA COUR

Michel Zink

Le lieu du tragique, c'est la cour. Selon une formule trop rebattue, "la tragédie, c'est une reine qui a des malheurs". Les pièges du destin sont plus effrayants quand ils se referment sur les grands, la chute des puissants est plus pitoyable, leur sort plus exemplaire que ceux du commun: "La tragédie est l'imitation d'une action noble", "d'hommes nobles".[1] Ce tragique qui s'abat sur les maîtres du monde, la tragédie comme forme littéraire n'en a pas le monopole. Il appartient tout autant à l'écriture de l'histoire. Aristote le dit. Tacite ou de Gaulle le savent. Le tragique dissimulé sous les fastes de la cour et qui marque jusqu'à ses petitesses, ses intrigues, ses pauvres ambitions, ses misérables trahisons, c'est celui qui transparaît dans le fiel de Saint-Simon. Et la tragédie shakespearienne est tragique parce qu'elle est investie par l'histoire, et par l'histoire des rois.

Que de parrainages écrasants pour Froissart, dont je m'apprête à parler ici! Froissart n'est ni Tacite, ni Saint-Simon, ni le général de Gaulle. Il est encore moins Shakespeare, et la comparaison est d'autant plus cruelle pour lui qu'elle est possible, puisque le personnage et la chute de Richard II, qui vont nous occuper un instant, l'autorisent.[2] Il n'a certainement pas lu la *Poétique* d'Aristote. Comme il paraît excessif, saugrenu peut-être, de lui prêter même le sens du tragique! Cet homme d'humeur liante et facile, aimant l'aisance et le confort, aisément flatté du cas qu'on fait de lui, aisément ébloui par les "grandeurs d'établissement"; cet historien qui ne sait que placer les drames de son temps sous le signe de la prouesse et d'un avènement de la chevalerie;[3] ce poète dont les confidences oscillent entre la mièvrerie d'une éducation sentimentaie et la satisfaction d'une réussite professionnelle; ce romancier qui poursuit inlassablement jusqu'à leur conclusion heureuse le récit gratifiant des exploits et des amours: que sait-il du tragique?

S'il en sait quelque chose, c'est dans les cours qu'il a pu l'apprendre. Il a pu y voir la machine infernale pousser les rois à œuvrer à leur propre perte et à celle de leur lignée. A sa manière, il le montre. Le roi de France Jean II le Bon fait arrêter les amis

---

1 Aristote, *Poétique*, 6 (1449b) et 5 (ibid.).
2 Voir Peter F. Ainsworth, *Jean Froissart and the Fabric of History. Truth, Myth and Fiction in the 'Chroniques'* (Oxford: Clarendon Press, 1990), pp. 172–73. On trouvera dans cet excellent livre des analyses et des informations nombreuses sur les principaux points du présent exposé.
3 Voir le prologue du livre I des *Chroniques*, sur lequel on reviendra plus loin.

de son propre fils, le dauphin Charles, sous les yeux et à la table de celui-ci, pour les faire exécuter dans l'heure: meurtre du fils à peine déplacé, geste sanglant qui, sans le toucher, l'atteint.[4] Ce meurtre du fils, le comte de Foix Gaston Phébus le commet, en tuant de sa main son unique héritier légitime.[5] Son héritage n'ira pas à son sang, puisque son bâtard Yvain ne pourra s'assurer de la succession qu'il lui destinait.[6] La pomme empoisonnée que Valentine Visconti (selon Froissart!) destine au dauphin cause la mort de son propre fils.[7] La folie atteint la France et son roi.[8] Celle de Charles VI est aggravée par l'irresponsabilité de sa cour. Sa personne est menacée par la frivolité d'une mascarade indécente, le bal des ardents, et par la criminelle imprudence de son frère.[9] L'Angleterre voit deux de ses rois humiliés, déposés, assassinés.

Mais n'est-ce pas trop prêter à Froissart que de le croire sensible au tragique de tels événements et soucieux de les mettre en valeur? Sa tendance ne le pousse-t-elle pas toujours vers l'édulcoration? N'épargne-t-il pas les grands plus qu'il ne les accable? Chez lui, Edouard III ne viole pas la comtesse de Salisbury. Certes, George Diller a montré qu'en la circonstance la version défavorable au souverain, celle de Jean le Bel, est peut-être une fable de la propagande française.[10] Mais ailleurs? Jean le Bel peint avec une férocité allègre le double remariage du vieux roi Philippe VI de Valois et de son fils, le futur Jean le Bon, tous deux veufs: ce sont des mariages consanguins pour lesquels ils finissent par arracher le consentement du pape; ils se disputent d'abord la même femme, que le père, dont la mort est toute proche, finit par prendre pour lui en usant de son droit régalien, tandis que le fils est accusé à mots couverts d'avoir empoisonné sa défunte épouse et se distingue par son avidité et ses malversations financières.[11] Pas un mot de ces turpitudes dans la version de Frois-

---

4 Froissart présente implicitement l'épisode et les lettres de défi que les parents des victimes (Philippe de Navarre pour Charles le Mauvais emprisonné, Geoffroy d'Harcourt pour son neveu exécuté) adressent à Jean le Bon comme une constellation de signes néfastes annonciateurs du désastre de Poitiers, quelques mois plus tard: *Œuvres de Froissart*, éd. Kervyn de Lettenhove, 28 tomes (Bruxelles: Académie Royale de Belgique, 1867–77), t. 5, pp. 358–60. On citera ici les *Chroniques* de Froissart dans cette édition (abrégée dorénavant en "Kervyn") de préférence à celle de la Société de l'Histoire de France (éd. S. Luce, G. Raynaud, L. et A. Mirot, 15 volumes, Paris, 1869–), car cette dernière, inachevée, ne donne pas le Livre IV dont nous allons surtout nous occuper. Toutefois, on fera parfois allusion à la division du texte de Froissart en chapitres telle qu'elle apparaît dans le ms. Paris BN F. fr. 8329 que reproduit la vieille édition Buchon (*Les Chroniques de sire Jean Froissart*, éd. J.A.C. Buchon, 3 tomes (1835, nouvelle édition Paris: F. Wattelier, 1867). Enfin, on donnera chaque fois la référence à l'édition de Buchon en même temps qu'à celle de Kervyn, car la première, plus maniable et moins rare, est souvent commode pour une consultation rapide des *Chroniques* de Froissart (ici: Buchon, t. I, pp. 323–25, chap. XX du Livre I).
5 Kervyn, t. 11, pp. 89–100 (Buchon, t. II, pp. 400–04, chap. XIII du Livre III).
6 Kervyn, t. 14, pp. 339–50 (Buchon, t. III, pp. 119–31, chap. XXIII du Livre IV).
7 Kervyn, t. 15, pp. 260–61 (Buchon, t. III, p. 243, chap. L du Livre IV).
8 Kervyn, t. 15, pp. 21–48 (Buchon, t. III, pp. 153–63, chap. XXIX du Livre IV).
9 Kervyn, t. 15, pp. 84–92 (Buchon, t. III, pp. 176–79, chap. XXXII du Livre IV).
10 George T. Diller, *Attitudes chevaleresques et réalités politiques chez Froissart. Microlectures du premier livre des "Chroniques"* (Genève: Droz, 1984), "V. Le destin du comte et de la comtesse de Salisbury dans les *Chroniques*," pp. 77–156.
11 Chap. LXXXIV, éd. Jules Viard et Eugène Déprez, *Chronique de Jean le Bel* (Paris, 1905),

sart.[12] Et pourtant, quel prélude elles lui offraient au conflit qui peu après oppose ce fils devenu roi à son propre fils! De même, sous sa plume, le drame de la cour de Foix n'est qu'une suite de malentendus et de hasards malheureux: le jeune Gaston ignorait que la poudre que lui avait remise son oncle était du poison destiné à faire périr son père, et le coup de couteau mortel que celui-ci lui porte était accidentel. D'autres chroniqueurs affirment au contraire que le jeune Gaston s'apprêtait au parricide et que son père l'a tué délibérément. Chaque fois Froissart paraît un peu trop porté à admettre et à diffuser la vérité officielle. La vision traditionnelle qu'on a de lui en paraît confortée: celle d'un esprit superficiel, ne recueillant que l'écume des événements, respectueux des valeurs établies, fasciné comme une midinette par les familles royales, parcourant l'existence avec un point de vue sur le monde et une image du monde qui sont ceux de *Points de vue Images du monde,* aussi incapable en un mot de saisir le tragique de l'existence que les ressorts de l'histoire.

Que cette vision soit fausse, que Froissart ait évolué au cours de sa vie jusqu'à porter sur les hommes en général et les princes en particulier un regard plus lucide et plus sévère, bien des indices le montrent, et d'abord le pessimisme qui marque à la fois l'ultime rédaction du livre I et le livre IV. C'est un point que les exégètes les plus récents des *Chroniques* ont bien mis en évidence. Mais il y a encore autre chose. Si l'on prête le souci d'une composition à cet ouvrage en apparence si peu composé, qui paraît se laisser porter par la succession des événements et le déroulement de leur collecte, on observe que les *Chroniques* partent du tragique de la cour pour y revenir au moment de s'achever – ou de s'interrompre. On soupçonne qu'elles le font délibérément. Ce n'est pas non plus un hasard si cette cour est celle d'Angleterre, qui a vu naître Froissart écrivain et à laquelle il est revenu sur ses vieux jours offrir un dernier tribut poétique. Une fois de plus l'œuvre et l'image de l'auteur qui s'y dessine prennent sens l'une par l'autre.

Telle est l'idée directrice du présent exposé. Les questions posées par la fin des *Chroniques* de Froissart, la petite énigme qu'elle constitue, peuvent s'éclairer si l'on prête attention à la symétrie entre le début et la fin de l'ouvrage, au type de réflexion qu'elle suppose, au contenu comme à l'écriture des derniers chapitres. Froissart part de Jean le Bel, le copie ou l'imite, se l'approprie, le prolonge, le dépasse, et pour finir profite des fausses répétitions de l'histoire pour clore son ouvrage sur un épisode analogue à celui qui l'a ouvert et qu'il empruntait à son devancier. Cet épisode ne serait donc pas le dernier par hasard – parce que la mort aurait arrêté la main de Froissart ou pour toute autre raison – mais de façon méditée. Et cette méditation porterait sur la mort des rois et les jeux du destin.

La difficulté avec Froissart est qu'il est trop connu sans l'être assez. Résumer pour des médiévistes les passages cruciaux des *Chroniques* est aussi ridicule que de leur raconter *Le Chevalier au Lion.* Mais c'est pourtant un auteur qu'il est permis de ne pas avoir bien lu: son ignorance, au jeu "d'Humiliation" cher à David Lodge,

---

t. II, pp. 182–87. Voir Michel Zink, "The Time of the Plague and the Order of Writing: Jean le Bel, Froissart, Machaut," dans *Contexts: Style and Values in Medieval Art and Literature,* éd. Daniel Poirion et Nancy Freeman Regalado, *Yale French Studies,* 1991, pp. 270–71.
[12] Kervyn, t. 5, p. 252 (Buchon, t. I, p. 283, chap. Premier de la deuxième partie du Livre I). Froissart note seulement que la dispense du pape a été nécessaire pour les deux mariages.

rapporte moins de points que celle de Chrétien de Troyes. Il faut donc malgré tout rappeler d'un mot ce qui pour beaucoup ici va de soi.

Après un prologue qui leur est propre, qui varie au demeurant avec les rédactions et sur lequel nous reviendrons, les *Chroniques* ont pour entrée en matière un développement emprunté à Jean le Bel, comme le seront les premiers chapitres. Chacun sait, dit le chanoine de Liège, dont Froissart répète les propos, qu'il y a en Angleterre une alternance de bons et de mauvais rois. Cette observation introduit le récit de la fin misérable d'Edouard II, dont le règne est encadré par ceux de deux grands rois, Edouard Ier, son père, et Edouard III, son fils. Ce récit, scabreux et sanglant, constitue l'épisode initial de la chronique de Jean le Bel comme de celle de Froissart. Dans le premier cas, il y a à cela des raison assez naturelles. Familier de Jean de Beaumont, frère cadet du comte Guillaume Ier de Hainaut, Jean le Bel l'a accompagné en 1327 dans son expédition contre les Ecossais au service de la reine Isabelle et de son fils le jeune roi Edouard III après l'emprisonnement et la mort d'Edouard II. Sa chronique est le récit de ses souvenirs. Placer en prologue à ce récit celui de la fin misérable d'Edouard II est un choix qui s'impose à l'auteur de toutes les façons. Ces événements précèdent immédiatement ceux qui forment la matière de ses souvenirs. L'expédition de Jean de Beaumont trouve une justification immédiate dans les circonstances dramatiques qui ont vu le tout jeune roi accéder au trône et dans les menaces qui pèsent sur sa mère et sur lui. Elle est aussi l'application de la promesse faite deux ans plus tôt par le même Jean de Beaumont à la reine Isabelle de lui venir en aide en cas de besoin, promesse formulée lorsque la reine s'était enfuie d'auprès de son mari et s'était réfugiée sur le continent auprès de son frère, le roi de France Charles IV, puis du comte de Hainaut. Elle est ainsi étroitement liée aux péripéties qui ont marqué la fin du règne d'Edouard II. Enfin, commencer par ce règne et par le mariage du malheureux souverain avec la fille de Philippe le Bel, c'est remonter aux sources du conflit dynastique franco-anglais. Le récit a donc une double justification, au regard de sa suite immédiate et des souvenirs de l'auteur et au regard des débuts de la guerre de Cent Ans, matière des développements ultérieurs de la chronique.

Il en va un peu différemment chez Froissart. Ce récit qu'il recopie presque textuellement sur son prédécesseur ne figure peut-être en tête de son ouvrage que pour cette seule raison. Mais le contexte et les circonstances lui donnent une coloration tout autre. Froissart est sans doute né en 1337. Il est venu pour la première fois en Angleterre en 1361. En commençant sa chronique, à l'imitation de Jean le Bel, en 1325, il remonte plus de dix ans avant sa naissance. L'histoire d'Edouard II ne peut avoir chez lui pour justification de servir d'introduction à ses propres souvenirs. Sa seule fonction est d'éclairer les causes des "guerres de France et d'Angleterre", dont Froissart dit dans son prologue qu'elles sont le sujet de son ouvrage. Jean le Bel, dans le sien, définissait son sujet comme le règne d'Edouard III, perspective plus étroite, plus annalistique, exigeant moins de recul. Froissart laisse entendre qu'il remonte à une sorte de préhistoire de son sujet afin que les événements dont il traitera soient compréhensibles et en reçoivent un sens.

Du coup le poids historique et politique de l'épisode initial en est accru, en même temps qu'il invite à une réflexion sur l'histoire et sur le destin des rois et des peuples. Réflexion dont on trouve l'aboutissement dans la version de Rome, l'ultime rédaction du Livre I, où tout ce début remanié s'écarte du texte de Jean le Bel pour aller dans le sens de la brièveté synthétique, et pour mettre l'accent sur les caractères du peuple anglais. Quant à la remarque sur l'alternance d'un bon et d'un mauvais roi en Angleterre, mise en relation avec une vision élargie de l'histoire, elle prend un sens plus fort que chez Jean le Bel. Mais ce sens, cette force et leurs effets sont encore multipliés si l'on saute à l'autre bout des *Chroniques* et que l'on confronte cet épisode initial à celui qui les clôt par hasard ou, comme je le crois, de propos délibéré.

La fin des *Chroniques* de Froissart coïncide presque entièrement avec la fin de Richard II,[13] fin qui présente des analogies évidentes et bien connues avec celle d'Edouard II. Si on fait remonter cet épisode ultime, comme le récit lui-même y invite, à l'aggravation du conflit entre le roi et le duc de Gloucester, son oncle, qui aboutit à l'enlèvement et à l'assassinat de ce dernier, il occupe plus du quart du livre IV, qui traite pourtant d'événements d'une extrême ampleur. Toute la fin de l'ouvrage lui est consacrée, à l'exception de deux excursus relatant les négociations franco-impériales de Reims autour de la soustraction d'obédience, et surtout, un peu plus haut, du long épilogue du désastre de Nicopolis, avec le rachat et le retour des prisonniers. Mais ces développements sont placés de telle façon que, quels que soient en eux-mêmes leur importance et leur intérêt, il paraissent n'être là que pour rendre plus dramatique le récit des affaires d'Angleterre. L'entrelacement est ici tout entier au service du suspens.

Qu'on en juge. Le duc de Gloucester et le roi chevauchent sur le chemin de Londres:

> Là sus ung certain passage estoit en embuche le conte Mareschal moult fort accompaignié. Quant le roy deubt cheoir sus celle embusche, il se départy de son oncle, et chevaucha plus fort que il n'avoit fait par avant, et mist son oncle derrière. Et tout prestement vescy le conte Mareschal, lequel, à tout une quantité d'hommes moult bien montés et en point, sailly au devant du duc de Glocestre et le prist et dist: "Je mets la main à vous de par le roy." Le duc fut fort espovanté et non sans cause, et percheu bien que il estoit trahy. Si encommença de cryer à haulte voix après le roy. Je ne scay se le roy l'ouy ou non, mais point ne retourna, et chevaucha toujours moult devant luy, et ses gens le sieuvoient.
> Nous nous souffrirons ung petit à parler de ceste matière pour racompter de messire Jaques de Helly et de messire Jehan de Chastelmorant.[14]

Et, s'interrompant à ce moment dramatique, avec un sens aigu du feuilleton "à suivre",[15] Froissart passe à l'ambassade française auprès de Bajazet. Trois chapitres et de nombreuses pages plus loin, les captifs, parmi lesquels le futur duc de Bour-

---

[13] Il ne s'agit pas ici de revenir sur la question de l'exactitude, des erreurs ou des lacunes du récit de Froissart au regard de la réalité des événements ni même de mentionner l'abondante bibliographie touchant la chute et la mort de Richard II. Signalons seulement que Kervyn fournit en annexe à son édition un dossier abondant réunissant des extraits des chroniques et des documents essentiels (t. 16, pp. 241–410).

[14] Kervyn, t. 16, pp. 28–29.

[15] Le manuscrit suivi par Buchon va au devant de l'impatience du lecteur en l'assurant que la digression sera brève: "Nous nous souffrirons un petit à parler de celle manière et assez tôt y retournerons" (Buchon, t. III, p. 293, chap. LVII du Livre IV).

gogne Jean Sans Peur, enfin rentrés en France, il revient au malheureux duc de Gloucester. Mais cette longue interruption lui est un prétexte pour rappeler alors les relations entre le roi et son oncle et pour résumer les épisodes précédents:

> Vous sçavés, si comme il est icy dessus contenu, en notre histoire où je parle des haynes couvertes lesquelles estoient engendrées de long temps et par plusieurs cas dentre le roy Richart d'Angleterre et son oncle le duc Thomas de Glocestre, lesquelles haynes le roy ne voulut plus porter, ne celer, mais y voulut ouvrer de fait, et mieulx aymait comme il disoit et que conseillé estoit, qu'il destruisist autruy que il fust destruit. Et bien vous ay recordé comment le roy Richart fut ou chastel de Plaissy à trente milles de Londres, et par belles paroles et doubles comme celluy qui vouloit estre au dessus de son oncle, l'amena et mist hors de son chastel de Paissy et le conduisy jusques assés près de Londres sus ung vert chemin qui tourne droit sur la rivière de la Tamise, et estoit entre dix et onze heures. Et avés ouy comment le conte Mareschal qui là estoit en embusche, l'arresta de par le roy et le tourna devers la rivière de la Tamise. Et avés ouy comment le dit duc cria après le roy pour estre délivré de ce péril, car tous ses esperis sentirent tantost, en cel arrest faisant, que les choses se portoient mal à l'encontre de luy, mais le roy, par laquelle ordonnance et commmandement tout se faisoit, fist le sourd des oreilles et chevaucha toujours devant luy, et vint celle nuit ens ou chastel de Londres. Le duc de Gloucestre son oncle fut autrement logié, car, voulsist ou non, de fait et de force, on le fist entrer dedens une barge en une nef qui gesoit à l'ancre emmy la rivière de la Tamise.[16]

Il faudrait avoir le temps de s'arrêter sur l'extraordinaire talent littéraire de Froissart. Cette façon ramassée de réunir en quelques lignes, à la faveur d'un résumé rendu lui-même nécessaire par une interruption habile, les longues années de haine recuite du roi à l'égard de son oncle et l'instant du guet-apens. Les variantes légères et significatives avec le récit entamé plus haut, qu'il poursuit pourtant avec exactitude. La première fois, il nous a dit que pour aller plus vite, pour éviter les encombrements et la ville de Brentwood, on a pris par un autre chemin, qui n'était pas la grand'route de Londres. Cette fois, il précise que c'était "sus ung vert chemin qui tourne droit sur la rivière de la Tamise": un chemin peu fréquenté, où l'herbe pousse, et qui longe la Tamise, où attend le bateau qui doit conduire le prisonnier à Calais. La première fois, il feint de se demander si le roi a entendu ou non les appels du duc de Gloucester. Cette fois, il révèle que Richard fait la sourde oreille ("fist le sourd des oreilles"), puisque aussi bien tout était préparé sur son ordre, et il ajoute un trait d'humour noir, sur les conditions différentes dans lesquelles les deux hommes ont été logés cette nuit-là.

Il faudrait tout citer, tout commenter. Tout est admirable. Tout montre, ici et jusqu'à la fin du livre et de l'œuvre, le soin et l'efficacité avec lesquels Froissart rend, sur un ton presque neutre, la haine, la peur, la trahison, la dissimulation, la servilité, la violence, l'humiliation, les retournements de situation, les ricanements du destin, la glu du piège où se prend celui-là même qui l'a tendu. Vraiment, Froissart n'est plus le jeune homme euphorique, ébloui par la cour de la reine Philippa et par le panache chevaleresque. L'écrivain, l'historien, le moraliste ont beaucoup appris sur l'homme, sur l'homme de cour, sur la faiblesse des puissants. L'histoire de la chute de Richard II, il ne la recopie pas sur Jean le Bel, comme celle

---

16 Kervyn, t. 16, pp. 71–72 (Buchon, t. III, p. 308, chap. LXI du Livre IV).

d'Edouard II, avec la satisfaction simple de voir les méchants punis et avec tout ce qu'il faut de détails croustillants et horribles. Il la raconte de lui-même, et mieux.

Il la raconte mieux, car il a appris à maîtriser de façon moins voyante, mais plus réfléchie et plus profonde les éléments de la dramatisation et les indices du sens. On vient d'en voir un exemple. Il en est d'autres, plus massifs. Par exemple l'usage qu'il fait des monologues et des discours. Ceux-ci sont absents du style de Jean le Bel, qui se contente, à la manière habituelle du temps, de quelques échanges de propos un peu gourmés et un peu redondants au regard des informations que livre la narration. Chez Froissart, mais surtout dans sa dernière manière, ils scandent l'action et l'éclairent, anticipent sur l'événement de façon à laisser le lecteur sous l'oppression d'une menace.

Ainsi, la tragédie de Richard II – non celle de Shakespeare, mais celle de Froissart – s'ouvre sur un long discours du duc de Gloucester à l'adresse d'un chevalier, son confident, discours qui révèle autant le caractère du duc que ses griefs à l'égard du roi. Et d'abord sa haine des Français: son entrée en matière est pour se réjouir du désastre de Nicopolis, qui a fourni la matière des chapitres précédents. Froissart trouve là, pour passer de la croisade aux affaires d'Angleterre, une transition en réalité fort artificielle. Mais à la lecture il n'y paraît point:

> De la perte que les François avoient eu et receu en Turquie, il estoit plus resjouy que courrouchié. Et avoit pour ce temps delés lui un chevalier qui s'appelait messire Jehan Laquingay, le plus espécial et souverain de son conseil. Si se devisoit à luy, ainsi que depuis fut bien sceu; et disoit à la fois: "Ces fumées des François sont et ont esté bien abattues et deschirées en Honguerie et en Turquie. Tous chevalliers et escuiers estrangiers qui se boutent en leur compaignie, ne scèvent que ils font, mais sont mal conseilliés; car ils sont si plains de pompes et oultre-cuidances que ils ne pèvent advenir à nulle bonne conclusion ne amener à effect choses nulles que ils emprendent. Et trop de fois est ce cas advenu et apparu durant les guerres entre monseigneur mon père, nostre frère le prince de Galles, et euls; ne oncques ils ne porent obtenir place, ne journée de bataille contre les nostres. Je ne sçay pourquoy nous avons trièves à euls . . ."[17]

Vivacité des propos sous l'apparent décousu desquels s'ordonne une pensée d'autant plus forte qu'elle est obsessionnelle et dont les arguments vont être développés dans le très long discours dont ma trop longue citation n'a reproduit que les toutes premières lignes. Reprenons la guerre contre la France. Les trèves signées et respectées par Richard II sont un scandale, son mariage avec la fille de Charles VI un désastre, les taxes dont il accable les marchands et les libéralités déplacées auxquelles il en emploie le produit une injustice et une erreur, son expédition d'Irlande une niaiserie. "Pour le présent, il n'y a point de roy en Angleterre, qui vueille, ne qui ayme, ne qui désire les armes."[18] Mais les arguments sont à la fois étouffés et poussés jusqu'à l'exaspération par les propos d'humeur. L'humeur d'un vieillard irascible. Comme tous les hommes âgés, le duc vit dans le passé lointain, qu'il embellit, et il néglige le passé proche: les faciles victoires sur les Français, dont le souvenir le grise, remontent à la grande époque du règne de son père, aux débuts de

---

17 Kervyn, t. 16, pp. 1–2 (Buchon, t. III, pp. 283–84, chap. LVI du Livre IV).
18 Kervyn, t. 16, p. 3 (Buchon, t. III, p. 284, chap. LVI du Livre IV).

la guerre, aux campagnes de son frère, le Prince Noir. Que les choses aient changé ensuite, que, non seulement sous Richard II, mais plus encore dans les quinze dernières années du règne d'Edouard III, les Anglais aient connu des revers importants qui peuvent justifier une politique de rapprochement avec la France: tout cela, il l'oublie. Faute de contradicteur, ces objections sont évidemment absentes du discours, mais la violence des propos suggère leur partialité. Un ton de tribun habile à éveiller la colère par le prétexte des humiliations subies. Une éloquence emportée jusqu'à l'injure, une expression imagée et familière jusqu'à la grossièreté:

> Je suis le darrain né de tous les enffans d'Angleterre; mais, se je povoie estre ouy et creu, je seroie le premier à renouveller les guerres et à recouvrer les tors fais lesquels on nous a fais et fait encoires tous les jours, par la simplesse et lâcheté de nous, et par espécial de nostre chief le roi qui s'est alyé par mariage à son adversaire: ce n'est pas signe qu'il le vueille guerroier. Nennil, il a le cul trop pesant, il ne demande que le boire et le manger, le dormir, le dansier et l'espringuier.[19]

Et le flot se déverse jusqu'à l'apostrophe finale, sorte de distique ou de ritournelle: "Lacquingay, Laqcuingay, tous ce que je vous compte, je vous dy vray."[20]

En même temps, le danger réel que le duc de Gloucester représente pour Richard II apparaît lorsqu'il prédit, à juste titre, avec jubilation un soulèvement populaire, que de son vivant il s'emploiera au reste activement à provoquer parmi les Londoniens.

Ce discours est le premier – et sans doute, il est vrai, le plus travaillé – d'une série nombreuse et variée. Certains sont l'expression collective de la voix publique qui juge et condamne les décisions et le comportement du roi. Ce chœur rend ainsi sensible et audible la montée des murmures et le danger que la désaffection de l'opinion, s'ajoutant au mécontentement des grands, fait courir au roi. Voilà que, justifiant *post mortem* la prédiction du duc de Gloucester, les chapitres successifs commencent à tous se conclure par les plaintes menaçantes des Londoniens contre celui qu'ils appellent "Richard de Bordeaux", d'après le lieu de sa naissance – manière de signifier qu'il n'est pas né sur le sol même de l'Angleterre, qu'il est à demi français, voire – insinuation qui se précisera plus loin – que sa naissance est suspecte. Ainsi, le développement consacré à l'assemblée de Reims sur la question du schisme, s'écarte des affaires d'Angleterre. Mais la fin, par un nouvel effet de transition très habile, y ramène le lecteur en montrant Richard II aligner sa position sur celle du roi de France. On entend alors la voix du clergé: "Ce roy est tous françois. Il ne vise fors à nous déshonnourer et destruire".[21] Puis celle des Londoniens, informés par les prélats:

> «Ce Richart de Bourdeaulx honnira tout, qui le laira convenir. Il est de cuer si françois qu'il ne le puet celler. Il accroit, mais il sera l'un de ces jours payé si estrangement que il ne pourra venir à temps à luy repentir; et aussi ne feront ceulx qui le conseillent.»[22]

---

[19] Kervyn, t. 16, p. 3 (Buchon, t. III, p. 284, chap. LVI du Livre IV).
[20] Kervyn, t. 16, p. 5 (Buchon, t. III, p. 285, chap. LVI du Livre IV).
[21] Kervyn, t. 16, p. 135 (Buchon, t. III, p. 331, chap. LXVII du Livre IV).
[22] Kervyn, t. 16, pp. 135–36 (Buchon, t. III, p. 331, chap. LXVII du Livre IV).

Et Froissart conclut lui-même en confirmant la terrible fin qui attend le souverain:

> Et aussi aucuns accidens soudainement luy vindrent sus le col, si grans et si horribles
> que les pareils il n'en sont point ouys, ne les semblables tant que l'histoire dure, excepté
> le noble roy Pierre de Lusegnan, roy de Cyppre et de Jhérusalem, que son frère et les
> Cyppriens murdrirent villainement.[23]

A la fin du chapitre suivant, si l'on se réfère au découpage de l'édition Buchon et
du manuscrit qu'elle suit, Froissart réitère l'annonce de ce destin tragique en rappelant les prophéties qu'il a entendues à la naissance de Richard et qui prévoyaient
que la couronne passerait à un Lancastre.[24] A la fin du chapitre d'après, Richard II,
après avoir organisé un tournoi auquel la plus grande partie de sa noblesse s'est
dispensée d'assister, part en expédition en Irlande. Les commentaires des Londoniens concluent le chapitre:

> «Or s'en va Richard de Bourdeaulx le chemin de Bristo et d'Irlande; c'est à sa
> destruction. Jamais n'en retournera à joye non plus que ne fist Edouard son tayon, qui
> se gouverna si follement qu'il le compara, et par trop croire le seigneur Despensier.
> Aussi Richard de Bourdeaulx a tant creu povre conseil et mauvais que ce ne se peut
> celler ni souffrir longuement, que il ne conviègne qu'il le compère.»[25]

Pour la première fois, le destin de Richard II est comparé à celui d'Edouard II. Ce
parallèle qui s'impose avec une telle évidence, Froissart se garde bien de le prendre à
son compte. Pour brouiller les pistes, et peut-être pour mettre le lecteur en appétit, il
a même affirmé plus haut, on l'a vu, que le destin de Richard II est le plus terrible de
toutes ses *Chroniques*, voire de l'histoire de la chrétienté, et proposer comme seul
point de comparaison la mort de Pierre Ier de Lusignan, alors que le sort d'Edouard
II s'en rapproche beaucoup plus, que sa déposition comme sa mort ont été à la fois
plus cruelles et plus ignominieuses, et que son histoire ouvre les *Chroniques*. Au
chœur des sujets révoltés devait être réservé de proclamer la ressemblance entre les
deux rois indignes.

Enfin, dans le chapitre LXX de Buchon, la voix publique ne cesse de faire
entendre ses menaces. Les Londoniens plaignent le sort du comte de Northumberland et de son fils, injustement bannis, et prédire que le tour des mauvais conseillers
du roi viendra un jour: "Si convient que les gentils chevalliers le compèrent trop
chièrement, et après le comparront ceulx qui présentement les jugent."[26] Puis le
désordre et l'insécurité croissants qui règnent dans le pays, les méfaits et les rapines
des milices privées, entraînent des récriminations générales. On rappelle le règne
glorieux d'Edouard III, sous lequel l'ordre régnait: "De son temps, il n'estoit
homme, tant fuist hardy, qui osast prendre en Angleterre une poulle ou ung oeuf sans
payer."[27] On le compare à celui de son successeur, dont on flétrit le goût pour le luxe
et les plaisirs, auquel on reproche sa francophilie, qu'on soupçonne de vouloir rendre
Calais aux Français. Et pour finir, à la fin de ce chapitre, les Londoniens reprennent à

[23] Kervyn, t. 16, p. 136 (Buchon, t. III, p. 331, chap. LXVII du Livre IV).
[24] Kervyn, t. 16, pp. 142–43 (Buchon, t. III, pp. 333–34 – fin du chapitre LXVIII du livre IV).
[25] Kervyn, t. 16, pp. 151–52 (Buchon, t. III, p. 336 – fin du chapitre LXIX du livre IV).
[26] Kervyn, t. 16, p. 154 (Buchon, t. III, p. 338 – chap. LXX du livre IV).
[27] Kervyn, t. 16, p. 157 (Buchon, t. III, p. 339 – chap. LXX du livre IV).

leur compte, en un long discours collectif, les arguments qu'avait développés le duc de Gloucester pour le bénéfice de Lackinghay, augmentés de tous les griefs nouveaux: la mort du duc de Gloucester lui-même, celle du comte d'Arundel, le bannissement d'Henri de Lancastre, du comte de Northumberland et de son fils. La conclusion est qu'il faut rappeler Henri de Lancastre, enfermer Richard dans la tour de Londres et le déposer, le discours – et dans le manuscrit Paris BN F. fr. 8329 le chapitre – s'achevant sur la mention de ses "œuvres infâmes".[28] Alors l'action se déclenche, et l'archevêque de Canterbury part en mission secrète sur le continent pour aller chercher Henri de Lancastre – le comte Derby, comme dit Froissart, Bolingbroke, comme dit Shakespeare.

Tous ces discours, dont l'artifice se dissimule d'autant moins qu'il s'agit souvent de discours collectifs, rendent palpable la montée des périls autour du roi. Ils constituent un exposé passionné et neutre des reproches qui lui sont faits. Passionné, puisqu'ils sont supposés faire entendre la voix même des opposants. Neutre, puisqu'ils évitent à Froissart de prendre parti en son nom propre. Placés avec une habileté réfléchie aux moments importants du récit, et en particulier en fin de chapitres, ils en soulignent les enjeux et le sens, en jouant d'une symétrie répétitive, en même temps qu'ils introduisent un élément de variété. Ils constituent, comme on l'a dit, des éléments de dramatisation. Mais ce sont aussi des éléments du tragique. Les erreurs de Richard II y trouvent en effet un écho, qui certes les dénonce, mais qui en même temps les amplifie et les répercute, les renvoie en direction de leur auteur, contre lequel elles se retournent et qu'elles finiront par abattre. Ils assurent le fonctionnement du piège qui fait du roi la victime de ses efforts pour se sauver.

Au dernier acte, tout se retrouve et tout se paie en une succession de scènes particulièrement oppressantes où se manifestent la lâcheté et la terreur du roi déchu, sa docilité face à un vainqueur qui le traite tantôt avec une mansuétude apparente, tantôt avec brutalité, mais toujours de la façon la plus insultante. Le repas qu'Henri lui conseille de prendre avant de se mettre en route pour Londres, que Richard fait docilement servir, dont il ne peut avaler une bouchée et qu'Henri refuse de partager sous prétexte qu'il a déjà déjeûné. Le lévrier qui abandonne son maître, qui est encore le roi, pour celui qui le sera bientôt.[29] Le discours – encore un, et le plus atroce – qu'Henri de Lancastre tient à Richard de Bordeaux, lui jetant à la tête qu'il est indigne de porter la couronne et jetant le doute sur la légitimité de sa naissance avec une argumentation soigneusement injurieuse: le bruit court que Richard n'est pas le fils du Prince Noir, mais "d'un clerc ou d'un chanoine français" que la princesse de Galles aurait connu à Bordeaux; ce bruit, Richard l'a accrédité lui-même par une conduite indigne de ses ancêtres putatifs et qui n'a cessé de trahir sa naissance réelle.[30] Après avoir rappelé ses crimes, Henri conclut qu'il "allongera sa

---

[28] Kervyn, t. 16, p. 161 (Buchon, t. III, p. 340 – fin du chapitre LXX du livre IV).

[29] Kervyn, t. 16, pp. 184–88 (Buchon, t. III, chap. LXXV du livre IV, pp. 349–50).

[30] Kervyn, t. 16, p. 200 (Buchon, t. III, chap. LXXVII du livre IV, pp. 354–55). Contrairement à ce qu'écrit Peter Ainsworth, le témoignage de Froissart ne dément nullement cette accusation. Il déclare bien, et à plusieurs reprises, qu'il était présent à Bordeaux lors de la naissance de Richard, mais non qu'il assisté à sa conception; *Jean Froissart and the Fabric of History* (Oxford, 1990), p. 213!

vie, en nom de pitié, tant qu'il pourra" en demandant pour lui la vie sauve aux Londoniens et aux héritiers de ceux qu'il a fait mourir. A tout ce discours outrageant, à cette pitié méprisante, Richard répond seulement, s'adressant à l'homme qu'il a naguère banni et déshérité, et qui est en train de le détrôner – bien plus, à qui il offre sa couronne dans l'espoir de sauver sa vie:

"Grant merchis, cousin," dist le roy Richart, "je me confie plus en vous que en tout le demourant d'Angleterre."[31]

Ce n'était donc pas innocemment que, de discours en discours, les Londoniens appelaient leur roi "Richard de Bordeaux", tandis qu'on répétait à Henri de Lancastre qu'il était "du droit estoc et génération saint Edouard qui fut roy d'Angleterre."[32] Mais tout cela n'apparaît au grand jour qu'au dernier moment, et dans la bouche du nouveau roi, soucieux de légitimer son usurpation.

Je me suis laissé entraîner par ce récit saisissant au point d'en être plus qu'il ne faudrait l'esclave. Mais j'en viens à son épilogue et à celui des *Chroniques* de Froissart. Car leur rencontre et leur double suspens sont d'une force suffisante pour me ramener à ma démonstration trop longtemps oubliée.

Henri de Lancastre avait déclaré à celui qui était encore le roi Richard II qu'il "allongerait sa vie tant qu'il pourrait." Le roi Henri IV n'a pas "allongé" bien longtemps la vie de Richard de Bordeaux. L'ultime soulèvement des partisans de ce dernier, les préparatifs militaires des Français irrités par la déposition du gendre francophile de leur roi ne l'y incitaient guère, et ses conseillers le poussaient à faire bon marché de sa promesse. Froissart est sur ce point d'une éloquente discrétion:

Si fut dit au roi: "Sire, tant que Richart de Bourdeaulx vive, vous, ne le pays ne serés à seur estat." Respondy le roy: "Je croy bien que vous dittes vérité; mais, tant que à moy je ne le feray jà morir, car je l'ay pris sus. Se luy tenray son convenant, tant que apparant me sera que fait il me ara trahison." Si respondirent les chevaliers: "Il vous vauldra mieux mort que vif; car tant que les François le sçauront en vie ils s'efforcheront tousjours de vous guerroier; et auront espoir de le retourner encoires en son estat, pour la cause de ce que il a la fille du roy de France."
Le roi d'Angleterre ne respondy point à ce propos; et se départy de là et les laissa en la chambre, et il entendy à ses faulconniers; et mist un faulcon sur un poing, et il se oublia à le paistre.[33]

Ainsi s'achève l'avant-dernier chapitre des *Chroniques* de Froissart. Le dernier s'ouvre sur ces mots:

Depuis ne demourèrent gaires de jours que renommée couru parmy Londres que Richart de Bourdeaulx estoit mort. La cause comme ce fut, ne par quelle incidence, point je ne le sçavoie au jour que je escripvy ces chroniques. Le roi Richart de Bourdeaulx mort, il fut couchié sur une littière sur ung chariot couvert de baudequin tout noir . . .[34]

31 Kervyn, t. 16, p. 201 (Buchon, t. III, p. 355, chap. LXXVII, du Livre IV).
32 Kervyn, t. 16, p. 166 (Buchon, t. III, p. 342, chap. LXXI, du Livre IV).
33 Kervyn, t. 16, p. 232 (Buchon, t. III, pp. 366–67, chap. LXXXI du Livre IV).
34 Kervyn, t. 16, p. 233 (Buchon, t. III, p. 367 chap. LXXXII du Livre IV).

Mais le récit des obsèques, qui commence alors, s'interrompt bientôt. Froissart tire du destin de Richard II une leçon à l'usage des princes sur les retournements de fortune et rappelle les circonstances dans lesquelles son propre destin a croisé celui du roi Richard. Il achève ensuite le récit des obsèques, mentionne le renouvellement des trèves entre la France et l'Angleterre, signale la fin misérable du comte Maréchal, l'ancien familier de Richard II, observe les autres bouleversements qui se sont produits – dit-il – à la même époque (déposition de l'empereur Wenceslas et du pape Benoît XIII), et son récit s'arrête court, semble-t-il, sur la soustraction d'obédience des Liégeois à l'anti-pape Boniface.

L'impression que le lecteur retire de tous les éléments réunis dans ce chapitre ultime est que Froissart réunit et noue les divers fils de ses *Chroniques*, mais qu'il en laisse, une fois le nœud fait, les extrémités pendantes, qu'il dote son œuvre d'une conclusion, sans pour autant clore le récit.

La façon dont il traite la fin de Richard II est emblématique de ce mélange du conclu et du suspendu. Suspens de la décision du roi Henri IV, qui refuse d'ordonner l'assassinat de son prédécesseur et même d'y consentir explicitement, mais qui donne clairement à entendre qu'il laissera faire en détournant les yeux au moment où on le lui conseille et en se laissant ostensiblement absorber par une occupation à la fois passionnante et futile. Suspens du récit qui s'interrompt sur cette image et reprend au chapitre suivant et quelques jours plus tard alors que Richard II est déjà mort. Suspens, ostentatoire lui aussi, de l'information et du jugement de l'auteur sur les conditions de cette mort: la rumeur en circule dans Londres, et cette rumeur est véridique, mais Froissart déclare ne rien savoir de plus sur ses circonstances. Ou plus exactement n'en avoir rien su quand il écrivait ses *Chroniques*, comme si maintenant, dans un temps ultérieur, il le savait, mais hors du cadre de son œuvre, *off the record*. Silence si criant que dans la marge du manuscrit Paris BN fr. 8323 un annotateur, peu sensible à ces effets littéraires, le reproche à Froissart et donne longuement sa version des derniers moments du roi déchu, dont il est un partisan (le texte même du manuscrit contient d'ailleurs plusieurs ajouts favorables à Richard II et hostiles à ses adversaires).

Au récit escamoté de la mort de Richard Froissart substitue celui, détaillé, de ses obsèques. C'est la conclusion la plus radicale qui soit – "on jette un peu de terre sur la tombe et en voilà pour jamais" – mais c'est une conclusion décevante, au sens ancien comme au sens moderne du mot, une information qui est de toutes les façons un leurre: les funérailles de Richard II sont celles du roi qu'il n'était plus et tous les détails fournis sur elles n'apprennent rien de plus sur sa mort. Leur gratuité même montre que Froissart n'est plus ébloui par les fastes des cours et qu'il sait très bien signifier que leur éclat comme la description qu'il en fait sont les masques de l'indicible. Ce récit même des funérailles, substitué ostensiblement à l'impossible récit de la mort, est interrompu, on l'a dit par une brève moralisation appuyée sur le témoignage personnel et les souvenirs de Froissart.

Enfin, au-delà de l'épilogue du règne de Richard II, le chapitre et avec lui les *Chroniques* tout entières s'achèvent sur un suspens tel qu'elles paraissent plutôt s'interrompre. Depuis Cologne, le légat de Boniface écrit aux Liégeois pour tenter de les persuader de revenir à son obédience:

"On lisy les lettres, et fut dit au message: 'Ne retourne plus pour tels choses, sur la peyne d'estre noyé; car autant de messages qui vendront icy pour telle matière, certes nous les jetterons en Mouse.' "[35]

On n'en saura jamais plus. Ce sont les derniers mots des immenses *Chroniques* de Froissart: une menace suspendue. Est-il étonnant qu'on les juge généralement inachevées?

Et pourtant, l'accumulation des interruptions, du suspens, du non-dit, forme bien une conclusion, et même une conclusion que tous ces accidents et ces syncopes de la narration ont pour effet de rendre plus frappante. On l'a vu pour ce qui est de la fin de Richard II. Après tout, le récit en est conduit jusqu'à son terme. Bien plus, Froissart tient même à informer son lecteur du sort du comte Maréchal, le familier du roi déchu, l'exécuteur des basses œuvres lors de la mort du duc de Gloucester, celui qui avait tendu à Henri de Lancastre un piège qui s'était en partie retourné contre lui:

> Je ne vous ay encoires pas déclairé, ne dit que le conte Mareschal par lequel toutes ces tribulations estoient avenues en Angleterre, devint, après qu'il eut passé mer, mais je le vous diray. Il se tenoit à Venise, et quant telles nouvelles luy vindrent que Henry duc de Lancastre estoit couronné roy d'Angleterre et que le roy Richart de Bourdeaulx estoit mort, il prist ces choses en si grant desplaisance qu'il s'en accoucha au lit, dont il entra en une maladie et en hideur, et puis en frénaisie, tellement que oncques puis n'en leva, ainchois en moru tantos après.[36]

On dirait l'épilogue des *Vacances* de la comtesse de Ségur. Pourquoi la fin lamentable du comte Maréchal est-elle importante? Parce que le chapitre précédent a relaté celle des derniers partisans de Richard II et que seul celui-ci, exilé, manquait à l'appel. Le récit est traité comme une conclusion au point de vouloir mener jusqu'à son terme le destin de chacun de ses acteurs. Peut-être aussi, dans le parallèle à peine suggéré mais toujours présent entre Edouard II et Richard II, le comte Maréchal joue-t-il le rôle d'Hugues le Dépensier (Hugh Despenser), le mauvais conseiller, l'âme damnée, et qu'il fallait montrer le châtiment de l'un comme de l'autre.

Car la symétrie entre le début et la fin de *Chroniques* est, encore une fois, évidente. Symétrie entre le destin des deux misérables rois, tous deux victimes de leur brutalité et de leur faiblesse, tous deux déposés et assassinés dans leur prison, et de surcroît tous deux mariés à une fille du roi de France nommée Isabelle – bien que ces deux reines ne se ressemblent guère. Symétrie jusque dans le détail qui veut que la révolte contre Richard II éclate alors qu'il est à Bristol, où Edouard II avait été arrêté. Symétrie des deux récits, renforcée sur le tard, comme si celui de la fin de Richard II influait rétrospectivement sur celui de la fin d'Edouard II. Dans les premières rédactions du livre I, en effet, Froissart, comme le faisait Jean le Bel, ne dit rien de la mort du roi. Pourtant, dans la version de Rome, contemporaine du livre IV, il en fait mention, mais une mention discrète:

---

35 Kervyn, t. 16, p. 240 (Buchon, t. III, p. 371 chap. LXXXII du Livre IV).
36 Kervyn, t. 16, p. 238 (Buchon, t. III, p. 370 chap. LXXXII du Livre IV).

Si demandai de che roi, pour justefier mon histore, que il estoit devenus. Uns
anciiens esquiers me dist que dedens le propre anee que il fu la amenés, il fu mors, car
on li acourça sa vie.[37]

Froissart se met lui-même en scène dans le rôle de l'enquêteur soucieux d'étayer
ce qu'il avance, de *justifier son histoire*, en s'informant auprès d'un *ancien écuyer* –
la source anonyme et commode qu'il invoque chaque fois qu'il s'agit de secrets
d'Etat dangereux – mais en même temps il se réfugie dans le vague et ne dit rien de
l'atroce vérité. Il ne procède pas autrement, on l'a vu plus haut, pour signaler la mort
de Richard II. Il affirme ne rien savoir de ses circonstances et transforme cette
ignorance en mérite en prenant la pose de l'historien scrupuleux qui ne livre que des
informations sûres. Les années passant et le métier venant, le vieux chroniqueur a
appris les pouvoirs de l'euphémisme, et aussi, depuis le livre III, le parti qu'il peut
tirer de son propre personnage, mis en scène au bon moment. Ces procédés, qu'il met
en œuvre dans l'épisode ultime, il y a alors aussi recours pour récrire l'épisode
initial, précisément là où les deux épisodes se rejoignent et se reflètent.

Cette récriture ponctuelle, à l'échelle des microlectures de Froissart chères à
George Diller, suggère que la chute de Richard II, si évidemment parallèle à celle
d'Edouard II au début des *Chroniques*, a pu lui paraître digne d'en marquer la fin.
Une fin capable de rehausser le début et de le charger de sens. L'entrée en matière
reprise de Jean le Bel sur l'alternance en Angleterre d'un bon et d'un mauvais roi,
qui visait primitivement la succession Edouard Ier – Edouard II – Edouard III,
englobe désormais Richard II, successeur d'Edouard III, et trouve un écho dans le
terrible discours d'Henri de Lancastre, qui voit dans l'indignité morale du roi la
marque de sa bâtardise, ou au moins – mais aussi bien: plus encore – une bâtardise
morale. Aux observations initiales sur les traditions de la monarchie anglaise depuis
le roi Arthur répond à la fin le rappel insistant des prophéties de Merlin qui an-
nonçaient le destin de Richard II. Au prologue, propre à Froissart, qui dans la plupart
des rédactions a pour noyau une réflexion sur la prouesse, répond en conclusion la
fin d'un roi lâche. L'œuvre à laquelle son prologue a fixé pour objet le récit des
"guerres de France et d'Angleterre" commence par l'histoire tragique d'un roi
d'Angleterre qui, marié à la fille du roi de France, fournit à son fils un prétexte pour
revendiquer le trône de ce pays. Elle se termine par l'histoire tragique d'un roi
d'Angleterre, marié à la fille du roi de France, dont la destitution et la mort vont
réveiller, on le pressent, ces guerres franco-anglaises. Enfin, le prologue nostalgique
du livre IV et l'hommage rendu, si longtemps après sa mort, à la reine Philippa ne
donnent-ils pas la tonalité d'un livre largement consacré aux malheurs de la
couronne d'Angleterre?

Au fil de ses *Chroniques*, et à mesure qu'elles tendent à devenir le récit de son
enquête, Froissart, disions-nous, a appris à se mettre en scène dans les moments
cruciaux. L'épisode ultime lui en fournit l'occasion, et de toutes les façons. Relatant
son voyage en Angleterre de 1395, au cours duquel il avait été reçu par Richard II, il
n'avait pas manqué de souligner qu'il était à Bordeaux lors de la naissance du roi et

---

[37] *Froissart. Chroniques. Dernière rédaction du premier livre. Edition du manuscrit de Rome
Reg. lat. 869* par George T. Diller (Genève: Droz, 1972), chap. XIII, l. 111–14, p. 90.

qu'il était présent à son baptême.[38] Dans le dernier chapitre, il interrompt le récit de ses funérailles pour y revenir longuement et avec la plus grande solennité. Il ne s'agit plus cette fois de s'attendrir sur ses souvenirs de jeunesse, mais de méditer sur les coups de la fortune:

> Or considérés, seigneurs, roys, ducs, contes, prélats, et toutes gens de lignage et de puissance, comment les fortunes de cestuy monde sont merveilleuses et tournent diversement.[39]

Froissart, se présentant de la façon la plus formelle ("moi, Jean Froissart, chanoine et trésorier de Chimay"), rappelle alors qu'il a été l'hôte de Richard II, dont il a reçu un présent généreux, et que, présent à Bordeaux quand il est né, il a entendu prédire qu'il serait roi; mais aussi que la première année où il était en Angleterre, c'est-à-dire en 1361, un chevalier avait en sa présence fait état des prophéties de Merlin contenues dans le *Brut* pour prédire qu'aucun des fils d'Edouard III ne règnerait, mais que la couronne reviendrait à la maison de Lancastre. Cette dernière prophétie, il en a déjà fait état plus haut, alors qu'Henri de Lancastre est réfugié à la cour de France. Il l'introduit alors de façon analogue par un témoignage solennel ("je, Jean Froissart, auteur et chroniseur de ces chroniques, en mon jeune âge, ouïs une fois parler . . .") et par des considérations sur la fortune, particulièrement fortes, car elles montrent que Richard II a causé sa propre perte et qu'on ne peut rien contre le destin:

> Les fortunes de ce monde sont bien merveilleuses, et la fortune fut bien terrible et merveilleuse en celle saison pour le roy d'Angleterre, et si très dure que merveilles est à penser et le acquist et acheta; car bien y euist pourveu s'il voulsist, et estoit trop fort de eslongier ce qui devait être.[40]

Formule frappante: le roi aurait pu se sauver s'il l'avait voulu, mais il ne pouvait le vouloir, car il ne pouvait échapper à ce qui devait être. N'est-ce pas là l'essence du tragique?

Cependant, si Froissart se met en scène pour donner du poids à ces réflexions comme à ces prophéties, il le fait aussi pour montrer que son propre destin a croisé à plusieurs reprises celui du roi, et cela au moment où vont s'achever ces chroniques qui au fil de leur rédaction ont de plus en plus tendu à devenir ses mémoires. Il ne cesse de rôder dans les dernières pages. Il juge ainsi utile de préciser que l'archevêque de Canterbury, lors de sa mission secrète auprès d'Henri de Lancastre exilé, est passé par Valenciennes, sa ville natale:

> Et descendy à l'hôtel au Cygne sur le marchié, et là s'arresta et y fut par trois jours, et s'i rafreschy. Et ne chevauchoit point comme archevesque de Cantorbie, mais comme un moisne pélerin, et ne descouvroit à nul homme du monde son estat, ne ce que il avoit empensé à faire. Si se départy de Valenchiennes au quatriesme jour . . .[41]

---

38 Kervyn, t. 15, p. 142, (Buchon, t. III, p. 198, chap. XL du Livre IV).
39 Kervyn, t. 16, p. 233 (Buchon, t. III, p. 368, chap. LXXXII du Livre IV).
40 Kervyn, t. 16, p. 142 (Buchon, t. III, p. 333, chap. LXVIII du Livre IV).
41 Kervyn, t. 16, pp. 162–63 (Buchon, t. III, p. 341, chap. LXXI du Livre IV).

L'incognito et le déguisement du prélat sont signalés à l'occasion de cette étape à Valenciennes, pendant cette étape. Qu'en conclure, sinon que lors de cette étape également incognito a été percé et identité découverte par un compatriote de Froissart? Comment le chroniqueur serait-il sinon informé de détails sans importance pour la mission de l'archevêque, comme le nom de l'hôtel où il est descendu? Et mentionnerait-il ce nom sans le plaisir particulier que l'on éprouve à retrouver des lieux familiers dans un contexte inattendu?[42] Il est vrai qu'il aime à citer les noms des hôtels où il descendait lui-même, comme le livre III le montre bien: l'hôtel de l'Etoile à Tarbes, l'hôtel de la Lune à Orthez.

Mais voici autre chose: on se souvient du savant suspens ménagé lors de l'arrestation du duc de Gloucester par l'introduction à cet endroit de chapitres consacrés à l'épilogue de Nicopolis. Juste avant de "retourner aux besoingnes d'Angleterre", et sans rapport avec son sujet, Froissart signale la mort de Guy de Blois, son protecteur et son mécène, en rappelant ce qu'il lui doit et ce que lui doivent ses *Chroniques*.[43] Avec la mort du grand seigneur ruiné, dont l'héritage sera dispersé, quelque chose s'achève pour l'homme et l'écrivain Froissart, même si Guy de Blois n'était plus guère en mesure de l'aider. Et il mentionne cette mort juste avant de se plonger dans le récit de la chute de Richard II et de terminer sur lui son œuvre.

Tous ces indices suggèrent que la mort de Richard II est une sorte de conclusion et que Froissart considérait son œuvre comme achevée. Mais ces indices, il faut le reconnaître, sont ténus et doivent beaucoup à l'interprétation. Ils se heurtent en outre à l'objection que le dernier chapitre repart sur d'autres événements et se termine abruptement. Toutefois, les événements brièvement mentionnés in extremis, en des termes qui ne permettent pas de supposer qu'ils devaient recevoir plus loin le développement qu'ils mériteraient, ne sont pas, dans la perspective d'une moralisation, sans rapport avec le drame qui a secoué l'Angleterre. C'est en tout cas ainsi qu'ils sont présentés:

> Comme vous povés entendre, advinrent ces meschiefs et ces tribulations sus les plus grans seigneurs d'Angleterre en l'an de grâce mil CCCC un mains.
> Aussi fut le pape Bénédict, qui se tenoit en Avignon et que les Franchois avoient de grand'volonté mis sus et sousteunu une grant espace, en ce temps déposé.
> Pareillement fut le roy d'Allemaigne déposé pour ses meffais et démérites.[44]

---

[42] Ce n'est cependant pas la seule fois où Froissart donne ce genre de détail. Ainsi, dans son récit du règlement de l'affaire de Gand en 1385, il précise que Jean Boursier, l'émissaire du roi d'Angleterre, et ses hommes "s'en vinrent en l'ostel que on dit La Valle" (Buchon, t. II, p. 343, chap. CCXL du Livre II), et plus loin que les ambassadeurs gantois arrivèrent "à Tournai à cinquante chevaux et se logierent tout ensamble à l'ostel au Saumon, en la rue Saint Brisse" (SHF, t. XI, p. 298; Buchon, t. II, p. 345, chap. CCXLI du t. II). Comme dans le cas qui nous occupe, il s'agit sans doute pour lui de montrer qu'il est bien informé. Quant à l'hôtel de la Lune où il logeait pendant son séjour à Orthez, la mention qui en est faite relève de la complaisance aux souvenirs personnels qui marque le récit du voyage en Béarn et à partir de là toute la fin des *Chroniques*. Les deux raisons ont pu se combiner pour le pouser à faire état de l'hôtel du Cygne à Valenciennes.
[43] Kervyn, t. 16, pp. 70–71 (Buchon, t. III, pp. 307–08, chap. LIX du Livre IV).
[44] Kervyn, t. 16, pp. 238–39 (Buchon, t. III, p. 370, chap. LXXXII du Livre IV).

On a observé depuis toujours que Benoît XIII n'a été chassé d'Avignon par Boucicaut qu'en 1403 et n'a été définitivement déposé qu'en 1408. On en a déduit que Froissart vivait encore à ce moment-là, bien que son récit s'arrête en 1400. On peut surtout en conclure qu'il force la chronologie de façon à rendre concomitantes les dépositions du roi d'Angleterre, de l'empereur et du pape, et à finir ainsi sur leur triple chute qui justifie son avertissement à l'adresse des princes et ses réflexions sur l'instabilité de la fortune.

Quant à la toute dernière scène et aux tout derniers mots – la réponse des Liégeois au légat du pape Boniface –, il est permis de leur trouver une double résonance. D'une part, le dernier mot de toutes les *Chroniques* est "Meuse", comme si Froissart, si présent dans son œuvre, voulait terminer sur le nom de la grande rivière de chez lui, qui coule à quelques kilomètres de Chimay. Parti de Valenciennes sur l'Escaut, après avoir couru le monde et écrit tant de pages, il se retrouve à Chimay et met le point final sur la Meuse. D'autre part, achever, comme on l'a dit, sur le suspens d'une menace, et donc sur la perspective d'événements ultérieurs, c'est signifier que la fin des *Chroniques* n'est pas la fin de l'histoire. Car le destin symétrique d'Edouard II et de Richard II ne doit pas faire croire que la boucle est bouclée. Rien ne s'achève, rien ne recommence, tout se poursuit. Seule l'œuvre se termine. Elle construit donc les indices de sa clôture, mais elle ne veut pas laisser ignorer leur artifice. Elle dément ainsi le nœud tragique qu'elle feint d'avoir noué, mais pour susciter l'oppression d'un autre tragique: celui du "bruit et de la fureur" d'une histoire sans fin.

Froissart, cet homme aisément réputé superficiel, finit ainsi par manifester un sens profond de la dramatisation et de l'éloquence de l'histoire. Un sens du suspens et de l'euphémisme terrifiants. Un sens des situations shakespeariennes. Non pas la simplicité du nœud tragique racinien, mais le foisonnement de l'histoire, indéfiniment poursuivie de roi en roi et de succession en succession – *de rei en rei e d'eir en eir* –, comme le disait ce *Roman de Brut* dont il invoque deux fois le témoignage,[45] et aussi le foisonnement trompeur du destin, qui laisse croire que les chemins et les issues sont multiples, alors qu'il n'est qu'étouffement et resserrement vers l'inévitable. Un tragique, enfin, qui est celui même de la fonction royale, parce qu'il est un tragique de la destitution et de la dégradation.

[45] Wace, *Roman de Brut*, t. 2.

DOMESTICATING DIVERSITY: FEMALE FOUNDERS IN MEDIEVAL GENEALOGICAL LITERATURE AND *LA FILLE DU COMTE DE PONTIEU*

Donald Maddox

For both monarchy and nobility, genealogies played important accessory roles in consolidating power and prestige in feudal society, and they were not infrequently instrumental in ensuring the functionality of its institutions. Initially used as a means of recording royal and dynastic lineages, they were gradually appropriated to serve similar ends in other sectors of feudal culture. Royal lineages were recorded as early as the seventh century in the genealogies of Irish chieftains and Frankish dynasties.[1] Early in the tenth century, the higher aristocracy began to make use of genealogical documents, and by the mid-eleventh century they could also be found within the lesser aristocracy.[2] Historians have in fact maintained that by the twelfth century genealogy had become a distinct genre.[3] If this be so, it was by no means a discrete genre, one of its most salient properties being its adaptability to serve the ends of other generic types, literary as well as historical. Indeed, the case at hand well illustrates the genre's flexibility, for I wish to examine one extremely influential genealogical schema that found expression in medieval historical documents and literary texts alike. After detailing the schema's principal features and briefly sketching its fortunes as a vital adjunct of other types of text, I shall take up in greater detail an example of how it is implemented in a thirteenth-century prose work, *La Fille du comte de Pontieu*.

In essence, this particular schema traces a given lineage back to a distinguished or otherwise remarkable female ancestor who had entered the line through an alliance. In many of the pattern's occurrences, this figure had married into a system where patrimonial succession through male heirs was the norm. One might assume that in such a system she would have enjoyed only a marginal status at best. Of capital

---

[1] See Léopold Génicot, *Les Généalogies* [Typologie des sources du moyen âge occidental, 15] (Turnhout: Brépols, 1975), pp. 14–15.

[2] On kinship structures in these social sectors, see Georges Duby, "Structures de parenté et noblesse dans la France du Nord aux XIe et XIIe siècles," in *Hommes et structures au Moyen Age* (The Hague and Paris: Mouton, 1973), pp. 267–85.

[3] See Génicot, *Les Généalogies*, pp. 11–44; and Gabrielle Spiegel, "Genealogy: Form and Function in Medieval Historical Narrative," *History and Theory* 22 (1983), pp. 43–53. Cf. Bernard Guenée, *Politique et histoire au Moyen Age: Recueil d'articles sur l'histoire politique et l'historiographie médiévale* (Paris: Publications de la Sorbonne, 1981), p. 357.

importance in this schema, however, is the fact that her lineage was in some way more powerful or prestigious than that of her spouse, thus significantly enhancing his bloodline.[4] In consequence, genealogies predicated on this type of schema typically portray the singular female ancestor as having been not only responsible for a major upturn in the line's fortunes, but also the sponsor, wittingly or no, of its halcyon days.

An early genealogy that adheres to this model is the *Historia comitum Ghisnensium* of 1194, by Lambert of Ardres.[5] Having traced the counts of Guines back through eight generations, and faced with the absence of factual information concerning the line's founding, Lambert simply resorts to the conventions of heroic fiction to liquidate the deficit (Duby, "Structures," pp. 78–82). He invents a scenario in which a Scandinavian adventurer named Sifridus allegedly won the county of Guines in battle from the Count of Flanders in 928 and then secretly impregnated his daughter. He claims that the Count of Flanders subsequently adopted and knighted their illegitimate son, who later founded the house of Guines (Duby, "Remarques," pp. 297–99). Such casual supplementation of genealogy with fiction was not uncommon. Lineal memory could easily falter after going back only two or three generations (Duby, "Structures," p. 270). To compensate for the silence of the past, the anemia of historic factuality was sometimes remedied by transfusions drawn from the pulsing arteries of folklore, legend, and myth. Even the genealogies which were to a certain extent factually accurate could thus shade almost imperceptibly into fiction. Consequently, from the eleventh century through the later Middle Ages, the motif of the fictitious female ascendant, ancestor or founder, was one important component of some genealogies and genealogically informed texts.[6] There were also instances where noble ancestry was traced back through this individual to Carolingian stock, as did the counts of Flanders themselves. In a tenth-century genealogy by Arnoul of Flanders, Arnoul's grandfather, Count Baldwin Iron-Arm, is said to have married one Judith, daughter of King Charles the Bald, thus injecting the noble Flemish vein with royal Carolingian blood.[7] The importance of this schema should not be underestimated. Gabrielle Spiegel has observed with regard to it that "the

---

4   Cf. Duby, "Remarques sur la littérature généalogique en France aux XIe et XIIe siècles," in *Hommes et structures au Moyen Age*, p. 292: "Ainsi s'introduit dans la conscience de la haute aristocratie un schéma de parenté que l'on peut définir brièvement: filiation strictement agnatique, le titre – à l'instar du titre royal – se transmet de père en fils; mais comme il arrive parfois que le titre ou la vocation à la puissance s'hérite par l'effet d'une alliance . . . le fil généalogique en remontant vers le passé peut subir des décrochements, abandonner la lignée patrilinéaire moins illustre pour, *à partir de telle aïeule dont les descendants ont conscience de tirer un héritage plus éclatant, remonter de fils en père cette lignée plus honorable*" (my emphasis).
5   *Historia comitum Ghisnensium, Monumenta Germaniae Historica, Scriptores*, vol. XXIV.
6   K.F. Werner, "Untersuchungen zur Frühzeit des französischen Fürstentums," *Die Welt als Geschichte* 20 (1960), pp. 116–18; Génicot, p. 42 n. 36; Duby, "Remarques," p. 296.
7   *Genealogia nobilissorum Francorum imperatorum et regum, Monumenta Germaniae Historica, Scriptores*, vol. IX, p. 303. On this document, see Génicot, "Princes territoriaux et sang carolingien: La *Genealogia Comitum Bulonensium*," in *Etudes sur les principautés lotharingiennes* (Louvain, 1974), 217–306; Duby, "Remarques," p. 292; idem, "Structures de parenté et noblesse," pp. 280–81.

characteristic genealogical myth of eleventh and twelfth century families involves the rape or seduction of a daughter of the Count of Flanders, who in marrying the social upstart that abducts her establishes the social prestige of the family, thereafter established along agnatic lines."[8]

Although the fortunes of this schema have been examined primarily in historical documents, alliances whose benefits accrue to an agnate are also featured in numerous works of courtly literature from the twelfth through the fourteenth centuries. Rape and seduction are only two of the many motifs that serve to depict the appropriation of a feminine "other" to illustrate a lineage. In Chrétien de Troyes's *Cligés*, for example, the prestige of Alexander's Constantinople is greatly increased by virtue of his marriage into the Arthurian line, via Soredamors, Gauvain's sister and Arthur's maternal niece.[9] Soredamors effectively "gilds" the Byzantine blazon with Arthurian luster by bearing Cligés, who will recover the patrimonial Empire from his conniving paternal uncle Alis, then effect a second beneficial cross-cultural alliance by marrying Fénice, the daughter of the German emperor.[10] In the Prose *Lancelot*, the motif of deceptive impregnation proves vital to fulfillment of the agnatic teleology of heroes: although he is to be excluded from the grail quest on account of his sinful union with Queen Guenevere, Lancelot is nonetheless a descendant of King David and destined to engender the grail hero Galahad. Deceived into the belief that he is lying with the queen, Lancelot is made to lie with the daughter of King Pellés, the "Roi Pescheor" and lord of Corbenic. It is she who provides Lancelot's lineage with the requisite virginity for his engenderment of Galahad.[11] In many instances, the desired female "other" is endowed with supernatural qualities: in *Le Bel Inconnu*, for example, Guinglain learns that he is the son of Gauvain, but also that his mother is a beneficent fairy who had provided covert sponsorship of his chivalric initiation.[12] In the late fourteenth-century *Roman de Mélusine*, we find a virtual replay of Lambert d'Ardres' chronicle of the counts of Guines: the founding of the Lusignan dynasty is attributed to the descendant of a Breton nobleman and the eponymous fairy whose fertility and prodigious engineering feats ensure the line's initial prosperity.[13] Hence a model adaptable to both historiographic and literary designs and attuned to the significant pivotal role played by matrilineal inflections in an essen-

---

[8] Gabrielle M. Spiegel, "Maternity and Monstrosity: Reproductive Biology in the *Román de Mélusine*," in *Melusine of Lusignan: Founding Fiction in Late Medieval France*, ed. D. Maddox and S. Sturm-Maddox (Athens: University of Georgia Press, 1996), p. 107.

[9] Chrétien de Troyes, *Cligés*, ed. A. Micha (Paris: Champion, 1965), vv. 44–2585.

[10] See D. Maddox, "Kinship Alliances in the *Cligés* of Chrétien de Troyes," *L'Esprit Créateur* 12 (1972), pp. 3–12.

[11] *Lancelot*, ed. A. Micha (Geneva: Droz, 1979), vol. 4, LXXVIII, 45–58, pp. 201–11. On this passage, see Elspeth Kennedy, *Lancelot and the Grail: A Study of the "Prose Lancelot"* (Oxford: Clarendon, 1986), pp. 279, 284–85.

[12] *Le Bel Inconnu*, ed. G. Perrie-Williams (Paris: Champion, 1929), vv. 3212–42. See Laurence Harf-Lancner, *Les fées au Moyen Age: Morgane et Mélusine, la naissance des fées* (Paris: Champion, 1984), p. 333; and Lucy Paton, *Studies in the Fairy Mythology of Arthurian Romance* (New York: Burt Franklin, 1960), pp. 176–78.

[13] Jean d'Arras, *Le Roman de Mélusine*, ed. Louis Stouff (Dijon: Bernigaud & Privat, 1932). See Harf-Lancner, pp. 155–78; and the essays on this romance in *Melusine of Lusignan*.

tially agnatic line. As Spiegel sums it up, "in eleventh- and twelfth-century genealogies and genealogical histories, as in the *Roman de Mélusine*, the social capital of the family resides on the female side" ("Maternity," p. 107).

Mindful of this genealogical schema valorizing female "social capital," I wish now to consider how it is implemented in *La Fille du comte de Pontieu*.[14] Although this relatively brief prose text has been called the first *nouvelle* in French, it defies more specific classification and has the look of a generic hybrid.[15] At times it is reminiscent of chronicle.[16] One also notes sporadic features of folktale, adventure romance, epic, and pilgrimage narrative. However, the single generic type that most effectively unifies this diversity of *matières* is genealogy, which constructs the network of kinship relations that informs the narrative in its entirety, from the first mention of the Count of Pontieu in the opening sentence, to Saladin who, when he is finally named at the very end of the story, is identified as a descendant of the Count's daughter. Genealogy thus provides the fundamental infrastructure of textuality; the logic of lineal relations unifies the events recounted and conditions textual closure. This is characteristic of the way in which medieval genealogies tend to furnish organizational principles for blending generically diverse materials.[17]

Let us therefore examine the story's genealogical infratext as laid out in Figure I. This diagram shows the full complex of lineal relations. The principal nexus of this kinship network is of course the count of Pontieu's daughter, who becomes a vital biological genetrix on behalf of three noble Picard houses, as well as a mediatrix of the Islamic East and the Christian West.[18] M1a and M1b designate, respectively, her

---

[14] *La Fille du comte de Pontieu, nouvelle du XIIIe siècle*, ed. Clovis Brunel (Paris: Champion, 1926).

[15] On its status as "nouvelle," see Brunel, p. iii: "on doit la considérer comme la plus ancienne nouvelle en prose française. Elle apparaît déjà avec le caractère très net de ce genre littéraire." However, a more recent critic of the *nouvelle* as genre expresses skepticism that any one of the story's three versions fits into "un genre littéraire précis." Roger Dubuis, *Les Cent nouvelles nouvelles et la tradition de la nouvelle en France au Moyen Age* (Grenoble: Presses Universitaires, 1973), p. 526.

[16] On features suggestive of chronicle in this version, see Joan Crow, "The Art of the Medieval Conteur: A Study of *La Fille du Comte de Pontieu*," *French Studies* 30 (1976), pp. 1–18; Evelyn Birge Vitz, "Story, Chronicle, History: *La Fille du comte de Pontieu*," *Medieval Narrative and Modern Narratology: Subjects and Objects of Desire* (New York: New York University Press, 1989), pp. 96–125. Also useful in this regard: Hayden White, "The Value of Narrativity in the Representation of Reality," *The Content of the Form: Narrative Discourse and Historical Representation* (Baltimore: The Johns Hopkins University Press, 1987), pp. 1–25.

[17] With respect to genealogy and chronicle, for example, Génicot remarks that "Les genres coexistent; ils échangent des données; *la généalogie sert d'armature* à la chronique et la chronique enrichit la généalogie; ils ne se confondent pas." *Le Généalogies*, p. 23, emphasis mine. Spiegel has characterized genealogy as a "perceptual grid" for shaping narrative accounts of social reality ("Genealogy," pp. 46–47).

[18] According to Danielle Régnier-Bohler, these qualities would make the count's daughter akin to a variety of other "feminine figures" in medieval French brief narratives (mostly *lais* whose primary functions of procreation and "alimentation" of lineage would partake of a "mythic" coherence, the cultural specificity of which is unfortunately never defined: "Figures féminines et imaginaire généalogique: Etude comparée de quelques récits brefs," in *Le*

FIGURE I. *La Fille du comte de Pontieu* Genealogical Table

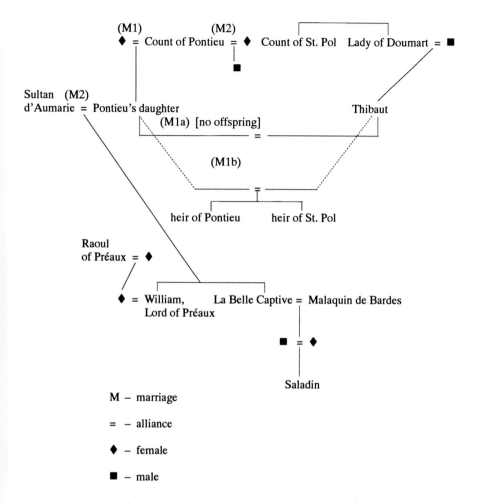

marriage and later remarriage to Thibaut of Domart, M2 her marriage to the Sultan of Almeria.[19] Her four offspring, two from each marriage, consist of three sons and a daughter, and their respective fortunes prove highly consequential. Each of her three sons acquires a noble title: her two sons by Thibaut inherit Pontieu and St. Pol, while William, her son by the sultan, becomes Lord of Préaux. Her male offspring thus develop the potential for constituting a powerful Picard dynasty. Meanwhile her daughter by the sultan will be the maternal grandmother of Saladin.

Récit bref au Moyen Age, ed. D. Buschinger (Université de Picardie: Centre d'Etudes Médiévales, 1980), pp. 73–95.
[19] The precise location of this sultanate is uncertain, though it is unlikely that OF "Aumarie" designates the Spanish port of Almeria. On this, see Gaston Paris, "La Légende de Saladin," *Journal des Savants*, May 1893, p. 358.

By far the most striking feature of this diagram of kinship relations is the prominence accorded to our schema. While, as we saw, one primitive version of this genealogical myth featured the daughter of a count of Flanders, here it is the daughter of the Count of Pontieu who, cast in the same role, brings the prestige of the house of Pontieu into the sultan's line. Moreover, the schema is repeated, always at crucial junctures: the Count's daughter produces a daughter, la Belle Captive, whose daughter is the mother of Saladin; the latter consequently receives Pontieu genes in a threefold cascade flowing from a matrilineal wellspring. Elsewhere, the title St. Pol descends to the son of Thibaut and the Count's daughter via the same type of schema: while Thibaut's father is not named, his mother is the Lady of Domart. As the sister of the Count of St. Pol, she brought the distinction of that line into Thibaut's obscure patrilineal heritage. Once again, female social capital benefits an agnatic system: there were no direct descendants in the St. Pol line; it thus passed from the Count of St. Pol to his sister's son, Thibaut, who eventually passed it down to his own son. As St. Pol brings distinction into the agnatic line of Thibaut via his mother, so in turn is the prestige of St. Pol augmented through Thibaut's marriage to the daughter of the Count of Pontieu. It is also through an advantageous alliance that William, the Count's daughter's son by the sultan, acquires a noble title, through marriage to the daughter of Raoul of Préaux. Already the heir of Pontieu blood via his mother, William's marriage into the Préaux line constitutes a second instance where the sultanate of Almeria is linked to European nobility through a marital alliance with the daughter of a feudal lord. This consistent recurrence of our schema of beneficial alliances on the distaff side considerably overshadows the most significant father-son filiation: the Count of Pontieu's son from his first marriage dies prematurely, leaving the Count's daughter with a clear title to the House of Pontieu.

Of what significance is the recurrence of our schema in this text? In order to appreciate the larger significance of genealogy in this case, we must remember that *La Fille du comte de Pontieu* was never a truly independent story, but rather a modular tale that figured in a number of multitextual schemes. From its earliest appearance, moreover, the story of Pontieu's daughter provides an etiological basis for the widespread legend of Saladin's "Europeanization."[20] In the thirteenth-century manuscript BN fr. 25462, containing what Brunel calls the "rédaction primitive" of *La Fille* (p. iii), the latter, one of fifteen works, immediately precedes a prose version of the *Ordre de chevalerie*, in which Saladin is depicted in a very positive light as an initiate into the arts of chivalry.[21] The trend toward Saladin's

---

[20] Much has been written about the medieval metamorphoses of Saladin's image, from early negative depictions following the fall of Jerusalem in 1187, to later portrayals of a sensitive, cultivated, "westernized" diplomat. For a useful recent review of much of this material, see Giuseppe Ligato, "Continuità ed eccezioni nella leggenda di Saladino," *Quaderni Medievali* 36 (1993), pp. 6–29.

[21] For a description of this manuscript, see Henri Omont, *Catalogue de manuscrits français de la Bibliothèque Nationale*, II (Paris: Leroux, 1902), pp. 602–04, and Robert F. Cook and Larry S. Crist, *Le deuxième Cycle de la Croisade: Deux études sur son développement* (Geneva: Droz, 1972), pp. 129–30. On the prose *Ordre*, see Hilding Kjellman, "Les Rédactions en prose de l'*Ordre de chevalerie*," *Studier i modern spraakvetenskap* 7 (1920), pp. 139–77.

rehabilitation is already evident in this version of *La Fille*; it ends with a reference "au courtois Salehadin,"[22] and there is no evidence whatsoever that this "courtly" descendant of the house of Pontieu is perceived as the great enemy of Christendom who in 1187 subverted the accomplishments of the earliest Crusades.[23] The other thirteenth-century version of *La Fille* is interpolated into the *Estoires d'Outremer et de la naissance Salehadin*, which further enhances the legend of Saladin's European forbears with liberal quantities of romance.[24] During the fifteenth century *La Fille* was again rewritten and amplified, this time as the second element of a cyclical triptych that begins with *Le Roman de Jean d'Avesnes*, the grandfather of our heroine, and culminates in the prose *Saladin*.[25] The author of the latter work marshaled the cumulative wealth of legendary material concerning Saladin, as well as the resources of epic and romance, in order to create the image of an exemplary heroic figure who well exceeds the constraints of historical fact.[26] Variously operant in these different adaptations of our story is a cyclical principle familiar from French epic cycles, whereby multiple texts create genealogies in retrograde fashion, moving backward in time from the hero through generations of his ascendants.[27] In these cyclic contexts, *La Fille du comte de Pontieu* was repeatedly rewritten to serve as a vast genealogical analepsis in the biography of Saladin. As a flexible component of the later medieval revisionism associated with the image of Saladin, the fundamental narrative in these versions of *La Fille* implies that Saladin's courtliness derived from his European ancestry, and that this is perhaps what also explains his martial success against the Crusading West. Such familiarization of alterity might thus have lessened in collective memory the negative impact of the monumental defeat of 1187.

It is nonetheless apparent that the establishment of an apocryphal kinship tie between Saladin and European feudalism was not the sole purpose of this text. If it is strongly implied that Saladin's legendary courtliness and refinement were due to the fact that Pontieu blood coursed through his veins, we also perceive the house of

---

22 Brunel, ed., p. 44. The version from the *Histoire d'outre mer et du roi Saladin*, refers to him as "le boin roi Salehadin," ibid., p. 44.

23 For detailed comparison of the two versions edited in parallel by Brunel (one from BN fr. 25462, the other extant in BN fr. 770 and 12203) see Crow, "The Art of the Medieval Conteur," pp. 2–16.

24 This work is extant in two manuscripts, BN fr. 770 and 12203; an edition of the former appears in Brunel, pp. 1–44. See Margaret Jubb, "The *Estoires d'Outremer*: History or Entertainment?," in *France and the British Isles in the Middle Ages and Renaissance*, ed. G. Jondorf and D.N. Dumville (Woodbridge: The Boydell Press, 1991), pp. 173–82, and Crow, pp. 1–18.

25 *Jehan d'Avennes, romanzo del XV secolo*, ed. A.M. Finoli (Milan: Cisalpino, 1979); Larry S. Crist, *Saladin: suite et fin du deuxième Cycle de la Croisade* (Geneva: Droz, 1972).

26 Of this text, Jubb observes: "we see the ultimate result of the christians' veneration for Saladin. . . . The Saracen's *vaillance, largesse*, and *courtoisie* have exalted him in the popular imagination to the stature of an exemplary, all conquering Alexander." Margaret Jubb, "The *Estoires d'Outremer*: History or entertainment?," in Jondorf and Dumville, pp. 173–82, cit. p. 181.

27 On this, see D. Maddox and S. Sturm-Maddox, "Introduction: Cyclicity and Medieval Literary Cycles," in *Transtextualities: Of Cycles and Cyclicity in Medieval French Literature* (Binghamton: Medieval and Renaissance Texts and Studies, 1995).

Pontieu as the nucleus of a powerful noble dynasty. In this regard, the heroine is a precursor of Mélusine, whose sons effectively constitute a dynastic world order under the aegis of the Lusignan.[28]

We have yet to confront the story's greatest enigma, however, which is this: why are the lineal relations, which are elaborated according to a rather canonic model, assimilated to a such a bizarre plot, replete with so many ironic and implausible elements? The pilgrimage to Compostella had been arranged so as to ask God to provide the couple with an heir; it had resulted only in the brutal gang rape of the wife and her homicidal rage toward her husband, followed by her progressive exclusion, first to a convent while Thibaut completed the pilgrimage alone, then to solitude in the marriage bed, and finally to a solitary voyage in a sealed barrel. Eventually, however, she does conceive, twice, in fact, but in a Saracen sultanate. After these blessed events, her father, stepbrother and first husband just happen to arrive in Almeria one day, and she, after recognizing them, saves them from harm. They return to Picardy with her, where she and Thibaut finally achieve the fertility they had initially sought in vain. All of which brings to mind the poet's immortal query: "Christ! What are patterns for?"[29]

To address this question, we need to recognize that the "perceptual grid" of genealogy in this account is elaborated concurrently with a second, equally important perceptual grid, whereby a series of pilgrimage narratives serves as the vehicle of the network of signifiers pertaining to lineage.[30] Each of the three major parts of the story is significantly marked by a pilgrimage to one of three major destinations of medieval pilgrims: Compostella; the lands of the Crusades; and Rome.[31] While at the outset the Compostellan venture furnishes the initial crisis leading to the marital rift between Pontieu's daughter and Thibaut, it also makes possible her eventual marriage to the sultan. In the second segment, father, son and son-in-law take the cross in service of God: "Fisent leur pelerinage molt saintement en tous les lius u il seurent c'on deoit Diu servir" (p. 22). The count also fulfills a year of expiatory service as a Templar, before the fateful voyage that takes the trio off course and onto the shores of Almeria. Once reunited, finally, the Picard family returns to France by way of a third major venue of pilgrims, Rome. There they receive appropriate papal counsel,

---

[28] In *Mélusine of Lusignan*, in addition to the article by Spiegel, see also Jane H.M. Taylor, "Mélusine's Progeny: Patterns and Perplexities," pp. 165–84.

[29]   For the man who should loose me is dead,
         Fighting with the Duke in Flanders,
         In a pattern called a war.
         Christ! What are patterns for?   Amy Lowell, "Patterns"

[30] On pilgrimage as a narrative schema, see Edmund Reiss, "The Pilgrimage Narrative in *The Canterbury Tales*," *Studies in Philology* 67 (1970), p. 298; Donald R. Howard, *Writers and Pilgrims: Medieval Pilgrimage Narratives and their Posterity* (Berkeley and Los Angeles: University of California Press, 1980); Donald Maddox, "Pilgrimage Narrative and Meaning in Manuscripts L and A of the *Vie de Saint Alexis*," *Romance Philology* 27 (1973), pp. 143–57. On the ethnocultural implications of pilgrimage, see Victor Turner and Edith Turner, "Pilgrimage as a Liminoid Phenomenon," in *Image and Pilgrimage in Christian Culture* (Oxford: Blackwell, 1978), pp. 1–39; and, on medieval pilgrimages, pp. 172–202.

[31] For pertinent historical background, see Jonathan Sumption, *Pilgrimage: An Image of Medieval Religion* (Totowa, New Jersey: Rowman and Littlefield, 1976).

and, of capital importance, the heroine's marriage to Thibaut is resanctifed. While these successive pilgrimages serve as a structuring device for the major segments of the intrigue, they are also the vital indices of a providential design: implicit is the idea that a higher power is in covert control of the entire course of events, including the implausible reversals that seem to imperil the story's coherence. Thibaut and his wife will produce offspring and heirs, but this blessing is deliberately deferred until Ponthieu's daughter can become fertile within the Saracen sultanate. Thus does God give her womb a generative function, but in service to two distinct genealogical developments, Christian on the one hand, Saracen on the other, according to an intricate double design that was neither anticipated nor understood by those involved. We are reminded throughout the narrative that events happen "as it pleases God"; the lady's alienation from Ponthieu, no less than her return, are purported to be under divine aegis, while in Rome the pope qualifies the Christian family's reunion as a "miracle."[32] The story thus acquires the kind of irony familiar from hagiography, as for example the irony of a Saint Alexis, to whose parents God granted a son, but only according to His mysterious *talent* and not according to their purely temporal desire for a noble heir.[33] While each of the three pilgrimages provides the locus at which a different type of divine sanction is attributed, together they also imply that the bizarre and implausible turns taken by the intrigue are in harmony with a covert reality of a higher order, one whose intricate design involves the use of genealogy and pilgrimage so as ultimately to assimilate Saladin, the principal agent of an alien and inimical ideology, to the ideological sphere of feudal Christendom.

Yet the brutal gang rape of the heroine, followed immediately by her desperate attempt to murder her husband, are anomalous elements whose gratuitous violence would seem to exceed basic requirements for a means of merely effecting the couple's separation. They are nonetheless consonant with the way in which our schema frequently involves some form of sexual transgression, as in Sifrid's rape of the Count of Flanders' daughter; Baldwin Iron-Arm's adulterous seduction of the daughter of Charles the Bald; Lancelot's unwitting fornication with the daughter of King Pellés; or a mortal's procreation with a creature of enchantment, whether it be a fairy (Guinglain's mother), or a hybrid fairy-monster (Mélusine). The prominence of the motif of sexual transgression is perhaps attributable to the fact that our schema normally involves an exogamous union of two parties whose alliance in some way poses grave problems. Whether the new couple bring about a confrontation of social strata, a cross-cultural conflict, or a merger of mortal and supernatural beings, potentially contradictory value-systems are involved, and the alien feminine embodiment of "social capital" is typically viewed with ambivalence. While she is indeed deemed desirable for her potential to bring power and prestige into the line, the fact that she is also socially or culturally "other," or under some type of prohibition or

---

[32] (p. 40). These factors prompt Vitz to see God as the "Subject" of this narrative, in "Story, Chronicle, History," p. 118. I would argue that they offer evidence that God is, rather, the *destinateur* – the addressor – that overdetermines the narrative progression, as well as being the arbiter of the various sanctions meted out to the human "subjects" in the story.

[33] *La Vie de Saint Alexis*, ed. C. Storey (Oxford: Blackwell, 1968), p. 25.

conditional constraints, makes conventional matrimonial protocols highly problematic, if not unthinkable. Consequently, abduction, seduction, rape, and other forms of transgression present expedient alternatives, if not the sole means available, for effecting the improbable union. Although La *Fille du comte de Pontieu* involves both sexual and ideological transgressions, it is unique in that it separates the moment of the initial sexual transgression, the incident of rape, from its culmination in the daughter's relinquishment of her Christian marriage, thus effectively breaking the motif down into successive phases: rape is followed by paternal repudiation, then by a form of abduction when sailors take possession of the heroine, and finally by her forced marriage to the sultan.[34] As in examples of our schema cited previously, the woman's alterity, though appropriated transgressively, is here accommodated and effectively neutralized as an ideological impediment; diversity is domesticated by the decree that this marriage must be consequent upon her apostasy.[35]

In its construction of two culturally diverse nuclear families through a single genitrix, the story provides a remarkable specimen of medieval *imaginaire généalogique*, with its distinct propensity to alloy biology with mythology. Moreover, it attests to an eagerness to revalorize the scandalous by recognizing a positive divine sanction in the fruits of a marriage predicated on transgression of sacrosanct Christian vows. In essence, this particular case of mythopoeic creativity partakes of a mentality that could be characterized as courtly. The pertinence of the term obtains in what the story implicity excludes from the realm of the admissible. Expelled therefrom, notably, is the primitive epic idealization of a pure family, a pure class, or a pure race, and along with it the attendant anxiety generated by those rare, monstrously treacherous figures instrumental in the transgression of cultural boundaries held to be inviolable.[36] In its place we find confident, beneficial attribution, both of a Christian bloodline to no less than a Saladin, and of a Saracen bloodline to the Picard descendants of Raoul de Préaux.[37] In *La Fille du comte de Pontieu*, then, the feudal aristocracy's oft-implemented model of genealogical enrichment through alliances with female "social capital" becomes the vehicle for exaltation of a positive image

---

[34] The tumultuous itinerary of the Count's daughter, involving various types of abuse and exploitation to which she must submit at the hands of the men she encounters along the way, is itself a type of narrative schema found in other contexts, one of the most remarkable medieval examples being Boccacio's story of the tribulations of Alatiel (*Decameron*, II, 7).

[35] (p. 20). In "The Christian Mother and the Saracen Son," a paper presented at the MLA Annual Convention in San Diego, December, 1994, Peggy McCracken discusses the differing motivations of the daughter's conversion to Islam in each version of *La Fille* and suggests that they all express an underlying anxiety concerning maternity's potential for the corruption of lineage.

[36] We find an early epic prototype of such boundary-transgression in the figure of Ganelon. See Pierre Van Nuffel, "Problèmes de sémiotique interprétative: l'Epopée," *Langues Romanes* 27 (1973), pp. 150–62; and Louis Marin, *Sémiotique de la Passion: Topique et figures* (Paris: Bibliothèque des Sciences Religieuses, 1971).

[37] Contemporaneous portraits of Saladin appear in numerous other texts. Cf. Gaston Paris on the "récits légendaires sur Saladin [qui] lui sont favorables. Les uns se contentent de célébrer ses vertus, les autres s'efforcent de le rapprocher des chrétiens en lui attribuant une disposition, plus ou moins suivie d'effet, à reconnaître et à professer la foi des chrétiens." In "La légende de Saladin," p. 289.

of what Natalie Zemon Davis has recently called "métissage culturel."[38] Repeatedly dramatized in this story, cultural interbreeding provides a means of ultimately rendering an otherwise pernicious collective trauma comprehensible in terms of a Christian view of salvation history. *La Fille du comte de Pontieu* thus joins many other late medieval texts – *chansons de geste*, romances, pseudo-chronicles, didactic treatises, and so forth – that endorse a monumental shift away from the exaltation in early epic of Saracen-bashing and wholesale ethnic cleansing.[39] From medieval courtly literature comes a powerful sense of the positive potential of interethnic exchange and cultural diversity, as well as realization that if the roots of courtly literature lie deep in the feudal imagination, the deepest are perhaps those that pertain to the vexed questions of lineage and genealogy.

[38] Natalie Zemon Davis, "Métissage culturel et médiation historique," *Le Monde*, June 18–19, 1995, p. 11 (excerpts from the seventeenth Conférence Marc Bloch, organized by the Ecole des Hautes Etudes en Sciences Sociales, Paris, June 13, 1995).

[39] Or "génocide joyeux," to use Jean-Charles Payen's term. Jean-Charles Payen, "Une poétique du génocide joyeux: Devoir de violence et plaisir de tuer dans la *Chanson de Roland*," *Olifant* 6 (1979), pp. 226–36. See also Peter Haidu, *The Subject of Violence: The "Song of Roland" and the Birth of the State* (Bloomington: Indiana University Press, 1993).

"DAME CUSTANCE LA GENTIL": GAIMAR'S PORTRAIT OF A LADY AND HER BOOKS

Jean Blacker

Gaimar's *Estoire des Engleis* is the earliest extant Old French verse chronicle, predating Wace's *Roman de Brut* by nearly twenty years.[1] Though composed very soon after Henry I's death in 1135, the *Estoire* traces English history from the coming of the Danes in the sixth century through the reign of Henry I's predecessor, his elder brother, William Rufus (1087–1100). Each of the four manuscripts of the *Estoire* is Anglo-Norman; one contains a 98-line, unusual dedicatory epilogue, accepted as authentic, while two others have a 22-line, more conventional dedication; a fourth manuscript does not contain a dedication.[2] In an article that addresses sources, patronage, and dating of the text, as well as providing a new edition of the epilogue with a translation, Ian Short has demonstrated that the longer epilogue, found in British Library MS Royal 13 A xxi, can be broken down into at least seventeen parts, including the naming of the author, praise of the patron, enumeration of sources, *auctoritas* of sources, and self-valorization through the disparagement of a rival (pp. 324, 326). In this rhetorically complex epilogue which almost takes on a life of its own apart from the main text, Gaimar portrays his patron, Constance FitzGilbert, almost as much through what he does not say as through what he does. While mindful of how Roberta Krueger's recent study has demonstrated that we should not take portrayal of female patrons in romance at face value – since the positive portrayals of female patrons are often undermined by negative portrayals of female figures in the texts themselves – I would like to examine Gaimar's presentation of Constance FitzGilbert in this historical narrative for what it may reveal both about female patronage (and patronage in general) and about perceptions of female patronage.[3]

Historical sources – other than Gaimar's *Estoire des Engleis* – indicate that

[1] Gaimar, *L'Estoire des Engleis*, ed. Alexander Bell, Anglo-Norman Text Society 14–16 (Oxford: Blackwell, 1960; repr. ed. New York: Johnson Reprints Corporation, 1971); Wace, *Le Roman de Brut de Wace*, ed. Ivor Arnold, 2 vols., Société des Anciens Textes Français (Paris: SATF, 1938–40).
[2] Bell, ed., pp. xiv–xxiii, and "The Epilogue to Gaimar's 'Estoire des Engleis'," *Modern Language Review* 25:1 (1930), pp. 52–59; Ian Short, "Gaimar's Epilogue and Geoffrey of Monmouth's *Liber vetustissimus*," *Speculum* 69:2 (1994), pp. 323–43; all citations from the 98-verse epilogue are from the latter article.
[3] Roberta L. Krueger, *Women Readers and the Ideology of Gender in Old French Verse Romance* (Cambridge: Cambridge University Press, 1993).

Constance FitzGilbert and her husband, Ralf, were related by marriage to the Clare family, but were members of the lesser nobility themselves; their principal residence may have been near Washingborough (Short, p. 336). Charters reveal that, in Lincolnshire, Ralf founded the Augustinian priory of Markby, and was also a benefactor to the Cistercian house of Kirkstead and to the Cistercian nuns of Stixwould priory; outside of Lincolnshire, the FitzGilberts were benefactors to Southwick priory in Hampshire (Short, p. 336). Constance, who may have brought the lands of Empshott and Eastleigh (Hampshire) into her marriage with Ralf, could have been a member of the de Venoiz family and thus possibly a descendant of Miles, a marshal of Duke William of Normandy.[4] With Ralf, Constance appears making grants to Pontefract priory and giving the chapel of Empshott to Southwick priory.[5]

In the first half of the epilogue newly edited by Ian Short (p. 325), Gaimar says that Constance asked him to translate a history for her, thus giving her credit for her interest in the subject, and himself credit for having undertaken the project (6430–31); it should be pointed out that Gaimar never hesitates to give himself credit when he thinks credit is due. Lady Constance is characterized as "gentil" (6430), but not as "bele," a point to which I will return later. Gaimar mentions the length of time he devoted to the project, "Gaimar i mist marz e averil/ e tuz les dusze mais" (6432–33) – according to Short, from March of 1136 through April of 1137 (p. 338) – and the high level of effort he expended in hunting down sources, "purchaça maint esamplaire" (6435). Then the poet-historian pays Constance his highest compliment – he couldn't have done it without her: "Si sa dame ne li aidast, / ja a nul jor ne l'achevast" (6439–40). Gaimar proceeds to illustrate the pains Constance took to borrow sources for him, naming Walter Espec of Helmesly (patron of Ailred of Rievaulx, hagiographer and author of the *Battle of the Standard*) and Robert of Gloucester (eldest illegitimate son of Henry I, and patron of historians William of Malmesbury and Geoffrey of Monmouth), who loaned a Latin book to Ralf which Constance then borrowed; it is significant that Constance is addressed as the patron, however, and not Ralf:

Ele enveiad a Helmeslac	She sent to Helmsley
pur le livere Walter Espac.	For Walter Espec's book.
Robert li quens de Glöucestre	Robert, earl of Gloucester
fist translater icele geste	Had this account translated
solum les liveres as Waleis	According to the books that the Welsh
k'il aveient des bretons reis.	Had on the kings of Britain.
Walter Espec la demandat,	Walter Espec asked for it,
li quens Robert li enveiat,	Earl Robert sent it to him,
puis la prest Walter Espec	And then Walter Espec loaned it

---

[4] Lewis C. Loyd, *The Origins of Some Anglo-Norman Families*, ed. Charles Travis Clay and David C. Douglas, Publications of the Harleian Society, 13 (Leeds, 1951; repr. Baltimore: Genealogical Publishing Company, 1975), p. 109, and Dorothy M. Williamson, "Ralf son of Gilbert and Ralf son of Ralf," *Lincolnshire Architectural and Archaelogical Society, Reports and Papers* 5:1 (1953), pp. 19–27, p. 25.

[5] Judith Weiss, "The Power and Weakness of Women in Anglo-Norman Romance," in *Women and Literature in Britain, 1150–1500*, ed. Carol M. Meale (Cambridge: Cambridge University Press, 1993), pp. 7–23 (p. 19).

a Räul le fiz Gilebert.	To Ralf FitzGilbert.
Dame Custance l'enpruntat	Lady Constance borrowed it
de son seignur k'ele mult amat.	From her lord whom she greatly loved.[6]
(6441–52)	

Gaimar continues by explaining his own painstaking efforts, naming Walter, arch-deacon of Oxford as the source of the "good book of Oxford," the same Walter from whom Geoffrey of Monmouth claims to have borrowed his main source for the *Historia regum Britanniae*.[7] Gaimar also names a Winchester chronicle, which likely represents the general tradition of the Anglo-Saxon Chronicle and "an English book of Washingborough," which could refer to what is now called the *Peterborough Chronicle* (Short, pp. 328–33). It is worth noting that Gaimar does not mention Geoffrey of Monmouth by name, though the Latin book allegedly commissioned by Robert of Gloucester to be translated "solum les liveres as Waleis" is quite possibly the *Historia Regum Britanniae* in one of its earlier versions, and thus raises interest-ing questions about the status of Geoffrey of Monmouth's source which he says he translated "quendam Britannici sermonis librum vetustissimum" (Wright, p.1; Short, p. 340). To round off his list of who's who in English and British historiogra-phy, Gaimar names Nicholas de Trailly, canon of York, who was also nephew of Walter Espec, the aforementioned royal justice and patron of historical texts; Gaimar claims that Nicholas would vouch for the truth of what he is saying about his sources, should the poet meet with skepticism in this regard: "e ki ne creit ço ke jo di/ demand a Nicole de Trialli" (6475–76).

Thus, in the first half of the epilogue, Constance FitzGilbert's name is embedded in an account of historical sources – books of a very valuable kind – and is noted for her social rank and whom she knows, if not personally, then through her husband Ralf, "k'ele mult amat" (6452). She has already been very helpful to the poet, and he does not ask anything further of her, not yet at any rate.

Whereas Gaimar devotes the first half of the epilogue to sources and circum-stances of production, looking back on what he has done in the past, he devotes the second half of the epilogue looking forward to what he might do in the future: the second half of the epilogue is dominated by an exposition of the shortcomings of a verse biography of Henry I, by a poet named David; this poem is no longer extant, nor can we identify David with any certainty.[8] Gaimar criticizes David's poem and intimates that, if given a commission, he could do a better job recounting Henry's life than David:

Ore dit Gaimar, s'il ad guarant,	Now Gaimar says, that if he has a protector,
del rei Henri dirrat avant,	He will go ahead and tell about King Henry,

---

[6] All translations of the Old French passages are my own.

[7] *The Historia regum Britannie of Geoffrey of Monmouth, I: Bern Burgerbibliothek MS 568*, ed. Neil Wright (Cambridge: D.S. Brewer, 1984).

[8] Bell, ed., p. xi; P.A. Becker suggests that the poem was in Latin and that David was the bishop of Bangor (1120–39) (*Der gepaarte Achtsilber in der französichen Dichtung*, Abhan-dlungen der Philologisch-historischen Klasse der sächsischen Akademie der Wissenschaften, 43, no. 1, Leipzig: D.S. Hirzel, 1934, p. 39).

ke s'il en volt un poi parler	For if he is willing to speak a bit
e de sa vie translater,	And translate concerning his life,
tels mil choses en purrad dire	He will be able to tell such thousands of things
ke unkes Davit ne fist escrivere.	That David never had written down.
(6477–82)	

This can be seen as an indirect request of Constance to commission a biography of Henry I, or possibly an attempt to obtain royal patronage, since Henry's second queen, Adeliza of Louvain, is named as the patron of David's poem:

ne la räine de Luvain	Nor did the Queen of Louvain
n'en tint le livere en sa main.	Ever hold [such a] book in her hand.
Ele en fist fere un livere grant,	[Of David's work] she had a great book made,
le primer vers noter par chant.	Whose first verse she had inscribed
(6483–86)	with musical notation.

Although Gaimar gives David credit for having organized his song well – "Bien dit Davit e bien trovat/e la chançon bien asemblat" (6487–88) – Gaimar claims that David neglected to depict the lighthearted gaming and merrymaking, the *gab* and *druerie*, of Henry's court, slipping in a bit of flattery of the monarch in the process:

Mes des festes ke tint li reis,	But concerning the festivities the king held
del boschaier ne del gabeis,	Romping [in the woods] and joking,
del dounaier e de l'amur	Courting and lovemaking
ke demenat li reis meillur	Displayed by the best king
ke unkes fust ne jamés seit,	Who ever was, or ever will be,
e crestien fust e beneit,	And who was Christian and blessed,
ne dit gueres l'escrit Davi.	David's writing scarcely says anything.
(6495–6501)	

Given that Henry is known to have fathered at least twenty-one illegitimate offspring – though fewer during the years he was married to his second queen, Adeliza, 1121 until his death in 1135, than during the early years of his reign – David might have made the diplomatic choice in omitting this topic.[9] Gaimar then repeats and embellishes his criticism of David's work as a preface to a suggestion that David might still be able to correct his omissions by writing a sequel ("car s'il en volt avant trover/son livere en pot mult amender" 6515–16):

Ore dit Gaimar k'il tressailli,	Now Gaimar says that he'll leave off
	[talking more about this now],
mes s'il uncore s'en volt pener,	But if he still wants to bother,
des plus bels faiz pot vers trover:	He can make verses about the finest deeds:
ço est d'amur e dosnaier,	That is, of love and courting,
de boscheier e del gaber	Romping [in the woods] and joking
e de festes e des noblesces,	And festivities and splendid entertainment,
des largetez e des richesces	Largesse and riches,
e del barnage k'il mena,	And the prowess he displayed,
des larges dons k'il dona:	The generous gifts he gave:

---

9   Chris Given-Wilson and Alice Curteis, *The Royal Bastards of Medieval England* (London: Routledge & Kegan Paul, 1984), pp. 60–73.

d'içо devereit hom bien chanter,	One ought to sing well about this,
nïent leissir ne trespasser.	Not letting anything slip by.
(6502–12)	

To conclude the main part of the second half of the epilogue, Gaimar jokingly threatens that he will keep David in his prison until he writes the song properly: "jamés istrat de ma prison/si eit parfeite la chançon" (6519–20). Gaimar's poem closes with a reference to Troy, implying that the *Estoire des Engleis* was once part of a larger whole, possibly the second half of what is considered his now-lost *Estoire des Bretuns*:[10]

Treske ci dit Gaima[r] de Troie:	Gaimar recounts from Troy to this point:
il començat la u Jasun	He began where Jason
ala conquere la tuisun,	Went to conquer the [Golden] Fleece,
si l'ad definé ci endreit.	And in this spot he has concluded it.
De Deu seium nus beneit! Amen.	May we all be blessed by God! Amen.
(6522–26)	

Although we have no way of knowing whether Constance was the patron of the first part of the Troy narrative, both the Latin book Gaimar says she borrowed from Robert of Gloucester and the "good book of Oxford" likely contained Arthurian material for the *Estoire des Bretuns*, material not within the scope of the *Estoire des Engleis*. The first of the two other sources mentioned but not directly in connection with Constance, "l'estorie de Wincestre" (6461), would have been more directly pertinent to the narrative of Anglo-Saxon history in the *Estoire des Engleis*; the second of the two sources, "de Wassingburc un livere engleis" (6463) which Gaimar says traced the Roman emperors and English kings, appears possibly to have been pertinent to both the *Estoire des Engleis* and the *Estoire des Bretuns*.

Constance appears in the second half of the epilogue, again in relation to books. Gaimar says that Constance had a copy made of David's biography of Henry I (6489), further evidence of her interest in serious reading material, perhaps even too serious for its lack of festive material according to Gaimar; Constance paid one silver mark for the book (6491–92), which in today's currency would be in excess of £2000 or $4000 (Short, p. 342n85). In addition, Gaimar says that Constance read the book often in her room, "en sa chambre sovent le lit" (6490).

This passage in particular is important for several reasons: first, it contains one of the earliest records of women's book ownership; second, it records the direct commissioning and purchase of books by women, at a time when women often received books through bequests from husbands or other family members;[11] third, it records female literacy (it is possible that Constance had the book read to her, although Gaimar does not use the construction "faire lire"); and fourth, it records women's

---

[10] A. Bell, "The Munich 'Brut' and the 'Estoire des Bretuns'," *Modern Language Review* 34 (1939), pp. 321–54.

[11] Susan Groag Bell, "Medieval Women Book Owners: Arbiters of Lay Piety and Ambassadors of Culture," *Signs* 7:4 (1982), pp. 742–68, p. 748.

interest in historical material in a period shortly before women are most frequently singled out as consumers of romances.[12]

Constance's connection with books in Gaimar's text becomes all the more noteworthy when compared with the portrayal – or at least mention – of other female patrons in Old French texts from the first half of the twelfth century. Four of the earliest of these texts – each of which happens to be Anglo-Norman – Benedeit's *Voyage of Saint Brendan*,[13] Philippe de Thaon's *Bestiaire* and *Livre de Sibile*,[14] and Sanson de Nanteuil's *Proverbes de Salemon* –[15] contain a short passage referring to a female patron.

Of the six manuscripts of the *Brendan*, four contain an 18-verse dedicatory prologue addressed to Queen Adeliza ("Aaliz") of Louvain, and one contains the same prologue but with the name of Henry I's first queen, Matilda (Short and Merrilees, pp. 4–5). This prologue is very conventional: the poet establishes himself in the role of servant, whereas the patron is seen as a conduit of divine and temporal justice:

Donna Aaliz la reïne,	Lady Adeliza, the queen,
Par qui valdrat lei divine,	Through whom God's law will prevail,
par qui creistrat lei de terre	Through whom terrestrial law will grow stronger,
E remandrat tante guerre	And all this warring will end
Por les armes Henri lu rei	Through the might of King Henry
E par le cunseil qui ert en tei,	And by the counsel to be found in you,
Salüet tei mil e mil feiz	Greets you a thousand times and a thousand [more],
Li apostoiles danz Benedeiz.	The disciple, Dom Benedeiz.
Que comandas ço ad enpris	He has undertaken this which you bid
Secund sun sens e entremis,	According to his talents and set about,
En letre mis e en romanz,	To put into Latin and into French,
Esi cum fut li teons cumanz,	Thus as it was your command,
De saint Brendan le bon abéth.	About Saint Brendan, the good abbot.
(1–13)	

The poet claims to need the patron's protection, to shield him from the mockery of others (14–18). Note that no terms are used to qualify the patron except "la reïne," that is, her rank; no references are made to interests nor to physical characteristics.

Philippe de Thaon also addressed the first version of his *Bestiaire* (c. 1120–35) to Adeliza:

[12] As, for example, by M. Dominica Legge, "The Influence of Patronage on Form in Medieval French Literature," in *Stil- und Formprobleme in der Literatur, Vorträge des VII. Kongresses der Internationalen Vereinigung für moderne Sprache und Literaturen in Heidelberg* (Heidelberg: Carl Winter, 1959), pp. 136–41.
[13] Benedeit, *The Anglo-Norman Voyage of St. Brendan*, ed. Ian Short and Brian Merrilees (Manchester: Manchester University Press, 1979), cf. editors' translation of prologue, p. 80.
[14] Philippe de Thaon, *Les Bestiaire de Philippe de Thaün*, ed. Emmanuel Walberg (Lund: Möller; Paris: Welter, 1900) and *Le Livre de Sibile by Philippe de Thaon*, ed. Hugh Shields, Anglo-Norman Text Society, 37 (London: ANTS, 1979).
[15] Sanson de Nanteuil, *Les Proverbes de Salemon by Sansun de Nantuil*, 3 vols., ed. C. Claire Isoz, Anglo-Norman Text Society, 44, 45, 50 (London: ANTS, 1988, 1994), passage cited from prologue, vol. I, p. 6.

Pur l'onur d'une geme	For the honor of a jewel
Ki mult est bele feme	Who is a very beautiful woman
E est curteise e sage,	And courteous and wise,
De bones murs e large:	Of excellent conduct and generous:
Aaliz est numee	She is named Adeliza
Reïne est corunee,	She is crowned queen,
Reïne est d'Engletere. (5–11)	She is Queen of England.

After referring to Adeliza as a "jewel" and as a beautiful, courtly, and wise woman, of "good values" and generous, Philippe provides a false etymology for her – in Hebrew, her name means "praise of God" (13–18).[16] Perhaps this flattery was more appropriate in the *Bestiaire*, a secular text, than in the *Brendan*, a narrative about a saint; nonetheless, the flattery and mention of, or emphasis on, physical beauty was to become common in dedications to female patrons in romances beginning in the second half of the twelfth century.

Between the time Philippe addressed the first version of his *Bestiaire* to Adeliza and the second version or reissuing, to Henry II's queen, Eleanor of Aquitaine (c. 1154), he addressed the *Livre de Sibile* to Henry I's daughter, Empress Matilda. In the 14-verse dedicatory passage, the poet wishes for the empress's entry into Paradise; from the empress, he wishes to gain for himself in abstract terms "her gift, her love, and her reward," and in concrete terms, his inheritance which he claims has been taken wrongly from him:

Le Livre de Sibile	The Book of Sybil
La roïne nobile,	The noble queen,
Issi [ai] translaté	Here [I have] translated [it].
Od l'aïe de Dé	With the help of God
E pur l'empereïs,	And for the Empress,
Ki soit en paraïs.	May her soul be [one day] in Paradise.
Deus m'en otroit sun dun,	May God grant me her gift,
S'amur, sun guer[e]dun,	Her love, her reward,
E ki sun grant barnage	And [may] her great prowess
Me rende m'eritage,	Render me my heritage,
Dunt sui desherité	Of which I am disinherited
E a mut tort mené. (1207–18)	And cut off from quite wrongly.

Note the lack of physical description of the female patron on the one hand, and also on the other, the lack of mention of her possible interest in the subject, in books, or in related matters.

Possibly because his bid to Matilda for restoration of his inheritance may have been unsuccessful, Philippe addressed the second version (or re-issuing) of the *Bestiaire* to Queen Eleanor.[17] In this 24-verse dedicatory prologue, the female patron (or rather, desired patron) is characterized as "a treasure of wisdom, honor and beauty," and of "largesse":

---

[16] M. Dominica Legge, *Anglo-Norman Literature and Its Background* (Oxford: Oxford University Press, 1963; repr. Westport, CT: Greenwood Press, 1978), p. 25 and n. 1.

[17] The epilogue from the revised *Bestiaire* is edited from Oxford MS Merton College 249 by Shields, ed. (*Sibile*), pp. 18–19.

Dus gart ma dame Alienor,	God preserve my lady Eleanor,
La reïne chi est censor[18]	The queen who is a treasure
De sens, de onur e de beuté,	Of wisdom, honor and beauty,
De largesce e de beuté! (10–14)	Of largesse and beauty!

Here, the patron is seen as the conduit, if not of divine justice, then at least of temporal justice; the poet begs the queen to have the king restore his maternal inheritance and, in exchange, Philippe offers Eleanor the bestiary book (18–25). The phrasing, "Cum vus purreiz al livre oïr" (30) ("As you could hear in the book"), implies that the queen was not reading herself, but was in the listening audience, possibly an audience of one.

The description of physical beauty of the patron in the *Bestiaire* functions not only as flattery of the patron, but also as enhancement of the poet's stature, through recognition of the worthiness of the patron, a female patron's worthiness perhaps being enhanced by her physical beauty. Eleanor is portrayed in a more traditional way than Constance: Eleanor, who is said to be fortunate to have married Henry (14–15), is asked to get her husband to do something for the poet ("Dame, se vus plest, aideiz mei/ De sul preiere vers le rei" (18–19)) – the emphasis is on the king and the king's power here. In the *Estoire*, Constance is said to use her husband as a contact, granted, but it is she who remains in the foreground, the final link between what the poet needs and the poet. It should be added that Constance does the procuring, so to speak, for a scholarly purpose, not a material one (at least not directly material, though Gaimar may have hoped to gain fame and fortune through his writing).

Sanson de Nanteuil dedicated the *Proverbes de Salemon*, c. 1140–54, to Alice de Condet. Alice, a member of the upper nobility whose first husband was Richard FitzGilbert of Clare, was thus related to Constance and Ralf FitzGilbert by marriage.[19] Before naming his patron, Sanson says that she had asked him many times to make his translation; he says that he is mindful of his lady whom he loves and fears:

E a s'enor at translaté	And to her honor he has translated,
Sanson de Nantuil, ki sovient	Sanson of Nanteuil, who remembers
De sa dame qu'il aime e creient,	His lady whom he loves and believes,
Ki mainte feiz l'en out preiéd	Who beseeched [him] many times
Que li desclairast cel traitéd.	To explicate this text for her.
(194–98)	

Sanson names Alice, calling her a "noble damme enseigné e bele" (202), and declares that her fame has spread far and wide throughout "sa contree" (205–6). He also mentions that she takes great pleasure in religious writings, that she gladly owns them and reads them:

| Pur ço l'en fist translatïun | For this he made this translation, |

---

[18] MS error for *tensor* "treasure"? (Shields, ed., p. 18n2).

[19] Ian Short, "Patrons and Polyglots: French Literature in Twelfth-Century England," *Anglo-Norman Studies XIV: Proceedings of the Battle Conference 1991*, ed. Marjorie Chibnall (Woodbridge: The Boydell Press, 1992), pp. 229–50 (p. 243), and "Gaimar's Epilogue," p. 336.

Qu'il conut sa devotïon,	For he knew her devotion,
Kar des escriz ad grant delit,	For she takes great joy in writings,
Molt volonters les ot e lit.	She gladly owns and reads them.
(209–12)	

Even if this last declaration of his patron's interest in religious books represents wishful thinking rather than a reflection of actual circumstance, Sanson has provided a dedication which is in some ways a middle ground between the flattering declaration of Eleanor's beauty in Philippe's rededication of the *Bestiaire* and Gaimar's extended discussion of books and Constance's relation to them. The portrait of Alice, albeit scanty, has a triple focus – on rank, education, and beauty, in that order. It is more conventional in its stance of the poet as servant fearful of his mistress, but less so in its mention of the female patron's education and interest in books.

Although it is found in a Continental French romance at the beginning of the second half of the century, one last dedication to a female patron merits mention here, since it stands in such stark contrast with that of Gaimar's dedication to Constance in his Anglo-Norman history. Benoît de Sainte-Maure dedicated the *Roman de Troie*, c. 1155–60, to a "riche dame de riche rei" (13468), who has been identified as Eleanor of Aquitaine by many scholars.[20] This 14-verse dedication is packed densely with praise and covers little other ground:

De cest, veir, criem g'estre blasmez	I truly fear being blamed for this,
De cele que tant a bontez	By her who has so much goodness
Que hautece a, pris e valor,	Who has rank, worth and reputation,
Honesté e sen e honor,	Honesty, wisdom and honor,
Bien e mesure e sainteé,	Goodness, *mesure*, and holiness,
E noble largece e beauté;	And noble largesse and beauty;
En cui mesfait de dames maint	In whom the misdeeds of many ladies
Sont par le bien de li esteint;	Are extinguished by her goodness;
En cui tote sciënce abonde,	In whom every form of knowledge abounds,
A la cui n'est nule seconde	To whom there is no equal
Que el mont seit de nule lei.	In the world according to any law.
Riche dame de riche rei,	Rich lady of a rich lord
Senz mal, senz ire, senz tristece,	Without evil, wrath, sadness,
Poisseiz aveir toz jorz leece!	May you have happiness always!
(II, 13457–470)	

The female patron, in whom all knowledge is said to be plentiful, and who has no equal, is qualified by a litany of virtues: "bonté," "hautesce," "pris," "valor," "honesté," "sen," "honor," "bien," "mesure," "largesce," and "beauté"; she is also noble and holy. As pointed out by Krueger, these compliments for the female patron can be construed as left-handed (pp. 4–7). Half-way through this passage, which in Krueger's words, "works as much to undermine female authority as to

[20] Benoît de Sainte-Maure, *Le Roman de Troie*, ed. L. Constans, 6 vols., Société des Anciens Textes Français (Paris: SATF, 1904–12). The scribe of Paris, Bibliothèque de l'Arsenal MS 3340 interpreted Benoît's reference to a lady as the Virgin Mary: "Riche fille de riche rei/ De vos nasquié tote leece/ Le jor de la Nativité:/ Vos fustes fille et mere Dé" (13467–70, vol. 6, p. 25).

acknowledge a powerful patron" (p. 4), Benoît praises the patron to the detriment of others of her sex (II, 13463–464), "her goodness erasing the misdeeds of many others." Nonetheless, the patron occupies center stage in the last reference as well, that of her knowledge in abundance.

In contrast to the romances discussed by Krueger, Gaimar's *Estoire des Engleis* does not present a female patron whose portrayal is opposed by dubious characterizations of female figures.[21] Gaimar's portrayal of Constance, realistic or idealized or somewhere in between, is positive, and she, and her contemporaries – as well as Gaimar himself – had much to gain from that. The longer, highly detailed epilogue (98 verses) – as opposed to the very conventional short one (22 verses) which names Adeliza in passing and Constance not at all[22] – fulfills several functions on behalf of the work, of vernacular historiography, of the author, and of the patron: first, it places the *Estoire des Engleis* within the context of a larger work, by claiming an earlier portion dedicated to a narrative of antiquity, serving to place English history within a more universal framework; second, through the narrative about sources, it articulates the synthetic methods of historical writing of the period, bringing all sources onto an equal footing (Latin, Old English, and Old French); third, the longer epilogue brings Gaimar's efforts into focus, for his present and quite possibly future benefit; and

---

[21] On portrayal of female characters (historical and fictional) in Gaimar, see A. Bell, "Gaimar and the Edgard–Ælfthryth Story," *Modern Language Review* 21 (1926), pp. 278–87; A.R. Press, "The Precocious Courtesy of Geoffrey Gaimar," in *Court and Poet: Selected Proceedings of the Third Congress of the ICLS, Liverpool, 1980*, ed. Glyn S. Burgess (Liverpool: Francis Cairns, 1981), pp. 267–76; Jean Blacker, *The Faces of Time: Portrayal of the Past in Old French and Latin Historical Narrative of the Anglo-Norman* Regnum (Austin, Tx.: University of Texas Press, 1994), pp. 87–91, and "Anglo-Saxon Women Redressed: Anglo-Norman Courtly Heroines in Gaimar's *Estoire des Engleis*," unpub. paper.

[22] Epilogue from MSS Durham, Cathedral Lib. C iv 27 and Lincoln, Cathedral Lib. 104, as edited by A. Bell, ed., Appendix, p. 207:

Ci vuil ore finir m'estoire,	I want to finish my narrative now,
Del rei Henri ne frai memoire	I will not make a record of King Henry
Kar Aeliz la bone reine	For Adeliza, the good queen
A qui Deu doinst grace divine	To whom may God grant divine grace,
En ad traitié un livre grant;	Had a great book made about it;
Pur ço [si] fin le mien a tant.	For this [reason] I am finishing mine forthwith.
L'estoire des Engleis ci finist.	He [Gaimar] finishes the history of the English.
Beneie les tuz Jesu Crist	May Jesus Christ bless all
Qui lur entente i mettrunt	Who will turn their attention to it
E qui as autres la dirrunt	And [those] who will tell it to others
Qui ne la sevent [ne l'] unt oie;	Who don't know it or haven't heard it;
Deu del ciel tuz les beneie	May God in heaven bless them all
Kar a tel chose deit l'um entendre,	For one must be attentive to such a thing,
U il n'i ad rien que reprendre	Where there is no means to reproach,
Ne vilain[i]e ne mençonge;	Nor baseness nor lies;
N'est pas [cest livre ne] faible ne sunge,	This is not fable nor dream,
Ainz est de veire estoire estrait	It is taken thus from the true story
Des anciens reis e de els fait	Of the ancient kings and their deeds,
Qui guvernoent Engleterre,	Who governed England,
Alcuns [en pais], alcuns en guerre.	Some [in peace], some in war.
Issi cuvint, ne pot el estre.	Thus it must have been; it could not have been otherwise.
Beneie vus Deu le rei celestre.	May God, the heavenly King, bless you.

fourth, it underscores a female patron's interest in and relationship to writing, reading, and ownership of books.

Whereas the shorter epilogue contains a conventional cursory reference to a royal patron, the longer epilogue provides many more details about historical craft and a portrait, albeit sketchy, of a woman much closer to the poet in social station than the queen. In part, the longer epilogue can be seen as an attempt to demonstrate the values of the lesser nobility and the secular clergy to the royal entourage.

While Gaimar seeks to gain prestige through protestation of hard work, he does not complain of the toil, but rather name-drops to illustrate the important people, including Constance, to whom he is connected in his literary-historical labors. He mentions books and book owners, however, more often than he does specific authors, except for David, though works such as the Anglo-Saxon Chronicle were anonymous. In addition to illustrating the interests of the lesser nobility and those who wrote for them, Gaimar's epilogue can be seen to serve as advice for fellow historians: production of historical works requires use of multiple sources, so don't be afraid to consult many, and be certain to find a resourceful lady who knows her books.

Gaimar does not place Constance FitzGilbert on a pedestal as a courtly lover places his lady, to be worshipped, praised, served, feared (and hence, possibly resented), but rather he places her at the lectern and in the inner circle of educated and influential patrons of historical texts, French, English and Latin on an equal footing. Gaimar's portrayal of Constance FitzGilbert is one of a dynamic woman of means who does what she can to further knowledge; if this can be construed as a male fantasy, it certainly ranks among the most feminist of the period.

In conclusion, though we see a reference to Constance in her chamber, we do not really see her in corporeal terms: whatever beauty of the physical body she may have possessed is irrelevant in Gaimar's hierarchy of values: although Constance's body is gendered in the most literal sense of the term, its importance for Gaimar – and, by extension, for his audience – originates in its ability to co-operate with her mind to appreciate, gather, buy, and read books. This portrait has the lady in her chamber, not with her weaving or among friends, however, but in solitary pleasure with her books, one of which immortalizes her in memorable fashion.

ALTERITY AND SUBJECTIVITY IN THE *ROMAN DE MELUSINE*

Sara Sturm-Maddox

The representation of subjectivity in literature, as much recent discussion has empha-sized, is not unlike the representation of subjectivity generally: because the construc-tion of identities cannot be divorced from ideology, that construction in literary texts may be examined both for its "literariness" and for its suggestiveness with regard to a broader cultural discourse. I propose here to consider the pertinence of such questions to a late-fourteenth-century romance, the *Roman de Mélusine* by Jean d'Arras,[1] and in particular Jean's representation of the eponymous heroine, Melusine herself.

In the exordium of the *Roman de Mélusine*, Jean d'Arras, before affirming that the object of his work is to relate "how the noble and powerful fortress of Lusignan was founded by a fairy" (*M* 5), has already reported accounts of fairies who meet and marry mortals – accounts that set the stage for the encounter of Melusine's fairy mother and mortal father as well as her own with her future husband. But even before that, he has prompted us to consider reports, not only of fairies, but of other supernatural creatures as well – lutins, shape-shifters – who involve themselves in the lives of mortals, some doing good and some harm, and admonishes us repeatedly that, as all of these creatures are part of God's *merveilles*, our mortal understanding cannot penetrate the secrets of their existence.

Thus Jean sets up a distinction between fairy and mortal that implies the impossi-bility of access by the latter to the subjectivity of the former. The distinction at first appears merely to formalize in Christian terms a disparity readily apparent in the *lais* of an earlier century, in which that lack of access is a given, both for the fairy's mortal partner and for the reader; we do not expect, conventionally, to be privy to the thoughts or emotions of fairies. These creatures, who appear to act according to the promptings of their own sovereign will, often seem curiously impassive. When they predict what will befall them and their human lovers in the case of the latter violating their conditions, they stress the consequences for the lover rather than for them-selves: "You would lose me forever," says Lanval's new *amie*; "Never could you see me, or possess my body" (vv. 147, 149–50).[2] The fairy who accords her love to Graelent, acquiescing only after being taken by force, reflects that this young man is

---

[1] Jean d'Arras, *Mélusine. Roman du XIVe siècle*, ed. Louis Stouff (Dijon: Bernigaud et Privat, 1932; repr. Geneva: Slatkine Reprints, 1974), cited by page number as *M*; translations mine.
[2] For *Lanval* see *Les Lais de Marie de France*, ed. Jean Rychner (Paris: Champion, 1971);

probably the best match to be made; on the other hand, although she foresees that she will suffer great pain as a result of Graelent's violation of her interdiction against revealing their love, the eventual consequences appear to be suffered by him alone.[3] In *Tydorel*, it is left to the reader to imagine the sorrow or regret of the fairy knight as he leaves his lady, never to return. The affection of fairy lovers for their human companions is similarly left to the reader's deduction when they sometimes – but not always – return to save the lover from death or disgrace.[4] As Micha remarks of the fairy lovers of both genders in the *lais*, "tous ces personnages semblent commandés par une volonté occulte ou agir en vertu d'une prescience inexplicable."[5]

The status of the "founding fairy" of Lusignan is in this regard complex, and somewhat vexed. She is born of a fairy mother and a mortal father, and her mother proclaims that had she and her sisters not vengefully shut their father up forever within a mountain, they would soon have been drawn away from the "ways of nymphs and fairies" by the force of his human seed. Now, not only is that progress arrested, but each receives a specific punishment from their mother: Melusine's is a periodic serpentine transformation. Nonetheless, her mother tells her, "if you find a man who wishes to take you as his wife, who will pledge to you that he will never see you on Saturday, or seek you out then or speak of it to anyone, you will live out a natural life-span as a normal woman, and die naturally. In any case, a very great noble lineage will issue from you, which will do many great deeds. And if you are separated from your husband, know that you will return to the former torment, without end until the High Judge sits in judgement" (*M* 12–13).

These words not only program Melusine's story throughout the text; they also make of her a most unusual fairy protagonist, in that they enable the reader to deduce her motives at each phase of that story. And Jean d'Arras avoids repeating the identification of Melusine as "a fairy:" from the scene in which her mother speaks of the "ways of nymphs and fairies" until the moment when her husband Raymondin's public disclosure of her intermittent serpentine transformation necessitates their separation, she is designated as "la dame."[6] During that long section of the text in which her story is conjoined with that of Raymondin, moreover, she appears progressively as a "normal" woman, although admittedly an extraordinary one. As

for *Graelent* and *Tydorel* see *Les lais anonymes des XIIe et XIIIe siècles*, ed. Prudence Mary O'Hara Tobin (Genève: Droz, 1976); translations mine.

[3] Robert J. Nolan notes that the Celtic stories with which *Mélusine* is often associated "stress the superiority of the woman over the man and her indifference when they are separated"; see "The Origin of the Romance of Melusine: A New Interpretation," *Fabula* 15 (1974), p. 193.

[4] Lanval's lady vindicates him by a show of her incomparable beauty, but it is not in response to her invitation that the knight departs with her; Graëlent is saved only through the intercession of the fairy's compassionate companions; in *Guingamor*, the knight is rescued by her companions, but his fate remains uncertain.

[5] Alexandre Micha, *Les Lais féeriques des XIIe et XIIIe siècles* (Paris: GF-Flammarion, 1992), p. 11.

[6] Here her presentation conforms to that of "les fées amantes" in earlier lay and romance; see Laurence Harf-Lancner, *Les Fées au Moyen Age: Morgane et Mélusine. La naissance des fées* (Paris: Champion, 1984), pp. 35–38.

Douglas Kelly emphasizes, the lack of monstrous marks on the last two of her ten sons suggests that in the course of her long maternity she progressively approaches the "human" state.[7]

If we consider as "representation of subjectivity" the varieties of *focalisation interne* – the focus on internal process through the description of psychological states indicative of an inner life of the characters – inventoried by Michèle Perret in the *Roman de Mélusine*,[8] we might expect in this larger context that that representation would have its role in what Kelly calls the "domestication of the marvelous" – that Melusine's life as an apparently "normal" woman would be rendered in a manner not unlike that of the other protagonists. But in fact we shall be obliged to conclude that it is the representation of subjectivity – or the lack of it – as much as her extraordinary accomplishments or her semi-serpentine transformations that sets Melusine apart. It is significant that Perret's examples concerning Melusine's subjectivity are all drawn from the "pre-history" of her story – when she is with her fairy peers, mother and sisters – and from its ending, when she is about to leave Lusignan and the world of humans. From the time she first encounters Raymondin until the days that immediately precede their separation, Melusine's thoughts and feelings are far less frequently indicated than those of other personages.

In that first critical encounter, the young nobleman has inadvertently killed the Count his uncle, and is exposed to grave danger of punishment. Melusine recounts to him the tragic event which he has not revealed, and then informs him that only she can help him escape the present peril; *with* her aid, she tells him, he can become the most lordly and powerful man of his entire lineage (*M* 25–26). A similar role is often attributed to fairy lovers: Lanval, unjustly excluded from Arthur's largesse, receives from his fairy mistress the wherewithal to resume a splendid life among his peers; in *Tydorel*, the fairy knight fathers the child that the queen had not conceived in her marriage. Raymondin is no exception: he readily accepts Melusine's conditions, of which the first is that he agree to marry her.

The scene, however, bears further scrutiny. Raymondin's reaction is singularly pragmatic: "he thought to himself that he had better take a chance on believing the lady, for one can only cross the cruel threshold of death a single time" (*M* 26) – a canny calculation that affords the reader an uncommon insight into his mental process. Melusine's comportment, on the other hand, betrays only her fairy prescience, which recalls that of her fairy mother: in the initial encounter of her father and mother, King Elinas is immediately "so overcome by love that he did not know how to behave," we are told, while the fairy, "who knew very well that he was in love with her," appears totally impassive, concerned only to obtain his consent to

---

7 "The Domestication of the Marvelous in the Melusine Romances," in *Melusine of Lusignan: Founding Fiction in Late Medieval France*, ed. Donald Maddox and Sara Sturm-Maddox (Athens, GA: University of Georgia Press, 1996), p. 44.

8 "Writing History/ Writing Fiction," in *Melusine of Lusignan*, p. 202. Perret cites Kate Hamburger who includes among the indices of fictionality "everything that gives access to the subjectivity of the characters: verbs of feeling and thinking attributed to third parties without need of justification, interior monologues, and free indirect style . . ." [*Fiction et diction* (Paris: Seuil, 1991), p. 76].

her interdiction.[9] Melusine in turn expresses no emotion until Raymondin has consented to marry her according to her terms, and at that point her controlled response contrasts sharply with his effusiveness. After detailing her first instructions, she addresses him as "mon amy" and presents him with rings having magical protective powers. In response, he "kissed her very amorously, as her to whom he completely entrusted himself; for he was by then so overwhelmed by love that he took everything she said to be the absolute truth" (*M* 27).

It is necessary to underline this contrast because some readers have found in Melusine's attachment to her husband a distinctive trait of her characterization, suggesting for example that "one fundamental difference between Melusine and her ancestors is the depth of her love for her mortal husband and desire to lead a 'human' life with him."[10] But although we may infer her love from all that she does on his behalf, such conclusions can only be *textually* justified on the basis of the small segment of her story immediately preceding her departure from Lusignan. Until that point the reader is reminded instead of her desire to escape her fairy condition through the marriage: on their wedding night when, before the marriage is consummated, she again cautions her husband about violating her interdict, then continues: "Since I have come so far in this, I shall have to wait for God's will and trust in your promise."[11] Certainly her statement is poignant, but it does less to affirm her love for Raymondin than to remind us of her preoccupation with her own story's end which cannot yet be foreseen.

Similarly for her often-cited love for her children, her "unusual depth of maternal love" (Hosington, pp. 202–203). Again, we may infer that love from her painstaking advice and admonitions, from her provisions for their well-being, from the material and magical gifts she gives them as they leave Lusignan. The affective element of that function, however, the maternal as differentiated from what we might call the dynastic concern, is once again not primary until after Raymondin's fatal revelation.

Were we to consider only Raymondin and Melusine, we might suspect that here as in numerous other texts it is the female protagonist's gender that denies her interiority or casts it only through the eyes of the male protagonists.[12] Not so, however, for in this text the construction of subjectivity cannot be readily differentiated according to gender. Although male characters, with the exception of Melusine, dominate the text, other female characters are equally endowed with thought and

[9] Declarations of love by fairies are often laconic: "I have come from afar to seek you, for I love you more than anything else in the world" says the fairy in *Lanval* (v. 116); the mysterious knight in *Tydorel* tells the lady "I have come here on account of you, whom I greatly love and desire" (vv. 58–59).

[10] Brenda M. Hosington, "Mélusines de France et d'Outremanche: Portraits of Women in Jean d'Arras, Coudrette and Their Middle English Translators," in *A Wyf Ther Was: Essays in Honour of Paule Mertens-Fouck* (Liège: Univ. de Liège, 1992), pp. 199–208; here p. 202.

[11] The only exception to this "non-erotic presentation of their wedding night," as Kevin Brownlee observes, is their indirect designation at the end of the scene as "les deux amans." See "Melusine's Hybrid Body and the Poetics of Metamorphosis," in *Mélusine of Lusignan*, p. 98, note 18.

[12] For examples see Valeria Finucci's introduction to *The Lady Vanishes: Subjectivity and Representation in Castiglione and Ariosto* (Stanford: Stanford University Press, 1992).

emotion, however brief their appearances or limited their roles. To Melusine's even-tual daughters-in-law are attributed extremes of emotion: Hermine, hearing news of her future husband's arrival, "felt such great joy in her heart that she didn't know what to do . . . and she was so absorbed in these thoughts that she didn't sleep at all the whole night" (*M* 116). What these depictions lack in subtlety they make up in hyperbole: "And the maiden was so joyful at this news that she had never before known such great joy. And know that she loved Guyon so much that she could not possibly have loved him more" (*M* 130). Throughout the romance, emotions, thoughts and even complex interior processes are reported of the other characters. They are repeatedly said to be sorrowful, joyful, fearful, enraged.[13] Collectively and individually, as Rupert Pickens has observed, they are *very* often amazed and astonished;[14] they plan, they scheme, they consider the consequences of their ac-tions; Raymondin's anguish after inadvertently killing his uncle is doubled in his son Geoffrey's crisis of conscience leading to his confession to the Pope (*M* 22, 28–29; 274). Interestingly, Jean d'Arras's attention to such representations is evident in his care on occasion to distinguish between a character's contrived appearance – that contrived for the textual audience – and the "real" reaction that he as narrator validates for his own audience, as here of Hermine: "She made a show of feeling great sorrow in her heart – as indeed she did" (*M* 116). Not so for Melusine.[15]

The distinction may pass almost unnoticed, because Melusine is not left without a voice; even a casual reader will note that in direct discourse she is at least the equal of other protagonists, often in lengthy monologues of considerable dramatic force. But her discourse does little to reveal interiority. Instead, it consists most often of practical advice offered to her husband and sons: she tells Raymondin how to measure out the parcel of land he will be given, on which Lusignan will be founded, and instructs him in fine detail how to reclaim his heritage in Brittany; she admon-ishes various of her sons as they set off to conquest and crusade, in terms that systematically rehearse the feudal ideals of noble conduct.

[13] Jean d'Arras frequently employs the same formula that reports events and circumstances, "et sachiez que . . .", to introduce inner processes, whether these be communal emotion – "et sachiez que le peuple du pays estoit moult doulent" (*M* 123) – or individual responses: "Et quant Uriien oy ces paroles, si pensa un pou; et sachiez que il fut moult doulens de ceste requeste pour ce que il avoit grant voulenté d'aler aval le monde pour veoir le pays et acquerre honneur" (*M* 120); "Et sachiez que, se Guyon eust eu loisir, qu'il lui eust dit aucques sa pensee" (*M* 127).
[14] For the frequence of "pronominal verbs denoting the mental and emotional processes of wonderment" and their shades of meaning see Rupert T. Pickens, "The Poetics of Paradox in the *Roman de Mélusine*," in *Melusine of Lusignan*, p. 49.
[15] A suggestive contrast is afforded by "Mélusine sicilienne" in Geoffroi d'Auxerre's *Super Apocalypsim*, where emotions are attributed to the fairy despite the fact that the particular form of interdiction in this tale entails her total silence. Not only does she affirm by signs and nods to her sceptical interlocutors her belief in God; as Harf-Lancner notes, "elle adopte, dans la demeure du héros, une attitude fort expressive: 'en diverses occasions, elle restait assise, silencieuse, à leurs côtés, pleine de gratitude et d'empressement. Elle mangeait et buvait avec eux, et en toute chose se montrait presque aussi à l'aise que si elle s'était trouvée parmi des compatriotes, des parents, des amis' " (*Les Fées au Moyen Age*, p. 146).

This prominence of advice in Melusine's discourse contributes centrally to her celebrated function in the romance as nurturer and founder, "Mélusine maternelle et défricheuse."[16] What it also underlines, however, is her relative omniscience concerning what the male characters – her husband, her sons, her husband's relatives or the nobles – have done or will do, an omniscience in which the reader recognizes fairy attributes that replicate those of her mother; "She knew it well" is a typical reaction recorded for both.[17] What she knows, moreover, she frequently conceals even from husband, comrades, or retinue, beginning with her initial encounter with Raymondin when she offers her companions an explanation for his apparent rudeness: "she said that as a coverup," the narrator tells us, "so that the others would not perceive what she herself noted, for she knew very well who the young man was" (*M* 24). Most striking is that no notion of her feelings is offered on the occasion of Raymondin's original betrayal, when he spies upon her and sees her bathing in her half-serpent form. Because she does not mention the occurrence, he concludes with relief that she knows nothing of it. "He was mistaken," explains Jean d'Arras, "for she knew everything; but since he had not revealed it to anyone, she tolerated it at the time and gave no sign of it" (*M* 331–32). Through such authorial comment, Jean repeatedly draws attention to an inner life even as he denies the reader access to its content.

Thus the disparity in the representation of subjectivity, throughout the long segment in which Melusine in other respects earns for herself the apparent status of "normal" woman, continues to set her apart. For her intratextual audience – her own ever-present public – her lack of communicativeness has an obvious function: it maintains an air of mystery whose inevitable consequence is duly recorded as curiosity and as "talk" about her, just as there had been talk and curiosity about her fairy mother.[18] As a result, Melusine retains her status as a figure to be interpreted, to be "read." Curiously, Raymondin himself does not attempt to "read" her until the voyeuristic scene provoked by his brother's report of others' speculation, with the disastrous consequences recorded in the text.[19]

The withholding of indications of subjectivity also prepares the impact of the

---

[16] See Jacques Le Goff and Emmanuel Le Roy Ladurie, "Mélusine maternelle et défricheuse," *Annales: Economies, Sociétés, Civilisations* 26 (1971), pp. 587–622.

[17] When Elinas follows Presine, love-struck, the lady "congnut assez qui il estoit et comment il avendroit de son emprise," and calls him by name (*M* 8); and when the daughters take vengeance on Elinas and return to tell her: "Haa, dist Presine, qui bien le savoit . . ." (*M* 12). When conventional conversational gambits fail to elicit Raymondin's disclosure of his crisis, Melusine announces that she knows it all: "Quant celle voit que il se celoit si fort contre lui, si lui a dit: Remondin, par Dieu, riens ne vous vault le celer; je scay bien comment il vous va . . ." and tells him his own story (*M* 25).

[18] Presine and Elinas "menerent longtemps bonne vie ensemble, Mais ly pays du royaume d'Albanie estoient moult esbahiz qui celle dame estoit, combien qu'elle gouvernast saigement et vaillaument" (*M* 9).

[19] When he does at last confront the need to "read" her, he confronts it as a question of good or evil. For the argument that he in fact misreads her, see Laurence de Looze, "La fourme du pié toute escripte: Mélusine and the Entrance into History," in *Melusine of Lusignan*, pp. 132–33.

closing pages of Melusine's story, in which her affective state acquires extraordinary prominence. The transition between the two is effected by the account of her visit to Lusignan that immediately precedes Raymondin's public revelation of her serpentine transformation. The passage in question is initiated by a letter sent by Raymondin's men to inform her that one of her sons has burned an abbey with all the monks, including his own brother, within; it tells too of Raymondin's apparently inconsolable grief. "Alas!" exclaims the narrator in reporting the decision to send the letter, "It was such a terrible thing to do! for it plunged both husband and wife into great torment and enormous grief" (*M* 254). The fact that Melusine learns of these catastrophic events only through the letter is in itself highly significant: "she takes it, breaks the seal, and reads it. And when she realizes the awful deed, she feels great sorrow." Thus, just at the point when her inner life is about to attain singular prominence in the narrative, the trait of prescience that has served heretofore as reminder of her "difference" is explicitly withdrawn.

In the depiction of Melusine's brief stay in Lusignan before she proceeds to face Raymondin, we find Jean d'Arras at his narrative best. We are not told, but may well infer, that she goes first to Lusignan because of her particular attachment to the place, the first fortress and first city she had founded in Poitou. Here we have a Melusine in a very agitated – and thus wholly uncharacteristic – state, an extraordinary prelude to what is to follow. "She stayed two days there," Jean d'Arras reports, "and seemed very dejected, and all the time she was constantly coming and going, up and down throughout the area, covering every bit of it, and from time to time uttering truly grievous laments and heavy sighs" (*M* 254) – a phrasing which effectively anticipates her behavior in her soon-to-be-assumed monstrous, serpentine state.

But Jean d'Arras goes on: "The story and the authentic chronicle – which I maintain to be true – says that she knew well the great sorrow that was about to befall her, and as for me I firmly believe it. But that never occurred to her retinue, who thought her behavior resulted from her displeasure that her son Geoffrey had burned his brother and the other monks, and by the great anger that she knew Raymondin felt about it." Here her fairy prescience is reintroduced, but now for the first time it serves to heighten the report of her emotion and, through the incomprehension of her retinue, the way in which she is singularly isolated through her essential difference: not the all-capable, self-possessed Melusine we have come to expect, but a figure both vulnerable and very much alone in her distress.

This modulation of focus sets up the scene that follows Raymondin's revelation of her serpentine transformation, the second transgression of her interdiction that seals her destiny according to the terms set by her fairy mother. "When Melusine heard that word," the narrator tells us, "she felt so much sorrow in her heart that she fell down in a faint . . .". The nobles and their ladies "raised the lady to a sitting position, and wet her face with cold water, and made such efforts that she regained consciousness. As soon as she could speak, she looked pitifully at Raymondin and then said . . ." (*M* 256). Just as Raymondin's lament after his voyeuristic transgression is remarkable in that it contains no comment whatsoever on the serpentine form he has observed, we find now that Melusine recovers from her faint, not as a now-unmasked fairy who tends to assume a very unusual form which might be considered diabolical, but as "la dame," and it is as such that she will speak for the

remainder of the scene that precedes her transformation and departure.[20] Now Raymondin resumes his lament, and its most characteristic feature, as Kevin Brownlee
notes, "is the catalogue of courtly and ethical virtues attributed by Raymondin qua
courtly *amant* to Mélusine qua courtly *dame*," a discourse whose "net effect . . . is
to intensify Mélusine's human side at the very moment that her hybrid corporeal
identity has been most graphically presented in the text up till now" (p. 83). But the
prior withholding of the attribution of interiority to Melusine makes her participation
in the final scene even more remarkable, as she now exclaims to Raymondin "What
misfortune for me that I ever saw your graceful body, your bearing, or your handsome face, or ever desired your beauty, since you have so falsely betrayed me!" (*M*
256). Most important from the point of view of the construction of subjectivity is
that this passage establishes what Brownlee terms Melusine's status as desiring
subject *retrospectively*.[21]

It is particularly suggestive in this regard that Melusine's lament is not just for
Raymondin. In this one scene we witness the creation of a whole affective life
retrospectively created for Melusine, as she evokes the things most dear to her: "Ah,
sweet country, I have had in you so much solace and delight, and would have had in
you a full measure of well-being, had it pleased God that I not be so dreadfully
betrayed. Alas! I used to be called 'lady,' and everyone attempted to do just what I
wanted. Now I shall be less than the poorest chambermaid! And those who always
showed great joy in seeing me will flee from me, and feel fear and repulsion when
they see me" (*M* 259). It is now too that her maternal emotions are first underscored.
Only moments prior to her departure, Melusine pronounces the word "fée" – in its
only occurrence in the latter part of the romance – only to negate it for the benefit of
her children; she seeks, she tells the noble company present, to preserve her children
from the reproach of being the offspring, not only "of a serpent or a fairy," but also
"of a bad mother" (*M* 259–60).[22]

Even more striking is the depiction of Melusine *after* her metamorphosis. After
launching herself from the castle window and assuming the form of a flying serpent,
she circles the tower uttering a cry "so marvelous and so sorrowful that everybody
wept from pity; they could tell very well that she was leaving only under constraint
and against her will" (*M* 260). Here the emphasis falls precisely but paradoxically
on an inner life that can be read by all, while it had been closed and concealed to
them before. Further demonstration of her affection for her children follows: while
her last two sons are infants, she returns, as she had promised, to care for them, and
is seen by their nurses in her female form each evening, "holding the children beside

---

[20] Here, Harf-Lancner notes, "la conduite de l'assistance fait écho à la réaction du héros"
(*Les Fées au Moyen Age*, p. 175). In other "contes mélusiniens," she points out, the hero has
"un mouvement d'horreur et de recul devant le spectacle qu'il a surpris" (p. 172).

[21] Just before she leaves, Melusine "as female (courtly) desiring subject is thus definitively
established in the text at the very moment of her disappearance in this capacity. All of this
functions, of course, as part of the romance's larger program of valorizing Mélusine by
'neutralizing' the threat of her female erotic desire; and, most particularly, within the context
of her fairy identity" (p. 90).

[22] See Harf-Lancner, *Les Fées au Moyen Age*, pp. 41–42.

the hearth, giving them as much comfort as she could" (*M* 261). Years later, as foretold, she returns in serpentine form to the Tour Poitevine of Lusignan to herald the death of Raymondin, and two of her sons who are present weep because they recognize the serpent uttering "grievous laments and such heavy sighs" as their mother. She in turn, seeing them weeping, "bends toward them with a terrible mournful cry . . ." and again, "when she saw her children weeping, she felt great sorrow, and let out a great, marvelous wail . . . and then it seemed to all those present that she wept very tenderly" (*M* 288).

Finally, we should not neglect Melusine's final scene in the romance, in which the suggestion of subjectivity is indirect but quite extraordinary. It occurs on her return to Lusignan before the domain is to pass into the hands of Jean de Berry (*M* 308ff.). Creswell, the current governor, and his mistress are abed when a serpent enters, and goes about the bed "thrashing with its tail" on it, "without doing them any harm." Then the serpent transforms itself into a woman, dressed "in the old-fashioned way," and sits before the fire before becoming a serpent again and departing. No attribution of feeling is necessary now for us to perceive her distress and melancholy, her fidelity to hearth and home.

What then are we to make of all this? Suggestive is Valeria Finucci's remark concerning Renaissance fictions that "epic narratives construct exemplary rulers by linking the fashioning of selves to the fashioning of kingdoms" (p. 7). In Jean d'Arras's text, where the fashioning of the patrimony is attributed to a woman, there is some attention to the fashioning of Melusine as an exemplary matriarch endowed with energy and vision, one dedicated to the advancement of her husband and her sons and at the same time beloved by the common people for her piety and generosity – altogether a reassuring representation of femininity consistent with feudal ideals. Yet we have noted that during the long segment in which she is as it were naturalized or "domesticated" in the romance, the lack of access to her subjectivity maintains the reader's awareness of her essential "otherness." For Melusine's identity is constructed differently from that of the other characters in Jean's romance; she is never as it were fully fashioned, because her fairy otherness renders her status resistant to our comprehension, just as Jean d'Arras had warned in his exordium. The distinction between fairy and mortal creatures, set forth in the exordium, is manipulated by Jean throughout Melusine's story to serve the ends of his particular feudal fiction. The result is the void at the center of the Lusignan project: the reader's discomfiture at the close of the romance results in large part from the impossibility of attributing a fixed identity to Melusine. That impossibility leaves the world that she has created, not the enduring legacy that Jean d'Arras's text purports to celebrate, but one whose foreseen decline has already begun.

PASSELION, MARC L'ESSILIE ET L'IDEAL COURTOIS

Michelle Szkilnik

Comme C.E. Pickford l'a bien montré dans son étude sur l'*Evolution du Roman Arthurien en prose vers la fin du Moyen Age*,[1] le roman arthurien exerce encore un charme certain sur les lecteurs de la fin du Moyen Age. L'idéal courtois incarné par Lancelot séduit suffisamment pour que de grands seigneurs prenant pour modèles les héros de romans cherchent à émuler dans la réalité les personnages de la fiction. Dans les romans en prose du XIVe et du XVe siècles, une myriade de personnages illustrent les éminentes valeurs chevaleresques que sont noblesse, générosité, pitié, loyauté, fidélité à la dame. Dans *Perceforest*,[2] Lyonnel, Nestor, Gadiffer, et bien d'autres préfigurent les qualités qui s'épanouiront chez Lancelot et les compagnons de la Table Ronde. Dans *Ysaÿe le Triste*,[3] Ysaÿe fils de Tristan, adoubé par Lancelot, se consacre à rétablir les valeurs courtoises tombées en désuétude.

Pourtant à côté de ces dignes précurseurs ou successeurs de Lancelot apparaissent des héros de stature comparable mais au comportement bien différent. Epris de justice, aussi vaillants aux armes que les héros plus "traditionnels," ils représentaient sans doute également un modèle, comme le confirment les rôles globalement positifs qui leur sont réservés. Passelion dans *Perceforest* tue l'infâme Bruyant sans Foy. Marc l'Essilié, fils d'Ysaÿe le Triste, abat des dizaines de mauvaises coutumes et se rend célèbre par son amour de la justice. Mais à ces qualités courtoises s'ajoutent des traits de caractère qui le sont beaucoup moins: infidélité à la dame, légèreté de moeurs, sens de l'humour douteux, violence, cruauté, implacabilité. Les excès de tels personnages, qui les marginalisent à nos yeux, mais pas aux yeux de leurs compagnons, le défi qu'ils semblent lancer à la société courtoise dans laquelle ils sont pourtant bien intégrés, nous invitent à reconsidérer l'idéal dit courtois. Marc et Passelion témoignent-ils simplement de la décadence des valeurs traditionnelles? Ou bien révèlent-ils une face de la chevalerie qui pour être le plus souvent cachée n'en

---

[1]   Paris: Nizet, 1960, en particulier chap. III, pp. 232–37.
[2]   *Perceforest*, première partie, éd. Jane H.M. Taylor (Genève: Droz, 1979); quatrième partie, éd. Gilles Roussineau (Genève: Droz, 1987), 2 tomes; troisième partie, éd. Gilles Roussineau (Genève, Droz, 1988–1994), 3 tomes. Sauf indication contraire, toutes mes références seront prises à la quatrième partie de cette édition. PF1 = *Perceforest*, quatrième partie, volume 1, PF2 = volume 2.
[3]   *Ysaÿe le Triste, Roman Arthurien du Moyen Age tardif*, éd. André Giachetti (Rouen: Publications de l'Université de Rouen, 1989). Toutes les références à ce roman seront prises dans cette édition. Y = *Ysaÿe*

existe pas moins chez tous les représentants de cette classe? Telles sont les questions auxquelles je voudrais apporter quelques éléments de réponse.

Dans ces chroniques du royaume de Grande-Bretagne qu'est le roman de *Perceforest*, Passelion occupe une place particulière. Fils de Priande et d'Estonné, Passelion appartient à la seconde génération des héros. La première, celle des fondateurs, comprend outre le père de Passelion, Estonné, l'empereur Alexandre, Perceforest, Gadiffer le roi d'Ecosse, Tor le Comte de Pédracq. La seconde génération s'avère aussi brillante que la première: Lyonnel du Glat, Nestor, Gadiffer le jeune, Bethidès, Troïlus, les douze chevaliers aux voeux ont tous l'étoffe de héros arthuriens. Notons tout de suite que le Tor et Estonné se mêlent aux jeunes héros et qu'il y a donc ici une sorte de brouillage des générations. En effet, Estonné épouse la soeur de Troïlus, Priande, et leur fils Passelion est en fait contemporain des héros de la troisième génération, les fils qui, après la bataille du Franc Palais, la destruction de la Grande-Bretagne et la mort de tous les illustres chevaliers de la seconde génération, s'engageront à restaurer le pays. Outre le rôle prépondérant qu'il joue dans le processus de restauration, ce qui distingue Passelion de ses contemporains, c'est qu'il est donc entré dans le roman avant la bataille du Franc Palais, qu'il a non seulement connu l'élite des chevaliers du Franc Palais mais même lutté à leurs côtés, malgré son jeune âge. Il appartient ainsi à deux mondes, ce qui explique l'autorité que semblent lui reconnaître les chevaliers de la troisième génération. Du reste lui a été adoubé avant la destruction de la Grande-Bretagne et il est donc pratiquement le seul à pouvoir à son tour faire chevaliers les héros de la troisième génération.

Bien d'autres éléments suggèrent la nature extraordinaire de Passelion. Sa naissance par exemple: son père Estonné vient d'être lâchement assassiné par Bruyant sans Foy. Priande, la mère de Passelion, en train d'accoucher au moment du meurtre, a une vision qui lui révèle ce qui vient d'arriver. L'enfant, impatient de sortir du ventre maternel pour venger son père, déchire alors le côté de sa mère et vient au monde une arbalète et une flèche de chair à la main (PF1, 157–60). Incroyablement précoce, d'une force exceptionnelle, le jeune Passelion est adoubé à l'âge de deux ans. Il accomplit alors ce à quoi il aspirait depuis sa naissance: il venge son père en tuant Bruyant sans Foy (PF1, 299–300). Si Passelion peut réaliser de tels exploits, c'est aussi parce qu'il est protégé par Zéphyr, une sorte de bon génie qui avait déjà pris en affection Estonné. Naissance merveilleuse, protection surnaturelle, force exceptionnelle, tout prédispose Passelion à devenir un héros de premier plan, un second Lancelot, ou plus justement son illustre prédécesseur.

Pourtant un trait de caractère perceptible dès sa naissance le rend différent de ce parangon des valeurs courtoises qu'est Lancelot. Passelion est violent, d'une violence parfois inquiétante. Sa naissance en porte témoignage. Qu'il veuille venger son père est sans doute tout à fait louable dans une société qui accorde tant d'importance à l'honneur du lignage, mais que penser de son impatience qui provoque la mort de sa mère? Comment interpréter l'arc et la flèche qu'il serre dans son poing à sa naissance, si fort qu'il faut les lui arracher (PF1, 161)? Cet arc et cette flèche durciront à l'air et c'est avec ces armes que Passelion tuera Bruyant. Mais pourquoi pas une épée, plus caractéristique du chevalier? Serait-ce parce que Passelion est plus un chasseur qu'un chevalier? Son agressivité, symbolisée par les armes avec lesquelles il naît, se manifeste bien entendu à l'égard de l'assassin de son père. Encore au berceau, il ne peut entendre parler de Bruyant sans se mettre en colère: "se ceans aucun parle de Bruiant devant lui, il maine telle vie que a peine le puet on appaiser," confie sa nourrice (PF1, 200, si on parle de Bruyant devant lui, il pique une telle colère qu'on a bien du mal à le calmer). A un âge où les enfants ordinaires ne répondent qu'à ce qui affecte leur bien-être matériel, il semble porter le plus vif intérêt aux récits de bataille et adopte une attitude farouche qui impressionne tous les témoins (PF1, 265–67). Cette ardeur belliqueuse se tourne parfois contre ses amis. Quand Zéphyr vient pour la première fois examiner le nouveau-né, Passelion lui décoche un bon coup de pied (PF1, 162). Lors de l'amusante scène de l'adoubement, Passelion, qui ne connaît pas les rites, s'emporte contre Lyonnel qui lui a donné la colée et le frappe de son épée. Sa réaction fait rire les chevaliers qui se mettent alors à le taquiner. Passelion distribue les coups et blesse les chevaliers jusqu'au sang. Tous interprètent sa violence comme le signe de son grand coeur (PF1, 278–81). Son tempérament farouche est perçu comme une qualité bien que les termes employés soient parfois ambigus: "Il estoit tant mauvais et impaciens" (PF1, 280, il était très méchant et impétueux); il allait devenir "un homme fier et tres criminel" (PF1, 281, un homme farouche et redoutable). Un épisode néanmoins frappe et trouble les compagnons de Passelion: après avoir tué Bruyant de son arc et sa flèche, Passelion lui arrache le coeur de ses propres mains et le déchire à pleines dents (PF1, 301). Sans doute Lancelot enfant pouvait-il aussi s'emporter violemment et à cette occasion "quanqu'il tenoit as dens et as mains tout depechoit" (il mettait en pièces tout ce qui lui passait par les mains ou les dents[4]). On se souvient aussi des coups dont il roue son maître. Mais c'est la noblesse de son coeur qui dicte cette réaction à Lancelot, scandalisé par les propos et l'attitude de "vilain" de son maître, alors que Passelion semble, lui, assouvir un désir beaucoup plus primaire où le goût du sang se mêle à la soif de vengeance.

Passelion est ensuite confié à la fée Morgue qui se charge de l'élever mais a fort à faire avec ce mauvais garçon, libertin et amateur de tours pendables et cruels. Les témoins ou les victimes de ses tours (celles qui survivent au moins) ne s'indignent que modérément. Morgue se plaint à Zéphyr mais avoue que les bêtises de son pupille la font souvent rire (PF2, 696–97). Quant à Zéphyr, il est tout prêt à excuser Passelion, voire à l'assister et à encourager son libertinage, soutenant par exemple que si Passelion viole toutes les filles du voisinage, c'est pour compenser les meurtres qu'il a commis (PF2, 701). Si sa brutalité dépasse de beaucoup celle de Lancelot et surtout paraît beaucoup plus gratuite, le portrait de Passelion enfant n'en fonctionne pas moins en relation avec celui de Lancelot, comme si l'auteur du *Perceforest* voulait exploiter certaines virtualités du personnage de Lancelot, en particulier ce tempérament violent qui semble s'émousser chez l'adulte et ne se déchaîne de toutes façons qu'à l'encontre des vilains. Comme s'il voulait s'amuser à démontrer qu'en partant presque des mêmes prémisses, on pouvait créer un héros respecté, admiré, un héros de la stature de Lancelot, qui soit néanmoins, et presque à l'excès,

---

4 *Lancelot, Roman en prose du XIIIe siècle*, éd. Alexandre Micha (Genève: Droz, 1978–1983), t. VII, p. 72.

l'opposé de Lancelot. Passelion n'est clairement pas courtois, ni à l'égard des autres chevaliers – il refuse par exemple d'aider un chevalier coincé sous son cheval (PF2, 848) –, ni surtout à l'égard des femmes. Il est intéressant de le comparer dans ce domaine non à Lancelot, l'homme d'une seule femme, mais au coureur de jupons qu'est Gauvain. Que le "Soleil de la Chevalerie" profite de sa réputation pour obtenir les faveurs des femmes, voire les solliciter de manière pressante, bien des textes en offrent la preuve. Néanmoins il y a loin entre séduire une femme par des paroles douceureuses et la violer sans autre forme de procès. Là encore le texte du *Perceforest* me semble ambigu dans sa présentation des faits, suggérant à la fois qu'il y a viol et pourtant que les femmes sont consentantes.

Morganette, Gaudine, Caniffre finalement aiment être forcées et qui plus est, alors que dans la plupart des cas les aventures de Gauvain restent stériles, Passelion, lui, est un formidable géniteur. Chacune de ses maîtresses d'une nuit lui donnera un enfant. Le libertinage de Passelion est donc doublement justifié: à une époque où la Grande-Bretagne est dépeuplée et manque de chevaliers, engendrer des fils est de la plus haute importance. On retrouve ici sur le mode sérieux la boutade de Zéphyr qui excusait Passelion de violer les servantes sous prétexte qu'on avait besoin de valets. D'autre part son attitude se justifie narrativement: puisque *Perceforest* veut se rattacher aux cycles arthuriens du XIIIe siècle, il faut que ses personnages soient d'une manière ou d'une autre les ancêtres de ceux du *Lancelot* ou du *Tristan*. Passelion est à l'origine de quatre lignages prestigieux: avec Morganette, fille de la fée Morgue, il est l'ancêtre et de Merlin et de la Dame du Lac, avec Gaudine, celui d'Iseut, avec Marmona, celui de Claudas de la Déserte. Notons qu'il *n'est pas* l'ancêtre de Lancelot (c'est son cousin Benuïc qui a cet honneur), mais qu'il comptera parmi ses descendants le farouche ennemi de Ban de Benoïc, Claudas, comme si dans l'impossibilité de se mesurer à Lancelot dont il n'est pas le contemporain, Passelion arrangeait néanmoins une confrontation à distance. Rappelons aussi que Claudas est présenté dans le *Lancelot* comme un chevalier magnifique et valeureux qui pourrait figurer parmi les plus grands, n'était son acharnement à l'égard du lignage de Ban. Est-ce parce qu'il compte Passelion parmi ses ancêtres que Claudas est affligé de cette violence orgueilleuse qui le perd?[5] En étant en outre le lointain ancêtre d'Iseut, Passelion ne s'amuse-t-il pas aussi à secréter une rivale à Guenièvre comme pour prendre parti dans le débat qui anime le *Tristan* en prose: quelle est la plus belle dame, d'Iseut ou de Guenièvre? Enfin que dire du fait qu'il soit l'ancêtre de la Dame du Lac, sinon qu'il a son mot à dire dans l'éducation et la formation de Lancelot? On voit combien la relation entre les deux personnages est complexe. Elevé sous les mêmes auspices que Lancelot, mais opposé du grand héros courtois par son attitude violente et anti-courtoise, personnage original, nouveau en apparence, Passelion a pourtant besoin de Lancelot pour se définir. Lancelot ne reste-t-il pas finalement le modèle? L'évolution de Passelion semblerait le suggérer. Alors que Lancelot est né courtois, Passelion doit le devenir. Il doit apprendre la politesse, la clémence, la générosité, la patience, toutes qualités caractéristiques du chevalier courtois. Il doit

---

5 Merci à Elspeth Kennedy qui, durant la discussion qui a suivi ma communication, m'a suggéré cet autre rapprochement entre les deux personnages.

consentir à brider son orgueil. Tout au long du roman, il reçoit ainsi diverses leçons de morale, de son père mort, de Zéphyr, de chevaliers qu'il affronte, voire de femmes, jusqu'au jour où il finit par éprouver enfin, à son grand étonnement, les souffrances de l'amour véritable. Mais la contre-partie de cette sophistication sociale du personnage n'est-elle pas son affadissement? Quand Passelion rejoint enfin les rangs des chevaliers courtois, s'il s'impose par son autorité naturelle comme leur chef, et remporte le prix du premier tournoi organisé après la bataille du Franc Palais, n'a-t-il pas presque épuisé ses possibilités narratives? Ce n'est plus lui qui va être chargé des aventures suprêmes, il occupe ensuite les secondes places, comme si seule son inquiétante violence pouvait être réellement productive du récit et de ses prolongements fictifs.

Si Passelion engendre de nombreux enfants dans le cadre du roman de *Perceforest*, il peut aussi se targuer d'avoir une postérité littéraire de taille. Le roman d'*Ysaÿe le Triste* semble s'être en effet inspiré de lui pour concevoir ses deux principaux personnages: Ysaÿe, le héros éponyme, et Marc son fils. Comme Passelion, Ysaÿe est un orphelin, sur qui veillent des puissances féériques. Il naît lui aussi dans des circonstances extraordinaires: convaincu que Tristan est blessé à mort, Iseut donne naissance à son fils dans la souffrance et le désespoir. S'il ne déchire pas le flanc de sa mère, l'enfant vient au monde une épée de chair à la main. La ressemblance ne doit toutefois pas occulter l'évidente différence entre l'arc de Passelion et l'épée d'Ysaÿe: l'épée est l'emblème du chevalier aussi valeureux que courtois qu'Ysaÿe deviendra. Sans franchement récuser la paternité littéraire de Passelion ni renier le père que la fiction lui prête (Tristan), le fils de celui qui savait si bien manier l'arc-qui-ne-faut semble ainsi prendre ses distances par rapport à ces figures quelque peu controversées, à ces francs-tireurs du monde courtois. Préférant l'épée à l'arc, lui s'inscrit d'emblée dans la lignée des authentiques chevaliers courtois.[6] Si la scène de son adoubement s'avère aussi mémorable dans son incongruité que celle de l'adoubement de Passelion, le symbolisme qui s'en dégage est différent: le petit enfant Passelion révélait à l'occasion de cette cérémonie son impétuosité et la violence de son tempérament. Ysaÿe choisit de se faire adouber par le squelette de Lancelot pour se ranger clairement sous l'égide de celui qu'il reconnaît comme un modèle.

C'est à Marc, le fils, que Passelion lègue ses traits de caractère. Extrêmement violent dès sa petite enfance – il noie son cousin dans un puits, torture les petits enfants, souille la nourriture etc. (Y 193–94) – Marc est redouté de tous quand il atteint l'âge adulte mais on lui reconnaît un sens aigu de la justice. Impulsif, agressif, il lui arrive de tuer ses propres amis dans le feu de l'action et de rejeter ensuite le blâme du meurtre sur la victime (Y 266). Son attitude envers les femmes contraste avec celle d'Ysaÿe fidèle tout au long de ses péripéties à son amie Marte. Certes, Marc ne viole pas les dames comme Passelion mais il n'hésite pas à trahir la promesse qu'il a faite à la belle Orimonde pour séduire d'autres demoiselles. Comme

---

[6] Voir mon article "L'ombre de Lancelot dans *Ysaÿe le Triste*," *Mélanges offerts à Alexandre Micha*, éd. M. Zink et D. Buschinger (Wodan, 1995), pp. 363–69.

Passelion, il engendre du reste fils et fille au hasard de ses aventures amoureuses.[7] Ses infidélités lui valent de se trouver dans des situations ridicules,[8] comme le libertinage jouait de mauvais tours à Passelion. Toutefois là s'arrêtent les ressemblances car le roman de *Perceforest* et celui d'*Ysaÿe* ne réservent finalement pas le même rôle à leurs personnages. Passelion reste dans *Perceforest* un héros marginal. S'il propose une alternative au modèle traditionnel représenté par presque tous ses compagnons, il se définit essentiellement par opposition: il est d'abord un anti-Lancelot, pour être mieux ramené par la suite à la norme. En ce sens l'idéal courtois reste intact et c'est toujours à lui qu'on mesure les héros.[9] Le roman d'*Ysaÿe* me semble aller plus loin. En répartissant entre père et fils les caractéristiques héritées du personnage de Passelion, l'écrivain suggère l'existence de deux types sans doute étroitement liés mais aussi inscrits dans le contexte historique des générations. Né et élevé dans le monde arthurien (même en pleine dégénérescence), fils de Tristan et "filleul" de Lancelot, Ysaÿe appartient encore à la génération des pères, ceux qui révèrent Lancelot comme le modèle de toute chevalerie (Y, 44–45) et déplorent la disparition des valeurs d'antan (Y, 409). Marc, le fils, n'a eu aucun contact avec le monde arthurien. C'est plutôt au monde de l'épopée qu'il est confronté, aux Sarrasins qui viennent attaquer le royaume de son oncle. S'il voyage ensuite en compagnie du nain Tronc à travers les royaumes aventureux du monde arthurien, cette expédition est présentée comme une expérience de caractère presque anthropologique. Sans doute Marc entend-il bien se couvrir de gloire en courant les aventures et en découvrant les merveilles de Bretagne, mais il y a aussi chez lui la curiosité d'un étranger intéressé sur le plan intellectuel par les moeurs de peuples différents:

> Lé oel de creature et lez orelles ne sont oncques asasyés de veir ou d'oïr les grans mervelles qui sont ou monde, et pour tant a creature humaine piés pour ce qu'elle soit portee es lieus, se estre peut, es quelz et desquelx les merveilles veues ay oÿ recorder, et pour tant ont esté pluiseurs chevaliers et pluiseurs boins philozophes nommés sy comme vous tous sçavés. Sy sui josnes et en men venir, et sy ne say de riens parler fors de che que on fait en cest païs (. . .) sy m'est prinse vollentés d'aller lez estranges royaumes visiter. (Y 371–72)

> (Les yeux humains et les oreilles ne se rassasient pas de voir et d'entendre les grands prodiges que recèle le monde, et si les hommes ont des pieds, c'est pour les porter, si possible, là où se trouvent les merveilles dont j'ai entendu parler. C'est la raison pour laquelle on cite en exemple plusieurs chevaliers et plusieurs bons philosophes, comme vous le savez tous. Je suis jeune et en pleine formation. Je ne connais rien d'autre que les moeurs de ce pays. J'ai envie d'aller visiter les royaumes étrangers.)

Cette découverte tardive du monde arthurien fait de lui un héros qui ne correspond plus au modèle courtois sans s'y opposer pour autant comme Passelion. Ainsi le

---

[7] Cf. l'énumération p. 489.
[8] Voir sa mésaventure dans la forêt aux Dames où il est rossé par une troupe de nains ressemblant étrangement à Tronc pp. 452–54.
[9] Les déviations par rapport à la norme se manifestent évidemment dès lors que la norme est érigée. Ainsi a-t-on pu parler d'une dégradation du personnage de Gauvain par exemple, qui très vite au XIIIe siècle apparaît comme de moins en moins conforme à l'idéal qu'il est supposé incarner. Voir Keith Busby, *Gauvain in Old French Literature* (Amsterdam: Rodopi, 1980).

roman d'*Ysaÿe* présente-t-il en succession deux types héroïques, l'ancien et le nouveau, incarnés respectivement par le père et le fils.

Mais comment interpréter le fait que dans sa seconde partie le roman ne s'intéresse presque exclusivement qu'à Marc? Ne faut-il pas voir là le type du fils éclipsant celui du père? Marc le justicier violent, peu sentimental, érigé en nouvel idéal? Sans doute non, car la fin du roman rétablit un équilibre entre les deux modèles. Père et fils se distinguent pareillement dans la dernière bataille contre les Sarrasins, chacun épouse finalement sa dame au cours de la même cérémonie et si Ysaÿe est couronné roi de Blamir, on a bien l'impression que père et fils règnent de concert. Par ailleurs, bien que le texte précise que les deux couples sont féconds, seuls les enfants illégitimes de Marc sont nommés. Ainsi contrairement à ce qui se passe avec Passelion, Marc n'est ni ramené à la norme courtoise, ni écarté par le roman. Son triomphe est consacré mais à égalité avec celui de son père, signe que, ultimement, le roman ne choisit pas entre les deux modèles chevaleresques.

La présence dans des romans que les critiques rattachent généralement à la tradition courtoise, de personnages comme Marc et Passelion nous invite à nous interroger sur nos définitions. D'une part elle témoigne de la rencontre de deux genres, l'épopée et le roman, qui se combinent de manière particulièrement évidente aux XIVe et XVe siècles, quand des héros d'un genre se manifestent dans l'autre – Tronc, le valet d'Ysaÿe et de Marc n'est autre qu'Aubéron.[10] Une certaine expression de la violence (et non la violence elle-même) qui surprend par sa nouveauté pourrait en fait venir de l'épopée, voire d'autres traditions comme celle du roman d'Alexandre. D'autre part, ces héros violents, qui ressemblent pourtant si bien à leurs comparses courtois avec qui ils sont du reste liés par le sang, éclairent d'un jour nouveau certains traits de l'idéal chevaleresque. Si Passelion peut à la rigueur passer pour un chevalier précourtois, mal dégrossi, que le temps, l'expérience et la volonté du narrateur peuvent corriger et polir pour le conformer à un idéal resté intact, Marc, lui, fait éclater la notion même d'idéal courtois. Tous les grands héros qui l'ont précédé pouvaient bien sûr faire preuve de temps à autre de faiblesses; mais précisément leurs possibles infidélités, leur cruauté occasionnelle étaient analysées en terme de défaillance. Ce que le personnage de Marc suggère cependant, c'est qu'il ne s'agit peut-être pas de défaillances mais de traits constitutifs du comportement chevaleresque. Violence et cruauté ne sont que l'autre face de la justice, l'implacabilité accompagne nécessairement la générosité, amour et infidélité vont de pair. La célébration des valeurs chrétiennes s'accommode de l'apologie des armes et de la violence, le service dû à la société, de la poursuite d'une gloire personnelle. Ce qui nous paraît des contradictions choquantes ne l'était peut-être guère pour le public du Moyen Age, surtout dans le contexte de la guerre de Cent Ans, époque durant laquelle est écrit le roman

---

[10] Voir aussi dans *Valentin et Orson*, roman du XVe siècle, l'improbable rencontre du roi Pépin et du roi Arthur qui se conclut par l'exécution d'Arthur après séjour à la prison du Châtelet.

d'*Ysaÿe*. En plaçant sur un pied d'égalité ses deux héros, le roman d'*Ysaÿe* laisse peut-être entendre qu'ils incarnent les deux faces d'une même attitude. Les qualités inquiétantes de Marc ne le sont que pour nous qui habitués à la vision romantique et réductrice de la chevalerie que nous a léguée le 19e siècle crions à la dégradation d'un idéal qui n'existe en réalité que pour nous.

THE POLITICAL SONGS IN THE *CHRONICLES* OF PIERRE DE LANGTOFT AND ROBERT MANNYNG[1]

Thea Summerfield

The verse chronicle which was written by Pierre de Langtoft in Anglo-Norman in the last years of the reign of Edward I is best known for the songs relating to the Scottish wars which it contains. When, in the 1330s, Robert Mannyng translated Langtoft's *Chronicle* into Middle English, these songs were for the most part retained. Scholarly interest has largely been limited to the question of the original language and social *milieu* of these songs. In this article I propose to focus on the formal and thematic relationship between the songs and the main text of the two chronicles. It will be shown that both Langtoft and Mannyng made use of a widely-known discourse of abuse for their own ends in their historiographical poems.

For his *Chronicle*, Langtoft used mono-rhymed alexandrine *laisses*. It deals with the kings of Britain and England from Brutus up to Edward II, giving special emphasis to the question of English rights to Scotland. In the section on the reign of Edward I the depiction of Anthony Bek, the bishop of Durham, is striking, while throughout there is much emphasis on the benefits which have been derived from good relations between Durham and Westminster. At the time of writing, Anthony Bek was severely embroiled with Edward I and in danger of losing his temporalities.[2] It is likely that Langtoft's *Chronicle* was written to offer Edward I an entertaining survey of English history which also gave historical proof of the benefits which might be expected, especially with relation to Scotland, from good relations between the king and the bishop of Durham.[3]

1   References are to T. Wright, *The Chronicle of Pierre de Langtoft in French verse from the earliest period to the death of king Edward I* (London: Rolls Series, 1866), vol. II; translations by Wright; parallel references are given to the recent, partial edition of Langtoft's *Chronicle* by Jean-Claude Thiolier, *Pierre de Langtoft: Le Règne d'Edouard Ier* (Créteil: CELIMA, Univ. de Paris XII, 1989). Unless otherwise stated all references are to Thiolier's *Rédaction II*; on *Réd. I* see below, n. 6. References to Mannyng's *Chronicle* are to the edition by Idelle Sullens (Medieval and Renaissance Texts and Studies vol. 153; Binghamton N.Y., 1996).

2   The friendship between the two men, and their subsequent quarrel, is described in Bek's biography by C.M. Fraser, *A History of Anthony Bek* (Oxford: Clarendon Press, 1957) and "Edward I and the Regalian Franchise of Durham," *Speculum* 31 (1956), pp. 329–42.

3   See Thea Summerfield, "Context and Genesis of Pierre de Langtoft's *Chronicle*," in *Literary Aspects of Courtly Culture. Selected Papers from the Seventh Triennial Congress of the International Courtly Literature Society, Amherst, Mass. 1992*, ed. Donald Maddox and Sara Sturm-Maddox (Cambridge: D.S. Brewer, 1994), pp. 321–32.

The nine songs, which are often called "the political songs" after the title of Wright's 1839 edition of political poetry in which they were included,[4] are a feature of Langtoft's account of the reign of Edward I only.[5] With very few exceptions the extant manuscripts display variation and revision only "on a very limited scale and of the simplest kind."[6] Two songs (nos. 1 and 8) are entirely in Anglo-Norman, like the rest of Langtoft's *Chronicle*, three (nos. 2, 4 and 5) are in English, and four (nos. 3, 6, 7 and 9) have stanzas in Anglo-Norman, followed by a number of stanzas in English. English stanzas never precede the Anglo-Norman ones, nor are these poems macaronic in the sense that Anglo-Norman and English are used alternately, either as stanzas or as lines. In this respect they are unlike other songs on political subjects written in the thirteenth and early fourteenth centuries.[7] All the songs, whether in English or Anglo-Norman, deal with particular aspects of the Anglo-Scottish war in the reign of Edward I; most are anti-Scottish, but two are – at least ostensibly – anti-English.

Theories of the origins of these songs, and the extent to which they were recorded *verbatim*, range from partly translated anonymous oral compositions[8] to the work of

---

[4] T. Wright, *The Political Songs of England, from the Reign of John to that of Edward II* (London: Camden Society, 1839).

[5] For an elaborate if tendentious description of Langtoft manuscripts, see Thiolier's edition, pp. 35–208. In Wright's edition of Langtoft's *Chronicle* the songs can be found on the following pages (st. = number of stanzas, AN = Anglo-Norman, Eng. = English): **no. 1**: p. 222 (2 st. AN); **no. 2** pp. 234–36 (4 st. Eng.); **no. 3** p. 244 (4 st. AN, 2 Eng.); **no. 4** p. 248 (4 st. Eng.); **no. 5** p. 252 (2 st. Eng.); **no. 6** pp. 254–58 (16 st. AN, 2 Eng.); **no. 7** pp. 260–64 (10 st. AN, 4 Eng.); **no. 8** pp. 266–68 (12 st. AN); **no. 9** p. 364 (2 st. AN, 2 Eng.); compare, in Thiolier's edition, pp. 291, 305–07, 315, 319, 323, 367–68, 369–71, 372–73, 420.

[6] V.J. Scattergood, "Revision in some Middle English Political Verses," *Archiv für das Studium der neueren Sprachen und Literaturen* 126, vol. 211 (1974), pp. 287–99, here p. 289. Major variations occur in Cambr. G.G.1.1, which has three extra stanzas (see Wright, *Pol. Songs*, p. 318 and Thiolier, p. 378n) and in the closely related manuscripts Coll. of Arms Arundel XIV and Oxford Bodleian Library Fairfax XXIV. These two manuscripts are considered by Thiolier to represent a first redaction, but see also T.M. Smallwood, "The Text of Langtoft's *Chronicle*," *Medium Ævum* 46 (1977), 219–30 and Thea Summerfield, "The Matter of Kings' Lives. The Design of Past and Present in the early fourteenth-century verse chronicles by Pierre de Langtoft and Robert Mannyng," Diss. Utrecht, pp. 19–20 and 179, n. 44. As far as the tail-rhyme songs are concerned, the so-called first redaction deviates in the following respects: song no. 1 (on John Balliol) (Thiol. p. 291) not included; song no. 2 (Thiol. pp. 305–07): similar to song no 2 in Red. II; song no. 3 (Thiol. p. 315): import of the AN tail-rhyme stanzas rendered as part of the *laisse*; no English stanzas included; song no. 4 (Thiol. p. 319): 4 English stanzas as in Red. II, but longer lines; last four lines different; song no. 5 (Thiol. p. 323): similar to Red. II. At this point these manuscripts end.

[7] See, for example, "A Song of the Times" (ed. Wright, *Pol. Songs*, pp. 133–36), "The Song against the King's Taxes" (ed. Wright, *Pol. Songs*, pp. 182–87), "Song on the Times" (ed. Wright, *Pol. Songs*, pp. 251–52), and "On the King's Breaking his Confirmation of the Magna Carta" (ed. I.S.T. Aspin, *Anglo-Norman Political Songs* (Oxford: Blackwell, for the Anglo-Norman Text Society, 1953), pp. 56–66. All these songs are contemporary with the songs in Langtoft's *Chronicle*.

[8] R.M. Wilson, "More Lost Literature in Old and Middle English," *Leeds Studies in English* 5 (1936), p. 43, Thiolier p. 17; see also M.D. Legge's rejection (p. 279).

a professional minstrel[9] or even of Langtoft himself.[10] Certainly there is contemporary evidence that songs on the subject of the Anglo-Scottish wars were made up by the two sides,[11] nor were such songs necessarily popular effusions; professional minstrels were involved in the composition of songs aimed at celebrating military feats and raising the army's morale, as is illustrated by the famous case of Roger Baston. He was commissioned in 1314 by Edward II to celebrate the expected relief of Stirling Castle, and was forced to sing the praises of the Scots instead after the painful defeat of the English at Bannockburn.[12] His long, learned poem in Latin is in a different category, however, from the songs in Langtoft's *Chronicle*.[13]

The songs in Langtoft's and Mannyng's *Chronicle* are invariably in tail-rhyme, whichever language is used: three short lines of two stresses each with a varying number of unstressed syllables, rhyming a-a-b/ c-c-b/ d-d-e/ f-f-e. They vary considerably in length; the English songs are never longer than four stanzas, while the Anglo-Norman songs fall into two groups: short songs of two or at most three stanzas (nos. 1, 3, 9) and extremely long songs, of 16, 10 and 12 stanzas respectively (nos. 6, 7 and 8). Whereas, as the numbers given them here indicate, the short Anglo-Norman songs occur at irregular intervals, very much like their counterparts in English, the long songs appear in a cluster, separated from one another by one *laisse* only.

There is a striking dissimilarity in tone and style between the English songs and the short Anglo-Norman songs on the one hand, and the long Anglo-Norman songs on the other. In the English songs violent, earthy anti-Scottish sentiments are expressed in a heavily alliterating distinctive Northern discourse of abuse. The Scots are presented as barely human, living like pigs in huts and hovels ("hodred in the hottes"); they are seen as fools and silly wretches ("sottes and wirches unwarre") who deserve little better than being stripped to their bare backsides after their death on the battlefield ("the fote folke/ put the Scotes in the polke,/ and nakned their nages" (the foot-people put the Scots in the poke and made bare their backsides)).[14] Nothing should be left them, according to Langtoft, but the footwear which came to denote all that is Scottish and, therefore, hateful and primitive: "his rivyn riveling"

---

[9] R.H. Robbins, "Poems dealing with contemporary conditions," in *A Manual of the Writings in Middle English: 1050–1500*, ed. A.E. Hartung (New Haven, Conn., 1975), vol. V, p. 1401.
[10] T. Turville-Petre, "Politics and Poetry in the Early Fourteenth Century: The Case of Robert Manning's *Chronicle*," *Review of English Studies* NS 39 (1988), pp. 8–9.
[11] References can be found especially in vernacular chronicles such as the Prose *Brut*. See V.J. Scattergood, *Politics and Poetry in the Fifteenth Century* (London: Blandford Press, 1971), p. 23 and Ranald Nicholson, *Edward III and the Scots: The Formative Years of a Military Career, 1327–1335* (Oxford: Oxford University Press, 1965), p. 23.
[12] R.H. Robbins, *Historical Poems of the XIVth and XVth Centuries* (New York, 1959), p. xl.
[13] It has been included in the *Scotichronicon*. See *Scotichronicon by Walter Bower in Latin and English*, ed. D.E.R. Watt (Aberdeen: Aberdeen University Press, 1991), vol. VI pp. 367–77.
[14] "hodred . . .": Langt/Wright II 236; Thiol. 817; "sottes . . ." Langt/Wright II 252; Thiol. 1000; "the fote folke . . ." Langt/Wright II 248; Thiol. 956–58.

(Langt/Wright II 264; Thiol. 1154).[15] The shorter Anglo-Norman poems, especially those on John Balliol (no. 1) and William Wallace (no. 9) also express violent feelings; Balliol is called by the abusive name of "ray Jon musard" and the delight in the dispersal of Wallace's body to the four corners of Britain is evident.

The long Anglo-Norman songs are a different matter; on the whole they are of a piece with the dignified language of the mono-rhymed alexandrines which constitute the body of Langtoft's *Chronicle*. Particularly in the long Anglo-Norman songs sophisticated references and apostrophes of Edward I may be found. Where they merge with stanzas in English, the difference in tone is as striking as the difference in language.

A good example is offered by song no. 6, quoted here in truncated form. It numbers sixteen stanzas of Anglo-Norman tail-rhyme, followed by two English stanzas. Having stated that Edward has now succeeded in establishing English rule in Scotland in the last two lines of the preceding *laisse*, king Edward I is addressed directly in the Anglo-Norman stanzas, and urged to judge the Scottish prisoners with the severity which, in Langtoft's view, they deserve. The song ends with two stanzas in English, which do not revile the Scots in general, but only the unfortunate John Balliol, who had enemies not only in England, but also in Scotland. He is referred to here by his nickname "Toom Tabard," which refers to his surcoat which had been stripped of the Balliol arms, signifying the formal surrender of his kingship in July 1296.[16]

> Ore ad le rays Eduuard Escoce enterement,
> Cum Albanak le avayt al comencement.
>   (. . .) Eduuard, parmy tuz vos resuns,
>   Voilliez pensez des arsouns
>   Du temple Deu omnipotent,
>   A Hexelesham, où cel host
>   De la croice fesaint rost,
>   Figure de humayn salvement.
>   Herodes i fert, l'emphle mourt,
>   En ceste angusse Rachel plurt;
>   Eduuard, or fa la vengement. (. . .)
>   For boule bred in his bok,
>   Wen he tint that he tok
>   Wiht [sic] ye kingedome.
>   For he haves overhipped,
>   His tipet is tipped,
>   His tabard is tom.[17]
>   (Langt/Wr. II 254–56; Thiol. 1034–62, 1034–35, 1054–62, 1084–89).

[15] How rivelings were made is described by John Elder in his *Proposal for Uniting Scotland with England* (1542). It was printed in *The Bannatyne Miscellany*, ed. David Laing, vol. I, part I (Edinburgh, 1824) and is quoted by Priscilla Bawcutt, "A Miniature Anglo-Scottish Flyting," *Notes and Queries* 233 no. 4 (Dec. 1988), 441–44. The word is also used in its derogatory sense by Robert Mannyng, Skelton and Dunbar (Bawcutt, pp. 442–43) and by Laurence Minot (*Laurence Minot: Poems*, ed. T.B. James and J. Simons, Exeter Medieval Texts and Studies (Exeter: Univ. of Exeter Press, 1989), p. 29).
[16] See R. James Goldstein, *The Matter of Scotland: Historical Narrative in Medieval Scotland*, Regents Studies in Medieval Culture (Lincoln and London: University of Nebraska Press, 1993), p. 46.
[17] Now has king Edward Scotland entirely/ As Albanak had it at the beginning./ . . ./ Edward,

The reference to Herod and Rachel in the Anglo-Norman part of this song is probably intended to rouse an echo in the audience's mind of reports of Scottish atrocities involving young children. Such stories were incorporated in the writs and requests for prayers disseminated by Edward I to muster material and spiritual support for his war in the North.[18] Edward's letters to Pope Boniface VIII in which the king justifies his claim to Scotland also tell a tale of Scots "slaying children in the cradle and women lying in childbed (. . .)," and of "small school-children of tender years learning their first letters and grammar" being burnt in their school when the Scots blocked the doors and set the building on fire.[19] Langtoft was intimately acquainted with this correspondence, having made a faithfully translated, rhymed account of it, in which these atrocities are included (Langt/Wright II, 418; Thiol. p. 482).

The change from alexandrines to tail-rhyme has a strong funnelling or tapering effect. As a result the songs serve most effectively to channel and concentrate the message and the passion which inform Langtoft's *Chronicle*, by creating a sharp focus on issues which are, in different ways, of prime importance to its political arguments. Here a difference can be detected between the English and the short Anglo-Norman insertions which we find scattered throughout the section on Edward I, and the long Anglo-Norman songs (nos. 6, 7 and 8) which appear in a cluster.

In the cluster of the three long Anglo-Norman songs and the single *laisses* between them, all the arguments and thematic strands which surface at significant points throughout Langtoft's *Chronicle*[20] come together: the enemy has been overcome, Merlin's prophecy that Britain would be united under one king is repeated, and the continued support of the three saints John of Beverley, Cuthbert and Thomas Becket is guaranteed. The last song of this triad is concluded in the same vein as the preceding *laisse*: all that remains for Edward now is to achieve victory over *li faus Phelippe de Fraunce* and then to go on crusade (Langt/Wright II 266–68; Thiol. 1178–1213).

The English songs, which follow the Anglo-Norman stanzas here and in other

---

among all your reasons,/ Deign to think of the burnings/ Of the temple of God Almighty,/ At Hexham, where that army/ Made roast of the cross,/ Figure of man's salvation./ Herod there strikes, the child dies;/ In this anguish Rachel laments;/ Edward, now do the vengeance./ . . ./ For truth when John de Baliol/ Left his book at the school,/ He was very ill deceived./ For bale bred in his book,/ When he lost what he took/ With the kingdom./ For he has overhopped,/ His tippet is tipped,/ His tabard is empty.

[18] Edward I's method of raising money and support have been extensively studied. See, for example, D.W. Burton, "Requests for Prayers and Royal Propaganda under Edward I," in *Thirteenth Century England III*, ed. P.R.J. Coss and S.D. Lloyd (Woodbridge: The Boydell Press, 1991), 25–35; W.R. Jones, "The English Church and Royal Propaganda During the Hundred Years War," *Journal of British Studies* 19 (1979), 18–30; M. Prestwich, *War, Politics and Finance under Edward I* (London, 1972).

[19] E.L.G. Stones, *Anglo-Scottish Relations, 1174–1328: Some Selected Documents*, 2nd edn. (London: Nelson, 1970), pp. 106–07.

[20] See my article "The Arthurian References in Pierre de Langtoft's *Chronicle*," in *Text and Intertext in Medieval Arthurian Literature*, ed. Norris Lacy (New York: Garland 1996), pp. 187–209.

places in the *Chronicle*, and the short Anglo-Norman songs underpin the message of the *Chronicle* in a different way, not by concentrating recurring themes, but by an emotive appeal to instincts of revenge. These taunting verses belong to the Scottish *flyting* tradition, well-known to modern readers of Dunbar's poetry, but at the time also a part of every-day life in Scotland.[21] It would be a mistake, however, to consider the anti-Scottish sentiments in Langtoft's *Chronicle* as contained within the limits of the English insertions. The vernacular vocabulary of abuse spills over into the main, Anglo-Norman, text in Langtoft's passionate plea for severe punishment of the Scots:

> Nostre rays sir Eduuard ayt la male rage,
> S'il ne les preygne et teygne si estrait en kage,
> Ke ren lur demorge après sun tayllage,
> For soul les rivelinges et la nue nage.[22]

(Langt/Wright II 232; Thiol. 769–72)

The thematic unity between the text of Langtoft's *Chronicle* on the one hand, and the songs, whether in English or Anglo-Norman, on the other, is supported by the structural integration of the tail-rhyme songs. The first of the tail-rhyme songs, on John Balliol in Anglo-Norman, can be seen to be firmly anchored in the body of the text; its first line is, in fact, the second half of a sentence beginning in the main text, while its last line smoothes the transition to the remaining text of the *Chronicle*:

> Pur le grant honur ke Eduuard le sené
> Fist à Jon Bayllof, tel est la bounté
> Dount li rays Eduuard/ Dur ray Jon musard/ Est rewerdoné.
> De Escose sait cum pot;/ Parfurnyr nus estot/ La geste avaunt parlé.[23]

(Langt/Wright II 222; Thiol. 645–52)

However, integration is more often achieved by poetic means. As can be seen in the part of song no. 6 which was quoted above, the rhyme of the *laisse* in *-ent* is continued from the *laisse* in the third rhyme-word of the tail-rhyme insertion, thus reducing the two preceding rhyme-words to a kind of internal rhyme, to change only (to *-ome*) in the English stanzas with which they merge, after which a new *laisse* (in *-er*) is started.[24] With a single exception,[25] all the Anglo-Norman songs or parts of songs have been integrated into the text in this manner.

The poetic integration occasionally appears to extend even to the English songs,

[21] See Priscilla Bawcutt, "The Art of Flyting," *Scottish Literary Journal* XI no. 2 (1983), pp. 5–24.
[22] May our king Edward be struck with madness,/ If he does not take them and hold them so close in cage/ That nothing remain to them after his taxing,/ Except only their rivelings and their bare buttocks.
[23] For the great honour which Edward the wise/ Did to John Baliol, such is the goodness/ With which king Edward/ By king John the fool/ Is rewarded./ Of Scotland be it as it may/ We must continue/ The history before told.
[24] Note that, although the end-rhyme changes with the transition to the English stanzas, a lexical link (*liver* > *bok*) smoothes the transition.
[25] The single exception is song no. 9, on the occasion of the execution of William Wallace.

at least on paper. This is the case in songs no. 2 and 3. Song no. 2, on Edward's efforts at Berwick, is entirely in English and numbers four stanzas. The last words of each stanza (*he, be, the, se*) continue the monorhyme on *é* (*espé, chaunté, rymeyé*) of the preceding *laisse*. After the English insertion a new *laisse* begins (on *-ouns*). Song no. 3 has six stanzas, four in Anglo-Norman followed by two in English. It is begun after a call to arms:

> Vous ne avez altre vaye ke valer ws dayt;
> Ore armez-vus, si aloums, nul alme se retrayt.
> De nos enemys/ Kant serount pris/ Mercy nul en ait.
> (. . .)
> Unkes Albanye/ Par coup d'espeye/ Fist si bon esplayt.
> On grene/ That kynered kene/ Gadered als gayt;
> I wene/ On summe it es sene/ Whar the byt bayt.[26]
> (Langt/Wright II 244; Thiol. 903–22)

Again, the end of the English song also marks the end of the *laisse*. Although it is impossible to know whether, in recitation, the continuation of the mono-rhyme was as effective as it looks on paper, there can be little doubt that an attempt at unity between the chronicle text and the insertions is being made here.[27]

Two of Langtoft's songs express anti-English sentiments. Langtoft introduces one of them (no. 2) as such, stating that the Scots had sung mocking songs about Edward I at Berwick. During the siege of that city in 1296, Edward had taken part in person in digging the earthworks around the city:

> Li rays Edduard la teent conquis par espé,
> Le [Berwick] fet environer de fosse large e lee.
> En reprouvant le Escot, ke ad de ly chaunté
> Et par mokerye en Englays rymeyé:
> Pykit him,/ An dykit him,/ On scoren sayd he;
> He dikes, he pikes,/ On lenche als hym likes,/ Hu best may be.
> Skatered be the Scottes,/ Hoderd in thar hottes,/ Never thay ne the.
> Ryth if I rede,/ Thai tumbled in Twede,/ Thet woned by the se.[28]
> (Langt/Wright II 235–36, Thiol. 806–21)

Langtoft is not the only chronicler to mention Edward's personal involvement; Rishanger's *Annales Angliae et Scotiae* and the Prose *Brut* also refer to an abusive,

---

[26] You have no other way likely to avail you;/ Now arm yourselves, and let us go, let no soul hold back./ Of our enemies,/ When they shall be taken,/ Let no one have mercy./ (. . .)/ Never Albany/ By sword's blow/ Did so great exploit./ On green/ That sharp race/ Are gathered like goats;/ I am of opinion/ On some it is seen/ Where the bit punishes.

[27] Such careful poetic integration has also been found elsewhere; see Anne Ladd, "Attitude towards Lyric in the *Lai d'Aristote* and some later fictional narratives," *Romania* 96 (1975) 194–208, esp. 206–07.

[28] King Edwards holds Berwick conquered by the sword,/ causes it to be surrounded with a wide and broad foss,/ in reproval of the Scot, who had sung of him,/ and in mockery made rhymes upon him in English:/ Let him pike,/ and let him dike,/ in scorn said they;/ he dikes and he picks,/ in length as it pleases him,/ how best may be./ Scattered are the Scots,/ huddled in their huts,/ never do they thrive./ Right if I read,/ they are tumbled into Tweed,/ who dwelt by the sea.

vernacular song being sung on the occasion, with very similar wording.[29] However, having quoted the anti-English song which was sung on the occasion, making very clear that these are not his own sentiments by the inclusion of "sayd he," Langtoft redresses the balance by turning the abuse around and adding two stanzas of undiluted contempt and hatred at the address of the Scots.

The second anti-English song (no. 3) is incorporated in the words of a messenger from the Scots, reporting back to the then king of Scotland, John Balliol. As Maureen Boulton has pointed out in her book *The Song in the Story*,[30] changing the metre to mark the words of a messenger is a common literary device. Here the messenger speaks first in mono-rhymed alexandrines, and switches to tail-rhyme (four stanzas in Anglo-Norman and two in English) after the rousing words "ore armez-vous" (to arms!). The whole song is carefully integrated poetically. By their encapsulation in a more remote mode of transmission (reported speech, a message), the anti-English sentiments expressed in the two anti-English songs are made innocuous and can at the same time be expected to have fuelled indignation in the English, anti-Scottish, camp.

What happenend when, in the 1330s, Robert Mannyng translated Langtoft's *Chronicle*? We are in the lucky circumstance of being able to compare the two texts with reasonable certainty, as it can be established on the basis of textual variants that Mannyng used a manuscript close to the extant Langtoft manuscript BL Royal 20 A XI.[31] Mannyng substituted Langtoft's mono-rhymed alexandrines by fairly irregular lines of five or six stresses in rhyming couplets. Internal rhyme is introduced from a seemingly arbitrary point in the story of the Norman Conquest onward (Mann/Sullens II 1720). The deviant rhyme and metre of the insertions is preserved everywhere. The Anglo-Norman songs, whether long or short, are translated into Mannyng's own English dialect, while the northern English songs are retained as they are found in BL Royal 20 A XI with on the whole very little variation.[32] Mannyng's translation of Langtoft's song no. 3, which was quoted above, is a good example of the effect of his translation. First the Anglo-Norman is translated, with an

---

[29] For the reference to Rishanger, see Legge, 1963:353. Rishanger states: "Confestim unus e Scotis alta voce coepit convitia et verba probrosa Regi Angliae inferre, patria lingua; – *"Kyng Edward, wanne þu havest Berwic, pike þe, wanne þu havest geten, dike þe"* (Rishanger, *Chronica et Annales*, ed. H.T. Riley (London, RS, 1865), p. 373). The Prose *Brut* states: "And Kyng Edward went him toward Berwick, and bisegede þe toun; and þo þat were wiþin (. . .) saide, in despite and in reprofe of him: 'Wenes Kyng Edward, wiþ his longe shankes, forto wyn Berwik, al our unþankes? gas pikes him! and when he haþ hit, gas diche him!' (*The Brut or The Chronicles of England*, ed. Friedrich W.D. Brie (London: Oxford University Press for the EETS, OS 131, 1960), p. 189).

[30] Maureen Barry McCann Boulton, *The Song in the Story: Lyric insertions in French Narrative Fiction, 1200–1400* (Philadelphia: Univ. of Pennsylvania Press, 1993), 143–80.

[31] See Summerfield "The Matter of Kings' Lives," p. 107 and n. 15.

[32] No. 2 and no. 7 have two extra English stanzas; no. 8 has been replaced by the song beginning: "Now tels Pers . . .," quoted below; no. 9, on William Wallace, has two extra stanzas (probably Mannyng's own elaboration) in the part which Mannyng translated from Anglo-Norman; the two English stanzas which follow are similar to the version in the Langtoft manuscript used.

additional line of little import to complete the couplet, next the English song-stanzas are transcribed:

> I knowe non oþer wise, what way may ʒow auale.
> Armes now ʒow alle þat non him withdrawe!
> How it may best falle, I haf ʒow said þe sawe.
>> Whan ʒe haf þe pris . of ʒour enmys . non salle ʒe saue,
>> (...)
>> þer on þat grene . þat kyndrede kene . gadred als þe gayte,
>> right als I wene . on som was it sene . þer þe bit bayte.[33]
>>> (Mann/Sullens II 6680–88)

On the whole, Mannyng follows Langtoft faithfully. Where Langtoft links song no. 1 to the main text, so does Mannyng ("turne we ageyn to rede/ & on our geste to spede" (Mann/Sullens II 6426–28)); the reported song on Edward's digging at Berwick is presented as such ("þei bad him pike & scorned him in þer song") and continued as by Langtoft, by the anti-Scottish song "for scatred er þi Scottis . . ." (Mann/Sullens II 6598–6603). Major deviations are found only among the three long songs, nos. 6, 7 and 8. They concern simplifications and the expression of a different opinion.

Song no. 6 lacks a number of Anglo-Norman stanzas containing Langtoft's loftier invocations, probably because they were considered too learned for Mannyng's rural audience.[34] A remarkable substitution can be found in a passage replacing Langtoft's jubilant celebration of English and Scottish unity, expressed first in a *laisse*, to continue, on the same theme and with the same end-rhyme, in a long Anglo-Norman tail-rhyme song (no. 8). Mannyng substitutes a song of his own making for this entire episode, stating in twenty-six lines of tail-rhyme, and in no uncertain terms, that he disagrees with his source-text:

> Now tels Pers . on his maners . a grete selcouth.
> He takis witnes. þat it soth es . of Merlyn mouth.
> (...)
> he sais Scotland . is in his hand . for now & ay.
> At myn inwitte . it is not ʒit . alle at our fay.[35]
>> (Mann/Sullens II 6827–28, 6835–36)

The passage ends with a prayer that the war may soon be over (Mann/Sullens II 6851–52). So what Mannyng does here is to substitute new contents, in which he expresses his own considered opinion, while retaining the form. It would seem that Mannyng regarded the Anglo-Norman stanzas as part of Langtoft's *Chronicle*, to be faithfully translated like the rest of the *Chronicle*, unless he had cause to pursue a

---

[33] I know of no other way which might be of avail to you./ Arm yourselves, all of you, let no one withdraw./ How it can best be done, I have told you./ When you have got the better of your enemies, none will you spare. (my trans.)

[34] See Summerfield, "The Matter of Kings' Lives," pp. 112–15, 151.

[35] Now Pierre tells,/ in his manner,/ a very strange thing;/ he says / that it is true/ what Merlin has testified./ (. . .)/ He says Scotland/ is now in his [Edward's] hands/ for now and always./ By my knowledge/ it is not yet/ completely at our command. (my trans.)

more personal agenda in a given episode, while the English stanzas of the songs may on occasion be supplemented by an additional couple of stanzas.

The songs in the two *Chronicles* serve to highlight key notions in the text. Existing short songs appear to have been used, and, where necessary, adapted. The longer songs were composed by Langtoft, using the poetic framework of the traditionally abusive songs. Mannyng retains the short, English songs with few variations, while translating those in Anglo-Norman. However, where he disagrees with what he finds in his source, he follows Langtoft's example of grafting his own ideas onto the root-stock provided by the discourse of abuse.

ROMANCE AFTER BOSWORTH

Helen Cooper

This paper is concerned with a moment when romance and history intersected, that moment being the Tudor takeover of the English throne at the Battle of Bosworth, in 1485. The battle marked the most extreme break in the more or less continuous lineal descent of the crown since 1066, when King Harold was killed at Hastings – the last English king to die defending his crown before Richard III himself. Henry Tudor, the victor of Bosworth, was a great-great-great-grandson of Edward III, but through the originally illegitimate line of the Beauforts; although they were later legitimized, the renewal of that legitimation under Henry IV explicitly excluded them from any right of inheritance of the throne. Moreover, if Henry's claim had been a dynastic one, then it would have been self-cancelling, for his lineal claim came through his mother, Lady Margaret Beaufort; and she, still being very much alive, would have been the rightful inheritrix. Henry went on to marry the prime Yorkist heiress, Edward IV's daughter Elizabeth; but he waited a good many months before he did so, getting himself crowned in the interim, in order to make it quite clear that his title to the throne was his own, by conquest, and not in right of his wife.[1]

To make matters worse in the eyes of those seeking dynastic legitimacy, Henry was not even a Plantagenet; and "Tudor" (correctly pronounced, as it was often spelt, "Tidder") was just about as outlandish a name as one could find in fifteenth-century England, having the respectability neither of English or Anglo-Norman. The Welsh were generally thought of as a wild people on the margins of civilization, properly subjugated by the cultured English.

The outcome of the battle of Bosworth was therefore more than just another move in the violent magnate power games that constituted the Wars of the Roses. It was with some reason that Henry set about trying to make it seem right and necessary, and in conformity with deep cultural ideals: the ideals embodied in romances, and dynastic romances in particular.

I do not intend to say much here about his pushing of his British ancestry, King Arthur included; nobody was ever really likely to take that as anything that strength-

---

[1] It has been argued that the delay of the marriage was necessary in order to get a papal dispensation, as the two were related (see e.g. S.B. Chrimes, *Henry VII* (London: Methuen, 1972), pp. 65–66); but this never seems to have prevented the interim marriage of any prince who had strong political reasons for taking swift action. The delay is of a piece with the act of parliament confirming him as king, which makes no mention of Elizabeth – or indeed of any title to the crown other than the fact that he held it (ibid., p. 62).

ened a fifteenth-century claim to the crown. It might be a reminder that Welshness could correlate with Britishness, and therefore the greatness of the British past, but its propaganda value was essentially no more than a myth of origin. Henry's naming of his eldest son Arthur was part of that, not implying any actual claim that Arthur would indeed return; that was just the sort of visionary Celtic nonsense that confirmed the worst suspicions of the English about the Welsh. And there was no question of *descent* from Arthur, who had died without direct heirs; embarrassingly for the English, Uther Pendragon's next heirs were the descendants of the daughter who married Lot of Lothian, and that line of argument suggests that the royal line of Scotland had a claim to the English throne. And that is not just the speculation of a modern scholar; it was a live issue in fourteenth- and fifteenth-century Scottish and English historiography.[2] I would, however, mention what might be termed a prophetic reference to Bosworth – or at least to the Tudor takeover – in Arthurian romance. In the Roman war section of Malory's *Morte Darthur*, Arthur has a dream in which he sees a dragon overcome a fierce beast that represents a tyrant threatening his kingdom. In the Winchester manuscript, as in the sources of the alliterative *Morte Arthure* and ultimately Geoffrey of Monmouth, the beast is a bear; in Caxton's print, completed just three weeks before the battle of Bosworth but prepared when a Tudor invasion had become a live possibility, it is changed to a boar.[3] Bosworth itself was allegorized later as a battle of dragon against boar, for instance in the early sixteenth-century poem *Scottish Field* in the Percy Folio Manuscript.[4] It may be pushing speculation too far to suggest that Caxton, whose patron Earl Rivers had been executed by Richard as the first action in his own assumption of power, might have been expressing a covert hope for just such an outcome; but at least one Malory scholar has seen in it "a bold political allusion,"[5] and certainly it would be surprising if the parallel between the prophetic vision and contemporary events had not been widely perceived by its early readers. A narrative does not have to be true history, nor even to be written for the occasion, for it to have historical relevance.

Arthur, however, was simply too far distant to be of much help in legitimating the Tudor usurpation. More interesting is a series of rewritings of the events of 1485 as dynastic romance, with the consistent implication that it was something right, proper, and in accordance with God's ordering of the world. These texts do not, even so, offer a single view of things. The romances written closest to the court itself offer

---

2   See Robert Huntington Fletcher, *The Arthurian Material in the Chronicles*, 2nd edition expanded by Robert Sherman Loomis (New York: Burt Franklin, 1966), pp. 241–49. The tradition runs from John of Fordun (1385) to Hector Boece (1527) and his translators.

3   *The Works of Sir Thomas Malory*, ed. Eugène Vinaver, 3 vols. (3rd edn. revised by P.J.C. Field, Oxford: Clarendon Press, 1990), pp. 196–97 (the Caxton text, from Book V chapter 4, is given below the Winchester text).

4   *Bishop Percy's Folio Manuscript: Ballads and Romances*, ed. J.W. Hales and F.J. Furnivall, 3 vols. (London: N. Trübner, 1867–68), 1.199–234:

> On this side Bosworth in a bancke : thé bred forth their standards
> with a dragon full dearfe : that adread was therafter,
> rayled full of red roses : and riches enowe.
> there he bickered with a bore : that doughtie was called.   (24–27)

5   P.J.C. Field, "Caxton's Roman War," *Arthuriana* 5.2 (1995), 31–73 (37).

narrative analogies to the takeover that present it as a rightful restoration of the true lineage. As one moves away from the court in terms of geography, class, and cultural models of courtliness, to productions by provincial gentry, the narratives become closer to history, but diverge so far from models of royal propaganda that they can even be read as a form of resistance.

That romance can be used in such ways at all would seem at first glance unlikely. It is famously – or notoriously – a genre that is ahistorical, implausible, resistant to the specifics of time and place. Even worse, the point where it offers the most obvious potential for political commentary is in its insistence on a God-given dynastic order: whatever disruptions there may be to the true line, the usurper will always eventually be overthrown by the rightful ruler or his heir, who will come back, even from apparent death, to reclaim his true inheritance. That was a quality of romance that made it problematic for every ruler of the fifteenth century, all of whom were opposed by claimants of dispossessed lines, from the usurper Henry Bolingbroke to the usurper Henry Tudor. It was, all the same, a motif that could cut both ways, for Richard III was himself a usurper even in Yorkist eyes, and Henry Tudor was the only remaining Lancastrian claimant.

The first work to suggest that Henry might be just such a true claimant restored was one commissioned by his mother, the redoubtable Lady Margaret Beaufort, around 1489: *Blanchardyn and Eglantine*, a translation by Caxton of a French prose romance. That it might be making such a suggestion is so understated that it cannot have served much propaganda function in the country at large, despite its dissemination in printed form; but it is the only secular work that the pious Lady Margaret ever commissioned, and it was presumably for reasons of politics rather than entertainment.[6] To summarize its complex action, the young Blanchardin, son of the king of Frise, leaves his royal home to pursue a life of chivalry, in the course of which he falls in love with Eglantine; during his prolonged absence his father's kingdom is overrun by Saracens and the king himself captured; and eventually Blanchardin drives out the invaders, is recognized as the true heir, succeeds his father, and marries his beloved. The events are the sort that make up dozens of romances, but they also have a loose potential to be mapped onto the events of Henry's own life: his strategic retreat from England to Brittany parallels Blanchardin's leaving his home for the exercise of prowess, the Yorkist tenure of the throne parallels the temporary abeyance of rightful rule in Frise, the imprisonment of Henry VI is equivalent to that of Blanchardin's father, and Bosworth and Henry's assumption of the crown could be regarded as an analogy to Blanchardin's restoration of the true line of succession in his own person as heir.

These general parallels become suddenly more specific, though, in the one significant change that Caxton makes to his source, and that is in the naming of the heroine. In the French she has a byname only, *la pucelle orgueilleuse d'amours*, the

---

[6] See Michael K. Jones and Malcolm G. Underwood, *The King's Mother: Lady Margaret Beaufort, Countess of Richmond and Derby* (Cambridge: Cambridge University Press, 1992), pp. 181–82.

maid proud in love. Caxton renames her as Eglantine, most insistently in the dedication to Lady Margaret. And the eglantine was not just a flower of general appropriateness for a heroine: the similarity of the word to "England" or "Angleterre" had led to the equation of the eglantine with the English rose. There is a striking use of the image, for instance, in a French political morality play dating from the end of the Hundred Years' War.[7] The winning of Eglantine can thus merge with the idea of marrying the English princess, especially one whose own heraldic badge was the white rose of York. So one finds a lyric closely contemporary with Caxton's translation that figures Elizabeth of York as the white rose in a courtly garden:

> In a gloryus garden grene,
> sawe I syttyng a comly quene;
> among the flouris þat fresshe byn,
> she gadird a floure & set betwene.
>   þe lily-whiʒte rose me thouʒt I sawe . . .[8]

And here for comparison is Blanchardin, walking in a garden and lamenting his separation from his beloved:

> In beholdyng vpon the fayre flouris wherof nature had fayre appareylled the gardyne, & amonge other he sawe a rosier tree laden with many a fayr rose that had a smel ful swete/ emonge whiche one was ther that of flagraunt odoure & of beaulte passed all the other; wherfore vpon her he dyde arrest his eyen, & said in this maner/ "Ha, noble rose, preelect & chosen byfore all other flouris that ben about the/ how be it they be right fayre/ thou puttest into my remembraunce thurgh the fayrnes that I see in the/ the right perfyt & excellent beaulte of myn owne goode lady . . ."[9]

We may, I think, legitimately suspect that such parallels were not lost on Lady Margaret when she commanded Caxton to "reduce and translate" the work "into our maternal and Englysh tonge," nor on Caxton when he chose a name for his heroine (p. xx). And the pre-existence of the work would increase its political value: the biography of the romance hero, the dispossessed heir who wins back his throne and marries the princess, brings with it all the confirming ideologies of courtly self-representation without their even having to be invented specially for the occasion.

That a text originally written in a more innocent political context can acquire a sudden historical specificity is demonstrated again by another romance translation: *Oliver of Castille*, translated by Henry Watson in 1518 from a French work composed in the mid-fifteenth century. This was printed by Wynkyn de Worde, who had

---

[7] This is the unedited *Moralité du Petit et du Grand* found in Paris, Bibliothèque Nationale MS fr. 25467; for a summary, see Helen Cooper, *Pastoral: Mediaeval into Renaissance* (Ipswich: D.S. Brewer; Totowa, NJ: Rowman and Littlefield, 1978), pp. 82–83.

[8] Ed. Rossell Hope Robbins in *Historical Poems of the XIVth and XVth Centuries* (New York: Columbia University Press, 1959), pp. 93–94. Henry Tudor himself could be represented as the red rose of England: see for example the following poem in Robbins, "I loue, I loue, & whom loue ye?" (pp. 94–95), and *The Rose of England*, one of the group of ballads connected with the Stanleys in the Percy Folio MS (on which see below); *Bishop Percy's Folio MS* 3.187–94.

[9] *Caxton's Blanchardyn and Eglantine*, ed. Leon Kellner, EETS ES 58 (1890), 122.27–123.6

himself at one stage been printer to Lady Margaret; she herself had died in 1509, but the royal connection is still interesting. The romance itself is considerably more of a hotchpotch than *Blanchardin*, but it is only the very end that is of concern here. The co-hero, named, like the first Tudor Prince of Wales, Arthur, has married the grand-daughter of the king of England; and in due course news comes

> that the Kynge of Englande grandfader of his wyfe was decessed. And that the Duke of Glocestre that was cousyn germayne to the Kynge of Englande/ had made hym to be crowned kynge of the realme. Wherfore he [i.e. Arthur] sente in to Englande for to knowe and it were by the consente of the noble men of the countree And for to knowe yf that he sholde not be receyued for kynge as reason wolde. It was answered to hym naye/ Wherfore he assembled a grete company of folke/ and with grete puyssaunce came and descended in Englande/ and dyde so moche by force of armes/ after dyuers grete batayles/ that he that sayd hym kynge was taken and put in pryson/ where as he neuer yssued oute after. After he made hym to be crowned kynge as reason wolde/ and ye Englysshemen receyued hym for theyr lord.[10]

The story must have sounded very familiar in 1518. Yet one of the most intriguing things about this is that the usurping wicked duke of Gloucester is present from the very earliest manuscript copies of the French original,[11] dating from some years before a duke of Gloucester's actual usurpation of the English throne. One need not ascribe any particular prophetic powers to the original author – English dukes of Gloucester had figured largely in recent history, and so it was an obvious title to select to add verisimilitude to a section of narrative set in England – but even more strongly than *Blanchardin*, the episode suggests that Henry's taking of the throne was an act of recovery, a restoration of right, not a violent disruption of the true line of descent.

It may have been more politic, all the same, to make the translation in 1518 than it would have been in 1485: by then Henry VII had been dead nine years, and Henry VIII, Henry's son by Elizabeth of York and younger brother of the Arthur who died young, was on the throne. For the Arthur of *Oliver of Castille* claims the throne in right of his wife; he himself has no claim without her. It was not an argument that Henry VII allowed anyone to believe, but by 1518 it had ceased to be a live issue: Henry VIII was the heir to both the Lancastrian and the Yorkist lines, and any other remaining Yorkists had been put to death on a variety of flimsy excuses. If Henry VII was to be presented as according with a romance model, it must be one that cast him as the ruler in his own right, even when there was on offer a wicked duke of Gloucester to be overcome.

Outside court circles, however, a rather different reading of the Tudor takeover was being developed, and it was one that made Henry less of a central figure. The key text here is a ballad-type poem known as *Lady Bessy* – Lady Bessy being

[10] *The Hystorye of Olyuer of Castylle*, ed. Gail Orgelfinger (New York: Garland, 1988), pp. 206–7 (sig. U(1)r in the facsimile intro. Robert Edmund Graves (London: Roxburghe Club, 1898)).

[11] I am grateful to Danielle Régnier, who has been editing the as yet unpublished French original, and to Jane Taylor for supplying this information.

Elizabeth of York herself. It survives in two closely similar manuscript texts, one Elizabethan, the second the famous mid-seventeenth-century Percy Folio manuscript; a third manuscript of the late seventeenth century, which gives a somewhat different but possibly partly authentic text, is now untraceable, though its text had been printed before it disappeared.[12] The poem tells of the events of 1484–85 in so far as they concerned Elizabeth, who, in this version, is herself the subject of a prophecy that she will become queen:

> Shee tooke a booke in her hande,
>   & did read of prophecye,
> how shee shold bee Queene of England,
>   but many a guiltelesse man first must dye.[13]

With the initially reluctant help of Lord Stanley, she accordingly sends an envoy to Henry Tudor to promise him marriage, along with three mule-loads of treasure to assist him in an invasion; she is present to watch the aftermath of the battle of Bosworth, addresses some bitter words to the corpse of her uncle Richard, and promptly marries Henry:

> Great solace it was to see,
>   I tell you, masters, without lett,
> when the red rose of mickle price
>   & our Bessye were mett.
> a Bishopp them marryed with a ringe,
>   they two bloods of hye renowne.
> Bessye sayd, "now may wee sing,
>   wee tow bloods are made all one."
> the Erle of Darbye he was there,
>   & Sir william Stanley a man of might;
> vpon their heads they sett the crowne
>   in presence of many a worthy wight.[14]

It is, in fact, very much a fanciful, romance version of history – history rewritten as romance – in which Elizabeth herself is cast as the dispossessed heiress, Henry Tudor merely as her knight in shining armour.

Rather amazingly, a number of historians have suggested that there may be some truth in all this, even though every detail that can be checked is demonstrably wrong (the one exception – and it is an interesting one – being the names of Lord Stanley's followers). Its nineteenth-century editors suggested that the poet must have been none other than the envoy sent by Elizabeth to Henry, a squire named Humphrey Brereton of Malpas,[15] since no one else could have known all the details of the events; and the attribution has tended to acquire the status of fact in historians of

---

[12] *Bishop Percy's Folio MS*, 3.319–63; the other texts are printed in *The most pleasant Song of Lady Bessy*, ed. J.O. Halliwell, Percy Society 20 (1847). The earliest manuscript, of c. 1600, is preserved among the papers of John Stowe, in London, British Library MS Harley 367.

[13] *Bishop Percy's Folio MS*, 3.327 (165–68).

[14] Ibid., 3.363 (1063–74).

[15] Malpas is indicated to be Brereton's place of origin, ibid., 3.347 (676).

Bosworth who mention the poem.[16] The careful description of a wart on Henry's face, for instance, by which the envoy is told how he can recognize his target, is taken as confirmation of the truth of it all. This, of course, overlooks the role played in imaginative narrative by authenticating detail – the detail included or invented precisely to add a specious verisimilitude to an otherwise implausible story. But the mere fact of the poem's existence is interesting enough, and worth pausing on.

A certain amount is known, or can be plausibly reconstructed, about its origins. It has some connection with the Stanley magnate family, the most famous of whom, Lord Stanley, was Lady Margaret Beaufort's third husband, therefore stepfather to Henry Tudor. On Richard's orders, he brought a substantial force to Bosworth, but his refusal to order them into battle, combined with his brother Sir William Stanley's last-minute intervention on Henry's side when it looked fairly clear that he was going to be the winner, ensured a Plantagenet defeat. Lord Stanley is presented as Elizabeth's confidant within the poem, and he and his followers provide its crowd scenes. The ballad, moreover, is one of a group of poems in the Percy manuscript that were written to celebrate the exploits of the Stanleys, or, where exploits had signally failed to happen (as at Flodden Field), to invent them.[17] It borrows some stanzas from another of these poems, *Bosworth Field*, which was almost certainly written before 1495 and which gives a remarkably accurate account of the battle and its participants;[18] *Bosworth Field* is indeed a Border-type ballad, concerned to record the heroic actions and pitiful slaughter on both sides, and avoids all the romancing of the story of the later *Lady Bessy*.

Who wrote it, if not Humphrey Brereton himself? I would not want to diverge far from earlier suggestions: I would go for some member of the family or, perhaps more likely, the household of the Breretons of Malpas, who were a cadet branch of a baronial Brereton family.[19] If the author was busy inventing a heroic past for the Stanley magnates, possibly his patrons, then why not for his own gentry family at the same time? A Humphrey Brereton had in fact existed at the right date – indeed, two of them did, being first cousins. Neither made any entrance into political history, and it is almost impossible to discover anything at all about them. Other family members, however, did perform some services: a distant cousin from the baronial branch of the family, named Andrew Brereton, was one of a number of people rewarded in 1486 to the tune of an annuity of twenty pounds; closer to home, Randle Brereton, brother of one of the Humphreys, became a knight of the body to Henry VII, and chamberlain of Chester. And one of his sons, William Brereton, became a groom of the chamber

---

[16] These range from James Gairdner, in his *History of the Life and Reign of Richard III* (revised edn., Cambridge: Cambridge University Press, 1898), p. 345, to Michael Bennett, *The Battle of Bosworth* (Stroud: Alan Sutton; New York: St Martin's Press, 1985), p. 174. Gairdner also ascribes *Bosworth Field* to the same author, p. 359.

[17] The fullest study is by David Lawton, "*Scottish Field*: Alliterative Verse and Stanley Encomium in the Percy Folio," *Leeds Studies in English*, NS 10 (1978), 42–57.

[18] On the date, see Charles Ross, *Richard III* (London: Methuen, 1981), Appendix 2, pp. 234–37. The text is printed in *Bishop Percy's Folio MS*, 3.233–59.

[19] The fullest information on them is given in George Ormerod, *The History of the County Palatine and City of Chester*, 2nd edn. revised by Thomas Helsby, 3 vols. (London: Routledge, 1882), 2.686–87.

to Henry VIII, and was one of those executed in 1536 on a charge of adultery with Anne Boleyn.[20]

To press speculation further, one wonders whether there might be some connection between that last fact and a distinctive feature of *Lady Bessy* that the historians have rather surprisingly missed: that its author was a Yorkist. Many of the authors of the Percy Folio Stanley poems go considerably further than this one does in their support of Richard III, or at the very least in their refusal to follow the Tudor model of demonizing him. *Scottish Field* opens with a eulogy of Richard's heroism at Bosworth, completely gratuitous from the narrative point of view:

> Richard that rich Lord : in his bright armour,
> he held himselfe no Coward : for he was a King noble.[21]

Bosworth Field is remarkably even-handed in its allowing of kingship to both Richard and Henry, and almost the worst that it says about Richard is that he was misled by evil counsel. *Lady Bessy* contains much more of the standard anti-Richard propaganda, but it still refuses to follow the Tudor line on the takeover. There is little here about Henry's own right to the crown. The late version of the poem records how implausible a king called Tudor was felt to be – the people of Shrewsbury mock him with his name as he passes the city,

> They called him Henry Tydder, in scorn truely,
> And said, in England he shou'd wear no crown.[22]

Indeed, the invention of the prophecy of Elizabeth's being queen, her invitation to Henry to invade, and their marriage the moment Bosworth has been won, all insist that the Tudor claim to the throne resided principally in Henry's marriage to the dispossessed heiress. The poem may therefore suggest some disaffection with the regime; it certainly suggests that the Breretons ought to be in favour with the Tudor monarchs. Both could perhaps be connected with a response to the execution of William Brereton.

What I have described here is a series of texts, emanating from the circles closest to the king – his own mother, with her own claim to be on the throne occupied by her son – out to an associate of a provincial gentry family writing for a local magnate. Each text rewrites the events of 1485 in a different way, from the Tudor romance of

[20] On the baronial Breretons, see Ormerod, 3.81–91, and on Andrew's annuity, *Materials for a History of Henry VII*, ed. William Campbell, 2 vols., Rolls Series (1873–77), 2.30. Two other Breretons received trivial sums at the same date, but no Humphrey appears in the royal records. The Sir William Brereton mentioned in yet another of the Percy Folio Stanley poems, *Flodden Field* (1.313–40 (69)), is more likely to have been the man of that name who belonged to the the baronial family (see *Dictionary of National Biography*, q.v. Brereton, Sir William, d. 1541) than the executed courtier from the Malpas branch, who would probably have been too young for the events of the poem (assuming, though it is not a safe assumption, historical accuracy on the part of the poet).

[21] *Bishop Percy's Folio MS*, 1.213 (28–29).

[22] *The most pleasant Song*, p. 34; the later version sometimes appears to contain better readings, or preserve more historically accurate details, than the Percy-Stowe text.

the dispossessed prince to the Yorkist romance of the dispossessed princess. But each one rewrites it as romance: the genre that insists on the return to a righteous equilibrium after disruption, on the restoration of the true heir as the ultimate happy ending. To Henry Tudor, surveying the carnage of the battle of Stoke fought against a Yorkist pretender; to his unloved wife Elizabeth, forced to play second fiddle to the king's mother Lady Margaret; to Prince Arthur, whose early death put paid to any notion of a second king of that name; to William Stanley, Lord Stanley's brother, whose intervention at Bosworth ensured a Tudor victory but who was executed by Henry a few years later; to William Brereton, beheaded on a false charge by the son of the union of the roses – to all of them, romance may not have seemed such a plausible reading of events.

III. NEGOTIATING A COURTLY VOICE

COURTLINESS IN SOME FOURTEENTH-CENTURY ENGLISH PASTOURELLES

John Scattergood

The pastourelle, in its typical manifestation, involves a confrontation in formal poetic terms; after a brief first-person introduction the main body of such a poem is usually taken up by the alternating speeches of two characters. But the formal confrontation is simply a reflex of larger confrontations which operate in terms of both gender and class: a knight, or occasionally a cleric, but in any case a male representative of one of the official cultures, encounters, in her context, a shepherdess or other rustic woman with whom he speaks in debate. The narrator, the "I" of the poem, is always the man. Typically he tries to seduce her: he is often successful, but sometimes he fails abjectly and comically, usually because of her outraged or witty refusal, but sometimes because of an intervention by other men (a member of her family, or her lover) from her own social context, who interrupt and sometimes drive off the intrusive stranger. In addition to the differences of gender and social assumptions of the two speakers, there are ethical and moral differences, and sometimes differences in their modes of discourse: when this happens the courtly language of the man is played off against the coarser, more demotic speech of the woman.

But the class differences in which the genre deals have become involved in theories about the origins of pastourelles. Michel Zink, in a thorough and sceptical review of the scholarship, isolates some of the problems: ". . . si la pastourelle est, comme tout le monde le reconnaît maintenant, un genre savant, est-elle le résultat de la transformation savante d'un genre populaire? Ou bien est-elle dès l'origine un genre aristocratique, inspiré des *Bucoliques* de Virgile, soit directement, soit par l'intermédiaire des traités médiévaux? Ou encore tire-t-elle sa source, non de la poésie latine antique, mais de la poésie latine cléricale du Moyen Age?"[1] It is significant that there are more questions than answers, and more hypotheses than assertions. Simply on the basis of content, it is sometimes difficult to know whether a particular pastourelle represents an aristocratic critique of the peasant lower classes, or whether it represents a satiric view of courtly mores and behaviour from a lower-class perspective. In its earliest manifestation this type of lyric appears in eleventh- and twelfth-century Provence, and earlier scholars were clear that it was a courtly genre. Audiau says: "Malgré son apparence, la pastourelle est un genre

---

[1] See Michel Zink, *La Pastourelle: Poésie et Folklore au Moyen Age* (Paris: Bordas, 1972), pp. 50–51. See pp. 42–52 for a discussion of this whole question.

strictement aristocratique, ou pâtres et bergères parlent le langage courtois des troubadours, sans se départir entièrement de leurs allures lourdaudes,"[2] and Jeanroy
calls it "l'amusement d'une société élégante."[3] Later scholars, however, have seen
the situation in a more complex light. Pierre Bec, for example, though he admits that
"la pastourelle occitane médiévale . . . est devenue un divertissement poétique
aristocratisant" in origin thinks it was a popular form, because it occurs so frequently in folk literature: "D'origine vraisemblablement popularisante, comme le
preuve le maintien de sa typologie fondamentale dans les folklores d'oc et d'oil . . ."
Circumspectly, perhaps, he calls it "un genre hybride."[4]

I

Though the number of pastourelles extant in English is much smaller than the
number in either Provençal or northern French literature – Helen Sandison counts
thirteen early poems, in addition to a few Tudor songs – some of the same problems
as to the nature of the genre occur.[5] The best known poem of this sort in English,
perhaps the only one to have any modern currency, is a nursery rhyme which begins,
in its most common form:

> Where are you going to, my pretty maid?
> I'm going a-milking, sir, she said . . .[6]

The investigations of Iona and Peter Opie reveal that this rhyme is of popular origin.
They print a version which Thomas Tonkin, a Cornish antiquary, heard sung in 1698,
and which William Pryce quoted in 1790:

> Whither are you going, pretty fair maid, said he,
> With your white face and your yellow hair?
>
> I am going to the well, sweet Sir, she said,
> For strawberry leaves make maidens fair.
>
> Shall I go with thee, pretty fair maid, he said, &c.
>
> Do if you will, sweet Sir, she said, &c.
>
> What if I do lay you down on the ground, &c.
>
> I will rise up again, sweet Sir, she said, &c.

---

[2] See Jean Audiau and Rene Lavaud, eds., *Nouvelle Anthologie des Troubadours* (Paris:
Libraire Delagrave, 1928), p. 11.
[3] Alfred Jeanroy, *Les Origines de la Poésie Lyrique en France au Moyen Age* (Paris:
Champion, 1889; 4th edn. 1965), I, 38.
[4] Pierre Bec, ed., *Anthologie des Troubadours* (Paris: Union Générale des Editions, 1979), p.
52.
[5] *The "Chanson d'Aventure" in Middle English*, Bryn Mawr College Monographs, vol. XII
(Bryn Mawr, Pennsylvania: Bryn Mawr College, 1913), pp. 46–67. See especially p. 61, n. 57.
[6] See *The Oxford Dictionary of Nursery Rhymes* (Oxford: Oxford University Press, 1951),
pp. 281–82. For the material in this and the next paragraph I am much indebted to this fine
book.

What if I do bring you with child, &c.

I will bear it, sweet Sir, she said, &c.

Who will you have for father for your child, &c.

You shall be his father, sweet Sir, she said, &c.

What will you do for whittles for your child, &c.

His father shall be a taylor, sweet Sir, she said, &c.[7]

The opening of the poem, with its implied rustic setting, the alternating speeches, the difference in gender and class between the speakers, immediately recalls the manner of the medieval pastourelle, as does the development of the argument – though, in the event, the attempted seduction remains hypothetical. What emerges most strikingly from the confrontation is the clear-eyed practicality of the maid, who is not averse to submitting to her would-be seducer nor bearing his child, but insists on his facing his responsibilities in that event – if the implication of the last two speeches is, as I think, that he will have to settle down to a trade ("taylor") in order to provide "whittles" for the child, which here could mean a "cloak" or a "blanket" or "babyclothes" or a "shawl or wrap" (*OED whittle* sb. 1). This is the earliest extant version, but there are many regional variations which have come down to, at least, the earlier part of the twentieth century.

The current version handles the issue of social class rather differently. The man's request to accompany the pretty maid is graciously granted, and his proposal of marriage is accepted "if you please," which, it emerges, has an unexpected literal force. Further questions from the man also reveal that the pretty maid is only a farmer's daughter, and that her "fortune" consists solely in her good looks. This new information produces the sort of reversal common in the closure of pastourelles, but with an interesting twist because it is the man who changes his mind, to be immediately dismissed in a forthright and witty way – if it does not please him to marry her, she has no wish to marry him either:

Then I can't marry you, my pretty maid.
Nobody asked you, sir, she said.

The point of this ending appears to be to expose the mercenary self-interest of the upper-class man, in contrast with the self-sufficient integrity of the simple country girl. In the opinion of Iona and Peter Opie this is a nineteenth-century rewriting of the earlier folksong: it certainly sets forth a particular ideological view of class relations in Victorian England which idealised the virtues of the rustic poor. From 1909 comes a version in the form of a sea-shanty entitled "Heave away, my Johnny," which preserves what may have been the original narrative introduction incorporating the "walking out" and "springtime" motifs:

As I was walking out one fine morning
All in the month of May,

---

[7]   Ibid., p. 282.

> I overtook a fair pretty maid,
> And unto her did say . . .[8]

This adds weight to the argument that this nursery rhyme is really, in origins, a pastourelle which has survived remarkably intact, in a formal sense, in the popular tradition.

And it is to the popular tradition, according to Helen Sandison, that earlier English pastourelles belong: ". . . the 'sage and serious' English poets have delivered the pastourelle from much of its aristocratic bias; they have made it seem less like a bit of conventional pretense offered for the amusement of a courtly singer and his courtly audience, and have given it more of the sincerity that marks the popular ballad."[9] There are a number of aspects of this generalisation which need to be examined – not least that of the issue of "pretense" and "sincerity" – but it the context of the present argument what is important is the overall accuracy of the statement.

It has to be said, in the first place, that a good many of the early pastourelles are evidently popular: they are written in some variant of ballad-stanza, and use plain demotic language. The closest in general movement to the classic pattern is *Crow and Pie* from Oxford, Bodleian Library MS Rawlinson C 813, a Tudor miscellany dating from about 1530, which, however, belonged to a Staffordshire gentleman who held various local posts of importance, and was MP for Newcastle-under-Lyme in 1545. In the traditional way, the first person narrator (who changes into a third person narrator in stanza 5), a "corteor," riding through a forest, meets "a fayre mayde" to whom he speaks of love.[10] She initially answers him "all yn scornyng." But, in a reduced version of courtly language, he asks her to have "rewe" on him, and, in the traditional way, offers presents – a gold ring, and a purse of velvet. She replies that she is afraid of her mother, that she is worried that she will lose her good name if she has anything to do with him, and fearful that he will prove unfaithful. The poem is not clear about whether she changes her mind, or whether the man overcomes her by force, but a sexual encounter does take place:

> He toke hur abowte the mydell small
> And layd hur downe upon the grene . . .

After the event she asks him to marry her, to give her the presents he promised, and (recognizing the possibility that she may be pregnant) to tell her his name and where he lives – but he answers everything evasively. She dismisses him with "Crystes curse," and consoles herself by saying that, though she may have been violated, she is "noder dede nor slowe," and that she trusts "to recover my harte agayne." She ends with a moral for the benefit of other maidens:

---

8 Ibid., p. 283.
9 Sandison, *The "Chanson d'Aventure" in Middle English*, p. 66.
10 *The Welles Anthology: MS Rawlinson C 813*, ed. Sharon L. Jansen and Kathleen H. Jordan (Binghamton, New York: Medieval and Renaissance Texts and Studies, 1991), pp. 216–19 (no. 48).

> ... lett no man downe yow throwe;
> For and yow doo, ye wyll yt rewe ...

This is a particularly unpleasant poem, not at all "l'amusement d'une société élégante." It is not expressed in ideological terms, but, nevertheless, it lays bare the power relations and systems of exploitation in its society in terms of class and in terms of gender. What starts as a pastourelle becomes something of a "betrayed maiden's lament."

In other poems also, the pastourelle opening and the initial encounter lead on to narratives which develop far beyond the traditional lines of the genre. In *Christopher White*, the speaker, a rich Edinburgh merchant, walking out one morning, overhears a "well fair mayd" lamenting that her lover Christopher White has been banished.[11] The merchant seeks to persuade her to love him instead, and offers his wealth as an inducement. She initially refuses him in words which turn out to be prophetic:

> If I be ffalse to Christopher White
> Merchant, I cannott be true to thee.

But, impressed by his wealth, she consents to marry him and to live in Edinburgh. While her husband is away at sea, however, she writes to her former lover, sends him money, and asks him to come to Edinburgh. He gets pardon from the king, returns, and absconds with the merchant's wife and much of the merchant's silver and gold. When the merchant returns he ponders what has happened, ruefully admitting that his wife had warned him of her possible infidelity earlier. This poem also concludes with a cautionary moral:

> Looke that you love your old loves best,
> For infaith they are best compaany.

In *John of Hazelgreen*, the poet, on a May morning, overhears a maiden lamenting about her thwarted love for Sir John of Hazelgreen. The speaker tells her that Hazelgreen is married and offers to take her with him and marry her to his eldest son so that she will be "a gay lady".[12] She protests that she is "too mean", but allows him to buy her clothes in town (in the various versions, Biggar Cross, Edinburgh, or Luckenbooths), and to take her to his house. They are greeted by his eldest son, who turns out to be young Hazelgreen. He marries the maiden, and his father (who is presumably the Sir John Hazelgreen who is married) endows them with the family lands – a sentimental ending totally different from what is usual in the genre.

---

[11] *The English and Scottish Popular Ballads*, 5 vols., ed. F.J. Child (New York: Dover Publications, 1965), II, 439–40 (no. 108).

[12] Ibid., IV, 159–64 (no. 293). I quote from the "A" version.

II

It is hard to date ballads such as these: they are frequently much older than the earliest texts which preserve them, and obviously had an earlier oral currency in popular tradition. The earliest English pastourelles, which date from the first half of the fourteenth century, have little in common stylistically with ballads: they are written in intricate stanza forms deriving from French, and use a much more elaborate linguistic register.

"Nou sprinkes the sprai . . ." is preserved on one of the end flyleaves of London, Lincoln's Inn MS Hale 135, a copy of Bracton's *De Legibus Angliae* which belonged to Alan de Thornton, who was in the employ of the Abbot of Ramsey.[13] It is written in a hand, different from that of the main part of the book, which was responsible for a number of memoranda concerning swans, dated 1302–1305. Despite its survival in such a learned context, it has been associated with popular poetry by R.M. Wilson who says it "reads much more like a popular *carole* than a literary composition . . ."[14]

Its literary relations, however, seem to me to make this unlikely: though no definite source has been found, it bears close similarities to two earlier pastourelles. In "L'autrier cavalcava . . .", by the troubadour Gui d'Ussel, the poet overhears a "pastorella" singing a lament, "Lassa! mal viu qui pert son jauzimen." [Alas! One who has lost her joy leads a sad life.][15] He approaches her immediately:

> Lai on il chantava
> Virei tost mon fre . . .
>
> (I made my way quickly to where she was singing . . .)

He dismounts from his horse, greets her, and asks her about her sad song. She tells him that her lover has abandoned and forgotten her. The poet reveals that his lady has also left him for another. The shepherdess then proposes that they console each other and turn their suffering into joy and gaiety:

> E tornem lo deconort
> C'avem avut en joi et en deport . . .
>
> (And let us change the sorrow that we have had into joy and gaiety . . .)

– an idea which the poet has no difficulty in accepting. The general movement of this poem, and some of the phrasing, has found its way into a French pastourelle beginning "L'autrier defors Picarni . . ." Here again the poet overhears the sad singing of the "pastoure":[16]

---

13 See *The Early English Carols*, 2nd rev. and enlarged edn., ed. R.L. Greene (Oxford: Clarendon Press, 1977), p. 274 (no. 450) for the text, and p. 313 for the account of the manuscript.
14 *Early Middle English Literature*, 3rd edn. (London: Methuen, 1968), p. 263.
15 See Audiau and Lavaud, *Nouvelle Anthologie*, pp. 287–90 (no. LXXI). The translations are mine.
16 For a text see K. Bartsch, ed., *Altfranzosische Romanzen und Pastourellen* (Leipzig, 1870),

> ... lasse, ke ferai?
> jeu ai perdu mon ami ...

> (Alas! What shall I do? I have lost my love ...)

Again, like Gui d'Ussel, he turns towards her immediately:

> Si tost com j'oi le cri
> celle part tornai ...

> (As soon as I heard the cry I turned in that direction ...)

He finds her "deles un arbre foilli." In response to his questions, she tells him that Robins, her lover, has made her unhappy, and, as in the troubadour lyric, the poet successfully woos her. The English poem, again, follows much of the general development of its predecessors, with what may be echoes in the wording: the girl's lament begins "wai es him i louue-longinge/ sal libben ai"; and the poet's approach is rendered

> Son icche herde that mirie note,
> Thider i drogh...

But though part of the English author's design early in his poem is evidently to recognize his literary antecedents, it seems equally clear that he intends also to find his own way as the confrontation develops. The "litel mai" of his poem is not someone who speaks "le langage courtois des troubadours" but has her own demotic manner. Nor does she suffer her abandonment with patience, but articulates a forceful wish for revenge:

> The clot him clingge ...

> Mi lemman me haues bi-hot
> Of louue trewe;
> He chaunges a newe.
> Yiif i mai, it shal him rewe
> Bi this dai ...

It has sometimes been suspected that a conclusion to this poem has been lost – presumably one in which (as in its predecessors) the poet and the girl indulge in what Audiau called "consolations réciproques."[17] Certainly, the unofficial way that the text has been preserved lends weight to such a view. As it is, however, the fact that the expected completion of the typical pattern of the genre does not occur and the sexual desires of the participants remain unsatisfied serves to sharpen the sense of what the poem says about "louue-longinge." The refrain, which is in the first person of the poet, associates, in a conventionally decorous way, the coming of spring, and lovesickness, "that slepen I ne may." But the sentiments, and particularly the

---

II, 7. See Sandison, *The "Chanson d'Aventure" in Middle English*, pp. 47–48 for a detailed comparison.

17 See *Nouvelle Anthologie*, p. 287 (this is the modern title he gives to the poem).

language of the "litel mai," serve to expose in a much more forthright way the violent and destructive emotions which are sometimes released by betrayal and disappointed love.

III

Dating probably from somewhat later, but in any case before 1340, come three pastourelles from London, British Library MS Harley 2253. Two of these are what Helen Sandison terms "undeveloped" versions of the genre.[18] "An Autumn Song" begins with a meditation on the season when the rose and lily fade, and on the way in which women, no matter how eminent or beautiful, are taken by death – all of which leads on to the entirely orthodox observation:

> Whose wol fleysh lust forgon
> ant heuene blis abyde,
> on Iesu be his thoht anon,
> that therled was his side. (7–10)[19]

This prefaces what looks like an introduction to a conventional pastourelle, as the poet rides out seeking enjoyment:

> From Petresbourh in o morewenyng'
> as y me wende o my pleyyng . . . (11–12)

But the moral concerns raised in the opening stanza deny the poem its expected development. Both the season and the poet's mental state are wrong for this sort of poem: instead of looking for a gratifying encounter he thinks about his "folie" (13), and about the "synne" with which he has fed his flesh "ant folewed al my tyme" (23); and he worries about the fate of his soul after death. Instead of meeting a secular woman he meditates on the Virgin Mary, and on her capacity for healing the spiritually sick:

> On o ledy myn hope is'
> moder ant virgyne,
> we shulen into heuene blis
> thurh hire medicine. (27–30)

Fittingly he closes with a prayer. But throughout, though the poem deviates from the orthodox pastourelle, the poet remains conscious of the genre and keeps before the reader the value system he is subverting: the Virgin Mary is pre-eminent "from Catenas into Dyuelyn" (34), normally a geographical way of praising a secular lady, and a little later she is invested with a pair of adjectives – "gent ant smal" (45) –

[18] *The "Chanson d'Aventure" in Middle English*, p. 61, note 57.
[19] Quotations are from *The Harley Lyrics*, 3rd edn., ed. G.L. Brook (Manchester: Manchester University Press, 1964), pp. 60–62 (no. 23). In this and in other quotations from Middle English I have used modern equivalents for the letters "yogh" and "thorn."

more often applied to courtly heroines. In the same way, the opening of "The Fair Maid of Ribblesdale" also seems to promise a pastourelle:

> Mosti ryden by Rybbesdale,
> wilde wymmen forte wale,
> ant welde whuch ich wolde,
> founde were the feyrest on
> that euer wes mad of blod ant bon,
> in boure best with bolde.   (1–6)[20]

But the conditional form of the verbs ("mosti," "founde were") ushers in a poem in which action always remains as a perpetual possibility never to be fulfilled. What is important as the poem develops, though, are the superlatives ("feyrest," "best"), because the poet envisages a woman idealized in a relatively formal head-to-foot *descriptio* – though he never meets her. This poem also ends on a religious note, again expressed conditionally, but of a very different kind from that in the previous poem:

> He myhte sayen that Crist hym seye,
> that myhte nyhtes neh hyre leye'
> heuene he heuede here.   (82–84)

Here, the religious dimension (anticipated in lines 46–48, 70–72) does nothing to subvert the secular ethos of the poem: the love of a beautiful woman is proposed as a heavenly bounty granted on earth.

From the same folio of the manuscript (fol. 66v) as contains the last poem discussed comes a pastourelle, usually called "The Meeting in the Wood" because of its setting, which is developed in a fully articulated form – the most complete example of the genre in English from the fourteenth century. It is in many ways a virtuoso piece, heavily rhymed and alliterated, and with elaborate stanza-linking. But the story it tells is the familiar one of the narrator's successful seduction of a country girl, and its movement contains many of the usual and expected elements. He greets her and asks her who she is, but is initially rebuffed: "Heo me bed go my gates lest hire grewede" (7).[21] He offers her fine clothes, but she replies that it is better to wear the clothes she has ". . . then syde robes ant synke into synne" (16). What breaks her resolve, however, is the prospect of being married (or betrothed) to a man she does not love and who is violent:

> Betere is taken a comeliche y clothe
> In armes to cusse ant to cluppe
> then a wrecche ywedded so wrothe;
> thah he the slowe ne myhtu him asluppe . . .   (37–40)

As Rosemary Woolf has shown, the ending of the poem owes something to the

---

chanson des transformations, in which the woman thinks of shape-shifting in order to escape her importunate suitor.[22] But here the girl rejects this as a possibility:

> Mid shupping ne mey hit me ashunche.
> Nes Y neuer wycche ne wyle.   (45–46)

She capitulates, but the poem ends on an ambiguously hopeful note: "Luef me were gome bute gyle" (48). The predicament of the lower-class mistress of an upper-class lover is here explored in a particularly disabused and chilling way. She knows that if she listens to him and accepts his offers he will probably quickly abandon her, which will not only cause her personal unhappiness but will also bring on the disapproval of her family and probably social ostracism too:

> Such reed me myhte spaclyche reowe
> When al my ro were me atraht,
> Sone thou woldest vachen an newe
> Ant take another wi inne nyye naht.
> thenne miht I hongren on heowe,
> In vch an hyrd ben hated ant forhaht.
> Ant ben ycayred from alle that Y kneowe
> Ant bede cleuyen ther Y hade claht.   (29–36)

The poem exposes a joyless and uncomfortable social reality.

In many pastourelles this theme is implicit, and at times it is articulated explicitly with clarity and force. In Johan d'Esteve's "L'autrier el gay temps de pascor . . .," for example, written about 1275, the shepherdess tells the poet in no uncertain terms that she has no intention of submitting to his blandishments because she does not intend to allow herself to have the name of a dishonoured woman:

> Mainada
> Blasmada
> No vuel e mi aja parsso.

(I do not wish at all to be regarded as a dishonoured girl)[23]

All the evidence suggests, however, that the problem of class in relation to amorous liaisons was one which exercised intelligent minds more generally within the courtly tradition.

Perhaps the most striking example in narrative verse appears in Marie de France's *Equitan*, in the dialogues between the king and the seneschal's wife.[24] After he has declared his love for her she asks for time to think about what he has said, and meditates on the problem of their differences in wealth and social rank, which, she thinks, rather like the girl in "The Meeting in the Wood," would make it more likely that he would eventually abandon her, to her detriment:

[22] See "The Construction of *In a fryht as y con fare fremede*," *Medium Ævum* 38 (1969), 55–59.

[23] For the text of this poem see Jean Audiau, ed., *La Pastourelle dans la Poésie occitane du Moyen Age* (Paris: Boccard, 1923), pp. 80–86 (no. XV).

[24] Marie de France, *Lais*, ed. A. Ewert (Oxford: Blackwell, 1944), pp. 26–34.

> Vus estes rei de grant noblesce;
> Ne sui mie de teu richesce
> Que a mei vus deiez arester
> De druerie ne de amer,
> S'aviez fait vostre talent,
> Jeo sai de veir, ne dut nient,
> Tost me avriez entrelaissee,
> Jeo sereie mut empeiree.   (121–28)

> (You are a king of great nobility. I am not rich enough for you to fix on me your passion and love. If you had your way with me, I know for sure and have no doubt that quickly you would leave me, and I should be greatly harmed.)

At this stage in the relationship this fear does not concern her as much as the thought that their love may not be equal, since her husband is the king's vassal, and love is not honourable if it is not equal: "Amur n'est pruz se n'est egals" (137). But she returns to worries about social inequalities and inequalities of wealth at the end of her speech:

> S'aukuns aime plus hautement
> Que a sa richesce nen apent,
> Cil se dute de tute rien.   (143–45)

> (If someone sets his love higher than is appropriate to his wealth, he is fearful of everything.)

And to some degree it is concern about these matters which brings on the horrific dénouement. The seneschal's wife, knowing that Equitan is under pressure from his courtiers to marry, again fears abandonment:

> Femme prendrez, fille a un rei,
> E si vus partirez de mei;
> Sovent l'oi dire e bien le sai.
> Et jeo, lasse ! que devendrai?   (215–18)

> (You will take a wife, the daughter of a king, and you will part from me; I have often heard this said and I know it well. And I, alas! What will become of me?)

It is surely significant that she dwells on the status of the woman she thinks may be his wife ("fille a un rei"). Though on one level their love is equal, the social inequalities of the relationship impose themselves constantly and are an ever present point of tension. Out of the lady's fear, and Equitan's wish not to marry anyone but her, comes the desperate plan to kill the seneschal, which rebounds so disastrously on the plotters.

A more extended treatment of this subject, however, appears in the imaginary dialogues of Andreas Capellanus's *De Arte Honesti Amandi* – though it is sometimes difficult to judge the seriousness of what is being proposed.[25] In his chapter on the love of peasants Andreas does not spend much time on subtle analysis, but makes a

---

[25] Quotations and references are from *Andreae Capellani Regii Francorum De Amore Libri Tres*, 2nd edn., ed. E. Trojel (Munich: Eidos Verlag, 1964). The translations are from John Jay

few brief, stark observations, fittingly, he says, because ". . . it rarely happens that we find farmers serving in Love's court, but naturally, like a horse or mule, they give themselves up to the work of Venus as nature's urging teaches them to do." Implicit in all that he says is the assumption that courtly love demands leisure, and is more appropriate to those who do not have to work for a living. "For a farmer," he says, "hard labour and the uninterrupted solaces of the plough and mattock are sufficient" (p. 149). It is not appropriate for them to concern themselves much with the theory of love, lest it mean that they neglect their proper functions, which are the provision of the means of life for their society. But in the Fourth and Sixth dialogues, in both of which the man is of distinctly higher rank than the woman, appears material which is relevant to the present argument.

In the Fourth Dialogue the limits of the discussion are defined by the typically unanswerable question:

Cuius scilicet sit mulieris magis laudanda probitas, utrum nobilis sanguine an illius, quae cognoscitur generis nobilitate destitui? (p. 71)

(In which woman does a good character deserve more praise – a woman of noble blood, or one who is known to have no nobility of family?) (p. 62)

The argument, in which many of the usual points about the nature of true nobility are rehearsed – whether it is inherited through lineage or acquired through the practice of virtue – is inconclusive. Both the nobleman and the woman of mean estate agree that goodness of character is more admirable in love than birth and beauty, and he gives this as a reason for his quest for her love:

. . . quod nec sanguinis generositas nec decora multum species pertinet ad amoris emittendam sagittam, sed amor est ille solus, qui hominum ad amandum corda compellit, et saepius ipsos instanter cogit amantes alienigenae mulieris amorem exigere, id est ordinis et formae nullatenus aequalitate servata. Amor enim personam saepe degenerem et deformem tanquam nobilem at formosam repraesentat amanti . . . (pp. 74–75)

(. . . neither excellence of birth nor beauty of person has much to do with the loosing of Love's arrow, but it is love alone that impels men's hearts to love, and very often it strongly compels lovers to claim the love of a stranger woman – that is, to throw aside all quality of rank and beauty. For love often makes a man think that a base and ugly woman is noble and beautiful . . .) (p. 65)

But though she admits the general truth of what he says, she still feels that he ought to seek love from somebody more like himself in class:

Non videtur multum tuae nobilitati congruere ad plebeiae mulieris ordinem declinare vel ex plebeia amorem appetere . . . In proprio igitur ordine requiras amorem et in alieno genere constitutam non oneris impetere, ne propter talem valeas praesumptionem digne pati repulsam. (p. 74)

(It does not seem very appropriate to your nobility to condescend to a woman of the plebeian class or to seek for love from her . . . Seek, therefore, a love within your own

Parry's *The Art of Courtly Love, by Andreas Capellanus* (New York: Columbia University Press, 1941).

class and do not try to attack a woman in another one, lest you meet with a well-deserved rebuke for your presumption.)   (p. 64)

She reasons that if a man of her own class is of as much virtue and goodness as a nobleman he deserves her love more, because he has not had the advantages of noble birth. In the Sixth Dialogue, however, the woman's fears are less theoretical. Like the girl in "The Meeting in the Wood" she feels that to get involved with a man of higher rank is risky. "It is better," she says, "to refrain from entering into such an affair than to suffer so much that we have to end it after it has begun" (p. 85). And she is explicit about the factors which put pressure on such an affair:

> . . . etsi omnia nostris succederent amplexibus prospera, si illud vulgi devineret ad aures, omnes aperte meam famam reprehensione confunderent, quasi ultra modum propriae naturae metas excesserim. Praeterea maioris altitudinis homo feminam ordinis inferioris fideliter non solet amare, sed, si amet, cito eius fastidit amorem et ipsam pro levi causa contemnit . . .   (p. 114)

> (Suppose everything did turn out prosperously for our embraces, if the affair came to the ears of the common people they would ruin my good name by blaming me openly on the ground that I had gone far outside my natural limits. Besides, it is not usual for a man of higher rank to love faithfully a woman of a lower one, and if he does he soon comes to loathe her love, and he despises her on slight provocation.)   (p. 86)

Like the seneschal's wife in Marie's *lai* and like several of the women in pastourelles she fears social disapproval and abandonment. The problem of relationships between upper-class men and lower-class women was clearly one which was of some interest to a broad range of courtly writers and readers, and it looks likely that the author of "The Meeting in the Wood" was himself familiar with its main points and expected his readers to know about them also.

IV

In Chaucer the most direct treatment of this nexus of ideas appears in *The Wife of Bath's Tale*, which, of all his stories, has most in common with the movement of a pastourelle.[26] It opens with an encounter in the fields between a member of the knightly class from King Arthur's court, who is on horseback returning from hawking, and a "mayde" who is on foot – one of the classic pastourelle situations:

> And so bifel that this kyng Arthour
> Hadde in his hous a lusty bacheler,
> That on a day cam ridynge fro ryver,
> And happed that, allone as he was born,
> He saugh a mayde walkynge hym biforn,
> Of which mayde anon, maugree hir heed,
> By verrey force, he rafte hire maydenhed . . .   (III [D] 882–88)

In this particular context, the comments of Michael Riffaterre are apposite: "A

[26] Quotations are from *The Riverside Chaucer*, ed. Larry D. Benson (Boston: Houghton Mifflin Co., 1987).

shepherdess, alone and defenceless in the solitude of the woods and meadows, is a natural symbol of feminine vulnerability, so much so that the development of a poetic genre, the medieval *pastourelle*, is but a narrative expansion on *rape*." [27] This is not true in absolute terms – not all pastourelles involve rape, which is, in terms of the genre, comparatively rare: indeed, in many of the poems the man's attentions are welcomed. But it is salutary to be reminded that rape, or, at least the use of some force, is implicit in several of the encounters described. The ambiguities of *Crow and Pie* have already been described, but there are other instances. In Giraut d'Espanha's "Per amor soi gai . . .," after the girl's initial refusal of the knight's advances and offer of a costly tunic, and after she has explained that she has parents and hopes to have a husband who will respect her, the poem, which switches abruptly from first-person to third-person narration, is resolved as follows:

> – E quant el l'en vit anar,
> Met se apres ela,
> Pres la per la blanqua man,
> Gieta en l'erbeta;
> Tres vetz la baizet;
> Anc mot non sonet;
> Quan venc al quartet:
> "Senher, vos mi ren."   (37–41)

(And when he saw her go away, he set out after her, and took her by her white hand, and threw her onto the grass; three times he kissed her; but she uttered no word; but on the fourth occasion: "Sir, I give myself up to you.")[28]

This turn of events is not something which Andreas would have found outrageous or surprising. In his chapter on the love of peasants he has the following recommendation:

Si vero et illarum te feminarum amor forte attraxerit, eas pluribus laudibus efferre memento, et, si locum inveneris opportunum, non differas assumere, quod petebas et violento potiri amplexu. Vix enim ipsarum in tantum exterius poteris mitigare rigorem, quod quietos fateantur se tibi concessuras amplexus vel optata patiantur te habere solatia, nisi modicae saltem coactionis medela praecedat ipsarum opportuna pudoris. (p. 236)

(. . . and if you should, by some chance, fall in love with some of their women, be careful to puff them up with lots of praise and then, when you find a convenient place, do not hesitate to take what you seek and embrace them by force. For you can hardly soften their outward inflexibility so far that they will grant you their embraces quietly or permit you to have the solaces you desire unless you first use a little compulsion as a convenient cure for their shyness.) (p. 150)

For him, peasant women can be raped, forced into sexual compliance. Indeed, he seems to be saying that it is necessary to treat them in this way. That is not how

---

[27] See "Compulsory Reader Response: the Intertextual Drive," in *Intertextuality: Theories and Practices*, ed. Michael Worton and Judith Still (Manchester and New York: Manchester University Press, 1990), p. 61.
[28] For a text, see Audiau, pp. 98–100.

matters are viewed in Chaucer's poem, however, for there is a public outcry, an appeal to King Arthur, and the knight is initially condemned to death, though the sentence is later commuted.

As the poem develops, however, and as the knight seeks the answer to the question, "What thyng is it that women moost desiren" (905), the poem goes back to subjects often raised in pastourelles – class differences and their relation to virtue. The knight finds the answer to the question put to him after another encounter with a woman in the countryside, though his intentions on this occasion are far from amorous:

> And in his wey it happed hym to ryde,
> In al his care, under a forest syde,
> Wher as he saugh upon a daunce go
> Of ladyes foure and twenty, and yet mo;
> Toward the whiche daunce he drow ful yerne,
> In hope that som wysdom sholde he lerne.
> But certeinly, er he cam fully there,
> Vanysshed was this daunce, he nyste where.
> No creature saugh he that bar lyf,
> Save on the grene he saugh sittynge a wyf –
> A fouler wight ther may no man devyse . . .   (989–99)

She demands as her reward for helping him solve the riddle that he should marry her, but the knight objects on three grounds – that she is "loothly," "oold," and is "comen of so lough a kynde" (1100–1101), that is, that she is ugly and old, and that the difference in social class between them is so great that he would feel disparaged by the union. She answers with a lengthy lecture on the nature of true nobility, in which she argues, with overwhelming convincingness, that nobility is dependent on virtuous actions and independent of class. It looks as though Chaucer appreciated that the confrontations with which pastourelles begin could provide a way into the discussion of serious social and philosophical matters.

Chaucer's use of some of the devices of the pastourelle in this context is interesting in that it suggests that, for him and his audience, the genre, though it involved the confrontation between upper-class men and lower-class women, did not have popular associations, and did not deal in trivialities. It is very much in line with what can be deduced from the surviving early fourteenth-century English poems of this sort, where the literary associations and the nexus of ideas discussed place them firmly in a courtly context.

V

What seems to have happened in English, though the evidence is not substantial, is that the pastourelle was originally a courtly genre, which over the centuries became *déclassé*: most post-medieval examples, as has been shown, are what could be called popular poetry – nursery rhymes or ballads.

It is also fairly clear that the genre has survived most successfully and persistently, though often in a very altered form, in regional and provincial contexts. Some of the ballads already cited, like *Christopher White* and *John of Hazelgreen*, are Scottish, and Hugh Shields and Tom Munnelly have collected various ballads current in Ireland between 1968 and 1985, some of which bear some of the marks of this type of poem.[29] *Stock or Wall* has a very traditional opening line "As I roved out one evening down by a narrow lane . . ." and involves a dialogue in which the girl sets various puzzles for the man, which he successfully solves and so attains her love. Another begins:

> Johnny Scott a-hunting went
> To the wildest hills and woods;
> To the fairest young lady in all England
> Young Johnny had a child . . .

and the rest records the winning of his lady, against considerable opposition, so that she can be his wife. In *There was a Shepherd's Boy* the encounter in the countryside involves a straightforward invitation by the girl, but in the sexual encounter at her father's house, "Sure the boy he wasn't able." In *Rosemary Lane* there is no sexual encounter, because in the dialogue the man and woman set each other tasks, which are impossible to perform, before either will consent to love the other. All these are updated and altered versions of ballads known to F.J. Child and collected by him. One which is not in his collection is *The Factory Girl*, which is known to pre-date 1843 but is still sung.[30] It is clear from the opening, where the factory is located in what is still a fairly rural setting, that it "belongs to the early epoch of industrialization."

> As I went out walking one fine summer morning
> The birds in the bushes did warble and sing;
> I spied lads and lasses, and couples were sporting,
> Going down to yon factory their work to begin.

The narrator approaches "one among them more fairer than any" and, in the dialogue which follows, he declares his love, seeks to impress her with his gold and silver, his "fine houses adorned with ivy," and offers to make her a lady, but all to no avail. She explains that she is an orphan and a "hard-working factory girl," and that for somebody of her social class "love and temptation are our ruination." She tells him to find a "lady" who would be more suitable for him, and, at the sound of the factory bell (summoning her to work), disappears and leaves him disconsolate. The traditional confrontation in terms of gender and class is here updated in a poem which proclaims the virtues and good sense of urban working-class women.

A notable modern exception to these popular examples of the pastourelle is Thom Gunn's "An Amorous Debate."[31] This poem begins, in the traditional way, with a

---

[29] For texts see *Early Ballads in Ireland: 1968–1985*, ed. Hugh Shields and Tom Munnelly, European Ethnic Traditions (Dublin: Folk Music Society of Ireland, 1985), nos. 1.4, 1.7, 2.8, 2.11.

[30] See Hugh Shields, "A Latter-Day 'Pastourelle': *The Factory Girl*," *Ceol: A Journal of Irish Music* 1.3 (1963), 5–10.

[31] From *Jack Straw's Castle* (London: Faber and Faber, 1976), pp. 57–58.

brief natural description and an introduction to the characters – here heavily ironised by the phrase "gleamingly discoursed":

> Birds whistled, all
> Nature was doing something while
> Leather Kid and Fleshly
> lay on a bank and
> gleamingly discoursed . . .

He appears to be a motorcyclist, and his leathers (which she removes) appear to be the equivalent of the medieval knight's armour. In addition, through a metaphor ("a very/ Mars unhorsed"), the medieval knight's mode of transport is alluded to. Though there is dialogue, there is not really a seduction: both are keen to make love, and, if anything, most of the initiatives come from the woman. The man has only one speech, and this is two words long: "Let's fuck." The debate, which obviously is rather cursory, does not treat any of the usual subjects handled by the writers of medieval pastourelles, but is conducted in the terms of perceived twentieth-century gender differences – the man's desire for sex is not accompanied, the woman feels, by a willingness to open himself fully and sensitively to the experience. She detects "reserves" in him, a kind of "obduracy." Even when he is naked she feels that he is "still encased in your/ defence." But her arguments and her physical presence change him, and the poem closes with a wonderful image of joining:

> And they melted one
> into the other
>   forthwith
> like the way the Saone
> joins the Rhone at Lyon.

This has partly been prepared for in the lines "Then she laid the fierce/ pale river of her body/ against his . . ." but the specificity of it is still surprising. Partly, of course, the mention of two French rivers and a French city alert the reader to the origins of the pastourelle genre. But there is probably more to it than this. The image appears to derive from a high style poem, which is not a pastourelle, in Maurice Sceve's sequence *Delie* (1544):[32]

> Plus tost seront Rhosne, & Saone desionctz,
> Que d'auec toy mon coeur se desassemble . . .
>
> Plus tost verrons & toy, & moy ensemble
> Le Rhosne aller contrement lentement,
> Saone monter tresuiolentement,
> Que ce mien feu, tant soit peu, diminue . . .   (no. 17)

> (Sooner will the Rhone and Saone be unjoined, than my heart will separate itself from you . . . Sooner we shall see you and me together, the Rhone flow backwards peacefully, and the Saone flow upstream very violently, than this fire of mine by any means shall diminish . . .

---

[32] Quotations are from *The Délie of Maurice Scève*, ed. I.D. McFarlane (Cambridge: Cambridge University Press, 1966), p. 128.

Gunn appears partly to need the allusion and the intertextual relations it suggests in order to help him locate his poem: though he may be dealing with a modern situation and a contemporary sexual issue, and though his characters may speak in a twentieth-century demotic idiom, he wishes to make it plain that he is using what was at one time a learned, courtly genre, and is conscious of the implications and larger perspective that that brings with it. His modern man and woman, in an unchanging natural landscape, re-enact an age-old scene, but they have no part of the world of courtliness and grace which is called up by the self-conscious literariness of his poem.*

---

* Here, as often when I write about lyrics, I am much indebted to my colleague Dr Hugh Shields for his help with Provençal and Old French. In this article I am further indebted to him for his expertise on Irish ballads and folk songs in English.

AMOR IN MARIE DE FRANCE'S *EQUITAN* AND *FRESNE*: THE FAILURE OF THE COURTLY IDEAL

June Hall McCash

In her recent excellent book, *Shaping Romance*, Matilda Bruckner suggests that "Marie's textual identity would not be completely changed by reordering her collection within the boundaries set up by the General Prologue, 'Guigemar,' and 'Eliduc.' Although the immediate effects of juxtaposition would certainly shift, the network of intertextuality that is not tied to any linear ordering would still operate, as orchestrated by Marie's choice of twelve *lais*."[1] Certainly, efforts to find a key to Marie's work and ascertain why the tales are ordered as they are have frustrated many a scholar, but, while I agree with Bruckner that there is a complex tracery of intertextuality within the *Lais*,[2] I am not as convinced as she that their order, with the exception of the two frame *lais*, *Guigemar* and the tale that I prefer to call by the title Marie gave to it, *Guildeluëc ha Guilliadun*, which open and close the collection, is relatively unimportant. Surely it is significant, for example, that the three bird *lais*, *Yonec*, *Laüstic*, and *Milun* are grouped together in the text, for they are thematically related, with each depicting an unhappily married woman who finds a chance for happiness with someone other than her husband. In all three the bird involved provides a key to the woman's liberation. The liberation is psychological in the case of the *Laüstic*, where the broken body of the nightingale encased in a reliquary becomes an enduring symbol of the lovers' love. The messenger-swan of *Milun* frees the lovers from isolation and opens the door to their communication, as it faithfully carries their declarations of love back and forth for twenty years. And the goshawk in *Yonec* provides a liberation from the emptiness of a marriage, allowing for the woman's sexual fulfillment and release from her barren state.

While I am not yet prepared to lay out a pattern of logical progression in all twelve *lais*, if indeed one can ever be found, I do think that one can make a similar

---

I am grateful to the Research Committee of Middle Tennessee State University for a grant that enabled me to prepare this article.

[1] Matilda Tomaryn Bruckner, *Shaping Romance: Interpretation, Truth, and Closure in Twelfth-Century French Fictions* (Philadelphia: University of Pennsylvania Press, 1993), p. 162.

[2] The intertextuality referred to by Bruckner is similar to the "intertwining" suggested by Sarah Spence, in "Double Vision: Love and Envy in the *Lais*," in *In Quest of Marie de France, A Twelfth-Century Poet*, ed. Chantal A. Maréchal (Lewiston/Queenston/Lampeter: Mellen, 1992), p. 263.

case for the importance of the ordering of the tales of *Equitan* and *Fresne* immediately after *Guigemar* in the Harley manuscript. *Equitan* seems to probe issues left unresolved in *Guigemar*, and *Fresne*, as we shall see, explores a different solution to a fundamental problem raised in *Equitan*. Taken together, these two tales announce early in the collection and expand in their telling the implications of the two frame *lais*.

It is my belief, as I have stated elsewhere, that the opening tale *Guigemar* presents the wound of love, for which the final *lai*, *Guildeluëc ha Guilliadun*, offers a key to its definitive cure.[3] The love longing of this world, Marie suggests, can only bring suffering; whereas that same love embraced within the love of God, can bring ultimate and immutable fulfillment. In her general prologue, she has suggested that the efforts put into a difficult task, such as probing the hidden meanings of her book, help one to "esloignier/ E de grant dolur delivrer"[4] ("ward off and rid oneself of great suffering").[5] Her *surplus de sens* leads the reader to conclude that, once all the *lais* are taken into consideration, love that is merely of the flesh is, in the end, inadequate for ultimate joy, and that even happy love affairs that lie within the reach of Fortune's wheel can only cause eventual pain. Only by giving oneself up to total selflessness and to complete trust in divine Providence, she seems to suggest, can one find enduring satisfaction.

Equitan contains a number of what I believe are deliberate echoes from *Guigemar*, with the repetitions serving to connect the two tales in a way that allows Marie to reinforce and intensify in the second *lai* the problem she introduced only subtly in the first. For example, only in these two tales is there any mention of the *plaie d'amour*. In addition to the physical wound Guigemar receives when his arrow rebounds from the horn of the white stag, he is also struck by a second affective wound of love as a result of his first encounter with his beloved:

> Mes Amur l'ot feru al vif;
> Ja ert sis quors en grant estrif,
> Kar la dame l'ad si nafré,
> Tut ad sun païs ublié.   (379–82)

> (But love had now pierced him to the quick and his heart was greatly disturbed. For the lady had wounded him so deeply that he completely forgot his homeland.)   (49)

---

3   See my article, "The Curse of the White Hind and the Cure of the Weasel: Animal Magic in the *Lais* of Marie de France," in *Literary Aspects of Courtly Culture*, ed. Donald Maddox and Sara Sturm-Maddox (Cambridge, England: D.S. Brewer, 1994), pp. 199–209. It should be noted that the conceit of the wound of love has meaning both within courtly love and religious contexts. See Dolores Warwick Frese, "Marie de France and the 'Surplus of Sense': A Modest Proposal Concerning the *Lais*," in *De Gustibus: Essays for Alain Renoir*, ed. John Miles Foley et al. (New York and London: Garland, 1992), pp. 216–33.

4   *Les Lais de Marie de France*, ed. Jean Rychner (Paris: Champion, 1983), lines 26–27. Subsequent references to the *Lais* are be to this edition and will be given within the text.

5   *The Lais of Marie de France*, trans. Glyn S. Burgess and Keith Busby (London: Penguin, 1986), p. 41. Subsequent translations are from this edition, and page numbers will be noted within the text.

Similarly, during his first meeting with the seneschal's wife Equitan experiences a wound from the arrows of Love:

> Amurs l'ad mis en sa maisniee:
> Une seete ad vers lui traite,
> Ki mut grant plaie li ad faite:
> El quor li ad lanciee e mise!   (lines 54–57)

> (Love admitted him into her service and let fly in his direction an arrow which left a very deep wound in him. It was launched at his heart and there it became firmly fixed.)   (p. 57)

The hunt is also a common motif in the two *lais*. Both Guigemar and Equitan set out initially upon a hunt. In Guigemar's case, it is an innocent and literal hunt that leads him ultimately to love, whereas Equitan's is a calculated *chasse* for amorous conquest, with the literal hunt as only an initial pretext. Both men end their hunt afflicted by the wound which will, as the metaphor is elaborated, require reciprocal love as a *guérison*. Each lover must therefore persuade a reluctant lady to cure him of his wound by giving him her love. In *Guigemar* the debate is by no means fully developed. The lover in a most direct and rather naïve manner asks for the unnamed lady's love:

> "Dame, fet il, jeo meorc pur vus!
> Mis quors en est mult anguissus:
> Si vus ne me volez guarir,
> Dunc m'estuet il en fin murir.
> Jo vus requeor de druërie:
> Bele, ne m'escundites mie!"   (lines 501–06)

> ("My lady," he said, "I am dying because of you; my heart is giving me great pain. If you are not willing to cure me, then it must all end in my death. I am asking for your love. Fair one, do not refuse me.")   (pp. 49–50)

Equitan's approach to the seneschal's wife, although recounted by indirect discourse, is almost identical.[6]

> Sun curage li descovri;
> Saveir li fet qu'il meort pur li.
> Del tut li peot faire confort
> E bien li peot doner la mort.   (lines 113–16)

> (. . . he disclosed his feelings to her, letting her know that he was dying because of her and that she was well able to bring comfort to him or to cause his death.)   (pp. 57–58)

Presenting the lady with a life-or-death plea, the lover in each case throws himself on her mercy. Though it would be a flattering proposal to any woman, both women

---

6   Philippe Ménard suggests that "l'aveu d'Équitan n'intéresse que très peu Marie de France: elle le rapporte en quatre vers et au style indirect." ("La déclaration amoureuse dans la littérature arthurienne au XIIe siècle," *Cahiers de civilisation médiévale* 13 [1970], p. 37). It may be not so much a lack of interest on Marie's part as the lack of necessity to repeat what we have already heard in greater detail in the initial *lai*.

hesitate. Guigemar's lady is taken aback by the suddenness of his proposal, responding:

> ... "Amis,
> Cist cunseilz sereit trop hastis
> D'otrïer vus ceste priere:
> Jeo ne sui mie acustumiere.["]   (lines 509–12)
>
> ("Friend, such a decision would be over-hasty: I am not accustomed to such requests.")   (p. 50).

His reply is that of an impatient and certainly inexperienced man who does not wish to engage in a long debate on the issue, as he informs her that only a woman of easy virtue likes to prolong the courtship to make her favors more valued, but that the "dame de bon purpens" [presumably one not accustomed to such courtly dalliance] will not behave haughtily toward a man who pleases her, but will readily give her love and experience its joy. The two lovers, he underscores, will enjoy the love only so long as no one discovers it. Hence, Guigemar sets forth the limited nature of such earthly love and the fragility of its bliss.

Equitan, by contrast, is a more experienced lover, adept at the amorous repartee of *fin'amors*.[7] He seems to enjoy the little *débat amoureux* with the seneschal's wife and clearly knows all the right things to say. She, in turn, raises appropriate objections of the sort that Andreas Capellanus would later catalogue in his *De amore*. Refusing to yield without discussion, she points out their unequal stations and the importance of equality as a basis for love:

> "Amurs n'est pruz, se n'est egals.
> . . .
> S'aukuns aime plus hautement
> Qu'a sa richesce nen apent,
> Cil se dute de tute rien!
> Li riches hum requide bien
> que nuls ne li toille s'amie
> qu'il voelt amer par seignurie!"   (lines 137, 143–48)
>
> ("Love is not honourable, unless it is based on equality.... If anyone places his love higher than is appropriate for his own station in life, he must fear all manner of things. The powerful man is convinced that no one can steal away his beloved over whom he intends to exercise his seigneurial right.")
>   (p. 58)

Equitan's courtly response is designed to win his lady's love. First of all, he tells her, any woman regardless of her station who is "sage,/ Curteise e franche de curage"

---

7 Several authors have identified *Equitan*, along with *Chaitivel*, as the *lais* that best portray the concept of *fin'amors*. According to Ernest Hoepffner (*Les Lais de Marie de France* [Paris: Boivin, 1935], esp. pp. 154–58) and R.B. Green ("*Fin'amors* dans deux lais de Marie de France: *Equitan* et *Chaitivel*," *Le Moyen Age* 81 [1975], pp. 265–72), they are in essence an attack on courtly love. Moshé Lazar, on the other hand, sees *Equitan* as a *lai* expressing *fin'amors* as an ideal (*Amour courtois et Fin'amors dans la littérature du XIIe siècle* [Paris: Klincksieck, 1964], esp. pp. 195–96).

(lines 155–56) is worthy of a prince's love. But in any case, says he, it is she who will hold the higher rank in love, and he who will be her vassal.

> "Ne me tenez mie pur rei,
> Mes pur vostre humme e vostre ami.
> Seürement vus jur e di
> Que jeo ferai vostre pleisir.
> Ne me laissiez pur vus murir!
> Vus seiez dame e jeo servanz,
> Vus orguilluse e jeo preianz."   (lines 170–76)

("Do not regard me as your king, but as your vassal and lover. I swear to you in all honesty that I shall do your bidding. Do not let me die because of you. You can be the mistress and I the servant; you the haughty one and I the suppliant.")   (p. 58)

In only three of the tales, these two included, do the lovers *exchange* tokens of their love and fidelity. Guigemar gives to his lady a *ceinture* that only he can unlock, while as her gift to him she makes in his *chemise* a knot that only she can untie. Whereas the emphasis of the gifts of Guigemar and his lady are on fidelity to the love relationship, those exchanged by Equitan and the seneschal's wife, more conventional *anneaux*, would seem to underscore the love itself.

> Par lur anels s'entresaisirent,
> lur fiaunces s'entreplevirent.
> Bien les tindrent, mult s'entramerent,
> puis en mururent e finerent.   (lines 181–84)

(By an exchange of rings they took possession of each other and pledged their faith. They kept this faith well and loved each other dearly. It was later to be the cause of their death.)   (p. 58)

Such exchanges of love tokens are surprisingly rare in the *lais*, with only one other instance, an exchange of rings between Guilliadun and Eliduc as he is departing for his homeland, in what is perhaps a deliberate ironic echo of the other two tales. Otherwise, Milun's lady sends him a ring; Guilliadun on another occasion sends a ring and girdle to Eliduc; and the lady in *Chaitivel* gives her four suitors love tokens to bear in tournaments. But there is no indication in these instances of a reciprocal gift.

Such echoes between the two initial *lais* are not, I think, coincidental. Marie is showing us in *Equitan* the logical next-step of *Guigemar*, thereby warning her readers of the dangers and destructiveness of the courtly ideal of love, against which she allows her lovers to be measured.[8] Having drawn her reader in with a seemingly

---

8   Jean Flori argues in his article "Seigneurie, noblesse et chevalerie dans les *Lais* de Marie de France" that *Equitan* "nous fournit un exemple inversé du 'modèle courtois' traditionnel puisqu'ici l'amant devient le seigneur du mari." (*Romania* 108 [1987], p. 188). This model of courtly love is in large measure based on Georges Duby's notion that *l'amour courtois* was an educational game in which powerful lords permitted their wives a position "illusoire, ludique, de primauté et de pouvoir" (see Georges Duby, *Mâle Moyen Age* [1988], p. 80), aimed at controlling the throng of unruly *iuvenes* that populated the medieval world. If such was the

innocuous tale of first-love that seems, if one does not read too closely, to end
happily, she then shows the potentially destructive nature of such a love if carried to
the logical next step. Writing of thematic irony in *Guigemar*, Joan Brumlik has
underscored the unsatisfying ending of the *lai*, which ends in the death and destruction of innocent people for the egocentric satisfaction of the lovers' desires.[9] We are
here but a step away from the willful act of intended murder in *Equitan*. Critics have
tended to justify the siege of Guigemar but condemn the murderous plot of Equitan.
But what wrong had Guigemar's rival Meriaduc done other than love the lady and try
to keep her for himself? If he is a stand-in for the "wicked" husband, the *mari* in
Guigemar does not seem to play so brutal a role as the cruel man in *Laüstic*. Finding
another man in his wife's bed, he allows him to go free, though he places additional
restrictions on his wife's movements by imprisoning her in a tower. This confine-
ment, however, is little more than an intensification of previous restraints. Prior to
Guigemar's arrival she was already under constant surveillance in an enclosure for
which there was only a single point of entry, guarded day and night. In fact, Guigemar seems more cruel than he in causing the deaths of the townspeople whose only
crime is having Meriaduc as their lord. In both *Guigemar* and *Equitan*, the self-
centered love of the protagonists leads to the death or plotted death of the innocent.
Further, *Guigemar* does nothing to resolve that little unmentioned problem at the
end, the lady's still-living husband, an issue that leads directly to the dilemma of
Equitan. What happens if the lovers wish to marry?

If the first two *lais*, taken together, are cautionary, as I think they are, then one
must pose the following question: given the love-longing that is a part of human
nature and the societal pressures condoned within the courtly milieu to engage in
love relationships, is there an alternative to such self-interested and potentially
destructive loves? In presenting the third *lai*, *Fresne*, and in juxtaposing it with the
second, *Equitan*, Marie seems to provoke the reader to think through the problem
and to work toward a solution. Despite obvious surface differences (e.g., *Equitan*
deals with the story of two men and one woman, while *Fresne* recounts the tale of
two women and one man; *Fresne* is a two-generational story that takes place in
several settings, while *Equitan* is limited to only one locus and a single generation),
there are extraordinary structural similarities in Marie's depiction of the two love
relationships that seem to invite a comparison of the two tales.

---

case, and I am frankly skeptical of Duby's thesis, it would place the husband in the role of
puppeteer, pulling the strings of an acquiescent wife and her young suitors. Nothing in the
literature suggests such a scenario. In fact, some texts that purport to deal with *fin'amors* even
call into question whether or not the lady had to be married, though she sometimes was, as she
is in both *Guigemar* and *Equitan*. As for the husband figure in most medieval texts, he tends to
be either hostile to the lovers or ignorant of their existence, as is the case of virtually all the
husbands in the *Lais* of Marie de France. In his article "Triadic Structure in the *Lais* of Marie
de France," Donald Maddox has demonstrated that the husband is most often excluded from
the relationship by the structure of the *lai* (in *Assays: Critical Approaches to Medieval and
Renaissance texts*, ed. Peggy A. Knapp [Pittsburgh: University of Pittsburgh Press, 1985], pp.
19–40).
[9]   See Joan Brumlik, "Thematic Irony in Marie de France's *Guigemar*," *French Forum* 13
(1988), pp. 5–16.

In both *lais* the lover falls in love with his lady *de lonh*, by merely hearing of her extraordinary qualities and beauty. Both ladies are described not only in terms of physical beauty and education, but, more interestingly, in terms of their formation by Nature. The two lovers respond similarly. Equitan desires the seneschal's wife without ever having seen her:

> Li reis l'oï souvent loër;
> . . .
> Sans veüe la coveita. (lines 38, 41)
>
> (. . . the king [had] often heard her praised. . . . They had never met, but he conceived a desire for her.) (p. 56).

Similarly, Gurun falls in love after merely hearing about the qualities of Fresne:

> De la pucele oï parler,
> Si la cumença a amer. (lines 247–48)
>
> (. . . he had heard tell of the maiden and began to love her.) (p. 64)

It is interesting to note that in the first case, Marie places the focus on desire by her choice of the verb *coveita*, whereas in the second she chooses instead the verb *amer*, which would seem to privilege Gurun's love over Equitan's in terms of courtliness. As the tales progress, however, Gurun seems to fall far short of the ideal and appears, in some respects, far worse than Equitan as a faithful lover and man of honor. He uses the church, and not merely a loyal retainer, as a means to satisfy his desire for Fresne. He also seems less faithful to the love relationship than Equitan, in that he promises Fresne that he will never fail her: "Certes jamés ne vus faudrai" (line 287), then, without hesitation or discussion, he breaks his promise by marrying her sister. Equitan on the other hand may be a man initially motivated by *coveitise* but he seems thereafter genuinely to fall in love with the seneschal's wife and is ready to do anything, however foolish, not to lose her. When his vassals urge him to take a wife, unlike Gurun, he refuses, telling his beloved:

> "Bele amie, n'eiez poür!
> Certes, ja femme ne prendrai
> Ne pur autre ne vus larrai." (lines 222–24)
>
> ("My fair one, do not be afraid. I shall certainly never take a wife or leave you for another.") (p. 59)

Initially, then, both lovers set out upon a calculated seduction, accomplished by means of deception. In the case of Equitan, he deceives his loyal seneschal who continues to occupy himself with the affairs of the kingdom, while Gurun will deceive the abbess who has nurtured and protected Fresne since childhood. In both cases, the lover loves the lady "lungement" until the same crisis arises to menace the relationship.[10]

---

10 "*Lung tens* durat lur druërie" and "Li reis l'ama mult *lungement*" (*Equitan*, lines 185, 197). See also "Pur sa franchise ne l'amast/ E ne cherist e honurast./ *Lungement* ot od li esté . . ." (*Fresne*, lines 311–13).

Marie juxtaposes the two *lais*, I believe, with one purpose in mind – to force the reader to contrast the two approaches to exactly the same crisis. Equitan and the seneschal's wife love each other loyally and well, until whispers begin to circulate among the courtiers that the king should take a wife. Similarly Fresne and Gurun seem to have loved each other greatly and for a long time when his vassals begin to bring pressure on their lord to marry. Fresne accepts with serenity her lover's decision, made, as I have suggested above, without discussion or apparent regret, to yield to the demands of his barons and contract a marriage with another woman, who will, of course, prove to be his beloved's twin sister. Equitan, on the other hand, dangles before his class-conscious beloved a "what-might-have-been" scenario:

> "Si vostre sire fust finez,
> Reïne e dame vus fereie.
> Ja pur nul humme nel lerreie."   (lines 226–28)
>
> (". . . if your husband were dead, I should make you my queen and my lady.
> I should not be deterred from this for anyone's sake.")   (p. 59)

A matter easily solved, she suggests. Like David and Bathsheba, the two plot to murder the hapless husband, a plot, foiled by their own foolishness, that leads to their deaths.

How can the reader account for the difference in the two reactions? What is the source of Fresne's complete serenity in the face of a real rival as opposed to the panic and ultimate treachery of the seneschal's wife at the mere possibility of one? Certainly of the two lovers Equitan has shown himself most true to his beloved. Yet what appeared to be the perfect courtly relationship suddenly turns to destructive behavior on the part of the lovers. The answer clearly does not lie in the loyalty of the love or in the reassurances given.

The behavior of Fresne has often been compared with that of the patient and long-suffering Griselda as well as with the character of Marie's own creation – Guildeluëc. The *lais* of *Fresne* and *Guildeluëc ha Guilliadun*, as Bruckner and others have noted, are the only two in which names are given to the female protagonists and in which women's names are used as titles. Each is paired with another by virtue of her name, with a phonemic echo binding the names of Guildeluëc and her rival Guilliadun and a botanical connection linking those of Le Fresne and La Coudre. Marie's other female characters, by contrast, tend to be caught up in a conventional world that depersonifies them, makes them types insufficiently distinguished to be worthy of names.[11]

In the first pair of tales under discussion, two men duel for the love of one woman; whereas in the second pair, two women are claimants to the affections of one man. Yet how different the outcomes are. The women seem to be capable in ways that the men are not of drawing love into a larger circle, without seeking to exclude the other woman, who will in the course of the *Lais* come to be recognized or accepted as a sister, whereas the tendency of the male lovers is to eliminate the

---

[11] It is interesting to note that even the two protagonists who would be readily identifiable by medieval audiences, Guenevere and Yseut, remain unnamed in the Lais. See June Hall McCash, "Images of Women in the *Lais* of Marie de France," *Medieval Perspectives* II (1996), pp. 96–112.

rival by death or destruction. Guigemar's self-serving "love" for the unnamed wife of someone else, while it may bring him momentary satisfaction, seems ultimately selfish in its willingness to sacrifice all others for his own gratification with a lady whom he was not even sure he recognized only a short while before. Similarly the "love" between Equitan and the seneschal's wife, while it seems at first to accord to what Jean Flori has labeled "amour vrai," which he sees as the love ideal in the works of Marie de France,[12] or with the medieval ideal of *fin'amors*, quickly shows itself to be exclusive and vicious as the two plot the death of the seneschal, who is described as a "Bon chevalier, pruz e leal" (line 22). Given the frequent negative image of the seneschal in courtly literature, Marie's positive depiction of Equitan's seneschal breaks the stereotype and underscores the fundamental goodness of one who does nothing to deserve the disloyalty of his lord and of his wife.

By contrast, the loves of Fresne and Guildeluëc, no less profound and moving, derive their strength from a greater source. They demonstrate, contrary to misogynistic views so often propounded in the Middle Ages, the nobility of which women are capable and which Marie seeks to emphasize. Both women are connected, albeit differently, with a life devoted to God and the world of the convent, which many literary historians believe to have been the abode of Marie herself, for at least a portion of her life. Fresne has been reared in a nunnery by the abbess and undoubtedly given the religious upbringing that allows her to center her life beyond the vicissitudes of this world. Similarly, Guildeluëc finds the life of the cloister and her new role as the bride of Christ preferable to remaining the wife of a disloyal husband, although she in no way condemns Eliduc for the displacement of his love. Neither Fresne nor Guildeluëc are destroyed by the shifting affections of the male figure in her life, for each has found a stronger, more stable center elsewhere. Instead, both are able to accept the situation without renouncing love, as Fresne does when, without malice or rancor, she prepares the marriage bed for her sister and her own lover. Similarly, Guildeluëc willingly steps aside to permit the earthly passion of her husband and his new love to run its course, then equally willingly accepts Guilliadun as a beloved sister in her convent. Fresne's love for Gurun, like Guildeluëc's for Eliduc, is a reversal of the values of the courtly world, where love demands exclusive rights and where jealousy, if Andreas Capellanus is a faithful recorder of the love values of twelfth-century aristocracy, is an important ingredient. Both women ask nothing of love but the joy of loving. They demand nothing, not even the exclusive right to be near the beloved. They are wholly unselfish in the name of love, recognizing that earthly affections are but a small part of a larger plan and that love can exist even without the physical presence of the beloved. Fresne and Guildeluëc are larger-souled characters than any of the males depicted in the tales, more accepting of a rival, whom they come to recognize as a sister, and more able to raise their love to a higher moral level.

To return to the initial issue as to whether any order at all would suffice for the tales, I can only pose the question: would the effect of these first three tales be the

---

[12] Jean Flori, "Amour et société aristocratique au XIIe siècle: L'exemple des lais de Marie de France," *Le Moyen Age* 98 (1992), p. 22.

same if they were not juxtaposed? I think not. Marie leads us gently and by stages into the secular world and its courtly ideals, showing us, first through the beguiling tale of *Guigemar* and then through the more overtly destructive *Equitan*, where such love can lead.[13] In *Fresne*, however, she gives us an early glimpse of an alternative type of love that will be more fully developed only in the final *lai* of her collection, *Guildeluëc ha Guilliadun*. Her use of female characters to lead her readers along a higher path intriguingly foreshadows Dante's use of the female guide to Paradise.

[13] Emanuel Mickel has argued that the first three tales of the *Lais* "present three distinct types of love. The first, *Guigemar*, presents a love that is neither charity nor cupidity, but a love begun as a 'passio' and ennobled by the loyalty of the couple. The second, *Equitan*, is clearly a love of cupidity and the third, *Le Fresne*, evidently the noblest of the three, presents a love of charity which transcends all obstacles and suffering." (See "A Reconsideration of the *Lais* of Marie de France," *Speculum* 46 [1971], p. 43.) It is my contention, rather, that the first two *lais* work together as cautionary tales, in which Marie warns her readers against being drawn in by such a tale as *Guigemar*, which seems on the surface to be a straightforward story of a young man's initiation into love, without considering the ethical problems raised by the unsettling ending of the story. The caution is made more explicit in *Equitan*.

SECONDARY CHARACTERS IN *EQUITAN* AND *ELIDUC*

Joan Brumlik

An inquiry into the role of secondary characters in *Eliduc* and *Equitan* emerged from a desire to know whether Marie's readers might assume, in her various scenes, either the presence of people not specifically alluded to, or their absence. These two *lais* were chosen because of their apparent differences, of which the most obvious are length and generic affinities, the former a short romance and the latter more of a *fabliau*. *Eliduc* is long and complex in its treatment of personal conflicts which are ultimately resolved within a religious context. *Equitan* is brief, its conflicts resolved violently, more in fabliau tradition. Notwithstanding these differences, the two *lais* are essentially alike in the placing and function of secondary characters. As a further consideration in my choice of *lai*, I wished to avoid texts in which the *merveilleux* is a major element, for these stories present problems of their own.

Marie plays with her audience from the very beginning of *Equitan*. She praises the Breton nobles of long ago for their *pruësce*, their *curteisie*, and their *noblesce* (lines 3–4), not in matters of love but with regard to the songs they composed so as to record events for posterity.[1] Equitan in particular, Marie tells us, should not be forgotten, therefore we expect to hear of someone rather exemplary, someone as *preux*, *courtois*, and *noble* as were the Bretons who wished to make their subject matter memorable.

We learn immediately that Equitan is indeed *curteis* (line 11) and that he is both king and administrator of justice in the realm. Furthermore he is very worthy and much loved in his country: ". . . de grant pris/ E mut amez en sun païs" (lines 13–14). The word *amez*, however, is not without moral ambiguity, since we are promptly told that what Equitan loves most of all is *deduit* and *druërie* and that his chivalric exploits serve solely to further his amorous undertakings: "Pur ceo maintint chevalerie" (line 15). This would suggest that his *pris* and his *courtoisie* might also be subservient to these same undertakings. Nowhere else does Marie undercut her introduction, not to mention her hero, in this way.[2]

---

[1] Line numbers refer to *Les Lais de Marie de France*, ed. Jean Rychner (Paris: Champion, 1966).

[2] Roger Dubuis maintains that Equitan's *druërie* is simply his quest for the right woman. He feels that in Marie's eyes *druërie* is "le couronnement, inéluctable et souhaitable, de la véritable courtoisie," as demonstrated in both Guigemar and Equitan (p. 411). I take Dubuis's well documented point that defining *druërie* requires attention to the context, for the word has many modalities in the *Lais*. However, within a context which pokes fun at courtly love I think there is no doubt that the king is portrayed as a dedicated womanizer. "La notion de druërie

Once Marie has replaced our original horizon of expectations regarding the noble Equitan, we are not surprised to learn that except in times of war, Equitan leaves to his loyal seneschal the ruling of the kingdom and the meting out of justice, so that he may the better enjoy himself:

> Ja, se pur ostïer ne fust,
> Pur nul busuin ki li creüst,
> Li reis ne laissast sun chacier,
> Sun deduire, sun riveier.   (lines 25–28)

> (Never, except in time of war, would the king have forsaken his hunting, his pleasures or his river sports, whatever the need might have been.)[3]

To add insult to injury the king takes as his lover his seneschal's wife. In the course of the wooing and the subsequent affair, all the conventions of courtly love are deployed and subverted to amuse Marie's audience. When the king is urged to take a wife, the seneschal's wife, determined to marry him, draws the king into a plan to kill her husband. He is to die in a scalding bath, a method which announces its failure by its very extravagance.

The love affair is marked by the utmost secrecy as the king provides an incongruous device for keeping the outer world at bay. When he wants to be alone with the seneschal's wife, the king claims that he wishes to be bled *priveement* (line 190) and must be undisturbed. In the palace space reserved for the lovemaking there are no secondary characters. There is no one to guard the door or keep watch, nor is there anyone around who would notice the comings and goings of the seneschal's wife, or the total absence of bloodletters.[4] Similarly, for the courting of the seneschal's wife, the king goes hunting *priveement* (line 43), in the region where the seneschal lives, and spends the night: "El chastel u la dame esteit" (line 46). After a sleepless love-sick night he goes hunting only to turn back, feigning ill-health and thereby causing great concern to the seneschal. No sooner are we thus abruptly made aware that the seneschal is present for this royal visit and has in fact been hunting with his king, than he promptly disappears from the text to await his final appearance. The long conversation between the wife and the king takes place in complete privacy, as they agree to the terms of their affair and their deaths are foretold.

---

dans les *Lais* de Marie de France," *Le Moyen Age* 98, 5th series, vol. 5 (1992), 391–413. Closer to my view is Judith Rice Rothschild: "Marie de France's *Equitan* and *Chaitivel*: *fin'amors* or *fabliau*?" in *The Worlds of Medieval Women: Creativity, Influence, and Imagination*, vol. II of *Literary and Historical Perspectives of the Middle Ages* (Morgantown WV: West Virginia University Press, 1985), 113–21 at p. 115. Rothschild notes that the audience is beautifully misled by Marie's insistence on the nobility of those who consider Equitan worthy to be remembered.

3   The translations are from *The 'Lais' of Marie de France*, trans. Glyn S. Burgess and Keith Busby (Harmondsworth, Middlesex: Penguin Books, 1986).

4   We know that bloodletting in the Middle Ages was increasingly done by women. See Audrey Davis and Toby Appel, *Bloodletting Instruments in the National Museum of History and Technology* (Washington: Smithsonian Institution Press, 1979), pp. 8–9. However, I do not think that Marie intended the reader to make the assumption that the seneschal's wife was a bloodletter for she makes a point of having no one present who might notice the woman.

For the murder of the seneschal, the lovers' security disappears. Both men are to be bled, after hunting.[5] At the king's suggestion they arrange to bathe together three days later. On the fateful third day, the king and the seneschal are together in the seneschal's bed chamber until the seneschal leaves. Ironically, he goes out "[p]ur deduire" (line 278). The baths are then set up and the seneschal's wife joins the king in her husband's bed, also *pur deduire* as it transpires: "Sur le lit al seignur cuchie-rent/ et deduistrent e enveisierent" ("They lay down on the lord's bed and took their pleasure," lines 281–82), although she is ostensibly there "pur la cuve" (line 284), to keep an eye on the tub of scalding water. The only secondary character in the *lai* now appears, the woman enlisted to guard the door (lines 285–86). As the reader anticipates, she cannot hold the door against the seneschal. The naked king, caught in the act, jumps into the boiling water feet first. He is immediately followed by the seneschal's wife, pushed in head first after him by her husband.

The woman at the door has been created to add to the suspense of the dénoue-ment. She is not intended to prevent the return of the seneschal, simply to make it more dramatic. By her very function in the story she is an indication that the lovers' sanctuary no longer exists. She guards a door which separates two arenas, one in which social conventions are flouted, and the other in which social conventions are observed.

There are as well several references in the *lai* to *la gent*, people generally. In all references they are associated with the royal dwelling but specifically excluded from any knowledge of the love affair. For example, Marie tells us that the love affair lasted for a long time without people knowing: "Lung tens durat lur druërie/ Que ne fu pas de gent oïe" (lines 185–86). There are also those who are informed as to why the king had to be left undisturbed, and later those who are critical of the king's refusal to take a wife. These people thus represent the conventional world kept in ignorance of the king's love affair. When the seneschal's wife plots the murder, she refers to those who would be summoned to bear witness to the sudden and unex-pected death of the seneschal in his bath: "Quant morz serat e escaudez,/ vos hummes et les soens mandez,/ Si lur mustrez cumfaitement/ Est morz al bain sude-inement" ("When he has been scalded to death, summon your vassals and his. Show them how he suddenly died in the bath," lines 257–60). Thus, in theory, when the king has murdered his seneschal, he will, with no pangs of conscience, go public to exculpate himself, reassuming his role as *jostise* by judging himself to be innocent.

In the economy of Marie's *lais*, individual secondary characters are rare and functional. This is particularly so where illicit love is portrayed as known to few, if any, secondary characters. One has only to think of the lovers' secluded paradise in *Guigemar* or the secrecy which surrounds the adventures of Milun and his lady, up to and including the birth of a child.

---

5   When the king and the seneschal are bled together, the suggestion is that the bloodletting is necessary for the king: "Seiner se fet cuntre sun mal," line 265. This might be a reference to the king's love-sickness when he turned back from the hunt, giving illness as the excuse. That the seneschal and his king are bled together when the seneschal is suffering from no known illness suggests a social aspect to being bled, just as for bathing. To be bled privately would then be most unusual.

Eliduc has been chosen for the second part of my discussion since it is the longest and most complex of the *Lais*, offering a substantially larger number of individual characters as well as groups of people, for example Eliduc's friends or the hostile courtiers. Like *Guigemar*, the story is initially set in a well-populated world. The hero is already happily married: "mut s'entreamerent lëaument" (line 12). He is also well regarded by his king until the latter turns against him and banishes him from the kingdom. His world is well peopled: he has vassals loyal to him (lines 72–73) and friends who are mentioned three times (lines 56, 74, and 77). A communal morality is evoked in Marie's proverbial "he who is loyal to his lord and loves his good neighbors is wise and sensible" ("Cil est sages e vedzïez/ Ki lëauté tint sun seignur,/ Envers ses bons veisins amur," lines 64–66). Even in the negative context of banishment, Eliduc is depicted as surrounded by loyal people, not least of whom his wife Guildeluëc, to whom he promises fidelity when he leaves. Secondary characters in the first section consist primarily of groups of people among whom Eliduc moves easily and is respected, notwithstanding the disfavor into which he has fallen vis-à-vis the king and some of the courtiers.

Upon his arrival in Exeter, Eliduc offers his services to a king at war with a neighbor. The king has his *conestable* see to an escort and arrange for lodging. Subsequently, the townspeople, the king's men and volunteer knights form a solid backdrop of support for Eliduc. When the war is over, with a year's contract ahead of him as *gardein* (line 270) of the kingdom, as he was in Brittany, Eliduc pledges loyalty to the king. He will ultimately prove disloyal both to his wife and to the king of Exeter. Simultaneously the well-populated world around him is suddenly and increasingly reduced, as secondary characters fall away.

At the beginning of the *lai*, when the emphasis was on his qualities as caretaker of the kingdom in Brittany, Eliduc was introduced to us as "pruz e curteis, hardi et fier" ("worthy and courtly, brave and fierce," line 6). A second description of him clearly announces his new role as a lover: "Elidus fu curteis e sage,/ beaus chevaliers e pruz e large" ("Eliduc was courtly and wise, a fine knight, worthy and generous," line 272). The daughter of the king sends for him through her chamberlain. The very image of the warrior-knight, Eliduc makes the trip on his *destrier*, accompanied by a fellow knight. The accompanying knight and the princess's chamberlain are immediately dropped from the text, although the chamberlain is to reappear. A more significant absence from the text generally is the queen. She is mentioned only once, in the introduction to the *lai*, when we are told that Guilliadun is the daughter of a king and queen (line 16). Without a mother or an entourage, Guilliadun is presented as vulnerable to Eliduc's charm, to her own youth and inexperience, and to the suggestions of her chamberlain, the go-between.

Eliduc steadfastly refuses to tell her that he is married, letting events take their course. He is now portrayed as completely alone, isolated from his companions. The father's position is not clear. We know that he has already refused one suitor, the king with whom he was warring when Eliduc first arrived, and that he has encouraged his daughter to honor Eliduc.[6] When Eliduc is summoned by his Breton king to return

6 In "The Celtic Origins of the Chess Symbolism in *Milun* and *Eliduc*," Maria A. Rebbert

home, the king of Exeter reluctantly accepts Eliduc's departure on the understanding that Eliduc will return to resume his position. Their conversation over, Eliduc asks for permission to speak to Guilliadun, and a *dameisel* is summoned to admit him to her. He has appeared from nowhere and disappears immediately. Marie uses the *dameisel* both to isolate the king from any knowledge of his daughter's love for Eliduc, and to leave the couple completely unchaperoned. As a result, overwhelmed by Guilliadun's grief at the news of his departure, Eliduc promises to return and take her away with him.

The town and its inhabitants, Eliduc's lodgings, peopled by his host and his companions, and the castle itself have been progressively reduced to the space that is Guilliadun's chamber, and to the classic grouping of two lovers and a go-between. Eliduc's military life is replaced by one of solitary and inconclusive soul-searching. For the couple in love, the outside world disappears entirely.

Once back in Brittany, Eliduc rapidly settles the war as the time for his return to Exeter approaches. He lies to his wife, telling her that he must return to Exeter because the king needs him. He chooses a minimum of people to accompany him. Two are nephews, a detail which allows us to see Eliduc as part of a larger family group. He also takes with him his chamberlain and his squires. All are sworn to secrecy. The loyal friends around him at the time of his first departure are not mentioned prior to the second leave-taking.

Eliduc's two voyages to Exeter give us considerable geographical detail. As a result we can chart Eliduc's second journey to and from Exeter. We know that he arrives in Totnes and takes lodging far from the port area for fear he would be known. At nightfall he and his chamberlain leave Totnes and ride north to Exeter where his chamberlain enters the city alone to fetch Guilliadun and bring her to him at some distance outside the city gate, where he is waiting at the edge of a fenced-in wood. By giving substance to the physical and geographical world from which Eliduc must hide, Marie emphasizes the enormity of his betrayal of the girl and of his wife, not to mention his betrayal of the king whose lands he was to keep safe. As well, Marie emphasizes his disregard for the safety of the men who are accompanying him, those who are the closest and most loyal to him. He subsequently murders a sailor for revealing that he is a married man. With Guilliadun apparently dead as a result of this indiscretion, Eliduc can get no advice from his companions. They are not hostile to him, they simply cannot help him maintain the secrecy and the privacy he vainly tries to reconstruct. He takes Guilliadun's body to a forest chapel where he leaves it in front of the altar, returning daily to mourn her loss and his own lack of responsibility, recognizing belatedly that were it not for him she

tells us that in Celtic literature, chess games between a lover and the father or the husband of the lady determined the lover's success or failure in his suit. She also suggests (p. 154) that even for a twelfth-century Anglo-Norman audience, Eliduc would have been playing chess with the father had he wished to be a suitor. That he has not been invited to play would perhaps indicate that Eliduc is not a contender in the father's eyes. It is thus significant that he and the girl leave the game and go off together. The girl then confesses her love for him. *In Quest of Marie de France: A Twelfth-Century Poet,* ed. Chantal A. Maréchal (Lewiston, Queenston, Lampeter: The Edwin Mellen Press, 1992), pp. 148–60.

would one day have been queen (line 943). As a result of Guildeluëc's concern for her husband, she discovers Guilliadun and brings her back to life by means of a flower which she has seen a weasel use to restore life to its companion.[7] She then withdraws into an abbey so that Eliduc and Guilliadun may marry and be restored to the community. Later, following the wife's example, they too will devote the remainder of their lives to God. In this *lai* more than any other, Marie develops the theme only touched upon in *Equitan*, that the private is, in the long run, almost inevitably made public.

When Marie creates the spaces in which illicit love is presented as sanctioned, she peoples them sparcely or not at all. Sometimes such spaces are invaded by husbands as in *Equitan* and *Guigemar*. *Guigemar* is particularly interesting in this regard for the cast of characters in the lovers' private sphere is originally restricted to the husband's niece and a eunuch, the guardian of the key to the elegant prison which, it is said, the lady never leaves (lines 245–54). The niece is not mentioned after her role as go-between has been accomplished, but we have already been told that she stays with the wife only when the husband is away.[8] After the lovers have spent a year and a half together, the public world invades their sanctuary. We are suddenly made to realize that the wife has duties to attend to elsewhere, that she may be fetched out of her prison to look after them. The person who enters her domain is the husband's chamberlain, not the eunuch. Further, the chamberlain can see the couple through a window. The private space disintegrates altogether, its stock characters dismissed, replaced by an everyday figure belonging to the outer world of the husband. In *Guigemar*, Marie is unmistakably clear in her depiction of the illusory nature of the space in which illicit love appears sanctioned.

In *Yonec* and *Lanval* the lovers' enchanted space is contiguous with every-day space, rather like the space created by two circles which overlap. In *Lanval*, the hero's lady goes to him whenever he desires her, wherever he is. Ultimately, he will go with her to Avalon, which, as William Calin observes, might well have been viewed at Marie's time as equivalent to death for the alienated hero.[9] In *Yonec* the bird-lover appears in the lady's space, her bedroom, until that space is violated by the suspicious husband and his sister, and the lover killed.

The space lovers occupy, whether a private space created merely by a rejection of

[7] See Peggy McCracken, "Women and Medicine in French Narrative," *Exemplaria* 2 (1993), 239–62. She provides much information concerning both the weasel and healing flowers (pp. 256–60).
[8] Rycher gives the following punctuation in the lines explaining the terms of the girl's stay with the imprisoned wife: "Od li esteit quant il errout./ De ci la ke il reparout,/ Hume ne femme n'i venist,/ Ne fors de cel murail n'issist" (lines 251–54). Burgess and Busby translate with no full stop until *reparout*: "The two loved each other dearly, and when the husband was away, the girl remained with her until his return. No one, man or woman, could have gained access to this spot or escaped from this walled enclosure" (p. 46). Only by assuming, as does the translation, that at all times no one except the eunuch or the husband's niece might enter or leave, can Guigemar's stay with the lady for a year and a half, undiscovered, be consistent with the terms of her imprisonment.
[9] *The French Tradition and the Literature of Medieval England* (Toronto, Buffalo, London: University of Toronto Press, 1994), p. 27.

conventional mores, as is the case in *Eliduc* and *Equitan*, or by a manifestation of the *merveilleux* to the same effect, as in *Lanval* or *Yonec*, is not portrayed as resolving problems in Marie's lays. Thus in *Eliduc*, the hero, upon his final return home, divides his activities between his public and his private life, his royal duties and the chapel. Again one can suggest two circles which overlap, the circle in which Eliduc belongs, with his wife and people, that is to say, the circle of social inclusion, and the circle of exclusion to which he condemned Guilliadun from the time he refused to tell her he was married. Eliduc cannot resolve the problem, not only because he believes Guilliadun dead, but because her apparent death reflects the reality of his dilemma: he cannot incorporate her into his public sphere. It is his wife whose love for him and pity for the girl will ultimately bring the latter into the community. She then withdraws into an abbey, allowing the lovers to marry. The only *merveilleux* in this *lai* is the flower which restores life. Yet one might well argue that it too is placed in the overlap of two circles, a natural remedy as well as a manifestation of the *merveilleux*, but above all a measure of the wife's love for her husband and for the girl herself.

We are accustomed, in our daily lives, to the concept, if not always the fact, of privacy. To be alone or to want to be alone is not of itself suspect. The medieval aristocrat's life was, on the contrary a public one, as John Bowers tells us in his discussion of the ordeal in Marie's *lais*:

> ... privacy in the modern sense was a true anomaly in these intimate, granular communities except in the sense of "collective privacy" sustained by all members of an extended household. Since any activity that a man and woman needed to keep private could be considered antisocial, suspicion naturally arose that such activities needed to be brought to light as sinful or criminal.[10]

To conclude, it goes without saying that Marie's placing and omission of people is deliberate. It would seem from these two examples that if a given scene is sparsely peopled, we may assume no one present other than those specifically mentioned in the text as occupying that space; and that where the public at large is present, informed, and not divided in its opinion, public sanction may be assumed to be accorded. Thus Eliduc, initially both praised and blamed, is cast as a potentially flawed character.

Both the private and the public take many forms in Marie's work, and of these I have discussed only a few. Much has been written about the role of fantasy or wish-fulfilment in the form of the *merveilleux* in such works as *Yonec* and *Lanval*. While there is no doubt that a personal fantasy is private, there are public aspects in these very private worlds that have yet to be looked at. As mentioned at the outset, I chose *Eliduc* and *Equitan* for this paper because these two *lais* are not problematic in this regard. My conclusions, however limited in scope, may suggest an approach to further study, not only of Marie's other *lais* generally, but of the public and private domains of the *merveilleux* itself.

---

[10] John M. Bowers, "Ordeals, privacy, and the *lais* of Marie de France," *The Journal of Medieval and Renaissance Studies* 24 (1944), 1–31 at p. 1.

THE OPTIMISTIC LOVE-POET: PHILIPPE DE BEAUMANOIR

Leslie C. Brook

Philippe de Beaumanoir (or Philippe de Rémi) bequeaths to us the minor inconvenience of answering to two different names, as well as that of being both a father and a son. Over the past decade the general opinion concerning the authorship of their writings has changed, so that now the literary compositions, and notably the two romances, *La Manekine* and *Jehan et Blonde*, are attributed to Beaumanoir *père* (died 1266), while the son (1253–1296) is still the undisputed author of the *Coutumes de Beauvaisis*.[1] However, whereas the two romances have attracted some attention in recent years, and continue to do so,[2] Philippe's lyric output has remained relatively ignored. In Paris, Bibliothèque Nationale MS fr. 1588, which contains the literary works, the two romances are followed by a *Salu d'Amours* (fols 97r–103v), a *Conte d'Amours* (fols 103v–106v), a fabliau entitled *Conte de fole larguece* (fols 107r–109v), a series of *fatrasies* (fols 109v–110v),[3] a *Lai d'Amours* (fols 110v–112v), an *Ave Maria* (fols 112v–113v), a second set of *fatrasies* (fols 113v–114r), and an incomplete *Salu à refrains* (fol. 114v). The poems which need to be considered in an analysis of Philippe's love poetry are the *Salu d'Amours*, the *Conte d'Amours*, the *Lai d'Amours* and the fragmentary *Salu à refrains*. In addition A. Jeanroy identified a group of *chansons* in a thirteenth-century *chansonnier* (Paris, Bibliothèque Nationale MS fr. 24406), which he considered to be also the work of Philippe de Rémi.[4] Two of the eleven *chansons* in this group actually bear the name "Phelippes de Remi" integrated into the verse.

The love poems in the manuscript containing Beaumanoir's romances are all a

---

[1] The romances and poems are to be found in Hermann Suchier, *Philippe de Rémi, sire de Beaumanoir: Oeuvres poétiques*, SATF, 2 vols. (Paris: Firmin Didot, 1884–85), and Sylvie Lécuyer, *Jehan et Blonde de Philippe de Rémi*, CFMA (Paris: Champion, 1984). The *Coutumes* have recently been translated by F.R.P. Akehurst, *The "Coutumes de Beauvaisis" of Philippe de Beaumanoir* (Philadelphia: University of Pennsylvania Press, 1992).

[2] Recent studies of note include Marie-Madeleine Castellani, *Du Conte populaire à "l'exemplum": "La Manekine" de Philippe de Beaumanoir* (Lille: Université de Lille III, 1988), M[argaret] Shepherd, *Tradition and Re-Creation in Thirteenth Century Romance: "La Manekine" and "Jehan et Blonde" by Philippe de Rémi*, Faux Titre, 48 (Amsterdam-Atlanta: Rodopi, 1990), and Jean Dufournet et al., *Un Roman à découvrir: "Jehan et Blonde" de Philippe de Remy (XIIIe siècle)*, Collection Unichamp, 29 (Paris: Champion, 1991).

[3] An essay on the *fatrasies* occurs in Dufournet, pp. 185–206, contributed by Dufournet himself.

[4] A. Jeanroy, "Les Chansons de Philippe de Beaumanoir," *Romania* 26 (1897), pp. 517–36. These poems will form the subject of a separate study.

mixture of lyric and pseudo-autobiographical narrative. Philippe projects himself as
smitten with love, which is inspired by the lady's beauty, and he proclaims his
sufferings and doubts, but finds a way of pleading his cause, either by letter or face to
face. The outcome is then either the expectation of a successful response or the actual
confirmation of it, so that his approach is always positive and forward-looking. The
most complex and imaginative of these poems is undoubtedly the *Salu d'Amours*,
since he brings into play a range of allegorical figures representing attitudes and
reactions to love, who struggle to gain his allegiance, before he is eventually urged
by Loialté to try to please his lady by addressing poems to her, explaining his plight,
in the hope of touching her pity. The *Salu* itself then becomes the principal poetic
offering, and in fact in the manuscript there are two miniatures, each portraying the
poet addressing his lady: in the first of them he is reading his poem to her, or
presenting it to her, in the second he is pictured with his hands together, beseeching
her, while she is depicted with her hands apart, palms upwards, as if in a gesture of
surprise.[5]

The narrative of the *Salu d'Amours*, which is framed by an introduction and
concluding *envoi*, serves to bring his lady up to date with events as he describes how
he came to fall in love with her in the first place and the trials he has endured since
then which have led up to his address to her. Success, then, will depend upon his
powers of persuasion, on his ability to move and convince his lady reader of his
sincerity and the depth of his suffering. And there is an *a priori* assumption that a
well-turned poem can bring success: the opening of the *Salu* (lines 1–5) explicitly
states this in general terms:

> Phelippes de Biaumanoir dit
> Et tiemoigne que biau voir dit
> Qui sont par amours envoiié
> Ont maint vrai amant ravoiié
> De mal en bien, de duel en joie.[6]

> (Philippe de Beaumanoir states and bears witness that good, sincere poems,
> sent in the name of love, have moved many a true lover from bad to good
> fortune, from sorrow to joy)

This general assurance at the beginning of the poem of a potentially happy outcome
through the agency of poetry is stylistically not unlike that of Guillaume de Lorris
concerning the reliability of dreams as an indicator of future reality at the start of the
Roman de la Rose. The other interesting point in these opening lines is that Philippe
assumes that suffering is an integral part of being in love, a stage preceding joy. In
this way, the hoped-for reward is seen to be earned: *service* implies pain loyally
endured in the cause. The whole introductory section (lines 1–46) almost functions
as a lyric poem in its own right, since following the general statement above, he

---

[5] The first miniature occurs at the head of the poem, the second between lines 616 and 617,
after Traïson has delivered the ten penalties.
[6] All quotations from Philippe's poems are taken from the Suchier edition, with occasional
modifications of spelling after consulting the MS.

explains to his beloved that prompted by Amours he is sending her his *salus* (line 9; itself both greeting and narrative poem), which will set out "une partie/ De la grieté qui m'est partie" ("part of the grief that is my lot," lines 17–18), urging her to read it and heed it, as it shows how much he is tormented by a mixture of desire and doubt, a victim of hesitation and an inner conflict which only she can resolve. A second introduction reiterates his feelings and sketches out the circumstances which led him to his present situation and the imposition of the ten penalties in the document drawn up by Traïson, which he hopes that his lady will alleviate. The main body of the text then explains in detail to her and to us how he came to fall in love with her, how he was accused in the court of Amours of the presumptuous gesture of taking her hand in a courtly dance, and was consequently imprisoned; how he there allowed himself to be judged by Traïson and her friends, who deceitfully imposed upon him the *lettre* containing the penalties which reflect his pain and anxieties; and how eventually Loialté and her friends arrived at Amours's court and suggested ways of lessening the suffering: Pitié, assisted by Amours, is to be despatched to plead with the lady, and Philippe is to be cheerful, not sad, but address poems to her to please her, and in particular his (present) *salu*, acquainting her with his plight.

In telling us all these details and plans, the lady will know what to expect, for she is both reader, with us, and *destinataire* of his devotion.[7] The final two sections of the *salu* (lines 971–1048) function as a conclusion, in which in a direct address to her he confirms that his narrative explains the existence of the *salu* he is composing, making a plea for her clemency, pointing to the injustice of the *chartre* "qui pour moi laidir fu ditee" ("which was written to harm me," line 997), and promising fidelity unto death: "se vous mes maus volés souffrir,/ Duskes a mort me voel pouroffrir" ("if you are willing to endure my ills, I will offer myself to you unto death," lines 1009–10). He discreetly acknowledges her right to respond as she sees fit, "de bien, de joie u de doloir" ("favourably, to joy or sorrow," line 1044), but it is clear that an adverse response would be seen as unjust. It is not a question of whether she will respond favourably, but when; and as if to reinforce the idea that poetry is the vehicle by which to impress and persuade, he writes two poetic virtuoso passages in the concluding lines. The first is a long anaphoric section (lines 975–97: "Tantes fleurs sont, seront et furent,/ Et tantes goutes d'yauwe plurent . . ." ("so many flowers are, will be and have been, so many drops of water have fallen")), the second a twelve-line sequence full of word-play on "fin," "fine," "desfine," "finer" and "afiner" (lines 1021–32), in a manner reminiscent of Yvain's speech to Laudine when declaring his love (lines 1975–86), the more so as there is a further passage containing a pun on "merci" (lines 1004–07).

Philippe's positive attitude appears early on in the poem (lines 75–78), when in the second introductory section he states in his address to his lady that he wants to serve her to merit her goodwill:

---

7   There is a change in narrative perspective between the closing lines of the narrative section and the address to the lady. In the narrative section she is referred to in the third person: "Et que je *li* face proiiere/ Qu'*ele* piteusement regart . . ." (lines 968–69), and in the following section she becomes "vous" (line 974, etc.).

> Tousjours pens, tousjours voel penser
> Et en pensant moi apenser
> Comment je vous porai servir
> Pour vostre bon gre desservir.

> (I constantly think and wish to think, and in so doing decide how I might serve you, to merit your goodwill)

This is an anticipatory answer to Traïson's charge in the narrative that in taking the lady's hand in the dance he was unworthy, not having ever performed for her any service "dont ele se lot" ("that she may rejoice in," line 169). There are optimistic indications, too, even in that part of the narrative in which he is under attack. He willingly surrenders to Amours when Traïson orders him to, because, as he says, "on amende en son estre" ("one improves in her company," line 182); the name of his prison is Pensee (line 214), his gaoler is called Espoir (line 216), and he acts as a friend. On the other hand among the ten penalties are such feelings as doubt, jealousy and despair, the latter of which will tell him that his love came about through folly born of melancholy, and melancholy will dispense words of discouragement, pointing out the impossible social gap between Philippe and the object of his love (cf. *Jehan et Blonde*). However, it is when he is at his lowest ebb, with Traïson's friends mocking him after tricking him, that Loialté and her friends arrive to lift his low spirits, which are not dwelled on, and immediately the vocabulary becomes optimistic again (lines 635–44, my italics):

> Et a tous jours mais traïs fusse
> Se je *secours* eü n'eüsse.
> Mais Dix qui trop het Traïson
> Ne vaut souffrir que sa reson
> Fust tenue de chief en chief,
> Qu'*alegiés* ne fuisse du grief,
> Si m'envoia pour mon *secours*
> Loialté, qui i vint le cours.
> Avoec li vint si bele route
> Que la cours en *resclarci* toute.

> (And I would have remained betrayed, had I not received *succour*; but God, who hates Treason, would not permit her edict that I should not be *relieved* of suffering to be respected everywhere, and sent for my *succour* Loyalty, who came by the shortest route, together with such fair company that the court became *resplendent*.)

Amours returns the greeting of Loialté and her friends "liement" ("joyously," line 649) and there follows "grant joie" ("great joy," line 651) between Amours and the new arrivals. A little further on (lines 678–80) there is confirmation that the sight of his allies cheers him up:

> Il me fu mout bel et mout gent,
> Et si me remist en confort
> Qu'Amours les conjoï si fort.

> (It pleased me greatly and comforted me that Love greeted them so heartily.)

They speak positively of helping to relieve his pain. Sens says: "S'Amours veut croire mon ditié,/ Il metra en son mal mecine" ("If Love will heed my song, he will give balm to his pain," lines 708–09), and generalizing, adds "Cascuns max doit avoir termine" ("every ill must have its end," line 710). Esperance, by definition, is equally reassuring (lines 711–14):

> Dist Esperance: "Ne s'esmaie!
> Car on garist bien de tel plaie,
> Et, s'Amours plest, il en garra,
> Et nostre aïde li parra."

> (Said Hope: "Don't be anxious; such a wound will heal, and, if Love wills, he will get better, and our help will be forthcoming.")

Sapience (another name for Sens), addressing Amours says (lines 733–36):

> Et mout seroit grant courtoisie
> Se li estoit amenuisie
> La paine dont morir l'estuet
> S'ayde valoir ne li puet.

> (And it would be a great courtesy if his pain were lessened, which will kill him if help is to no avail.)

Loialté, in her long speech (lines 807–918), proposes a time-limit to the suffering caused by the penalties, but that limit is to be in the gift of the lady; and while Pitié is to be sent to persuade her, Esperance is to give comfort to Philippe. Moreover, Loialté also testifies (lines 875–84) to the value of poetry in winning hearts:

> Avancié se sont maint amant
> De biau trouver, par saint Amant!
> Car ja soit çou que femme n'aint,
> Quant ele set c'on ne se faint
> Et c'on trueve dités pour li,
> Ne puet que ne pense a celi
> Qui pour li sueffre si grant soing.
> Et quant ele set son besoing,
> Plus tost a amer l'entreprent
> Par les biaus dis dont ele esprent.

> (Many a lover has made progress through fair verse, by St Amant! For although a lady may not love, once she knows that a lover is not pretending, and that he is writing poems for her, she cannot help but think of him, who suffers so much on her account. And when she learns of his need, she soon begins to love him because of the fair words which inflame her.)

All this optimism and assurance does comfort him: "Et moi, ce vous puis je bien dire,/ Fui plus soués de mon martire" ("And I can assure you that I felt more relieved of my martyrdom," lines 925–26). It is precisely the narrative movement of the poem which allows development in his feelings. This buoyancy nevertheless puts considerable pressure on the lady to conform eventually to his wishes; hence his final optimistic "Quant vous plaira, j'arai salu" ("When it pleases you, I shall receive favour," line 1045).[8]

---

8   For a further analysis of this poem, see my "Allegorical narrative in Philippe de Beauma-

Without having quite the same poetic complexity and density, the *Conte d'Amours* makes use of similar attitudes to love, in particular suffering, in the face of which the lover never abandons hope. As it is not a *salu*, there is no letter sent to the beloved, nor does it use allegory as a way of ensuring narrative progression and analysis of feeling to the same extent as in the *Salu d'Amours*. The two most striking differences between the *Conte* and the *Salu*, though, are that the *Conte* substitutes an actual meeting between Philippe and the lady for the letter, and the poem ends with confirmation that he eventually succeeded in persuading her to respond favourably to his love.

It is with this confidence and confirmation in mind that he is able at the outset of the poem to assure his readers that his tale will encourage all (men) who suffer for love. He does not describe the circumstances under which he fell in love: he merely informs us in the third stanza that the lady's beauty caused him torments from the moment he saw her (3.5–6), but that he determined to confront her with his suffering without delay. The emphasis is then on his meeting with her ("A li ving et li dis . . ." ("I came to her and said"), 4.1), beginning with a lengthy pleading of his cause (stanzas 4–14). He asks straight away for her "merchi" ("Pour Dieu je vous requier et prie/ Que vous aiiés de moi merchi" ("In God's name I beseech you to have pity on me"), 4.2–3), claiming that he will die without it. It is within her power to bring him "Deduit, doleur, joie u pesance" ("Delight, sorrow, joy, or grief," 5.12); she is the only "mire" ("doctor") for his "grief plaie" ("grievous wound," 7.11). Using an extended metaphor, he describes himself as swimming in the sea of her beauty, finding a ship of Hope, but refused respite aboard by a sailor, who is "Doutance la puans" ("Foul Doubt," 11.4). He also unoriginally claims to be in her prison ("mue," 12.1), "en paine et en plour" ("in pain and tears," 12.2), to which she has the key to release him and the medecine to cure his ills ("Et la mecine de l'ardour/ Dont mes cuers art, frit et tressue" ("And the balm to cure the fever with which I burn and am racked"), 12.11–12). He ends by offering her the stark choice – joy or death for himself; if it is death, he prefers to know quickly ("Assés vaut miex morir briement" ("It is better to die quickly"), 14.3).

Stanzas 16–29 then consist of a dialogue between them, in which she vigorously refuses to yield to his pressure, and gives a good defence of her innocent position. She tells him she is not interested; she does not want him to suffer for her, and does not accept responsibility if he insists on doing so rather than turning his heart elsewhere. She will not grant her love, and none should blame her for this ("Si ne m'en devroit nus blasmer," 19.3). He unsuccessfully tries to soften her attitude by reiterating that a refusal would mean death for him; and as the discussion proceeds, he is able to protest steadfastly that he cannot remove his heart from her, and make flattering remarks which underline his determined loyalty. Eventually she adamantly refuses any hope of him gaining her love and drives him away, "esgarés" ("in despair," 29.9).

At the point at which he leaves her there is unfortunately a sizeable lacuna in the manuscript, caused by a missing folio which would have contained over twelve

noir's *Salu d'Amour*," in *Literary Aspects of Courtly Culture*, ed. Donald Maddox and Sara Sturm-Maddox (Cambridge: D.S. Brewer, 1994), pp. 171–78.

stanzas of the poem. When the story resumes, it is clear that Pitié has appeared to him in a dream, and that thanks to her encouragement hope has returned to his heart. However, he waits until the end of May before returning to his lady. This evidently represents a suitable time-lapse, which will enable the lady to measure his loyalty and constancy. This time when he kneels before her and explains his continued plight she is better disposed (37.8). She now acknowledges that she has caused his sufferings and promises amends: "Des grans tou[r]mens que fais vous ai/ Vous bail amende" ("I will grant relief for the great torments that I have caused you," 38.4–5); Pitié has softened her heart, and she has now come to love him. Accepting her offer of amends, he kisses her, whereupon she tells him he can have five hundred kisses! (40.3). Following this success Philippe describes his sense of continuing rapture. Although love is fickle to its adherents, it is hope that brings eventual victory to lovers: "Se ne fust la grant souatume/ D'espoir, nus n'en eüst victo[i]re" ("Were it not the sweetness of Hope, none would ever gain victory," 43.12); and he hopes that his love will now endure (45.4).

Thus the narrative shift in the *Conte d'Amours*, when compared with the *Salu d'Amours*, allows for a concentration on describing how first the lady refused, but then was won over by a combination of pity and the demonstration of sincerity through protracted suffering. Eventually the lady was persuaded to think that she owed him a favourable response, but this is made to correspond to her feelings: love, not mere duty.

The *Lai d'Amours* uses a different format from the previous two poems discussed. It consists of 152 alexandrines, each of which is really an octosyllabic followed by a quadrisyllabic. The narrative focus concentrates again on the pleading stage of the relationship, with only the eventual promise of reward this time, provided that his love remains constant and true. The first third of the text (to line 52) is a hymn to the lady's beauty, the rest a dialogue of persuasion and resistance, with an ultimate softening by the lady, in a manner reminiscent of the dialogues in Andreas Capellanus's *De Amore*.

In the part of the poem which describes the lady's beauty in some detail, Philippe concentrates on her facial features and neck, but with some briefer allusion to the rest of her body and limbs, including some fantasising about her hidden private parts (lines 45–49) – again, an echo of Andreas Capellanus. Only she can cure him of the torments of his obsessive thoughts. He determines to confront her and plead for her favour, and the interview occupies the remainder of the poem. He begins by claiming to be sent to her by Amours as her prisoner, and to be completely in her power, having been captivated by her beauty, which constantly haunts his thoughts and prevents him from eating! (lines 53–62). It is again in her power to grant him joy or death: "Si me poés mettre en la voie/ de morir// Ou de grant joie recueillir/ a tousjors mes" ("You can set me on the path either to death or to great joy for evermore," lines 65–66). In reply the lady refuses to believe that he is hers "cuer et cors" ("heart and soul," line 70); she has not asked for his service; his attitude is all pretence ("Vous me dites tout par faintise," line 72), and he cannot expect love in return for that. She thereby tacitly accepts that love could be granted if his love proved true. However, she does not want to be in love with him or with anyone – a risky defiance! – as she has heard ("ce m'a on dit," line 77) that it is too painful an experience. She concludes that his words are insincere, uttered "par gabois" ("jest-ingly," line 79) to try her out.

Her charge enables Philippe to protest that this is not so, and that his heart is utterly hers. This leads to an exchange (lines 86–92) which is once more faintly reminiscent of that between Yvain and Laudine:

> Pour çou m'estuet par estavoir – priier merci,
> Se le vous pri comme a celui – qui mon cuer a.
> – Je l'ai, voire? Qui l'esraça – de vostre cors?
> – Je le vous dirai: li esfors – de vo biauté,
> Vostre cors li bel acesmé – et vostre sens.
> – Mes sens qu'i a mesfait? Mes sens – ne mes savoirs
> Onques n'i misent leur pooirs, – que je seusse.

> (And so I must beg your mercy, and I do so as to the one who has my heart. I do? Who tore it from your body? I will tell you: the strength of your beauty, your graceful body and your wisdom. What wrong did my wisdom do? My wisdom and reason were never involved to my knowledge.)

If his heart were deposited with her, she would promptly return it, "Car je ne voel riens retenir/ del vostre a tort" ("For I do not wish to retain wrongly anything of yours," line 95). When Philippe then asks her to return his heart, i.e. respond favourably to his feelings, she insists that he take it back without her adding any of her own affection to it; but he claims that it would be impossible to take it back unless she returns his love. He also insists that his heart is ready to serve her and therefore deserves reward, for if his service proves to be to no avail, then it would be to the lady's shame (line 111). Despite this pressure put upon her to make some more hopeful response, the lady defends herself well, claiming that she does not see why she should be obliged in any way, just because the heart had foolishly been placed in her service. It is not her fault if he suffers, and she asks to be left alone. This request allows Philippe to make one last appeal: if he continues to serve loyally as a true lover, could he ever achieve love in return "par priiere ne par clamour?" ("through prayer and plea?" line 126). It would not matter to him how long he suffered, provided that in the end he could be merry and feel joy (line 130). Somewhat unexpectedly the lady then relents, and replies that if he loves her as he says, her heart might eventually be won over, but she would need to test him first, to avoid being mocked ("Ne voel pas que vous me gabois," line 139). Philippe has at last elicited the response he wants, and he thanks her, adding "Des or enduerrai mes max/ en bon espoir.// Quant il vous plaira, mon doloir/ metés en joie" ("Henceforth I shall bear my ills with hope; when it pleases you, you will turn my sorrow to joy," lines 147–48). He is prepared to suffer and wait, in expectation of an eventual reward. Persistence has won him a chance to impress and flatter; the hope of success, but no firm promise, will keep his love burning.

Of the *Salut à refrains*, only the first eight stanzas survive. It occupies the verso of the last folio of the manuscript, and evidently the remainder of the poem was never incorporated into it. Nevertheless the fragment gives us some indication of the poem's content: Philippe presents himself as addressing his loved one, sending her his *salus*, and awaiting a reward for his sufferings (1.1–3):

> Douce amie, salus vous mande
> Cil qui de vous atent l'amande
> Des grans tourmens qu'il a sousfers.

> (Sweet love, he sends you this declaration, awaiting relief from the great torments that he has endured.)

He then proceeds to express the conventional suffering caused by her beauty, which will lead to death if she does not respond positively, alongside references to "espoir" (1.7) and "esperance" (3.7); but the fourth stanza implies a fresh standpoint, for it would seem that the lady has already been informed of his love. Stating that there can be no greater experience for a woman than love, he adds (4.4–6) that he is sure she feels it:

> Et je croi bien de li [= Amors] savoir
> Que ele l'a, et si set bien
> Que je l'aime sur toute rien.

> (And I believe that I have learned from Love that she does feel love, and that she knows well that I love her above all else.)

In the following stanzas he continues to express his constant "dolour" (5.5) and true love for her, begging her mercy (stanza 7). The last extant stanza (8) is particularly interesting, for it expresses not only hope, based on a feeling of deserved reward, but also an anxiety, because of the social distance between himself and his love:

> Jolis me font amors sans faille.
> D'autre part rai une bataille
> Qui mout me destraint durement.
> Car je sai bien certainement
> Qu'en trop haut lieu ai m'amour mise;
> Mais il a tant en li franchise
> Que, s'il li plaist, merci avrai.
>   Se pour bien amer doit nus avoir
>   Joie, je l'arai.

> (Love makes me merry indeed; and yet I feel a conflict that pains me much, for I know full well that I have placed my love too highly. But he is so generous that if he pleases, I shall receive mercy. If anyone deserves to have love returned through his own true love, I do.)

Conclusion

All four of these poems are really variations on the same theme, which suggests that poetic form and style of expression were at least as important to Philippe as content. The narrative element is in any case invariably rather banal, and it is in the *Salu d'Amour* that he expresses the situation in its most developed and sophisticated form. In all of these poems, love has been inspired by beauty, giving way to anguish and torments which only the lady object can cure. Not content to endure these sufferings, Philippe seeks positively to alleviate them by a direct appeal to the lady, either by letter or in person. Because of the depth and enduring nature of his love as he imagines it, he feels he has a right to a favourable response, even if there are social differences. Suffering is seen as a stage towards redemption earned by merit and sincerity; the lady ought to reward him because he is worthy and loyal, and thereby lovable. The key to success is his contact with the lady, and his reliance on the word, either in poetry or through rhetoric, to persuade. Once he can engage her in dialogue or get her to pay attention to his dilemma by letter, his problem is already half solved, even if he is initially rejected, for time is on his side, and he has only to wait until her heart changes, convinced of his genuineness and softened by pity, or Pitié. What is unthinkable for him is that any rejection should be final, for then he would be writing a story of a lost love, and the mood of the poem would be entirely different. Thus the lady becomes the victim of male persuasion, responding in the way that Philippe's creative fantasy wishes. His optimistic tone is possible because he does not create her as a figure like Alain Chartier's *La Belle Dame sans mercy*, who, as Anne Berthelot has recently pointed out, refuses to enter into the male dialogue.[9] The only escape for woman lies, as she says, in the "refus catégorique de communiquer" (Berthelot, p. 14). Philippe's creations in these poems do not have this resistance, so the texts either hint at or confirm a happy outcome and an end to the lover's frustration.[10]

[9]   Anne Berthelot, "La *Belle Dame sans mercy*, ou la dame qui ne voulait pas jouer," in *La 'Fin'amor' dans la culture féodale*, Actes du colloque du Centre d'Etudes Médiévales de l'Université de Picardie Jules Verne, Amiens, mars 1991 (Griefswald: Reineke-Verlag, 1994), pp. 13–21.
[10]   The situation is rather different when Jehan falls in love with Blonde in the romance *Jehan et Blonde*. Jehan becomes stuck in despair, and twice nearly dies, as he sees the social gap between himself and Blonde as hopeless. Nevertheless, after Blonde fails to keep her promise to become his *amie*, which she had made to prevent him from dying, Jehan does approach her for the hoped-for response, only to be plunged back into despair when she tells him that she was not serious, but was only trying to restore his health. It is finally the working of Pitié that induces her to return Jehan's love and rescue him a second time from death's door (lines 425–1331).

THE LADY SPEAKS: THE TRANSFORMATION OF FRENCH COURTLY POETRY IN THE FOURTEENTH AND FIFTEENTH CENTURIES

Maureen Boulton

In the courtly lyric poetry of the twelfth and thirteenth centuries, the lady is central but paradoxically absent. It is she who is at once the inspiration and the *destinataire* of the lover's songs. Repeatedly addressed in the songs, the poet's lady seems never to answer, and the insistent invocations only draw attention to her silence.[1] Of course the female voice is not entirely absent from medieval lyric poetry. The Occitan songs of the *trobairitz* are perhaps the earliest examples of this tradition. Yet, with the exception of a group of dialogue poems, they do not so much respond to the pleas of the courtly singer as appropriate, even as they adapt, his rhetoric for their own purposes.[2]

In the thirteenth and fourteenth centuries, the rhetoric of courtly love found new

---

[1] E.g. *Dame, Douce dame, Bele dame, Bele douce dame, Bele.* There are of course exceptions, but they are of the briefest. Among others, the Châtelain de Couci says he was laughed at (*Chanson attribuées au Chastelain de Couci*, ed. Alain Lerond [Paris: PUF, 1964], no. V, v. 19), and asked to sing (no. VIII, v. 1) by his lady. Gace Brulé quotes his beloved as asking him rudely "Quant irez vos outre mer?" in song XXXIX, v. 21 (*Chansons de Gace Brulé*, ed. Gédéon Huet [Paris, 1902; repr. New York and London: Johnson Reprints, 1968]).

[2] On the modification of courtly rhetoric by female poets, see Joan M. Ferrante, "Notes Toward the Study of Female Rhetoric in the Trobairitz," in *The Voice of the Trobairitz. Perspectives on the Women Troubadours*, ed. William D. Paden (Philadelphia: Univ. of Pennsylvania Press, 1989), pp. 45–60. See also Angelica Rieger, *Trobairitz: der Beitrag der Frau in der altokzitanischen höfischen Lyrik. Edition des Gesamtkorpus*, Beihefte zur Zeitschrift für romanische Philologie, 233 (Tübingen: Niemeyer, 1991). In contrast, Frank M. Chambers, "Las Trobairitz Soiseubudas," in *The Voice of the Trobairitz*, pp. 63–72, maintained that most of the female interlocutors in the dialogue poems respect the code of courtly behavior.

One might also cite the *pastourelle*, where female response is an essential part of the genre. In many of these poems, the knight's pretensions are deflated by the shrewd insight of the witty shepherdess, whose critique of the courtly code is most pointed. Joan Ferrante, "Male Fantasy and Female Reality in Courtly Literature," *Women's Studies* 11 (1984), pp. 67–97, has argued that the women in these poems attack male fantasies with words: they "show up the difference between what men claim and what they actually want, between what they say and what they do." Yet the *courtoisie* of the *pastourelle* is often only a sham – a technique of seduction – and the shepherdess rightly exposes its deception. But however "bele," the shepherdess is not a "dame." Consequently, her criticism, which does not address the genuine article, also comes from outside the courtly sphere.

life in the discursive treatments of the *dits amoureux*.[3] This new genre, which by its very name distinguished itself from the *chanson*, is characterized by discontinuity, by its enunciation in the first person, and by its didactic intent. One of the most famous *dits*, the *Roman de la Rose*, is essentially a narrative elaboration in the first person of the themes of the courtly lyric, and many of its successors preserve its "male-centered" quality. Nevertheless, the expansive treatment permitted by the *dit* allowed poets to subject the rhetoric of *courtoisie* to widely varied techniques, ranging from incorporation of uncourtly genres (*refrains*), to metric experimentation, and combinations of different modes of discourse (including prose and lyric poetry).[4] In three *dits* of the late fourteenth and early fifteenth centuries, we see the lady's response to a lover's lyrical declaration treated as a central theme of the work, rather than (as in the romance) simply as an element of the plot. Guillaume de Machaut and Christine de Pizan – perhaps significantly, in works described as "Livre"[5] – allow the lady to use the same forms (lyric poems and prose letters) as the lover, while Alain Chartier's *Belle dame sans merci* counters stanza for stanza each of her lover's arguments. In Machaut's *Livre dou Voir Dit* and in Christine's *Livre du Duc des Vrais Amans*, the lady's presence and participation profoundly alter the courtly drama, for she is not simply the reflection of the poet's desire, but speaks for herself, responds to her poet-lover's declarations, and even composes poetry inspired by her own love. In so doing, she transforms the courtly ethos which is the foundation of these works. Unlike the shepherdesses of the *pastourelles*, these ladies encounter honorable suitors and seem to accept the conventions of the code. The criticism of courtliness in these works is expressed indirectly, through the interaction of the participants. Consequently, the fissures in the courtly code that these works expose to view anticipate Alain Chartier's great courtly debate of the fifteenth century.

Composed by Machaut circa 1363–65,[6] near the end of his career, the *Voir Dit* purports to be the "true account" of his love affair with the young Peronne (whom he calls "Toutebelle").[7] The work is composite in form, consisting of more than

---

3   On the *dit*, see Jacqueline Cerquiglini, "Le Clerc et l'écriture: le *Voir Dit* de Guillaume de Machaut et la définition du *dit*," in *Literatur in der Gesellschaft des spätmittelalters*, ed. Hans Ulrich Gumbrecht, Begleitreihe zum *GRLMA*, I (Heidelberg: Winter, 1980), pp. 151–68; and James Wimsatt, *Chaucer and the French Love Poets: The Literary Background of the Book of the Duchess* (Chapel Hill: Univ. of North Carolina Press, 1968), pp. 2, 30–69.

4   See M.B.M. Boulton, *The Song in the Story. Lyric Insertions in French Narrative Fiction, 1200–1400* (Philadelphia: Univ. of Pennsylvania Press, 1993), esp. pp. 181–271.

5   On Machaut's title, see Jane H.M. Taylor, "Machaut's *Livre du Voir-Dit* and the Poetics of the Title," in *Et c'est la fin pour quoy sommes ensemble. Hommage à Jean Dufournet. Littérature, histoire et langue du moyen âge*, 3 vols., Nouvelle bibliothèque du Moyen Age, 25 (Paris: Champion, 1993), 3, pp. 1351–61. Before Machaut, most works called "Livre" were manuals or treatises. Both Machaut and Christine insisted on the veracity of their works.

6   See Nigel Wilkins, *Guillaume de Machaut, La Louange des Dames* (Edinburgh, 1972; New York: Barnes and Noble, 1973), pp. 10–12 on the date.

7   In the absence of the edition by Paul Imbs, now undertaken by Jacqueline Cerquiglini, one is obliged to use that of Paulin Paris, *Le livre dou "Voir Dit" de Guillaume de Machaut* (Paris: Société des Bibliophiles français, 1875). One of the passages omitted by Paris was printed by Antoine Thomas, "Guillaume de Machaut et l'Ovide moralisé," *Romania* 41 (1912), pp. 382–400. On the shortcomings of the edition, see William Calin, *The Poet at the Fountain:*

nine thousand lines of narrative verse, forty-six letters in prose, and sixty-three lyric poems, some of which have musical notation. In this work, Machaut reversed the relationship between love and poetry conventional in the *chansons* of the twelfth and thirteenth century. Where the *trouvère* sang because of his love,[8] it is poetry that inspires love in the *Voir Dit*. The first *rondeau* quoted in the work begins the "affair" that is the subject of the work, and thus generates the work as a whole.[9] It also gives a clue to the peculiar characteristics of that work: the love affair begins with a declaration, but by the lady. In her *rondeau*, Toutebelle describes herself as "Celle qui onques ne vous vi" (she who has never seen you) and specifies the origin of her love in the good things that everyone has said of him.[10] This declaration denies the usual origin of love in sight and reverses not only the relationship of poetry and love, but the relationship of lover and lady. The lady's voice intrudes here upon the lover's solitary melancholy. And this new voice is not the conventional one of *Esperance*, or even of a kindred spirit as in Machaut's *Fonteinne Amoureuse*. Toutebelle is altogether more unconventional than *Esperance*, and frequently contradicts the poet.

Toutebelle is not simply a poet's muse, or even the moving force in the literary work, but like the poet himself, a complex character. Toutebelle not only sings in the *Voir Dit*, she also speaks, or rather, writes in prose. In Letter XII (Paris, pp. 114–15), she excuses herself for not having written as often as she had hoped, and goes on to explain:

> Et cellui jour il convient partir, ma suer et moy, pour aler a .IIII. lieus long; et suis certeinne qu'il sera avant le lundi au soir ou le mardi au matin que nous retournions . . . Et eschivasse volentiers ceste alee, se je osasse ne peusse bonnement . . .
>
> (And that day, my sister and I must leave to go four leagues away; and I am certain that it will be Monday evening or Tuesday morning before we return. . . . And I would willingly avoid this trip if I dared or if I could.)

Machaut allows her to appear not only as Toutebelle, but also, in effect as Peronne – a social being with family and responsibilities.[11]

In contrast to his earlier works, the *Remede de Fortune* and the *Fonteinne*

Essays on the Narrative Verse of Guillaume de Machaut, Studies in Romance Languages, 9 (Lexington, Ky: University of Kentucky Press, 1974), pp. 17–18 and Jacqueline Cerquiglini, *"Un Engin si soutil." Guillaume de Machaut et l'écriture au XIVe siècle* (Paris: Champion, 1985), p. 9. On the work, see in addition Paul Imbs, *Le Voir Dit de Guillaume de Machaut: étude littéraire* (Paris, 1991).

[8] E.g., "Par amors ferai chanson," Richart de Semilli in *Chanter m'estuet. Songs of the Trouvères*, ed. Samuel N. Rosenberg and Hans Tischler (London and Boston: Faber & Faber, 1981), pp. 254–56.

[9] The songs and letters give rise to further creation and allow the love to exist. The "affair" is essentially literary; one song calls forth another, a letter requires an answer, and the progress of the "affair" is mirrored by the writing of the book. Given the perfection of the correspondence, the meeting of the lovers could scarcely be other than difficult.

[10] "Car pour les biens que de vous dit/ Tous li mondes communement/ Conquise l'avez bonement/ Celle qui onques ne vous vi." (Paris, p. 7; vv. 176–79).

[11] Even if Peronne d'Armentières is really the author of Toutebelle's letters and poems in the

amoureuse, where the timid, unsure lover who complains of his treatment by Love or Fortune finally receives encouragement from his lady, the *Voir Dit* begins with the desired encouragement. The starting point here – the acceptance of the lover by the lady – is in most *dits amoureux* never reached, except perhaps in a dream. However, this very acceptance places the poet-lover in a difficult predicament. Since Toute-belle loves him through his poetry, he is still bound by the conventions of the courtly lyric tradition: he must celebrate the merits of his lady which inspire his love and lament the exquisite pain caused by his "doux mal"; hope, of course, sustains him in his languishing state, and is also the source of his joy. Given the starting point of the *Voir Dit*, however, it is difficult for Guillaume to assume the stance of the *fin' amant*: he has little to ask for and less to lament.

The reversal of the opening continues in later exchanges and eventually in the lovers' encounters. Guillaume writes in a letter a statement ("I prefer to languish for you than to enjoy any other"[12]) that could have come from any number of *trouvère chansons*, but Toutebelle hastens to assure him of her love and reproves him:

> Et, mon dous cuer, je vous pri sur toute l'amour que vous avez à mi, et si acertes comme je puis, que vous ne vueilliez pas mettre vostre cuer à meschief, ne croire les paroles que vous m'avez escriptes; car en l'ame de mi, je ne le pensay onques, ne que vous me vosissiés ne daignissiés faire ce que je ne vorroie faire à vous, que j'aim plus que moi, n'autruy. (Paris, p. 62, Letter IX)

> (And my sweetheart, I beg you on the love that you have for me, and I assure you, that you should not wound your heart, nor believe the words that you have written; for in my soul I never thought that you would wish or deign to do what I would not do to you, for I love you more than myself or anyone else.)

When she reproaches his lament, her reasssurance constitutes a criticism not only of his weakness, but of the subject of much courtly poetry. During one of their few meetings, he composes a languishing *ballade* for her,[13] while Toutebelle's response signals her willingness to cure his complaint:

> Dont doucement me reprenoit
> Toutes les fois qu'il m'avenoit,
> Et disoit: "Vous vous estes plains,
> Dous amis; dont viennent cils plains?
> Par ma foi je vous gariroie
> Tout maintenant, se je savoie." (Paris, pp. 100–101, vv. 2399–2404)

> (She sweetly reproached me every time it happened, and said: "You have complained, sweet friend; whence comes this plaint? By my faith, I would cure you right now, if I knew how.)[14]

Voir Dit, it is Machaut who anthologized them, and who is thus responsible for the particularization of her character.

[12] Et s'aim mieulz languir pour vous que de nul autre joïr. (Paris, p. 60).

[13] "Le plus grant bien qui me viengne d'amer,/ Et qui plus fait aligier mon martire,/ C'est de mes maus complaindre et doulouser" (Paris, p. 100, vv. 2372–75): "The greatest good that comes to me from loving, and which most consoles my suffering is to complain and be sad for my woes."

[14] A similar exchange occurs on pp. 117–19, vv. 2783–87, 2804–06. Cerquiglini, *Engin*, pp.

Such immediate and positive answers to his complaints make it difficult for the poet to maintain his melancholy, and Toutebelle fails to realize that a cure of the poet's pain would stifle his muse. If the poetic vein lies in complaint, satisfaction might well end all composition.

The poet thus exposes the central paradox of courtly poetry – that love must remain unrequited in order to inspire. Were the lady to grant what the poet-lover so ardently pleads for, his eloquence would be silenced. Could it be that the *fin' amant* fears that his lady's answer might actually be affirmative? Machaut certainly suggests as much in the machinations of his narrator to stave off the willing encouragement of his lady. In this work, Machaut has allowed the lady not only to speak, but to speak first, and his work shows how difficult it is for a poet to contend with an independent voice apparently not bound by the same conventions – as she hardly could be, for the conventions did not allow her to speak. On the other hand, the poet cannot abandon those conventions because they are the only ones permitted by the controlling lyric mode.

Christine de Pizan's *Livre du Duc des Vrais Amans*, composed between 1403 and 1405, orchestrates three female voices. In her prologue, Christine explains that she composed it at the request of a patron whose story she tells.[15] Since she cast her narrative in the form of a *dit amoureux*, her own voice as poet is submerged (but does not dissolve) in the masculine voice of her narrator-poet-lover. At first glance, the formal structure of the *Duc des Vrais Amans* resembles that of the *Voir Dit*, for the Duke's account of his love is punctuated by nineteen lyric poems (sixteen *ballades*, two *rondels*, and a *virelai*) and eight prose letters; one of the poems and several of the letters are ascribed to the lady. If the elements are familiar, Christine combined them in a new configuration which is where her own voice emerges.

The work can be divided into four sections: the first and longest is the Duke's account of falling in love which ends (v. 2328) when he writes to declare his love to the lady. The second part develops this love affair, for the lady responds compassionately to the Duke's misery. This section ends (v. 3166) when she receives a long and severe letter from Dame Sebille de la Tour, to whom she turned for assistance. The third section shows the separation of the lovers in the later stages of the affair. The book concludes with a lyric cycle, the "Balades de plusieurs façons," including a

143–50 discusses the role reversals of poet and lady at some length. On Toutebelle, see Sarah J. Williams, "The Lady, the Lyrics and the Letters," *Early Music* 5 (1977), pp. 462–68. On the narrator figure in Machaut's *dits*, see Calin, "Machaut as Narrative Poet," in *Machaut's World: Science and Art in the Fourteenth Century*, ed. Madeleine Pelner Cosman and Bruce Chandler (New York: Annals of the New York Academy of Sciences, 314, 1978), pp. 177–87; and Cerquiglini, *Engin*, pp. 107–38.

[15] The older edition by Maurice Roy, *Oeuvres poétiques* SATF (Paris: Firmin Didot, 1896), pp. 59–208; is now replaced by the critical edition by Thelma S. Fenster, *Christine de Pizan. Le Livre du duc des vrais amans* (Binghamton: MRTS, 1995), which gives the date as 1403–05. Translations are from Thelma S. Fenster, *The Book of the Duke of True Lovers. Christine de Pizan*, with lyric poetry translated by Nadia Margolis (New York: Persea Books, 1991). For a study, see Liliane Dulac, "Christine de Pisan et le malheur des *Vrais amants*," *Mélanges de langue et de littérature médiévales offerts à Pierre Le Gentil* (Paris: SEDES, 1973), pp. 223–33.

complainte, four *rondels*, and three *virelais* as well as nine *ballades*, which alternate between lover and lady.

Christine maintains in this work the traditional relationship between love and poetry. The first section begins as a conventional *dit*: the Duke presents himself as a poet-lover who describes his first love and whose lines reflect his shifting emotions, which are otherwise given only the briefest of descriptions.[16] The early stages of the love affair take place against the backdrop of a tournament that the Duke arranged for the purpose of meeting his lady. During this period, he is content to dream of her beauty and to imagine speeches to her in private, while he dances with her in public. We see him enjoying her company, but he keeps his feelings to himself. Only when the idyll is broken and the lady is summoned home by her jealous husband does desire torment him. The elaboration of this initial, pleasant, stage of love occupies more than a third of Christine's work. The effect of this gradual development is to give some background to the expressions of desire and to root the Duke's passion in a companionable friendship. Although the lady appears in this section only through the filter of her admirer's gaze, Christine has radically modified her image. Not remote or forbidding, the Duke's lady appears friendly and encouraging in a variety of social settings. Despite the relatively conventional nature of his *ballade*-laments, the Duke seems to perceive this difference, for he complains of the cruel necessity which deprives him of her company, rather than of her cruelty. Mirrored in his eyes, the lady's reflection shows no hint of hardness or caprice.

In the second part of the work, the Duke suffers the torments of desire. When he falls ill from his suffering, a cousin comforts his young relative with practical advice. He urges the Duke to declare himself, sensibly pointing out that the lady (not as bold as Toutebelle) can hardly take the initiative. This well-wisher even visits her to explain the situation. With the way prepared, the Duke finally writes to the lady and requests:

> vueillez en pitié ouÿr et recevoir la douleureuse complainte de vostre servant, lequel, comme contraint, ainsi comme cellui qui est a mort et prent remede perilleux pour estre ad fin ou de mort ou de vie, tres doulce dame, a vous qui par vostre escondit me pouez paroccire et par le doulz reconfort de vostre octroy remettre en vie, je viens requerir ou mort hastive ou garison prochaine. (Letter I, pp. 137, lines 4–10)

> (please listen with compassion and receive the plaint of your servant, who, as one under duress, like a man near death who takes desperate measures either to end his life or to live once more, very gentle Lady, to you who by your refusal have the power to kill me, and who, by the sweet comfort of your acquiescence, can restore me to life, I have come to ask for a speedy death or imminent healing. (p. 89))

He reinforces his request in the two *ballades* enclosed with it. Up to this point in the work the role of the lady has been largely conventional: she has unwittingly inspired love in a young poet-lover, and is seen exclusively through his eyes. Her reply to the Duke's conventional plea, however, is a drastic departure from convention. In answering his letter she changes the work, for at last she appears clearly and speaks in her own voice. This is one of very few occasions where the object of *fin' amors*

---

16 Cf. Dulac, "Christine," p. 227.

responds to the misery of the lover. Not a *belle dame sans merci*, she is, on the contrary, touched by his suffering:

> Si sachiez que s'il est ainsi que pour cause de moy aiez tant de mal, il m'en poise de tout mon cuer; car ne vouldroie estre achoison de grevance a nulluy, et plus de vous me peseroit, en tant que vous congois, que d'autre quelconques.
>
> (Letter II, pp. 141–42, lines 5–9)

> (Understand that if you suffer so much because of me, all my heart is heavy, for I would not want to be the cause of grief to anyone. It saddens me more in your case than in another because I know you. (pp. 92–93))

As for love, she returns his esteem and emotion as far as is consistent with her honor:

> Mais, se ainsi estoit qu'amour de dame donnée honnourablement et sans villain penser vous peust souffire, sachiez que je suis celle qu'Amours a ad ce menée qui vous vueil asmer trés or et trés ja. . . . Si vueil que vous chaciez de vous toute merencolie et tristece, et soiez liez, jolis et joyeux. Mais sur toutes riens je vous charge et enjoing que secret soiez. (Letter II, p. 142, lines 17–20, 32–43.)

> (If it were the case, though, that the love of a Lady honorably given and without low thoughts might satisfy you, know that I am she whom Love has led to this, who wants to love you from this very moment on. . . . So I want you to chase away all melancholy and sadness and be happy, gay, and joyful. But above all I charge and enjoin you to be discreet. (p. 93))

If she is not a coy beauty, neither is she Machaut's bold Toutebelle; she is prudent, yet compassionate and honest.

The prospect of happiness does not silence the young lover, who encloses a *ballade* in his letters. A dangerous idyll of clandestine meetings follows this exchange, one of which is reported in detail. Another meeting is rendered poetically by the quotation of the two *ballades* the pair exchange. The second of these is particularly interesting, because it was composed by the lady, but the Duke's narrative (typically) does not inform us of the circumstances of its composition, only of its delivery:

> Avant que je me partisse
> De la tres doulce faitisse
> De ma balade os responce
> Qui me donna plus d'une once
> De joye tres amoureuse,
> Car la belle savoureuse
> En la lisant, me lia
> Ses bras au col; il y a:
>   Benoite soit la journée,
>   Le lieu, la place et demeure,
>   Doulx amis qu'ad ce menee
> Fus. (3090–3101)[17]

> (I had a response to my ballade before I parted from that very sweet creation, who gave me more than an ounce of very loving joy, for that beautiful,

[17] The opening lines are perhaps modelled on Machaut's "Je maudi leure et le temps et le jour," *Poésies lyriques*, ed. Vladimir Chichmaref, 2 vols. (Paris: Champion, 1909), I, CCXIII.

exquisite one, in reading it, put her arms about me, thus: Blessed be the very day. The site, the place and repair – Gentle friend – where, led this way, I was. (pp. 108–09))

This is the only poem composed by the lady within the narrative, but its inclusion prepares the way for the series of poems attributed to her at the end of the text.[18] These poems, together with her letter, allow the lady more of a voice in the work, and consequently present her as a more developed character, rather than merely the projection of the lover's desire. Like the Duke and Toutebelle, she turns to poetry in response to the vicissitudes of love.

The lady unintentionally destroys the idyll when she writes to the Dame Sebille de la Tour to enlist her aid: that lady exposes the inconsistencies of courtly ideology and directs a cold blast of common sense on the lovers' passion. She insists that the danger for the lovers, and especially for the lady, is real. In the next section of the letter she examines the supposed merits of courtly love – that it ennobles the lover, that the lady acquires a faithful servant – and demonstrates that these claims disappear in the harsh light of reality. Her letter ends with a warning of the moral dangers of love outside of marriage. Rather suprisingly, the lady Sebille encloses a *ballade*, which simply restates in lyric form some of the arguments of the letter. Sobered by these strictures, the lady tries to break off her affair and sends Sebille's letter to explain what has happened. Although he respects her decision, the Duke gives such rein to his misery in the *ballade* enclosed with his letter that she relents. Nevertheless, once awakened to the dangers of their situation, they cannot recapture their idyll. When he is obliged to travel they resort to exchanging poetry: "And so we wrote many a lyric about our affair: now of grief, now of surcease. I recited ballades that I composed about our various states: lais, complaintes, other poems, of which there was one happy one for every ten sad ones – that's the say of a foolish heart that Love leads astray. My Lady sent me some in return, whenever she could appropriately do so."[19] The series of lyrics appended to the *Duc des Vrais Amans* are, in effect, explained by these lines. As the lovers seem not to meet again, there is nothing to report, and the poems explain themselves as they continue the development of the plot.

The sequence of poems also represents in its layout the growing separation and alienation of the lovers. The first two *ballades* – dialogues between lover and lady – include them together in these poems which describe their parting.[20] In the remaining *ballades* and the three *virelais* each voice speaks in turn, and communication is possible, if slow. When she wonders if he has found another lady, he reassures her.

---

[18] See Anne Paupert, "Le 'Je' lyrique féminin dans l'oeuvre poétique de Christine de Pizan," in *Et c'est la fin pour quoy sommes ensemble*, 3, pp. 1057–71.

[19] Pp. 130–31. "Si fu mainte chançon faitte,/ Puis de dueil, puis de repos,/ De nostre fait; a prepos/ De divers cas je disoie/ Balades que je faisoie,/ Lais complaintes, autres diz,/ Dont un joyeux entre dix/ Doloreux avoit: C'est guise/ De fol cuer qu'Amours desguise,/ Ma dame m'en renvoioit/ A son tour quant lui seoit." (vv. 3504–14).

[20] See Charity Cannon Willard, "Lovers' Dialogues in Christine de Pizan's Lyric Poetry from the *Cent Ballades* to the *Cent Ballades d'Amant et de Dame*," *Fifteenth Century Studies* 4 (1981), pp. 167–80.

He tries to visit her, but it is too dangerous. There follow four of his *rondeaux*, with nothing from her, when he is obliged once more to depart. In contrast to the rest of the work, the lady speaks last, in a long *complainte*, in which she expresses her growing conviction that he has abandoned her:

> Mais riens n'y vault ma complainte
> N'estre de plours pale et tainte
> Car jamais, fors d'amour fainte
>   Ne m'amera
> Puis qu'aultre amour a attainte
> Et la moye a hors empainte. (p. 217, vv. 145–50).

> (Nothing's gained by my complaint/ Nor my face tear-stained and faint,/ For he'll ne'er, except in feint,/ Love me the same. Since another he's attained, And my love cast off, disdained. (p. 150))

With prolonged separation, even the consolation of correspondence is denied them, and each voice is isolated in its pain.

The lady's voice in the *Duc des Vrais Amans* does not oppose her lover's, nor does she set out to expose any hypocrisy in the courtly game. On the contrary, she accepts its conventions and believes in its idealism. And surely she is right to do so, for her lover is worthy of her trust. But Christine was interested in the effect of this ideology on the young people who must act it out: she projected the courtly situation into the future and her conclusions were discouraging. She portrayed a young man's idealistic love, generously returned by his lady, and showed how it inevitably led her to risk social and moral disaster. Even for these high-minded lovers who manage to avoid catastrophe, such love brings happiness to neither. Like Dame Sebille who used a *ballade* in her denunciation of courtly love, Christine used the conventions of the *dit amoureux* for the purpose of undermining its ideology.

Alain Chartier's *Belle Dame sans Merci* (probably written in 1424)[21] differs from the works of Machaut and Christine, in that the narrator does not recount his own story, but reports a dialogue he heard as an eavesdropper between a lover and his lady. The form of the poem – one hundred huitains – is that of a *complainte*.[22] Except for the narrative frame (24 stanzas at the beginning and four at the end), the lady has a virtually equal voice to the lover's: stanzas 29–96 alternate between the two speakers. This lady speaks a different language from that of her predecessors. Shunning the encouragement of Toutebelle, this lady is no less astute or witty, but she is cynical. Modern readers find her forthrightness attractive. William Kibler has observed "there is nothing quite so appealing as a young woman who vivaciously states that her eyes are for looking, that she may flirt openly with whom she wishes,

---

[21] *The Poetical Works of Alain Chartier*, ed. J.C. Laidlaw (London and New York: Cambridge University Press, 1974). On the work see Daniel Poirion, "Lecture de la *Belle Dame Sans Mercy*," in *Mélanges . . . Le Gentil*, pp. 691–705; William W. Kibler, "The Narrator as Key to Alain Chartier's *La Belle Dame sans mercy*," *The French Review* 53 (1979), pp. 714–23; and Joseph Brami, "Un Lyrisme de Veuvage. Etudes sur le *je* poétique dans la *Belle Dame Sans Mercy*," *Fifteenth Century Studies* 15 (1989), pp. 53–66.

[22] Daniel Poirion, *Le Poète et le prince. L'évolution du lyrisme courtois de Guillaume de Machaut à Charles d'Orléans* (Paris: PUF, 1965; repr. Geneva, 1978), pp. 406–09.

and that she is free and intends to remain so."[23] As the phenomenon of sexual harassment is publicly exposed, who would deny the lady her right to decline advances?

The lover opens the dialogue with three stanzas which resemble in their themes a courtly *chanson*: he describes his misery, asks how she can see his pain unmoved, and begs only to be allowed to serve her. The narrator introduces her reply by noting her impassivity (vv. 217–20). She does not bother to explain *how* she can be unmoved. She merely asks why he does not seek his own peace of mind (vv. 221–24). By implication, since loving her is something he has chosen to do, he has only himself to blame for his misery.

In the following stanzas (29–96), as he uses the images of *fin'amors* to press his suit, she throws them back in his teeth. When he complains of Doulx Regard (xxix), she snaps: "Les yeulx sont faiz pour regarder." When he says he will die of love (xxxiii) she has two answers: first she doubts his claim, but if it is true that love can wound so grievously "Mieulx en vault un dolent que deulx" (272). She rejects not only his love, but the very possibility of love, and especially the rhetoric of *fin' amors*.

Eventually, it becomes clear that the lady refuses love because she cannot believe or trust the words of lovers:

> Amours est cruel losengier
> Aspre en fait et doulx a mentir   (313–14)
>
> (Love is a cruel deceiver, bitter in deed and sweet in lies)
>
> Vous et autres qui ainsi jurent
> Et se condempnent et maudient,
> Ne cuident que leurs sermens durent . . .   (345–47)
>
> (You and others who so swear, and condemn yourselves, and curse, do not think that your oaths will last.)

The fear of deception, of betrayal, of false oaths, seems to keep her from relenting. She is not vindictive enough to wish his death, but she maintains that she will not be gullible enough to allow anyone to boast of her conquest (704). She names "Male bouche" directly as the source of her mistrust:

> Male bouche tient bien grant court:
> Chascun a mesdire estudie,
> Faulx amoureux au temps qui court
> Servent tous de gouliardye.   (713–16)
>
> (Slander holds great court: each studies to malign, false lovers in the time that passes serve everyone with lechery.)

The lady is perhaps cynically realistic, but is also paralyzed by her distrust. This confrontation of courtly idealism and actual hypocrisy is, according to Daniel Poirion, central to the work.[24] When the lady mercilessly rebuts all of the lover's

---

23 Kibler, "The Narrator," p. 716.
24 *Poète et le Prince*, p. 260.

arguments and demolishes his disclaimers, the lover is caught in an acute predicament: if he follows her advice to love elsewhere, he would, in effect, justify her suspicion. In the end, when words will not avail to prove his loyalty, he vindicates himself, as he said he would, by dying for love.

In Chartier's poem, the Belle Dame is a citizen of the modern (fifteenth-century) world – unsusceptible to conventional flattery, suspicious of promises, unwilling to trust to loyalty, whose existence she seems to doubt. Confronted with such a lady, the courtly ideal must, like the lover, die of frustration. At the same time, it is wrong to dismiss the lover as a weepy fossil; the lady herself is to be pitied, for she is unable to recognize true *courtoisie* when she sees it.

The tone of Chartier's poem is quite different from the two earlier works. Where Machaut took some delight in exposing the paradoxes of courtly love, and Christine condemned it as a dangerous snare for young people, Chartier views it nostalgically, as a noble ideal that no longer functions in his world.

NICE YOUNG GIRLS AND WICKED OLD WITCHES: THE "RIGHTFUL AGE" OF WOMEN IN MIDDLE ENGLISH VERSE

Jessica Cooke

In the life cycle, as in the Garden of Eden, it is the woman who has been the deviant.[1]

Almost always with attractive women there is an element of deception – in literature, that is. A heroine fails to live up to the high ideals which a romantic male assumes to be a necessary corollary of her beauty, and thereby deceives him, or, more accurately, un-deceives him, which is worse.[2]

It is rightly lamented that "the records of women of the past are sparse, and every kind of ingenuity is needed to reconstruct even fragments of their lives."[3] This study will explore one particular subject rendered inaccessible because it pertains to women, namely the stages of the female life cycle as represented in Middle English poetry. Exploration of the ages of man and the human life cycle in medieval and renaissance English literature led me (not unreasonably, as it seemed) to look for evidence of the medieval ages of woman – with very little reward.[4] It appears that by comparison with the high degree of representation of the stages in man's life in the medieval texts, that of the life of woman hardly exists at all. In addition, such evidence as exists for the portrayal of the ages of woman is mostly marginal or sublimated, rarely explicit. A belief implicit in the texts seems to suggest itself, that while youth was often described as the most joyous time of life for man, other periods of men's lives were considered to be equally, if not more, valid. By comparison, it appears to have been held that the only really valid or worthwhile time of life for women was youth: "hir rightful age."[5] Female old age was portrayed with such distaste as to suggest that it was considered worthless, or even malign. Old men in medieval literature are variously described as ugly and disagreeable, certainly, but

---

1   Carol Gilligan, "Woman's Place in Man's Life Cycle," in *Feminism and Methodology*, ed. Sandra Harding (Milton Keynes: Open University Press, 1987), pp. 57–73 (59).
2   E. Talbot Donaldson, *Speaking of Chaucer* (London: The Athlone Press, 1970), p. 47.
3   Joan Thirsk, foreword to *Women in English Society*, ed. Mary Prior (London: Metheun, 1985), p. 2.
4   See Jessica Cooke, "The Beginning of the Year in Spenser's *Mutabilitie Cantos*," *Notes and Queries* 240 (1995), pp. 285–86; and Jessica Cooke, "Januarie and May in Chaucer's *Merchant's Tale*," *English Studies*, forthcoming volume.
5   Chaucer, *The Romaunt of the Rose*, 405. All references in Chaucer are cited from *The Riverside Chaucer*, ed. Larry D. Benson (Boston: Houghton Mifflin Company, 1987).

not as intrinsically useless, evil or unnatural. Indeed, they very often represent venerable wisdom at best, and querulousness at worst, as with Elde in *The Parlement of the Thre Ages*.[6] The assumption that the beauty of young women must be accompanied by corresponding goodness provided authors (then and now) with a device by which the protagonists in texts are deceived again and again.

Further, the under-representation of the ages of woman in the texts has largely been perpetuated by the critics, presumably because the emphasis on different issues in research necessarily tends to echo that in the primary texts (Prior, p. xv). While acknowledging that this omission in the scholarship is perhaps to have been expected, I suggest that the development of a methodological approach with which to examine the stages of life of female characters in the texts would prove valuable. I have chosen to concentrate largely (though not exclusively) on certain poems produced around the reign of Richard II, because it has so often been noted that the Ricardian poets were deeply interested in the ages of man.[7] Certainly, the Ricardian poets as a group utilised the topos unusually thoroughly,[8] and where the ages of man are most in evidence, it seems most likely that faint resonances of the ages of woman might also be perceptible. But while this project is yet in its infancy, my arguments must of necessity be tentative.

Though it is assumed that the word "man" in the generic sense can be taken to designate "humanity," it appears that the word "man" in the ages of man topos did not designate "mankind" but specifically, "the male of the species." Mary Dove examined the way in which the theme of the ages of man was incorporated into medieval English texts, and, concerning the medieval schemes dividing a man's life, she pointed out that: "Where woman's experience of the ages is explicitly recognised, it is recognised in terms of its deviation from a masculine norm. The supposition that man's experience of the ages is normative is remarkable tenacious in writings belonging to the Ages of Man tradition."[9] Not only is this supposition tenacious in medieval writings, it is similarly pervasive in modern scholarship, where all too often, "a study deals with only one sex but presents itself as if it were applicable to both sexes,"[10] resulting in overgeneralised and unrepresentative conclusions. The androcentricity of medieval literature ensured that maleness was considered the norm by which all else was measured, and in this context, women constituted a deviation from normality, as less than men, different from men, or un-men. It is essential then, that any study which attempts to address female characters in the texts cannot merely assume that their experience must duplicate that of the

6   *The Parlement of the Thre Ages*, ed. Thorlac Turville-Petre in *Alliterative Poetry of the Later Middle Ages* (London: Routledge, 1989), pp. 67–100.
7   See J.A. Burrow, *Ricardian Poetry* (London: Routledge and Kegan Paul, 1971), pp. 117–18.
8   See also Philippa Tristram, *Figures of Life and Death in Medieval English Literature* (London: Paul Elek, 1976), p. 92.
9   Mary Dove, *The Perfect Age of Man's Life* (Cambridge: Cambridge University Press, 1986), p. 20.
10 Margrit Eichler, *Nonsexist Research Methods: a practical guide* (Boston: Allen and Unwin, 1988), p. 6.

male characters,[11] but instead, must identify and acknowledge the bias in research (however unconscious) in order to eliminate it. Once this is achieved, new challenges present themselves, such as how to identify the "implicit" or "marginal" evidence as exists for the ages of woman in Middle English texts, lacking the "explicit" evidence for women's experience in the ages of man literature.

The medieval schemes divided the life of man most often into three, four, six or seven stages,[12] where the earliest stage or stages of babyhood and early childhood are not specifically gendered, but described in a way which could apply both to boys and girls. However, the subsequent ages are nearly always described in terms of the growth to manhood and male maturity. Female maturity, while bringing the possibility of physical perfection, was believed not to reach the same level of rational perfection.[13] Implied is the argument that while only the earliest and latest stages of a man's life were deficient, *all* the ages of a woman's life were seen to be imperfect or lacking by comparison with the strongest and most vital middle period of a man's life (Dove, p. 22). Aristotelian philosophy defined woman as an incomplete male, retaining the genitalia within her body, the conditions of whose conception must have lacked the heat necessary to create a male (Robertson, pp. 144–45). Because the purpose of a woman was to be beautiful in order to attract a mate and produce children, not to be rational, it follows that a woman was only useful in the generative stages of her life, when she was young. Achieving their functional phase at a stage earlier than men, women also lost their fundamental purpose with the onset of menopause. It has been suggested that "One of the consequences of the ages of woman's life being perceived in this way was that it came to be regarded as a fact that the course of woman's life was shorter than man's" (Dove, p. 23). In some way, the loss of their generative function seems not just to have rendered them less useful to their community, but (frighteningly, in our eyes) also to have reduced their status to the position of non-people, whose right even to life is questionable. Such a position seems extreme to modern tastes, and is impossible to verify because we know so little about the expectations placed upon old women by their community in the pre-modern period. Most notorious is the evidence of the witch-trials (later than the period here under discussion, but relevant nonetheless), which suggests that old women who were unmarried or widowed were far more likely to be accused of witchcraft than any other group.[14]

---

[11] Sara Mills, ed., *Gendering the Reader* (Hemel Hempstead: Harvester Wheatsheaf, 1994), pp. 14–15.

[12] J.A. Burrow, *The Ages of Man: A Study in Medieval Writing and Thought* (Oxford: Clarendon Press, 1986).

[13] Elizabeth Robertson, "Medieval Medical Views of Women and Female Spirituality in the *Ancrene Wisse* and Julian of Norwich's *Showings*," in *Feminist Approaches to the Body in Medieval Literature*, ed. Linda Lomperis and Sarah Stanbury (Philadelphia: University of Pennsylvania Press, 1993), pp. 142–67 (144–45).

[14] Marianne Hester, *Lewd Women and Wicked Witches: A Study of the Dynamics of Male Domination* (London: Routledge, 1992), p. 193: "Women over the age of forty were vulnerable to witchcraft accusation, partly because they were no longer carrying out their main role (according to Puritans), that of childbearing . . . In addition, age had 'mystical power' associated with it which could be used to do evil."

Two non-Ricardian texts which include rare explicit portraits of the ages of woman are the *Secretum Secretorum* and the fifteenth-century alliterative poem *Death and Liffe*.[15] Of the existing copies of the Arabic pseudo-Aristotelian *Secretum Secretorum* in Middle English,[16] the translations of the "long form"[17] include a comparison of the seasons with the four ages of woman, described as "a refreshing departure from the overwhelmingly masculine character of such descriptions elsewhere" (Burrow, *The Ages of Man*, p. 30). However, the importance of this rare explicit treatment of the female life cycle has not always been recognised.[18] Spring is personified as a beautiful young woman, adorned with jewellery and clothed in robes of many colours "to be shewyd to men yn þe feste of weddynge" (Steele, p. 73),[19] while summer is described as a woman of perfect age, and fully grown in body. The female figures of spring and summer are portrayed approvingly as pleasing to the eye, but once the youth and beauty have departed from autumn and winter, they are described as no longer having worth. Autumn's transitional, insecure stage between youth and age is emphasised, "Wherfor hit is no mervaile yf beute she hath loste" added Yonge (Steele, p. 245). The final season of winter is represented by an old woman, but in a tone approaching disgust with this stage of the female life cycle. She is described as almost naked, barren, broken, decrepit and miserable, needy and nearing death. Yonge concluded of winter (Steele, p. 246):

> In this tyme the world semyth like an olde katte, al overcome wyth age and travaill, that lyve ne myght, for she is al dispoylit of beute and of streynth and vertue.

The nakedness of winter is seen to be hideous and obscene beyond the mere symbolism of the bare ground in winter when the summer growth has died back. The underlying message is that with the departure of youth and beauty goes also the purpose of woman, whose sole purpose then is to die. It is interesting that in Yonge's version, not only is the old woman bereft of her beauty and strength, but also her *vertue*, perhaps suggesting that once a woman's purpose has gone, her continued existence becomes morally dubious. By contrast, old men are not described as intrinsically useless or evil, retaining their additional faculty of intellect.

The female personifications of death and life in the early fifteenth-century poem *Death and Liffe* also provide a rare glimpse of the female ages of old age and

---

[15] *Death and Liffe* ed. I. Gollancz in *Select Early English Poems*, 9 vols. (London: Humphrey Milford, 1913–33), vol. 5.

[16] See R. Steele, ed., *Three Prose Versions of the Secreta Secretorum*, EETS, e.s., 74 (London, 1898); M.A. Manzalaoui, ed., *Secretum Secretorum: Nine English Versions*, EETS, o.s., 276 (Oxford: Oxford University Press, 1977).

[17] See M.A. Manzalaoui, "The Pseudo-Aristotelian Kitab Sirr Al-Asrar: facts and problems," *Oriens* 23–4 (1974), pp. 147–257.

[18] Tristram, p. 98. This otherwise informative and interesting study often falls into the methodological trap outlined above, omitting to specify the gender of the stages of life under examination.

[19] James Yonge altered the female Spring character in his source to the far more common personification of a young man in his version of 1422, *The Governaunce of Prynces*, in Steele, pp. 243–44.

youth.[20] Dame Liffe is described (57–97) as a young, happy and beautiful woman, to whom kings and princes swear loyalty, and for whom plants and animals flourish. Complementing her vitality and beauty are her rich clothes and ornaments of green and gold, the conventional colours of youth, just as the personification of spring was adorned with rich clothes and jewellery. Thus, beauty, youth and intrinsic goodness in woman are implicitly associated. By comparison, Dame Death is described (151–76) in terms of a hideous old woman, emaciated, with hollow eyes, a grey complexion, and a hook nose hanging to her stomach like that of a witch. Her partial nakedness, reminiscent of winter in the *Secretum Secretorum*, seems to suggest that old women's bodies, having lost their beauty, should be muffled up from sight. She is not only frightening and hideous, but also sorrowful (151, 177–78): the protraction of life beyond usefulness is seen to be futile, ugly, unnatural, evil and sad. Just as youth, beauty and goodness are implicitly combined in the portrait of Liffe, so female old age and evil are associated in that of Dame Death.

Now to progress to certain of the Ricardian poems: *Sir Gawain and the Green Knight*[21] has been studied for its representation of the ages of man (Burrow, *Ricardian Poetry*; Dove, p. 138; Tristram, p. 88), often equating Youth, Middle Age and Old Age with Gawain and Lady Bertilak, Sir Bertilak, and Morgan le Fay. But solely to view Morgan in particular as a manifestation of ungendered old age precludes fuller awareness of the implications that arise from her character as an old woman.[22] Further, the attribution of the two women to different non-gendered age categories denies their specific presentation to Gawain as two halves of a whole portrait of womanhood rather than two isolated stages of life.[23] In effect, it is Gawain's failure to recognise the affinity between them upon their first meeting, and his concentration on their outward differences instead, which sets him off on the wrong path of assumptions in Hautdesert.[24] The contrastive tone of the *descriptio* of the two ladies echoes Gawain's dual reaction of attraction to the young woman and repulsion by the old, and it is this "antithesis of Youth and Age"[25] that has been the focus of concentration to the detriment of the view that the two ladies form a unit,

---

[20] I have chosen to examine these figures in particular not because they are female personifications of abstract qualities, of which there are very many in Middle English literature, but because they effectively represent two stages in the female life cycle.

[21] J.R.R. Tolkien and E.V. Gordon, eds., *Sir Gawain and the Green Knight*, second edition revised by Norman Davis (Oxford: Clarendon Press, 1967).

[22] For example Tristram, p. 91, described Morgan: ". . . whose plot has in it all the meanness and envy characteristic of Elde."

[23] Ibid., pp. 91–92: "The difference between Morgan la Fay, and the brilliant youth of Sir Bercilak's lady beside her . . . alerts one to the recognition that her plot typifies the jealousy and vindictiveness felt by those on the brink of the grave for those who have life before them." While this is true for many other figures of Elde in Middle English texts, if it were true for Morgan, not only would she be working against Gawain, but also against the young and beautiful Lady Bertilak, with whom instead she works hand in glove. She hates Arthur, Guinevere and their court because of her grievances against them, not because of their youth.

[24] See Ian Bishop, "Time and Tempo in *Sir Gawain and the Green Knight*," *Neophilologus* 69 (1985), pp. 611–19 (615–16).

[25] Derek A. Pearsall, "Rhetorical 'Descriptio' in 'Sir Gawain and the Green Knight'," *Modern Language Review* 50 (1955), pp. 129–34 (131).

surely a theme stronger and more relevant in the poem. Their identical actions and purpose are carefully documented by the poet: from the outset they take him between them to sit and talk (977–80).

> Watz neuer freke fayrer fonge
> Bitwene two so dyngne dame,
> Þe alder and the yonge;
> Much solace set þay same.   (1315–18)

While the young lady is described as fair in every capacity (943–44), the gratuitous brutality of the portrait of Morgan as a hideously ugly old woman has often been remarked.[26] That Gawain will learn her evil motives cannot be the reason for this brutality: he will learn the same of Lady Bertilak. It has been argued that the poet made "an attack on the lady not for being an adversary, but simply for being old" (Burrow, *A Reading*, p. 64), but I would argue further that she is attacked specifically for being an old *woman*. Morgan cannot be unwelcome in such a setting simply because the poem is only otherwise about young people: Bertilak is clearly older than most, though his precise age seems deliberately obscure.[27] The hostile tone of her description is strikingly similar to that of the personification of winter in the *Secretum Secretorum* and to the physical description of Dame Death. While Lady Bertilak's apparel is designed to display her beauty to the best advantage like that of spring and Dame Liffe, Gawain and the audience are spared an otherwise even more repulsive sight by the fact that Morgan remains almost absurdly covered up with clothing.

Famed for his courtesy, Gawain tries to divide his attention equally between the two ladies, but the preceding *descriptio* ensures that the outward physical manifestation of Morgan's great age suggests a correspondingly evil inner self, and that knowing equally little about the young lady, her portrait of physical beauty suggests inner goodness. With this dual picture, the poet appears to take advantage of the implicit belief in the usefulness of young women and the uselessness of old ones, in order to increase the suspense of the Hautdesert section, and to heighten Gawain's shock upon discovering that, in the event, both women have the same intention, to test the honour of the knights of the Round Table through Gawain, and if possible, to breach that honour. Prompting the expectation of corresponding goodness, Lady Bertilak's youth and beauty consequently act as a *disguise* to shield her intention, and accordingly, her method of assault employs her youth and beauty in the bedroom scenes, while the old woman represents the more malign, aloof force as the instigator of the testing of Gawain, and the manipulator of Arthur's Camelot.

Gawain expresses no anger that Bertilak was involved in the plot, but he is appalled by the revelation that Lady Bertilak was his "enmy kene": that a beautiful young woman contradicted his assumptions and deliberately deceived him is some-

---

[26] J.A. Burrow, *A Reading of Sir Gawain and the Green Knight* (London: Routledge and Kegan Paul, 1965), p. 63; Albert B. Friedman, "Morgan le Fay in *Sir Gawain and the Green Knight*," *Speculum* 35 (1960), pp. 260–74 (267).

[27] See Eiichi Suzuki, "A Note on the Age of the Green Knight," *Neuphilologische Mitteilungen* 78 (1977), pp. 27–30.

how below the belt. In his diatribe against women, he remembers how other men were blinded by the beauty of women to their hidden agenda. Only now does he recognise in the duality of the two women affinity of purpose rather than just disparity in appearance:

> And comaundez me to þat cortays, your comlych fere,
> Boþe þat on and þat oþer, myn honoured ladyez,
> Þat þus hor knyght wyth hor kest han koyntly bigyled.   (2411–13)

In order to reconcile the fact that Morgan le Fay is much older than her brother Arthur, an interesting reason is offered, as far as the perceptions of old women are concerned. "When Morgan was a healing nurse she was beautiful, but as her knowledge of the wicked arts of sorcery grew, she became progressively uglier. From this we may reasonably infer that Morgan's ugliness in Sir Gawain is to be taken as an indication of her evil nature and sinful purposes" (Friedman, p. 267; also noted by Tolkien and Gordon, p. 130). The converse of this suggestion almost immediately springs to mind on a general level: if a woman is old and ugly, she must be wicked. The gratuitous viciousness of Morgan's plot, calculated to frighten Guinevere to death, has caused puzzlement, but viewed in the context of the medieval ages of woman, is attributable accordingly not just to the envy of old age, but to the fact that she is an old woman.

Of all the Ricardian texts, the *Canterbury Tales* appears to provide the most literary evidence for the ages of woman, including as it does so many inharmonious marriages in which the husbands and wives are placed at incongruous stages in the life cycle. This study can only highlight a very few instances of this evidence. In her *Prologue* (*The Canterbury Tales* III D 1–856) the Wife of Bath insists that she will not assume the expected modes of behaviour appropriate to the different stages of her life, but instead:

> I wol bistowe the flour of al myn age
> In the actes and in fruyt of mariage.   (113–14)

Further, she is an expert on the trouble in marriage "in al myn age" (174), in all the stages of her life, and she concludes that, having won the battle, her husband Janekyn tells her to: "Do as thee lust the terme of al thy lyf" (820). Rarely are we given so many references to the span of woman's life in this way, presumably because the Wife herself is a rare example of a woman no longer at the "productive" stage of youth. Her very presence forcefully challenges the assumption that old women are useless. As in her *Prologue*, a major theme of the Wife's *Tale* (*The Canterbury Tales* III D 857–1264) is the relative merits of female age and youth. Returning to Camelot, the knight ". . . saugh upon a daunce go/ Of ladyes foure and twenty, and yet mo" (991–92), towards which he approached "ful yerne" (993), but who disappear, and are replaced instead by a ferociously ugly old woman, "A fouler wight ther may no man devyse" (999). Though not explicitly stated, the dancing ladies would appear to be young, but their transformation into an old woman serves to suggest that their multiple and youthful appearance was merely a disguise designed to draw the knight, just as Gawain was drawn to Lady Bertilak. The crone's self-deprecating tone – "Thise olde folk kan muchel thyng . . ." (1004) – contrasts sharply with her shape-shifting abilities and uncanny knowledge. When the knight complains about her aged appearance on their wedding night, she, apparently unwittingly, defines an underlying inconsistency in the treatment of old men by comparison with old women, in an ironically bewildered argument:

> ye gentils of honour
> Seyn that men sholde an oold wight doon favour,
> And clepe hym fader. (1209–11)

While appearing to remind the knight that nobles should honour old people, her use of "fader" suggests that only old men, and not old women, should be treated with respect; that she herself is an old woman highlights the inconsistency in this code of conduct. With her choice to him "To han me foul and old til that I deye,/ And be to yow a trewe, humble wyf . . . Or elles ye wol han me yong and fair,/ And take youre aventure of the repair . . ." (1220–21, 1223–24), she is correcting his assumptions (and those of the audience) that a young and beautiful woman is not necessarily a good one, and an old woman, though ugly, is not necessarily a bad one. His delight that she chose to transform herself into an apparently young and submissive wife suggests that he has not learned the lesson that appearance has little to do with character, and though outwardly different she is still the same person. The suggestion that "The loathly lady triumphs over age and ugliness by transforming herself through her own will into radiant youth"[28] ignores the fact that she can change herself into anything she wants at any time while remaining essentially the same, rendering the knight's preference despite her warnings about young wives rather ironic.

Like the young wives about whom the crone warned the knight, May in the *Merchant's Tale* (*The Canterbury Tales*, IV E 1245–2418) has a hidden agenda which is masked by the youth and beauty of her outward appearance,[29] and which only gradually becomes apparent. Though she is ruthless and duplicitous, her youth acts as her shield, proffering the semblance of goodness. The rare autobiographical account of the Wife's own earlier marriages provides an insightful commentary to the similar experiences of May, which, told from the perspective of Januarie, would only otherwise appear cold and remote. Januarie has fallen into the same trap as the Wife of Bath's knight, believing that a young and beautiful wife will automatically be a good, submissive wife, rhapsodising about the generative quality of the young woman he will choose. Following the opinion in Innocent III's treatise *De Contemptu Mundi*[30] that by thirty, women were old, he believes that "thise olde wydwes" would cause too much harm and mischief:

> I wol noon oold wyf han in no manere.
> She shal nat passe twenty yeer, certayn. (1416–17)

---

[28] Bernard F. Huppé, *A Reading of the Canterbury Tales* (New York: State University of New York, 1964), p. 134.
[29] Donaldson, p. 52, explored how ". . . January first pictures to himself her physical charms, and then, as if by inference from these, her fine moral qualities . . ."
[30] *Patrologia Latina* 217, ed. J.-P. Migne (Paris, 1889), pp. 701–46.

But his belief that young women are more benign and easy to control has already been contradicted by the Wife of Bath who declared that she was at her most manipulative and deceptive when she was *young*, married to her first three husbands, whom she characterised as "good," "riche" and "olde." Far from the expected submission, her youth and beauty provided her with the mask, the energy and the weapon with which to gain complete control over these husbands, for whose gullibility in believing that a young wife will necessarily be good she ridiculed them as: "sire olde lecchour," "olde dotard shrewe" and "olde barel-ful of lyes." Though her opinion of Januarie's assumptions is never made explicit, May's silence seems to be as eloquent as the Wife's ranting. Projecting into the future of the tale, May (like Alison) might well recall her marriage to rich old Januarie as "good," but only because her youth provided a sufficiently attractive disguise with which to gain mastery over both Januarie and his riches.

The final text this study will examine is the *Romaunt of the Rose* (Benson, pp. 685–767), which, it may be argued, is hardly Ricardian in origin, except that it influenced the poetry of that period so much as to have become an integral part of it in Chaucer's translation, and that, as such, it contains one of the most powerful vilifications of female old age. The malignance attributed to female age is apparent in the inclusion of a female Elde (349–412) in a sequence of portraits depicting evils on the wall enclosing the Garden of Love. Thus associated with "Hate," "Vilanye," "Coveitise," etc., female old age is castigated not only as an enemy to love, but almost as a sin against nature. Heavy emphasis is placed on her uselessness now that her physical beauty is gone, "A foul forwelked thyng was she,/ That whylom round and softe had be" (361–62), and that: "Iwys, great qualm ne were it none,/ Ne synne, although her lyf were gon" (357–58). This is the logical conclusion of the belief in the uselessness of old women, and the underlying sentiment behind many such hostile portraits, but rarely is it so explicitly expressed. Even more telling is the assertion:

> I trowe that she
> Was fair sumtyme, and fresh to se,
> Whan she was in hir rightful age. (403–05)

Likening the woman's youth to her *correct* or *proper* age implicitly designates all her other ages to the realm of incorrectness and impropriety, providing explicit proof for the belief that the only appropriate age for women was youth.[31]

To say that Lady Bertilak, the young Wife of Bath, and May all follow a hidden agenda which is belied by their appearance is not to say that female youth and beauty necessarily hide wickedness in medieval literature, but that they hide the independent purpose of the individual. By contrast, the maturity and independence of the Wife exempt her from having to hide her intentions under the mask of youth and

---

[31] In his translation of *The Romance of the Rose*, by Guillaume de Lorris and Jean de Meun (Princeton: Princeton University Press, 1971), Charles Dahlberg offered "her prime," the best part of her life, by comparison with Chaucer's connotatively different "hir rightful age," the only proper part of her life.

beauty. Like Morgan le Fay, Alison's transcendence of her youth may subject her to the view that old women are useless or wicked, but she proves that with age comes autonomy. There is clearly much work yet to be done on the theme of the medieval ages of woman, but I hope to have indicated how, in the absence of explicit evidence, the medieval fictional texts can help us to understand the way in which the ages of woman were perceived.

READERS, WRITERS, AND LOVERS IN *GRIMALTE Y GRADISSA*

Diane M. Wright

Grimalte y Gradissa, the fifteenth-century Spanish courtly romance by Juan de Flores,[1] presents a fictional account of the activities of reading and writing through the appropriation of Giovanni Boccaccio's *Elegia di madonna Fiammeta* (c. 1343). In spite of the textual debt to *Fiammetta* Flores diverges from Boccaccio's text in several important ways. He does not maintain the introspective pseudo-autobiographical narrative in which the Italian Fiammetta relates to her private diary the story of her love affair with Pamphilo and his subsequent desertion of her. With the publication of her book implied in *Grimalte y Gradissa*, she is no longer anonymous as she was in the Italian text. Her story is public knowledge as "famosa scriptura" [famous writing] and no doubt has even entered into the oral tradition since Flores informs us that the Italian lovers are known in all the towns and villages. Rather than the near complete use of a first person narrator as in the Italian work, Flores's *Grimalte y Gradissa* contains diverse forms of discourse including speeches, narration, letters, and poetry that present the characters from numerous perspectives.[2]

Barbara Weissberger was the first to observe that Flores's characters are aware of themselves as readers and writers, whose readings of the work called *Fiometa* condition their responses.[3] She notes as well Flores's exploration of reader incitation, that is, reading as a stimulus that causes readers to recreate or create new roles for themselves outside the text, over a hundred years before the theme's inclusion in Cervantes's *Don Quijote*. As Weissberger further recognizes, *Grimalte y Gradissa* is a fictionalization of the profound impact of the printed word on a society still strongly dependent on oral forms of discourse. The responses of the fictional readers and writers in Flores's work illustrate that the dynamics associated with reading and

---

[1] All subsequent references to *Grimalte y Gradissa* are from Juan de Flores, *Grimalte y Gradissa*, ed. Carmen Parrilla (Santiago de Compostela: U of Santiago, 1988) and will be cited by page number (p.). The English translations appear in brackets and are my own.

[2] See Alan Deyermond, "El punto de vista narrativo en la ficción sentimental del siglo XV," in *Actas del I Congreso de la Asociación Hispánica de Literatura Medieval, Santiago de Compostela, 2 al 6 de diciembre de 1985*, ed. Vicente Beltrán (Barcelona: Promociones y Publicaciones Universitarias, 1988), pp. 45–60.

[3] Barbara Weissberger, "Authors, Characters, and Readers in *Grimalte y Gradissa*," in *Creation and Re-creation: Experiments in Literary Form in Early Modern Spain. Studies in Honor of Stephen Gilman*, ed. Ronald Surtz and Nora Weinerth (Newark, Del.: Juan de la Cuesta, 1983), pp. 61–76.

writing in a society adjusting to the printed word, and whose habits of thought remain linked to orality, is social-rhetorical in nature and is an essentially ethical activity.[4]

The fictionalization of readers and writers begins with Flores, real reader of Boccaccio, who as writer inscribes himself within the text as the character Grimalte and who effaces Boccaccio from the work by conferring authorship on Fiometa. Alonso de Córdoba who supplied the poetry in the printed editions is yet another real reader, no doubt, of both the Italian and Castilian works. All the characters, from the protagonists to the villagers, partake in the "communal memory" of a shared text, that of *Fiometa*, as a model for behavior. A shared text and memory do not necessarily suggest that each reader will respond in the same manner, but depend, for example, on whether the reader, like the protagonist Gradissa, identifies with *Fiometa's* intended readers, the "enamoradas damas" [enamored ladies] or like Grimalte, comprehends the work as an agent of seduction.[5]

Similarly, the act of writing is also social-rhetorical in nature, but also, for the writer and lover, desire becomes the source of rhetorical inventiveness. Fiometa is the author of her story and Grimalte is also given the task of writing. Through the process of rewriting Fiometa's ending, Grimalte comes to understand better Fiometa's story although he remains an intrusive male reader who can never be entirely sympathetic to her situation. Grimalte's desire for Gradissa leads to the creation of the final product ultimately read by Gradissa and the outside reader, the work entitled *Grimalte y Gradissa*.

Reading as Social-Rhetorical Activity

The scholarly work of Mary Carruthers and Brian Stock[6] has shown that in orally residual cultures like fifteenth-century Spain, judgement was not based on an introspective analysis of psychological motivations but rather was viewed as an ethically conceived social-rhetorical process whose measure was constituted by the examples set by past models. Carruthers posits

> Character indeed results from one's experience, but that includes the experience of others, often epitomized in ethical commonplaces, and made one's own by constant recollection. (p. 179)

---

4 See Walter Ong, *Orality and Literacy: The Technologizing of the Word* (New York and London: Methuen, 1982).

5 A special thank you to Louise Haywood whom I met during the ICLS Conference and who later sent me a copy of her article, "Gradissa: A Fictional Female Reader in/of a Male Author's Text," *Medium Ævum* 64 (1995), pp. 85–99, which provides an analysis of the levels of fictionality in *Grimalte y Gradissa* as well as a treatment of women readers and writers in a male-authored text. Although our respective studies coincide on several points, my focus is on the social-rhetorical and ethical dimensions of reading and writing, touching on gender as it relates to this issue.

6 Mary Carruthers, *The Book of Memory: A Study of Memory in Medieval Culture* (Cambridge: Cambridge University Press, 1992) and Brian Stock, *The Implications of Literacy: Written Language and Models of Interpretation in the Eleventh and Twelfth Centuries* (Princeton: Princeton University Press, 1983).

Hence, individuals perceive themselves according to, and are guided ethically by, the past communal standards (shared experience) already established according to the actions, good or bad, of others in order to give meaning or authenticate personal experience. Carruthers indicates that what was necessary was "a recollecting subject, a remembered text, and a remembering audience" (p. 182). Furthermore, Stock remarks that writing influenced the means by which individuals established personal identity both with respect to the inner self and the external world:

> And the writing down of events, the editing so to speak of experience, gave rise to unprecedented parallels between literature and life: for as texts informed experience, so men and women began to live texts. (p. 4)

Boccaccio's original work in which Fiammetta repeatedly measures herself in reference to the experience of famous classical personages, thus making their experience her own, bears out the idea that texts can inform and provide deeper understanding to one's experience.[7] Flores's own version of Fiammetta (Fiometa) responds in much the same way. She identifies with Troy's Cassandra, "Entiendo que si Casandra te oyera como yo triste, te oí, también pasara mi pena" (p. 98) [I understand that if Cassandra were to hear you as I, saddened, heard you, she would also experience my pain][8] and later, Panfilo cautions her that her death would not compare in fame to that of the Roman Lucrecia.[9] Both Boccaccio's Fiammetta and Flores's Fiometa differ from the way a modern woman would perceive herself:

> A modern woman would be very uncomfortable to think that she was facing the world with a 'self' constructed out of bits and pieces of great authors of the past, yet I think in large part that is exactly what a medieval self or character was. (Carruthers, p. 180)

Other characters in *Grimalte y Gradissa* also give meaning to experience from "the bits and pieces of great authors of the past." Grimalte, similar to Fiometa before him, authenticates and validates his situation when he compares his grief for Fiometa's death to the grief felt upon the destruction of Troy and its citizens: "ni las fijas de Príamo lloraron tanto por Héctor ni desolación de Troya, ni mucho menos Ecuba se mostró tan dolorida quando el cruel fuego de Grescia abrasava sus palacios" (p. 138) [Priam's daughters did not cry so for Hector nor for Troy's ruin,

---

[7] Cf. Boccaccio's heroine who validates her experience through an identification with classical figures: "Pasiphae, Phaedra, and I too still had a husband when we fell in love. Husbands themselves most of the time fall in love while they have a wife; look at Jason, Theseus, the strongest Hector, and Ulysses" (20) in Giovanni Boccaccio, *The Elegy of Lady Fiammetta*, ed. and trans. Mariangela Causa-Steindler and Thomas Mauch (Chicago: The University of Chicago Press, 1990).

[8] Cassandra was the daughter of Priam of Troy. Parrilla explains that the allusion to Cassandra in Flores's text is an instance of *amplificatio* and Flores in downplaying Cassandra's powers of clairvoyance magnifies the deceit suffered by Fiometa (p. 195).

[9] "Mira exemplo en los antiguos romanos que menospreciavan la vida por el famoso muerte. Pues si aquella muerte que muy aparejada <te> veo te viniese, no te daría tal loor como aquella de Lucrecia, que para siempre quedará su memoria" (pp. 87–88). [Consider the example of the ancient Romans who valued life less than a famous death. And if that death that fittingly I see might come to you, I would not give you such praise as that (given to) Lucrecia, who forever will remain in memory].

nor much less did Hecuba show herself so anguished when the cruel fires of Greece were burning its palaces]. In turn, Grimalte envisions his own quest to find Panfilo in terms of Jason's search for the Golden Fleece.[10] Another, inverse use of the classical model is the implication by Grimalte of Panfilo as "otri Alexandre" (p. 66) [another Alexander] emphasizing Panfilo's infamy due to his ignoble treatment of Fiometa. Classical heroes and heroines prove the most frequent models of emulation through which the characters validate and confer meaning upon their actions and those of others. The communal memory stimulated by the example of classical figures also provides a common point of shared experience as well between the characters and the extra-diegetic listener/readers in keeping with the humanist spirit of fifteenth-century Spain.

Characters as Readers

John Dagenais in his monograph on the ethics of reading aptly summarizes the vital dynamics of reading in manuscript culture:

> Texts were acts of demonstrative rhetoric that reached out and grabbed the reader, involved him or her in praise and blame, in judgements about effective and ineffective human behavior. . . . They required the reader to take a stand about what he or she read.[11]

Flores exploits the fundamental ethical and active nature of the reading process on the level of fiction. Not only the protagonists but the villagers become involved in Fiometa's story, assigning praise and blame and allowing the text to shape their relationships with members of the opposite sex. Grimalte explains that the news of Panfilo's treatment and desertion of Fiometa had spread from village to village thereby causing the women to take on for themselves the role of Fiometa and to blame Panfilo for her disgrace: "Y muchas Fiometas en cada villa hallé, porque quien se quería fingir ella bien se pasava sus tiempos escarneciéndose de mí" (p. 30) [And I found many Fiometas in each village, because whoever desired to feign being her spent her time well mocking me].

Later Grimalte relates that the popular reaction generated by Fiometa's story was such that even old men were now hopeful of igniting anew the spark of desire, and when they do not succeed, blame Panfilo for their amorous failures:

> Así entre las gentes no ay otro razonar sino de vos, y aun los viejos, con esperança de resusitar nuevos amores, si algunos disfavores resciben de aquellas a quien requestan,

---

[10] "Que no menos crimen <era> a los de aquél buscadores, que en el viejo y antiguo tiempo la demanda a los del vellecino dorado. Pero yo, menospreciando el peligro de mi vida, aunque no armado de las armas de Jasón, de la victoria cobrar a éste me esforçava" (p. 161) [That it was no less a crime to those who sought him, than in the old and ancient time the quest to those who sought the golden fleece. But I, belittling the danger to my life, even though lacking the arms of Jason, I strove to gain victory over him].

[11] John Dagenais, *The Ethics of Reading in Manuscript Culture: Glossing the "Libro de buen amor"* (Princeton, New Jersey: Princeton University Press, 1994), p. xvii.

no creen que defectos suyos los priven de ser amados, mas antes piensan (que) vuestras culpas los embaraçan. (p. 66)

[So amongst the people there is no other talk but of you, and even old men, with hopes of reviving new loves, if they receive some disfavor from those whom they woo, do not believe that their own defects might deprive them of being loved, but rather think that your guilt impedes them.]

Grimalte's report to Panfilo that he is being blamed for failed seduction attempts is one demonstration of the power of texts, whether in oral or written form, to change attitudes and perceptions of those outside the work. Fiometa's story has become the organizing principle around which the characters order their love affairs.

The contrast in the characters' responses to Fiometa's story is exemplified further by the protagonists of Flores's work and illustrates the significance that gender plays in the reading process. Although both Grimalte and Gradissa have read Fiometa's work which was addressed to the "enamoradas damas," they respond in distinct ways. Gradissa, as the intended, ideal reader, identifies completely with Fiometa, casting herself so perfectly into the role that she shares in Fiometa's pain: "las agenas tristesas tanto la apassionaron que ella no menos llagada que aquella otra se sentía" (p. 2) [the other's grief moved her so that she felt herself no less wounded than that other lady]. Gradissa reads the work as an *exemplum,* whose example she will heed to guide her own response towards Grimalte: "Porque quando entera vuestra me ayáis, soy cierta que seréis a mí un Panfilo a Fiometa" (p. 5) [Because when you possess me entirely, I am certain that you will be a Panfilo to my Fiometa]. By reading her own autobiography into Fiometa's story and by requiring Grimalte to rewrite it, she is acknowledging the power of writing to effect change.

Gradissa as the ideal, active reader of *Fiometa* further illustrates reading as a rhetorical activity. She reads rhetorically in the sense that she reads to be persuaded just as she would listen to a speech in order to be convinced. Her reading of Fiometa's book successfully moves her to distrust men giving her further cause to reject Grimalte's advances and setting upon him the quest to reunite the former lovers. Not satisfied solely with changing the fate of Fiometa, she demands that Grimalte in courtly service rewrite the story, imposing on it a different, happier ending. She emphasizes that he should record his quest in such a way that she will want to identify with Fiometa:

vos pido que todas las cosas que entre ella y su Pánfilo pasaren, por estenso escritas me las enbiéis...Y vos, trabajad que Fiometa le aya tal y tan próspero, que yo me desee ser ella. (p. 9)

[I ask that you send me in extensive writings everything that occurs between her and her Panfilo . . . And you, must strive that Fiameta will find him such and so prosperous, so that I shall desire to be her.]

Only through the written word used rhetorically to persuade will Gradissa allow herself to be won.

Grimalte, on the other hand, reads Fiometa's story from the distinctly masculine point of view of the seducer. Like the village men, he identifies with Panfilo and therefore seriously misinterprets Gradissa's reaction to Fiometa's story in expecting the work to aid him in seducing her. As he explains to Fiometa the work had the opposite effect:

> pensando un día cómo mejor la serviese, un libro llamado Fiometa le levé en que liese . . . De manera que quanto yo más de piedad la tentava, tanto más a crueldad la convertía. (pp. 26–27)
>
> [thinking one day how best to serve her, I brought her a book called Fiometa to read . . . So that the more I tempted her with compassion, so more I converted her to cruelty.]

Grimalte, as an intrusive male reader who is confident that he has carefully understood Fiometa's story, offers an interpretation severely lacking in empathy for Fiometa:

> Y si dezís que los engaños de Pánfilo me an sido enemigos, devíades pensar, *si bien su istoria leístes*, quan pocas passiones rescibió en el seguimiento de Fiometa, mas ella muy más contenta que él alegre, pocas dilaciones dieron a sus desseos. Pues todas aquellas cosas que con pequeños trabajos se alcançan, no duelen tanto perderlas como aquellas que con grandes afanes se resciben, y así como aquel que ligeramente la ovo, ligero la dexa perder. (p. 13; my *emphasis*)
>
> [And if you say that Panfilo's deceits have been an enemy to me, you ought to consider, if you read her story well, how few delights he received in the pursuit of Fiometa, but she (was) much more content than he happy, (for) few delays did they give to (the consummation of) their desires. For all those things that are gained with little effort, do not hurt so much when they are lost as those that with great toil are achieved, and so he who lightly possessed her, easily allows himself to lose her.]

In effect, he considers her an easy conquest for Panfilo, justifiably abandoned by him. Unlike Gradissa, Grimalte is not the ideal reader to whom the work is directed. Later in the work, after he has accompanied Fiometa in search of Panfilo, he does attempt to sympathize with her after she is again deserted by her faithless lover. Nevertheless, Grimalte continues to echo the same uncourtly words of Panfilo before him. Grimalte's failure to understand Fiometa's story reflects his failure to identify with Fiometa's intended readers, the enamored ladies.[12]

Characters as Writers/Lovers

In *Grimalte y Gradissa*, the social-rhetorical nature of reading and writing is further compounded by a consideration of the relation of desire to rhetorical inventiveness. A number of medieval medical treatises endow the imagination with a vital role in erotic passion and, as complementary studies by Toril Moi and Mary Wack have

---

[12] A prime example of Grimalte's failure to identify with Fiometa is illustrated when he meets her for the first time. He does not recognize her, and addresses her as "señora" [lady] inquiring if she has seen Fiometa. Fiometa's reply expresses surprise that he would not know her: "¡Qué yerro es el preguntar en las cosas que parescen manifiestas! Porque a cualquiere deve ser claro yo ser aquella Fiometa sin ventura que buscáis" (p. 33) [What error it is to ask about things that seem apparent! Because it ought to be clear to anyone that I am that unfortunate Fiometa whom you seek].

shown, passionate love figures as a source of creativity that endows the lover with the rhetorical prowess to dominate language.[13] Moi notes that since the lover's desire is produced by language it then seeks satisfaction in verbalization. Wack also notes, "Paradoxically, then, the lover's imagination is potentially both physically destructive and rhetorically productive" ("Imagination," p. 110). The lover's pain and frustration are released through a steady stream of words. If the lover can successfully convince through words, then he avoids physical suffering and death. The true measure of the male lover's desire and ultimate success in love is inextricably dependent upon his rhetorical competence.

As noted already, the stimulus for rhetorical production in *Grimalte y Gradissa* originates with Boccaccio's *Fiammetta*, a work that appears in the former as written by Fiometa herself. The Italian work, as presented by Boccaccio and continued by Flores, is the written product of Fiammetta's frustrated desires when her lover, Pamphilo, deserts her. For her, the act of composition is therapeutic in alleviating her intense suffering after Panfilo has left her: "Porque en quexar sus fatigas más senzillas las sentiesse" (p. 2) [Because in lamenting her burdens more simply she felt them]. Writing as a social process allows Fiometa to share her pain with a chosen group, the "enamoradas damas." As Fiometa explains, "por fazer menos graves busqué con quien se doliesse de mí, y por la tener hallada más senzillos los siento y alividados" (p. 36) [in order to make them less heavy, I searched for someone to sympathize with me, and on account of having found her I (carried) them more easily and felt alleviated]. Writing also serves an exemplary purpose in that by recording her story, other women could heed her fate and not fall prey to men: "tomó remedio manifestar sus males a las damas enamoradas, porque en ello tomando exemplo, contra la maldad de los hombres se apercibiessen" (p. 2) [she found remedy in making known his evil ways to the enamored ladies, because by heeding her example in this, they might be warned against the wickedness of men]. For Fiometa, suffering caused by desperate love was on the one hand rhetorically productive in the engendering of a written text as a form of release, and on the other ethically conceived as a warning to female readers who would read the text after it was produced.

Similarly, Grimalte, now charged with putting his quest to reunite Fiometa and Panfilo in writing, can ease his suffering through rhetorical invention. His role of writer and courtly lover is further united with that of go-between since he must act as "tercero" [go-between] between Fiometa and Panfilo, when shame prevents Gradissa from taking on the "writer's" task herself.[14] Grimalte reluctantly accepts

---

[13] See Toril Moi, "Desire in Language: Andreas Capellanus and the Controversy of Courtly Love," in *Medieval Literature: Criticism, Ideology and History*, ed. David Aers (New York: St. Martin's Press, 1986), pp. 11–33, and Mary Wack, "New Medieval Medical Texts on *Amor Hereos*," in *Zusammenhänge, Einflüsse, Wirkungen. Kongressakten zum Ersten Symposium des Mediävistenverbandes in Tübingen, 1984*, ed. J.O. Von Herausgegeben et al. (Berlin and New York: Walter de Gruyter, 1986), pp. 288–98, and "Imagination, Medicine, and Rhetoric in Andreas Capellanus' 'De Amore'," in *Magister Regis, Studies in Honor of Robert Earl Kaske* (New York: Fordham University Press, 1986), pp. 101–15.

[14] "y bien quisiera ser yo aquella tercera si el freno dela verguença no me templara" (p. 8) [and well I would wish to be that go-between if the reins of shame did not temper me].

the role of author and go-between in order to prove his love to Gradissa. Ultimately, Grimalte's written account becomes a testimony to his lack of rhetorical prowess in reuniting the Italian lovers and in seducing Gradissa.

After Gradissa charges Grimalte with the task of resolving the story of Fiometa and recording it in writing, he complains in very uncourtly fashion that she is only trying to be rid of him and bewails the fact that he must produce a written account. He does not believe himself as capable a writer as Fiometa:

> que bien conocéis vos que la gracia con que Fiometa quexa sus males caresce de mí para recontaros aquellos. Y aún sería muy gran dichoso si la Fortuna quisiese que el loor que hasta aquí ella tiene merescido por su gentil razonar, que agora por mi rudeza no lo pierda. Pues a mí no sería posible que la memoria ni el sentido me bastase a recontar las cosas tan bien dichas como a ella las oyese. Que si Dios a mí de sus gracias alguna parte me diera, yo soy cierto que vos ya fuérades mía, sin aver de ir agora a los estraños reinos a conqueriros. (pp. 14–15)

> [that well you know that the charm with which Fiometa laments her misfortunes is lacking in me to recount them to you. And it would be even more fortuitous if Fortune desired that the praise, which until now she has merited because of her gentle words, should not now be lost due to my clumsiness. But I could not possibly have enough memory or sense to recount so well as she the things as I heard from her. Or if God granted me some part of her eloquence, I am certain that you would already be mine, without me having to go now to foreign lands to conquer you.]

Although Grimalte as reader of Fiometa's tale fails to recognize the exemplary intention of the work that Gradissa discovers in her reading, he admires and praises Fiometa's rhetorical skills as writer (stimulated as they were by her desire for Panfilo). His apparent admiration for the *form* while misreading the *content* has the effect of causing him to doubt his writing and rhetorical abilities. Up to this point his verbal skills have failed to seduce Gradissa and it appears he has even less faith in his mastery of the written word. But what Grimalte fails to note is that his misreading of *Fiometa* will undoubtedly influence his future rewriting.

The act of writing, of authorship with a particular end in mind, of a happy reunion between Panfilo and Fiometa, has the consequence of drawing Grimalte personally into their story. Grimalte, having regarded Fiometa's text as a means to an end, the seduction of Gradissa, writes with this same purpose in mind.

As Grimalte plays go-between, and through the process of recording the story of Fiometa and Panfilo, he becomes so involved in their lives that his descriptions border on the voyeuristic when he observes and describes moments of great intimacy between them. Fiometa and Panfilo's reunion is so exuberantly recalled by Grimalte that it appears he has been successful in reuniting them:

> que no creo jamás dos enamorados de voluntad mejor oviesse, ni con más lindos modos entenderse. Sin duda, quanto más yo mirava, tanto de mayores gracias en mis ojos eran representados, porque me parescía que el mesmo Dios de los amores los enseñava.
> (pp. 76–77)

> [I don't believe that there were ever two lovers more willing, nor who understood each other with more pleasant ways. Without a doubt, the more I watched, the greater were their blessings represented in my eyes, because it seemed to me that the very god of love was instructing them.]

The scene Grimalte so enthusiastically describes bears the mark of his passionate desire as lover. He does not describe so much as interpret the events colored by his unfulfilled passion for Gradissa. As Grimalte observes Panfilo and Fiometa's amorous encounter, he recalls his own hopeless situation with Gradissa and grieves:

> ¡O quán atento yo los mirava, pensando que de sus gracias alguna deprendiese! . . . contento me hazía el mirarlos, que tanto vencido estava en dulçor de sus amores, trayendo a la memoria los míos, que los amores dellos me davan sentible pena. (p. 77)

> [O how attentively I watched them, thinking that I might learn something from their pleasure! . . . it pleased me to watch them, that so defeated was I by the sweetness of their love, calling my own to mind, that their love caused me great pain.]

His intrusion into Panfilo and Fiometa's ardent meeting leads to pain as it reminds him of his own unrequited passion.

The final speeches between Panfilo and Fiometa reveal that Grimalte's ardent reporting of their reunion was more rhetorical invention than reality. Influenced by his imagination and desire for Gradissa, he loses control as writer and cannot control the final outcome as Panfilo rejects Fiometa and departs. Grimalte has failed as go-between as the two former lovers separate forever, and he has failed as author as well. He cannot write a better story than Fiometa. Fiometa dies shortly thereafter and Grimalte delivers the sad news to Gradissa who again assumes her position as reader, this time of Grimalte's text.

Although Gradissa is Grimalte's intended reader, she fails to read his text as the *exemplum* of the loyal lover but continues to read along gender lines as she shares in the pain of Fiometa's desperate end. She even accuses Grimalte of having been deceived by what she considers Panfilo's false repentance, when Grimalte reports that Panfilo had promised to exile himself as penitence for having been the cause of Fiometa's death. She is proven wrong when Grimalte locates Panfilo living as a wild man in the wilderness of Asia. Grimalte joins him in his act of repentance and three times a week a hellish vision of Fiometa emerges to haunt them. Unable to provide Gradissa with a happy ending, the only recourse for his lack of rhetorical prowess is to imitate Panfilo's repentant behavior.

In sum, the exploration of the activities of reading and writing as fictionalized in *Grimalte y Gradissa* opens up exciting possibilities for imaginative fiction as the boundaries between fiction and life, and between autonomous literary works is defined and redefined. *Grimalte y Gradissa* presents different types of readers and writers who use reading and writing both to persuade others and to give meaning to personal experience. The written work becomes the *locus* of shared experience which guides the characters' behavior in matters of love and desire. Flores also illustrates how gender differences produce divergent readings and responses to the same work: the women identify with Fiometa and the exemplary aspects of her story, and the men emulate Panfilo, employing the work as an instrument of seduction. In spite of Grimalte's attempts to lead his tale to a happy conclusion, the written product of his rhetorical profuseness, stimulated by desire and released through language, records his ultimate failure so that it is the power of the pen that wields the final blow.

SHOTA RUSTAVELI AND THE STRUCTURE OF COURTLY LOVE

G. Koolemans Beynen

The subject of this paper is Shota Rustaveli's poem *Vepxist'q'aosani*, usually translated as *The Knight in the Panther Skin*, henceforth *KPS*. The literal translation is: In the Leopard Skin.[1] The poem has about 6500 lines and was written around AD 1200 in Georgia, in the Caucasus. We know little about the author and his other works, if any, but the poem is undoubtedly a masterpiece and arguably the high point of Georgian literature. It treats the characters' maturation by gaining control of their emotions and especially of love, the highest emotion, which exalts people, brings out the best in them, is most difficult to control and therefore offers more than any other emotion opportunities for personal growth.[2] Emotional control of one's love is reached with the help of one's beloved and friends, to whom people need to communicate their problems. People are contrasted with the leopard, which cannot communicate and, hence, control its feelings. Otherwise people and leopards are similar, a theme also found in Georgian folklore.[3]

[1] Modern translations include: *The Lord of the Panther-Skin*, trans. R.H. Stevenson, UNESCO Collection of Representative Works: Series of Translations from the . . . USSR (Albany: State University of New York Press, 1977); *The Knight in the Panther Skin*, trans. Katharine Vivian (London: The Folio Society, 1977); and *The Man in the Panther's Skin*, trans. Marjorie Wardrop (London, 1912; repr. Moscow: Progress Publishers, 1966). Donald Rayfield's *The Literature of Georgia* (Oxford: Clarendon Press, 1994) discusses Rustaveli's poem in the context of Georgian literature. Prince Theimouraz Bagration's *Shota Rustaveli: A Man in his Time* . . . (New York: The Georgian Association in the USA, 1968) provides the cultural and historical background for the poem. The author thanks the International Research and Exchanges Board of Washington DC, Petrozavodsk State University and the National State Library of Karelia for their help in writing this paper. Earlier variants were read for the University of South Africa Medieval Association, March 27 1990, and at the Sixth International Conference on the Cultures of Caucasia, May 16 1993 at the University of Chicago.
[2] A.G. Baramidze, "Shota Rustaveli," *Vestnik Akademii Nauk SSSR*, no. 6 (1966), pp. 135–39, p. 136.
[3] G. Koolemans Beynen, "The Symbolism of the Leopard in the *Vepxist'q'aosani*," *The Annual of the Society of the Study of Caucasia* 2 (1990), p. 39.

The Narrative

The poem begins when King Rostevan of Arabia is succeeded by his daughter Tinatin since there is no male successor. He becomes depressed, convinced that no one in the younger generation is his equal. Avtandil, his commander-in-chief and Tinatin's secret lover, arranges a hunting match and wins, which cheers up the king. Then a mysterious knight in a leopard skin rides by, rebuffing all efforts to contact him. This sends the king into another depression from which his daughter Tinatin cures him with a few well-chosen words. Tinatin then tells Avtandil to find the knight.

After three years Avtandil finds a cave where the knight dwells with a maiden. When the knight leaves, Avtandil tries to force the maiden to reveal his identity. He is unsuccessful until he tells her that he is in love and on a quest for his beloved.

The mysterious knight is Tariel, the son of Saridan, the king of one of the seven kingdoms of India. Saridan gave his kingdom to Parsadan, the king of the other six, for the sake of a united India. Parsadan thereupon made Saridan his commander-in-chief and adopted Saridan's son Tariel, since Parsadan was childless.

Then a daughter, Nestan-Daredzhan, was born to Parsadan, who made her his successor in Tariel's place. The two eventually fell in love, Tariel succeeded his father as Parsadan's commander-in-chief and subjugated the Khatavians, a powerful neighboring tribe, to prove to Nestan-Daredzhan his love.

Parsadan suddenly betrothed Nestan-Daredzhan to the Prince of Khvarazm. She was furious, blamed Tariel and forced him to kill the prince, after which Tariel had to flee. Parsadan blamed his sister Dabar, who had raised Nestan-Daredzhan. Dabar kidnaped Nestan-Daredzhan and then committed suicide. Nestan-Daredzhan disappeared and after several years of fruitless searching, Tariel retreated with her maid Asmat to a cave where Avtandil found him.

Avtandil then took over the search for Nestan-Daredzhan. He eventually located her among the Kadzhi, a tribe of sorcerers, with the help of Patman, the wife of the Dean of Merchants of the town Gulansharo. He then slept with Patman. Tariel liberated Nestan-Daredzhan with the help of his friends and the poem ends with all heroines and heroes reigning happily in their respective countries.

Love and Friendship

The poem is particularly attractive because love and friendship are both presented as the moving forces of mankind's actions. This results in a poem where we find the emotional intensity of love along with a strong element of camaraderie.

Gol'tsev argues that the poem celebrates friendship and not love. For proof he turns to Avtandil's quest for Tariel: although Tinatin merely asked him to find Tariel, Avtandil searches three years and then goes on to include Nestan-Daredzhan in his search. This, Gol'tsev claims, shows that Tariel has replaced Tinatin in Avtandil's list of priorities.[4] But when Avtandil includes Nestan-Daredzhan, he does so because as

<hr />

4   Viktor Gol'tsev, *Shota Rustaveli*, 2nd edn. (Moscow: GIXL, 1956), pp. 101, 105.

a human being he feels obliged to assist a suffering fellow human being in need of help. He returns to Tinatin when his help is no longer needed, i.e. after uniting Nestan-Daredzhan and Tariel, which shows that Tinatin had been foremost in his mind. Moreover, love is central in the poem, since Avtandil's friendship for Tariel is derived from his love for Tinatin, since it is ordered by her.

Avtandil provides us with a good instance of the socializing and maturing power of love: love, in Rustaveli's conception, leads from a devotion to one's beloved to friendship for a fellow lover, then to relations with people associated with the friend, and then to all mankind. It takes a person out of an egoistical cocoon and activates his interest in others, first in one person and then, through this one person, in others and then eventually in all society.

The KPS *and Courtly Literature*

The *KPS* seems at first a typical courtly work: a hero is sent by his beloved on a quest and heroes are inconsolable in the absence of their beloveds, weeping rivers of tears. But Bowra notices in addition to its "cult of ideal love" also "a special heroic outlook."[5] Dronke notices "a full exposition of *amour courtois*" while hinting at some additional element when he states that it "transcends the boundaries between popular and courtly poetry."[6] Both then notice a special quality, and it is the purpose of this paper to define this further by discussing (1) the place of the *KPS* in Courtly Literature, (2) the problem of adultery in the *KPS* and Courtly Literature, and (3) Zhirmunski's typology for Epic and Courtly Literature.

The *KPS* has three parts, each with a different courtly structure: (1) a short introduction in which the poet dedicates the poem to Queen Tamar, and where only the poet and his Queen play a part, (2) a large narrative part where our four heroines and heroes are the main actors, and (3) a short epilogue with a dedication to King David, the Queen's husband, who is the only one addressed.

The introduction has a typical courtly character: Rustaveli declares his love for Queen Tamar and laments that she is unaware of his feelings. This causes him to call her "cruel like a leopard," which introduces the leopard theme in the poem (Beynen, p. 39). There is no mention of the Queen's husband, so that Courtly Literature is presented as a verbal play without consequences, especially since the Queen's husband will be mentioned in the epilogue and must have been aware of Rustaveli's poem and his real, invented or conventional emotions. The epilogue is too short to be of any importance for our discussion of Courtly Literature.

The main part of the poem is about the love between Tariel and Nestan-Daredzhan and, to a lesser degree, Avtandil and Tinatin's love. The absolute devotion of the heroes to their beloveds, the quest on which Avtandil embarks on Tinatin's request, and the strong emotions which result in floods of tears place the

---

5   C.M. Bowra, *Inspiration and Poetry* (London: MacMillan, 1955), p. 57.
6   Peter Dronke, *Medieval Latin and the Rise of European Love-Lyric, Vol. I: Problems and Interpretations* (Oxford: Clarendon Press, 1968), pp. 15–16.

poem clearly in the corpus of Courtly Literature. On the other hand, the poem has features not typical of Courtly Literature; these features can shed light on the problem of actual or implied adultery in courtly works.

The seemingly excessive weeping has long been considered a hallmark of Courtly Literature.[7] It is present in the *KPS* as well. Whatever its reason, it is compatible with the task that faces all heroines and heroes in the *KPS*: control of their emotions. The Russian folklorist Vladimir Propp noted that in folklore excessive characteristics, for example, twelve heads or eight legs, should not be taken literally but indicate more abstract characteristics: a dragon with twelve heads is an extremely dangerous dragon, and not one with additional heads. Similarly, a horse with eight legs is a very fast horse.[8] Excessive weeping should be interpreted similarly: the emotions are unusually powerful. Their strength indicates the strength of the hero: the stronger the emotions, the stronger the hero who manages to control them.

It should be noted that the emotional outbursts of the heroes follow a socially codified pattern: their behavior not only expresses their emotions but does so in a socially sanctioned way. Tariel behaves therefore in the first part of the poem in a way that is both immature and mature: it is immature in his inability to control his strong emotions, but it is mature in that he expresses his immaturity in the only socially acceptable way: like a *midzhnuri*, someone possessed by love.[9]

The poem is especially interesting since females play a dominant role both in the poem and in the social reality contemporary to it: it was written during the rule of Queen Tamar, one of the great rulers in Georgian history, and both heroines are the successors to their fathers, like Queen Tamar.

The Two Heroes

One feature that makes the *KPS* unique is the presence of two heroes. There are, to be sure, other such pairs as well: Roland and Oliver or Achilles and Patroclus (Bowra, p. 60). The Ossetian scholar Abaev has discussed such two-hero groups and calls it the 'Patroclus motif.'[10] In such groups we find a friendship which holds the two back and keeps them from being productive in the sense that they do not fulfill their beloveds' wishes, win battles or conquer territories. When one hero dies, marries, or otherwise disappears, the remaining hero becomes productive. This is not the case in the *KPS* where, indeed, Tariel goes through an unproductive period, but this period does not end with the death of Avtandil. Rather, it ends when Avtandil discovers the whereabouts of Nestan-Daredzhan. Abaev does not discuss Roland and Olivier, where both heroes die before they can become productive.

---

[7] C.S. Lewis, *The Allegory of Love: A Study in Medieval Tradition* (New York: Oxford University Press, 1958), p. 1.

[8] Vladimir I.A. Propp, *Istoricheskie korni volshebnoi skazki* [The Historical Roots of the Magic Tale], 2nd edn. (Leningrad: Leningrad State University Press, 1986), p. 247.

[9] S.V. Lominadze, oral communication, Moscow, August 1993.

[10] V.I. Abaev, "Le Cheval de Troie," *Annales: Economies, Societes, Civilisations* XIII, 6 (November–December 1963), p. 1059.

Abaev's suggestion is hence not very helpful, all the more since we find in the *KPS* not only two heroes but two heroines as well. In some courtly works we also find two major male characters who are, however, antagonists. One is the husband of the beloved or the poet's competitor, while the other is the poet or lover. The first character, e.g. King David in the epilogue to the *KPS*, King Arthur, or King Mark in *Tristan and Isolde*, is not necessary for the love relation and may be absent or merely implied. This character is also more mature or established: he is married to the poet's beloved, has more experience in social life and warfare, and has usually a high social position, such as a kingship. The second male character is the poet or poor knight who tries to win the love of his beloved. In addition, he is socially less mature or established: he is not married, has less social or military experience, and often no stable income. The presence of these two antagonists leads to a competition.

Here we find then the first feature which makes the *KPS* unique: although we find here two male characters, one more and the other less mature and established, there is no competition between them. This is caused by the presence – and this is the second feature – of two heroines of whom each has the same degree of maturity or socialization as her lover.[11] The presence of the two heroines has eliminated the competition for the single female that characterizes Courtly Literature; instead, the presence of both an established and a less established male-female pair fosters male-female co-operation, since the couples of equal maturity are drawn together by their similar problems. This co-operation is reinforced by the fact that the couples declare their love early in the poem. The males spend therefore little time on conquering the affection of the heroines so that both couples can concentrate on eliminating the problems that stand in the way of their happiness.

In the *KPS* then the absence of male competition and the co-operation between male and female characters of equal maturity results in a general atmosphere of co-operation.

Avtandil's Adultery

The male competition in some courtly works has resulted in at least the suggestion of adultery. One would then expect no adultery in the *KPS*, since competition has been replaced by co-operation. It is therefore surprising to find a significant adulterous episode. Even more surprising is that it is the more established male character, Avtandil, who commits the adultery. In Courtly Literature the adultery, if any, is the result of the less established character reaching his goal.

The adulterous episode begins when Avtandil follows Nestan-Daredzhan's spoor to the town of Gulansharo. There he befriends the wife of the Dean of Merchants, Patman, with whom he is about to spend the night when they are interrupted by an intruder who, Patman fears, will blackmail her. Avtandil kills him at her request. Patman then tells him the story of the blackmail, during which she happens to

---

[11] The terms 'mature,' 'established,' and 'socially established' will be used as synonyms in this paper.

mention Nestan-Daredzhan and her whereabouts: she is a prisoner in a Kadzhi fortress. Patman and Avtandil then spend the night together, and send Nestan-Daredzhan a letter the next morning.

This episode is hard to explain. One can defend Avtandil's behavior by arguing that his adultery served to get more information about Nestan-Daredzhan. But such a justification of the means by the end does not agree with the rest of the poem, where the heroes prove their superiority by accomplishing seemingly impossible tasks. Also, Avtandil could have got the desired information by merely suggesting he would sleep with Patman, or he could have gone to the market of Gulansharo and got the information there, since, after all, that is where Patman got her information too. Also, the adultery occurs *after* Avtandil has acquired the information and can therefore not serve as the reason for receiving it, all the more since he had already embarked on his adultery *before* Patman had even mentioned Nestan-Daredzhan.

We propose the following explanation for Avtandil's adultery. Most courtly works show only the initial stage of male-female relations, where the less established hero conquers his beloved and reaches maturation. These works do not deal with what will happen after the hero's maturation, i.e. when his beloved and he start living happily ever after. And here we have a third feature that makes the *KPS* unique: it shows not only the maturing of the less established Tariel, but it also describes the life of the mature and more established Avtandil. In Tariel we see the growth of an immature person who learns to control himself; in Avtandil we see the mature and established hero whose characteristics are as follows: (1) like a Good Samaritan of Courtly Literature he helps those who are less established and less mature, and (2) though on the average Avtandil's behavior is on a high moral level, it does not stay level: there are occasional high points and lapses. One such high point is his assistance to Tariel; one such lapse is his adultery with Patman.

In traditional courtly works, adultery, its suggestion, or possibility is an objective declaration of the social acceptance of the less established hero: his acceptance by his beloved, who through her marriage or social position is a recognized member of society, testifies that he, too, is now an established member of society, if only as her lover or admirer. In the *KPS*, adultery is a temporary negative deviation from the high level on which the mature hero conducts his life; there is a positive deviation as well: his help of Tariel.

While the standard courtly model shows the social maturing of the less established hero, in the *KPS*, we find a 'dual-track' model: we watch one hero mature, we see a second hero maintain a varying level of maturity. Initially the two heroes belong to two different types: an established and a less established one; at the end of the poem they have both become established and mature.

Not only the two male heroes but the two heroines display this pattern, resulting in a 'four-track' model. While, for example, the second Isolde in the Tristan legend remains a shadowy figure who does not develop, in the *KPS* we find one mature and established heroine and a second one who proceeds through the same maturation process as the initially less established hero: she emerges at the end as a mature and established person.

A Typology of Courtly Love

The introduction to the *KPS* is based on the basic courtly model: a less established male poet and his established beloved. The latter may have a husband, who is then the former's competitor, but he is not mentioned. This model is displayed in figure 1:

Male	Female	
	Queen Tamar	More established
Shota		Less established

Figure 1. The basic courtly model, consisting of a less established male and his established beloved. The names of the participants in the basic love relation are in bold print.

The above model has open slots for a more established male and a less established female. The slot for the male is filled in the epilogue of the *KPS* by King David, and, for instance, in various Arthurian romances, by King Arthur, while Queen Guinevere is the established female and Lancelot the less established male, as is shown in figure 2.

Male	Female	
King Arthur	**Queen Guinevere**	More established
Lancelot		Less established

Figure 2. The first expansion of the basic courtly model by the addition of a more established male. The names of the participants in the basic love relation are in bold print.

A third model results when the slot for the less established female is filled. The best known instance of such a model is found in *Tristan and Isolde*, where Tristan tries to forget Isolde in his relation with "Isolde with the White Hands." The primary love relation still obtains between Tristan and the first Isolde only; only their names appear in bold print.

The Russian scholar Zhirmunski names several Middle-Eastern biographies and works of fiction with the same structure: the hero tries to forget his beloved in the arms of another woman. Curiously, in all these works the two females have the same name, as in the Tristan legend. One exception is the Turkish popular novel Tahir and Zuhra: the second female is named 'Khadicha' instead of 'Zuhra.'[12]

---

12 Viktor M. Zhirmunski, "Literaturnye otnosheniia vostoka i zapada kak problema sravnitel'nogo literaturovedeniia [The Literary Relations between East and West as a Problem in Comparative Literature]," *Sravnitel'noe literaturovedeniie: vostok i zapad* (Leningrad: Nauka, 1979), pp. 43–44. This is the second version of Zhirmunski's article, where he has

Male	Female	
King Mark	**Isolde I**	More established
Tristan	Isolde II	Less established

Figure 3. The second expansion of the courtly model by the addition of a less established female. There is still only one love relation, as indicated by the bold print.

Rustaveli's *KPS* contains on the one hand a variation of the Tristan model, on the other hand it is unique in that it has two basic love relations.

Hence, the definition of the male in the courtly love relation as socially less mature and less established, as in figure 1, creates the possibility of another male, who is established and socially mature. This possibility is realized, for instance, in Arthurian romances and displayed in figure 2. Similarly, there is an opening for a less established female character, and we find this in the Tristan legend and in several Middle-Eastern works, as displayed in figure 3. In the *KPS* these additions have lost their secondary status and now participate in a love relation of their own, as shown in figure 4.

Male	Female	
Avtandil	**Tinatin**	More established
Tariel	**Nestan-Daredzhan**	Less established

Figure 4. The third and maximal expansion of the initial model: the bold print indicates that now two love relations exist between both the established and the less established pairs.

The above analysis implies a typology that places the *KPS* at the end of a development in Courtly Literature: both slots open in figure 1 have been filled and love relations exist now between all four participants. Moreover, not only the less established hero but the less established heroine, too, mature and become established at the end of the *KPS*.

Zhirmunski (Zhirmunski 1946, p. 167), however, places the *KPS* at the beginning of Courtly Literature and after Epic Literature, as do Stevenson[13] and Bowra (p. 47). He does not provide arguments for his thesis, but these can be supplied from the works of Stevenson, Dronke and Bowra: Epic Literature exalts devotion to one's king, family, or fatherland; Courtly Literature praises the devotion to one's beloved;

omitted his remark about the place of the *KPS* in Epic and Courtly Literature; the first version was published in *Trudy iubileinoi nauchnoi sessii LGU*: sektsiia filologicheskikh nauk (Leningrad, 1946), pp. 153–78.
[13] R.H. Stevenson, "Epic: Georgian: VEPKHISTQAOSANI or THE MAN IN THE PANTHER SKIN," in *Modern Encyclopedia of Russian and Soviet Literature* (Gulf Breeze, Florida: Academic International Press, 1977–), pp. 220–29, p. 226.

the *KPS* has all of the above and must therefore be a transition between Courtly and Epic Literature.

There are, however, structural differences between the *KPS* on the one hand and Epic and Courtly Literature on the other that argue against a transitional position: patriotism and love are in the *KPS* structurally different from patriotism in Epic Literature and love in Courtly Literature. First, patriotism, or, more generally, the devotion to one's fatherland, kingdom, or tribe is an axiomatic given in Epic Literature where the hero's motivations are noble but lack the intensity of motivations based on love. In the *KPS* patriotism is secondary and derived from the devotion to one's beloved (Baramidze, p. 137). Patriotism is in Epic Literature an independent virtue: the two male heroes are fellow soldiers whose devotion is limited to their country, commanders and fellow soldiers; in the *KPS* it is an extension of an emotion that begins as the love for one person and then expands to embrace all humanity: beloved, friend, countryman and fellow human. Second, love is in Courtly Literature a similarly limited emotion: it is limited to the beloved, and certainly never extends to the second male, the competitor. This is substantially different from the co-operative relation we find in the *KPS* where the presence of a second heroine changes the competitor into a fellow lover. The interest in a fellow lover then serves in the *KPS* as the stepping stone for the heroes' interest in their fellow men, rulers, fatherland and finally in all good people.

The implication of Zhirmunski's typology is that patriotism begins in Epic Literature as an emotion limited to the hero's group, then changes in the introduction to the *KPS* to an emotion limited to one's beloved, grows to embrace all of mankind at its end, and then shrinks in Courtly Literature back again to its form in the introduction to the *KPS*. We propose a simpler hypothesis: an emotion which is limited to one's group in Epic Literature becomes individualized in Courtly Literature as an emotion limited to one beloved person. In the *KPS* this emotion grows, first when it extends to a fellow lover, then to all who help in the quest originally ordered by the one beloved, and at the end of the *KPS* love has transcended tribalism and nationalism to include all good people.

Conclusion

In Courtly Literature, the presence of one female and first one and then two males leads to a competitive relation between the males, and the emphasis is on the social development of the less established male. The additions of (1) the second heroine, and (2) a second love relation introduce a new dimension in the *KPS*, where now each male is associated with a different female. Also, in the *KPS* the heroes are already certain of the love of their respective beloveds, so that they concentrate on a general maturation process instead of conquering the affections of their beloveds. The presence of the two heroines eliminates the need for competition, which results in a more general process of maturing not restricted to one male only. The *KPS* also addresses what the heroine and hero will do after they have become established: help those who have not yet become established, and accept that occasional deviations from the courtly ideal will occur. The *KPS* represents a more developed model of

Courtly Literature, even though Zhirmunski has proposed that it represents an initial form. Two factors explain the maximal expansion of the Courtly Literature model on Georgian soil. First, Shota Rustaveli's genius which realized that not only males but females, too, develop and mature, and, second, the presence of Queen Tamar who, we surmise, must have developed before Shota's eyes from a little girl into a mature ruler.

IV. TEXTS AND READERS

THE TOURNAI *ROSE* AS A SECULAR AND A SACRED EPITHALAMIUM

Lori J. Walters

Tournai, Municipal Library, MS 101 (which I will refer to as the Tournai *Rose* or MS Tou) contains the most complete version of Gui de Mori's *remaniement* of the *Roman de la Rose*, emendations by an anonymous editor, and an extensive and idiosyncratic program of illuminations. I propose to examine the ways in which this manuscript can be considered both a secular and a sacred epithalamium, a work commemorating the wedding of a real-life couple as well as one celebrating the soul's pursuit of divine love. For convenience's sake, I will refer to the person(s) who planned the overall conception of the manuscript (including transcription of the text, rubrication, illumination, etc.) as the planner (this person may in fact be identical to the anonymous editor).[1] In this study I will examine the following hypothesis: in his desire to indicate the soul's quest for higher forms of love, the planner incorporated references to the Song of Songs and Franciscan spirituality into the iconographic cycle. In so doing, he suggested a long-standing rivalry between the Canticle and the *Rose*.

Gui expands the scope of the *Rose* by references to monastic authors (Hugh of St. Victor in particular), to authors belonging to the Parisian university milieu (Gui begins his new prologue with a translation of a much-quoted line from Aristotle's *Metaphysics*), and to poets who wrote in the tradition of Ovid in Latin and the vernacular. The nature of the epithalamium lends itself well to the synthesis of classical and Christian currents in Gui's *remaniement*. The undisputed master of the classical genre, Catullus was cited along with Ovid and Gallus by Jean de Meun in his well-known midpoint passage (vv. 10465–10650, Lecoy edition) in which Jean places himself in the tradition of the Latin elegiac poets. Gui develops the character of the *Rose* as an epithalamium to a greater extent than his predecessors. In trans-

---

[1] For a discussion of the concept of the manuscript planner or conceptualizer ("concepteur"), see Beat Brenk, "Le texte et l'image dans la *Vie des saints* au Moyen Age: rôle du concepteur et rôle du peintre," *Texte et image: Actes du Colloque international de Chantilly*, 13–15 octobre 1982 (Paris: Les Belles Lettres, 1984), pp. 31–40; Jonathan J.G. Alexander, *Medieval Illuminators and Their Methods of Work* (New York and London: Yale University Press, 1992); Sandra Hindman, "The Roles of Author and Artist in the Procedure of Illustrating Late Medieval Texts," *Text and Image, Acta*, vol. X, ed. D.W. Burchmore (Center for Medieval and Early Renaissance Studies, State University of New York at Binghamton, 1986), pp. 27–62; Sandra Lewis, "Images of opening, penetration and closure in the *Roman de la Rose*," *Word and Image* 8 (1992), pp. 215–42. I thank Jeffrey Hamburger for his comments on a version of this paper. Its deficiencies remain of course my own.

forming Guillaume de Lorris and Jean de Meun's secular art of love into one more acceptable to a clerical audience, Gui produced a *Rose* that was less misogynistic and more sympathetic to marriage than the original text. As Sylvia Huot has noted in her monumental study, *The 'Romance of the Rose' and its Medieval Readers*, through his omissions, additions, and restructuring of the discourses of Reason, Ami, La Vieille, Nature, and Genius, Gui turned Jean's digressive text into a more linear work with a more pronounced didactic intent. Reduced by 90%, Genius's speech no longer contains the blatantly pornographic passages or allusions to the Lover's sexual organs, although Gui does allow him to pluck the Rose. Most importantly for our purposes, Gui bridges the gap between Reason and the God of Love, proposing a reasonable type of erotic attachment consistent with the aims of Christian marriage.[2] While including most of Gui's additions and adopting Gui's system of editorial marks, a system that provides invaluable insights into the most conspicuous stages of the text's recasting, the anonymous editor reintroduces most of Gui's omitted passages. His restoration of the bawdy sections of Genius's discourse is the most striking indication of his desire to turn Gui's clerical *Rose* into a more secular one. The text present in the Tournai *Rose* thus includes Gui's *remaniement*, which is monastic in character but more sympathetic to marriage than the original *Rose*, and the editor's modifications that restore much of the secular cast to the *Rose*.

Whereas Huot does not consider the iconographic program of MS Tou, I aim to show how the illustrated manuscript containing the composite text just described can be seen as a wedding song that functions on several levels. The pictorial cycle illustrates both Gui's additions to the *Rose*, such as his creation of an eleventh anti-courtly vice, pride, and many of Gui's original omissions later restored by the anonymous editor, such as the Pygmalion episode. The planner's play on the monastic, scholastic, and Ovidian strands in the hybrid text represented in the manuscript allows the pictorial cycle to be read on three basic levels that are not present in standard iconographic cycles of the *Rose*:

1. a search for earthly love culminating in the sacrament of marriage,
2. a satiric commentary on the monk or priest "Gui de Mori" engaged on an erotic love quest (in addition to the usual satire of the mendicant orders),[3]
3. a cleric's search for higher forms of love.

The planner's implicit indication of positive and negative quests of the Rose may have been inspired by the tendency to interpret things *in bono* and *in malo* exhibited by both Guillaume de Lorris and Gui de Mori. For example, to Guillaume's original exposition on the five good and five evil arrows of love (vv. 907–79), Gui adds an extended interpolation that occupies fols. 13r–14r of MS Tou. Although I will at

---

[2] See Sylvia Huot's discussion of Gui de Mori in *The 'Romance of the Rose' and Its Medieval Readers: Interpretation, Reception, Manuscript Transmission* (Cambridge: Cambridge University Press, 1993), esp. pp. 85–129.

[3] See my "Illuminating the *Rose*: Gui de Mori and the Illustrations of MS 101 of the Municipal Library, Tournai," *Rethinking the 'Romance of the Rose': Text, Image, Reception*, ed. Kevin Brownlee and Sylvia Huot (Philadelphia: University of Pennsylvania Press, 1992), pp. 176–200, for a discussion of Gui's critical treatment of a cleric's erotic quest.

the negative clerical erotic quest of level 2, in this study I will concentrate on levels 1 and 3, which concern the Tournai *Rose* interpreted as a secular epithalamium celebrating a real-life marriage and a spiritual epithalamium indicating a variety of sacred truths.[4]

The emphasis on the exemplary nature of romantic love in Gui's *remaniement* finds its place in a manuscript undoubtedly produced as a wedding or a betrothal gift or as a gift for an already married couple. The bas-de-page decoration on fol. 5r (fig. 1), the first page of the text of the Tournai *Rose*, has the God of Love, enthroned in a tree, shooting arrows at a young woman and a young knight located on either side of him. In the tree to the right of the kneeling male figure hangs a shield bearing a coat of arms that identifies him as a younger son of the Pourrés family, well-known members of the Tournaisian bourgeoisie. With its sympathetic view of marriage and its acknowledgment of the existence of many loyal and virtuous women, Gui's *remaniement* is a more logical choice for a manuscript commemorating a wedding than the original text of the *Rose*.

This first illuminated page of the *Roman de la Rose* in MS Tou suggests both a positive secular and a positive clerical quest. The young lovers illustrated in the bas-de-page decoration will undertake a love quest culminating in a church-sanctioned wedding that ideally will produce progeny. The clerical figure approaching the wall of the garden in the large illustration at the top of the page will engage on a quest for divine or sacred love as befits a monk or priest (there is also satire directed against such a cleric who would undertake an erotic quest). Images similar to the one found in the bas-de-page illustration on fol. 5r appear in a variety of manuscripts of sacred and profane works to indicate positive or negative quests.[5]

These positive secular and clerical quests can be related to two groups of religious allusions prominent in Gui's *remaniement*: Song of Songs commentaries and works of Franciscan spirituality. The most important textual reference to the tradition of the Songs is to Hugh of St. Victor's *De Arra animae* (*The Divine Fiançailles*) quoted by Gui in his prologue and in a passage on fol. 55v. Gui also transmits the tonality of the Song in recasting passages from Aelred de Rievaulx's *De amiticia spiritualis*,[6] a

---

[4]   This article is part of a larger study on the Tournai *Rose*, which bears the working title *Gui de Mori and the 'Book of the Rose': The Tournai Manuscript of the 'Roman de la Rose' and Its Contexts*.

[5]   A negative secular quest is indicated in the Ormesby Psalter, Oxford, Bodleian Library, MS Douce 366, fol. 131r. With its very prominent phallus-dagger, vulva-ring, and cat and mouse, this image was decoded by Lucy Feeeman Sandler as a "bawdy betrothal." A negative clerical quest is evoked in an early fourteenth-century Flemish Book of Hours; Cambridge, Trinity Coll. MS B. II.22, fol. 30r. A man and a woman kneel before the God of Love in an obvious satire of the erotic quest of a monk and a nun. A positive secular quest is indicated in Paris, Bibliothèque Nationale, MS fr. 2186, the *Roman de la Poire*, a reworking of the first part of the *Rose*. The *Poire*'s romance characters are exemplary lovers with a didactic purpose similar to those found in the Tournai *Rose*, containing Gui de Mori's reworking of Robert de Blois's didactic romances. Although according to Michel Pastoureau a positive identification of the couple depicted in the illustrations, believed to be those for whom the manuscript was produced, is not possible, the heraldic markings on their clothing suggest that they were associated with the French royal house.

[6]   The most important appear in Chapter 39 of MS Tou, entitled "D'amisté" (On Friendship).

Figure 1. *Roman de la Rose*, Tournai, Bibliothèque Municipale, fol. 5. A large
miniature precedes the new prologue to the *Rose* composed by Gui de Mori.
It depicts a tonsured cleric who approaches the enclosure surrounding the garden.
In the marginalia at the bottom of the page, the God of Love seated in a tree shoots
an arrow at a knight and a lady who are kneeling on either side of him.

Figure 2. *Roman de la Rose*, Tournai, Bibliothèque Municipale, fol. 1.
The table of contents is headed by a miniature of the Virgin Mary crowned and seated. She holds the Infant Jesus on her lap; a male and a female figure kneel on either side of them.

treatise concerning the disinterested love that should exist between monks. Structural analogies also link MS Tou with the Songs. Thanks to the presence of the short anonymous continuation (found on fols. 40v–41r), a seventy-two verse conclusion in which the Lover obtains possession of his coveted rosebud for one evening and has hopes of recovering it in the future, the Tournai *Rose* evokes the dialectic of desire and momentary consummation characteristic of the Songs.

An extraordinary passage added by Gui to Faus Semblant's speech indicates Gui's indebtedness to Franciscan ways of thought. Gui repeats many of the defenses of the mendicant orders found in the papal bull, *Exiit qui seminat*, pronounced by Nicolas III in 1279. In this passage Gui redefines the Rose quest as the proper observance of the Franciscan rule:

> Pourcoi tout religions
> Dont il voelent la flor garder
> Aparust en eaus regarder
> Souvrain povre souvrainement
> Vivre doivent estroitement
> Et se il ensi le faisoient
> On querroit miex ce qu'il diroient
>
> (That is why all religious orders
> Whose monks want to preserve the flower,
> [i.e., maintain the essence of their religious beliefs]

Have to keep ever present before them[7]
The most excellent poor one/ the poor most excellent one above all
They have to live strictly
If they acted thus,
Their teachings would be taken more seriously.)   (fol. 105v)

Like Bonaventure before him, Gui realizes that the Franciscan order has to be reformed from within, which can only be accomplished by renewing the inspiration provided by the founder of the order. The Franciscan's ultimate vision, rather than the solipsistic one of Narcissus viewing his own face in the well, should be of the "souvrain povre," Francis of Assisi, called "Il Poverello," "the poor man of God," whose state of voluntary poverty was in direct imitation of Christ's. In his use of the term "la flor garder," Gui may be making an indirect reference to the "little flowers" of Saint Francis, anecdotes about the saint that circulated orally before making their first appearance in written form in the Latin *Actus Beati Francisci et sociorum ejus* (1328). By employing the expression "la flor garder," Gui melds typical *Rose* imagery and the imagery associated with the Franciscan order.

The planner incorporated references to the Song of Songs and Franciscan spirituality into the iconographic cycle of the Tournai *Rose*. The illustration that heads the table of contents of MS Tou (fig. 2) shows a seated Virgin and Child flanked by two kneeling figures. Framed by this miniature (the most overtly religious illustration that I have come across in *Rose* manuscripts of this period) and a colophon that speaks of both "perfect worldly joy" and the possibility of spiritual redemption (quoted by Huot, p. 123), the quest for the Rose becomes a narration celebrating the Church-sanctioned marriage of secular protagonists as well as a variety of divine quests more applicable to monastics. Although the table was added to the codex, the miniature is the work of Piérart dou Tielt, one of the two primary illuminators of the Tournai *Rose* (the other was the Master of the Ghent Ceremonial, who, according to François Avril, Conservateur général au Département des Manuscrits de la Bibliothèque nationale de France, executed only the miniature and bas-de-page illustration on fol. 5r). In a private consultation, Avril affirmed that the table is an integral part of the manuscript. One of his major reasons for believing so is that the kneeling figures in the miniature heading the table, the couple for whom the manuscript was produced or the donors, are the same pair depicted on their knees before the God of Love in the bas-de-page illustration on fol. 5r (the two pairs of figures do not look identical because different artists executed the miniatures).

The miniature of the Virgin and Child is associated with the monastic theme of mystical marriage and other closely related themes particular to the Song of Songs. In the *Mystical Marriage of Saint Catherine of Alexandria* (fig. 3), the Virgin and Child occupy center stage as they do in the opening miniature of MS Tou. The Virgin and Child also hold a prominent place in the iconography of the Song of Songs. In the thirteenth century, the Virgin and Child in various poses became established

---

[7]   The syntactic difficulties of the preceding three verses are obvious. Huot, p. 124, points out similar problems in the colophon (see my discussion *infra*).

Figure 3. *Mystic Marriage of St. Catherine* (shown with Saint Joseph and Saint Margaret of Antioch, who is reading from a breviary). Executed by the workshop of the Master of Frankfurt, Flemish, 1460?–1533; oil on panel; San Diego Museum of Art (Gift of Mrs. Cora Timken Burnett).

alongside the kiss, a popular iconographic motif in many *Rose* manuscripts including the Tournai *Rose*, as one of the favored illustrations gracing the beginning of the Song of Songs, which after the Psalms was the Old Testament book most often commented on in the later Middle Ages.[8]

Since the Song of Songs usually lacks an extensive illustrative cycle, it is helpful to compare the program of illuminations of MS Tou to the iconographic program of the Songs that appears in the *Rothschild Canticles*, an extensively illustrated book of mystical devotion probably produced for a well-born nun in Flanders or the Rhineland in 1300.[9] The illustration of the Song of Songs in the *Rothschild Canticles* comprises one of the most comprehensive cycles based on the Biblical source in medieval art. Although the metaphors of the Canticle form the pretext for much of the work's text and iconographic program, one set of six miniatures draws so closely on it as to constitute a distinct group. These six miniatures provide a transition between two groups of paradisaic subjects by connecting the theme of the *imitatio Christi* with the extended encounter between Christ and the soul in the enclosed garden, an image of paradise in this context.

A brief description of these miniatures will bring out analogies with the illustration of the Tournai *Rose* (see Hamburger, Chapter 5, for a more detailed treatment of the Songs miniatures, including reproductions of all the miniatures discussed here). In the upper register of the miniature on fol. 18v (fig. 4), the first in the series drawing closely on the Songs, Christ and the Sponsa embrace on the left; on the right, Christ leads the bride into the *hortus conclusus*. The left-hand scene recalls the emphasis on the kiss in the iconographic cycle of the Tournai *Rose* (seen, for example, in the bas-de-page illustration on fol. 36r); the right-hand scene is reminiscent of the scene where Oiseuse gives the Lover entry into the garden. The bottom register of the picture on fol. 18v shows the Sponsa thrusting a lance toward the full-length figure of a totally naked Christ (the curve of his leg preserves his modesty), who turns and indicates the wound in his side. This wound leads to the *cor salvatoris*, which according to Bonaventure functioned as the seat of love and mystical fulfillment. Although the representation of the wound of love in the *Rothschild Canticles* recalls the image of the God of Love shooting arrows at the Lover's heart in the illustration of most *Rose* manuscripts, there is an increased importance accorded the arrows and the stalking of the Lover by the God of Love in both the text and the pictorial cycle of the Tournai *Rose* (see discussion below of the miniature on

---

[8]   Alison Stones, "Illustrating Lancelot and Guinevere," *Lancelot and Guinevere: A Casebook*, ed. with an intro. by Lori J. Walters (New York: Garland, 1996), p. 126 and n. 10 on p. 150. The initial from Bernard de Clairvaux's commentary on the Songs (1200) shows a pair of kissing lovers. The image later becomes de-eroticized; for example, an adult Christ (exhibiting stigmata) and his mother Mary are shown embracing in the Passionary of Abbess Cunigunda (c. 1316–20; Prague, University Library, MS UK XIV A 17, fol. 16v).
[9]   My analysis is based on Jeffrey F. Hamburger's superb study, *The Rothschild Canticles: Art and Mysticism in Flanders and the Rhineland Circa 1300* (New Haven and London: Yale University Press, 1990). The manuscript had an original complement of 50 full-page miniatures, 160 smaller vignettes, 41 historiated initials, and extensive marginalia, as well as 23 tinted drawings added to the manuscript.

Figure 4. The *Rothschild Canticles*, fol. 18v. Upper left register: left-hand side, Christ and the Sponsa embrace; right-hand side, Christ leads the bride into the *hortus conclusus*. Lower left register: Sponsa thrusts lance toward the naked figure of Christ in the right register. Right register: Christ turns and indicates the wound in his side. Beinecke Rare Book and Manuscript Library, Yale University.

fol. 12r). In the illustrations of *Christus und die minnende Seele*,[10] an early four-teenth-century didactic work "in which the Song of Songs is converted into an edifying romance" (Hamburger, p. 84), the soul is depicted as shooting arrows at Christ.

The third miniature (fol. 21r) in the Songs group illustrates the embrace of Wisdom. In the upper register Christ instructs the Sponsa; in the lower register, Christ embraces Wisdom. This has analogies with the heightened importance of Lady Reason in Gui's *remaniement* as well as to the presence of images of the Sapiential Christ in the Tournai *Rose* (seen, for example, in the bas-de-page illustration on fol. 137r).

The fourth miniature (fol. 23r) depicts Christ's pursuit of his beloved, the soul. In the upper register, Christ, who seeks a reconciliation with his lover, asks her to return; in the lower register, the soul, overcome by a sense of unworthiness because of sin, at first flees his advances. This corresponds in a loose way to the extended

---

[10] This didactic work borrows some forms from romance and *Minnesang*. See most recently, W. Williams-Krapp, "Bilderbogen-Mystik: *Zu Christus und die minnende Seele* mit Editionen der Mainzer Uberlieferung," *Überlieferungs-geschichtliche Editionen und Studien zur deut-schen Literatur des Mittelalters: Kurt Ruh zum 75. Geburtstag*, ed. K. Künze, Texte und Textegeschichte, 31 (Tübingen: Niemeyer, 1989), pp. 350–64.

Figure 5. The *Rothschild
Canticles*, fol. 25. Upper
register: Christ puts his hand
through an opening in the wall
to touch the beloved. Middle
register: Christ leads the
Sponsa toward the garden.
Lower register: the lovers take
delight among the fruit and the
flowers. Beinecke Rare Book
and Manuscript Library, Yale
University.

pursuit of the Lover by the God of Love emphasized in the iconographic cycle of the
Tournai *Rose* (to be treated below).

The last miniature in the series (fig. 5; fol. 25r) portrays the final reconciliation of
Christ and the soul. The three registers present a play on v. 5.4 of the Songs, "My
beloved put his hand through the key hole, and my bowels were moved at his
touch." In the upper register, Christ puts his hand through an opening in the wall to
touch the beloved; in the middle register, Christ leads the Sponsa toward the garden;
in the lower register, the lovers take delight among the fruits and the flowers, an
image meant to evoke the consummation of their love. The last image recalls Gui's
remaniement in the Tournai *Rose*, which includes the short anonymous conclusion to
Guillaume de Lorris's section that occurs in only seven other *Rose* manuscripts.[11] If,
as Jeffrey Hamburger maintains, biblical allegory assumes the forms of medieval
romance in the *Rothschild Canticles*, in the Tournai *Rose*, a love story assumes the
forms of sacred allegory.

---

[11] See my "Author Portraits and Textual Demarcation in Manuscripts of the *Romance of the
Rose*," in *Rethinking the 'Romance of the Rose'*, pp. 359–73 and Leslie Brook, "The Anonymous Conclusion Attached to Guillaume de Lorris's *Roman de la Rose*," *Neophilologus* 79
(1995), pp. 389–95.

Figure 6. *Roman de la Rose*, Tournai, Bibliothèque Municipale, MS 101, fol. 12. The miniature portrays the interior of the garden. At the top of the illustration, the participants in the carol join hands. In the remaining scenes, the Lover makes his way through the garden followed by the God of Love.

Hamburger's analysis of the *Rothschild* Canticles is particularly germane to the analogy posited in the Tournai *Rose*'s iconographic cycle between the Lover and Saint Francis as an image of Christ. Since, as he notes, in the late thirteenth century Bernard and Augustine came to be regarded as exemplary lovers of Christ, it is easy to include Saint Francis, with his customary stigmata, in the group. Hamburger contends that the image of the Sponsa wounding Christ would have found a receptive audience in the convents of Flanders or Germany. He cites Gertrude of Hefta, who in her *Legatus divinae pietatis* describes a vision of Augustine that equates his wounded heart with a rose (p. 76).

The analogies between Francis and the Poet-Lover of the *Rose* are twofold. First, as author of one of the first lyric poems in the Italian vernacular, known as the "Canticle of the Creatures," or "Canticle of Brother Sun," Francis approximates Guillaume de Lorris's first-person speaker of the *Rose*, which represents the amalgamation of the lyric poet and the clerkly narrator figure. The suspicion that Francis should have sung in French[12] as well as in Italian only increases his similarity to the *Rose*'s Poet-Lover.[13] Second, writers sometimes compared Francis to a romance hero. In thirteenth-century Flanders, where Franciscan piety was especially strong, Francis passed for a hero of his time who could compete with the most popular romance protagonists. Jacob van Maerlant, the "father of Dutch poetry," active in the second half of the thirteenth century, likened Francis to a romance hero in his poetic version of Bonaventure's *Legenda Major*, the *Sinte Franciscus Leven*, in asserting that Francis rather than Tristan or Lancelot should be considered to be the true hero of the time.[14]

A detailed examination of the miniature on fol. 12r (fig. 6), which gives a pictorial summary of the major events taking place in the garden, will reveal how the Tournai *Rose*'s iconographic cycle can be read in terms of Franciscan spirituality. Although produced by a different artist (Piérart dou Tielt), it has both stylistic and thematic links to the initial miniature on fol. 5r (executed by the Master of the Ghent Ceremonial) depicting the outside of the garden. The upper register, which portrays thirteen personification characters participating in the carol of love, contains more figures than are usually seen in the representation of this episode. Masters of exploiting secular traditions for sacred purposes (Fleming, p. 179),[15] the Franciscans made important contributions to the domain of lyric poetry; in particular, they made the carol their own through the technique of *contrafactum*.[16] In the next scene, the Lover

---

[12] John Fleming, *An Introduction to the Franciscan Literature of the Middle Ages* (Chicago: Franciscan Herald Press, 1977). Fleming, p. 179, speculates that he may have sung in *langue d'oc*.

[13] We recall that the God of Love says that the budding love poet Jean de Meun "fleütera nos paroles/ par carrefors et par escoles/ selonc le langage de France," vv. 10611–13 [will sing out our words/ at crossroads and in the schools/ according to the language of France]; these verses are found on fol. 96 of MS Tou.

[14] *Sinte Francisus Leven*, ed. P. Maximilianus (Zwolle, 1954), I, p. 36.

[15] Fleming cites the case of a fourteenth-century English psalter (London, British Library, MS Royal 2b vii), "which illustrates, quite without irony, the true spiritual joy of the just (Ps. 72: 18f.) with a picture of friars and sisters carolling (p. 179)."

[16] Meaning "counterfeit," the technique of contrafactum sets new words to old tunes. In general, the term applies to a lyric text that borrows the rhyme scheme from another text.

Figure 7. *Saints James, Anthony, Francis and Ansanus*, Master of Panzano, Italian (Sienese), active second half of fourteenth century, tempera on panel, San Diego Museum of Art (Gift of Anne R. and Amy Putnam). Detail: Saint Francis indicates his wounded heart.

Figure 8. Fresco executed by Giotto or one of his followers, San Francesco in Assisi. Francis places a ring on the finger of Lady Poverty.

opens his arms to the animals assembled before him in a gesture characteristic of Francis. That this visual reminiscence of Saint Francis welcoming the animals, a reference to his "Canticle of the Creatures," one of the first lyric poems composed in the Italian vernacular, appears along with the prominent Franciscan motif of the carol in the miniature on fol. 12r suggests quite strongly that the Lover's journey is also meant to recall Francis's own spiritual pilgrimage and *imitatio Christi*. The following scenes of the chase and wounding of the Lover bring to mind Saint Francis's stigmata, which appeared on his heart as well as on his hands and feet. An example of the widespread fourteenth-century depiction of Saint Francis with a wounded heart is the painting done by the Master of Panzano, a Sienese artist active in the second half of the fourteenth century (fig. 7), which shows Francis indicating the wound in his heart.

Another motif associated with Francis was mystical marriage, expressed perhaps most poignantly in literature by Dante in *Paradiso* 11. The scene of the saint's espousal of Lady Poverty figures in a fresco executed by Giotto or one of his followers that participates in the series illustrating scenes from the saint's life found on the walls of the lower basilica of San Francesco in Assisi (fig. 8). Here Francis places a ring on the finger of the woman despised by all others, Lady Poverty. Gui adds an interpolation concerning poverty (found on fol. 9r of MS Tou) in which he claims that poverty often made a liar out of him. This representation of "Gui de Mori" as a reprehensible example of a Franciscan is part of of the implied author's satirical depiction of the monkly protagonist who has problems remaining true to his vows. It also points to the positive quest of a Franciscan whose vows would enable him to reach a better understanding of divine love. In MS Tou, in which the Francis-can-looking clerical quester has a positive valence as a figure of Saint Francis in his role as Lover of Christ, the search for the Rose becomes a Franciscan quest for spiritual enlightenment consonant with Gui's reinterpretation of the Rose quest as the proper observance of the Franciscan rule.

Huot's insights into the varied permutations of the original text of the *Roman de la Rose* in the context of different manuscript books give ample testimony to the manuscript's function as a crucible for literary experimentation. The present study of the Tournai *Rose*, the manuscript containing the most important version done by Gui de Mori, extends the significance of Huot's conclusions concerning his *remaniement*. If the text existing in the Tournai *Rose* is a prime example of an intergeneric hybrid, the locus of combination of Ovidian, scholastic, and monastic strands, the iconog-raphic cycle is the locus of crossover of standard cycles of *Rose* illumination and iconographic traditions more characteristic of devotional works and romance (I will treat the latter in depth in the book referred to in note 4). The planner of MS Tou incorporates two of Gui's major categories of religious references – allusions to the tradition of the Song of Songs and to works of Franciscan spirituality – into the pictorial cycle. He also illustrates sections of the *Rose* originally omitted by Gui – such as the bawdy passages dealing with the plucking of the Rose – in order to prove that even including these passages, the work can still be read as a positive spiritual quest in the tradition of the Songs. Of the three known renditions of the Songs in the French vernacular, Paris, Bibliothèque Nationale, MS fr. 14966 possesses a prologue in which the author, after having asked for the aid of the Virgin Mary, claims that his work is "plus honeste" than the *Rose* (fol. 1v). The invocation of the Virgin is reminiscent of the use of the miniature of the Virgin and Child at the beginning of MS Tou.[17] The author's statement lets us infer a long-standing rivalry between the *Rose* and the Songs, which can be expressed in the following way: which work is capable of functioning as a more fitting vehicle to convey a spiritual message? The planner of MS Tou is, I believe, trying to show that without any doubt the answer to that question is the *Rose*.

[17] For a short discussion of this version, see p. xvi of Cedric E. Pickford's introduction to *The Song of Songs: A Twelfth-Century French Version* (London: Oxford University Press, 1974).

THE *GESTA HENRICI QUINTI* AND THE BEDFORD PSALTER-HOURS[1]

Sylvia Wright

Contemporary portraiture almost never appears within biblical text in the Middle Ages; the few exceptions include the *incognito* portraits of Henry IV enacting the roles of biblical kings in his Big Bible of c. 1412.[2] But the Psalter-Hours of his third son John, Duke of Bedford (British Library, Add. MS 42131)[3] contains among the 300 two-line initials of its minor illumination a portrait gallery of family, friends, and even enemies whose faces appear at carefully selected texts which relate to their life stories or reputations.[4] This manuscript is the only one Bedford commissioned in London and the last of a group of works made for the early House of Lancaster by Bruges-trained pre-Eyckian artists.[5] Like the better known Parisian Book of Hours made in 1423 for his wedding,[6] the London work contains cryptic portraiture and commemorates a ceremonial event of dynastic significance: the triumphal royal entry of Henry V into London on 23 November 1415, following the victory at Agincourt. The main theme of its unique and complex decorative programme is the legitimacy of this troubled house.

The twenty-two author portraits so far identified in the Psalter-Hours suggest that writers at the early Lancastrian court were honoured for more than mere literary merit: all appear in contexts that allude to their recognition of the dignity of the royal house. Ten portraits of the poet John Gower illustrate texts which evoke his role as

[1] A grant from the Neil Ker Memorial Fund of the British Academy towards the cost of photography is gratefully acknowledged.

[2] S. Wright, "Bruges Artists in London: the Patronage of the House of Lancaster," *Flanders in a European Perspective: Manuscript Illumination Around 1400 in Flanders and Abroad, Proceedings of the International Colloquium in Leuven 7–10 September 1993*, ed. M. Smeyers and B. Cardon (Leuven: Peeters, 1995), pp. 93–109. The Bible and other related works, including the Bedford Psalter-Hours, will be the main subjects of a study of the patronage of the early House of Lancaster.

[3] R. Marks and N. Morgan, *The Golden Age of English Manuscript Illumination 1200–1500* (London: Chatto and Windus,1981), pp. 35, 104–7 and pls. 33–4.

[4] E. Millar, "The Luttrell Psalter and the Bedford Book of Hours," *British Museum Quarterly* IV (1929), pp. 63–9 and pls. XXXIX and XL.

[5] See Wright, "Bruges Artists." Three main artists sharing several assistants divided the illumination of eighteen large and three hundred small initials. Most illustrations are composite works with the successive stages of drawing, painting, shading and highlighting completed by various hands working by the batch.

[6] J. Backhouse, *The Bedford Hours* (London: The British Library, 1990).

prophet and moral authority; the last of these is inscribed with his name.[7] Gower had abandoned Richard as patron after a serious breach of kingly duty during the king's dispute with the citizens of London in 1392 when he removed the courts to York. The bond between sovereign and subjects was so badly damaged that Richard became the only English monarch to require a second inaugural royal entry.[8] Within a year Gower removed all dedications of his works to Richard and accepted the livery of Henry Bolingbroke. His characterisation of the king as a wayward child in the 1393 revised edition of the *Vox Clamantis* may have inspired the speech of Archbishop Arundel that brought about Richard's deposition in 1399. In 1400 Gower appended the *Chronica Tripartita*, a partisan account of the rise of Henry IV and the fall of Richard II, to the *Vox Clamantis* and dedicated it to Arundel.[9] This purported chronicle is the authority for their concealed portraits in Bedford's manuscript.[10] In each of the three portraits of Geoffrey Chaucer the poet wears a linen coif, headwear associated with the legal profession,[11] a likely reference to his training in law.[12] In the envoy of a begging poem written to Henry IV he had invoked the three-fold Lancastrian claim to the throne, addressing him as "Conqueror of Brutes Albion, which that by lyne and free eleccion been verray king."[13]

Portrait-subjects of the next generation of writers include Thomas Hoccleve (fig. 1), as a clerk in the Office of the Privy Seal, who appears at PS 48. He composed poetry flattering to the king for special occasions such as the belated funeral of Richard II in 1413;[14] he had no praise for the deceased, only a warm welcome to the new king Henry V as a champion of orthodoxy and fighter of heresy. The poem reflects royal policy of the first year of the reign which was devoted to stamping out the Lollard heresy with which Ricardian loyalists were closely allied. The pronounced triangular shape of his face agrees with his portrait in the Arundel manuscript where the poet presents his *Regiment of Princes* to Henry. The fleshy face of the Benedictine monk John Lydgate (fig. 2), of Bury St Edmunds, appears twice.[15]

---

[7] S. Wright, "The Author Portraits in the Bedford Psalter-Hours: Chaucer, Gower and Hoccleve," *British Library Journal* 18 (1992), pp. 190–201.

[8] G. Kipling, "Richard II's 'Sumptuous Pageants' and the Idea of the Civic Triumph," *Pageants in the Shakespearean Theatre*, ed. D.M. Bergreon (Athens: University of Georgia Press, 1985), pp. 83–103.

[9] G.C. Macaulay, *The Complete Works of John Gower: the Latin Works*, vol. 4 (Oxford: Clarendon Press, 1902), p. xl.

[10] The relevant portraits of Henry appear at PSS 7, 11, 14 and 15, and those of Richard at PSS 35, 43 51 and 142.

[11] Wright, "Author Portraits," fig. 6.

[12] J.H. Fisher, *The Importance of Chaucer* (Carbondale and Edwardsville: Southern Illinois University Press, 1992), pp. ix–x, 43ff. See also J.A. Hornsby, *Chaucer and the Law* (Norman, Oklahoma: Pilgrim Books, 1988).

[13] "The Complaint of Chaucer to his Purse," line 22. *The Riverside Chaucer*, ed. L.D. Benson (Boston: Houghton Mifflin Company, 1987), p. 656.

[14] *Hoccleve's Works, 1: the Minor Poems*, ed. F.J. Furnivall, EETS, ES 61 (London: Kegan Paul, 1892), pp. 47–9. Discussed recently by Derek Pearsall, "Hoccleve's *Regement of Princes*: the Poetics of Self-Representation," *Speculum* 69 (1994), pp. 386–410, esp. p. 391.

[15] The portrait on fol. 70 is illustrated in Millar, pl. XL bottom row, centre. For Lydgate portraits elsewhere see D. Pearsall, *John Lydgate* (Charlottesville: University Press of Virginia, 1970), pp. 33–4, 47 n. 34, illustrated frontispiece and between pp. 166 and 167.

Figure 1. Thomas Hoccleve, Bedford Psalter-Hours, PS 48. British Library, Add. MS 42131, fol. 118. *By permission of the British Library.*

Figure 2. John Lydgate, Bedford Psalter-Hours, Matins, Office of the Dead. British Library, Add. MS 42131, fol. 70. *By permission of the British Library.*

He had already begun writing the *Troy Book* (1412–20) in English at Henry's request; in later years he was effectively poet laureate. Two further author portraits are modelled after the Gower portrait formula.[16]

The most important author however, at least for the immediate purpose of the manuscript, is the priest of the royal chapel who in 1417 wrote the *Gesta Henrici Quinti* as part of Archbishop Henry Chichele's campaign to raise enthusiasm, prayers and funds for the second military expedition to France that would secure Henry's "French inheritance."[17] This biography in Latin served as the textual source for the concealed portraits of Henry V and its description of the 1415 triumphal royal entry and accompanying pageants furnished the imagery for the overall decorative

---

[16] One of them is illustrated in D. Turner, "The Bedford Hours and Psalter," *Apollo* 76 (1962), fig. 9.

[17] *Gesta Henrici Quinti: The Deeds of Henry V*, ed. and trans. F. Taylor and J.S. Roskell (Oxford: Clarendon Press, 1975).

programme of the manuscript. Although we do not yet know the author's name,[18] it may now be possible to describe his appearance. Four portraits of a slight, fair-haired secular priest in light blue vestments on an unusual light green background, located in each of the three sections of the manuscript and in the prayers and hymns at the end of the volume (fols. 9, 15v, 194, and 218v) must be his. Each one illustrates text that refers to regal majesty. The first appears in Matins in the Hours of the Virgin at PS 23, a celebration of Christ's ascension into heaven visualised as an earthly royal entry, ". . . Lift up your gates, O ye princes, and be ye lifted up, O eternal gates and the King of Glory shall enter in . . ."[19] At Lauds he seems to sing the words of PS 149, "let the children of Sion be joyful in their king." His only portrait in the psalter appears at PS 118.9 and reflects the Henrician court's interest in classical antiquity. The text reads, "I understand more than all my teachers because thy testimonies are my meditation. I have had understanding above the ancients . . ."

The medieval ritual of the royal entry[20] evolved from the late Hellenistic imperial entry[21] and the *Gesta* author's description of it suggests a knowledge of antique sources.[22] Henry's appearance among his people on 23 November 1415 is nothing less than an epiphany: both the *Gesta* author and the manuscript illuminators focus on the adoring crowds and their desire to see the face of the ruler as he processed across London Bridge, through Cornhill and Cheapside to St Paul's cathedral. Henry displayed both imperial dignity and Christ-like humility at his entry:[23]

> the king, wearing a gown of purple, proceeded, not in exalted pride and with an imposing escort or impressively large retinue, but with an impassive countenance and at a dignified pace . . . there following him . . . his prisoners. Indeed . . . it might have been gathered that the king, silently pondering the matter in his heart, was rendering thanks to God alone, not to man.

The royal entry with pageantry, the most elaborate public spectacle of a king's reign, usually coincided with a coronation. The king comes to his people as *christus*, God's Anointed, they receive him at the city gates to offer him their allegiance and he reciprocates by granting privileges and promising to provide justice. When Henry

---

[18] On the controversial identity of the author see A. Gransden, *Historical Writing in England: c. 1307 – early Sixteenth Century* (London: Routledge and Kegan Paul, 1982), pp. 198ff.

[19] All biblical quotations are taken from the Douai translation except where indicated.

[20] For an overview of the development of *Adventus* from classical to late medieval see E. Kantorowicz, "The 'King's Advent' and the Enigmatic Doors of Santa Sabina," *Art Bulletin* (1944), 207–31, reprinted in E. Kantorowicz, *Selected Studies* (Locust Valley, New York: J.J. Augustin, 1965). On the symbolism of English pageantry see Kipling, who disagrees in some respects with Kantorowicz. On records pertaining to French royal entries see B. Guenée and F. Lehoux, *Les Entrées françaises de 1328 à 1515* (Paris: CNRS, 1968). On the development of classical themes see L. Bryant, *The King and the City in the Parisian Royal Entry Ceremony: Politics, Ritual, and Art in the Renaissance* (Geneva: Travaux d'Humanisme et Renaissance no. CCXVI, 1986).

[21] For the origins in imperial liturgy see S. MacCormack, *Art and Ceremony in Late Antiquity* (London and Los Angeles: University of California Press, 1981).

[22] The imperial reception of the tetrarchs Diocletian and Maximian into Milan in 291 shares several points in common with the 1415 royal entry. Translated in MacCormack, pp. 25–6.

[23] G. Schiller, *Iconography of Christian Art*, trans. J. Seligman (London: Lund Humphries, 1972), v. 2, pp. 18–23.

Figure 3. David Enters Jerusalem, Bedford Psalter-Hours, PS 52.
British Library, Add. MS 42131, fol. 122. *By permission of the
British Library.*

V acceded to the throne over two years earlier on 9 April 1413 the chroniclers noted
no such celebrations.[24] It may be significant that Henry appears not to have symbolically claimed his kingdom until he had conquered the French at Agincourt. The
climax of the 1415 entry was the king's passage through a castle which had been
constructed over the Eleanor Cross in Cheapside. As he entered a choir of maidens
emerged from a gatehouse singing to him, "Welcome Henry ye fifte, King of
Englond and of Fraunce." The author explicitly compared the victorious Henry to
David "coming from the slaying of Goliath (who might appropriately be represented
by the arrogant French)" (p. 111). The artist chose this act of public acclamation to
illustrate PS 52 (fig. 3). While the English tradition emphasised the liturgical aspects
of the ceremony,[25] in Flanders, the homeland of the Master of the Great Cowchers,
the main artist, the royal entry had the force of a constitutional act.[26]

[24] C. Allmand, *Henry V* (London: Methuen, 1992), p. 411.
[25] Bryant, p. 82.
[26] Kipling, p. 102 n. 50

Pageantry themes could vary, but the king's appearance is invariably staged as an epiphany and his city becomes a sacred space:[27] in 1377 Richard at his coronation was received as the soul entering the heavenly Jerusalem and in 1392 the Second Coming aptly served as the prototype of the only repeat performance of an inaugural royal entry in English history.[28] The 1415 triumph of Henry V was based at least in part upon Christ's Entry into Jerusalem where he was recognised as King of the Jews. An angelic choir heralded Henry's arrival at London Bridge chanting the Palm Sunday antiphon, "Benedictus qui venit in nomine Domini."[29] All of the works created by the Master of the Great Cowchers for the House of Lancaster carry a legitimising theme; here it is expressed by the *vox populi* as the faces of the citizens peering out of the initials in the manuscript. A full paragraph of his textual source, the *Gesta*, is devoted to the description of the crowds who were "gazing from windows and other openings," and who were "very becomingly decked out in cloth of gold, fine linen and scarlet, and other rich apparel of various kinds" (p. 113). The artists portrayed this finery as gold embroidery, pearls and fur collars and Flemish and Italian hats. Many of the 290 portrait-head initials may refer to these faces in the windows, intended perhaps as *acclamantes*.[30]

Certain of the portrait-heads may portray the actors in the pageants of 1415. Three initials contain double portraits of young "boys in white linen" (p. 105) who played the parts of angels. Men in turbans who appear in twenty-five initials could have been the company of prophets "their heads wrapped and turbaned with gold and crimson" from the Cornhill pageant (p. 107). Twenty-six out of sixty-nine portrait-heads of kings have white or grey hair like the "men of venerable age" who played the kings of the English succession in Cheapside (p. 107). The character types of the pageants – apostles, patriarchs, angels and virgins – are also the groups of citizens of the heavenly city, identified in the liturgy of the funeral, who assemble to welcome the soul upon its arrival in heaven.[31] In Hubert and Jan van Eyck's Ghent Altarpiece, a direct descendant of the Wilton Diptych and the Bedford Psalter-Hours, these celestial citizens gather together to celebrate the Eternal Mass in the City of God, the post-apocalyptic New Earth.

Explicit labels at the pageant sites of 1415 reveal London as the "civitas dei." On a tower built over London bridge the legend, taken from PS 45.5, reads: "fluminis impetus letificat civitatem dei" (p. 105). On either side of the gateway into the castle over Cheapside were written words from PS 86: "gloriosa dicta sunt de te, civitas dei" (p. 109). St Augustine's fifth-century text *De Civitate Dei* not only served as the main source of knowledge about antiquity throughout the Middle Ages, but it also established the prevailing philosophy of human history. In the fourteenth century this text received considerable attention from certain English friars as part of a classicising movement;[32] it was also translated into French and illustrated for the

---

[27] Kipling, p. 90.
[28] Kipling, pp. 84, 85, 94 and 99 n. 4.
[29] Kantorowicz (1944), p. 207.
[30] Kantorowicz (1944), pp. 222f.
[31] Kantorowicz (1944), p. 207.
[32] B. Smalley, *The English Friars and Antiquity* (Oxford: Blackwell, 1960).

Figure 4. Henry V, Bedford Psalter-Hours, PS 3. British Library, Add. MS 42131, fol. 74. *By permission of the British Library.*

Figure 5. Henry V, Bedford Psalter-Hours, PS 4. British Library, Add. MS 42131, fol.74v. *By permission of the British Library.*

Figure 6. Henry V, Bedford Psalter-Hours, PS 11.
British Library, Add. MS 42131, fol.81. *By permission of the
British Library.*

Figure 7. Henry V, Bedford Psalter-Hours, PS 32.
British Library, Add. MS 42131, fol. 100v. *By permission of the
British Library.*

Figure 8. Henry V, Bedford Psalter-Hours, PS 107.
British Library, Add. MS 42131, fol. 180v. *By permission of the British Library.*

Figure 9. Henry V, Bedford Psalter-Hours, PS 120.
British Library, Add. MS 42131, fol. 198. *By permission of the British Library.*

Figure 10. Henry V, Bedford Psalter-Hours, PS 143.
British Library, Add. MS 42131, fol. 211. *By permission of the
British Library.*

Figure 11. John, Duke of Bedford, Bedford Psalter-Hours, PS
16. British Library, Add. MS 42131, fol. 84. *By permission of the
British Library.*

Figure 12. Emperor Sigismund, Bedford Psalter-Hours, PS 17.
British Library, Add. MS 42131, fol. 85. *By permission of the
British Library.*

Figure 13. Emperor Sigismund and Henry V, Bedford
Psalter-Hours, Te Deum. British Library, Add. MS 42131,
fol. 225. *By permission of the British Library.*

Figure 14. Giangaleazzo Visconti, Bedford Psalter-Hours, PS 36.
British Library, Add. MS 42131, fol. 105v. *By permission of the
British Library.*

Figure 15. The Anointing of David, Bedford Psalter-Hours, PS
1. British Library, Add. MS 42131, fol. 73. *By permission of the
British Library.*

nobility who regarded it as a source for Roman history.[33] Books XI–XXII treat the rise of two cities, one destined for salvation, the other not. At Communion, when the Real Presence was created at the Eucharist, the Christian community, the elect body of believers that Augustine designated as the City of God, could experience Grace – the foretaste of the eternal bliss that was the goal of all Christians and which would be continually available to them at the end of history. The Host, the wafer that becomes the body of Christ during communion, had become the visual and dramatic focus of the liturgy just as the Crucifixion was the pivotal act in human history. Christ's sacrifice made redemption from sin possible: it marks the transition from the era of the Old Law to the New Law of Grace. On Corpus Christi Day, the community celebrated its presence with processions and dramatic performances, reaffirming social unity through collective worship.[34] The Corpus Christi Plays were produced in cycles, enacting the salvation history of mankind.

The Real Presence of Christ is also celebrated at the royal entry. The king on these occasions becomes the antique *deus praesens* of the emperor in Christian form.[35] Civic communion is a recurrent feature in the late medieval royal entry; it is recorded in 1377 and 1392. In 1415 the pageant of the kings of the English succession alluded to the first manifestation of the Eucharist when the kings offered wafers and wine to Henry, "that they might receive him . . . just as Melchizedek did Abraham when he returned from the slaughter of the four kings" (p. 109, Gen. 14.18).[36] Pageants of majesty or God the Father often feature bright light which is also a symbol of imperial divinity.[37] In Cheapside in 1415 there "was enthroned a figure of majesty in the form of a sun . . . emitting dazzling rays, it shone more brightly than anything else." Here maidens taking gold leaves from chalices and sprinkling them upon the king's head draw attention again to the king's semi-divine nature. The concept of the English king's mystical body, the *character angelicus* that was "void of Infancy, Old Age, and other Imbecilities," existed in fact long before it was recognised in law in the later fifteenth century.[38]

The ardent desire to see the face of the ruler, which has its liturgical parallel in the desire to see the Host, is a recurring motif in the *Gesta*. In addition to his eager citizens, two images of giants on London Bridge were compared to a couple "bent on seeing the eagerly awaited face of their lord" (p. 103). Even the Emperor Sigismund at Calais "had waited for a long time at the shore to see his eagerly desired face" (p. 157). The motif of the ceremonial entry itself is repeated throughout the text, from Henry's ceremonial conquest of Harfleur, complete with an Episcopal procession with the royal chapel in copes and an enthronement (pp. 51–3), to

---

[33] S. Off Dunlop Smith, "New Themes for the City of God around 1400," *Scriptorium* 36 (1982), pp. 68–81.
[34] J. Bossy, "The Mass as a Social Institution," *Past and Present* 100 (1983), pp. 29–61.
[35] MacCormack, pp. 22–3.
[36] Augustine, *City of God* XVI, 22.
[37] MacCormack, p. 20 et passim.
[38] E. Kantorowicz, *The King's Two Bodies* (Princeton: University of Princeton Press, 1957), pp. 8f.

the diplomatic comings and goings of the nobility (pp. 131, 133, 139, *et passim*). The royal entry was the court ceremony *par excellence*. At the Council of Constance, the largest international gathering of the Middle Ages and possibly the intended audience of the *Gesta Henrici Quinti*, the splendour of the arrivals of princes, cardinals, dukes and envoys of universities and towns was noted and even illustrated in chronicles.[39]

The *Gesta Henrici Quinti*, written in 1417, is the earliest of five medieval biographies of Henry V.[40] It opens with the Oldcastle affair, establishing Henry's anti-heresy credentials at a time when Wycliffe's views were on trial at Constance. The obscure nature of the Bedford portraits may reflect a tradition of cryptography and literary symbolism associated with certain types of historical writing.[41] Deliberate parallels may have been intended with the life of Constantine; Hoccleve did once address him as "the liknesses of Constantyn,"[42] the first Christian emperor and an Englishman (his mother was born at York). This belief was seized upon in making the case for recognition of English nationhood at Constance.[43] The invasion and conquest of France fill chapters 3–14; chapter 15 covers the triumph in London; chapters 16–24 deal with the failure of diplomatic initiatives and finally Henry resolves to go to war in chapter 25.

The first portrait of Henry V (fig. 4) at PS 3 closely compares with the royal portrait in the Arundel copy of Hoccleve's *Regiment of Princes*,[44] leaving no doubt about the identity of the subject. A ribbon spiralling around the border bar adjacent to the text is inscribed "souverayne," and an illuminated line-filler, a toppled gold fleur-de-lys, denotes that he has achieved sovereignty over France. The psalm is the prayer of one who is troubled by thousands who rise up against him. Sir John Oldcastle, Lollard heretic and leader of assassination plots against Henry, had once been an intimate member of the royal household. The superscription for PS 3 labels it "a psalm of David fleeing from Absolom" and associates it with the rebellion against David that was led by his favourite son. Absolom was also the biblical pseudonym of Richard II whose supporters were closely allied with the Lollard rebels.

A copy (fig. 5) of this portrait illustrates Psalm 4 where the psalmist thanks the Lord for answered prayer and exhorts his people to make the "sacrifice of justice." In chapter 2 of the *Gesta*, just as Henry prepares to sail off to invade France, another plot was uncovered at Southampton. As a result another intimate associate of the king, Henry Scrope, was tried and publicly executed. A second copy (fig. 6) is at PS 11 where the psalmist bemoans the children of men who "have spoken vain things

[39] L. Fischel, "The Pictures of the Reichental Chronicle," in *Ulrich von Reichental, Das Konzil zu Konstanz, MCDXIV–MCDXVIII*, ed. O. Feger (Constance: Stamberg, 1964), pp. 90–6 and illustrations.

[40] Gransden, pp. 195f.

[41] A. Gransden, "Silent Meanings in Higden and Elmham," *Medium Aevum* 46 (1977), pp. 231–40.

[42] *Hoccleve's Works*, I, p. 41.

[43] Allmand, pp. 418–19.

[44] B.J.H. Rowe, "Notes on the Clovis Miniatures and the Bedford Portrait in the Bedford Hours," *Journal of the British Archaeological Association*, third series XXV (1962), pp. 56–65.

every one to his neighbour: with deceitful lips and a double heart have they spoken." Duplicity, along with arrogance, is the character trait most frequently ascribed to the French: *Gallicana duplicitas* (pp. 17, 135, 141, 174).

At PS 32 Henry (fig. 7) appears again urging the people to rejoice in the Lord. God will reward the nation for its struggles for they are "the people whom he hath chosen for his inheritance." The *Gesta* author likewise attributes this favoured nation status to England (pp. 79, 89–95, 121 *et passim*). The psalmist also observes that "the king is not saved by a great army; nor shall the giant be saved by his own strength." The *Gesta* author notes the disparity in numbers of the English and French troops (pp. 50–60, 65, 79, and 121) as further proof of God's favour.

At Psalm 107 the psalmist (fig. 8) is ready for battle. His heart is ready, he will sing unto his Lord among the nations, and he recites a list of the lands that are under his control and reflects the royal entry theme of the *Gesta*. Ambition abounds: "Over Edom I will stretch out my shoe: the aliens are become my friends. Who will bring me into the strong city? Who will lead me into Edom?" A more sensitive portrait of Henry (fig. 9) at PS 120 is painted in the manner of Herman Scheerre, with darker modelling around his eyes. The text is a prayer of thanksgiving to his Lord, the keeper of Israel, which concludes "May the Lord keep thy coming in and going out."

The portrait series in the psalter ends like the *Gesta* with Henry resolved to go into battle. At PS 143 Henry (fig. 10) wears chain mail and a helm topped with the golden circlet which he wore at Agincourt.[45] This psalm is the prayer before battle: "Blessed be the Lord my God who teacheth my hands to fight and my fingers to war." The superscription of this psalm reads: "A Psalm of David against Goliath."

Bedford, who stayed in London as guardian of England during the military campaign, may have participated in planning the reception. His own portrait (fig. 11), however, relates to his role in the *Gesta*. PS 16 is the prayer of a man who, when surrounded by his enemies, was protected by the Lord. In the summer of 1416 he led the English naval forces at the battle of Harfleur (pp. 145–7). Although his hair is much longer in the Psalter-Hours the distinctive aquiline profile matches exactly that of the portrait in the Parisian Bedford Hours.[46] The psalmist seems to speak for Bedford when he wishes to distinguish himself from those "who have their portion in this life . . . and leave . . . their substance to their babes." His portrait at this psalm would seem to confirm his active role in the design of a manuscript filled with so many portraits. The psalm concludes, "As for me I will behold thy face in righteousness: I shall be satisfied when I awake, with thy likeness."[47]

Emperor Sigismund (fig. 12) was in England from May to September 1416. He came to negotiate peace, but instead entered into a pact of friendship. On his departure his retinue scattered broadsides praising England, "bendicta anglia – quia quasi angelica natura gloriosa laude Ihesum adorans es . . ." and wishing her victory (p. 157). The emperor's face was internationally known and many portraits of him

[45] Allmand, pp. 88–9.
[46] Backhouse, frontispiece.
[47] King James Bible translation.

survive. Both of the Bedford portraits agree with identifiable models. The portrait (fig. 12) at PS 17, a psalm of friendship, resembles this likeness in the Augustinian Church at Constance where he wears a crown over his green turban.[48] A final portrait of Henry V also includes Sigismund (fig. 13) wearing the open imperial crown. It illustrates the Te Deum, the hymn that was sung at Bedford's victory and at the royal entry in 1415. The composition is reminiscent of antique coins and medals.

Various stylistic factors in the manuscript and its apparent sources suggest the influence of the humanist movement in Italy where the rediscovery of classical antiquity was creating the basis for a new aesthetic. Although the Latin style of the *Gesta* has been praised, no claims of humanist influence have ever been made for it. While an early impulse toward the new humanism among English friars is manifested in their interest in St Augustine,[49] humanism in England is often considered to begin in 1418 with the visit of Poggio Bracciolino whom Henry Beaufort met at the Council of Constance.[50]

There is, however, firm evidence in the Bedford Psalter-Hours of Italian, specifically Milanese, influence through the Master of the Great Cowchers. Although the Master could have come into contact with antique or Italian motifs through his contacts with the Boucicaut workshop, certain images are not so easily explained. For example, a portrait of Giangaleazzo Visconti (fig. 14) by the Master of the Great Cowchers at PS 36 seems to have been modelled after one in the Visconti Hours.[51] The same dignified profile and pronounced streaky black and white rendering of the duke's hair supports the identification which the inscription "milano" on his collar confirms. The Bedford Psalter-Hours has many features in common with the Visconti Hours. The arrangement of the device, helm and shield in the margins of fol. 74 of the Bedford Psalter-Hours and on the back of the Wilton Diptych is essentially the same as that on fols. BR. 23, 128 of Visconti's book. The proliferation of calligraphic ornament, which in the English example contains many clues to the meaning of the complex decorative programme and the identity of those portrayed in it, resembles the script that also serves as ornament in the Visconti Hours. Like the House of Lancaster, Giangaleazzo came to power as a usurper and his particular devotional requirements were similar. Henry V's adoption of a religious symbol as a personal emblem must have been influenced by practice at the court of Milan: the dove, symbol of the Holy Spirit, dominates the centre of the opening miniature of the book and appears frequently thereafter.

The Bedford Psalter-Hours has been labelled "the last great manuscript in the true medieval tradition"[52] and most of the large illustrations are indeed typical of

---

[48] B. Kéry, *Kaiser Sigismunds Ikonographie* (Munich and Vienna: Anton Scholl & Co., 1972), figs. 23–4.

[49] For the fourteenth-century commentaries see Smalley, pp. 45–65, 88–100, and 121–32.

[50] R. Weiss, *Humanism in England during the Fifteenth Century* (Oxford: Blackwell, 1957), p. 13.

[51] M. Meiss and E.W. Kirsch, *The Visconti Hours* (London: Thames and Hudson, 1972), pl. BR 115.

[52] Turner, p. 267.

London work c. 1415–20. But the Master of the Great Cowchers, a *pasticheur*, has shown a disregard for established conventions of illustration of Christianity's oldest prayerbook, the psalter. Although most of the visual elements of the psalter imagery derive from traditional illustration and the conventional format is maintained, the iconography has been disturbed by addition of more up-to-date images and moving the images to illustrate different texts. Uniquely in the history of psalter illustration, the eight large miniatures that mark the liturgical divisions have been converted into a continuous narrative: it reads as a royal biography, the life of King David based on the Usurpation Narrative of I Kings.

The Anointing of David (fig. 15) has been moved from its usual position at PS 26 to illustrate the first psalm. God has chosen the young David to replace an incompetent king who is still in power and Samuel the national priest anoints him; at the same moment God sends his blessing along a golden ray from heaven (I Kings 16.1, 11–13). The golden horn which contains the oil and a symbolic gold crown which dominates the image may refer to another Lancastrian tradition. The Legend of the Holy Oil, the oil with which all three Lancastrian kings were anointed, was provided by the Virgin Mary in order to enable one particular king to win back the lands in French possession.[53] The Jesse Tree border may allude to the pageant of the kings of the English succession while the heraldic devices of the duke which are suspended from it link the duke's lineage with that of Christ, an association which Lydgate found blasphemous when he saw John of Gaunt at the base of a Jesse Tree in a later royal entry pageant.[54]

A tiny detail in the background of three of the eight large psalter miniatures seems to have heraldic significance. A man carrying a sack of grain moves up the hill towards a windmill, a scene which was well known in fifteenth-century wall-painting.[55] Because it changes grain into flour, the mill came to symbolise the process of Transubstantiation that occurs when the communion wafer becomes the body of Christ.[56] In Parisian manuscripts windmills occur frequently in the background of Infancy cycles where the meaning seems to pertain to the advent of the New Law; in the Boucicaut Hours of 1405–8, for example, there is a windmill in the background of the Visitation, behind the pregnant holy women, which may symbolise the Incarnation.[57] A more political meaning may have been attributed to the windmill by the Orosius Master, who juxtaposes an idol with a windmill in the

[53] T.A. Sandquist, "The Holy Oil of St. Thomas of Canterbury," *Essays in Medieval History Presented to Bertie Wilkinson*, ed. T.A. Sandquist and M.R. Powicke (Toronto: University of Toronto Press, 1969), pp. 330–44.

[54] *The Minor Poems of John Lydgate*, part 2, EETS OS 192 (London: Oxford University Press, 1934), 62. P.H. Parry, "On the Continuity of English Civic Pageantry: a Study of John Lydgate and the Tudor Pageant," *Forum for Modern Language Studies* 15 (1979), p. 231.

[55] J. Salmon, "The Windmill in English Medieval Art," *Journal of the British Archaeological Association*, ser. 3 5–7 (1941), pp. 88–102.

[56] A. Lindet, "Die mystiche Mühle," *Die christliche Kunst* 31 (1934–35), pp. 129–39. A, Lurie, "A Newly Discovered Eyckian John the Baptist," *Bulletin of the Cleveland Museum of Art* 67 (1981), pp. 86–119; and J.S. Pierce, "Memling's Mills," *Studies in Medieval Culture* 2 (1966), pp. 111–19.

[57] Illustrated in M. Meiss, *French Painting in the Time of Jean de Berry: The Boucicaut Master* (London and New York: Phaidon, 1968), fig. 30.

Building and Destruction of Troy.[58] In 1406–8 the Egerton Master gave prominence to a windmill in his illustration of the *Ara Coeli* legend in which the Emperor Augustus sees a vision of the Virgin and Child and converts to Christianity.[59] In England this model of redemption and historical transition took on a political cast. When Henry V adopted the windmill as one of his personal badges[60] he presented himself as the pivotal point between two eras. The three appearances of the windmill in the psalter signify Henry's sovereignty over the land. Like Visconti's emblem of the blazing sun that fills the sky of the opening page of the Visconti Hours, the tiny windmill stands on the highest hill, directly behind David.

At PS 26[61] David kills a bear and lion that were destroying his father's flocks (I Kings 17.34–6). The dying beast in the background is not part of the biblical story, but might have heraldic significance. The yale, a mythical beast that was Bedford's heraldic device, could swivel its horns at will and fold one back if injured in battle.[62] The political subtext of the illustration of David killing Goliath (I Kings 17.1–7, 40–50) at PS 38 is less cryptic. The left sleeve of the giant's coat-armour bears the inscription "(f) RANC (e)" in tiny script concealed in the embroidered decoration. Background details drawn with a fine brush include, along with the tiny windmill in white lead, a gallows with pendant corpse, an Italian motif, which has been sketched in black ink.

At PS 52 (fig. 3), David's royal entry, the tiny windmill again rises above the land; in the background are the cities out of which women came, "singing and dancing with timbrels of joy and coronets" (I Kings 18.6). David's arrival at the gates of Jerusalem is rare in psalter illustration; a more likely source for the composition is the Bruges *Speculum Humanae Salvationis*, produced c. 1410. The women who talk among themselves about David are secular cousins of the angels of the Wilton Diptych[63] (I Kings 18.6).

Saul, increasingly jealous of David's popularity, throws a javelin at David at PS 68 (I Kings 18.10–12). He offered his daughter Merab to David, but married her to someone else. Another daughter, Michal, fell for David and Saul decided to give her to him as a "stumbling block" (I Kings 18.21). The royal wedding at PS 80 depicts a mature bearded David who takes the hand of his bride. The royal marriage, particularly in the context of the narrative, may refer to difficult negotiations with the French and, particularly, the vexing *gallicana duplicitas* which served as the main justification for Henry's return to war.

At PS 97 a middle-aged David leads a procession to restore the ark (II Kings 6).

58 M. Meiss, *French Painting in the Time of Jean de Berry: the Limbourgs and their Contemporaries* (London: Thames and Hudson, 1974), fig. 400.
59 M. Meiss, *Painting in the Time of Jean de Berry: the Late Fourteenth Century and the Patronage of the Duke* (London and New York: Phaidon, 1967), pp. 233–5 and figures.
60 W. St John Hope, "The Funeral Monument and Chantry Chapel of Henry V," *Archaeologia* 65 (1913–14), pp. 139–44.
61 Marks and Morgan, pl. 34.
62 *The Book of Beasts*, ed. and trans. T.H. White (Gloucester: Alan Sutton, repr. 1984), pp. 10–11.
63 Wright, "Bruges Artists," p. 97.

In his old age, at PS 109, an elderly David composes the psalms in an image as old as psalter illustration itself while two scribes in contemporary scribal dress record his words. One of them may be an *incognito* portrait of Hoccleve who, in his portrait at PS 48, wears the same scribal costume. Here the model of good kingship is found in contemporary England. The literary circle around Henry V commanded such esteem that it could be imagined as the model for biblical history.

MEDIEVAL EQUIVALENTS OF "QUOTE-UNQUOTE": THE PRESENTATION OF SPOKEN WORDS IN COURTLY ROMANCE

Frank Brandsma

Imagining the oral delivery of a medieval courtly romance will probably bring most medievalists to the assumption of a clerk reading the text aloud from a manuscript to a more or less attentive group of listeners, both male and female, probably predominantly the latter. In a way, the presentation and aural reception of romance may not have been that much different from giving and listening to a paper at an academic conference. In both situations a written text is transformed into spoken words and transmitted by sound to listeners. It depends as much on the presentation as on the written text whether the audience will understand and appreciate the "paper." For instance, the listeners may expect to be able to register by ear when one of the speaker's long phrases has ended and when a new one begins. Ideally, they are able to *hear* the punctuation of the text that is being read.

It has become a convention to provide extra audible help for the listeners when the text becomes complicated. The relationship of cause and effect, which in writing may be indicated by a colon, will be more easily understood by listeners when it is made explicit by a word like "because." The special status of the word "because" is marked by inverted commas, but it is hard to make an audience hear this. When it comes to quoting, these inverted commas are an even more severe problem. It has, however, been solved by the well-known convention of the two-handed, two-fingered scratch in the air, often combined with the audible signals "quote" and "unquote," which of course one will never encounter in the published version of a given paper.

In the medieval situation the same problem arises, especially when the characters in a romance speak and are quoted. The presentation of spoken words – reported speech – in courtly romance is the central issue of this article. The modern analogy of the oral presentation helps us become aware of the complexity of the medieval reader's task when it comes to direct discourse. He (or she?) could not rely on punctuation, for there are few manuscripts of courtly romance that use, for instance, dots in a consistent and – in modern eyes – helpful way.[1] But perhaps medieval

---

[1] Cf. M.B. Parkes, *Pause and effect: an introduction to the history of punctuation in the West* (Aldershot: Scholar Press, 1992) and e.g. Françoise Gasparri, Geneviève Hasenohr and Christine Ruby, "De l'écriture à la lecture: réflexion sur les manuscrits d'*Erec et Enide*," in Keith Busby, Terry Nixon, Alison Stones and Lori Walters, eds., *Les Manuscrits de Chrétien de Troyes: The Manuscripts of Chrétien de Troyes*, Faux Tire 71, 72 (Amsterdam/Atlanta: Rodopi, 1993), vol. I, pp. 97–148.

manuscripts indicated reported speech in other ways, in order to make both performer (that is: the person who read the text aloud) and listener recognize the special
status of the words spoken?

The obvious method to discover these ways is to analyse and compare the presentation of spoken words in the medieval manuscripts and texts. It would be preferable
always to use the manuscripts, because a system of markers like paragraph signs and
initials may be specific to the manuscript rather than to the text and also because a
single manuscript formed the basis for the oral delivery. However, the scant avail-
ability of the manuscript material has necessitated the use of diplomatic, and sometimes critical, editions for some of the texts discussed. In this line of research – to
give just one example – it is preferable to use Roques's edition of Chrétien's *Le
Chevalier de la charrete* instead of Foerster's, since the latter gives what he thinks
the best combination of variants from different manuscripts, whereas the former
follows the Guiot manuscript.[2]

In order to explore and compare the presentation of reported speech in courtly
romance, samples were taken from a number of Old French and Middle Dutch texts,
featuring, among others, Chrétien's *Le Chevalier de la charrete*, *La Vengeance
Raguidel*, the "Charrette"- and "Préparation à la Queste"-sections of the prose
Lancelot and their Middle Dutch translations, the Middle Dutch *Walewein* and
several romances from the Middle Dutch *Lancelot* Compilation.[3]

Instead of a given number of lines or pages, each of the samples contained a
sequence of one hundred units of reported speech, one hundred smaller or larger
speeches with their immediate context. The words of one character are at the heart of
each unit. This speech is usually preceded or followed – or even interrupted – by an
indication of the speaker and by a formula indicating that he or she is going to speak
or has said something. These elements I will call the *inquit-formula*. In the analysis

---

[2] *Les romans de Chrétien de Troyes édités d'après la copie de Guiot (Bibl. Nat., fr. 794). III.
Le Chevalier de la charrete*, ed. Mario Roques (Paris: Champion, 1983), Les classiques
français du Moyen Age 86; cf. also *Der Karrenritter (Lancelot) und das Wilhelmsleben
(Guillaume d'Angleterre) von Christian von Troyes*, ed. Wendelin Foerster (Halle: Niemeyer,
1899, repr. Amsterdam: Rodopi, 1965) and Chrétien de Troyes, *Lancelot or, The Knight of the
Cart (Le Chevalier de la Charrete)*, ed. and tr. W.W. Kibler (New York: Garland, 1984).
Kibler's edition "is based closely on Guiot, but departs from the former in a number of
instances in which readings from other manuscripts allow us a better glimpse of Chrétien's
purpose" (p. xxv).

[3] Editions/manuscripts of the Old French texts: Chrétien: ed. Roques (cf. note 2); *Vengeance*: Raoul de Houdenc, *Sämtliche Werke*, ed. Mathias Friedwagner. II, *La Vengeance de
Raguidel. Altfranzösicher Abenteuerroman* (Halle: Niemeyer, 1909, repr. Geneva: Slatkine,
1975); prose 'Charrette': *The Vulgate Version of the Arthurian Romances*, ed. H. Oskar
Sommer (Washington, 1908–1916, repr. New York: AMC press, 1979), vol. IV, pp. 155–227
(omitting pp. 182, lines 34–195, line 30); 'Préparation à la Queste': photographs of Paris, BN
122, fols. 109v–113r, corresponding with vol. IV, par. LXXIII, 1 – LXXVI, 1 of *Lancelot.
Roman en prose du XIIIe siècle*, ed. Alexandre Micha (Geneva/Paris: Droz, 1978–1983) and
pp. 59–71 of vol. V of Sommer's edition. For the Middle Dutch texts, see F. Brandsma, "De
presentatie van het gesproken woord in Middelnederlandse epische teksten; een steek-
proefsgewijze verkenning," in J.D. Janssens and J. van der Meulen, eds., *Bundel Leiden* (in
preparation).

of the units, it comes down to registering the distribution of these and similar elements in order to record their frequency in the different positions they may occupy.

The beginning of the unit may be marked by an initial or by words like the Old French "si" and "lors," whereas the unit's end is often indicated by similar signs before the next line.[4] If you are reading a text aloud and your eyes, scanning ahead, see an initial or a paragraph sign coming up, it is quite probable that the reported speech you are quoting will end right before that marker.

Both the inquit-formula and the actual speech may contain elements that enable the performer and listener to assess the status of a given word or phrase. The most important and flexible of these elements is the indication of the addressee, or in Bernard Cerquiglini's terms, the "allocutaire."[5] The person spoken to may be mentioned within the inquit-formula and also right at the beginning of a speech, and even at its end. Whether it belongs to the auctorial text or to the speech, in each of these positions the addressee marks the boundary between 'normal text' and spoken words. When the characters in a given text tend to begin their speeches by saying "Sir knight" or "Dear damsel," this may be interpreted as an expression of their courtliness, but it may also have a more technical function in the performance and aural reception of the text.

The presentation of reported speech is quite a structured and varied aspect of the style of a text. The units in verse romances show a bewildering variation with regard to the elements used, their position, the distribution of the direct discourse over the lines, the use of rhyme, etcetera, whereas in the prose texts the use of forms of punctuation makes up for the absence of rhyme.[6] However, the combination of one

---

[4]   Cf. Christiane Marchello-Nizia, *Dire le vrai: L'adverbe "si" en français médiéval*, Publications romanes et françaises CLXVIII (Genève: Droz, 1985). For the initials, paragraph signs etc., see Roger Middleton, "Coloured Capitals in the Manuscripts of *Erec et Enide*," in *Les manuscrits de Chrétien de Troyes* (cf. note 1), vol. I, pp. 149–93; Willem Kuiper, "Lombarden, paragraaf- en semiparagraaftekens in Middelnederlandse epische teksten", *Spektator* 10 (1980–1981), pp. 50–85 and Erwin Mantingh, "*Lanceloet, Perchevael, Moriaen* en de spin Sebastiaan. Luisteren met tussenpozen," in B. Besamusca en F. Brandsma, eds., *De ongevalliche Lanceloet. Studies over de Lancelotcompilatie*, Middeleeuwse studies en bronnen 28 (Hilversum, 1992), pp. 44–75.

[5]   Bernard Cerquiglini, *La parole médiévale. Discours, syntaxe, texte* (Paris: Editions de Minuit, 1981).

[6]   Cf. A. Hilka, *Die direkte Rede als stilistisches Kunstmittel in den Romanen des Kristian von Troyes. Ein Beitrag zur genetischen Entwicklung der Kunstformen des mittelalterlichen Epos* (Halle: Niemeyer, 1903, repr. Geneva: Slatkine, 1979). See also Jean Frappier, "La brisure du couplet dans *Erec et Enide*," *Romania* 94 (1965), pp. 1–21; J.D. Janssens, "Hoofsheid en het gesproken woord in de ridderroman," in J.D. Janssens, ed., *Hoofsheid en devotie in de middeleeuwse maatschappij. De Nederlanden van de 12e tot de 15e eeuw* (Brussels, 1982), pp. 42–70; Jean Rychner, *La narration des sentiments, des pensées et des discours dans quelques oeuvres des XIIe et XIIIe siècles* (Geneva: Droz, 1990); Evert van den Berg, *Middelnederlandse versbouw en syntaxis. Ontwikkelingen in de versificatie van verhalende poëzie ca. 1200 – ca. 1400* (Utrecht: HES, 1983); Evert van den Berg, "De Karelepiek. Van voorgedragen naar individueel gelezen literatuur," in A.M.J. van Buuren a.o., eds., *Tussentijds. Bundel studies aangeboden aan W.P. Gerritsen ter gelegenheid van zijn vijftigste verjaardag* (Utrecht: HES, 1985), pp. 9–24 and pp. 326–27; Evert van den Berg, "Vorm en

hundred units from each text in a sample makes it possible to quantify and generalize on the level of the sample and to express – and even visualize – the way a text presents spoken words in a series of numbers or figures, indicating how often a certain element was present in the units, how often the inquit-formula followed the speech, etc. Comparison of the samples may show characteristic features of texts and authors and perhaps indicate even more principal or structural differences between, for instance, verse and prose texts or between Old French texts and their Middle Dutch translations.

The connection of these more general differences with different modes of reception looms large here, but I wish to stress that the material so far does not allow for any convincing and straightforward generalizations with regard to reading versus listening. In the analysis and discussion of the material, I have assumed that the authors and scribes expected their texts to be read aloud to an audience, since that assumption best brings to light the function of elements like the addressee. It also makes the modern reader more aware of, for instance, the problems that arise when inquit-formulas are omitted in a rapid exchange of words or when within a unit the mode of speech suddenly changes from indirect to direct.[7] It is amazing how many problematic aspects show up when you look closely at something as common as direct discourse. Rather than stun the reader with an elaborate survey of the problems encountered, however, I will focus on some of the more general tendencies in the samples. I will first discuss an overall pattern that emerges in the samples of verse and prose texts and then go into some aspects of the Middle Dutch translations.

The basic structure for a unit of reported speech consists of the name of the speaker, an equivalent of the word "said" and the actual speech. If, in a dialogue, this unit is followed by a similar one, the inquit-formula of the second unit indicates the end of the words spoken by the first speaker. The regular alternation of speeches and their introductions provides structure to the dialogue, gives it a regular if somewhat dull rhythm, easily recognized by both performer and audience. The same goes when the inquit-formula and speaker are consistently given *after* the actual speech or right after its first words. However, although groups of identically structured units do occur, especially in Chrétien's *Charrete*, the poets tend to alternate different struc-

---

inhoud: ontwikkelingen binnen de ridderepiek ca. 1200 – ca. 1350," *De nieuwe taalgids* 85 (1992), pp. 405–21 and Christine Ferlampin, "Les dialogues dans le *Tristan en prose*," in J. Dufournet, ed., *Nouvelles recherches sur le Tristan en prose* (Paris, 1990), pp. 79–121.

7   See D.H. Green, "On the Primary Reception of Narrative Literature in Medieval Germany," *Forum for Modern Language Studies* 20 (1984), pp. 289–308. Green argues convincingly that authors may have taken into account that their works might be read aloud to a group as well as read (in the modern sense), in response to M.G. Scholz's *Hören und Lesen. Studien zur primären Rezeption der Literatur im 12. und 13. Jahrhundert* (Wiesbaden, 1980). If Green is right and if we are right in assuming that listeners need more audible help in order to understand the narrative, we may assume that the medieval authors aimed for listeners, for accommodation of their demands will have satisfied the readers as well. Cf. also D.H. Green, *Medieval Listening and Reading. The primary reception of German literature 800–1300* (Cambridge: Cambridge University Press, 1994). For the sudden change from indirect to direct discourse (and vice versa), see K. Heeroma, *Moriaen, Lantsloot en Elegast luisterend gelezen* (Leiden, 1973) and Norris J. Lacy, "Emergent Direct Discourse in the Vulgate Cycle," *Arthuriana* 4 (1994), pp. 19–29.

tures within dialogues, probably to liven up their tale. I will give an example, taken from the *Vengeance Raguidel*:

(unit A) [Mesire Gavains]speaker [dist]inquit-formula après:
          ["Tu i pués bien venir o moi,
          Ja n'i avras garde, je croi;
645   J'enterrai el castiel avant."]speech 1
(unit B) Et [cil]speaker [respont]inquit: ["Mauvais garant
          Avroie en vos, je n'irai mie.
          Alés i, n'en revenrés mie
          Si trovés le Noir Chevalier;
650   S'il n'est alés el bos chacier,
          Ja ne venrés demain midi."]speech 1
(unit C) ["Por Diu"!]speech 1 [fait]inquit [Gavains]speaker: ["mainne m'i
          Tant que je voie sa maison
          U tu me mostres visïon
655   Par de quel part g'irai plus droit."]speech 2
          Li vagiers dist qu'il le menroit
          Tant qu'il li mosterroit le tor
          U la forest est tot entor.
          Atant en .i. sentier entra.
660 (D)   ["Sire,"] speech 1 [fait]inquit [il]speaker, ["venes par ça,
          Car le castiax est ça a mont."]speech 2

[Sir Gawain then said: "You may well come with me, you will have nothing to worry about, I think; I will first enter the castle." And he said: "I have no great faith in you, I will not go. Go there and don't come back at all, find the Black Knight; if he has not gone into the woods to hunt, he will not come before noon tomorrow." "By God," said Gawain, "take me to where I can see his house or show me how I can come there by the most direct route." The cowherd said he would guide him until he would show him the tower surrounded by forest. Then he entered a path. "Sir," he said, "Go this way, for the castle lies uphill from here."]

The units and their components have been marked with brackets and labels. Their registration in the matrix is demonstrated in Table 1:

Table 1. Distribution of the components of the direct discourse in the *Vengeance* example

Units	Initials	Si, Lors, Doe etc.	Speaker	Inquit-formula	Addressee	'Starter'	Addressee	Speech 1	Addressee	Inquit-formula	Speaker	Addressee	'Starter'	Addressee	Speech 2	End
A: l. 642-645			X	X				X								
B: l. 646-651		Et	X	X				X								
C: l. 652-655						X				X	X				X	
D: l. 660-661							X			X	X				X	

Whereas in units A and B "speech 1" follows the inquit-formula, it precedes this formula in units C and D. In these units "speech 1" is reduced to a short introductory phrase: "Por Diu" and "Sire" respectively. The exclamation in unit C and the indication of the addressee in D have the same function: they mark the beginning of a new speech and, at the same time, the end of the previous one. The boundary between the speeches of units B and C is thus marked by the words "Por Diu," indicating that within this couplet another character begins to speak. Whereas the addressee is easily recognized and defined, the exclamation belongs to a more vague category of words and phrases that in Old French stretches from "Or" and "Oïl" through "Certes" and "Par foi" to "Si m'ait Diex," all words that are typically, but not exclusively, found at the beginning of phrases and speeches. One might call them *starters*. The mention of the addressee or the "starter" is quite common in verse as well as prose texts. In the samples an average of 20 per cent of the units has a starter, whereas 40 per cent mentions the addressee in this position.

The two patterns illustrated by units A B and C D occur in both verse and prose texts, but their frequency differs significantly. In verse texts, "speech 1" tends to continue with the rest of the character's words, resulting in one continuous flow of spoken words, in short: the pattern of units A and B. In prose texts, however, the narrator often interrupts this flow right after its beginning in order to state the speaker and the inquit. Thus the character's continuous words are quoted in two separate speeches, the first of which seems intended specifically to alert the audience to the more informative words which will follow the inquit-formula. Although taken from a verse text, the C and D units of the example illustrate this pattern adequately. In a dialogue with this pattern, the second speech of a unit immediately borders the first speech of the next unit. This "collision of speeches" may cause problems for the performer and the audience, when it comes to recognizing the change of speaker. I will come back to this aspect later on.

In the samples, the frequency for the relevant components attests to the structural difference. Verse texts score high with regard to giving speaker and inquit-formula *before* the actual spoken words and relatively low on having those components *after* "speech 1." They have a far higher percentage for "speech 1" than for "speech 2." In the prose texts, this pattern is exactly reversed, as Diagram 1 shows.[8]

Even though units with the prose pattern occur in verse texts as well, and vice versa, the preferences are striking: where the verse texts give the technical information the performer and audience need right at the beginning of the unit, the prose texts seem to hide these components and even blur the boundaries between speeches. The topic of the modes of reception, hovering over this investigation like a bird of prey ready to pounce on results like these, provides the alluring interpretation that the verse texts were meant to be heard and the prose texts to be seen, that is to say: read.

However, this interpretation is both premature, because it is based on just a few samples from two texts and on just one stylistic aspect, and insufficient, because it

---

8   The diagram shows basic patterns in verse and prose texts. Only the relevant elements of the analytic system are shown, in order to fit seven texts in one diagram. The results for Chrétien's *Charrete* and the prose *Charrette* are based on three samples of 100 units.

Diagram 1. Direct discourse in verse and prose texts

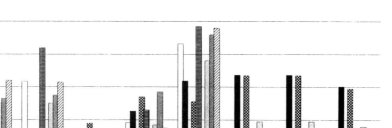

does not take into account the regularity of the prose pattern and the function of the introductory phrases therein. To a trained reader's eye, a "starter" or the mention of the addressee may have been as clear a signal for the change of speaker and for the format of the direct discourse that is to follow as an explicit inquit formula preceding the spoken words. Furthermore, in the manuscript and diplomatic edition consulted, the two prose texts use a system of punctuation in which a full stop usually – but far from exclusively – indicates a change of speaker. In combination with the fairly consistent use of the starter and/or addressee, this punctuation may effectively have helped a performer read the prose text aloud to an audience. Perhaps it took more care and preparation to provide an adequate and lively presentation of the direct discourse when reading from a prose text, but it was by no means impossible. On the contrary, the relatively high scores on the audible introductory elements (cf. diagram 1), in my opinion, indicate that the oral presentation of the prose texts was foreseen by their authors. So, at this point in the research, it seems best to let the merlin of the modes of reception hover some more . . .

Diagram 1 also shows an example of another kind of reception: translation into Middle Dutch verses. I will conclude this article with a discussion of several Middle Dutch translations and of the opportunities the method of stylistic analysis described above may provide here. In diagram 1, there are columns for the two Middle Dutch translations of the *Vengeance Raguidel*. These are translations in rhymed couplets. In Middle Dutch literature, this is the usual format for courtly romance; even the prose *Lancelot* is put into verse in Middle Dutch. The first *Vengeance* translation, dating from before 1250, has come to us only in fragments; the second version is an adaptation/abbreviation of this translation, incorporated in the *Lancelot* Compilation, which dates from the first decades of the fourteenth century. A comparison of the figures for the French *Vengeance* with those for its two versions in Middle Dutch shows that the translations score even higher than the *Vengeance* on the elements that are high in the verse pattern, and far lower on the low elements. The verse pattern, with its preference for a preceding inquit-formula and a single speech component, thus emerges even stronger in the Middle Dutch verse texts. This is not specific to the *Vengeance* and its translation, for the samples of all nine other Middle Dutch verse texts examined show the same pattern, often with even higher, respectively lower, scores. The Middle Dutch corpus consisted of indigenous romances like the *Walewein*, of translations of Old French verse texts like the translations of the *Vengeance*, Chrétien's *Conte du Graal* and *Renaut de Montauban*, and of translations of Old French prose texts from the *Lancelot-Grail* cycle. All of them strongly favour the verse pattern.[9]

Where the Dutch poets who translated a rhymed text were able to follow and even reinforce the pattern in their source, the translators of prose originals have completely restructured the presentation of direct discourse. In diagram 1, the columns for the 'Préparation à la Queste' (BN 122) and the *Lanceloet* represent samples taken from the same section of the story: they differ significantly! Similar results came in for Jacob van Maerlant's translation of the prose *Joseph d'Arimathie* and for the fragments of the Middle Dutch adaptation of the prose *Lancelot* that is called *Lantsloot vander Haghedochte*, "Lancelot of the Cave." The Dutch poets of these three texts have systematically returned the inquit-formulas, which were incorporated in the speeches in their prose source, to the beginning of the complete unit. They also sometimes changed direct discourse to indirect and strongly reduced the number of "colliding speeches."[10] The result is a far more standardized, straightforward presentation of the direct discourse, which may have been easier, if less lively and engaging, for both performer and audience.

One of the problems solved by this return to the verse pattern is that of the recognition of the units in a sequence. Punctuation is rare in the manuscripts of Middle Dutch verse texts, so the visual aid employed by the authors and scribes of their Old French sources was not taken over in any consistent way by the Dutch poets, although in the *Lanceloet* the change of speaker within a line is sometimes marked with a full stop. But if the rhythm of the sequence is clearly indicated by the inquit-formula before each speech, as it is in these three texts, punctuation is unnecessary: the units are well-defined in an audible, and not just visible way. To this clear structure, the manuscripts of the two Middle Dutch *Lancelot* texts add further help for the performer.

The *Lantsloot* manuscript abounds with paragraph signs. The episode chosen to

---

[9] For (a discussion of) the complete results of the samples from the Middle Dutch texts, see Brandsma, "De presentatie," see note 3.

[10] Several studies of Middle Dutch adaptations/translations describe the way the poets handled direct discourse, cf. F.P. van Oostrom, *Lantsloot vander Haghedochte. Onderzoekingen over een Middelnederlandse bewerking van de Lancelot en prose*, Middelnederlandse Lancelotromans I (Amsterdam: Noord-Hollandsche Uitgevers Maatschappij, 1981); Dieuwke E. van der Poel, *De Vlaamse Rose en Die Rose van Heinric. Onderzoekingen over twee Middelnederlandse bewerkingen van de Roman de la Rose* (Hilversum: Verloren, 1989); Bart Besamusca, ed., *Lanceloet. De Middelnederlandse vertaling van de Lancelot en prose overgeleverd in de Lancelotcompilatie. Pars 2 (vs. 5531–10740). Met een inleidende studie over de vertaaltechniek*, Middelnederlandse Lancelotromans V (Assen/Maastricht: Van Gorcum, 1991).

demonstrate this describes how a damsel leads Dodinel to a narrow plank across a stream and invites him to cross it:[11]

¶	Doe vraghede hi der joncfrouwe	¶	Then he asked the damsel
5500	Ende seide: "Bi uwer trouwe,		and said: "By your faith,
	Hoe hebdi mi hier brocht		why did you bring me here
	Ende wat hebben wi hier socht?		and what are we looking for here?
	Hoe soudic over dese brugge liden?		How could I pass this bridge? It is
5504	Men ne macher over gaen no liden."		impossible to ride or walk over it."
¶	Doe sprac si: "Ic seg u wat gi doet:	¶	Then she said: "I will tell you what
	Laet staen u part, gaet over te voet.		to do: leave your horse and go over
	Dats tbeste dat ic can verhoren;		on foot. That is the best solution;
5508	Ic sal allene gaen voren."		I will first go over alone."
¶	Doe seide hi ter goeder uren:	¶	Then he soon said: "I'll do it,
	"Ic neme dats mi mach gheburen!"		whatever may come of it!"
¶	Die joncfrouwe ghinc voren ...	¶	The damsel went over first ...

The example illustrates the way paragraph signs are used in this manuscript. They indicate the basic narrative structure and are also found before the beginning of units of direct discourse, thus indicating also the end of the previous unit. When reading from this manuscript, the performer can *see* at a glance where the words of the character he is quoting will end. Here, the paragraph sign – and sometimes the initial – is the medieval equivalent of our "unquote."

The final example is taken from the *Lancelot* Compilation and shows a similar system for the indication of units of direct discourse. In this episode Lancelot meets a damsel, who warns him that he has entered a dangerous forest:[12]

	ende Hi hadde groet wonder waerbi	(and) He wondered why she looked at him
	Sine so besach. Doe seide hi:	like that. Then he said:
16140	"Wat segt di, wat dunct u, joncfrouwe?"	"What do you say, what do you think, damsel?"
	ende Si seide: "Mi dunct, bi mire trouwe,	(and) She said: "I consider it, on my faith,
	Alte groet scade nu ter tijt	too great a loss at this moment
	Dat also scone lichame alse gi sijt	if as beautiful a man as you are
16144 al	Dus vart rechte vort te sire doet.	(all) thus goes straight to his death.
	Ende hets verlies alte groet,	And it's indeed a great loss,
	Want gine mocht niet gecomen wesen	since you couldn't have come
	In vreseliker foreest dan in desen."	into a more terrible forest."
16148 ende	Hi seide: "Ne vervart u niet,	(and) He said: "Don't be afraid,
	Bedi, joncfrouwe, men niet ne siet	because, damsel, one does not see
	Alle die ongevalle gescien	all accidents happen
	Daer hem die liede af ontsien."	that people fear."

[11] Cf. *Lantsloot vander Haghedochte. Fragmenten van een Middelnederlandse bewerking van de Lancelot en prose*, ed. W.P. Gerritsen, Middelnederlandse Lancelotromans II (Amsterdam: Noord-Hollandsche Uitgevers Maatschappij, 1987), lines 5499–5511.

[12] Cf. Frank Brandsma, ed., *Lanceloet. De Middelnederlandse vertaling van de Lancelot en prose overgeleverd in de Lancelotcompilatie. Pars 3 (vs. 10741–16263). Met een inleidende studie over de entrelacement-vertelwijze*, Middelnederlandse Lancelotromans VI (Assen/Maastricht: Van Gorcum, 1992), lines 16138–16154. In line 16139 the corrector has indicated the end of the sentence by placing a colon after "besach."

16152 ende Si seide: "God bescermes u,   (and) She said: "May God protect you,
      want Mi ware leet mesfielt u nu."   (because) I would be sorry if you were hurt."
      Ende hi sciet mettien van hare.   And then he left her.

There are two differences between this manuscript and that of *Lantsloot*. The marginal signs here are not just visible signs, they are abbreviations for words and may have been made audible when a performer read the text from this manuscript aloud to an audience. In fact, and that is the second difference, these marks were not made by a scribe but by a contemporaneous corrector. He added these words, and further on in the manuscript also used marginal dots and colons, in order to prepare the text for oral delivery, as Gerritsen has demonstrated.[13]

Thus, from the perspective provided by the statistical analysis of direct discourse, this unique manuscript offers us the chance to look over the shoulder of – or perhaps better: to listen with great attention to – a medieval reader and performer, and to witness the oral delivery of a medieval courtly romance.

T. A Sandquist + Michael Powicke
Essays Presented To Bertie Wilkinson
(U of Toronto Press, 1969)

"The Holy Oil of
[found in Royal 12.C.xii]

---

[13] Cf. W.P. Gerritsen, "Corrections and Indications for Oral Delivery in the Middle Dutch Lancelot Manuscript The Hague, K.B. 129 A 10," in J.P. Gumbert and M.J.M. de Haan, eds., *Neerlandica manuscripta. Essays presented to G.I. Lieftinck. vol. III. Litterae textuales* (Amsterdam, 1976), pp. 39–59 and W.P. Gerritsen, "A Medieval Text and its Oral Delivery," in W.P. Gerritsen and C. Vellekoop, eds., *Talks on Text. Papers read at the closing session of the NIAS theme group Orality and Literacy on May 27th, 1992* (Wassenaar: NIAS, 1992), pp. 73–81.

See June Hall McCash (ed.), *The Cultural Patronage of Medieval Women*
(U of Georgia: Athens, Ga, 1996);
"In Carmi Parsons, "Of Queens, Courts, & Books: Reflections on the Thirteenth-Century *Literary Patronage of 13C Plantagenet Queens*
p. 175–201
ances Underhill, "Elizabeth de Burgh; Connoisseur & Patron" (266–287)
[R]alph Hanna III, "Some Norfolk Women & their Books, ca. 1390–1440" (288–305)

COURTLY ROMANCES IN THE PRIVY WARDROBE[1]

Carter Revard

> Elizabeth Burgh
> p. 173: "...the first documented example of her book buying came in 1324, when she ured a scribe to copy the *Vitae patrum*, at a cost of 85.j, robin, or meals at table. (60) James Westfield Thompson, *The Medieval Library*, U Chic 1939 p. 645

London, BL MS Add. 60584 is the final account of John Fleet, First Keeper of the Privy Wardrobe, covering the period 16 July 1324 to 1 July 1341.[2] It offers keyhole glimpses of the English court, especially during the four years 1326–30 when Roger Mortimer of Wigmore, as Isabella's Minister of Courtly Love, held all but royal sway in England – showing, for instance, which members of the new court in 1327 were issued "romances" as part of their perks, and by sometimes naming the books issued giving insight into "the" audience for "romances." In 1982, Juliet Vale briefly but usefully discussed some of this evidence,[3] which the present paper examines further and relates to the lives of courtly readers, especially the two whose book-borrowing is most fully specified – that is, Isabella and Mortimer – in the spring of 1327.

---

[1] Research for this paper was aided by a grant from the British Academy's Neil Ker Memorial Fund, by travel funds from Washington University, St. Louis, by the staffs of the British Library, Bodleian Library, Olin Library of Washington University, the Huntington Library, and by archivists at the College of Arms, for which I am grateful.

[2] The manuscript, acquired by the British Library in 1979, was unavailable to T.F. Tout for his classic *Chapters in Medieval Administrative History*, 6 vols. (Manchester, 1920–1933), of which volume 4, pp. 439–84, provides the standard history of the Privy Wardrobe and Fleet's keepership (1323–44).

[3] Juliet Vale, *Edward III and Chivalry* (Woodbridge: The Boydell Press, 1982), pp. 49–50, note 122 pp. 128–9, and Appendix 9 p. 169. Vale reports (p. 169) that Fleet's account shows delivery to Roger Mortimer of four romances; I have found no such itemizing, but Fleet records for 8 December 1325 (fols. 3v, 4r, 4v) that the Abbot of Wigmore by the hand of Walter de Ludlow, Canon of Wigmore, delivered to the Tower at the precept of Hugh Despenser, Jr., items taken from Mortimer and other Contrariants including (fol. 3r col. 2, lines 8–18) a Register-book, paper, diverse Coffers, a Psalter in French, *three diverse Romances*, and diverse quires of *surgerie*, with (fol. 4v line 5) two pairs of coffers for *hernes* ("gear") painted with the arms of Mortimer and Genevile. On fol. 14v (last 11 lines), Fleet records delivery to Mortimer on 19 February 1327 (by the hands of Walter de Lingaigne, Canon of Wigmore, and Walter de Evesham, *clericus*) of household furnishings, *not* including any books; this list apparently runs over to fol. 15r, line 1, where it ends with mention of several masers. Then, with no apparent break and *just possibly* as still listing items delivered to Mortimer, on 15v, lines 2–13, Fleet records: (line 2) *Et in .j. cista sunt .lxvj. libri & alii diuersi quaterni in .j. sacco interius Cistam sub sigillo Thome Donfflete*; (line 3) *Item in aliis Cistis .iij. Missalibus .iiij. portiforibus .ij. gradalibus .j. Bibla . . . etc.* (see note 35 for further discussion of the question of whether fol. 15r records actual delivery to Mortimer or merely records books in stock).

Other readers of interest include Isabella's four Ladies at that time, all members of the Clare family, three of them widows of the Contrariants Bartholomew de Badlesmere, Roger D'Amory and Maurice Berkeley, and the fourth the widow of Piers Gaveston.[4] Two of them – Elizabeth de Burgh, later Countess of Ulster, and her sister Margaret, Countess of Cornwall – were co-heiresses with their sister Eleanor, wife of Hugh Despenser Junior, to the estates of their brother Gilbert de Clare, Earl of Gloucester (killed at Bannockburn in 1314). Quarreling over those estates between Despenser and their husbands was a major cause of the 1321–22 Contrariant uprising that widowed them.

A fellow Contrariant with Badlesmere, Berkeley, and D'Amory was Roger Mortimer of Wigmore,[5] who had surrendered in January 1322, before the Battle of Boroughbridge, on the promise of amnesty – but once in custody he was sentenced to death, which was then commuted to life imprisonment in the Tower of London. D'Amory and Badlesmere, captured at Boroughbridge in March, were executed soon afterwards; Maurice Berkeley was imprisoned in Wallingford Castle, from which he almost escaped in 1323, but where he died in 1326. Mortimer fared better: in 1323 he drugged his jailers, escaped from the Tower, and fled to France, where he was allowed to live with the tacit approval of the King of France, a source of rage and fear to England's Edward II and his favorites the Despensers, who in 1322–26 effectively governed England, grasping after the lands and properties of many Contrariants, and particularly oppressing the widows of D'Amory, Badlesmere and Berkeley – all, as remarked above, members of the Clare family.[6] But by early November 1326, Isabella and Mortimer had captured Edward and summarily executed the Despensers as well as Edmund, Earl of Arundel.[7] This done, they returned to London and gathered their followers into a court of friends and favorites – including not only the three Contrariant widows but the Countess of Cornwall, a fourth Clare widow and heiress – whose chambers (as Fleet's account roll shows) they lavishly supplied with clothes, furnishings and books from the Privy Wardrobe's stores.

---

[4] In her Appendix 9 (p. 169), a table of romances and other books listed by Fleet, and of the persons to whom these were delivered, Vale does not mention two of these women (Isabella de Clare, Lady Berkeley, and Margaret (Clare) de Dumville, Lady Badlesmere); nor does she identify as sisters the two women she does mention – Lady Elizabeth de Burgh and Margaret, Countess of Cornwall. She notes delivery of books and romances to Elizabeth de Burgh; Margaret Countess of Cornwall; Roger Mortimer; John Bohun, Earl of Hereford; Sir Nicholas de Stapleton; John Montgomery; William de Langley; Roger de Swinerton; and Queen Isabella.

[5] See May McKisack, *The Fourteenth Century* (Oxford, 1959) pp. 71–104; some corrections are in R.M. Haines, *Archbishop John Stratford* (Toronto, 1986), 156–213.

[6] Michael Altschul, *A Baronial Family in Medieval England: The Clares, 1217–1314* (Baltimore, 1965), pp. 172–4; also, Jennifer C. Ward, "Elizabeth de Burgh, Lady of Clare (d. 1360)," in Caroline Barron, *Medieval London Widows, 1300–1500* (London, 1994), 29–45; G.W. Watson, "Alice de la Marche, Countess of Gloucester and Hertford, First Wife of Gilbert de Clare, Earl of Gloucester," *Genealogist*, n.s. 38, 169–72; and Clare Æmilia Musgrave, *Household Administration in the Fourteenth Century, with Special Reference to the Household of Elizabeth de Burgh, Lady of Clare*, cited in Kate Mertes, *The English Noble Household, 1250–1600* (Oxford: Basil Blackwell, 1988), p. 220.

[7] Haines, *Archbishop John Stratford*, 164–88.

It is on what we may learn from Fleet's book-inventories and lists of book-deliveries to some of these new courtiers, that our discussion will now focus. Though Fleet usually does not note the titles of books given out, he does show that from January through March 1327 each great lady called to court, and some gentlemen, received and sealed indentures for "romances," chamber furnishings, dining apparatus, liturgical books and gear for chaplains, apparel, saddles and horse-trappings, and the like.

Fleet names (fols. 13v, 14v) as receiving books in early 1327 the four great ladies of the Queen. *Elizabeth (Clare) de Burgh* (1295–1360), granddaughter of Edward I and widow successively of John de Burgh, Theobald de Verdun, and Roger D'Amory, on 20 February 1327[8] received one Missal, three books of surgery, and *four books of Romance (De libr' de Romanc'.iiij.)* – titles not given. Elizabeth's sister and co-heiress *Margaret (Clare), Countess of Cornwall* (1292–1342), widow of Piers Gaveston and wife of Hugh Audley, on 3 March 1327 was given a Missal, two Breviaries, an Ordinal, two Graduals, two Tropers, one Psalter, one "book" of unspecified kind, and *four Romances (De libris .j. De Romaunc' .iiij.)* – titles also not given.[9] On 4 March 1327, the older half-sister of Elizabeth and Margaret, *Lady Isabella (Clare) Berkeley* (1263–1333), widow of Maurice Berkeley, received similar liturgical books and *six Romances (De Romaunc' .vj.)*. The fourth great lady, *Margaret (Clare) D'Umfreville Badlesmere* (1287–1333), was a cousin of the others, daughter of their father's younger brother – and widow successively of Gilbert D'Umfreville (d. 1303) and Bartholomew de Badlesmere (executed 1322). She had been imprisoned in the Tower from April to November 1322, cloistered with Minorite nuns until July 1324, and allowed to live with friends from then until Isabella called her to court.[10] There, on 22 March 1327, she received her furnishings, including *two romances (De Romanciis .ij., vnde diuersitat' coop'te' & colores omnium predictorum plenius notificant' in indentura prenotata)* – titles not given. Fleet mentions also (fol. 15v, lines 1–9) that the *damsels at court* were given furnishings, liturgical items, and *one Psalter, one Psalter partly in French, and four books of Romance*.[11]

This evidence (to reiterate) does not tell *what* books they received, but it does tell us that in February and March 1327, each lady called to court with Isabella and Mortimer was given books of *Romance*,[12] chamber furnishings, and liturgical books

---

8 Precept to deliver books and furnishings 13 December 1326; delivery to her attorney Robert de Lodelowe, goldsmith, 20 February 1327.

9 On 3 March she was represented by her "valets" John Plompton and William Wallingford; on 6 March by her attorney Laurence de la Welde, Canon of Tonbridge.

10 One reason she was treated severely was that during the Contrariant uprising she had refused Isabella admission to Leeds Castle (of which Margaret's husband Badlesmere was keeper). For her younger brother Master Richard de Clare and his links to Magister John Walweyn see note 23, below.

11 Fleet does not name the 1327 damsels; Queen Isabella's damsels of 1311–13 (and some of their page-boys) are named, but no books mentioned, in the *Household Book of Queen Isabella*, pp. xiii, 173, etc.

12 "Romance" being ambiguous, we cannot be sure (without their titles) just what sorts of books were given. On fol. 27v, listing books given Isabella in March 1327, Fleet uses Latin

and gear for her chaplains. Since three were Contrariant widows, the fourth
(Margaret Clare) widow of Piers Gaveston and wife of Hugh Audley, and all were
victims of Despenser maltreatment, their being brought to court both affirmed the
justice of the Contrariant cause and showed mercy to its victims – but also showed
that the great Clare inheritance, and the marriages of its widowed heiresses, were
tightly within the grasp of Isabella and Mortimer.

One set of romance-readers, then, are great ladies of wealth and noble blood,
caught in the political upheavals and violence of the age – much, one is tempted to
say, like Chaucer's widow Criseyde when Pandarus comes into her parlor and finds
her, among a circle of Trojan princesses and noblewomen, listening to a damsel read
the *Romance of Thebes*. Interestingly, though in 1327 Isabella, Lady Berkeley was
about sixty-four, the other three ladies were near Queen Isabella's age: Elizabeth de
Burgh about thirty-two, her sister Margaret about thirty-five, their cousin Margaret
Lady Badlesmere about forty. If the romances they read taught the doctrine of *amour
courtois*, they were by no means past putting it in practice.

But Fleet's accounts show that romance-reading was not so neatly gendered. On
28 January 1327 – just before the coronation of Edward III – Sir Thomas Wake of
Liddell was given by the King garments with the arms of Lancaster, furred with
miniver, and *three romances, two covered in white leather, the third in red leather* –
as well as (on 4 February 1327) the dosser with special embroidering which was
under the King's feet at his coronation (fol. 26v). Wake of Liddell was a very
important Lancastrian baron, obviously being given special favors by Isabella and
Mortimer in 1327, though the next year he would back Henry of Lancaster's abortive
rebellion against them. On 4 March 1327, another magnate, John de Bohun, Earl of
Hereford (son of a Contrariant killed at Boroughbridge), received chamber furnishings, liturgical vestments and books (two Missals, two Breviaries, two Epistolaries,
two Psalters, one Antiphoner, three Graduals, two Tropers, one Collects, two Prim-
ers, one Orisons, one Canon for Mass, one Psalter in French), *and* certain secular
books: *one Brut in Latin together with a Testament of King Henry, and one Romance*. It is worth note that the Earl's *Brut* was in Latin not French or English – and
that he seems to have returned it, for it turns up later in Fleet's accounts, still
accompanied by the *Testament of King Henry* (fol. 20r col. 1, fol. 32r col. 2).

Other noblemen were also given romances. Delivery was made on 14 March
1327, to two men serving as executors of the testament of Thomas, Earl of Lancaster,
of the usual chamber-furnishings and clothing – and of *three books of romances and
one Bestiary*. About April 1327, Sir John Montgomery was given items (for both

romancia or its French equivalents *roma(u)nc(i)e/roma(u)nz* to refer not only to *Reynard the
Fox* and *Méraugis et Sado* – books we would call "romances" – but also to a *History of the
Normans* and Vegetius's *On Military Matters*. For the last, Fleet's phrasing *tercius lib[er]
Romancie* might mean "a third book, a romance," or "a third book in French"; however,
when he adds that the book has a Latin title on its cover (*ext[erius] int[itulatus] de arte
Milicie*), we infer it is "*in* Romance" – a French translation. Sometimes Fleet uses *in gallico*
or (*in parte*) *romancie* to clarify that a text usually in Latin is here in French: fol. 3v, *De
psalteriis in gallico .j.*, "Of Psalters in French, one"; fol. 6v, *De psalteriis j.*, presumably "Of
psalters (in Latin), one," but in the following line *De psalter[iis] in p[ar]te romanc[ie] .j.* –
"Of psalters partly in French, one."

men and horses) to be used in tournaments or court entertainment (hastiludes), but he also received (then or on 28 February 1327) *two romances and one book of Registers* (fol. 23v): could he have used those romances in choosing names, costumes or disguises for persons taking part in those hastiludes? Another knight who received *four books of romances* (possibly in 1325, however) was Sir Roger Swinerton.[13] These facts show that *some* military men were given romances along with their gear and furnishings, though many knights received only military gear and liturgical books. Of the six named, each got on the average two romances, whereas the noblewomen averaged four.

But what of that other estate, the clergy, in these accounts? They are abundantly present, both small and great – bishops given legal and theological items,[14] valets and chaplains receiving furnishings and books for their courtly patrons: the Countess of Cornwall's items were received by her attorney Laurence de la Welde, Canon of Tonbridge;[15] Isabella, Lady Berkeley's romances by her chaplain and valet Baldwin

Portraits of some of these courtiers are found in

[13] ^Christ Church Oxford MS 92, a magnificently illuminated "mirror for princes" compiled by Walter de Milemete in 1326–27 for presentation to Edward III (*The Treatise of Walter de Milemete*, facsimile edition by M.R. James, Roxburghe Club vol. 162 (Oxford, 1913); see *Catalogue of Additions to the Manuscripts in the British Library, 1951–55, Part I*, pp. 51–3), contains portraits of some of the courtiers then receiving furnishings and romances. Painted in full armor, they are identifiable from coats or shields: Roger Mortimer of Wigmore on fol. 1v, Sir Thomas Wake of Liddell and the Earl of Hereford on fol. 60v, as described by James (xxx–xxxi): "Picture in text (Of the King's wars, etc.). The King crowned and armed on horseback in the midst of a group of eight men, six of whom are knights, the remaining two civilians in close caps, whom the King addresses. In the initial, the Holy Face. At bottom, a combat of two pairs of knights: a lady in a tower on left." Since the text advises the King at war to be prudent as well as valiant, the picture is meant to show him with his valiant knights going to war, but consulting even as he rides with two wise counsellors. On fol. 10r the manuscript's compiler, Walter de Milemete, addressing the young Edward III, says that by God's providence the King is literate and has been instructed by Milemete in literary and legal knowledge (*ueraciter credo ex dei prouidencia estis litterati & michi scientiis litteratibus & legalibus instructi*, fol. 10r). Milemete is doing for Edward III what Hoccleve, with the *Regement of Princes*, later did for Henry V: presenting to the King a "mirror."

[14] Brief mention may here be made of greater clerics given (or giving) theological, legal or liturgical books. On 27 November 1326, *John de Stratford*, Bishop of Winchester, delivered 11 legal tomes (taken from the captured king's retinue?), of which some reappear in Fleet's later inventories. *Alexander Bicknor*, Archbishop of Dublin, on 16 March 1327, received 12 diverse quires, 32 books of Holy Church, and one roll of charters (fol. 15v); for Bicknor, see J.F. Lydon, "The Enrolled Account of Alexander Bicknor, Treasurer of Ireland 1308–14," *Analecta Hibernica* 30 (1982), 9–46, and Haines, *Archbishop John Stratford*, pp. 150, 154, 168, 174, 186. *Adam Orleton*, a Mortimer associate, Bishop of Hereford 1317–27 and Treasurer of England briefly in 1327, received (fol. 25v, 10 December 1326) at Kenilworth, where he was persuading Edward II to abdicate, certain items – no books, however. (For Orleton's career, see R.M. Haines, *Church and Politics in Fourteenth-Century England* (Cambridge, 1978), and his *Archbishop John Stratford*.) Other clerics include *Walter de Islep*, Clerk of the Great Seal (fol. 21v, 25 March 1327), given numerous law books but no romances; and *Walter of London*, cleric and Almsman of the King, given items for alms distribution but no books (fol. 20v, 28 February 1329). London was Piers Gaveston's chaplain in 1308 (J.S. Hamilton, *Piers Gaveston, Earl of Cornwall 1308–1312* (Detroit, 1988), p. 149); twenty years later he is still at court, handing out alms as chaplain to the son of Edward II.

[15] Her attorney, like Mortimer's Walter Lingaigne, is an Austin Canon; such canons are

de Hengham and Adam de Odington; the liveries to Roger Mortimer of Wigmore on 28 February 1327 (fol. 14v) by Walter de Evesham, *clericus*, and Walter de Lingaigne, Canon of Wigmore Abbey, Mortimer familiars handling domestic gear and books.[16] The *clericus* Walter de Evesham had been Mortimer's "Chaplain and Almsman" before the Contrariant uprising, and after Mortimer's surrender in January 1322 Evesham accompanied Joan Mortimer and their children to Southampton. When the daughters were sent to nunneries and Joan remanded to Ludlow Castle, Walter continued in her service as Almsman. After Mortimer escaped from the Tower in August 1323 and fled to France, King Edward suspected that his followers were hatching invasion plots, and early in 1324 sent an inquisition-team to Ludlow to look into rumors that local people were supplying Mortimer with money for these. They summoned (among others) Walter de Evesham – who (of course) swore *he* knew nothing of such things.[17]

The shadowy presence in Fleet's accounts of such clerics hardly shows how important they surely were in book-matters. They handled administrative and familial business and correspondence, and sometimes copied books for their patrons – an activity which highlights the way Fleet's inventories categorize books and quires and *peciæ* as bound or unbound: for instance (fol. 15r), *.xxiij. libr' de Romanciis paruis & magnis ligatis in bordis*, and *.xj. peciis de Romanciis in quaternis ligatis & non ligatis*. It has been asserted that in the 1320s the Privy Wardrobe was primarily a storehouse, rather than a place where books were actually copied or made, but the fact that Fleet registers many instances of texts being in the form of *peciæ* suggests that readers might borrow "instalments," or borrow a given romance in the form of several *peciæ*. Moreover, there was no impermeable wall between the Great Wardrobe and the Privy Wardrobe: as the list of books delivered to Isabella shows (fol.

satirized for gladly serving ladies in *L'ordre de Bel Ayse* (Isabel Aspin, ed., *Anglo-Norman Political Songs* (Oxford: Blackwell, 1953), pp. 130–42, lines 115–16).

[16] In December 1325, during Mortimer's exile in France, the Despensers brought many of his possessions to the Tower (Fleet, fol. 3v) – and the man who delivered them was *Walter de Lodelowe, Canon of Wigmore*, perhaps from the Ludlows of Stokesay, possible patrons to the scribe of BL MS Harley 2253. Notably, a Canon of Wigmore named Walter de Lodelowe had earlier obtained for Wigmore Abbey (from its owner, John Purcell) the fine copy of *Ancrene Wisse* that is now CCCC 402. The Lingen family had close ties to Wigmore Abbey and the Mortimers: see E.J. Dobson, *The Origins of Ancrene Wisse* (Oxford, 1976), esp. Chapter VI, "Brian of Lingen," and Appendix III, "The Lingen Family," and (for corrections) Bella Millett, "The Origins of *Ancrene Wisse*: New Answers, New Questions," *Medium Aevum* LXI.2 (1992), pp. 206–228. In 1327 the family head was Sir John de Lingaigne (IV), born c. 1284, knighted 1306, tenant both of the Mortimers of Wigmore and the Mortimers of Richard's Castle; his wife Agnes was of Richard's Castle (perhaps the *Annote* of the Harley Lyrics), and he perhaps elder brother to Canon Walter de Lingaigne.

[17] London, PRO JUST 1/1389, 7 January 1324. Walter may have belonged to a family which included several clerics surnamed *de Evesham*: Thomas, in 1341, was named Master of the Rolls; his brother John, a Chancery clerk, in 1328 was presented by Roger Mortimer of Wigmore to Ludlow, remaining its Rector into the 1360s; and Reginald de Evesham appears in Fleet's accounts in 1326, attorning for Bishop Adam Orleton. (Documentation for these assertions is found in the Calendars of Close and Patent Rolls, Inquisitions Post Mortem, and the episcopal registers of bishops of Hereford, 1317–1360s, and of Archbishop Simon Langham.)

27v), the first four "diverse Romances" apparently came from the Privy Wardrobe, while the remaining five were delivered at the Queen's precept by Thomas Usfleet, Clerk of the Great Wardrobe.

The suggestion here is not that chaplains or canons were sitting in the Tower copying the *peciæ*, merely that if they borrowed such segments for their patrons, it would not be surprising if, before returning them, they copied some of them in quick cursive for later familial or personal reading. Isabella had her own scribes and illuminators;[18] so did Elizabeth de Burgh and Edward III.[19] It is noteworthy, however, that the texts held in the Tower were in such varied format and borrowed in that format.

To return to book-borrowers: besides familial chaplains and canons, there were the greater clerics, one being the noted bibliophile, tutor and confidant of Prince Edward (and later co-conspirator with him in overthrowing Mortimer), and future Bishop of Durham *Richard Bury*, who received (in 1328) various liturgical volumes and *six diverse books*.[20] (One would like to know which books Bury selected, but Fleet does not tell us.) Another interesting cleric was *Magister John Walweyn*, who sometime in 1328–29 received (fol. 18v)[21] two books: the *Romance de Achilles* and *De propheciis Sibille sapientis*. His interest is threefold: his close associations with the Mortimer court and Mortimer himself; the two books he borrowed; and his possible authorship of the *Vita Edwardi Secundi*, which was written – so Noel Denholm-Young has argued – by a *Magister* John Walweyn.[22] Denholm-Young noted that two contemporaries of this name (whom he calls *John I* and *John II*) had very similar careers; there was also, it seems, a third. The "Master John Walweyn" of Fleet's roll appears there after 1326, the year John I died – so he cannot be John I. And since John I is Denholm-Young's choice for author of the *Vita Edwardi Secundi*, Fleet's John II (or III?) seemingly could *not* have written it. Yet Denholm-Young's argument – that since the *Vita* breaks off in 1326, the year John I died, it cannot have been written by John II (Denholm-Young seems not to have known of a John III) – is by no means compelling. Given that Johns II and III share many other authorship-qualifications of John I, and surely were closely related to and perhaps inherited much of John I's lands and goods, one of them could be the author, or the redactor, of

---

[18] For book-production in Isabella's own household in the last year of her life (1357–58) see Edward A. Bond, *Archæologia* 35 (1853), pp. 453–60. *Elizde Burghs household in n. Cabovey+*

[19] See note 13 above. *Edw III in note 13, Elizde Burghs household in n. Cabovey+ Frances Underhill et al.*

[20] See N. Denholm-Young's essay, "Richard de Bury (1287–1345) and the *Liber Episto-laris*," in his *Collected Papers* (Cardiff, 1969), 1–41, and C.R. Cheney, "Richard de Bury, Borrower of Books," *Speculum* (1973), 325–8.

[21] Other items on fol. 18v are dated 4 November 1328 and 28 February 1329. The *Calendar of Memoranda Rolls (Exchequer) Preserved in the Public Record Office* (London: HMSO, 1968), p. 373, shows that in 1328 the King's livery for his Christmas feast included items for *Magister John Waweyn*, while the *Foedera* record (II, ii, 764) that on 6 May 1329, the King went to France with a retinue including *John Walwayn, clericus*. In the Mortimer-controlled court of those years, Walweyn perhaps was "his" man.

[22] Noel Denholm-Young, *Vita Edwardi Secundi* (London, 1957), pp. xix–xxviii; and *English Historical Review* (1956), pp. 189–211. For *John III*, see Joyce Horn, *Fasti Ecclesiae Anglicanae, 1300–1541, vol. II, Hereford Diocese*, pp. 15, 50.

the *Vita Edwardi Secundi*. Perhaps, indeed, Mortimer brought Walweyn to court not only as lawyer and diplomat, but as chronicler.[23]

As for the two books Walweyn borrowed, *De Achilles* hints at an interest in a conquering heroic figure who was by no means treated favorably in medieval romance (see, for instance, the account of his victim Hector in the "Nine Worthies" set pieces of such works as the *Parliament of Three Ages*). His other choice, *De propheciis Sibille sapientis*, shows interest in the succession of Holy Roman Emperors – a matter that played a considerable part in the machinations of Edward III in the early part of the Hundred Years War – and more generally an interest in prophecy, an area on which we may cite the work in recent years of Scattergood, Phillips, Smallwood and Hamilton.[24]

We turn finally to those book-borrowers of greatest interest, Isabella and Mortimer. Luckily, Fleet records the names of all nine books borrowed by Isabella, whose first choice was the *Roman de Renart* – a text with striking parallels to the 1322–27 domestic and political upheavals in France and England. Most dangerously, the seduction by Renart of Isengrim's wife Hersent, his later rape of her, and his trial at the King's Court for this – all given great play in several branches of the *Roman de Renart* – would evoke in any readers during the spring of 1327 memories of Edward's cuckolding by Isabella and Mortimer. D.D.R. Owen suggests[25] that whereas the "chief audience for the epic . . . was the nobility in their castles," and that of the "romance proper" was "the more refined society of the courts," for the *Roman de Renart* we should "look first of all to the expanding class of the bourgeoisie" – but Fleet's evidence shows that *Renart* was read by at least one French princess and queen of England, Isabella. Owen also points out that *Renart* was turned to some very specific political purposes. The warrior/diplomat Philippe de Novare, for instance, included in his prose *Mémoires* of the mid-thirteenth century a verse "branch" of his own composition, in which Philippe satirized his fellow participants in the power struggles of Cyprus and the Middle East, "using the names

---

[23] The Master John Walweyn in Fleet's accounts has ties not only to Roger Mortimer of Wigmore (note 21 above), but to the Clares and Bartholomew de Badlesmere: BL MS Egerton Roll 8724, part of a 1330s inventory of Mortimer's muniments in the Tower of London, records a charter by which *Richard de Clare, clericus*, gives to Bartholomew de Badlesmere and his wife Margaret the manor of *Pleshey* in Hertfordshire, and also the accompanying quitclaim and remission by *John Walewayn, clericus*, to *Magister Ricardus de Clare* of all Walewayn's right in that manor. Master Richard was brother to Margaret de Clare, wife of Bartholomew Badlesmere.

[24] For the *Prophecy of the Tenth Sibyl* see H.L.D. Ward, *Catalogue of Romances in the Department of Manuscripts in the British Museum*, vol. I (London, 1883), 190–95. On prophetic texts and their uses, see T.M. Smallwood, "The Prophecy of the Six Kings," *Speculum* 60.3 (1985), 571–92; Bernard Hamilton, "Prester John and the Three Kings of Cologne," in H. Mayr-Harting and R.I. Moore, *Studies in Medieval History Presented to R.H.C. Davis* (London, 1985), 177–91; J.R.S. Phillips, "Edward II and the Prophets," in W.O. Ormrod, *England in the Fourteenth Century* (Woodbridge, 1987), 189–201; and V.J. Scattergood, "Adam Davy's Dreams and Edward II," *Archiv für das Studium der Neueren Sprachen und Literaturen*, 206 (1970), 253–70.

[25] D.D.R. Owen, *The Romance of Reynard the Fox* (Oxford University Press, 1994), p. xi; subsequent quotations come from pages xii, xv, xvii–xviii.

of Reynard and his associates as pseudonyms for his fellow participants in the bitter hostilities." In the 1260s Rutebeuf's *Renart le Bestourné* attacked the friars; later, the *Couronnement de Renart* and *Renart le Nouvel* (c. 1289) and the early four-teenth-century *Renart le Contrefait* attacked courtly, clerical, and secular vice and hypocrisy by using the *Renart* framework and characters. Certain branches of the poem (XII, VII, XI) even before 1200 had (Owen remarks) been turned to "particu-lar" satire. Since redactors of *Renart* had done this for more than a hundred years, and were still doing it not long before Isabella borrowed some version of *Renart* to read, we cannot doubt that in 1327 readers would be "seeing" applications of the long beast-epic's situations, characters, and events to the current scene.[26]

Isabella's second choice was Raoul de Houdenc's *Le Roman de Méraugis de Portlesguez* (ed. M. Friedwagner, Halle, 1897), one of a group of romances de-scribed by Kathryn Gravdal as "Byzantine romances" (others include *Guillaume de Palerne* and Hue de Rotelande's *Ipomédon*) which "often incorporate trickster-like heroes," and yet "manage to remain within the boundaries of respectable romance, never seeming to transgress romance codes."[27] Méraugis is "a trickster knight in an extended tale of successive disguises" who "dons the mask of fool to gain admis-sion to his ladylove" and "plays a transvestite scene in which he successfully parades as a coy courtly lady." Gravdal discusses these as transgressive parody, mediating between folk material and chivalric romance; *Le Roman de Renart* and Douin de Lavesne's *Trubert* are central texts in this account. Not that Isabella had a predilection for romances of the "Byzantine" group: she surely knew the whole range of "romances."[28] We are viewing one snapshot of her tastes – books borrowed just after she and Mortimer had taken the reins in the English court.

As for Isabella's other books, the "History of the Normans" is identified by Juliet Vale as perhaps Wace's *Le Roman de Rou* (heavy on military combat), and her fourth book was a French translation of Vegetius's *On the Art of War* – practical reading, since Isabella in 1326 had taken a vigorous part in the invasion of England, over-throw of the king her husband, and execution of the hated Despensers, and against the Lancastrians in 1328 would clothe herself in armor and ride all night.[29] On the other hand, Isabella was much interested in the story of Perceval and the Holy Grail: her booklist here includes the *Romance of Perceval* (in her last year of life she had her scribes produce a manuscript of the *Holy Grail*), as well as *a French translation of the Old Testament*. I cannot identify three items on her list: *Les p[ro]loges de*

---

[26] *Renart* repeatedly in its various branches exposes the duplicity, corruption, and folly of courts and courtiers, as well as the clergy and peasantry of France and England.

[27] *Vilain and Courtois* (University of Nebraska Press, 1989), p. 121, notes pp. 168–9. Gravdal cites, for a discussion of the "Byzantine genre," Paul Zumthor, *Histoire littéraire de la France médiévale* (Paris, 1954), pp. 122 and 150.

[28] When she died in 1358 Isabella owned many romances, "some of the Charlemagne cycle, some of the Trojan war, a few belonging to the Arthurian group": T.F. Tout, *Chapters in Medieval Administrative History* (Manchester, 1920–33), V. 249.

[29] This is recorded in a continuation of the *Brut* chronicle cited by R.M. Haines, *Archbishop John Stratford*, p. 203.

[30] Could we possibly read this as *Les p[rivi]leges de gales* – perhaps a description of the Marcher barons' customs and the special rules that distinguished their feudal relations?

gales,[30] *De Heremit'* etc., and *Le Romans de guy & guerri.* Vale suggests that this last may have been a pairing of *Guy of Warwick* and *Fouke le Fitz Waryn* – and if the latter was indeed in the Tower and borrowed by Isabella in March 1327, we are not far from the scribe of MS Harley 2253, who left (in BL MS Royal 12.C.xii) the only remaining redaction of the romance of Fulk FitzWarin.[31]

The range of Isabella's reading is wide indeed: satiric moral and political humor in *Reynard the Fox*, exotic scenarios in *Méraugis et Sado*, moral tales in the Old Testament, heroic battles in the *Roman de Rou*, and practical military arts in *De Re Militari*. Yet one book found among Isabella's effects after her death, the *Trésor* of Brunetto Latini,[32] suggests a still wider dimension to her mind and interests. This being a small encyclopedia, she may have wanted it for any or all of its manifold contents. But in spring 1327, when the Privy Wardrobe contained a copy of the *Trésor* accessible to though not listed as borrowed by her, it had a political dimension which might especially have interested her. Jeremy Catto has recently shown such interest in the *Trésor* by Andrew Horn, a Londoner who "became prominent in the city about 1300, and, as chamberlain from 1320 to his death in 1328 . . . belonged to the administrative or judicial rather than the aldermanic world of London."[33] Catto notes that Latini "presented his scheme of knowledge as leading up to the science of politics, on which other branches of knowledge were to depend," and that (about when Isabella was borrowing books from the Tower) Horn copied extracts from the *Trésor*'s third book "on the conduct of a podestà in an Italian city, edited for the guidance of a mayor of London," as "a mirror both for princes and for communities." Close attention to current political situations was not new to her: in 1313, she had had her scribes copy the *Ordinances* imposed by the barons on her husband.[34] Surely, then, Isabella's 1327 book-selections reflect an alert intelligence keenly interested in a wide range of stories and ideas, literary modes and political and military matters.

We turn, finally, to Roger Mortimer's books. Fleet mentions (fols. 3rv, 4rv) *three romances* which were possibly Mortimer's before 1325, and lists a plethora of books which may have been delivered to him in February 1327 (fols. 14v, last 11 lines, 15r, lines 2–13).[35] If Isabella's interests were wide, what shall we say of Mortimer's? It

---

[31] E.J. Hathaway, P.T. Ricketts, C.A. Robson, Alan Wilshere, *Fouke le Fitz Waryn*, Anglo-Norman Text Society nos. 26–8 (Oxford, 1975), pp. xxxvii–lii; and C. Revard, "*Gilote et Johane*: an Interlude in BL MS Harley 2253," *Studies in Philology* 79.2 (1982), pp. 122–46 (a revised account, using later discoveries, is in progress).

[32] Cited by Vale, *Edward III and Chivalry*, p. 49 and notes 112–15, p. 128.

[33] Jeremy Catto, "Andrew Horn: Law and History in fourteenth-century England," in R.H.C. Davis and J.M. Wallace-Hadrill, *The Writing of History in the Middle Ages: Essays Presented to Sir Richard Southern* (Oxford, 1981), 367–91.

[34] F.D. Blackley and G. Hermansen, *The Household Book of Queen Isabella of England* (Edmonton, Alberta: University Press, 1971), pp. xxiv, 115–16.

[35] This may be only Fleet's inventory of books in stock just then. It seems unlikely that so many and such varied books should be handed over to Mortimer; but as mentioned above (note 3), in 1325 many of Mortimer's goods – of which three items were "diverse romances" – had been confiscated and delivered by the Abbot of Wigmore to the Tower. Is it possible that in February 1327 Mortimer was reclaiming some of his own things? Another point: the *three*

looks – *if* these books were actually handed over to him – as if he had borrowed a very large share of all Fleet's books: *66 books in one chest along with various quires* (which may be in that sack within the chest, under the seal of Thomas Dunfflete); many religious and liturgical volumes – a *Legenda Sanctorum* in Latin, a Bible in French, the *Epistles of Paul*. And instead of the four or six books of Romances borrowed by the ladies and noblemen, we see *23 books of romances small and large, bound in boards*, as well as *11 peciae of Romances, in quires bound and unbound*. This could only have been a borrowing not for one person but for a romance-reading group, whether in bowers or (as spring and summer came) in gardens, or in pavilions such as those Fleet's inventory lists a little lower on the same page (15r), in which some participants might sojourn during the *hastiludia* which Mortimer and Isabella would encourage in the coming year or so.[36]

Unfortunately, Fleet does not record the titles either of these twenty-three Romances or of those three delivered to the Tower in 1325. He does, however, tell us the title of one book perhaps given to Mortimer at this time: "a book containing eleven quires, unbound, *De Regimine Principum*". If Mortimer himself was a serious reader of or listener to this book, his interest would imply that in 1326–27 he was not only actively taking over a realm, he was thinking about the theory as well as the practice of government. If Isabella was perhaps looking at a book written by Dante's mentor Brunetto Latini, Florentine encyclopedist and political exile who returned to become a leader of Florentine "republican" government in the late thirteenth century, Mortimer was apparently taking from its Tower chest a book on the *Government of Princes* written by a Roman advocate of papal power over the monarchies.

What a monarch might have had in mind in reading that book (or two other "mirrors for princes" produced specifically for Edward III in 1326–27 – perhaps with encouragement from Isabella and Mortimer),[37] is imaginable if we look at a shrewd later king of England's uses of such a "mirror," as recently described by Derek Pearsall:[38] the government cleric Hoccleve, in "translating" and adding to the *Regement*, not only advanced his own financial and poetic interests, but provided for Henry V an excellent public-relations instrument. Mortimer, of course, was not a king, and even though as king he might have been no less impressive than Henry V, his few years in power were rather more like those of Henry IV or Richard III.

---

romances given to the executors of Thomas of Lancaster on 14 March 1327 correspond tantalizingly to the *three romances* included among gear of the Contrariants (Thomas of Lancaster, Roger Mortimer, Bartholomew de Badlesmere, the Earl of Hereford) delivered in 1325 to the Tower. Could those romances, rather than being Mortimer's, have been marked by heraldic or other signs as Lancaster's, and so in 1327 returned to his executors?

[36] For these see Vale, *Edward III and Chivalry*, pp. 60–61 and Appendix 12, pp. 172–4.

[37] See, above, notes 13, 19. Milemete's "Mirrors" and his claim to have instructed Edward in letters and law show a serious effort in 1326–27 to educate the new King in government both of himself and the realm. Manuscript illuminations integral with the texts of Ch. 92 and Add. 47680 display coats of arms of his knights and nobles (including Roger Mortimer of Wigmore) at court and on the battlefield, actively participating in the King's "ideal" government.

[38] "Hoccleve's *Regement of Princes*: The Poetics of Royal Self-Representation," *Speculum* 69 (1994), 386–410.

In any case, it appears that Fleet's evidence on books borrowed and – presumably – read by Mortimer and Isabella, and by the clerics, noblewomen and noblemen at court with them in 1326–30, points to a court with many readers of a wide range of texts – political, theological, legal, satiric, romantic, didactic, military, devotional, enigmatic and prophetic. The time they spent in wooing was no doubt their undoing – but they certainly read in books as well as looks, whatever folly the looking, or the booking, eventually led them into.

JOHN SHIRLEY AND THE EMULATION OF COURTLY CULTURE[1]

A. S. G. Edwards

"Courtly culture," particularly in its metropolitan manifestation in the later middle ages in England, was not the preserve uniquely of a noble class, but was available to those, like Geoffrey Chaucer, who were members of an upwardly mobile bourgeoisie.[2] The permeability of what were potential barriers of hierarchy between nobility and the merchant class has obvious implications for the literary historian of the later Middle Ages in England. In attempts to discriminate between "courtly" and "non-courtly" readership in metropolitan environments, solutions to the question of audience for particular works can prove elusive. The activities of the fifteenth-century London scribe John Shirley bring such problems into focus. The various manuscripts he copied, or with which he can be associated, reveal consciousness of a contemporary court culture, but also suggest attempts to present such a culture to an audience that had limited direct acquaintance with it. I wish to examine the kinds of new contextualizations that take place with such an apparent widening of audience outside even a loosely defined "courtly" one, in terms of text choice and forms of manuscript production.

Shirley has been defined variously as "one of England's earliest publishers,"[3] a literary agent,[4] the proprietor of a circulating library,[5] an antiquary preserving the past,[6] and most recently as "a kind of romance hero, reading and recording, setting

---

[1] I use the following Abbreviations:
IMEV: C. Brown and R.H. Robbins, *The Index of Middle English Verse* (New York: Index Society, 1943) and R.H. Robbins and J.L. Cutler, *Supplement to the Index of Middle English Verse* (Lexington, Ky: University of Kentucky Press, 1965), cited by number.
MP: *The Minor Poems of John Lydgate*, Parts 1–2, ed. H.N. MacCracken, Early English Text Society, ES 107, OS 192 (London: Oxford University Press, 1911, 1934), cited parenthetically by volume and pages.
[2] For discussion of this question see Sylvia Thrupp, *The Merchant Class of Medieval London* (Chicago: University of Chicago Press, 1948), pp. 234–87, and Rosemary Horrox, "The Urban Gentry in the Fifteenth Century," in *Towns and Townspeople in the Fifteenth Century*, ed. J.A.F. Thomson (Gloucester: Sutton, 1988), pp. 22–46.
[3] E.P. Hammond, *English Verse between Chaucer and Surrey* (Durham, NC: Duke University Press, 1927), p. 191.
[4] Derek Pearsall, *John Lydgate* (London: Routledge, 1970), pp. 74–5.
[5] A. Brusendorff, *The Chaucer Tradition* (London: Oxford University Press, 1925), pp. 216–17.
[6] R.F. Green, *Poets and Princepleasers* (Toronto: University of Toronto Press, 1980), pp. 130–33.

in order the author he transcribes."[7] Underlying all these assessments is an implicit recognition of the scale of his activities. We have from his hand several substantial collections: MSS British Library (henceforward BL) Additional 16165, Bodleian Library (henceforward Bodl.) Ashmole 59, Trinity College Cambridge R.3.20 and London Sion College MS Arc. L.40.2/E.44 (both probably originally parts of the same collection); the now fragmentary BL Harley 78 also comes from his hand. In addition, there is the proliferating number of manuscripts that seem to be derived from his collections: MSS BL Harley 2251 and 7333, Additional 29729 and Additional 34360, and Harvard English 530 are among the most substantial. Although most of these seem to have been produced within and for metropolitan circulation, at least one (no longer extant) seems to have provided the basis for a provincially produced manuscript, BL Harley 7333, done apparently by Augustinian canons in Leicestershire. In addition, there are other manuscripts or collections which may be connected to him by script and/or rubric.[8] There are also a number of other manuscripts that Shirley owned or annotated, some of which can be connected to his book-producing activities.[9]

The scale of this activity correlates with what might be termed Shirley's scribal logistics. His renting of premises in St Bartholomew's Hospital and his evident relationship with the scribe John Cok who copied a manuscript of *Piers Plowman* (together with Middle English devotional works) for him (Cambridge, Gonville & Caius MS 669*/646) indicate a level of organization which invites the assumption that Shirley had the sense of an audience of some size for his various compilations. What that audience was and what Shirley perceived its needs to be are questions that merit some exploration.

Shirley's earlier career was as secretary to Richard Beauchamp, earl of Warwick. Such a position not only gave entree of some sort to courtly circles but also to some sort of vernacular literary culture. We do not know a great deal about Beauchamp's library. He owned some vernacular books: BL MS Additional 24194, a copy of Trevisa's translation of Higden's *Polychronicon*, contains his arms; he also owned some manuscripts of prick-song[10] and a manuscript of Froissart.[11] He may also have owned the copy of Trevisa's translation of *De regimine principum* that is now Bodl.

---

[7] Seth Lerer, *Chaucer and his Readers* (Princeton: Princeton University Press, 1993), p. 130.

[8] Such as Venerable College of Rome MS A. 347 (including Lydgate's *Life of Our Lady* and *The Master of Game*) or Bodl. Rawlinson poet 32 (a copy of the *Libel of English Policy*). The hands of both of these are sufficiently close to Shirley's own to suggest that his may have provided the model for them. In addition, the rubrics in the Rawlinson manuscript seem conceived in the style of Shirley's; for a plate illustrating both script and rubric for the Rawlinson manuscript see the plate (of fol. 173) in *The Libelle of Englyshe Polycye*, ed. G. Warner (Oxford: Clarendon Press, 1926).

[9] For a recent list that does not, however, include all the manuscripts noted here, see Jeremy Griffiths, "A Manuscript Inscribed by John Shirley," *The Library*, 6th series, 14 (1992), 83–93.

[10] Andrew Wathey, "Lost Books of Polyphony in England," *Research Chronicle* 21 (1988), 11, no. 15; I owe this reference to the kindness of Dr Kathleen Scott.

[11] Bibliothèque Nationale MS f. fr. 831; see *The Lyric Poems of Jehan Froissart*, ed. R.R. MacGregor (Chapel Hill, 1975), p. 18.

Digby 233 and possibly a copy of Chaucer's *Boece*.[12] Other books may be connected with his family.[13]

Such a summary will have to stand as a contextualization of the immediate courtly book-owning circles of which Shirley would have been aware. Even in such an incomplete and cursory form it links him through his patron to the ownership and circulation of vernacular texts that were substantial both in content and form.[14] Shirley was evidently conscious not just of the ownership of such texts within courtly circles, but also of the emulative literary activity it could prompt: his earliest collection, BL MS Additional 16165, includes (fol. 245v) a virelai addressed by Beauchamp himself to his second wife, Isabella Despenser.[15] Isabella herself was a patron of Lydgate,[16] as was Beauchamp himself,[17] while his first wife, Elizabeth Berkeley, may have commissioned John Walton's translation of Boethius.[18] Elizabeth was also the daughter of Thomas, Lord Berkeley, the commissioner of a number of major vernacular translations (including Trevisa's *Polychronicon* and *De Proprietatibus Rerum*) and an evident bibliophile.[19]

Shirley's awareness of such kinds of courtly book owning is one that he seems to have tried to reflect in his own book-producing activities. For example, a number of his major prose transcriptions mirror texts that elsewhere survive in expensive, elaborate copies. Harvard English 530, a Shirley-derived manuscript, includes a political tract "The III Consideracions Right Necessarye to the God Governaunce of a Prince," also in University College, Oxford 85, a very handsome MS copied by an identified scribe, Ricardus Franciscus, and illuminated and illustrated by the Fastolf Master,[20] with whom he had other links. Franciscus copied a number of other

---

[12] See further Ralph Hanna III, "Sir Thomas Berkeley and his Patronage," *Speculum* 64 (1989), 878–916 (especially 897, 902, 911).

[13] For example, a Book of Hours and Psalter now in the Pierpont Morgan Library, New York, contains the signature of his son, Henry Beauchamp; for a description see Part I of the Dyson Perrins sale, Sotheby's, 9 December, 1958, lot 19; he also owned MS Garrett 34 (now in the Johns Hopkins Library), another psalter: see D.D. Egbert, "The 'Tewkesbury' Psalter," *Speculum* 10 (1935), 376–86. The signature "Beauchamp" occurs in Harvard Law School MS 21 (*Statuta Parliamentorum*) in a fifteenth-century hand.

[14] Beauchamp's manuscript of the *Polychronicon* was copied by the so-called Delta scribe, the copyist of a number of large and expensive manuscripts in the late fourteenth to early fifteenth centuries, including some of the *Canterbury Tales* and Gower; see A.I. Doyle and M.B. Parkes, "The Production of Copies of the *Canterbury Tales* and *Confessio Amantis* in the early fifteenth Century," in *Medieval Scribes, Manuscripts and Libraries: Essays Presented to N.R. Ker* (London: Scolar Press, 1978), pp. 163–210.

[15] "Balade made of Isabelle Countasse of Warr/ and lady despenser by Richard Beauchamp Eorlle/ of Warrewyke" (*IMEV* 1288).

[16] At her "instaunce" Lydgate is said to have translated *The Fifteen Joys of Our Lady* (*IMEV* 533; *MP* I: 260–67).

[17] Lydgate wrote *The Title and Pedigree of Henry VI* for him (*IMEV* 3808; *MP* II: 613–22).

[18] The only authority for her as the commissioner is a sixteenth-century print published in Tavistock in 1525.

[19] See the fine discussion of Thomas Berkeley in Ralph Hanna III, "Sir Thomas Berkeley and his Patronage." The inclusion of Trevisa's translation of *The Gospel of Nichodemus* in BL Additional 16165 (fols. 94–114) may also reflect Berkeley influence.

[20] For descriptions of University College Oxford 85 see J.J.G. Alexander and Elzbieta

manuscripts, some of elaborate vernacular texts, with miniatures.[21] The "Governaunce" tract also occurs in Trinity College Cambridge O.5.6, another handsome manuscript which contains a number of illustrations.[22] The University College manuscript also includes a Middle English version of the *Secreta Secretorum*, a version of which appears in Shirley's Bodl. Ashmole 59.

Both the University and Trinity manuscripts probably postdate Shirley's own. But they testify to an interest in these kinds of texts in milieux of evident affluence and prestige. They stand in obvious contrast to the forms of production of Shirley's own copies. None of Shirley's own manuscripts and virtually none of those derived from him contain any significant decoration in terms of borders, initials or illustrations. He does not seem to have envisioned the audience for his collections as one which might require texts of such elaborate – and expensive – kinds. There is a decorative hierarchy for such texts and Shirley's manuscripts always come at the bottom of it, a fact which may suggest something about his sense of the audience for them.

The same point about decorative hierarchies and their possible implications can be made about *The Master of Game*, which appears in Shirley's BL Additional MS 16165, in a copy in private hands with a inscription in Shirley's hand,[23] and in the Rome, English College MS A.347[24] which may be Shirley-related. Edward, duke of York's work has been characterized as "precisely the sort of book that would have appealed to courtiers" and one copy, BL Cotton Tiberius B.XII, which contains illustrations and partly erased coats of arms, entered the royal library.[25] Several other de luxe copies of this work survive, including Bodl. Bodley 546[26] and the Kerdeston fragment now in the possession of the duke of Gloucester in Kensington Palace.[27] Its circulation within Shirleyan book-owning circles suggests the operation of his emulative principle: the replication in modest formats of texts that elsewhere had circula-

---

Temple, *Illuminated Manuscripts in Oxford College Libraries* . . . (Oxford: Clarendon Press, 1985), no. 549; Margaret S. Blayney, *Fifteenth-Century English Translations of Alain Chartier's Traité de l'Esperance and Quadrilogue Invectif*, EETS 281 (London: Oxford University Press, 1980), pp. 39–41; M.A. Manzalaoui, ed., *Secretum Secretorum: Nine English Versions*, EETS 276 (London, 1977), pp. xxxix–xl (with plate).

[21] For the most recent listing of his manuscripts see Lisa Jefferson, "Two Fifteenth-Century Manuscripts of the Statutes of the Order of the Garter," *English Manuscript Studies* 5 (1995), 18–35, esp. p. 22. They include Pierpont Morgan MS M 126 (Gower, *Confessio Amantis*), Philadelphia, Rosenbach 439/16 (Lydgate, *Fall of Princes*).

[22] For a description see M.R. James, *The Western Manuscripts in the Library of Trinity College, Cambridge*, 4 vols. (Cambridge, 1900–04), iii, 310–11.

[23] I owe information about this copy to the kindness of Dr A.I. Doyle; I have not had an opportunity to examine it; I am much indebted to the owner for a copy of the inscription.

[24] Sometimes referred to incorrectly as "MS 1306."

[25] For a description of this manuscript (with plate) see James P. Carley, "The Royal Library as a Source for Sir Robert Cotton's Collection: A Preliminary List of Acquisitions," *British Library Journal* 18 (1992), 53–55 (p. 55).

[26] See the description and plates in O. Pächt and J.J.G. Alexander, *Illuminated Manuscripts in the Bodleian Library, 3* (Oxford: Clarendon Press, 1973), no. 923 and Plate LXXXVIII.

[27] For some account of this fragment see B. Danielsson, "The Kerdeston 'Library of Hunting and Hawking Literature' (early 15th c. fragments)," in *Et Multum et Multa: Beiträge zur Literatur, Geschichte und Kultur der Jagd Festgabe für Kurt Lindner*, herausg. Sigrid Schwenk, Gunnar Tilander, Carl A. Willemsen (Berlin: Walter de Gruyter, 1971), pp. 47–59.

tion as de luxe books, presumably to make such texts available to metropolitan, non-aristocratic, audiences.[28] Presumably, such a work was felt to be suitable for wealthy, prestigious members outside of the immediate court circle.

Similarly, Shirley's copy of the Middle English *Pilgrimage of the Life of Man* in the Sion College manuscript stands very much at the lower end of the range of surviving copies.[29] At the upper one would probably place Bodl. Laud misc. 740, copied for Sir Thomas Cumberworth, by a scribe and decorator whose services were employed elsewhere in such de luxe manuscripts as New York Public Library Spenser 19, the companion text, *The Pilgrimage of the Soul*.[30]

It would, of course, be naive and incorrect to offer a simplistic equation between levels of decoration and levels of audience. Not all books owned by members of courtly circles were expensive, nor were expensive books only owned by those in such circles. But some general correlation seems plausible.

The evidence afforded by some of Shirley's other prose texts tends to confirm this generally downmarket tendency in his copies. *The Three Kings of Cologne* occurs in a Shirley manuscript, Bodl. Ashmole 59, and a derived one, Harvard 530.[31] The work survives in Middle English in over twenty copies, most of them relatively

---

[28] The appeal of such texts for such metropolitan, non-courtly audiences is confirmed elsewhere: for example, a manuscript including *The Craft of Venery*, now in the collection of Paul Mellon, was copied by John Porter, MP c. 1450; for a description see *Bibliotheca Phillippica, Medieval Manuscripts: New Series: Third Part*, Sotheby's Sale Catalogue, 28 November, 1967, lot 107 (olim Phillipps 12086). Beinecke Library MS Wagstaff 163, which includes another copy of *The Master of Game* and other hunting texts, was possibly copied by John Whittocksmead (1410–82) also an MP; for description see Barbara E. Shailor, *Catalogue of Medieval and Renaissance Manuscripts in the Beinecke Rare Book and Manuscript Library Yale University, I* (Binghamton, New York: Medieval and Renaissance Texts and Studies, 1984), pp. 216–23. The identification of Whittocksmead comes in a review of this catalogue by A.I. Doyle in *Analytical and Enumerative Bibliography* 8 (1984), 249–54 (253).

[29] For a description see N.R. Ker, *Medieval Manuscripts in British Libraries: I: London* (Oxford: Clarendon Press, 1969), pp. 290–91.

[30] See Pächt and Alexander, *Illuminated Manuscripts in the Bodleian Library, 3*, no. 925 and Plate LXXXVIII and *The Pilgrimage of the Lyfe of the Manhode*, ed. Avril Henry, EETS 288 (Oxford: Oxford University Press, 1985), xlii–xlv; on the New York Public Library manuscript see Victor Hugo Paltsits, "The Petworth Manuscript of 'Grace Dieu' or 'The Pilgrimage of the Soul' An English Illuminated Manuscript of the Fifteenth Century," *Bulletin of the New York Public Library* 32 (1928), 715–20; and Rosemarie Potz McGerr, ed., *The Pilgrimage of the Soul: A Critical Edition of the Middle English Dream Vision* (New York: Garland, 1990), pp. lxxx–iv.

[31] A factor, at least in Shirley's mind, in the circulation of *The Three Kings of Cologne* may have been its recurrent associations with Chaucer: in addition to Ashmole 59 manuscript (which contains Chaucer lyrics) it appears elsewhere with Chaucer's works in BL Additional 36983 (with Chaucer's lyrics and various devotional and didactic works in Middle English), Magdalene College Cambridge Pepys 2006 (with Chaucer's lyrics and dream visions, together with Melibee), Stonyhurst College B.23 (with an extract from The Parson's Tale), Huntington Library HM 114 (with *Troilus & Criseyde*), and (in a Latin version) in Cotton Cleopatra D.vii (with Chaucer's lyrics). The assertion I have made elsewhere (in the Introduction to *Manuscript Pepys 2006: A Facsimile* [Norman, Okla: Pilgrim Books, 1985], p. xxii) that "the *The Three Kings of Cologne* do[es] not appear elsewhere with Chaucer texts" is notably incorrect.

[32] For a list see N.F. Blake, R.E. Lewis, A.S.G. Edwards, *An Index of Printed Middle English*

modest.[32] *The Gospel of Nichodemus*, which he also copied in BL Additional 16165, was quite popular in a variety of forms none of them especially distinguished in their manuscript presentation. For these texts there never seems to have been the range of decorative possibilities that existed for those I have just been discussing. The choices here seem to have been relatively safe unadventurous ones in which the form confirms the existing needs and resources of his audience, as well as the mode of presentation generally employed for vernacular devotional texts.

The verse sections of Shirley's collections (principally Trinity College, Cambridge MS R.3.20, BL Add. 16165, fols. 206v–257v) and Bodl. Ashmole 59, fols. 1–99v) contain almost exclusively shorter verse texts, often lyric, chiefly of the works of Chaucer and Lydgate, particularly Lydgate. In Shirley-derived manuscripts (principally BL Harley 367 and 2251, and Additional 29729 and 34360) he can be linked with occasional fairly brief narratives, such as the extracted Prioress's Tale in BL Harley 2251. It is only in BL Harley 7333, a large collection including the *Canterbury Tales*, that Shirley can be linked to any extended narrative sequence, and even here it is unclear how much of the Tales comes from him. (The recurrent annotation "nota per Shirley" breaks off in the Miller's Tale.) Such a preoccupation with lyric forms may reflect his sense of fashionable French fifteenth-century courtly lyric collections which were circulating in England and his attempt to establish an English equivalent for a different audience.[33] Such an interest in French culture is also reflected in his attempts to locate some of the verse he transcribes within cultural and courtly circles where French offers the cachet of the literary chic. He is the only authority for the information that "The Complaint of Venus" is translated from Graunson and (less compellingly) that "Fortune" is "translated out of ffrenshe." And Julia Boffey has traced his implausible efforts to graft onto the canon of the contemporary duke of Suffolk a group of French lyrics.[34]

The continuing courtly interest in French culture in the fifteenth century also finds its reflection in Shirley's prose translations from the French, demonstrated most clearly in the relationship between Cambridge University Library MS Ff.I.33, which Shirley owned, and which contains copies of *Le Secret des Secrés* and the *Livre de bonnes meurs*, and BL Additional 5467, a Shirley-derived manuscript containing direct translations from it.[35] Once again, the Additional manuscript is an extremely simple, unadorned copy. Shirley also owned another French text, BL MS Royal 20 B.xv, a version of Vegetius' *De Re Militari*. His evident preoccupation with the

---

Prose (New York: Garland, 1985), no. 290 (the Whalley manuscript noted there should be deleted).

[33] On such collections, and their circulation in England, see Julia Boffey, *Manuscripts of English Courtly Love Lyrics in the Later Middle Ages* (Cambridge: D.S. Brewer, 1985), pp. 138–40. She notes (p. 140) that "Shirley, as Beauchamp's secretary, must have known" his manuscript of Froissart's poems (on which see n. 11 above).

[34] Julia Boffey, "French Lyrics and English Manuscripts: The Transmission of Some Poems in Trinity College, Cambridge, MS R. 3. 20, and British Library MS Harley 7333," *Text* 4 (1988), 135–46.

[35] See B. Lindström, "The English Versions of Jacques Legrand's *Livre de Bonnes Meurs*," *The Library*, 6th series, 1 (1979), 247–54, especially pp. 252–53. (The Beaumont College manuscript noted there was sold at Christie's, 28 June, 1973, lot 49.)

dissemination of such works of courtly instruction is linked to his wider concern with French-derived literary models. And, once again, the unpretentiousness of the forms of the surviving translations may suggest that he envisioned an audience that was different from that for his source texts.

The manner of presentation of these collections is also significant. There survive two versified tables of contents in which Shirley enumerates the various delights that await his imagined reader, who is identified as "knight squyer or lady/ or other estat what euer they be." This reader is exhorted to

> . . . sendeth this boke to me agayne
> shirley I meane which is right fayne
> if ye ther of haue had plesaunce
> as in the reddinge of ye romance
> than am I glad by god on lyue
> as I were lord of tonnes fyue
> and so at your commaundement
> It shall bene eft when you list send
> wt all ye saruice þᵗ I can[36]

Seth Lerer has recently observed of this passage: "This is the language not of bibliographic but of knightly service . . . The rhetoric of lordship and service here aristocratizes the dynamic of scribal lordship and service – not necessarily because Shirley was working for commissioning aristocrats, but rather because Shirley constructs an aristocratic romance out of the processes of edition and transcription, reading and response" (Lerer, p. 131). The observation of the level of address and its relationship to audience is astute: such an exhortation invites the reader to share Shirley's own assertions about his audience, to assume that he is master of some sort of courtly library and that nobility was eager to read his plain booklets. It is an assumption designed for an audience that needed such reassurance, one that was possibly not all that Shirley asserted it to be.

For Shirley's versified tables of contents are related to one of the most distinctive aspects of his manuscripts: the often egregiously anecdotal rubrics which precede them, particularly for the poems by Lydgate and to a lesser degree those by Chaucer. Often these provide the main or only source for our knowledge of the occasion of these poems. The very circumstantiality of detail in some of these accounts has at times been held to lend them authority.[37] And there seems no way of directly challenging what they claim, though they may merit more scepticism than they have generally received. My more immediate concern is with the tonal and social consistency of the terms of reference they employ. Often the poems and other works he transcribes are contextualized in courtly environments. Chaucer's "Complaint to his Lady" is described thus: "here filowyng begynneþe a right lusty amerous balade made in wyse of compleynt of a right worshipfull knyght þat euer serued his lady"

---

[36] Hammond, *English Verse between Chaucer and Surrey*, p. 197, lines 81–89 (I have emended the nonsensical "weddinge" in line 84); cf. also p. 196, lines 96–100.

[37] See Brusendorff, *The Chaucer Tradition*: "[Shirley] must have been in touch with the Chaucer family through Lydgate, a fact which gives his information about the poet a special value" (p. 235).

(BL Additional 16165, fol. 190); Shirley's preface to the *Canterbury Tales* announces that it is intended for "all þos that beon gentile of birthe or of condiciouns" (BL Harley 7333, fol. 37); he provides the only authority for the royal occasion of some of Chaucer's lyrics ("This balade made Geffrey Chauciers . . . and sent it to his souerain lorde kyng Richarde the secounde" (BL Harley 7333, fol. 147v). When he turns to the more contemporary Lydgate his terms become more specific in their courtly reference: "And folowynge begynneþe a deuoute salme of þe sautier whiche Lydegate daun Johan translated at þe Chapell at Wyndesore at þe request of þe dean whyles þe kyng was at evensonge" (*MP*, I, 1); "Here begyneth verses of þe sauter whiche þat kynge Herry the V. whom god assoyle by gret devocion vsyd in his chappell at his hyȝe masses bytwene þe levacion and þe consewcracion of þe sacrament translatid by þe Monke Lydegat dan John" (*MP*, I, 209); "Here begyneth a balade whych Iohn Lydgate the Monke of Bery wrott & made at þe commaunde-ment of þe Quene Kateryn as in here sportes she wallkyd by the medowes that were late mowen in the monthe of Iulij" (*MP*, II, 809). What these and most of Shirley's other Lydgate rubrics have in common is their efforts to associate him intimately with the great and the good. Such association is not unreasonable given what we know about Lydgate's poetic career and its links to courtly circles (on which see Pearsall, *John Lydgate*). But it may be the case that Shirley is trading on Lydgate's reputation rather than reflecting it with any accuracy. Such rubrics as those I have just quoted suggest a tone of intimacy, insider information, not just between Shirley and Lydgate but extended to include the audience. The urbane nonchalance with which assertions are thrown out makes it seem churlish to wonder whether Lydgate *really* knocked off a poem at the request of the dean "whyles þe kyng was at evensonge" or whether Queen Katherine's meadows were *really* "late mowen." It may be that the truth matters less than the tonality: the establishing of a relationship of vicarious knowingness between Shirley, audience and text. In general his recurrent name-dropping seems part of a larger strategy of reminding his readers of the contexts of courtly culture out of which he would have them believe that these poems proceed. It offers his audience glimpses into the life and more importantly the literary tastes of these great and good that are directly linked to his own manuscript productions. The common element in a number of his rubrics is the stress on class, on the rank of those who (he says) commissioned these works, sometimes general as in the "great estates of þis lande" (*MP*, II, 682) who, we are told, commissioned his "Mumming at Hertford"; more often implausibly specific, as in some of the instances I have already quoted.[38]

The reason why Shirley would make such assertions may lie, once again, with the emulative nature of his manuscripts, with his attempts to replicate for a less socially defined audience the sort of things he wished to reassure them were read by the nobility. His rubrics were perhaps a form of social warranty, a guarantee that if you

---

[38] Occasionally there is a gap between Shirley's assertion and Lydgate's text: for example, the Shirley-derived manuscripts BL Harley 7333 and Harvard 530 are the ones to credit Lydgate with translating *Guy of Warwick* "at þe request of Margarite Talbot fournyval and Lisle" (*MP*, II, 516), a claim of which there is no mention in the poem itself.

were reading his texts you were not one of the "rude uplondissh people" whom (he tells us) the court chose to emulate on one literary occasion.[39]

Such apparent attempts to emulate different aspects of "courtly" books may shed a little light on the motives behind Shirley's activities and the various hypotheses that have been advanced to explain them. Certain explanations can be swiftly discounted. For example, the likelihood that Shirley's compilational motives were those of an antiquary (an argument urged by Green in *Poets and Princepleasers*) does not stand scrutiny. There is no impulse in Shirley's compilations to preserve rare records of some distant past. The greatest number of works he copies are those of a living poet, John Lydgate. The earliest datable texts Shirley copies are those of Chaucer, many of which were accessible through commercial scriptoria, with which Shirley himself evidently had links. The ways of presenting these texts do not seem so much compatible with antiquarian impulses as with attempts to present them in terms that satisfy the social and cultural curiosity of his audience.

I have always cherished the older view that Shirley's motives for his transcriptional activity were neither antiquarian nor romantic but primarily commercial. Some aspects of his book production may provide support for this view. It is clear that he intended them to circulate initially in the form of a series of smaller, separate, booklets, a form of production that Ralph Hanna has recently shown was employed in BL Additional 16165,[40] and which seems to have been the case with other of his collections. (Shirley seems to have been the earliest to employ this form of production systematically for collections of Middle English texts.) This may suggest that the motive underlying his manuscript production was a commercial one. Systematic, separate booklet production in the fifteenth century has been generally, though not invariably, linked to forms of speculative manuscript production through which the buyer could assemble a collection of such fascicles. I still think this is the most likely interpretation of Shirley's activities; but I think any view of his activities must also take account of an aspect of Shirley's character not always properly considered: he was a snob. A life of service on the fringes of the aristocracy had left him with a sense of court culture that he sought to refract on to his non-courtly audience by producing for them the sorts of works he felt were appropriate for a courtly audience, to reflect for them, in his manuscripts, a world of which they were not, in any full sense, a part.[41]

---

[39] In a mumming held "before þe kyng holding his noble feest of Cristmasse in þe Castel at Hertford" (*MP*, II, 765).

[40] Ralph Hanna III, "John Shirley and British Library MS. Additional 16165," *Studies in Bibliography* 49 (1996), 95–105. I am indebted to Professor Hanna for permitting me to read his work in advance of publication.

[41] I am much indebted for information and comment to Dr Julia Boffey, Dr Ian Doyle and Professor Felicity Riddy.

RICHARD HILL – A LONDON COMPILER

Heather Collier

Oxford, Balliol College, MS 354 was compiled by Richard Hill, an early-sixteenth-century London grocer. It is a commonplace book – an informally organised collection of material chosen according to personal taste or interest,[1] and was probably compiled over a period of about thirty years: the earliest date given in the manuscript is 1503 (written in the top margin of fol. 165), while the last entry in the Chronicle, although not actually dated, lists the names of the Mayor and Sheriffs of London that relate to the year 1536. Hill's book contains 247 separate and diverse items including 13 religious pieces in Latin, 3 French items relating to business, 12 extracts from Gower, as well as 108 Middle English poems both secular and religious, some of them unique to this manuscript; there are also 111 English prose items, ranging from veterinary recipes of a couple of lines to a London Chronicle of some 30 pages, from riddles and puzzles to a table for calculating the price of lead.[2] As such it has a wealth of information to offer us on the tastes, attitudes and experiences of an early-sixteenth-century Londoner. Hill's book is interesting because it represents the work of a compiler who is obviously outside court circles but still interested in the pageantry and ceremonial of the Lord Mayors of London, so in a sense it reflects the greatest cultural diversity imaginable.

As a sixteenth-century London grocer, Hill belonged to the middle stratum of society and his book might be said to proclaim these social origins even in format. It is a paper volume with most of its pages measuring approximately 292 x 108 mm. Although medieval manuscripts such as Hill's are often referred to as "holster books," this volume is also of a standard sixteenth-century account book size that

---

[1] G. Guddat-Figge in her *Catalogue of the Manuscripts Containing Middle English Romances* (Munich: Fink, 1976), p. 27 and A.G. Rigg in *A Glastonbury Miscellany of the Fifteenth Century* (Oxford: Oxford University Press, 1968), p. 26 describe MS Balliol 354 as the "typical" or "best" example of what a commonplace book should be.
[2] For the most thorough accounts of the manuscript, see: R. Dyboski, *Songs, Carols and Other Miscellaneous Poems from the Balliol MS 354, Richard Hill's Commonplace Book*, EETS ES 101 (1908, repr. New York: Kraus, 1981), pp. xxxiv–lix; R.A.B. Mynors, *Catalogue of the Manuscripts of Balliol College Oxford* (Oxford: Clarendon, 1963), pp. 352–54; S.J. Ogilvie-Thomson, *A Handlist of Manuscripts containing Middle English Prose in Oxford College Libraries*, The Index of Middle English Prose, Handlist 7 (Cambridge: D.S. Brewer, 1991), pp. 8–14. Quotations from the manuscript given in this paper are taken from Dyboski's edition unless otherwise stated.

could have been purchased either ready bound or as separate quires at the stationers' shops of sixteenth-century London.[3] In terms of its layout, there is something very ordinary, practical and functional about Hill's manner of presenting his texts and he obviously wasted little money on the book; his items are closely written on both sides of the paper (about 50 or 60 lines to the page) and the manuscript is undecorated.

Little interest is shown in the activities or personages of the court *per se*, but Hill includes two poems that focus on the English nobility: "The Lamentacion of the Duches of Glossester" (fols. 169v–170v) and "The Lamytacion of Quene Elyzabeth" (fols. 175r–176r) which is followed by two epitaphs, one in English and one in Latin, on the same queen. In general, Hill copied a large volume of prose material of a practical nature – medical recipes, notes on how to make harness polish or pickle herrings, tables and charts for calculating weights and measures, prices and dates, tips on gardening, checklists and handy notes on French vocabulary (useful for a grocer trading abroad). Like other Londoners of his class, Hill showed some interest in politics and pageantry, an interest which focussed not on the king and his noblemen, but on the Mayor and Aldermen of the city of London, men whose actions and decisions affected the ordinary Londoner's daily life, comfort and security: this was the power base that mattered to Hill and to others like him in whom the processions and ceremonies stirred a sense of metropolitan pride.

Nowhere is this focus on the Mayor rather than on the King more apparent than in the London Chronicle that Hill includes in his manuscript (fols. 232r–247r). The entry for each year is headed with the names of the Mayor and Sheriffs in office and then significant events are recorded. The usual method of compiling a London Chronicle was to copy an existing Chronicle with additions, omissions and alterations as dictated by personal taste, until the years covered came within one's own experience, when composition could become original.[4] The preference and prejudice of the authors are revealed in their selection and weighting of events. The Mayor is usually centre stage (Hill in his entry for 1485 puts more stress on the death of two Mayors due to "swetyng seknes" than on the death of King Richard III in battle;

---

[3] Guddat-Figge (pp. 30–36) offers a good general account of "holster books".

[4] A. Gransden, *Historical Writings in England*, vol. 2 (London: Routledge, 1982), pp. 220–48 discusses the development and the methods of compiling London chronicles. E. Kennedy, *Chronicles and other Historical Writing*, vol. 8 in *A Manual of the Writings in Middle English, 1050–1500*, ed. A.E. Hartung and J.B. Severs (Connecticut: Archon Books, 1989), p. 2845 lists 38 London chronicles surviving in manuscript and 40 in print. It has been very difficult to establish textual relations between the various chronicles because of the idiosyncratic ways in which their compilers moved between a variety of sources before beginning their original composition. The most useful attempts to sort out these relationships are: A.H. Thomas and I.D. Thornley, *The Great Chronicle of London* (London: George W. Jones, 1938), pp. 24–34 and most recently M.-R. McLaren, "The Textual Transmission of the London Chronicles," *English Manuscript Studies 1100–1700* 3 (1992), pp. 38–72. O.S. Pickering in "A London Chronicle in Yorkshire: An Addendum to Handlist VI of *The Index of Middle English Prose*," *Notes and Queries* 238 (New Series 40), pp. 305–07 suggested that a London chronicle was "typical of its genre in moving in and out of relationships with other chronicle manuscripts as it progresses."

entries for 1505, 1508, 1510, 1512, 1514, 1523, 1529, 1530, 1533 all concentrate on the Mayors and Sheriffs); considerable space is devoted to describing pageants and processions (e.g. Hill's long entry for 1536); and civic pride is also demonstrated by a preoccupation with repairs to the city and damage done (Hill notes for 1521 "newe ovyns *in* Sowthwark", for 1440 "a gret fyre at the Sterre *in* Bredstreet, & myche harme do*n*" and for 1506 "that nyght was blowen down the weder-cokk at Powles").

Tremendous interest is shown in commercial activities – the business of the Guilds (Hill notes for 1454 "This yere was the rydyng of the craft*is* layd downe, and rowed to Westmynst*er* in barges") and prices of goods (Hill for 1486 mentions the crowning of the king and the price of salt as matters of equal importance and frequently notes shortages and intervention by foreign merchants). There was considerable rivalry between the different Merchant companies to get their members elected to the top positions, for it meant that their craft had the ascendancy for the next year. Sometimes squabbles occurred, as Hill records in his chronicle for the year 1505 (fol. 235v): ". . . & this yere was a strif at Yelde-hall, for chosyng of the sheryf; for the taylors wold haue had M. Fitzwill*iam*, & the other Comens chose M. Grove, groc*er*." On occasions, the king intervened in the elections and insisted that the companies should elect his designated candidate. Hill records one such incident which occurred in 1506 and it is clear that the aldermen held out against the king's wishes as far as was possible: "Item this yere the Kynge sente down a lett*er* myssyve, th*at* M. Fitzwill*iam*, taylor, shuld be choson sheryff for the Comons/ but the Comons chase M. Johnson, goldsmyth; & th*er*fore the Kyng was gretly dysplesid; and he co*m*mandid the Comons to make a newe elecc*ion*/ & so the Comons mad a newe elecc*ion* the Xth day of Octobre and th*er* chase M. Fitzwill*iam* sheryff/ and the same M. Fitzwyll*iam* made a fest alone . . .". The final comment presumably indicates the display of disapproval shown by the aldermen boycotting the extremely popular Mayoral banquet. Hill often expresses an interest in this event, commenting on the fact that there was no banquet held to mark the inauguration in 1508 of Sir Larans Aylmer, who took over when William Brown died in office. Although the banquet was probably not held as a mark of respect, Hill seems displeased with the unusually subdued nature of the proceedings – "and he *in* a gray clok" he remarks, drawing attention to the difference between this and the "skarlet gown & clok, & a chayn of gold abowt his nekk" (entry for 1530) which he obviously expected, and he finishes the account with an expressive "No fest!" On fol. 103 he copies a list of "suche howshold stuff as must ned*is* be occupied at the mayres fest yerely kepte at the Yelde hall", so the festivities were evidently of interest to him.

During the ICLS conference John Scattergood pointed out to me that Dunbar in *A Treatice of London*, copied in Hill's manuscript on fols. 199v–200r, openly acknowledges the importance of the Mayor and the merchant classes by incorporating them in terms of fulsome praise into his description of the city. The merchants are "full of substance and myght" (line 7), "full royal to beholde" (line 34) and "Ryche . . . in substance that excellis" (line 45), while the whole of the last stanza is devoted to the Mayor:

> Thy famowse mayre, by princely gou*er*nance,
> With swerde of justice the ruleth prudently,

No lorde of Paris, Venys, or Florance,
In dignyte or honour goth hym nygh.
He is examplar, right lodester & gwy,
Pryncypall patrone & rose orygynall,
A-bove all mayres, as master most worthy.   (Lines 49–55, Dyboski, p. 102)

The occasion of that poem is itself an interesting instance of the civic authorities and the court working in conjunction. The poem was delivered as Hill notes "at Mr Shaa table when he was mayre," that was the civic banquet given to honour the Scottish ambassadors who were in England in 1501 to negotiate the marriage between James IV and Henry VII's daughter, Margaret. It is clear from the selection of material in the manuscript that the middle classes looked to this alternative court of the Mayor and his officials to provide them with colour, ritual and intrigue, and that the figures of the royal court were distant and shadowy, occasionally and momentarily of interest (1510 "Item, on Myd-somer nyght the Kyng cam prevyly to the Kyngis Hed in Chepe, in the rayme[n]t of on of his yemen of the garde, & a hawberd in his neke/ & so departid agayn after the washe.") but not the stuff of real life as they understood it.

Hill's compilation is a very useful yardstick for assessing the attitudes and preoccupations of the early-sixteenth-century middle-class Londoner, simply because of the huge amount of material he managed to copy. The interest the manuscript has for us lies not only in its representative value but in what it also reveals of Richard Hill as an individual. He gives some straightforward biographical details in his book, since on occasions it is used as a safe place for recording significant family events in much the same way as family Bibles were used. We are told in some notes (fol. 17r and fol. 176r) that Richard was born at Hillend, the family seat in Hertfordshire and was apprenticed to a London grocer, John Wyngar, who was elected Mayor in 1505 and was an influential man in the city. Richard married his employer's niece, Margaret, and they settled in London where they had seven children in nine years, five boys and two girls. The last two boys to be born, Simon and Robert, both died in infancy, while Elizabeth, their second daughter, died aged eight. The births, christenings and godparents of his children are listed in the manuscript together with details of how much was given as christening gifts – an average of 20 pence, but the priest, Master West, who was Elizabeth's godfather, only gave 8 pence, while Richard's sister Margaret gave 4 shillings and 6 pence when she was William's godmother. Hill also gives some details of his professional life (fol. 107r), such as the dates on which he was given the freedom of Antwerp and Bergham op Zoom, and how much he paid for his celebratory dinners (about 2 shillings).

As well as these facts about his life, the manuscript reveals to us glimpses of Hill's personality and attitudes. The activity of compiling may not be as direct a means of revealing one's personality as that of original composition, but like a shrewd second-hand dealer, a good compiler will select what is interesting and valuable from what is on offer and the items that he chooses will reflect something of his own tastes and interests. He will also reveal a little of his personality in the way that he handles the process of compilation, how accurately he copies, how much he adds to or subtracts from his source, or how much thought he puts into organising his material. By analysing Hill's treatment of his sources we can begin to build up a picture of the man behind the collection.

One of Richard Hill's most important sources is a printed book variously known as Richard Arnold's *Chronicle* or *The Customs of London*. It was printed first in Antwerp in 1502 by Van Berghen (STC 782) and a second edition came out in 1521, printed by Treveris in Southwark (STC 783).[5] Hill's commonplace book and Arnold's *Customs* have 33 items in common (Table 1, below). The items are scattered over some 200 pages in Arnold but are copied as units by Hill; that is, he groups together items of a similar nature such as the general household recipes (fols. 3v–5r) or the facts and figures about London (fols. 102r–106v). It is clear that Arnold's *Chronicle* acted as a source for Hill and not vice versa since the earliest date that can be assigned to Hill's manuscript is 1503 and Arnold's book first appeared in print in 1502. Such has been the conclusion of a number of scholars, but there has been no attempt to analyse either the nature of the copying or what it reveals about the process of compilation and textual transmission. For example, R.A.B. Mynors describes sections of Hill's book as "largely from Arnold" or "partly from Arnold," but he makes no attempt to be more specific as regards the nature of the copying or its context.[6] And even the most recent and most detailed description of the prose items to date, that by Ogilvie-Thomson, on occasions misconstrues the relationship between Hill's and Arnold's texts.[7]

A closer examination of the shared items reveals some interesting glimpses of Hill the compiler at work. In general Hill copies extremely accurately and closely so when he does deviate from Arnold's text it is worth trying to establish why. Sometimes there are practical reasons for such deviations. For example, the item "The Charg of euiri Ward *in* London at XV" (fol. 102) is much abbreviated in Hill. While the order of wards and the figures are identical, Hill leaves out the division into east and west side of Walbrook and does not have the two final sections, "The Particioun of the Brydg ward at a XV" and the "Fourme of the Same Particioun."

---

[5] Page references here are to the edition by F. Douce, *The Customs of London, Otherwise Known as Arnold's Chronicle* (London: Rivington, 1811), which brings together both of the original volumes and is yet to be superseded by any more recent edition. Titles of items are also from Douce and abbreviations have been given in full but indicated by italics.

[6] Mynors, pp. 352–53.

[7] Ogilvie-Thomson relied on D.C. Browning's transcript of the manuscript made in 1920. My comparison of Ogilvie-Thomson's description with the microfilm copy of the manuscript has revealed a few omissions and errors. For example, the fact that four of Hill's items also occur in Arnold's *Customs* is not noted, whereas the connection with Arnold is mentioned in reference to other shared items. Ogilvie-Thomson numbers the items as [12], [13], [14] and [17]. They are "The Charg of euiri Ward *in* London at XV" (*Customs*, p. 46); "The Ordinaunse for the Assise of Talewod and Belet in the Cyte of London by the Main and Aldirmen" (*Customs*, p. 97); "The Nombre of Parish Chirches, Townes and Bisshopriches and Sherys in Englande, and the Compasse of the Lande" (*Customs*, p. 139); and "The Fourme of Makyng of Lettres of Attorney" (*Customs*, p. 108). On two occasions the nature of the relationship between Hill's piece and Arnold's is, I believe, incorrectly described. The first of these Ogilvie-Thomson numbers as item [3]. It consists of twenty-two brief entries of a practical nature (listed as numbers 1–22 in Table 1) which she describes as "taken partly from Richard Arnold's *Chronicle of London*". In fact all twenty-two of the entries are taken from *Customs*. The second is the gardening treatise which Hill entitles "Of Graffyng" discussed below.

Table 1. The thirty-three items common to both MS Balliol 354 and Arnold's *Customs of London*

(The items are listed in the order in which they appear in MS Balliol 354.
Arnold foliation refers to the Douce edition of *Customs of London*.)

Item no.	Title	Hill fol.	Arnold fol.
1	To brewe Beer	3v	247
2	The Coestes to make Soep	3v	246
3	The Crafte to make a Watir to haue Spottis out of Wullen Cloth	3v	173
4	The Fourme and the Mesur to mete Land by	3v–4r	173
5	To make Veneger shortli if ye haue nede	4r	189
6	To make Percely to growe in an our space	4r	189
7	The mesurs of Reynysh Wyne too be bought by in Andwarpe and Dordreight, and also the mesurs and rekenyng of Wyne to be bought at Burdeux, and gawge of the same	4r	189–90
8	The Rekenyng of Wyne at Burdeux	4r	190
9	The Crafte to make Gunepoudir	4r	188
10	The Weyght of Essex Chese, and of Suffolke, in England; and the Weyght in Andwarp and in Barough	4r–v	263
11	The Costis for to make Hering and Sprottis at the Coeste	4v	263
12	To make Rede Sprottis at the Coste	4v	263
13	The maner to make Ynke	4v	238
14	To make a Pigell to kepe freshe Sturgen in	4v	189
15	The Ressaite to make Ypocras	4v–5r	187
16	Clarey	5r	187
17	The Crafte to make Ypocras and Braket and Clare	5r	187
18	For Clarre	5r	188
19	For Braket	5r	188
20	The Crafte to make Orchell	5r	188
21	The Crafte to make Corke for Diars	5r	187
22	The Weight and maner of beyng of Irne, and the difference of the Weyghtes vsed in England	5r	190–91
23	The Article conteyned in the Bull of Pope Nicholas, purchaced by the Curatis of the same cite of oblacions	5v–6v	178–9
24	The vij. Ages of the Worlde from Adam forward	101v	156–57
25	The vij. Ages of Man liuing in the World	102r	157
26	The Charg of euiri Ward in London at XV	102r–v	46–48
27	The Ordinaunce for the Assise of Talewod and Belet in the Cyte of London by the Mair and Aldirmen	103r	97–98

Item no.	Title	Hill fol.	Arnold fol.
28	The Nombre of Parish Chirches, Townes and Bisshopriches and Sherys in Englande, and ye Compasse of the Lande	103r	139–40
29	The Fourme of makyng of Lettres of Atturnay	106v–107r	108
30	The Ordinaunce for the Assise and Weight of Bred in the Cite of London	106v	49–56
31	The Craft of Graffyng and Plantinge of Trees and altering of Frutis as well in Colours as in Taste	109r–117v	164–170
32	A ballade of ye Notte-browne Mayde	210r–213v	198–203
33	The names off Balyfs, Custos, Mayers, and Sherefs of the Cite of London ...	232r–247r	xix–lii

On the other hand, Hill does have Arnold's last line, giving the total for a XV in England. The omission of the Bridge ward details is of some significance. There is no logical reason why Hill would have been any less interested in the Bridge ward than in any other area of the city; in fact he lived there in Bridge Street in 1521.

A similar question is raised with the item "The Ordinaunce for the Assise and Weight of Bred in the Cite of London" (fol. 106v), which is copied from Arnold and which Hill abandoned in the middle of a line. Hill appears to have become muddled before apparently deciding that he was not going to continue the task and crossing out what he had written so far. Since he takes the opportunity later in his manuscript (fols. 118r–122r) to copy a different version of the "Assise of Bred" and with it an "Ordinance for Bakers," presumably also from this new source, it was not the case that he had simply lost interest in the material. An examination of the Arnold text shows that in all probability these items are curtailed in Hill because of some localised damage to fol. 16 of his edition of Arnold. He was using a text in which the bottom quarter and the top right-hand corner of fol. 16r were illegible which would explain the omissions in "The charge of every ward . . .". Whatever the nature of the physical damage, it affected the text on both sides of the page and prevented him from being able to decipher "The assise of bred . . ." which Arnold has on fol. 16v. This example, while not important in itself, does give a sense of a real person behind the finished product. Hill was not just copying from Arnold, he was copying from a particular edition of Arnold which had been damaged, and he struggled with the copying, trying hard to decipher as much as he could before reluctantly giving it up as pointless. He leaves space after the items, presumably in the hope that he would come across the same material again, which, of course, he did in the case of the "Assise of Bred."

On other occasions Hill deviates from his copy text as a matter of personal preference rather than of necessity. For example Hill includes in his volume a treatise on gardening entitled *Of Graffyng* (fols. 109r–117r) which Ogilvie-Thomson numbers as items [22]–[24] and describes as "a condensed form of the text in *Customs*, pp. 164–170" (p. 10). A closer examination reveals that this is not exactly the case.

Arnold's treatise runs to about 3000 words while Hill's version is about 5000. Arnold does not acknowledge any sources but the material he presents is a truncated version of two very popular gardening treatises of the time; one by "Geoffrey" and the other by Nicholas Bollard.[8] Hill's version is also an amalgamation of the two standard gardening treatises, but he did not copy and condense the material in Arnold. There is room here for only the broadest sort of comparison but that should be enough to demonstrate the point.[9] Arnold starts with twenty-two items from "Geoffrey's" treatise and then, without marking a division of any sort, moves into Bollard's treatise. He includes only the following: Part 1, chapter 1, paragraphs 5, 6 and 7; chapter 2, paragraph 1 and the first line of paragraph 2; chapters 3, 4, 5 and 6; Part 2 is copied in its entirety but Part 3 is omitted.[10] Hill's approach is entirely different and, while he may well have got the idea for a gardening treatise from Arnold's book, he was certainly using sources other than Arnold for his compilation.

Hill starts with a statement of intent which itself bears testimony to the fact that this treatise is compiled, not simply copied or adapted from a single source: "Th*is* man*er* of tretise is manyfold & so co*m*myn th*at* at th*is* tyme I wold not shewe of her*e* most usuall settynge but of pr*e*vy works co*n*teynyng the same mater and after ev*e*rythyng in ordre appereth."[11] He uses much more of "Geoffrey's" treatise, keeping the personal and literary references throughout.[12] He marks the end of

---

[8] These are both discussed by W.L. Braekman in "Bollard's Middle English Book of Planting and Grafting and Its Background," *Studia Neophilologica* 57 (1985), pp. 19–39 where he points out that the two works always appear together in English manuscripts which he lists. It is not therefore evidence of any connection between Hill's gardening treatise and Arnold's that they both include material from the same two books. "Geoffrey" is otherwise known as Godfridus or Galfridus (Hill refers to him as "godfray").

[9] A much more detailed study of Hill's "Of Graffyng" than is possible here forms part of my forthcoming Ph.D. thesis.

[10] Braekman (p. 29) mentions an anonymous quarto printed c. 1520 entitled *The Crafte of graffynge and plantynge of trees* (STC 5953) which despite being damaged sounds very similar to Arnold's version of Bollard and may well be linked to it. I have not had the opportunity to examine it yet.

[11] The quotation is taken from the manuscript and abbreviations have been expanded and indicated by italics. Aberystwyth, National Library of Wales, MS Porkington 10 includes a gardening treatise (fols. 27r–32v) which opens with a similar introductory statement: "Here begynneth a shorte tretice for a man*er* to knowe wyche tyme of the yer*e* hit is best to to graffe or to plante treys and also to make, a tre to bere o manere fruyte of diverys colourys and odowrys w*i*th many other thyngys." This manuscript has even less of Bollard's treatise than Arnold does but rather more of "Geoffrey's" in which it comes closer to Hill's version. It is one of the very few manuscripts which has the Bollard material preceding the "Geoffrey" treatise. (See Braekman pp. 20–21 for a list of the English manuscripts.)

[12] MS Porkington 10 has a limited number of these references (e.g. the reference to Aristotle's "boke of plants" on fol. 31) but names nothing like the number of sources that Hill does. It includes some, but not all of the anecdotal style of reference that Hill uses. Interestingly, where Hill refers to Master Robert ("M. Robert saythe the same, make a hole with a wymble . . ."), Porkington has Master Richard ("Also Master Richard saythe to do the same thyngge make an hole with a wymbull . . ."). Towards the end of his treatise when Hill repeats some of the "Geoffrey" material (fol. 116v), he too names Master Richard. (See Braekman p. 39, n. 57 for a reference to another Richard with an interest in gardening books.)

"Geoffrey's" treatise, "Here endith the tretise after Godfray upon Paladys" (fol. 114r) and then begins Bollard's Treatise of which he copies all but paragraphs 2 and 3 of chapter 2 in Part 1 (he gives a brief paraphrase) and paragraphs 2, 3 and 4 of chapter 6 in Part 1. His version of Bollard therefore seems much closer to that given in London, British Library, MS Sloane 7 (fols. 92r–93r) than to Arnold's, even down to what Braekman (p. 21) describes as "a marked tendency towards condensing the wording of the text as much as possible . . . a terseness of diction . . ." which characterises MS Sloane 7. Hill marks the end of Bollard's treatise, "Explicit tractatus nich.ballard de oxinford" (fol. 115v), copies one five-line instruction on grafting from elsewhere and then copies fifteen more gardening instructions which correspond in both order and expression to those found on fol. 129 of London, British Library, MS Sloane 122.[13] He follows these with four more instructions which are found in London, British Library, MS Sloane 442 (fol. 4r)[14] and then recopies some of the material from "Geoffrey" with which he began his treatise. On this occasion he does so without ascribing it to a source and he gives a few more general directions on how to get quick results from gardening. Finally he signs the piece "Explicit Quod Hill." Since he does that only eight times in the whole manuscript this is sufficiently unusual to give us a sense of his personal contribution to the process of compiling the text. Hill's treatise is not "a condensed form of the text in *Customs*"; in fact Hill can have taken from Arnold little more than the idea of including a gardening treatise in his commonplace book, if indeed he was indebted to him at all for this item. Again this example of how Hill's relationship with his sources can be misinterpreted may not seem particularly important in itself. If we dismiss the method of compiling and the mechanics of copying as unimportant, however, we can arrive at the wrong conclusions about a piece and may form false opinions of the man behind the work.

Hill's use of Arnold's "London Chronicle" has been noted by a number of scholars but with some difference of opinion as to how far Hill actually copied Arnold. Flenley (p. 40)[15] states that "From 1413 . . . to 1490, it is almost identical with Arnold's printed record. From 1490, i.e. within Hill's own memory, it is independent though still quite brief, containing just the sort of notes that a Londoner engaged in commerce would make and gradually becoming fuller until it ends abruptly in 1536, halfway through an account of a procession." Kennedy (p. 2653) agrees with this: "the Chronicle is based on Arnold's Chronicle for 1413–90; then it gives an independent account of London events for the years 1490–1536," but W.P. Hills[16] takes an entirely different view (p.453) "the period 1414–1428 is all but identical. . . . After 1428 close correspondences in the Chronicles are rare, although a common source is suggested in a few instances." An examination of the two texts for the period 1414–89 bears Hills out. Hill did not copy Arnold's chronicle past 1428, although he may have used it or Arnold's source (perhaps Dublin, Trinity

---

13 Braekman (p. 23) prints these fifteen instructions from MS Sloane 122.
14 Ibid., p. 24.
15 Ralph Flenley, *Six Town Chronicles of England* (Oxford: Clarendon Press, 1911).
16 W.P. Hills, "Richard Hill of Hillend and Balliol MS 354," *Notes and Queries* 177 (1939), pp. 452–56.

College, MS 509 or London, British Library, MS Cotton Julius B.i). A very brief comparison of the chronicle in MS Cotton Julius B.i and Hill's chronicle reveals that Hill certainly had access to a London chronicle other than Arnold's, either this manuscript or one connected to it. A couple of examples should illustrate the point. For the year 1440 Hill and Julius B.i both give the Mayor as Robert Large, where Arnold has Stephen Brown, and both mention a fire at "Bredstret Sterre" which is not in Arnold's record. For 1441 both manuscripts are once again in agreement over the name of the Mayor, John Paddesley, while Arnold names Robert Clopton, and both refer to a joust at Smithfield, which is not mentioned in Arnold's book. In terms of the text my point is a small one, but it is worth knowing that Hill did not solely rely on Arnold's *Customs* as his source. He also used at least one other London Chronicle, presumably going to some trouble to find the manuscript sources to compare with Arnold's printed book.

These two examples have, I hope, gone some way towards explaining why I think it is inadequate to describe clusters of the items in Hill's manuscript as having been largely or partly derived from a single source. By generalising in this way, we miss out on the details in the differences which show us something of an independent mind at work. Thus much of the interest of the manuscript is lost since the value of a book of this sort surely lies in what it can reveal to us of the motives behind the compilation and assembly of the finished product. The inaccurate generalisations which often arise as a result of misunderstanding the compiler's use of his sources can lead to false assumptions about motive, preference and prejudice as revealed in the manuscript as a whole. With this in mind, I would like to finish on a note of caution. In his book *The Stripping of the Altars*[17] Eamon Duffy refers to Hill as "clearly a traditional Catholic, untouched by the reforming currents already evident in the City in the 1520s." Duffy bases his conclusion on the orthodox religious material in both prose and verse which Hill includes in his manuscript. He looks at what is there and finds it to be orthodox. I am inclined to wonder why it is there and to try and build up an image of the motives of the man behind the work. Why does Hill copy a long Latin treatise on confession which as Duffy states (p. 76) "is obviously designed for use by a priest"? The claim that Hill was a "traditional Catholic" can be borne out to the extent that there is no evidence of heresy in the material he copies, but that is not the same as proving that he was "untouched by the reforming currents."[18] If we put the material he copies together with the details provided in the manuscript about his professional and religious life, it becomes just as feasible to argue that Hill was very likely to have been touched by the reforming movement. As a member of the Grocers' Company, Hill belonged to a professional group well known in London for its sympathy with the reforming movement and which numbered among its ranks leading evangelicals such as John Petyt, Robert

---

[17] Eamon Duffy, *The Stripping of the Altars: Traditional Religion in England 1400–1700* (New Haven and London: Yale UP, 1992), p. 76.
[18] Susan Brigden in *London and the Reformation* (Oxford: Clarendon Press, 1989), p. 77 looks at the same material in Hill as Duffy does but comes to the entirely different general conclusion that Hill "had come into contact with reforming circles in the City."

Foreman and John Blage.[19] Not only was Hill interested in books but he had trading links with Antwerp which was where many of the reforming books were produced for the underground English market and Grocers were known to deal in books and stationery as well as foodstuffs.[20] The parishes to which Hill belonged – St. Andrew Undershaft, St. Margaret's Fish Street, St. Mary at Hill – seem to have attracted more than their fair share of suspicion from church officials.[21] And his good friend, Robert West, the priest who stood as godfather to Elizabeth, complained publicly in 1528 that only "flatterers and dissemblers" were allowed to preach at Paul's Cross "for they that say truth are punished." A year later that same Master West was "abjured for books and opinions contrary to the proclamation." (Foxe, vol. 5, p. 28).

None of the above details prove anything at all; they simply point to the danger when dealing with compilations such as this of concentrating solely on what is copied and undervaluing the motivation of the compiler. A manuscript such as Hill's poses other problems also because of the relatively late date of its copies, many of which are of little value to modern editors or of little intrinsic interest to modern readers. By shifting the focus to Hill, however, and the idea of the compiler behind the book, we can begin to uncover the complex worlds into which Middle English texts were released when they reached the hands of sixteenth-century copyists and readers.

[19] The Grocers' Company were the patrons of All Hallows, Honey Lane, to which in 1525 they appointed as rector Robert Forman who was well known for his involvement in the reforming movement. Three years later he was discovered organising a book-running operation from the church (Brigden, pp. 113 and 128). Petyt was an influential man who held many positions of importance in the City and had helped frame the anticlerical legislation with Cromwell in 1529. He was also a key figure in the underground book trade and patron of a number of evangelical preachers. including Forman (Brigden, p. 185). Blage was an agent of Cranmer's and a well-known activist in the reforming movement. Together with his apprentice, Richard Grafton, he was instrumental in getting a Bible in English (Brigden, p. 419; J. Foxe, *Acts and Monuments*, ed. S.R. Cattley and G. Townsend (London: Seeley and Burnside, 1837–41), vol. 5, pp. 350–58, 389, 443–44).

[20] Carol Meale discusses the importance of Flanders as a source of book imports in "Patrons, Buyers and Owners: Book Production and Social Status," in *Book Production and Publishing in Britain 1375–1475*, ed. J. Griffiths and D. Pearsall (Cambridge: CUP, 1989), pp. 201–38, as does Kate Harris in her essay in the same volume ("The Evidence for Ownership and the Role of Book Owners in Book Production and the Book Trade," pp. 163–99). G. Pollard mentions grocers' involvement in the book trade in "The English Market for Printed Books," *Publishing History* 4 (1978), pp. 7–48. Hill twice in the manuscript (fols. 4r and 204r) copies recipes for making a selection of different inks, so he may himself have been involved in supplying the book trade.

[21] Robert West was the priest at St. Margaret's, Fish Street in 1521 when he stood godfather to Elizabeth and in 1528, when he made this complaint, he was priest at St. Andrew Undershaft, where the Hill family were living by 1526. St. Margaret's most famous parishioner was Richard Hunne whose English Bible was set in the church for the use of any parishioner who cared to read it. In 1529 the parish priest at St. Mary at Hill, William Wegen, declared "Luther to be a good man" (Foxe, vol. 5, p. 28) and the parish boasted quite a number of well-known and unorthodox parishioners including John Sempe whose outspoken views had him imprisoned and John Gough the leader of the Christian Brethren and a book runner associated with Forman (Foxe, vol. 5, p. 447).

V. THE LIMITS OF COURTLINESS

OUR FOOD, FOREIGN FOODS: FOOD AS A CULTURAL DELIMITER IN THE MIDDLE AGES

Terence Scully

"There is no accounting for taste": *De gustibus non est disputandum.* So said a sage many long generations ago. The observation remains sound that much of what explains "taste" has to be laid at the door of plain old irrational prejudice. And prejudice is usually close to the heart of the distinction between cultures.

The clearest instance of this is perhaps in that variety of "taste" that determines what we like to eat. Some of us like East Indian food; some of us can't stomach it. Occasionally we may attempt to justify our prejudices in matters of food by referring to particular ingredients or practices – such as the gastronomic delicacy in Arabic cultures of eating the eyes of roasted goat kids. The natives may assure us that certain foods are very satisfying; but . . . no, thank you, we'll just stick with what we know and like. That's the food of *our* people.

In late-medieval Europe the same sorts of prejudice about foods were held and expressed in many quarters. People then as now had quite clear notions about which foods were *our* foods and which foods identified those who enjoyed them as "foreigners." Foods constituted – and perhaps always have constituted – one of the most forceful means of delimiting different cultures. Certainly for the aristocracy and those in the late Middle Ages who were wealthy enough to be able to afford to *choose* which foods they wished to eat, the distinctions between the familiar and the foreign in matters of food were clearly perceived.

In this study I should like to look briefly at medieval instances of the use of food as a measure of distances between cultures. The areas at which I should like to glance are twofold: the writings of travellers and chauvinists, and actual culinary recipes from *courtly* milieux. My sources may therefore in a sense be seen as divided between the opinions of amateurs and those of the professionals of medieval cookery.

Literary Comments

To some extent literary texts and travellers' narratives confirm prejudices that we can see expressed elsewhere against "foreign" tastes. Some writers display nationalistic biases in proclaiming that the foods they themselves are accustomed to eating are superior in nature to those preferred in other lands.

With jingoistic pride the fourteenth-century Catalan Francesc Eiximenis evokes the currently held opinion that ". . . the Catalan nation illuminates all other nations in decent dining and in temperate drinking; beyond any doubt it is true that Catalans have the most temperate lifestyle of any people on earth."[1] Catalans, for instance, drink wine and consume it in modest measure, whereas Englishmen and German barbarians are content with beer, mead or cider, all clearly contemptible beverages; though the French and the Lombards themselves recognize the merits of wine, they, lacking the Catalan sense of "temperance," always indulge in it to great excess! Eiximenis sets forth a long list of instances of crudity in the dining habits of these other European nations, their sloppiness and general lack of social finesse and grace at table, to say nothing of politeness, all of which demonstrates a clear patriotic hubris based extensively upon food and eating habits.

In the fourteenth century the French poet Eustache Deschamps never seems to tire of ranting against his personal *dislikes* in the matter of food.[2] And most significantly, with virtually no exception, it is the food habits of "foreign" lands that evoke his disgust. For instance, in Hainaut, Brabant and Brussels, the locals know nothing of the more refined condiments, cloves, saffron or grains of paradise: rather they smother everything in *mustard*! Mustard is served on roasts, on mutton, boar, hare, rabbit, bustard, fish (without distinguishing whether the fish under the mustard are from fresh water or the sea – on herring, carp, boiled pike or sole). Horror of uncivilized horrors, mustard is even mixed with fish bouillon and added to the drippings from a roast!

According to Deschamps, still looking at the table customs of those foreigners of the East, Flanders doesn't even have any wine worth drinking; the poet is sick of the all-pervasive stench of beer in these northern and eastern lands. In Bohemia, he must not only do without the good wine of France, but he cannot enjoy good French sea-fish. Besides that, when he is travelling in that region he must tolerate what appears regularly on Bohemian tables: atrocious black, tough salt meats, tough pork and beef, unappetizing tough salt fish, rotten white cabbage and leeks, turnips – all of this invariably seasoned with black pepper and (what else?) sweet mustard; and all of it washed down with (what else?) a bitter, sour beer. They are meals, growls Deschamps, "from which my bowels have ended up bursting" (*dont j'ai touz rompuz les boyaulx*)! And furthermore, he goes on to complain, in Bohemia "the proper organisation and serving of meals (*le service et l'arroy des més*) is completely unknown to any but God." In Germany the guest has no choice but to accept what is offered: salt fish, smoked pork (both of which are served without the benefit of a decent Jance Sauce!), along with a broth that he terms simply "pathetic" . . . and (what else?) beer. To top all of this off, writes Deschamps, like the Bohemians, the Germans have abominable table manners!

---

[1] ". . . La nació catalana era exempli de totes les altres gents cristianes, en menjar honest e en temperat beure; e sens tot dubte aquesta és la veritat: que catalans són los pus temprats hòmens en viure qui sien al món." Francesc Eiximenis (c. 1340–c. 1409), *Com usar de beure i menjar*, ed. Jordi J.E. Gracia, Clàssics Curial (Barcelona: Curial, 1977).

[2] *Œuvres complètes d'Eustache Deschamps*, 11 vols.: vols. 1–6 ed. Auguste Henri Edouard marquis de Queux de Saint-Hilaire; vols. 7–11 ed. Gaston Raynaud (Paris: Firmin Didot, 1878–1903; repr. New York: Franklin, 1966). References to food are passim throughout Deschamps' work.

So much for simple French prejudice! A generation or two later a French chronicler, Gilles le Bouvier,[3] attempted an objective summary of the distinctions in food habits between northern and southern Europe. Languedoc, he wrote, was rich in wheat and wine, in olive oil, dates and almonds; Provence produced "a great quantity of olive oil, almonds and figs"; Genoa, Tuscany, Naples and Sicily abounded in olive oil, citrus fruits, figs and wine. On the other hand, in the north, in Normandy, cattle and their products were abundant, as were apple and pear trees and people consequently drank much apple cider and perry; the Flemish likewise ate much meat, fish, milk and butter; the aggressive character of Scandinavians was determined by their lack of wine and their devotion on the other hand to beer and mead.

Andrewe Boorde (c. 1490–1549), Englishman that he was, distinguished clearly between ale and beer.

> Ale is made of malte and water; and they the which do put any other thynge to ale then is rehersed, except yest, barme, or godesgood, doth sofystical theyr ale. Ale for an Englysshe man is a naturall drynke. . . . Barly malte maketh better ale then oten malte [malted oats] or any other corne [grain] doth. It doth ingendre grose humoures, but yette it maketh a man stronge. . . .
> Bere is made of malte, of hoppes, and water: it is a naturall drynke for a Dutche man. And nowe of late dayes it is moche used in Englande to the detryment of many Englysshe men . . .[4]

By 1525, when hops (the plant botanically known as *Humulus lupulus*) were first introduced into England from Flanders, they had been added to beer in Netherlands brewing for several hundred years. Hops increase the durability of the beer and add a slightly bitter flavour to the mixture, a quality which Andrewe Boorde seems to despise. Beer is a cold drink, he goes on to say, which "doth make a man fat, and doth inflate the bely, as it doth appere by the Dutche mens faces & belyes." Then, as now, there was a lot of chauvinism bound up with taste.

Beer is continually cited by satirical writers in an effort to disparage Germans because of their contemptible taste and their gastronomic ignorance. The thirteenth-century Frenchman Henri d'Andeli, in his *Bataille des vins*, even goes so far as to have a priest excommunicate beer as a heathen beverage, unacceptable among good God-fearing and faithful Christians (lines 179–81). This beer is explicitly the product of the Oise, of Flanders and of England. His contemporary and compatriot, the Norman Henri d'Avranches, writes a similar diatribe against the English taste for beer: "I know not what monstrosity the depths of hell have created that some call *beer*; it becomes no thicker as it is drunk, nor thinner as it is watered; wherefore it is obvious that it must leave many dregs in the belly."[5]

---

[3] Gilles le Bouvier, dit Heraut Berry (1386–c. 1457), *Le livre de la description des pays*, ed. E.-T. Hamy, Recueil de voyages et de documents pour servir à l'histoire de la géographie depuis le XIIIe jusqu'à la fin du XVIe siècle, 22 (Paris: Ernest Leroux, 1908), pp. 52, 71, 81, 86, 102–8, 118–30.

[4] Andrewe Boorde, *A Compendyous Regyment, or a Dyetary of Helth*, ed. F. Furnivall, Early English Text Society, ES 10 (London: Kegan Paul, Tench, Trübner, 1870), p. 256.

[5] "Nescio quod stygiæ monstrum conforme paludi/ Cervisiam plerique vocant: nil spissius illa/ Dum bubitur, nil clarius est dum mingitur, unde/ Constat, quod multas feces in ventre

Occasionally a traveller will express amazement that foreigners are civilized enough to eat as well as the traveller would at home. An Italian, a prosperous and complacent Florentine, enumerated with wonder the servings of a meal he enjoyed in the German town of Villach in 1486: there he was regaled with three mock fish moulded out of milk, eggs and almonds, and garnished with almonds, raisins and candied aniseed; a pâté of fowl mixed with cinnamon and ginger; and fattened thrushes, chicken and other meat. He summed up his astonished pleasure by saying of the meal that "each course was better than the last" and that, all in all, the meal was just as if it had been *delivered* "straight from Florence"![6] What we should note in this reaction is that the traveller *expected* to find inferior, even unpalatable fare once he left home – and particularly, we may suspect, when he had to travel to Germany.

Such was indeed the result for another Italian forced to travel abroad. Bishop Liutprand of Cremona, venturing over to Byzantium, complained that the wine he was expected to drink there was utterly unfit for any civilized palate because, apparently according to the custom of the place, it was adulterated with pitch, resin and gypsum![7]

The popular twelfth-century Pilgrim's Guide to Compostela warns the travelling Christian, and particularly the French Christian, about the totally uncouth dining habits he is apt to find among the Navarrese:

> The whole extended family eats together, which means that servant and master, maid and mistress, all dip into one and the same bowl, in which the main dish and side dishes are all mixed up together. They don't use spoons for eating, but their hands! They all drink from the same beaker. If you saw and heard them eating you would think they were hounds or pigs.[8]

If Europeans could have so much contempt for other Europeans, what, then, about the food habits of the truly *foreign*? Speaking of the Mongols, Mandeville wrote:

> . . . They eat all sorts of wild meats and others, such as dogs, cats, foxes, mares, foals, rats and mice, and other animals wild and domestic, large and small. And they eat the heads, too, and all the inner and outer parts of the animal, and they remove nothing from any animal except for the gall. And they eat little bread, except at the court of the great lords, and in some places they have no peas nor beans, nor any other pottages except for meat broths. The eat little else than meats and the broth that are made from them. . . . The great men drink mare's milk or that of other animals, and another beverage that is made from a half lot of milk and water cooked together, for they have neither wine nor beer in their land. And they live very meanly, for they eat only once a day, and even so very little, whether at court or elsewhere. And certainly a single man

relinquit." Quoted by A. Héron in *Œuvres de Henri d'Andeli, trouvère normand du XIIIe siècle* (Rouen: Cagniard, 1880), p. 92.

[6] Quoted in Edith Ennen, *The Medieval Woman*, trans. Edmund Jephcott (Oxford: Blackwell, 1989), p. 192.

[7] Norbert Ohler, *The Medieval Traveller*, trans. Caroline Hillier (Woodbridge: The Boydell Press, 1989), p. 96.

[8] Quoted in Norbert Ohler, op. cit., p. 193. See also William Melczer, *The Pilgrim's Guide to Santiago de Compostela* (New York: Italica Press, 1993), p. 94.

from our country would eat more in one day than one of them would eat in two or three days.[9]

While visiting the island of Zipangu, Marco Polo, normally an open-minded observer of the "foreign", discovers a particularly distasteful culinary custom, of which he warns us.

> The reader should . . . be informed that the idolatrous inhabitants of these islands, when they seize the person of an enemy who has not the means of effecting his ransom for money, invite to their house all their relations and friends and, putting their prisoner to death, dress and eat the body, in a convivial manner, asserting that human flesh surpasses every other in the excellence of its flavour.[10]

Recipe Texts

It appears that, with very few exceptions in the late Middle Ages, compilations of culinary recipes were made in very large measure simply *because* those recipes represented the cookery of the aristocracy. Such recipes illustrated the best possible culinary practice of its time and place. The manuscript copies that were made of these recipe collections were intended, again with very few exceptions, for the libraries of aristocratic manors and castles. As the Catalan recipe collection, the *Libre de sent soví*, states in its preamble, cookery "is one of the refinements that should be understood and passed on to all sorts of persons – that is, to men and women of whatever estate."[11]

And yet, as the title of that fifteenth-century English recipe collection edited by Robina Napier puts it, this is above all "cookery for a princely household or any other stately household."[12] The evidence upon which we can draw is of a cookery that is firmly attached to the courtly class.

Distinctions, in the matter of late-medieval cookery, tend to be drawn not according to class – the upper class is simply assumed – but rather along the lines of nationalities and of recognized national taste. One of the earliest recipe collections, dating from about 1300, the French work known from its *incipit* as the *Enseignements*, concludes with a rather revealing statement: "Here ends the treatise on preparing all sorts of beverages [. . .] and all sorts of dishes *according to diverse customs in diverse lands*."[13] This happens to be written at the end of this cookbook.

---

[9] Malcolm Letts, *Mandeville's Travels. Texts and Translations* (London: Hakluyt Society, 1953), pp. 370–71. This is my translation of the French text of the Paris manuscript.

[10] *The Travels of Marco Polo* (New York: Orion, [1958]), p. 266.

[11] ". . . És una de les gentillesses que hom den seber e fer entendre a totes natures de gents, so és ha hòmens hi ha dones, de qualsevulla estament que sia." Rudolf Grewe, *Libre de sent soví (Receptari de cuina)* (Barcelona: Barcino, 1979), p. 61.

[12] *A Noble Boke off Cookry ffor a prynce housseolde or eny other estately houssolde. Reproduced verbatim from a rare MS in the Holkham Collection* (London: Elliot Stock, 1882).

[13] ". . . Soronc divers usages de divers pais." Grégoire Lozinski, *La Bataille de Caresme et de Charnage*, Bibliothèque de l'Ecole des Hautes Etudes (Paris: Champion, 1933), Appendix I, pp. 181–87, lines 226–28.

The beginnings, however, of recipe collections can afford the cook or the compiler the opportunity to vaunt local cuisine as worthy of comparison to that of all foreign cookeries. Such boasting is quite understandable, given that the cook existed to fulfil the wishes of his employer, who was his lord and master, and given that, for the cook, the household of his lord and master must unquestionably represent as close as he could make it the best of all possible worlds. In Savoy, for instance, the chief cook of the Duke opens his recipe collection by lauding the Duke's court as the cynosure of all courts, and by formally dedicating all his professional talents to keeping it so.[14]

Among the seven or eight thousand recipes contained in these 60 or 70 manuscript collections, we find a surprising number of dishes whose names embody a foreign placename.

These dishnames establish a distance between local usage and foreign usage in matters of food. The dishes are felt to be a product of a particular culture and to be closely bound to that culture; as a consequence their name often bears a reference to their geographic origin.[15] We find, for instance, in France a Subtle Broth of England; in Italy, an Aragonese Soup and a Pink Dish of Barcelona; in Naples, Egg Fritters *a la Fiorentina*; in France, a Flemish Caudle; in Aragon, a Good French Sauce; in Naples, both Partridge in the French Fashion and French Apple Pie; in Venice, a French Torte; in one Italian collection, a Good French Dish, a French Pottage, French Sauce and French Mustard.[16] A Catalan collection specifies that if you wish to make your mustard in the French fashion, you use vinegar rather than a meat broth.[17] A Tuscan collection offers a Genoese Mullet; a Venetian collection, a Hungarian Torte; a German collection, both Jerusalem Purée and Greek Eggs; English collections, Spanish Broth; French collections, Savoyard Broth; and English, French, German, Catalan and Portuguese books have a variety of recipes qualified everywhere as Lombard. Norse Pies turn up right across Europe, as do Parmesan Pies. Provençal Milk is known in France and Italy. Bohemian Peas are made in Germany; and Italian recipes show both a German Broth (*Brodo Todescho*) and German Scrambled Eggs (*Ova Menata alla Todesca*). And so forth.

By their very presence in these collection, these dishes with the "foreign" names must have been accepted as worthy of preparation and consumption within the culture represented by the cookbook.

Curiously, one national origin gave rise to some confusion. The confusion sprang from the similarity between the name German and the foodstuff almonds. As a result, several prepared dishes (particularly in English cookery) have alternate names such as *Hagas de Almaynne* and *Hagas de almondes*.[18]

---

[14] Terence Scully, *Chiquart's 'On Cookery.' A Fifteenth-Century Savoyard Culinary Treatise* (New York: Lang, 1986).

[15] In his article "Internationalisme, nationalisme et régionalisme dans la cuisine des XIVe et XVe siècles: le témoignage des livres de cuisine," *Manger et boire au moyen âge*, 2 vols. (Paris: Belles Lettres, 1984), vol. 2, pp. 75–91, Jean-Louis Flandrin sets out a partial listing of recipe names that incorporate placenames.

[16] Manuscript: London, Wellcome Institute for the History of Medicine, WMS 211.

[17] Rudolf Grewe, op. cit., p. 177, §162.

[18] Thomas Austin, *Two Fifteenth-Century Cookery-Books*, Early English Text Society, Original Series, 91 (London: Oxford University Press, 1888; repr. 1964), pp. 44 and 84.

At the end of the fourteenth century, the Parisian bourgeois who was responsible for the *Menagier de Paris* observes, with some wonder and disgust, the bizarre German custom of cooking a carp for twice the length of time that a good, sensible French chef would give it. "Note," he remarks, "that Germans say of the French that they run a very great danger in eating their carp cooked so little. And it has been seen that, if Frenchmen and Germans have a French cook who prepares carp for both groups – the carp being prepared in the French way – the Germans will take *their* share and will cook it just as long all over again, and the French, no."[19] Whatever the reasoning behind the German distrust of underdone carp, suspicion and mutual disdain clearly marked the two cooking practices.

In this regard, one of the most interesting documents comes from the hand of a German cleric and professional cook, Johannes von Bockenheim.[20] Working in Avignon and Rome for Pope Martin V, Bockenheim developed a set of recipes suitable for the whole diverse range of Christian nations represented from time to time at the papal court. Most interestingly, among the recipes that he wrote down in the 1430s, he identifies many as particularly suitable for some particular national taste. A particular mutton dish (§4) will be good for Alemanni and Germans (*erit bonum pro Alamanis et Germanis*); similarly Alemanni and Bohemians will delight in wildfowl in a pepper sauce (§25: *erit bonum pro Alamanis et Bohemis*); other Germans will, presumably, feel right at home eating a pork pie (§29), and German prelates will appreciate a particular almond sauce (§73). A curious assimilation of Alemannic taste and peasant taste is perhaps identified in a variant reading for a dish of pea sops (§58): *erit bonum pro rusticis* (var.: *Alamanis*). According to Bockenheim Saxons and Frisians will go for a meat-ball sauce on chicken (§53), whereas Frisians and Slavs will feel at home if served roast bits of small birds in a sauce (§20). A cheese-custard tart (§39) will be a sure hit with Swabians and Bavarians, as will a pie of lamb- and kid-tripe (§37) with Hungarians and Bohemians. Thuringians and Hessians (along with Frisians) can be counted on to like a spiced cheese pie and (along with Swabians) stockfish (§§40 and 69), while Rhinelanders will be pleased if served a fancy roast-and-boiled salmon (§62).

For the English, Bockenheim selects four apparently appropriate dishes: a beef pie, a cheese broth, a pie composed of layers of wildfowl and veal-and-mutton, and a chicken-and-meat-ball stew (§§31, 33, 35 and 44). For the French, who cannot have been very numerous at the court of Martin V during the schism, only one dish is specified, and that is the cheese broth, a taste for which they appear to share with the English (§33). On the other hand the Italians receive the lion's share of Bockenheim's attention, no fewer than ten dishes[21] being designated as likely to please them, along with a further seven which are qualified as *pro Romanis*.[22]

---

[19] Georgine E. Brereton and Janet M. Ferrier, *Le Menagier de Paris* (Oxford: Clarendon Press, 1981), p. 233, §178.

[20] Bruno Laurioux, "Le 'Registre de cuisine' de Jean de Bockenheim, cuisinier du pape Martin V," *Mélanges de l'Ecole française de Rome* 100 (1988), pp. 709–60.

[21] §§2, bread pudding; 8, ground meat; 11, ground kid bowels; 15, ground kid offal, in balls roasted on spit; 17, sauced pigeons; 21, stuffed pork belly; 30, meat pie; 32, meat broth; 57, stewed spinach; and 66, roast spinach.

[22] §§3, spit-roasted slabs of meat; 7, boiled veal and raisins; 9, stewed kid liver and lungs; 18,

While Bockenheim recognizes that many tastes in food are distinctly "foreign," he seems at least to respect all of them and to attempt to give them their due. The same cannot be said for all compilers of late-medieval recipe collections. The anonymous author who is responsible for the Neapolitan collection concludes his recipe for Saracen Sauce by advising the cook, "Make up little platefuls of this [Saracen] sauce – then serve it to a table of Saracens!"[23]

By the end of the Middle Ages the gastronomic snob Platina shows himself to be very aware of foreign alimentary and culinary practices.[24] To the recipes that he copies, translating from Italian into Latin, he appends such comments as: "The dish of my host Palellus yesterday did not displease me when, for a Roman-style meal, he served calves' feet, well washed, cooked in their own juice and sprinkled with spices . . ." (V, 15); ". . . My friend Gallus frequently eats this dish [a Catalan Dish of Partridge], for, although he is a very bitter enemy of the Catalans, he hates that race of men, but not their food" (VI, 33); ". . . Aquitania especially uses wild millet, while the Pontic race [inhabitants of the Black Sea region] prefers no food to it. It also abounds in the region around the Po" (VII, 8); concerning marzipan, "I remember that I have eaten nothing more pleasant with my friend Patricius at Siena, where they make it as a specialty" (VIII, 48); and concerning a dish of Salted Eggs, ". . . I can remember eating nothing more pleasant, with my friend Sophianus. I should think that this was brought from Greece, from which the best salted dishes are usually brought" (X, 67).

Platina may occasionally sneer contemptuously at foreigners, but rarely at their food. Concerning the gluttony he perceived as rampant in various Italian states, he writes (VIII, 1): "Not only in Rome, where great worldly displays are nourished at much expense, but even in certain Italian cities where wealth is concentrated, I have seen many who are so given over to their gullets and bellies that, with obesity and the frequency of varied foods, they have lost all desire to eat." And after praising a number of wines made in various Italian states, he concludes (X, 69): "I would not deny that others are worthy in reputation, in Piceno, in the Cisalpine region and in other parts of Italy, but it is enough only to make mention of these lest it be called unsatisfactory for our age, which produces better wines than men!"

Conclusion

Whether from sheer prejudice or based upon rational assessments of actual local usage, opinions formed and were firmly held in the late Middle Ages about foreign taste and its merit. Generally speaking, the amateurs, the consumers of medieval

cockerel pie; 22, roast pork liver (a most curious variant notes rather that this dish is appropriate for gluttons and pimps: *erit bonum pro glutonibus et lenonibus*); 26, peacock in a pepper sauce; and 52, cheese sops.

23 ". . . Et manda a tavola de Sarazini." Manuscript: New York, Pierpont Morgan Library, MS Bühler 19.

24 Bartolomeo Sacchi, *alias* Platina (1421–1481), *De honesta voluptate et valitudine*, ed. Mary Ella Milham (New York: Renaissance Society of America, [projected 1997]).

cookery and foodstuffs, often tended to be chauvinistic and to use food to distance themselves from the "foreign." The professionals of the kitchen, however, while they did identify foreign dishes quite clearly, accepted these dishes as being worthy of serving on their masters' board.

In sum, while a few foodstuffs and dishes tended to remain distinctly "foreign" and were clearly recognized to be one of the principal factors that determined just what was "foreign" in other cultures, a good and increasing number of them did travel across Europe from region to region, and were welcomed into local usage.

COURTLY COOKING *ALL'ITALIANA*: GASTRONOMICAL APPROACHES TO MEDIEVAL ITALIAN LITERATURE

Christopher Kleinhenz

Nowadays it is not uncommon for people to look back with nostalgia to the Middle Ages, to view this historical period as though it were a simpler, yet more glorious age, a time of knights errant and damsels in distress, of high adventures and magical interludes, when private morality and public social interaction were governed by adherence to the precepts of noble love, honor and loyalty, and courtly life was characterized by colorful tournaments and lavish feasts. Though uncritical and ahistorical, the romanticized view of the Middle Ages packaged in Hollywood and marketed by Madison Avenue appeals both to our imagination and to our natural instincts. In short, the attraction of the Middle Ages involves soul and body, spirit and matter, mind and stomach, as it were.[1] Capitalizing on this basic human desire for fine food and merry-making, contemporary entrepreneurs have promoted the popular notion that medieval people enjoyed seemingly endless rounds of delicious meals, sumptuous banquets and gargantuan feasts.[2] While perhaps partially true for

---

[1] For general treatments of food in history see, among others, the following: Alfred Gottschalk, *Histoire de l'alimentation et de la gastronomie depuis la préhistoire jusqu'à nos jours*, 2 vols. (Paris: Éditions Hippocrate, 1948), and Jean-François Revel, *Culture and Cuisine: A Journey through the History of Food*, trans. Helen R. Lane (Garden City, NY: Doubleday, 1982). For food in the ancient world, see, among others, Emily Gowers, *The Loaded Table: Representations of Food in Roman Literature* (Oxford: Clarendon Press, 1993). For food in the Middle Ages see the following studies, among others: *Essen und Trinken im Mittelalter und Neuzeit: Vortrage eines interdisziplinaren Symposions vom 10.–13. Juni 1987 an der Justus-Liebig-Universität Giessen*, ed. Irmgard Bitsch (Sigmaringen: Thorbecke, 1987); *Food in the Middle Ages: A Book of Essays*, ed. Melitta Weiss Adamson (New York and London: Garland, 1995); Bridget Ann Henisch, *Fast and Feast: Food in Medieval Society* (University Park: Pennsylvania State University Press, 1976); Constance B. Hieatt and Sharon Butler, *Pleyn Delit: Medieval Cookery for Modern Cooks* (Toronto: University of Toronto Press, 1976); Madeleine Pelner Cosman, *Fabulous Feasts: Medieval Cookery and Ceremony* (New York: Braziller, 1976); and Terence Scully, *The Art of Cookery in the Middle Ages* (Woodbridge: The Boydell Press, 1995), and *The Viandier of Taillevent: An Edition of All Extant Manuscripts* (Ottawa: University of Ottawa Press, 1988).

[2] For example, north of Chicago, there is an establishment called Medieval Times which is advertized in promotional brochures with phrases such as "Visitors enjoy a four-course feast served by wenches and serfs while knights on horseback compete in tournament games, jousting matches and sword fights" [*AAA Tourbook: Illinois, Indiana, Ohio*, 1995 edn., p. 70] and "Reenactment of an eleventh-century medieval banquet . . . in a climate-controlled castle" [*Illinois Visitor Guide*, 1993, p. 31].

the landed nobility and the wealthy urban merchants, this rosy picture of culinary delights does not, alas, reflect the day-to-day reality of the great majority of people in medieval Italy.[3]

In our consideration of the place and importance of food in medieval Italy we must first of all distinguish between the historical and the literary, the real and the imaginary. Historical documents may record the richness – or leanness – of the harvest and the rise and fall of grain prices.[4] Contemporary cookbooks – admittedly few but fascinating for their details – give invaluable instructions on preparing a wide assortment of delicacies:[5] from hors d'oeuvres of seasoned crane livers (*Del savore con la grua*, Faccioli, *Arte*, p. 52) to main courses of eel pie (*Del pastello di anguilla*, ibid., p. 45), stuffed peacock (*A empiere un pavone*, ibid., p. 40) and fish in aspic for twelve people (*Gellatina communa e bona de pesse*, ibid., p. 73), to tasty

---

[3] For food in its many historical, popular and anthropological contexts in Italy see, among others, the following studies: Emilio Faccioli, "La Cucina," in *Storia d'Italia*, vol. V, part 1: *I documenti* (Turin: Einaudi, 1973), pp. 983–1030, and Waverley Root, *The Food of Italy* (New York: Vintage Books, 1977); as well as those by Piero Camporesi, *Bread of Dreams: Food and Fantasy in Early Modern Europe*, trans. David Gentilcore (Chicago: University of Chicago Press, 1989), *Il paese della fame*, 2nd edn. (Bologna: Il Mulino, 1985), *The Magic Harvest: Food, Folklore and Society*, trans. Joan Krakover Hall (Cambridge, MA: Polity Press, 1993), and *The Anatomy of the Senses: Natural Symbols in Medieval and Early Modern Italy*, trans. Allan Cameron (Cambridge, MA: Polity Press, 1994). Food in medieval Italy has been the subject of several studies: Jean-Louis Flandrin and Odile Redon, "Les livres de cuisine italiens des XIVe et XVe siècles," *Archeologia medievale*, 8 (1981), pp. 393–408; Allen J. Grieco, "Savoir de poète ou savoir de botaniste? Les fruits dans la poésie italienne du XVe siècle," *Médiévales*, 16–17 (1989), pp. 131–46; Massimo Montanari, "Note sur l'histoire des pâtes en Italie," *Médiévales*, 16–17 (1989), pp. 61–63; *Mostra dell'antica cucina veneta* (Treviso – Ca' da Noal, 2–16 dicembre 1973), Ente Provinciale per il Turismo, Treviso (Treviso: Tipografia Longo & Zoppelli, n.d.); Odile Redon and Bruno Laurioux, "La constitution d'une nouvelle catégorie culinaire? Les pâtes dans les livres de cuisine italiens de la fin du Moyen Age," *Médiévales* 16–17 (1989), pp. 51–60; Lynn Thorndike, "A Mediaeval Sauce-Book," *Speculum* 9 (1934), pp. 183–90. See also John Larner, *Italy in the Age of Dante and Petrarch 1216–1380* (London: Longman, 1980).

[4] For studies on food-related topics including the economics of peasant life, the grain trade, and agriculture in the Middle Ages, see, among others: Fernand Braudel, *The Structures of Everyday Life: The Limits of the Possible*, vol. I: *Civilization and Capitalism, 15th–18th Century*, trans. Siân Reynolds (New York: Harper & Row, 1981) (especially chapters 2 and 3: "Daily Bread" and "Superfluity and Sufficiency: Food and Drink"); Giovanni Cherubini, *Agricoltura e società rurale nel medioevo* (Florence: Sansoni, 1972); Georges Duby, *The Chivalrous Society*, trans. Cynthia Postan (Berkeley: University of California Press, 1980) (especially chapter 14: "The Manor and Peasant Economy"); Giuliano Pinto, *Il Libro del biadaiolo: carestie e annona a Firenze dalla metà del '200 al 1348* (Florence: Leo S. Olschki, 1978); and Georges Yver, *Le commerce et les marchands dans l'Italie méridionale au XIIIe et au XIVe siècle* (Paris: Librairie des Écoles Françaises d'Athènes et de Rome, 1902).

[5] See, for example, the following: Anonimo Meridionale, *Due libri di cucina*, ed. Ingemar Boström (Stockholm: Almqvist & Wiksell International, 1985); *Arte della cucina. Libri de ricette, testi sopra lo scalco, il trinciante e i vini dal XIV al XIX secolo*, 2 vols., ed. Emilio Faccioli (Milan: Edizioni Il Polifilo, 1966); and *Libro di cucina del secolo XIV*, ed. Ludovico Frati (Bologna: Forni, 1970; reprint of Livorno, 1899 edn.); Francesco Zambrini, *Il libro della cucina del sec. XIV, testo di lingua non mai fin qui stampato* (Bologna: Commissione per i testi di lingua, 1968; reprint of the 1863 edition: Bologna, Romagnoli).

desserts of garlic cake (*Torta d'agli*, ibid., p. 95) and what would now be called "low-fat cheesecake" (*Torta de caxo e ova senza lardo*, ibid., p. 95). These practical guides introduce us to the largely foreign world of medieval taste: strange spices, uncommon sauces, and unusual meats. Although available in great variety in Italy, the ingredients for many of these recipes were, because of their cost, beyond the reach of the average person. The desire for the finer things in life – good food, nice clothes, and a comfortable home – burgeons naturally in a consumer society, and this is precisely what we find in the urban centers of medieval Italy, where the merchant class became the new aristocracy, supplanting the old feudal nobility. The adventures and exploits of the members of this social class were so vividly portrayed by Giovanni Boccaccio that his *Decameron* has been characterized as the "epopea dei mercatanti" (the "epic of the merchants").[6]

In their references to banquets, most literary texts focus less on the "realistic" depiction of the event and more on the imaginary feast, highlighting the desire for what is absent, and not representing what is – or was. This tendency is completely understandable, for it is doubtful that average people would consider their ordinary and monotonous fare at mealtime to be the stuff of literature. They would derive much greater pleasure in reading – if they could read – or in hearing about elegant feasts that would excite their imagination and whet their appetite, even though most of these gastronomical delights remained beyond their reach. As surprising as it may seem, the representation of food and banqueting in early Italian literature has not been systematically studied. The present essay will attempt to provide a brief introduction to the topic, one to which I intend to return in future work.

It is fair to say that food is always on people's minds, but not always in an open and conscious manner. One visible sign of prosperity in the Middle Ages was the girth of an individual: those who could afford to eat, did so, and often in great quantity. Fatness then became a sign of material wealth; conversely, leanness came to indicate poverty – either voluntary or involuntary –, asceticism, and thus greater spirituality. As so many other bodily functions, eating is a necessary and integral part of our being, but perhaps because it is so ordinary, this activity is rarely accorded a prominent place in literary works. References to food, eating and feasting play three principal roles in medieval Italian literature: (1) brief references to food serve a purely narrative function in the text in that they present in simple and unadorned terms what happened; (2) more elaborate gastronomical descriptions are directed toward one of three ends: (a) to impress upon the reader the special character of the event, often a major celebration, ritual, or ceremony, (b) to embellish an elaborate, already idealized portrait of a fantastic situation or society, and (c) to provide the proper cultural context for moral, social, or theological commentary on the event in question; and (3) culinary references assume the form of metaphors, both brief and extended, and these provide the rhetorical means for the convincing literary representation of philosophical subjects and transcendental truths. Given the limitations of space and the nature of the organization for which this essay was prepared (the

---

[6]   Vittore Branca used this felicitous phrase as a chapter title in his *Boccaccio medievale*, new and rev. edn. (Florence: Sansoni, 1970).

International Courtly Literature Society), I intend to concentrate on those representations of food and feasting that are most pertinent to what we may term "courtly
literature and culture" in Italy.

One aspect of the subject that rarely garners but certainly merits attention in
literary or culinary criticism may be expressed as a question: what did medieval
Italian peasants eat? In the general absence of historical records, we must turn to
literary evidence.[7] We find some indications in the verses of the *jongleur* Matazano
da Calignano who indulges in a vituperative discourse on the low birth and mean
existence of the peasant:[8]

> Là zoxo, in uno hostero,
> sì era un somero;
> de dré sì fé un sono
> sì grande come un tono:
> de quel malvaxio vento
> nascé el vilan puzolento.
> . . .
> Ora è stabilito
> che deza aver per victo
> lo pan de la mistura
> con la zigola cruda,
> faxoy, ayo e alesa fava,
> paniza freda e rava.   (vv. 83–88, 97–102)[9]

The anti-peasant remarks in this popular poem are the first in Italian literature.
However, these verses do not simply repeat the scornful view of peasants held by the
aristocracy, for, as is evident from other parts of the poem, Matazone is equally
critical of the noble class and thus clearly aligns himself with the middle-class urban
dwellers for whom he wrote. The style, tone and dialectal coloration of the composition leave no doubt concerning its intended – and undoubtedly appreciative – audience. To be able to perform their strenuous labors, peasants ate a great deal of highly
caloric, but rather uninteresting food that consisted primarily of grains and legumes,
and from this impoverished diet we can gauge the tremendous effect that the description of lavish meals with exotic foods must have had on the average person.

What did the nobles eat? How courtly was their cooking? Here we have more

---

[7] For the relatively little evidence we have, see the studies of Massimo Montanari, who
provides an overview of food production and eating practices in medieval Italy: *Campagne
medievali: strutture produttive, rapporti di lavoro, sistemi alimentari* (Turin: Einaudi, 1984)
and *L'alimentazione contadina nell'alto Medioevo* (Naples: Liguori, 1979).
[8] For the text of Matazone's poem, see *Poeti del Duecento*, ed. Gianfranco Contini (Milan-
Naples: Ricciardi, 1960), vol. I, pp. 789–801. For some discussion of the larger historical-an-
thropological context of the passage in Matazone concerning the birth of the peasant, see the
chapter on "Carnevale all'inferno," in Camporesi, *Paese della fame*, pp. 27ff. See also Paul
Meyer, "Dit sur les vilains par Matazone de Calignano," *Romania* 12 (1883), pp. 14–28.
[9] Larner (pp. 99–102) also cites Matazone's verses and provides a translation (p. 171), which
I have modified according to Contini's edition and commentary: "Down there, in a house,
there was an ass; from its behind it made a sound as loud as thunder: from that evil wind the
stinking peasant was born. . . . Now it is ordained that he [i.e., the peasant] must eat coarse
bread baked with rye, haricots, garlic and boiled beans, cold mash, and turnips."

evidence, as, for example, the precious historical record of the eighteen-course feast prepared for the wedding of Violante (the daughter of Galeazzo II Visconti) and Lionel (Duke of Clarence, the third son of Edward III of England) on the fifth of June, 1368, in Milan.[10] Petrarch was reported to be among the fifty guests at that sumptuous affair, although – surprisingly – he gives no account of the event.[11] Perhaps this orgy of conspicuous consumption did not sit well with his admittedly simple tastes, as he confesses them in numerous writings. In his letter to Francesco Nelli, written from Milan on December 7, 1359, Petrarch notes:[12]

> From my tender years I have only very rarely enjoyed sumptuous repasts, and I have been disgusted by long banquets and parties prolonged into the night. I have always liked what Horace came late to approve: "a short meal is best, and sleep on a grassy brookside bank."

Petrarch's apparent love of simple, humble fare reflects, as his literary allusions here and elsewhere suggest, certain classical attitudes toward food and physical well-being. The dichotomy found in this historical period between the rich and the poor, the well-fed and the famished, the opulent and the simple, is an integral part of the human condition and informs its literary representation.

In addition to the numerous narrative uses in literature of simple gastronomical references, we find some instances in which more elaborate descriptions of food and feasting figure in important ways to designate a type of ideal society, both for comic and for serious ends. While we do not possess detailed descriptions of fabulous meals or banquets in any literary work from the thirteenth and fourteenth centuries, the Viscontean "Grand Bouffe" described above would seem in many ways to reify the culinary dreams and gastronomical desires of generations of Italian authors.[13] In

---

[10] A detailed report of the banquet and its many courses is given in the *Annales Mediolanenses* (in *Rerum Italicarum Scriptores*, XVI (Milan, 1730), cols. 738–40); Giovanni de' Mussi provides a much more limited account in his *Chronicon Placentinum* (in *Rerum Italicarum Scriptores* XVI (Milan, 1730), cols. 509–10). For the description of the eighteen-course meal, together with the gifts presented at specific times during that celebration, see Larner, pp. 212–13. See also the suggestion made by Albert Stanburrough Cook (in *The Historical Background of Chaucer's Knight*, Transactions of the Connecticut Academy of Arts and Sciences, vol. 20 [1916], pp. 185–86) to the effect that "the feast in the *Squire's Tale* had borrowed other features from the banquet offered to Lionel and his train" (p. 185 note). We also possess an eyewitness account of another monumental feast – this time in sacred, not secular space – given by two cardinals for Pope Clement V in 1308. In *Petrarch and His World* (Bloomington: Indiana University Press, 1963), Morris Bishop describes this banquet in some detail (pp. 44–45).

[11] Petrarch is listed among the attendees in the *Annales Mediolanenses* as "Dominus Franciscus Petrarcha" (col. 739).

[12] *Fam.* XXI, 13. The translation is by Morris Bishop: *Letters from Petrarch* (Bloomington: Indiana University Press, 1966), pp. 175–76.

[13] The closest thing to a full description of a fabulous feast that we possess is found in a remarkable work, *Il Saporetto*, the sonnet cycle by Simone Prudenzani, a late-fourteenth/early fifteenth-century poet from Orvieto. The second section of this work opens with two sonnets (59–60) that describe a great feast at the court. See Santorre Debenedetti, *Il "Sollazzo" e il "Saporetto" con altre rime di Simone Prudenzani d'Orvieto*, in *Giornale storico della letteratura italiana*, Supplemento 15 (1913).

the *Decameron* Boccaccio presents for humorous ends one such fantasy. In the third novella of the eighth day, Calandrino, the gullible Florentine who is the perennial butt of practical jokes, is told the wonders of the fabled land called Bengodi

> nella quale si legano le vigne con le salsicce e avevavisi un'oca a denaio e un papero giunta; e eravi una montagna tutta di formaggio parmigiano grattugiato, sopra la quale stavan genti che niuna altra cosa facevano che far maccheroni e raviuoli e cuocergli in brodo di capponi, e poi gli gittavan quindi giú, e chi piú ne pigliava piú se n'aveva; e ivi presso correva un fiumicel di vernaccia, della migliore che mai si bevve, senza avervi entro gocciola d'acqua.[14]

The exquisite humor of this passage plays, of course, on the discrepancy between fantasy and reality and on Calandrino's extreme gullibility, elements that Boccaccio's fourteenth-century readers would recognize and appreciate. In Boccaccio's *Decameron* we are treated to the vast and rich array of human types and situations – it is the human comedy *par excellence* – and food and feasting play a major role in the narration, in large part because these are the measures of material success in society and in life. The desire for food – just as that for sex – predominates in the *Decameron*, and we see among Boccaccio's myriad characters those who have – and enjoy – and those who do not have – and live in perpetual desire. Calandrino is motivated by his inordinate love of food – and money and sex –, and these desires inform each of the *novelle* in which he figures. The role that food and feasts play in Boccaccio's *Decameron* has, however, been extensively studied, and thus we will not dwell on it here.[15]

On the more serious side, we note the inevitable conflict between the desire for luxury, for creature comforts, and the objective, usually harsh assessment of these material possibilities. Nowhere in medieval Italian literature is this contrast more acutely and accurately presented than in two sonnet cycles on the months of the year, one optimistic and joyful written by Folgore da San Gimignano and the other pessimistic and grim composed in response by Cenne da la Chitarra.[16] In his sonnets Folgore evokes the ideal fantasy world of the courtly *brigata*, whom he endows,

---

[14] Giovanni Boccaccio, *Decameron*, 2 vols., ed. Vittore Branca (Turin: Einaudi, 1992), II, 908. The translation follows that of Mark Musa and Peter Bondanella: Giovanni Boccaccio, *The Decameron* (New York: Norton, 1982), p. 484: ". . . where they tie up vineyards with sausages and where you can have a goose for a penny and a gosling thrown in for good measure, and that there was a mountain there made entirely of grated Parmesan cheese upon which there lived people who did nothing but make macaroni and ravioli which they cook in capon broth and later toss off the mountain, and whoever picks up more gets the most; and nearby there flowed a stream of dry white wine, the best you ever drank, without a drop of water in it."

[15] See, for example, Frank Capozzi, "Food and Food Images in the *Decameron*," *Canadian Journal of Italian Studies* 34 (1987), pp. 1–13; David Lampe, " 'Festa Grandissima': Food, Feast and Fantasy in *The Decameron*," *La Fusta* 8 (1990), pp. 7–17; and Laura Sanguineti White, *La scena conviviale e la sua funzione nel mondo del Boccaccio* (Florence: Leo S. Olschki, 1983).

[16] The texts of the sonnets by Folgore and Cenne follow Contini, *Poeti del Duecento*, vol. II, pp. 403–34. The translations are mine.

month by month, with a plethora of "gifts," those material, much desired, pleasure-giving objects representing all the best that the world has to offer. Each month has its special quality, its particular, seasonal "gifts," and, as might be imagined, food items and the pleasures of the table figure prominently in this courtly setting. We find, for example, the bounty of the hunt described in the sonnet for February,[17] or the plentiful variety of marine life in the sonnet for March.[18] In addition to the sonnet for July, dedicated almost completely to food items, the colder months bring with them increased attention to lavish feasts: in October it is said that "l'arrosto e 'l vino è buona medicina" (v. 11: "the roast and the wine are good medicine"); for the cold November days we find the hope that for the "fuoco spesso" (v. 9: "hot fire") and for "fagiani, starne, colombi e mortiti,/ levri e cavrïuoli a rosto e lesso" (vv. 10–11: "pheasants, partridges, doves and salamis, hares and roe-deer both roasted and boiled"). In December Folgore desires for the host to be "joyful and refined" ("inebrïato e catelano," v. 5), in order that "everyone may eat and drink their fill" ("morselli ciascun bëa e manuchi," v. 7) and that "the wine kegs be bigger than San Galgano" ("le botti sien maggior' che San Galgano," v. 8).

In his sonnet cycle Cenne da la Chitarra responds directly and realistically to Folgore's idealized vision of a perfect, harmonious society in which nothing – and especially food – is lacking. Cenne's cynical response *per le rime* is pure parody, but of a rather pedestrian variety, as the following examples demonstrate. Folgore's rich assortment of luscious fruit for June – "Aranci e cedri, dàttili e lumie/ e tutte l'altre frutte savorose" (vv. 9–10: "Oranges and lemons, dates and limes, and all other tasty fruits") – is transformed by Cenne into a decidedly bitter harvest of "Sorbi e pruni acerbi siano lìe,/ nespole crude e cornie savorose" (vv. 9–10: "Sorbs and bitter thorns are there with unripe medlars and 'tasty' bunchberries").

Folgore envisions his courtly group enjoying a wide assortment of fine foods for the month of July:

> e man e sera mangiare in brigata
> di quella gelatina ismisurata,
> istarne arrosto e giovani fagiani,
> lessi capponi, capretti sovrani;
> e, ci piacesse, la manza e l'agliata,[19]

and Cenne transforms these dishes into a most unappetizing meal:

---

[17] "E de febbrai' vi dono bella caccia/ di cervi, di cavrioli e di cinghiari. . . . E la sera tornar co' vostri fanti/ carcati de la molta salvaggina,/ avendo gioia ed allegrezza e canti;/ fin trar del vino e fummar la cucina . . ." (vv. 1–2, 9–12): "For February I give you good hunting: stags, roe-bucks and wild boars. . . . And when you return in the evening with your lads loaded down with game and full of joy, happiness and songs, may the kitchen smoke and wine be drawn."

[18] "Di marzo sì vi do una pischiera/ d'anguille, trote, lamprede e salmoni,/ di dèntici, dalfini e storïoni,/ d'ogn'altro pesce in tutta la rivèra . . ." (vv. 1–4): "For March I give you a fishpond full of eels, trout, lampreys, and salmon, sea bream, dolphins, sturgeon, and every other fish imaginable."

[19] Vv. 4–8: "Together with good friends both day and night feasting on wonderful galantine, roast partridges and young pheasants, boiled capons, exquisite kid; and beef with garlic sauce for those who like it."

carne di porco grassa apeverata;
e poi, diretro a questo, una insalata
di salvi' e ramerin, per star più sani,
carne de volpe guascotta a due mani
e, a cui piacesse, drieto cavolata.[20]

In opposition to Folgore's "finissimi cuochi" ("refined cooks," v. 6) for December, Cenne presents a "cuoco brutto" ("awful cook," v. 5). Folgore's fondest wish for November – that everyone may "sempre avere aconci gli appetiti" ("always have their appetite whetted," v. 12) – is countered by Cenne's dire prediction that the *brigata* would be "di vin e carne del tutto sforniti" ("completely out of wine and meat," v. 12), and so on. Where does reality lie? Probably somewhere between Folgore's idealized vision and Cenne's grim picture. Nevertheless, through extensive use of gastronomical references Folgore is able to embellish his portrait of an ideal society.

Reality is represented in many ways, and references to food are equally varied. If the popular misconception of the Middle Ages as a gastronomical paradise is even partially correct, then a casual observer might expect to find banqueting scenes and lavish feasts filling the pages of Arthurian romance. Contrary to these expectations, we rarely see a menu; no one seems to linger at table – indeed, fast food would apparently suit a knight's busy schedule. Entire meals are consumed in the short space of a sentence or two. While the two great Italian chivalric prose romances of the late thirteenth and early fourteenth centuries – the *Tavola Ritonda*[21] and the *Tristano Riccardiano*[22] – describe in some detail jousts and tournaments, they are usually very succinct in those passages concerning gastronomical activities and adventures. The text reports simply that "water was brought to the knights to wash their hands and then they sat down to eat" ("fu apportato loro l'acqua da lavarsi le mani, e sedettono a mangiare," *Tav. rit.*, p. 486) or that the "food was served in great abundance, and after it was brought in, everyone began to eat" ("le vivande sì vennerono a molto grande dovizia; e dappoi che le vivande fuorono venute, e tutta giente sì incominciarono a mangiare," *Tris. Ricc.*, p. 236). In fact, when scenes involving food do appear in these courtly romances, they generally serve to impart or to reinforce a moral lesson; they are not included simply to display the high life of the aristocracy, to suggest a certain elevated social status, or to evoke a courtly aura, and thus to provide entertainment for the masses. The general absence of elaborate courtly dining rituals[23] reflects the minor role of the "aristocracy" in the Italian

---

[20] Vv. 4–8: "Fat and highly seasoned pork; and then, after this, a salad of sage and rosemary, in order to remain healthy, badly cooked and tough fox meat, followed by cabbage mash, for those who like it."

[21] *La Tavola ritonda o l'istoria di Tristano*, ed. Filippo-Luigi Polidori, 2 vols. (Bologna: Romagnoli, 1864–1865). The translation is by Anne Shaver: *Tristan and the Round Table. A Translation of "La Tavola Ritonda"* (Binghamton, New York: Medieval and Renaissance Texts and Studies, 1983).

[22] *Il Tristano Riccardiano*, ed. E.G. Parodi (Bologna: Romagnoli-Dall'Acqua, 1896). This edition has been reissued with a new introduction and notes by Marie-José Heijkant (Parma: Pratiche, 1991). All translations from this work are mine.

[23] Except, of course, for the references to spiritual food and meals that accompany the

communes and thus the "foreign-ness" of these courtly customs to medieval Italian life. Two examples will suffice to show how references to food provide a cultural context for moral commentary in medieval Italian courtly literature.

In our first example, taken from the *Tavola ritonda*, a food-related reference is the major component in a carefully devised test of loyalty, in which a magical horn fashioned by Morgan the Fay ("la Fata Morgana") is used to assess the fidelity of a woman to her husband:

> . . . per la virtù di quello corno si poteano conoscere tutte le leali dame dalle misleali, e quelle che facevano fallo al loro marito; imperò che lo corno si è incantato per tal maniera, che ponendolo alla bocca ad alcuna dama pieno di vino, ed ella avesse fatto fallo a suo marito, i' niuna maniera del mondo non potrebbe inghiottirne niente; anzi lo vino se le spargerebbe per lo petto; sì forte le tremerebbe la mano: ma le liali dame berranno assai.[24]

When Isolt attempts to drink, her hand shakes so much that she spills the wine all over herself. Her husband, King Mark, then has the rest of the women take the test, and of the 686 who attempt it, only 13 pass it. The author of the *Tavola* provides the following explanation of this event:

> . . . delle seicentottantasei, non se ne trovò a quella prova liali se none tredici; e quelle non erano sofficienti per più loro cagioni, sì che era rimaso per quella cagione: ma la volontà aveano non di meno interamente come l'altre; ma perchè non erano convitate, però ristava. Ma credo che al paese ciò addivenisse per cagione che le dame vi sono molte grandi bevitrici, bugiarde e ghiotte, e bene pacchianti di roba, più che altre dame lussuriose: gli uomini begli, e vili di loro persone, e poco atanti nelle armi e poco valorosi; ma molto erano arroganti, avarissimi.[25]

Mark, however, does not carry out his threat to burn the 673 ladies, Isolt included, for reasons that are not necessary here. The importance of the passage for our purposes lies in the association of food – here wine – with debauchery and the context it creates for the authorial commentary. The author breaks into his narrative to underscore the traditional view expressed in courtly literature concerning the disreputable ways of the women – and men – of Cornwall. In his opinion, the 673 women failed the wine-in-the-horn test because they were excessive drinkers, glut-

---

description of the Holy Grail and the adventures of Arthur's knights who join the quest. See, for example, chapters 108–10 and 117–21 in the *Tavola ritonda*.

[24] *Tav. rit.*, ch. 43; p. 158. ". . . by the powers of this horn one could find out whether one's lady were loyal or disloyal, and which ones sinned against their husbands. The horn was enchanted in such a way that if it were filled with wine and held to the lips of a lady who had been false to her husband, by no effort in the world could she swallow anything from it, but her hand would tremble so much that the wine would spill on her breast; a loyal lady, though, could drink as much as she liked" (Shaver, pp. 102–03).

[25] *Tav. rit.*, ch. 43; p. 159. ". . . but of the 686 only thirteen proved loyal, and these not by their own desires; they had fully as much will as the others, but they had not been invited, so they remained true. I believe that such a thing happened in this country because the ladies were all such drunkards, liars, and gluttons, and were so fond of clothes, and more lecherous than other ladies. The men were handsome but cowardly, unskilled at arms and without valor, but they were very arrogant and greedy" (Shaver, p. 103).

tons and liars whose lust knows no bounds![26] While motivated in part by common medieval misogynistic attitudes, the author does not exclude the men of Cornwall from this specific criticism, thus adhering to the popular view of their uncourtliness. We might infer from this intervention that the author is consciously making a more general statement concerning the decline in morality in a materialistic and hedonistic society (perhaps the one in which he was living), and the food-oriented reference occasions this moral outburst.

The second example – the account of the death of King Mark in the *Tavola Ritonda* – presents the dire consequences related to excessive consumption of food. Mark's treachery in the death of Tristan has gained him the undying enmity of Arthur and his court. After a number of battles and sieges, Mark is taken captive, but, since the laws of chivalry do not allow the execution of a person in custody, he is imprisoned in a tower overlooking the tomb of Tristan and Isolt:

> . . . sì fanno fare dinanzi dal pillo, cioè alla sepoltura di Tristano, la più alta torre e la maggiore che fare si potesse; la quale torre era alta VIII cento LXXX piedi: e in cima della torre fanno fare una gabbia di ferro, e dentro vi missono lo re Marco in pregione; dicendogli che, perch'egli none avea guardato Tristano vivo, ch'egli lo guardasse morto. E lasciaro a coloro che furono messi sopra ciò, che lo re Marco fosse loro raccomandato, e che, mentre ch'egli vivea, ciascuno dì dovesse avere di tre maniere carne a grande abbondanza, e di fini vini e potenti, senza niuna acqua, e ciascuno mese gli mutassono due volte roba di lana e di lino; e comandarono che pane nè altra minestra nè altra vivanda non gli dessono; e che mai neuno, nè morto nè vivo, none lo cavassono. E così fue fatto. In tale maniera vivette lo re Marco XXXII mesi, e ingrassò tanto forte, che mai neuno uomo non si vidde sì grasso; e morì di grassezza.[27]

Everything about Mark is reprehensible, and the author takes pains to underscore his cowardly, unsympathetic, and essentially evil nature. Mark's grotesque end, as a result of overeating, is therefore just and appropriate and becomes both emblematic

---

[26] The episode also appears in the *Tristano Riccardiano* (chapters 76–77, pp. 154–57), with certain modifications. The number of women who undergo the test of loyalty is 365, of which only two succeed in drinking from the horn. Unlike the authorial commentary found in the *Tavola Ritonda*, the author of the *Tristano Riccardiano* does not offer any opinion on the character of the women of Cornwall. While this episode is common to most of the Tristan romances, the number of women who fail the test varies greatly: from 673 here to 365 in the *Riccardiano* to "one hundred or more" ("cent ou plus") of which four pass in the Old French *Tristan en prose*. The very high number here would seem to reinforce the moral intent of the author.

[27] *Tav. rit.*, ch. 137; p. 523. ". . . they had a tower built in front of Tristan's sepulchre, the highest and the best that could be made, 880 feet high. On top of it was built an iron cage, and here it was that King Marco was imprisoned. They said that since he had not protected Tristano while his nephew was alive, he could watch over him now that he was dead. They left him to those who were put in charge, saying that as long as he lived he was to be given [each day] three kinds of meat in great abundance and good strong wine with no water, and that each month he was to have two changes of wool and linen clothing. They commanded that he not be given bread or soup or any other food, and that no one ever let him out of the cage, even if he were dead. And so it was done. Thus, King Marco lived thirty-two months, and it is said that he became so fat that no one had ever seen a fatter man; they say he died of fatness" (Shaver, p. 333).

of and a moral commentary on the vile end that awaits traitors – and gluttons![28] Gluttony has traditionally been associated with original sin because of the scene in the Garden of Eden – and thus also with pride and with lust. It is this moral dimension of food that the author of the *Tavola ritonda* evokes throughout; he has no other interest in the description of festive scenes.[29]

We will conclude this survey with a brief look at one very large category of references to food and feasting: their use as metaphors to represent philosophical subjects and transcendental truths. The metaphorical allusiveness present in many literary texts is, of course, part of a long tradition. We recognize the critical importance that the combination of dining scenes and miraculous events in the Old and New Testaments has for medieval conceptions and representations of food and eating. These include the following scenes, among others: the Garden of Eden; Moses drawing water from the rock; manna falling from heaven; the feeding of the five thousand with the loaves and fishes (esp. John 6:1–13); the transformation of water into wine at the wedding feast at Cana (John 2:1–12); and, perhaps most significant of all, the institution of the Eucharist at the Last Supper (Matt. 26:17–29; Mark 14:12–25; Luke 22:7–23; and John 13:21–30). The visual depictions of these biblical episodes in medieval frescoes, panel paintings, and manuscript illuminations often provide a reasonably accurate historical record of dining practices during this period. The mystery of Transubstantiation and the spiritual union with the Divinity achieved in the rite of Communion demonstrate the non-material, divine nature of food as conceived and represented in the Middle Ages. In the *Divine Comedy* Dante incorporates this central Christian metaphor in his representation of the great feast in Paradise, of the heavenly manna that graces the wedding feast of the Lamb (cf. Rev. 19:9). At the beginning of canto 24 of *Paradiso* (vv. 1–9), Beatrice calls upon the souls of the blessed in the Heavenly Court[30] to assist the pilgrim Dante in his quest for divine Truth:[31]

---

[28] Mark's fate is mirrored in some representations of the punishment of gluttons in scenes of the afterlife and Last Judgment. For example, in the fresco by Taddeo di Bartolo (1393) in the Collegiata (Duomo) in San Gimignano, we see several rather portly gluttons standing around a table and being forced to look at the source of their problem – food on the table – by devils. Among the scenes from Hell depicted by Fra Angelico in his panel on the Last Judgment (c. 1430; San Marco, Florence), we see gluttons crowded around a table where they are forced to eat all sorts of disgusting things by devils. These devils are also the "cooks" who boil sinners in another section of this artistic representation of Hell. Cf. the acts of "eating" that occur among the traitors in Dante's *Inferno*: e.g., Ugolino (canto 33) and Lucifer (canto 34).

[29] In addition to the moral dimension that accompanies the appearance of food in the courtly narrative, scenes of eating and festivity can have a comic dimension as well. See my essay, "Perspectives on the Quest Motif in Medieval Italian Literature: Comic Elements in Antonio Pucci's *Gismirante*," in *Literary Aspects of Courtly Culture: Selected Papers from the 7th Triennial Congress of the International Courtly Literature Society*, ed. Donald Maddox and Sara Sturm-Maddox (Cambridge: D.S. Brewer, 1994), pp. 249–56.

[30] For Dante's view of the court, see my essay, "Dante as Reader and Critic of Courtly Literature," in *Courtly Literature: Culture and Context: Selected Papers from the 5th Triennial Congress of the International Courtly Literature Society, Dalfsen, The Netherlands, 9–16 August, 1986*, ed. Keith Busby and Erik Kooper (Amsterdam and Philadelphia: John Benjamins, 1990), pp. 379–93.

[31] All passages from the *Divine Comedy* are taken from Dante Alighieri, *La commedia*

O sodalizio eletto a la gran cena
del benedetto Agnello, il qual vi ciba
sí, che la vostra voglia è sempre piena,
    se per grazia di Dio questi preliba
di quel che cade de la vostra mensa,
prima che morte tempo li prescriba,
    ponete mente a l'affezione immensa
e roratelo alquanto: voi bevete
sempre del fonte onde vien quel ch'ei pensa.

Throughout the *Comedy* Dante employs alimentary images to suggest the right and proper sorts of nourishment, in sharp contrast to the gross material fare that weighs one down and effectively prevents one from rising to the divine. The gluttons in *Inferno* 6 lie on a foul, rain-drenched plain, reminiscent of an immense garbage dump, their souls constantly pelted by the foul mixture of rain and sleet, emblematic of their earthly excesses in eating and drinking. Just as their sin caused the bloating, disfiguring and ultimate disintegration of their earthly body, so here in Hell they are wasting away without the hope of ever achieving either corporeal or spiritual perfection. The emaciated souls of the gluttons on the sixth terrace of Purgatory (cantos 23–24) are, through temperance and proper nourishment, on their way toward salvation. The perfect incorporeal souls in Paradise subsist through their communion with the Eternal Fountain that satisfies all spiritual cravings.[32] The *Divine Comedy* stands as the supreme testimony to the power of the poet to use metaphors in his transformative vision of the world. As poet, Dante provides the food necessary for true understanding of the relationship of the individual to the universe, of the importance of proper nourishment not only for the physical, temporal body but also for the immaterial, eternal soul. In his treatise on philosophy, the *Convivio*, Dante intends, as the title indicates, to present a "banquet," a feast, the object of which is intellectual sustenance. Dante conceives the work as a multi-course "meal," featuring

---

secondo l'antica vulgata, 4 vols., ed. Giorgio Petrocchi, Società Dantesca Italiana, Edizione Nazionale (Milan: Mondadori, 1966–1967). The translation follows that of Allen Mandelbaum, *The Divine Comedy of Dante Alighieri: Paradiso* (New York: Bantam Books, 1986): "O fellowship that has been chosen for/ the Blessed Lamb's great supper, where He feeds/ you so as always to fulfill your need,/ since by the grace of God, this man [i.e., Dante] receives/ foretaste of something fallen from your table/ before death has assigned his time its limit,/ direct your mind to his immense desire,/ quench him somewhat: you who forever drink/ from that Source which his thought and longing seek."

[32] We must also note that Dante employs "kitchen humor" in certain parts of the *Inferno*. In cantos 21 and 22 the Pilgrim encounters the demons under the general leadership of Malacoda, whose activity in keeping the barrators under the surface of the boiling pitch is likened to that of cooks who use forks to keep meat under the surface of the boiling broth: "Non altrimenti i cuoci a' lor vassalli/ fanno attuffare in mezzo la caldaia/ la carne con li uncin, perchè non galli" (21:55–57: "The demons did the same as any cook/ who has his urchins force the meat with hooks/ deep down into the pot, that it not float"). In canto 22 Dante describes the two devils who fall into the hot pitch and are stuck together as being "cotti dentro da la crosta" (v. 150: "cooked/ beneath that crust"), as though they were two devils "baked in a pie"! For "kitchen humor" in the Middle Ages, see Ernst Robert Curtius, *European Literature and the Latin Middle Ages*, trans. Willard Trask (New York: Harper and Row, 1963), pp. 431–35.

fourteen *canzoni* prepared in different ways as the "meat" and extended prose commentaries explicating the literal and allegorical content of the poems as the "bread" (I, i, 14–15), and he clearly expresses his mission in the Introduction to the work:[33]

> E io adunque, che non seggio a la beata mensa, ma, fuggito de la pastura del vulgo, a' piedi di coloro che seggiono ricolgo di quello che da loro cade, e conosco la misera vita di quelli che dietro m'ho lasciati, per la dolcezza ch'io sento in quello che a poco a poco ricolgo, misericordievolmente mosso, non me dimenticando, per li miseri alcuna cosa ho riservata, la quale a li occhi loro, già è più tempo, ho dimostrata; e in ciò li ho fatti maggiormente vogliosi. Per che ora, volendo loro apparecchiare, intendo fare un generale convivio di ciò ch'i' ho loro mostrato, e di quello pane ch'è mestiere a così fatta vivanda, sanza lo quale da loro non potrebbe esser mangiata. E ha questo convivio, di quello pane degno, cotale vivanda qual io intendo indarno essere ministrata; e però ad esso non s'assetti alcuno male de' suoi organi disposto, però che né denti né lingua ha né palato, né alcuno assettatore di vizii, perché lo stomaco suo è pieno d'omori venenosi contrarii, sì che mia vivanda non terrebbe; ma vegna qua qualunque è [per cura] familiare o civile ne la umana fame rimaso, e ad una mensa con li altri simili impediti s'assetti; e a li loro piedi si pongano tutti quelli che per pigrizia si sono stati, che non sono degni di più alto sedere; e quelli e questi prendano la mia vivanda col pane, che la farò loro e gustare e patire. (I, i, 10–13)

Dante casts himself in the role of teacher in the *Convivio* in which he will introduce novices to the study of philosophy. In the *Comedy* he is both teacher and student, poet and pilgrim, the latter who gradually comes to full knowledge of the subject that the former has already mastered. Dante will enlighten individuals on the operation of Divine Justice and on the perfect order of the universe. Common to both works is the metaphor of the banquet that serves to nourish the intellectual and spiritual needs of humankind. Through this use of concrete imagery to speak of and represent ethereal concepts Dante displays his consummate artistry and command of his material, so that everyone can comprehend even the most abstract idea.

---

33 The text follows that of Maria Simonelli, Dante Alighieri, *Il Convivio* (Bologna: Pàtron, 1966); the translation is by Richard H. Lansing, *Dante's "Il Convivio" ("The Banquet")* (New York: Garland, 1990): "Therefore, I (who do not sit at the blessed table, but, having fled the pasture of the common herd, gather up a part of what falls to the feet of those who do sit there, and who know the unfortunate life of those I have left behind, for the sweetness that I taste in what I gather up piece by piece, and moved by compassion, though not forgetting myself) have set aside for those who are unfortunate something that I have placed before their eyes some time ago, by which I have increased their desire. Wishing now to set their table, I intend to present to all men a banquet of what I have shown them and of the bread which must necessarily accompany such meat, without which it could not be consumed by them. This banquet, being worthy of such bread, offers meat which I intend should not be served in vain. Therefore I would not have anyone be seated there whose organs are ill-disposed because he lacks teeth, tongue, or palate, nor anyone addicted to vice, for his stomach is so full of poisonous and contrary humours that it would not be able to retain my meat. But let come here all those whose human hunger derives from domestic or civic responsibilities, and let them sit at the same table with others likewise handicapped; and at their feet let all those place themselves who do not merit a higher seat because of their indolence; and let each group partake of my meat with bread, for I will have them both taste of it and digest it." (Lansing, pp. 4–5).

How shall we conclude this survey? The three basic categories we outlined at the beginning of this essay could be compared to a three-course dinner *all'italiana*. We recall that the three principal roles of references to food, eating and feasting in medieval Italian literature are (1) as brief mentions, (2) as more elaborate descriptions (directed toward three distinct ends), and (3) as metaphors. The first course is the appetizer, the *antipasto*: it announces the meal and gives some hint as to its content, but does not dwell at any length on its substance, nor is it a meal in itself; and such is the brevity of many references to food and eating in the text. The second course, which admits to three distinct parts, consists of the *minestra, carne,* and *contorni*: the great variety of soups and pasta dishes make us aware of the special character of the event, the succulent entrées provide the textual "meat" for commentary, and the salad and other accompanying side dishes serve to embellish and enhance the quality of the entrée. The third and final course is the *dolce*, the dessert which embodies the sublime character of the chef's imagination and power to present through the tangible reality of whipped cream, meringue and tortes the supreme metaphor of ineffable bliss. Buon appetito!

THE OUTSIDER AT COURT, OR WHAT IS SO STRANGE ABOUT THE STRANGER?

William MacBain

Medieval French romances are full of strangers. The hero himself is frequently portrayed as someone from another, often distant, land. Erec, a fully integrated stranger at the court of King Arthur, eventually returns to his own country to marry Enide, and take over the kingdom from his recently deceased father. Lanval, a less fortunate alien at the same court, leaves not only Arthur's realm but in all probability the entire planet when he leaps up behind his fairy mistress on her palfrey and heads for the otherworldly Isle of Avalon.

Sometimes the hero is introduced to us first in his home environment, from which he is later forced, by unhappy circumstances, to emigrate. He becomes a knight errant, and he goes off to seek his fortune in distant lands and at foreign courts. Marie de France's Eliduc, and later his son Ille, in the romance by Gautier d'Arras, do that with great success, and unlike the accident-prone Lanval who had to be virtually "beamed up" to Avalon, both adapted remarkably well to their changed environment, and made excellent settlers – even to the extent of entering into marital arrangements with local princesses of great beauty, and incurring severe psychological stress on account of earlier marriages they had contracted before leaving home.

In *Aucassin et Nicolette* the heroine is taken away from her royal parents when she is still a small child. She is bought by a Provençal "visconte" who has her baptized, and raises her as his god-daughter in considerable comfort and ease. She adapts so well that she cannot even recall who she really is until, abducted once more – and this time by her own unwitting father and brothers – she at last sees the walls of Carthage, and remembers that she is the daughter of the King and Queen of that great city. Despite the joyous welcome she receives from her family, she suffers reverse culture shock to an extreme degree, and elects to dress up as a minstrel and return to her adopted homeland, Provence, in search of the hapless Aucassin.

In none of the above cases, does the "stranger" ever appear to encounter a language barrier. He stands out on account of his good looks, his bravery, his fighting skills, sometimes for the quality, or color of his armor, but never as a result of his failed agreements, his faulty conjugations, his wrong tenses, his inappropriate vocabulary, or his bizarre accent – nor indeed for any of those things that make us feel so foolish when we venture beyond our customary linguistic borders. And yet we know that in the twelfth and thirteenth centuries, moving a mere thirty miles could place you in a different dialect zone. Even now, in spite of the homogenization brought about by radio and television, it is often possible to tell which area of

London or New York people hail from, to say nothing of what stratum of society they grew up in, or what kind of school provided their basic education. In country areas, where dialect roots go deeper and change is less rapid, the regional accent, and sometimes even the local vocabulary, are immediately apparent to a visitor from outside. How is it then that, in a period when linguistic differences were far more marked than at the present day, they are overlooked by the authors of our romances? Are we to suppose that medieval heroes, and heroines, so skilled in all matters befitting a knight or a lady, have also undergone a total immersion course in one or more foreign languages and dialects? Ille goes off to Rome and discourses at length with an Italian Pope and a German Emperor all, apparently, in his own native Breton with nary a second thought. Unlike our latter-day Presidents and Prime Ministers, he has no entourage of interpreters to help him out. Nicolette may have forgotten her family, but either she still speaks excellent Carthaginian, whatever that was supposed to be in the early thirteenth century, or else her father and brothers have acquired a perfect mastery of Provençal. Whatever problems exist in her two dysfunctional families, linguistic communication does not appear to be among them.

It would be tempting to think that the failure of authors and characters alike to remark on the linguistic problems of a given "stranger" is simply a corollary of courtly behavior. It would be indecorous to do so. But is this the case? Perceval[1] is recognized as naive and stupid on account of the *content* of his speech not, apparently, because of his dialect or accent. He is told by a well-intentioned mentor not to go around repeating advice given him by his mother.[2] And earlier, in his first encounter with a group of knights whom he mistakes for heavenly angels, he completely ignores the questions they put to him, and persists in seeking their answers to his own. The "uncourtly" derision which he encounters at the hands of these knights is no doubt attributable to their perception of him as not belonging to their class and thus unworthy of courtly respect. One of the knights goes as far as to remark that the Welsh are all by nature more stupid than animals grazing in a field.[3] He is perceived as belonging to the class of the twice subjugated (by the English first, then by the Normans), but there is no suggestion that he speaks a different language from that of the ruling class represented here by the group of knights.

Marie de France's Eliduc, unjustly exiled from his home country, Brittany, travels to the region of Exeter in England in search of employment as a free-lance knight (or

---

[1] References are to *Le Roman de Perceval ou le conte du Graal*, ed. William Roach (Geneva: Librairie Droz, 1959).

[2] – "Or ne dites jamais, biax frere,
Fait li preudom, que vostre mere
Vos ait apris rien, se je non.
Et sachiez que ne vos blasmon
Se vos l'avez dit dusqu'a chi;
Et des or mais, vostre merchi,
Vos proi que vos en chastiiez,
Car se vos plus le disiiez,
A folie le tenroit l'en;
Por che vos proi gardez vos en."
                  (*Perceval* 1675–83)

[3] "Sire, sachiez tot entrcsait
Que Galois sont tot par nature
Plus fol que bestes en pasture;
Cist est ausi come une beste.
Fols est qui dalez lui s'areste,
Sa la muse ne velt muser
Et le tans en folie user."
                  (*Perceval* 242–48)

high-class mercenary!). He is well received by the king of that area whose refusal to offer his daughter Guilladun in marriage to a local warlord has brought his realm under attack. No mention is made by Marie of any language barrier that might exist between Bretons and Anglo-Saxons or even Anglo-Normans, and no impediment of this order exists between Eliduc and the beautiful Guilladun. The reader is led to assume that everyone speaks not only the same language, but even the same dialect and without as much as a trace of a foreign accent. The same is true in other *lais* of Marie such as *Guigemar*, whose hero hesitates to make any amorous request of his "lady" for fear that she might take a dislike to him and run away, not, as one might imagine, because she is a respectable married woman, but rather "por ceo qu'il ert d'estrange terre . . ." (*Guigemar* 478).[4] Foreign he may be, but he has apparently not the slightest difficulty in communicating with her. It is as if both speak the same tongue, and indeed the same dialect. We do not know, of course, how far afield the enchanted yacht carried him: possibly just across the bay, but the subtext is that it is quite far, if not quite as remote or as magical as Lanval's Avalon. When he departs once more, his presence having been detected by the lady's evil husband who, unable apparently to enjoy the lady's favors himself, is bound and determined that no one else shall, Guigemar is magically transported once more to his home base, to be followed at a respectable interval by the lady herself. The recognition scene has a certain comic quality that, I am sure, Marie did not intend. Guigemar sees a powerful resemblance to the lost beloved, but since, in his experience, "Femmes se resemblent asez" (*Guigemar* 779), he has to make quite sure that his eyes do not deceive him. Both he and his lady must therefore go through the ritual of undoing the knot made by each in the other's symbolically "intimate" article of dress: the tail of Guigemar's shirt and the belt the lady wears around her waist. Again there is no attempt at "voice" recognition: no suggestion that she from across the sea sounds the least bit different from the ladies gathered at Meriaduc's castle, many of whom must surely have been rejected by the obstinately celibate Guigemar before his encounter with the white doe.

In what, then, does foreignness show itself if not in accent, clothing, or eccentric behavior? What is so "strange" about the stranger who arrives at the court, be it Arthur's or that of the Holy Roman Emperor? If we consider the case of Lanval, we see someone who in every respect seems to share the values of his fellow knights at Arthur's court, and yet he is very definitely perceived as an outsider. At the Feast of Pentecost Arthur distributes lands and lesser chattels such as wives to his principal vassals. In this way he rewards their faithful service by giving them the means to attain a certain economic independence, and also sexual satisfaction combined with the means of establishing a line of succession for the acquired fief. Only he "forgot" Lanval, albeit a member of his *meisniee*. One must surely ask why? It seems that when he arrived at court, the son of a foreign king, and therefore of very high rank, he had shown that most important of knightly virtues: generosity to others less fortunate than himself. In so doing he had gradually used up all of the resources with which his royal father had endowed him: "Tut sun aveir ad despendu . . ." (*Lanval*

---

[4] References are to *Les Lais de Marie de France*, ed. Jean Rychner (Paris: Librairie Champion, 1968).

30), and home being very far away, there was no way of replenishing his resources other than by receiving gifts from Arthur for his service, or by specifically requesting help, which he was loath to do. His fellow knights could have reminded Arthur of his plight, but most of them were apparently envious of him on account of those very qualities in which he excelled: his valor, his generosity, his good looks, and his "pruësce" (*Lanval* 21–23). Some pretended to like him, but had he suffered any "mesaventure" they would not once have pitied him. Clearly, there was no help to be had from that kind of source, nor from those who were openly envious of him. But what of the handsome Yvain, and his cousin Gawain, "li francs, li pruz," so loved by one and all? They, too, are silent, and surely not from envy. Marie goes out of her way to point out that not *all*, only *most* of the knights ("tuit li plusur") are envious of Lanval. But she gives no reasons why the more noble ones ignore him, and do not include him in their leisure activities. Surely it must be because he is perceived as an outsider, a foreigner, not one of them. Marie herself, speaking perhaps from personal experience, remarks on Lanval's sadness, saying: "Seignurs, ne vus esmerveillez:/ Hum estrange, descunseillez,/ Mut est dolenz en autre tere,/ Quant il ne seit u sucurs quere!" (*Lanval* 35–8). Things change once his fairy mistress has provided him with both sexual and emotional fulfilment (the wife factor!) and an inexhaustible dowry with which to resume gracious living and return to his former practice of dispensing largesse to those in need (the economic factor). And yet, while his own retainers and others down on their luck, such as strangers passing through, prisoners, and *jongleurs*, depend on him, he still appears to be side-lined by his fellow knights, those who have no need of his generosity. A few weeks after the Pentecost incident, at the midsummer Feast of St. John, the knights go off to sport in a meadow below the tower in which Arthur's Queen is currently resident. They have already left their quarters when, suddenly, it occurs to Gawain ("li francs, li pruz") that it might be nice to invite their "cumpainun" Lanval whom they have left behind. Gawain's reasons for this change of heart are that Lanval is "larges e curteis/ E sis peres est riches reis . . ." At this point all of the knights turn back to ask him to join them. (It would no doubt have been better for Lanval if they had not done so, but then we would have had no story, and that would have been a great pity!)

Lanval is now "accepted" by his peers. But soon he is to be isolated once more as a result of the Queen's accusation. The King, to whom he had given loyal and unrewarded service, opposes him, and the senior knights called to "judge" him in this matter appear to be more inclined to believe the Queen, and thereby accommodate the King. Do they know Lanval so poorly that they can imagine him to be capable of making unwanted advances to the Queen, and then behaving spitefully when rejected by her? His own "courtliness" prevents him from telling his side of the story. As a loyal vassal of Arthur, he can hardly inform him that it was the Queen who made unwanted advances to him, and he is more than a little embarrassed by the Queen's interpretation of the reason for his rejection of her proposition. She has accused him of being a closet gay, an accusation much easier to make than to disprove even in our supposedly enlightened times. It is also an accusation which, if it becomes public, may well lead to further ostracization, even when, as in Lanval's case, it is groundless. One can doubly understand Lanval's reluctance to explain his apparent rudeness to the Queen by unveiling the spiteful accusation which brought forth his angry retort that ". . ./Une de celes ki la sert,/ Tute la plus povre meschine,/ Vaut mieuz de vus, dame reine,/ De cors, de vis e de beaute,/ D'enseignement e de bunté!" (*Lanval* 297–302).

But Lanval, the isolated stranger with neither friend nor relative at court ("N'i aveit parent ne ami"), is not abandoned by everyone. Gawain pledges himself and all of his companions at the risk of losing their lands and fiefs in the event that Lanval should fail to show for his trial. It appears later that, by the time the trial date draws nigh, there are already one hundred who pity Lanval. Even the barons who must decide the case are troubled to see this "franc humme d'autre pais/ Ki entre eus ert si entrepris" (*Lanval* 429–30), and they try to find a way out for him. He must be able to prove that his mistress is indeed more beautiful than the Queen: in other words that his remark to the Queen was a statement of fact, and not a gratuitous insult uttered with malicious intent. As we all know, the fairy mistress relents and puts in an appearance at court, charming all of the barons, including the King himself.

And so Lanval is rehabilitated, has acquired friends and supporters, and has found his mistress again. But in reality he has become even more of an outsider than before. He is now truly out of the closet: not the one the Queen had imagined him to occupy, but another. His entire fortune depends on his mistress who is and always will be an alien being, someone from "outside the norm." She can hardly be expected to live at Arthur's court as if she were merely the wife of one of his vassals when in fact she outranks Arthur himself. Did Marie not inform us earlier that neither the fabulously wealthy Semiramis nor the Emperor Octavian could have purchased "le destre pan" of the tent in which she received Lanval! And even if her opulent lifestyle were to be discounted, how can she or Lanval go on living at the same court as the outraged Queen whose duplicity has now been unmasked? If Lanval is innocent, as all agree, then the Queen has lied, as the fairy herself has made abundantly clear: "De ceo qu'il dist, ceo saches tu,/ Que la reine ad tort eü:/ Unkes nul jur ne la requist" (*Lanval* 619–621). The only possible resolution of the situation is the departure of Lanval, and since Arthur's is the best court available in the real world, Lanval must depart with his fairy mistress to a different world, a superior world where he can live in peace and harmony with his beloved to whom he has proved his dedication and his fidelity. The final scene of the departure to Avalon symbolizes, to my mind, the rejection of the male-dominated society of Arthur's court in favor of one in which more feminine values are prized. Lanval is not embarrassed to sit as a passenger on his lady's palfrey, thus reversing the role of the knight in shining armor come to save the lovely maiden in distress. It is he who is in distress, and the lovely maiden has come to rescue him, and carry him off to a land where he may find himself to be even more of a stranger than at Arthur's court; but, alas, we are denied the sequel to the tale, no first, second, or third "continuations" of *Lanval* having survived into modern times!

An apparent exception to this rule of the monolingual universe is presented by the *Tristan und Isold* of Gottfried von Strassburg[5] where much is made not only of the

---

[5] References are to *Tristan und Isold*, ed. Friedrich Ranke, 6th edition (Berlin: Weidmannsche Verlagsbuchhandlung, 1962).

hero's language skills, but also of those of Isolt, and even Kurvenal. Isolt speaks both Latin and French in addition to her native Irish.[6] Kurvenal shares Tristan's ability in Irish, as does another of the sailors,[7] and in consequence of this ability they are seen as valuable interpreters for the monolingual Cornish barons, should they be harassed by their Irish enemies still smarting from the loss not only of the Morolt but also of their annual tribute of Cornish slaves.

It is Tristan, however, who is the true polyglot. He first displays his linguistic skills when, as a young boy, he ventures onto the ship of the Norwegian merchants and plays chess with them, impressing them not only with his fine manners but also with his linguistic versatility. Indeed they cannot tell what land he comes from.[8] This quality in Tristan is emphasized once again when he makes his initial appearance at the court of King Mark. He endears himself to Mark first by his singing, and then to all of the nobles at this cosmopolitan court since he can speak all of their languages.[9] It is curious, however, that when the wounded Tristan is picked up by the Irish as he is adrift near Dublin, he converses with them presumably in Irish, and yet claims not to know what country he has arrived in.[10] One can imagine his Irish interlocutors wondering how this can be. Is this an Irishman by a stroke of good fortune drifting unwittingly back to his own homeland? – or is he some foreign polyglot, fluent in so many languages that he speaks Irish without being aware that he is doing so?

On his second visit to Ireland, at a time when all men from Cornwall are liable to be put to death, he does not pretend to be Irish but announces that he is from Normandy and that he and his men are merchants.[11] This fabrication is intended to persuade his hearers that he is not from Cornwall, but since we know that he is from

6   diu schoene si kunde
    ir sprache da von Develin,
    si kunde franzois und latin
       (*Tristan* 7984–86)

7   so si Curvenal da vor
    und ander mit im an dem tor,
    den diu sprache si bekant.
       (*Tristan* 8715–17)

8   swaz vuoge er aber an der stete
    mit gebaerden oder mit spil getete,
    daz was in da wider alse ein wint:
    si nam des wunder, daz ein kint
    so manege sprache kunde;
    die vluzzen ime ze munde,
    daz siz e nie vernamen,
    an swelhe stat si kamen.
       (*Tristan* 2279–86)

9   "Tristan, ich horte dich doch e
    britunsch singen und galois,
    guot latine und franzois:
    kanstu die sprache? herre, ja,
    billiche wol." nu kam iesa
    der hufe dar gedrungen;
    und swer iht vremeder zungen
    von den bilanden kunde,

der versuohte in sa zestunde:
dirre sus und jener so.
hier under antwurter do
höfschliche ir aller maeren:
Norwaegen, Irlandaeren,
Almanjen, Schotten unde Tenen.
da begunde sich manc herze senen
nach Tristandes vuoge.
da wolten genuoge
vil gerne sin gewesen als er.
       (*Tristan* 3690–3707)

10   sus bin ich eine sider geswebet
    mit marter und mit maneger clage
    wol vierzic naht unde vierzic tage,
    swar mich die winde fluogen,
    die wilden ünde truogen
    wilent her und wilent hin;
    und enkan niht wizzen, wa ich bin,
    und weiz noch minre, war ich sol.
       (*Tristan* 7596–7603)

11   koufliute heizen wir binamen,
    ich und min cumpanie,
    und sin von Normandie.
    unser wip und unser kint sint da.
       (*Tristan* 8802–05)

Parmenie, and that this in itself would account for any foreign accent he might have, it seems superfluous to pretend to be from Normandy. No doubt he is also fluent in Norman, but why the pretense? Perhaps, like so many polyglots, he simply enjoys playing different roles and keeping his audience guessing as to the identity of the "real" Tristan.

In contrast to Tristan's linguistic versatility, the Cornish barons' ignorance of Irish is dramatically visualized on the occasion of the single combat between Tristan and the Seneschal who had claimed to be the dragon-slayer and thus the winner of Isolt's hand. The people assembled in the stadium marvel at the rich attire of the Cornish contingent, but also at their total silence. They did not know the language of the country![12] Gottfried, proud no doubt of his own outstanding grasp of both Latin and French, clearly considers the monolingualism of such high-ranking people a decidedly negative and possibly slightly comic feature. They cannot speak Irish, and they dare not betray their Cornish origins by speaking in their own language, so they remain silent while all of the other spectators discuss the pros and cons of the contest to come.

Returning briefly to Gautier's *Ille et Galeron*, there is one brief mention of what might be called foreign speech, and it is again pejorative, and perhaps even xenophobic, in nature. When the brave Romans led by the Breton Ille are defending the city against the Greeks, the latter are described as babbling unintelligibly "en lor latin" – their version of a language already incomprehensible to Gautier's courtly audience. This is a way, I believe, of distinguishing between the "us" of the audience and the "them" of the enemy. The latter appear less terrifying, despite their superiority in numbers, because they cannot even speak a civilized language!

What are we to make, then, of the lack of what might be called linguistic realism in some of the most courtly romances of the period, in contrast with the strong emphasis placed on it in Gottfried's *Tristan*?

In my opinion the poem by Gottfried is less exceptional in this regard than might be thought at first glance. The hero's linguistic versatility is paralleled by his musical ability, stressed on numerous occasions, and especially in his first visit to Ireland, when it is his "sweet music" that not only moves the men of Dublin to treat him kindly, but also endears him to the Queen, who proposes to exchange her healing powers for music lessons for her daughter Isolt. It is related also to Tristan's fondness for playing different roles: Cornish huntsman, merchant's son from Parmenie, wandering minstrel, Norman merchant, minstrel again in the tale of the harp and rote, pilgrim or beggar in the scene of Isolt's sacred oath, fool in the *Folie Tristan* episodes, and so on. But at no time is Tristan called upon to act as interpreter, or even to use his language skills to advance the story. His minstrelsy is much more signifi-

---

12   genuoge da jahen,
      ezn getrüege nie so manic man
      als ebenguotiu cleider an.
      dazs aber alle stille swigen,
      dem lantgesinde rede verzigen,
      daz geschah durch die geschiht:
      sin kunden der lantsprache niht.   (*Tristan* 10868–74)

cant in this regard. It brings him favor with King Mark at a time when he is as yet unaware that Tristan is his nephew; it facilitates his entry into the Irish court and buys him close contact with both the Queen and Isolt; it permits him to free Isolt from the knight of the rote. By contrast, his linguistic skills are simply an ornament. They are never specifically put to the test, although, as mentioned earlier, the lack of foreign language skills made the Cornish barons look, and probably feel, a little ridiculous.

It would be wrong to assume that medieval writers were unconcerned about linguistic differences. It is obvious that copyists did their best to minimize the dialectal features of the texts they copied in order to make them more universally intelligible, thus providing modern editors with the very difficult task of determining the date and region of the supposed *Urtext*. And again, in many "bourgeois" texts certain characters – in particular Anglo-Normans – are often lampooned for their pronunciation, no doubt to the great amusement of the crowd. In one semi-courtly text, *La vie d'Edouard le confesseur*,[13] the author asks the hearers' indulgence for Anglo-Normanisms which may have brought smiles to the faces of the majority "Continentals" at the court of Henry II and Eleanor of Aquitaine: "Un faus franceis sai d'Angletere,/ Ke ne l'alai ailurs quere. Mais vus ki ailurs apris l'avez,/ La u mester iert, l'amendez" (7–10).

Why, then, is linguistic diversity scarcely mentioned in most courtly texts? Why, indeed, is the stranger not stranger? Perhaps the answer is to be sought in the very exceptions noted above: Gautier's pejorative reference to the invading Greek hordes who "si s'escrient en lor latin" (*Ille et Galeron* 1810), the Cornish barons' ignorance of any language but their own – despite the presence of numerous "foreigners" at Mark's court, and Tristan's extraordinary linguistic versatility which marks him as superior in every respect to the "insiders" at court and thus a fit object of envy for "losengiers" and "felons" alike. The newcomer to court is in the vast majority of cases perceived by the audience, if not by the "insiders," as a superior being. He is generally more handsome, more accomplished, more courtly, and more competent in tourneys and in single combat situations. Erec, Lancelot, Yvain, Eliduc, and Ille all fall into this category. There can be no doubt that Lanval, too, qualifies in all areas except that of combat in which he is never put to the test. But we are told that he had served Arthur well before being omitted from what might reasonably be called the "Pentecost Honors List." The outsiders are heroes with whom the courtly audience is expected to identify. But it is hard to identify with someone who speaks fractured Francien or pidgin Picard. Linguistic inadequacy is by definition "comic," not heroic. One need only remember John F. Kennedy's stirring solecism, "Ich bin *ein* Berliner," or Jimmie Carter's "lust" for the Polish people, which may have provoked as much amusement as they did enthusiasm. In popular literature and film of the twentieth century, characters with foreign accents are generally portrayed as comic (Colonel Klink), evil (Dr Fu Man Chu), or superficial and untrustworthy (most characters having a slight French accent!). The Star Trek series is a treasure-

[13] *La vie d'Edouard le confesseur: Poème anglo-normand du XIIe siècle*, ed. Östen Södergard (Uppsala: Almquist & Wicksell, 1948).

chest of what might be termed "front-loaded" accents. Spock is characterized less by his Vulcan accent than by the content of his utterances and his totally emotionless delivery. He is "intriguing" not comic. Scotty, on the other hand, combines his national "dourness" with the plain common sense of the traditional Scottish engineer. His Scottish accent is neither high-class Edinburgh, like that of Miss Jean Brodie, nor low-class Glasgow, like that of many Scottish comedians from Sir Harry Lauder on down. He is portrayed as solid and likeable, but he is never going to get the girl. That role is reserved for Captain Kirk, who, like any aspiring Hollywood not-so-*jeune-premier*, naturally speaks "non-regional" American English.

Our medieval writers ask us to admire the "outsider-hero." If he is "different" from the insiders at court, it must be in his superiority over them, whether it be in his physical beauty (with the notable exception of the injured Ille), in the quality and visual impact of his armor or, as in Tristan's case, his many skills and accomplishments. His fundamental quality, however, must be his courtliness. In this, he must exceed all others since, in the long run, it is he who wins the lady – or as in the case of Eliduc and Ille, both ladies!

The latter-day creator of science fiction films expects us to suspend our work-a-day unimaginativeness while watching the movie. Of course the inhabitants of other planets, and in particular the sex-goddesses, do not really speak American – or Oxford-English. But if they spoke even another Indo-European or Asian language we in the awe-struck audience would never know what they were saying, and our hero-representatives on their intergalactic missions would be equally at a loss for intelligible words. In the same way, the creators of medieval romances expect their hearers to imagine a kind of European Union *avant la lettre*, one which extends moreover to North Africa and the Middle East, and in which everyone of a certain class converses in a *lingua franca* identified with that of the audience, be it Champenois, Picard, Anglo-Norman, or Middle High German. The native tongue of the hero is not to be stressed for fear of making him "negatively" different from his peers. By definition he must excel in all the qualities admired and idealized by the target audience. If, like Tristan, he has many languages at his command, those must be in addition to a total mastery of the language of the court to which he comes as heroic outsider, sweeping all before him, and winning the hand or heart of the most desired lady around, before returning in triumph to his home base, like Erec or Ille, or, in the case of Tristan – an exception to so many rules – to union with the beloved in death, and reconciliation with society.

"PSEUDO"-COURTLY ELEMENTS IN A CANONICAL EPIC

Sara I. James

It is a long-standing tradition in French literary medieval studies to hold that epic and courtly writings are exclusive; what is the source of this distinction, and what definition does it impose upon the term courtly? It will be the object of this paper to seek to reflect upon the point of intersection of these concepts. I will touch upon both their social and literary senses, basing my remarks upon the thirteenth-century epic group loosely called the *Geste de Monglane*, the adventures of whose eponymous hero were said to "ressemble[r] trop à celles des derniers chevaliers de la Table-Ronde," and were described as "fadaises, qui n'ont rien d'épique" by no less an authority than Léon Gautier,[1] and, more importantly, upon a parallel reading of Gautier's criticism in and of itself.

It is my suggestion that scholars of courtly literature have a vested interest in including the epic in their field of study, yet this view is relatively recent, and has in general emphasized a reworking of the definition of epic rather than that of courtly, as we see in the works of Calin, Cook, Kibler, Suard, et al.[2] The critical separation of the two is, I would argue, based upon the critical work of Gautier, and highly arbitrary. The critical element is, as we shall see, distinct from his summaries recounting epic action, and the two inherently contradict each other on a thematic level. Gautier, "notre père à tous," as Michel Zink has called him,[3] is the source both of vital, objectively recounted information concerning the content of the *chansons de geste*, and also of a definition of epic that persists to this day, and serves to exclude from the canon many of the very works it is based upon. I will use Gautier's

---

[1] Léon Gautier, *Les Epopées françaises: Etude sur les origines et l'histoire de la littérature nationale* (repr. Osnabrück: Otto Zeller, 1966), vol. 4, p. 142. Hereafter all references to Gautier's work will be given parenthetically, e.g. (4: 132) for volume 4 of *Les Epopées françaises*, page 132.

[2] See, for example, William Calin's "Rapports entre chanson de geste et roman au XIIIe siècle," *Essor et fortune de la chanson de geste dans l'Europe et l'Orient latin*, Actes du IXe Congrès International de la Société Rencesvals . . . (2 vols. Modena: Mucci Editore, 1984), vol. 2, pp. 407–24; Robert F. Cook's "Unity and Esthetics of the Late Chanson de geste," *Olifant* 11 (1986), pp. 103–14, and " 'Méchants romans' et épopée française: pour une philologie profonde," *Esprit créateur* 23 (1983), pp. 64–74; William Kibler's "La 'chanson d'aventures,' " *Essor et fortune de la chanson de geste . . .*, vol. 2, pp. 509–16; and François Suard's "L'épopée française tardive (XIVe–XVe s.)," *Etudes de philologie romane et d'histoire littéraire offerts à Jules Horrent*, ed. Jean-Marie d'Heur and Nicoletta Cherubini (Liège: n.p., 1980), pp. 449–60.

[3] Personal communication, 1991.

detailed and clear analyses of the poems in question as a point of contrast with his scathing criticism of the same, the better to outline the fundamental paradox at work here, a paradox that has informed epic studies over the past century and contributed to the genre's exclusion from the register of the courtly.

It has been one of the more compelling and elusive tasks of medieval studies to define the term "courtly." Leslie C. Brook nonetheless opens up new possibilities when he suggests that he "would be wary of theoretical definitions if they are going to be used to *exclude*."[4] Thus, far from restricting the field, any new definition should seek to broaden and shed light upon genres and general categories, bringing us closer to an understanding of these works in their original context.

Courtly literature is traditionally the domain of lyric love poetry, of a certain form of versification, and is clearly connected to a court through literary influence or patronage. Janet Smarr, in a recent issue of *Encomia*, recalled the three traditional questions, positive answers to which would generally establish a work's inclusion in the courtly canon: "1) Is the text about courtly material? i.e., is it about kings and queens, knights and ladies at a court, doing courtly activities (fighting, feasting, hearing minstrels, having love affairs, conspiring politically). . . . 2) Is the text aimed at a courtly audience? . . . 3) Is the text sponsored by a court?"[5] Although Smarr quite correctly points out that none of these criteria is watertight, taking into consideration as they do numerous variables such as genre, performance conditions, and audience, they all are nonetheless in some way linked to the term "court" through content and through what scholars suppose to have been the context. The context, of course, is an uncertain variable, unconfirmed in most cases, but construed from certain indications in the text, such as prologues or direct appeals to the audience. Such ground-breaking work as Edmond Faral's,[6] linking place and conditions of literary production to style, content, and ideology, is, let us recall, at one remove from Gautier's pioneering generation. The variety of work possible within this frame thus has of course allowed for a reexamination of what has and has not generally been considered courtly.

The epic, or *chanson de geste*, is a genre typically excluded from the courtly framework by critics. As even a quick skimming of Léon Gautier's *Epopées françaises* will prove, the snobbishness goes both ways: an alarming number of *chansons de geste* are not even given that title by the eminent specialist, but instead are referred to as "Romans," with a term such as "misérable" preceding, or "décadent" following. One reason for any unfortunate epic's exclusion from the Galterian canon is that it resembles a "courtly" work (although he himself did not use this term), too much so for comfort. Once again, the distinction between Gautier's clear recounting of events in poems, and his ideologically-driven assessment of them on literary grounds, cannot be over-emphasized.

And yet Reto Bezzola, in his seminal work on the origins of courtly literature, included the *chanson de geste* in courtly literature, on account both of its probable

4   Leslie C. Brook, "Courtly Reflections," *Encomia* 15 (1993), pp. 24–25.
5   Janet Smarr, "More Courtly Reflections," *Encomia* 16 (1994), p. 8.
6   Edmond Faral, *Les Jongleurs en France au Moyen Age* (Paris: Champion, 1964).

origins, discussed by Faral, and its socio-ideological purpose, an important connection long neglected by handbooks and manuals of medieval literature influenced by Gautier. For Bezzola, in fact, it was simply a matter of degree:

> [J]usqu'à quel point ces chansons de geste, que le XIXème siècle avait l'habitude de considérer comme des chants populaires, sont-elles de la littérature de la cour ou même de la littérature courtoise?[7]

> A qui ces poèmes épiques tout pénétrés de la conception de la féodalité avec tous ses droits et devoirs, du compagnonnage, du combat pour le suzerain et pour l'empire, pour la terre des aïeux et pour la chrétienté, auraient-ils dû s'adresser, sinon à cette classe féodale elle-même . . .? (Bezzola, 2.3: 489)

And yet the stigma remains, producing various unpleasant epithets for any epic that dare stray from the Roland fold. From Galterian tirades to the now accepted term "épopée romanesque," to use Guidot's term,[8] not forgetting Claude Lachet's designation "parodie courtoise d'une épopée" for the canonical *Prise d'Orange*,[9] critics have done everything possible to exclude certain poems from the realm of *chanson de geste* and liken them to romance or other typically courtly genres – without, God forbid, actually including them in the latter! As recently as 1992, Daniel Poirion's definition of the *chanson de geste* sought to distinguish "true" epics from the "decadent," while noting the survival of epic plots, themes and forms into the sixteenth century;[10] François Suard's work on the epic genre, published in 1993, uses the term "chansons d'aventure et de merveilles" to denote those epics that show the influence of courtly genres.[11]

I will examine certain thematic aspects of several poems of the *Geste de Monglane*, aspects which have been heavily abused, denigrated, and shuffled from one category to another: amorous intrigues; magical or fantastic episodes; and finally, what might be called attention to individual behavior on the part of our heroes and its stylistic presentation. The first two are considered the property of courtly literature; the third, as we shall see, while a generic attribute of the romance, can be attributed to a variety of developments in the *chanson de geste*. All of these elements contribute to making visible a broader spectrum of "courtliness," and in doing so force the question of epic's inclusion in courtly literature.

The poems to which I shall refer are the *Enfances Garin de Monglane*, *Garin de Monglane*, *Hernaut de Beaulande*, *Girard de Vienne*, and *Rénier de Gennes*. Because of the almost fluid nature of the *Geste de Monglane* – the content varying from

---

[7] Reto Bezzola, *Origines et formation de la littérature courtoise en Occident 500–1400* (Paris: Honoré Champion, 1967), vol. 2, pt. 3, p. 487. Hereafter all references will be given parenthetically.

8. Bernard Guidot, *Recherches sur la chanson de geste au XIIIe siècle d'après certaines oeuvres du cycle de Guillaume d'Orange* (Aix-en-Provence: Publications de l'Université de Provence, 1986), p. 589. Hereafter all references will be given parenthetically.

[9] Claude Lachet, *La Prise d'Orange, ou, parodie courtoise d'une épopée* (Geneva: Slatkine, 1986).

[10] Daniel Poirion, "Chanson de geste," *Dictionnaire des lettres françaises: Le Moyen Age*, ed. Geneviève Hasenohr and Michel Zink (Paris: Hachette, 1992), pp. 238–43.

[11] François Suard, *La Chanson de geste* (Paris: Presses Universitaires de France, 1993).

manuscript to manuscript, and edition to edition, where editions are available – this choice may be considered arbitrary. I consider it a fair sampling of works consistently included in any discussion of the *Geste*, and of those against which most of the charges of "misplaced" courtliness are levelled.

Interestingly enough, while condemning most love interests in *chansons de geste*, Léon Gautier spoke of love as one of several "lieux communs épiques" which included "tournois, amours, guerres contre les Sarrasins, etc., etc." (4: 107), almost reproducing Janet Smarr's listing of courtly activities. It is, of course, of paramount importance to this paper to note the almost identical nature of these two lists, one of supposedly epic traits, the other of supposedly courtly traits. The insistence upon the separation of these two literary phenomena which have so much in common has resulted in a distinction without a sharp difference that persists, generally unquestioned, after over a century.

In speaking of the *Enfances Garin* and *Garin de Monglane*, "oeuvres de la décadence" (4: 107, 126), Gautier condemns such typically forward young women as Germaine and Mabille, the latter "punie de ces impures et coupables pensées" (4: 145), concerning premarital sex with Garin. As for the queen Galienne's "mauvais discours" (4: 140), an impassioned speech recounting her adulterous thoughts for Garin, Gautier holds the poet personally responsible: "En un instant, elle est dépouillée de tout son ancien prestige, je veux dire de sa pudeur" (4: 138). Orable, later Guibourc, the chief female protagonist of the geste in question, has never been treated in such harsh terms.[12] Even within the context of these two poems, Gautier admits that such behavior, while it "dépasse toutes les bornes de la pudeur." is not rare, let alone alien to the noble epic. "Nous avons vingt scènes de ce genre dans la longue série de nos Chansons: il est permis de les trouver monotones" (4: 119). How to reconcile these contradictions? Not only is the epic habitually contaminated by some foreign genre or influence, but the traditional portrayal of the *dame courtoise* undergoes a radical change, no longer the haughty and inaccessible lady by any means. If indeed such epics are the results of courtly influence, then the notion of the distant, idealized lady of courtly literature is subject to significant revision.

The role of the marvelous and the fantastic in the *chanson de geste* is also hotly disputed. In speaking of the later prose version of the *Geste de Monglane*, Gautier attaches to *Hernaut de Beaulande* "tous les défauts des traductions du quinzième siècle: . . . *Amour* mis à la première place; des enchantements et des féeries ridicules;

---

[12] The character of Guibourc has been (deservedly) the object of many studies; among the more nuanced are Philip Bennett's "The Storming of the Other World, The Enamoured Muslim Princess and the Evolution of the Legend of Guillaume d'Orange," *Guillaume d'Orange and the chanson de geste: Essays presented to Duncan McMillan . . .*, ed. Wolfgang Van Emden and Philip Bennett (Reading: Société Rencesvals, 1984), pp. 1–14; and Jeanne Wathelet-Willem's "Guibourc, femme de Guillaume," *Les chansons de geste du cycle de Guillaume d'Orange: Hommage à Jean Frappier*, ed. Philippe Ménard and Jean-Charles Payen (Paris: SEDES, 1983), vol. 3, pp. 335–55.

la disparition complète de l'élément héroïque" (4: 204). Obviously, for our pioneer, the first two traits lead inevitably to the third.

Yet Gautier cannot remain internally consistent in this instance either; in speaking of the enchanter Perdigon, who appears in several of the poems of this cycle and saves the day, he says, "Le merveilleux va nous distraire un peu de tant de monotonie et de tant de médiocrité. Salut à l'enchanteur Perdigon!" (4: 150). "Ne nous étonnons pas de cette nouvelle apparition du merveilleux dans notre poésie nationale, et saluons-le avec joie!" (4: 157). Whether or not this is Gautier's playful side manifesting itself is hard to tell, but such a statement is clearly in opposition with his general claim that magic smacks of the Arthurian. It is not worthy of the *chanson de geste*, and should in and of itself be enough to label the work a "méchant roman d'aventures" or "féerie" (4: 134–35, 145).

One of the most significant aspects of the *merveilleux* in the cycle is the presence of giant-warriors, perhaps a throwback to the monstrous Sarrasins of the *Roland*. Rainouart of the Guillaume d'Orange poems is well-known; less so, perhaps, is the ancestor that the later poems seek to give him in the Monglane works: the giant Robastre. Armed too with a *bâton*, like Rainouart's *tinel*, he even becomes a monk in *Hernaut de Beaulande*, although his actions as such are about as conventual as those of Guillaume and Rainouart in their respective *moniages*!

Robastre, like Rainouart, does not seem to receive the same criticism as do other fabulous characters, perhaps because he is subordinated to the nature of the epic such as traditional criticism conceives it. "[I]l représente la force corporelle et sans intelligence au service d'une bonne cause," says Gautier of Robastre (4: 148). Joan B. Williamson has analyzed the particularly untamed and brutal nature of Rainouart, which is frightening and, at the same time, a sign that God has put a monster into the Christians' arsenal.[13] Strangely enough, it is not such elements that Gautier is condemning when he speaks of these Monglane poems as "des Romans de la décadence, pleins d'un faux merveilleux et, qui pis est, d'une fausse barbarie" (4: 173).

The words "faux," "fausse" seem here to be the key. Just as Gautier's seemingly random assessment of the semi-courtly *Girard de Vienne* as having a "caractère profondément épique" (4: 194) with no further explanation, implies a mysterious and contradictory set of criteria, so do his judgments of various violent incidents seem arbitrary. It would seem that the distinction between authentic, and non-authentic, or "faux," is based upon what Gautier perceives to be the necessity of such actions, or even the nobility of their motives; whatever is gratuitous is "barbaric," unconvincing, romanesque. As the title of his study indicates, the development of epic is the "histoire d'une littérature nationale," and as such deserves only the most elevated and justifiable instances of violence. In *Garin de Monglane*, the hero comes upon the thief who has stolen his horse, tied to a tree after having been caught by other miscreants. With a "férocité que rien n'excuse," our hero submits his victim to

---

[13] Joan B. Williamson, "Le personnage de Rainouart dans la *Chanson de Guillaume*," *Guillaume et Willehalm: Les épopées françaises et l'oeuvre de Wolfram von Eschenbach. Actes du colloque du 12–13 janvier 1985*, ed. Danielle Buschinger (Göttingen: Kümmerle, 1985), pp. 159–71.

torture before killing him (4: 143–44). Girard de Vienne, together with his brother, kills a seneschal for what we would nowadays call bad service in a restaurant; this "barbarie révoltante" (4: 186) is, however, certainly no worse than Rainouart's flinging a man against a tree and killing him, or Guillaume d'Orange's random murder of those who obstruct his path. In the second part of Girard's *chanson*, his nephew Aymeri tries to kill the queen for her disrespect to his family; much in the same way, Aymeri's son Guillaume nearly kills his own sister when she slanders Guibourc in the palace at Laon. "Moeurs sauvages, comme on voit," proclaims Gautier, "mais énergiquement épiques!" (4: 224).

> ... [C]es Sarrasins qui ont pénétré jusqu'au coeur de la France et sont maîtres d'une de nos meilleures provinces; cette brutalité sublime de jeunes gens uniquement élevés dans les armes et pour les armes; ces marchands assassinés à coups de poing; ce pillage féodal; cette joie naïve à la vue du butin. . . . tous ces traits nous paraissent profondément épiques, et nous nous trouvons enfin . . . face à face avec de véritables beautés! (4: 184)

Gautier's gleeful relief at some excusable ferocities in *Girard de Vienne* is new evidence of some profound conflicts on a basic thematic level. What is laudable? What is brutal? Obviously there is no modern pacifist approach here in the great critic's words, but rather, I believe, a statement about certain acts being inherently appropriate: violence and murderous giants are all very well for the sake of glory against the Saracens, and so anything within the immediate ideological context of the Guillaume d'Orange cycle is permissible.

What this does not take into account is the fact that such violence, the product of "des jeunes gens uniquement élevés dans les armes et pour les armes," is, strictly speaking, a courtly product. Such a mentality, as we would call it nowadays, would have been produced within the court hierarchy for the maintenance and furtherance of the system; those in the courtly audience would be the first to applaud such action, confirming as it did their feudal function; conversely, such an audience would be the best-equipped to judge any scene as appropriate or not, and in *their* perception of the difference lies what we would call distinction between various genres and registers. Bezzola himself sees in the unrestrained violence of the chronologically later epic something mimetic, reflecting the tumult of the outside world (Bezzola, vol. 2, pt. 3, pp. 506–8). In any event, the essential element is that there is no negative judgment upon these heroes *within* the text of the poem, only from without; the poet praises the heroes for their prowess, strength and resolve, while it is Gautier, the cultural outsider, who condemns.

This same reasoning applies also to the third set of criteria associated with courtly literature and condemned by later critics, what I have called individualistic and "un-knightly" behavior. This third section is rather loose, dealing as it does with random instances of our heroes' comportment and stylistic matters, rather than with a general theme; although it is perhaps continuing the vicious circle of generic broad-brushing, I am going to call these elements "courtly" for the sake of clarity.

The *Enfances Garin* is particularly susceptible to Gautier's criticism, containing as it does a long description of a tournament that recalls the detail found in *Le Petit*

Jehan de Saintré; the poet also permits himself a long digression on Amour, as god; and we see the princess Florette confide her love for Garin to her sister (4: 116). *Garin de Monglane* also sees an important role assigned to the courtly game of chess (4: 132). Later in the poem, Garin in his adventure-filled search for Mabille, who will become his wife, comes across a *jongleur* who gives him Mabille's dog; the dog will lead him to her. "Ses aventures," says Gautier, "ne ressemblent que trop à celles des derniers chevaliers de la Table-Ronde. On rougit d'avoir à raconter ces fadaises, qui n'ont rien d'épique" (4: 142). Garin endures many romanesque digressions and obstacles on his route, including devils conjured up by an adversary, but, after all is said and done, the dog indeed leads to recognition (4: 146–47).

Bernard Guidot, in speaking of the *Enfances Garin*, refers to the singular nature of what some might call psychological development in the poem. Unlike other heroes of the cycle, Garin does not simply act, he thinks, rationalizes, and explains his mental processes in detail (Guidot, pp. 294–95). At the same time, notes Guidot, the evil characters such as Ostrisse are pure Evil, lacking any psychological refinement (p. 568). We have, thus, within one poem, both the extensive interest in individual characterization and the allegorization that are part of courtly literature. It is in such a work, says Guidot, that a "morale individuelle" takes primacy over a group code (p. 296) – a rich irony for literature as dependent upon a group as that of the court! Yet could not a canonical work such as the *Roland* be cited as a prime example of allegorizing evil? The Saracens, in their monstrous form, certainly incarnate ungodliness, and in an unmitigated fashion.

Be that as it may, Guidot emphasizes the nature of what we see as contamination of concepts, the "courtly" and the "epic."

> L'osmose était inévitable entre ces deux mondes littéraires qui, au fond, s'adressent à un public identique. . . . Il s'agirait donc de l'insertion de recettes commodes dans un registre épique, d'un relâchement de la rigueur structurelle des oeuvres. L'aventure de la narration est calculée avec soin et finalement soumise, à long terme, à des objectifs épiques (Guidot, p. 589).

I would question the reference to relaxation of structural demands, since those to which most critics refer exist in relatively few epics; what is important here is the term "objectif," and it seems that this, too, is what Gautier understood to be the basis for judgment between "faux" and authentic. Whether it be an "unheroic" moment of weakness or love, or a magical digression, or any number of "non-canonical" traits, is the element in question subordinated to the plot, to the needs of the work in general? If the answer is yes, then in fact the issue of whether or not certain traits are or are not courtly is irrelevant. As we have seen, both Smarr and Gautier listed a practically identical group of traits as courtly, then as epic. The latter is a genre; the former is now understood to be an ideology, yet they are not incompatible. If we list then both epic and courtly literature under the general rubric of literature by, for, and/or about the court, that liberates us as critics to analyse works as quite possibly they were meant to be read, unconstrained by anachronistic definitions. It broadens, of course, our conception not only of the epic, but also of the courtly world and its interests. Could we not say that the very popularity and evident longevity of the cycle of Monglane, the cycle of Guillaume d'Orange, necessitates a variety of theme, tone and structure? To deny this would be to refuse "l'esthétique médiévale, qui ne répugnait pas au mélange des tons,"[14] to narrow our definitions, and to discourage what we should encourage: such enlightening work on the epic and the courtly as has already so enriched our discipline.

---

[14] Jean Frappier, *Les Chansons de geste du cycle de Guillaume d'Orange* (Paris: SEDES, 1955), vol. 1, p. 220.

THE PRODIGAL KNIGHT, THE HUNGRY MOTHER, AND THE TRIPLE MURDER: MIRRORS AND MARVELS IN THE *DOLOPATHOS* DOG STORY

Mary B. Speer

We all know people who can't tell jokes well. They may leave out information that is essential to making the punchline work, or mangle the punchline altogether, or overload the narrative with irrelevant material so that a sleek greyhound of a jest becomes a shaggy dog story. When the joke fails, we recognize that it does so because these people are incompetent narrators.

In Gaston Paris's major assessment of the Latin prose *Dolopathos*, a harsh critique that dominates his long review of the editio princeps published by Hermann Oesterley in 1873,[1] Paris charged John of Haute-Seille, the Cistercian monk who composed the romance between 1184 and 1212, with just such narratorial ineptitude, both in the frame narrative of his romance and in most of the intercalated tales. Several features of the *Dolopathos* particularly irritated Paris: John's independence from the source narrative that he claims to have heard but not seen – a source that Paris and other scholars believe to have been an oral performance of the *Roman des Sept Sages de Rome*;[2] his ostentatious use of quotations from classical literature and the Bible, which Paris dismisses as nothing more than "un vrai savoir d'écolier de cloître" (p. 491); and his transformation of secular folk material with a venerable Oriental heritage into propaganda for monastic Christianity. Dedicated to Bertrand, bishop of Metz, John's *Dolopathos* is indeed very different from the Seven Sages texts; it launched a distinct subfamily within the tradition, its chief offspring being Herbert's courtly reworking of the *Dolopathos* in Old French verse c. 1230.[3]

---

[1] *Romania* 2 (1873), pp. 481–503. I quote John's text from the edition by Alfons Hilka, *Johannis de Alta Silva Dolopathos, sive De rege et septem sapientibus*, vol. 2 of *Historia septem sapientum* (Heidelberg: Winter, 1913), and from the English translation by Brady B. Gilleland, *Dolopathos, or The King and the Seven Wise Men* (Binghamton, NY: Medieval and Renaissance Texts and Studies, 1981).

[2] On the affiliations of the Seven Sages texts, see my edition of the *K* and *C* verse redactions: *Le Roman des Sept Sages de Rome: A Critical Edition of the Two Verse Redactions of a Twelfth-Century Romance* (Lexington, KY: French Forum, 1989). For abundant information on the entire tradition, see Hans R. Runte, J. Keith Wikeley, and Anthony Farrell, *The Seven Sages of Rome and the Book of Sindibâd: An Analytical Bibliography* (New York: Garland, 1984) and annual updates in the *Seven Sages Newsletter* published by Runte.

[3] *Li Romans de Dolopathos*, ed. Charles Brunet and Anatole de Montaiglon (Paris: Jannet, 1856; repr. Nendeln: Kraus, 1977).

Despite Paris's low opinion of John's narratorial ability, the dedicatory letter, preface, and epilogue of the romance reveal an ambitious writer, eager to imitate the ancient philosophers who recorded the true deeds of famous men in order to instruct and please posterity, yet desirous of making his mark with new material. Though John apologizes for his "simple prose style" in a rather labored rendition of the modesty topos, he also emphasizes that he began this work while steeped in the classics, and he coyly announces that he is presenting an entirely new narrative of his own invention:

> Ego autem dum ueterum recolo studium, dum eorum ammiror ingenia, cuiusdam regis gesta, sub quo et cui mira contigerunt, subito in memoriam deuenerunt. Que quia adhuc scriptoribus intacta uel forsitan incognita permanebant, timens ne tanta tanti regis opera paulatim successu temporis a memoria hominum omni cum tempore laberentur, presumpsi ea quamquam elinguis et ydiota, quamquam nullius discipline scienciam assecutus, saltem qualicumque stillo describere. . . .   (Hilka, p. 3.16–24)

> [Once when I was deep in the study and admiration of the classics, I happened to recall the history of a certain king and the amazing things which happened to him during his reign. No writer had yet written about him, possibly because no one else had heard of his deeds, and I was worried lest the great history of this great king pass into oblivion as time went by. Although I am rather stupid and have no talent or training, I decided nevertheless to write about these things as best I could.   (Gilleland, p. 4)]

The unheard-of king is Dolopathos. Ruler of Sicily at the time of Caesar Augustus, he marries the sister of Caesar's wife and has one son, Lucinius, whose education he entrusts to Virgil. To do justice to this father-son pair situated precisely at the dawn of the Christian era, John greatly expands the frame narrative from the version he probably knew in the *Sept Sages*. He relates at some length Dolopathos's exemplary government, as well as Lucinius's ideal education. By contrast, the tale sequence initiated by the stepmother's false charge of rape when Lucinius returns to Palermo is reduced to eight tales, rather than the canonical fifteen: seven told by the Seven Sages of Rome and a final story recounted by Virgil himself. The queen tells no stories. John's extended post-trial narrative describes the conversion of the adult Lucinius to Christianity and his abdication to make a pilgrimage to the Holy Land. Clearly, this monk has transformed the *Sept Sages* model into a new form, a didactic *roman antique* narrated from a monastic perspective. Any changes in material he borrowed from the better-known secular tradition must be evaluated in light of these programmatic alterations.

The initial tale in John's abbreviated tale sequence is known as *Canis* "The Dog" in Seven Sages scholarship, "The Faithful Greyhound" among folklorists.[4] *Canis* is a well-documented folktale with a remarkably stable plot: while the master of the house is absent, his loyal pet – usually a greyhound in Western Europe – saves the

---

[4] Karl Goedeke gave short Latin titles to all the tales in the Seven Sages tradition: "*Liber de septem sapientibus*," *Orient und Occident* 3 (1866), pp. 385–423. *Canis* figures as type 178A in Antti Aarne and Stith Thompson, *The Types of the Folktale*, 2nd rev. edn. (Helsinki: Academia Scientiarum Fennica, 1961). J.-C. Schmitt provides a pioneering study of *Canis* versions in the Seven Sages tradition in *Le saint lévrier: Guinefort, guérisseur d'enfants depuis le XIIIe siècle* (Paris: Flammarion, 1979).

life of his infant son by killing a wild animal that has attacked the baby. Returning home, the master infers from the bloody signs of the struggle that the pet has killed the child; enraged, he slays the faithful animal, then is overwhelmed with remorse when he discovers his son, alive and well, in a room littered with the attacker's remains.

John's version of this dog story is both elaborate and distinctive; it is not surprising that Gaston Paris singled out his aberrant *Canis* for special attention when he denounced John's alterations of stories that Paris regarded as canonical and fixed in the *Sept Sages* tradition:

> L'auteur . . . éprouve le besoin d'allonger, d'arrondir[,] de motiver le récit qu'il a recueilli; mais il perd trop souvent de vue, dans sa préoccupation du détail, le sens et le but du conte. Ainsi, . . . le récit des aventures préalables du chevalier qui tua son chien est ennuyeux, inutile et même préjudiciable à l'effet. (p. 495)

Paris regards both content and meaning as fixed and "detail" as irrelevant; in his view, *Canis* is merely an exemplum illustrating the danger of acting in haste and nothing more. In an earlier study, however, I showed that in the verse *Sept Sages Canis* is not a neutral version, but a purposeful narrative designed both to reflect the events of the frame narrative and to respond to the preceding tale told by the queen. By a process of reception I call specular identification, the king is led to participate sympathetically in a story that mirrors his own situation.[5] My aim now is to show how John's *Canis* functions as a cautionary tale specifically tailored to fit his monastic romance. We shall see that in its privileged position as the first tale, it establishes themes that will be sounded again in later tales, themes crucial to John's dual goal of instructing while entertaining a readership of monks and ecclesiastical dignitaries. As in the *Sept Sages*, evaluating the precise details of the story – episodes, characters, choice of words – is essential to interpreting its meanings. And since John is a far more self-conscious and literarily ambitious narrator than the *K* redactor, we may expect his modifications to bear significance.

In John's romance, *Canis* is structured as a story with not one, but two calamities, the second far worse than the first and consequent upon it. Ignoring the advice of family and friends, an extravagant young knight first wastes his inheritance on chivalric trappings, unworthy companions, and frivolous pleasures in order to enhance his worldly reputation. Ruined, he leaves home secretly, taking with him only his wife and infant son, a horse, a dog, and a hawk; later, when he thinks the dog has killed his son, he murders the horse, dog, and hawk "in impetu ire et nimie turbationis" (Hilka, p. 47.28) ["in a fit of rage and madness" (Gilleland, p. 42)]. The

---

[5] "Specularity in a Formulaic Frame Romance: 'The Faithful Greyhound' and the *Roman des Sept Sages*," in *Literary Aspects of Courtly Culture*, ed. Donald Maddox and Sara Sturm-Maddox (Cambridge: D.S. Brewer, 1994), pp. 231–40. Yasmina Foehr-Janssens has also explored the variability of *Canis* as an exemplum: "Le chien, la femme et le petit enfant: Apologie de la fable dans le *Roman des Sept Sages de Rome*," *Vox Romanica* 52 (1993), pp. 147–63. Foehr's rich thesis on the Seven Sages traditions should lay to rest any doubt that subtleties of meaning and structure abound in these long understudied texts: *L'autre voie du roman: Le "Dolopathos" et la tradition du "Roman des Sept Sages"* (Paris: Champion, 1994).

narrator concludes the account of both disasters – the financial ruin and loss of reputation, then the still more dire destruction of the three animals that metonymically represent his knightly identity and also provide the young man's only means of keeping his family alive – with similar phrases that underscore the knight's guilt:

> . . . coactus est tandem dolens et contabescens suam quamuis sero recognoscere stulticiam. (Hilka, p. 46.5–6)

> [At last, sick and sorry, he was forced to recognize his stupidity. But it was too late. (Gilleland, p. 40)]

> Penitet commissi militem, sed sero. (Hilka, p. 48.1–2)

> [The knight was sorry for what he had done, but it was too late. (Gilleland, p. 42)][6]

This structural doubling, emphasized by a verbal echo, is an artful use of *gradatio* by an author versed in the classics. Structurally, John's version of *Canis* also works against its most obvious intertext, the parable of the Prodigal Son in Luke 15, where the Prodigal leaves home, wastes his inheritance in a distant country, then returns home to the loving father. In *Canis* we have no loving father, and for the prodigal knight no return is possible. The parable's comfortable closure – as far as the Prodigal is concerned – contrasts pointedly with our tale's more open ending. Far from being "the long and useless preamble" that Gaston Paris deplored, the first episode of this unusually bleak version of *Canis* is structurally and hermeneutically significant.

In addition to restructuring the narrative, John has completely remotivated the dog-killing protagonist. Instead of a mature head of household – in the verse *Sept Sages* a responsible lord of Rome – we have an orphaned prodigal knight: "quidam iuuenis secundum mortalium dignitatem nobilibus ortus natalibus" (Hilka, p. 45.11–12) ["a certain young man of noble birth, as mortals consider such things" (Gilleland, p. 40)], who desires to enhance his nobility and reputation through lavish spending. This presentation of the youth underscores the distance that separates the personage from King Dolopathos. The detached, critical voice of the narrator also establishes the modes of reception for the intradiegetic king as well as for the extradiegetic monastic readers. Rather than identify sympathetically with a protagonist whose life mirrors his own, the king must remain aloof from a character of negative exemplarity; both he and the extradiegetic audience should be alert to the narrator's contempt for the value-system that prizes noble birth, "as mortals consider such things," and worldly extravagance. Like the Prodigal Son, the young knight rapidly spends his inheritance in what John considers contemporary dissipations: courtly pleasures, such as knightly pursuits and thoughtless largesse,[7] and the dissolute company of actors and dancers.

---

6 Schmitt also notes the repetition (p. 81).
7 Throughout John criticizes the folly of noble largesse; Herbert, however, lauds that courtly virtue, notably in his version of Dolopathos's wedding festivities. On largesse and other differences between the two *Dolopathos* romances, see Speer, "*Translatio* as *Inventio*: Gaston Paris and 'The Treasure of Rhampsinitus' (*Gaza*) in the *Dolopathos* Romances," in *Transtextualities: Of Cycles and Cyclicity in Medieval French Literature*, ed. Donald Maddox and Sara

John fills out his sketch of the knight's character with two revealing quotations from the *Ars poetica* of Horace that underscore the knight's immaturity:

Ipse enim, ut moris est iuuenum,
   'Cereus in uitium flecti, monitoribus asper,
   Vtilium tardus prouisor, prodigus eris,
   Sublimis cupidusque et amata relinquere pernix',
militum seruientiumque turbam multiplicare studuit, per menses quoslibet mutare uestes, 'equis armisque nouis gaudere et aprici gramine campi.' (Hilka, p. 45.16–22)

[[In the way of young men,][8]
"[h]e was easily moulded to vice, harsh to his advisors, slow to foresee the useful, wasteful of his money, proud and greedy and fickle."
He desired to increase his followers of servants and knights, often to wear expensive clothing, and "to enjoy horses and new arms and the sport of the sunny field." (Gilleland, p. 40)]

Both quotations come from the section of Horace's letter where he advises the would-be playwright to create verisimilar personages when not deploying traditional characters. The writer "must note the manners of each age, and give a befitting tone to shifting natures and their years";[9] as models, Horace then provides capsule portraits defining the qualities that characterize the child, the youth, the man, and the old man. John has borrowed all but the first line of the five-line portrait of the young man, eliminating "imberbis iuvenis, tandem custode remoto" at line 161 ["The beardless youth, freed at last from his tutor"], perhaps because his married knight is likely somewhat older than an "imberbis iuvenis." John has divided the other four lines into two units that he inserts into his text in inverse order. The character weaknesses that close Horace's portrait come first here while the amusements favored by the young man exemplify those weaknesses. The diversions themselves are updated to fashionable knightly sports, with "new arms" replacing the hounds ("gaudet equis canibusque" line 162) of the model portrait.[10]

One consequence of John's reinvention of the *Canis* protagonist is that the motivation for his killing rage is located, with all the force of classical authority, in the character of a young man who is "spirited, of strong desires, but swift to change his fancies" (line 165). No longer do we see the murder – here a triple slaying – as an isolated and unexpectedly tragic result of extreme grief and overhasty action; now it arises from the essential folly of youth, which includes the failure to follow sound advice. Dolopathos is to understand that killing his son without good cause is an immature act, unworthy of a wise king.

Sturm-Maddox (Binghamton, NY: Medieval and Renaissance Texts and Studies, 1996), pp. 145–54; also Foehr-Janssens, *L'Autre Voie*, pp. 77–88.
[8]   Gilleland's translation omits this phrase.
[9]   "De arte poetica," lines 156–57, in *Satires, Epistles and Ars Poetica*, ed. and trans. H. Rushton Fairclough (Cambridge, MA: Harvard University Press/London: Heinemann, 1947).
[10]   Foehr-Janssens takes the quotation from Horace as evidence of John's desire to write courtly literature: "Il est dans la nature même du jeune homme, du moins en littérature, que d'être plein d'allant, amoureux de la chasse et des plaisirs, peu économe" (*L'autre voie*, p. 270).

A second consequence is that the character flaws attributed to the young man are linked inextricably to his noble rank and knightly identity; thus, the worldly values of knights as a class are stigmatized. To medievalists familiar with the depiction of secular chivalry in the *Queste del saint Graal*, it comes as no surprise that a twelfth-century Cistercian monk would paint so negative a portrait of a young knight. This portrait, moreover, plays a specular function within the romance, where young knights are repeatedly associated with rash judgment, self-indulgence, and suscepti-bility to dangerous feminine charms. Early on in the frame, we learn that in peace-time Dolopathos was obliged to establish intensive physical training to prevent the "manly strength" of his warriors from degenerating into "womanly softness" (Gilleland, p. 7; Hilka, p. 6.8–9). The treasonous denunciation of the virtuous king to Caesar was organized by jealous nobles who hated peacetime, and the stepmother who accuses Lucinius of dishonoring her is firmly supported by her noble family. In addition, the portrait of the irresponsible young knight is renewed in each tale told by the sages. The likeness with the young thief of *Gaza*, also a spendthrift knight who has exhausted his father's fortune in an effort to gain worldly glory, is particularly strong, as Paris observed (p. 495). But Foehr-Janssens reminds us that those two profligate knights belong to a "confrérie de jeunes hommes dépensiers et pleins de désir" (*L'autre voie*, p. 269). The young king of *Senex* executes the old men of his realm with shortsighted cruelty and surrounds himself with wicked young advisors; the young suitor of *Creditor* foolishly pledges a pound of his flesh to a moneylender in his eagerness to win a rich bride, then forgets to repay the loan on time. In *Viduae filius* a prince, en route to a battle, carelessly sets his hawk on a chicken that is the sole possession of a poor widow, then, when the widow's son retaliates by killing his hawk, flies into a rage and murders the peasant lad; the thief's sons of *Latronis filii*, though not knights, prefer riches to honor. In *Cygni* the young lord who marries a fairy and fails to protect his wife and children from his treacherous mother is presented as "adolescens quidam magnus secundum eos quos uulgo ex nobilitate sanguinis et ex rerum opulentia magnos uocamus" (Hilka, p. 80.28–29) ["a certain young man, great according to those who judge greatness by noble birth and wealth" (Gilleland, p. 71)]. The critical portrait of the young knight in *Canis*, evoking the Prodigal Son, supported by Horace's thumbnail character sketch, and presented by an anticourtly clerical narrator, is both reflected and reinforced throughout the tale sequence. To appreciate the severity of John's moralizing tone, one need only ob-serve what the knight becomes in the hands of the courtly Herbert, who glamorizes him with laudatory phrases and eliminates the critical narrator's interventions (pp. 168–69).

The antithesis of the foolish young knight is, of course, Dolopathos's son, Lu-cinius, Virgil's prize pupil and, presumably, the *beau idéal* of the cloister. Not only has he triumphed in learned disputations at school, but he follows his tutor's advice to remain silent and successfully resists the combined seduction efforts of the most beautiful women at court. Dolopathos is surely intended to recognize the superiority of Lucinius to this prodigal knight.

Let us now see how John handles the exile of the ruined knight and his murder of the three noble beasts. To avoid shame and mockery, he flees in the night. Only at this moment do we learn that he has a wife and child; they appear with no preparation and never become fully realized characters. The dog, likewise, is merely a dog, not a greyhound.[11] The sad little party wanders through many lands and finally one day, at sunset (propitious hour), arrives in a city where a compassionate burgher, a *civis*, like the man who hired the Prodigal Son to feed his swine, offers the knight, rent-free, a stone townhouse that has been unoccupied for five years. This offer of hospitality is expressed in the only direct discourse of the whole tale, no doubt to underscore the difference between extending charity to foreigners and practicing courtly largesse for self-aggrandizement.

While living in the burgher's house, the knight hunts for food daily with his dog or hawk; if he catches nothing, he and his family remain hungry until the next day. Unlike the Prodigal, he takes no menial job: "neque enim eum more rusticorum uiuere, fodere scilicet aut mendicare, sua generositas paciebatur" (Hilka, p. 47.7–8) ["his noble birth would not permit him to live like a rustic, namely to dig or to beg" (Gilleland, p. 41[12])]. On the crucial day, after twenty-four hours without food, the knight goes hunting with his hawk, leaving the dog at home. His wife, unable to bear a two-day fast, goes alone to a neighbor's house to request food. In her absence, a snake creeps out of a hole in the wall and attacks the child, with the traditional consequences: the dog kills the snake after a fierce fight, during which the baby's cradle is turned upside down. Returning with game, the knight infers from the overturned cradle and the bloody floor that the hungry dog has eaten the baby; enraged, he kills (in this order) the horse, the dog, and finally the hawk. Just as he is about to commit suicide, his wife comes home; she rights the cradle and begins to suckle her son. Then the couple find the dead snake and acknowledge the dog's faithfulness. The tale ends quickly, without any mention of the formal penance found in other versions: "Penitet commissi militem, sed sero" (Hilka, p. 48.1–2).[13]

There is much about this abrupt dénouement to disconcert even readers less eager to condemn it than Gaston Paris, who inveighed against "l'inepte idée de faire tuer au chevalier, outre son chien, le faucon et le cheval qui formaient sa seule fortune" (p. 488). The reasons for some changes are fairly clear. For instance, a snake is more likely to appear in a house that has stood empty for five years than in a busy palace, so this change, aside from the echo of the parable in the charitable burgher, seems justified on the grounds of verisimilitude. The meaning of the snake as a reflection of the seductive stepmother, an evil that comes from within the house itself, is unchanged.[14] The knight's despairingly destructive rage may be seen as the ultimate

---

11 Herbert sometimes translates *canis* as *chien*, but uses the traditional *lévrier* in important contexts: the departure (p. 171), the killing of the snake (p. 176), the knight's murder of the dog (p. 177), and the final recognition (p. 178).

12 I have modified Gilleland's translation, which reads "to live like a farmer or a laborer or a beggar."

13 For translation see p. 378 above. In most Seven Sages texts penance for the murder involves symbolic mutilation of the knight's body or equipment, or a pilgrimage; see *Sept Sages*, note to *K* 1375.

14 See Schmitt, pp. 78–79; Speer, "Specularity," pp. 237–39; and especially Foehr-Janssens, "Le chien," pp. 153–57.

culmination of his youthful folly; the sage fosters that interpretation in the moral that he attaches to the tale:

> 'Aduerte, o rex, quantum isti ira preceps nocuit, dum illud unde uiuebat impetuosus extinxit. Tu autem ne forte sicut et iste penitenda committas, noli precipitare sententiam.' (Hilka, p. 48.2–5)

> ["Take note, O King, how that hasty anger injured him when he impetuously killed the things by which he lived. Lest you perhaps do something for which you are sorry, do not summarily carry out this sentence." (Gilleland, p. 42)]

Paris contended that the triple slaying spoils the natural moral of the story, as if both the moral and the story were fixed for all time. I believe, however, that, by upping the stakes, John aimed to render the ending of *Canis* more dramatic, to complete the knight's fall to the bottom of Fortune's wheel. John has also given a new social twist to the moral by motivating the knight's rage as the wild impetuosity of a proud nobleman reduced to landless penury. By implication, a wise king of mature years should exhibit better judgment than an irresponsible young hot-head.

The hungry mother is a much more ambiguous personage than the prodigal knight. In John's *Canis* she first seems to be an extension of her husband, like the animals that accompany them; she offers no advice and lays no blame on the inadequate provider she married. Unlike her husband, though, she is not too proud to ask for food. Would her inability to tolerate a two-day fast be a sign of feminine or worldly weakness in the eyes of monks inured to spiritual discipline? Or if she is to be judged imprudent for leaving her baby unattended, could her action be justified as the effect of hunger in a nursing mother? John provides no entry into her character, no explanation of her actions other than hunger.

In the *Sept Sages* version of the tale, women play larger and more negative roles. The three nurses who abandon the baby to watch a bearbaiting are responsible for the initial misreading of the evidence in the bloody room; the lord's wife, alarmed at their account, passes on their reading to her husband, thus prejudicing his own interpretation of what he sees. In *Dolopathos*, however, the knight is not misled by any feminine intervention; rather, his fecklessness contrasts sharply with the competent nurturing of his wife, who has the good sense to look immediately under the cradle, then to feed her baby. This practical mother, in turn, is the inverse of the sensuously seductive stepmother.

Yet the very opacity of the mother in John's *Dolopathos* has troubled readers who wish either to understand or to exculpate her. In his translation, Herbert adds the information that she was newly risen from childbed when the family left home (p. 171), thus already a victim of her husband's folly. He makes her still more sympathetic by emphasizing her suffering from hunger and reinforcing his amplification with maxims: "Moult a de mal ki muert de fain" and "L'en dit ke besoigneus n'a loi" (p. 176). Herbert also describes the tenderness with which the mother puts her baby down for a nap before going to the neighbor's house. More recently, Jean-Claude Schmitt repeatedly asserts that she goes in search of food so that the baby will not starve (pp. 69, 76, 80, 83); therefore, "son départ n'est pas une faute" (p. 80). Cynthia Ho, who argues that "truant sympathies" undermine the antifeminist interpretations forced on the tales of the Seven Sages tradition, finds proof of her thesis in John's *Canis* because there "the silent wife escapes blame."[15] Foehr-Janssens, who invokes the medieval topos opposing the faithful dog to the untrustworthy woman, suggests that the mother is to be read as an antifeminist stereotype: "Il faut dire que l'amour du chien pour son maître dépasse de loin en persévérance et en loyauté tout ce que l'on pourrait attendre d'une femme!" ("Le chien," p. 155). John, however, seems to use the wife as a foil for her husband in the discovery scene and makes no explicit judgment about her.

If the process of specular identification functions with notable clarity in the *Canis* of the verse *Sept Sages*, it operates far less directly in the *Dolopathos*. Inversion and opposition are more common here, and loose ends like the abrupt ending and the hungry mother indicate that John did not intend to tie off all the narrative threads in the traditional manner.[16] Nor is the story exclusively oriented toward the neat lesson of avoiding overhasty action; it also provides a critique of courtly chivalry, although this can be fully appreciated only in the broader context of the frame romance that concludes with Lucinius's conversion and abdication – another open ending. The unfinished, indeterminate quality of John's *Canis* goes hand in hand with the incompleteness of his version of *Gaza*, the next tale, following which the sage expounds a deeper meaning that pertains to both stories, to pre-Christian antiquity, and to earthly life in general: "Tantis enim ignorantie tenebris mundus iste obuoluitur, ut sepe que iniquissima et falsissima sunt, iustissima et uerissima ab hominibus iudicentur" (Hilka, p. 56.4–7) ["The world has been muffled with such shadows of ignorance that often what is most unjust and false is judged by men to be the most just and true" (Gilleland, p. 49)].[17] As the tale sequence progresses, the stories will become more pointed, more closed, more overtly antifeminist; the indeterminacy of *Canis* and *Gaza* establishes the foundation for a complex tale sequence where mirroring and reappropriation lead finally to the discovery of the truth about the queen's accusation. But the greatest truth, of course, overcomes the shadows of ignorance only when Lucentius is enlightened with the news of the Light of the World.

To conclude: John's unusual version of *Canis* is anything but a carelessly told tale. This ambitious author has reinvented an old story to fit a particular slot in his romance, where it is charged with many layers of meaning. Although the sage who narrates *Canis* introduces the story modestly as "an ancient exemplum from the treasury of [his] heart," King Dolopathos's surprised reaction to it provides an unmistakable signal that readers are intended to recognize and admire John's innovations: "Quoniam, ait, *mirum nec a me adhuc quicquam simile auditum* narrasti, non possum tibi quod petisti negare" (Hilka, p. 48.12–13) ["Since you have told me *an amazing story and one that I have not heard before*, I cannot deny your request [to defer Lucinius's execution for one day]" (Gilleland, p. 42; emphasis added)]. The *Canis* we find in the Latin *Dolopathos* thus yields rich dividends to a deep comparative reading; working adroitly in a nexus of intertexts, John has artfully reshaped this *mirum* for delight as well as instruction.

---

[15] "Framed Progeny: The Medieval Descendants of Shaharizad," *Medieval Perspectives* 7 (1992), p. 94; see also pp. 96, 103.

[16] See Foehr-Janssens on open closure in the *Dolopathos: L'Autre Voie*, pp. 197–98.

[17] On John's *Gaza*, see Speer, "*Translatio*," pp. 138–45.

UNE RECLUSE FORT (PEU) COURTOISE: DESTIN D'UNE ANECDOTE DANS LE *ROMAN DES SEPT SAGES*

Yasmina Foehr-Janssens

Dans un article déjà ancien, Alfons Hilka a dressé l'inventaire des différentes occurrences d'un récit tiré du *Roman des Sept Sages de Rome* et intitulé Inclusa.[1] Cet apologue a connu une grande fortune narrative. Il propose des thèmes bien connus de la littérature narrative d'inspiration courtoise, lai ou roman. On y rencontre un mari jaloux, une malmariée et un jeune étranger, amoureux de la belle. Le récit débute par une résurgence narrative du motif de l' "amour de loin," suscité par un rêve, ou par la vision d'une image de beauté. Son intrigue repose sur la quête d'une épouse et donne lieu à de nombreuses descriptions d'objets et de parures magnifiques. Cette richesse thématique explique peut-être que le récit serve de toile de fond à deux romans importants: *Flamenca* et *Joufroi de Poitiers*.

Pourtant, dans les versions du *Roman des Sept Sages* qui le rapportent, Inclusa sert de machine de guerre contre les femmes et prend des allures de fabliau. Les sages de Rome, qui illustrent volontiers leurs arguments par des narrations enchâssées, prennent prétexte du bon tour joué par les amants pour fustiger la crédulité des maris et la duplicité des femmes. Cette histoire, très proche par son contenu du *Miles gloriosus* de Plaute, apparaît dans toutes les versions du *Roman des Sept Sages*, excepté celle connue sous le sigle L.[2] C'est dire qu'elle appartient au noyau central de cette oeuvre singulière apparue au XIIe s. dans la littérature occidentale. Notre récit occupe une position de choix dans le roman, puisqu'il clôt la série des fables enchâssées proposées au roi de Rome par les sages et la reine. Les premiers veulent dissuader le souverain de condamner son fils à mort. La seconde, au contraire, encourage la colère paternelle et espère un verdict sévère. Lorsqu'Inclusa se termine, seul le récit raconté par le jeune prince après un silence de sept jours relancera encore la dynamique des narrations secondaires.

---

[1] Cf. Alfons Hilka, "Die Wanderung der Erzählung von der Inclusa aus dem Volksbuch der *Sieben weisen Meister,*" *Mitteilungen der schlesischen Gesellschaft für Volkskunde* 19 (1917), pp. 29–72. Voir également l'article de Alexander D. Krappe, "Studies in the *Seven Sages of Rome,* XI: Inclusa," *Archivum romanicum* 19 (1935), pp. 213–26.

[2] *Roman des Sept Sages de Rome en prose, publié pour la première fois, d'après un manuscrit de la Bibliothèque Royale avec une analyse et des notes du Dolopathos* [. . .] par A.J.V. Le Roux de Lincy (Paris: Techener, 1838) [forme la deuxième partie de l'ouvrage de A. Loiseleur-Deslongchamps, *Essai sur les fables indiennes*]. Pour de plus amples renseignements sur le *Roman des Sept Sages de Rome,* on consultera la bibliographie spécialisée: Hans R. Runte, J. Keith Wikeley, Anthony J. Farrell, *The Seven Sages of Rome and The Book of Sindbad: an analytical bibliography* (New York et Londres: Garland, 1984).

Pour comprendre les raisons qui commandent le choix surprenant d'Inclusa comme exemple sapiential, nous étudierons la forme de ce récit ainsi que ses rapports avec d'autres anecdotes du recueil et avec l'histoire cadre. Notre étude s'appuie sur le témoignage de la plus ancienne version française des *Sept Sages*, représentée par la rédaction K (Paris, BN, MS f. fr. 1553) et le fragment C (Chartres, Bibl. Mun., MS 620).[3]

Dans le cadre de la littérature narrative d'expression française, les principes de la "fin'amor" font l'objet d'un débat largement ouvert à la controverse. S'il est de notoriété publique que les oeuvres de Marie de France, de Chrétien de Troyes et de Thomas d'Angleterre témoignent de cette fermentation intellectuelle, nous aimerions montrer que des textes de réputation plus didactique n'échappent pas à cette polémique et, bien plus, en vivent. Entre lai et fabliau, Inclusa offre un beau terrain d'exploration pour qui s'intéresse à la délicate définition de la "courtoisie."

Un jeune chevalier voit un jour en rêve une femme d'une grande beauté dont il tombe amoureux sur le champ. Un songe parallèle suscite le même "amour de loin" chez la belle, une jeune épouse enfermée dans une tour par son mari. La technique formulaire particulière à nos textes[4] permet d'exprimer avec force la réciprocité des sentiments des amants. Dans K, un même couplet d'octosyllabes sert à qualifier l'expérience amoureuse de l'homme aussi bien que celle de la femme:

> Il ne savait d'où elle venait, de quelle terre,
> sinon que son amour lui faisait la guerre.
>   (voir K, vv. 4231–32 et 4237–38, voir aussi C, vv. 1505–06)[5]

C varie un peu la formule pour retrouver, à propos de la jeune femme, une expression qui rappelle le lyrisme occitan:

> Et cette dame eut un songe à son tour
> et, pour cela, elle s'éprit du chevalier en retour

---

3 Ces textes ont été magistralement étudiés et édités par Mary B. Speer: *Le Roman des Sept Sages de Rome: a critical edition of the two verse redactions of a twelfth-century romance*, prepared by Mary B. Speer (Lexington: French Forum, 1989). On se référera également aux pertinentes études du même auteur: Mary B. Speer, "New light on the Chartres Prose fragment of the *Roman des sept sages*," *Scriptorium* 35 (1981), pp. 262–70; ibid., "Recycling the Seven Sages of Rome," *Zeitschrift für romanische Philologie* 99 (1983) pp. 288–303; ibid., "The prince's baptism in the *Roman des sept sages*," *Medievalia et humanistica* 14 (1986), pp. 59–80; ibid., "Editing the formulaic romance style: the poetics of repetition in the *Roman des sept sages*," *L'Esprit créateur* 27 (1987), pp. 34–52.

4 Mon analyse s'appuie sur les conclusions de l'étude que Mary B. Speer a consacrée au style de chacune des deux rédactions: "Editing formulaic romance style." L'auteur reprend les termes proposés par Jean Rychner à propos des fabliaux, pour qualifier C comme une "version dégradée" du *Roman des Sept Sages* en vers, et K comme un "remaniement dégradé" de la même oeuvre.

5 Les éditeurs du présent recueil ont souhaité rendre les contributions accessibles à un large public intéressé par la culture médiévale. C'est pourquoi nous présentons toutes nos citations en traduction française. Nous avons essayé de rendre dans la langue moderne la forme et la syntaxe de l'octosyllabe formulaire. Nos références textuelles se rapportent à l'édition de M.B. Speer, citée plus haut.

sans l'avoir jamais vu (*n'onques nou vit*),[6] mais il lui semble que,
quand ils se rencontreront,
ils se reconnaîtront facilement.   (voir C, vv. 1517–21)

Notre amoureux abandonne sa terre d'origine pour partir en quête de la belle inconnue. Il arrive un jour sur un rivage de Hongrie où il découvre la tour et la femme de ses rêves. Un chant d'amour entonné par la dame scelle leur reconnaissance mutuelle (K, vv. 4283–84).

Le chevalier, fort courtois et bon soldat, gagne bientôt les bonnes grâces du mari, le duc de Hongrie. Tant et si bien qu'il obtient le droit de bâtir une maison qui jouxtera la tour. Notre chevalier fait aménager une voie dérobée entre cette construction et la chambre de la dame de ses pensées. De cette manière, il peut se rendre auprès d'elle, en déjouant la surveillance du mari qui croit son épouse en sécurité. Dix portes solides défendent en effet l'accès à sa chambre. Grâce au stratagème du passage secret, le couple adultère peut organiser l'enlèvement de la belle. Celui-ci aura lieu sous les yeux et avec le consentement du duc, trop confiant "en la force et la puissance de sa tour" (voir K, vv. 4507–08, et C, vv. 1719–20). Le héros donne un jour un banquet en l'honneur d'une femme qu'il présente au maître des lieux comme sa fiancée venue de son lointain pays. Celle-ci n'est autre, bien sûr, que la malmariée. Le mari crédule accepte l'idée d'une ressemblance surnaturelle entre sa femme et la promise supposée de son hôte. Il pousse la bienveillance jusqu'à assister aux noces des amants et à accompagner au rivage les nouveaux mariés, bénissant ainsi le rapt de sa propre épouse!

Le drame de la jalousie tient une place prépondérante dans l'intrigue. On retrouve ici l'armature narrative qui sert de toile de fond à des lais tels que *Yonec* ou *Guigemar*. La tradition courtoise est unanime, dans sa diversité, à condamner le mari abusif.[7] La rivalité entre le jeune amoureux et l'époux ombrageux semble d'ailleurs induire une réflexion typologique sur les vices et les vertus. A la prodigalité de l'amant, dont l'exemple le plus fameux est sans doute celui de Joufroi, héros éponyme du *Joufroi de Poitiers*, s'oppose l'avarice du mari. Le désir libre et audacieux s'acharne contre les barrières que lui oppose la jalousie. En fait, tout porte à croire que ce conflit aligne dans un camp les qualités de la jeunesse et dans l'autre les traits figés de la vieillesse. Chez Marie de France, cette distribution des rôles se marque explicitement à l'initiale du lai de *Yonec* (vv. 11–28) ou dans *Guigemar* (vv. 213–17):

> Le mari était follement jaloux, comme le sont tous les vieillards naturellement, – chacun a horreur d'être cocu; – l'âge oblige à passer par là. (*Lais* de Marie de France, présentés, traduits et annotés par A. Micha (Paris: Flammarion, 1994), p. 45)

---

[6]   Le célèbre poème VI de Jaufré Rudel présente des accents que cette formulation rappelle, mais on pourrait songer aussi au poème IV de Guillaume IX (*Amigu'ai ieu, no sai qui s'es/ qu'anc non la vi*). Pour un exposé sur l'emploi de ce motif dans la littérature narrative, voir Philippe Ménard, *Le Rire et le sourire dans le roman courtois en France au Moyen Age (1150–1250)* (Genève: Droz, 1969), pp. 189–93. L'auteur montre que ce thème est souvent traité avec une certaine distance ironique.

[7]   On songera par exemple à l'intrigue d'*Eracle*. L'injure faite à l'épouse arbitrairement enfermée y est présentée comme la cause directe de l'infidélité de l'impératrice. Dans *Flamenca*, le discours d'Archambaut ne laisse aucun doute sur la gravité des ravages provoqués par la jalousie.

Notons tout de suite que cette configuration prend une dimension tout à fait particulière dans l'économie du *Roman des Sept Sages*. L'histoire cadre raconte un conflit entre deux générations, attisé par la présence de la jeune et belle reine, seconde épouse du roi Vespasien. Celle-ci n'est pas insensible aux charmes juvéniles de son beau-fils. Le prince, selon elle, a pour lui la jeunesse et la courtoisie (cf. K, v. 797), alors que son père "est déjà chenu,/ désormais il a trop vécu" (K, vv. 803–04). Les contes ne manquent pas de recomposer ces données de base pour en faire jaillir toutes les conséquences dévastatrices. Ainsi, après Inclusa qui retranscrit l'intrigue initiale dans les termes d'une aventure courtoise, le conte Vaticinum propose une nouvelle interprétation. Un jeune héros prédit à son père qu'il le surpassera en dignité. Le père, ulcéré par ce qu'il prend pour de l'outrecuidance, tente de tuer son fils en le précipitant dans la mer. Tout se passe comme si la jeunesse ne pouvait se défendre d'un comportement agressif vis-à-vis de l'âge mûr, comportement que celui-ci programme en fait, tout en supportant mal ses effets. "Est père," semble dire le conte Vaticinum, "celui qui adresse à son fils une demande de perfection, mais n'admet pas que, dans sa volonté de répondre, l'enfant en vienne en remettre en question la supériorité paternelle." Le quinzième conte résume par là une des thèses centrales du *Roman des Sept Sages*.

La suite du récit reprend d'ailleurs, à travers une curieuse fable animale, le propos d'Inclusa. Trois corbeaux harcèlent le roi du pays où réside le fils, rescapé de la noyade. Les oiseaux, deux mâles et une femelle, ne cessent de poursuivre le souverain de leurs cris perçants. Le jeune prophète expose leur cas. Le plus jeune des deux a vécu en concubinage avec la femme du premier, alors que, par temps de famine, son mari l'avait abandonnée. A présent, chacun des deux oiseaux revendique la légitimité de son union avec la femelle. Incapables d'aboutir à un accord, les oiseaux demandent justice au roi. Le verdict du souverain et de sa cour fournit une exégèse rétroactive d'Inclusa. Le mari qui enfreint le code de bonne conduite envers les femmes ne mérite pas de retrouver ses droits conjugaux:

> "Sire," disent tous les barons,
> "celui-là doit l'avoir selon la raison,
> qui la sauva pendant le temps de la pénurie,
> et l'autre, qui l'abandonna
> dans la carence, et la rejeta,
> la doit perdre, sachez-le bien." (voir K, vv. 4875–80; cf. C, vv. 1977–2006)

Ainsi, curieusement, les fables enchâssées semblent vouloir faire mentir la réputation du *Roman des Sept Sages*, souvent cité comme exemple de littérature misogyne d'inspiration cléricale. Notre tradition se révèle bien plus nuancée dans ses propos qu'il n'y paraît lorsqu'on s'en tient aux brutales condamnations de la perversité féminine qui émaillent les propos des sages.

On nous objectera avec raison qu'il ne saurait être question de réduire le propos du *Roman des Sept Sages* à l'éloge d'une jeunesse courtoise en butte à l'hostilité d'une vieillesse jalouse et cupide. Pour le roman de clergie, il y a une bonne vieillesse, celle qui s'appuie sur la science et les arts afin de trouver la sagesse. Les sept valeureux précepteurs du prince ont pour mission de rendre témoignage de ces vertus.

Mais les sages eux-mêmes ne sont pas toujours au-dessus de tout soupçon. Le conte Sapientes nous les dépeint en savants abusifs et envieux. Leur adversaire, le jeune Jessé, enfant prodige, offre, contre une science officielle devenue vénale, le secours d'une jeunesse clairvoyante et généreuse dans un scénario repris à la légende arthurienne.[8] De même, dans Medicus, le neveu d'Hippocrate est victime de la haine de son oncle qui finit par le tuer parce qu'il s'est montré supérieur à lui. Le conflit des générations ne cesse de se refigurer dans les contes.

La même subtilité régit le traitement de la jeune belle-mère du prince. La reine joue un rôle comparable à celui de la femme d'Arthur dans le lai de *Lanval*, puisqu'elle accuse faussement son beau-fils d'avoir voulu la séduire. Mais ses paroles ne recouvrent pas, peu s'en faut, une position anticourtoise. Malgré le châtiment qui punira en fin de compte sa luxure et son mensonge, toutes les valeurs qu'elle prône ne sont pas condamnées. On remarquera par exemple que la souveraine dénonce l'absence d'une formation chevaleresque dans l'éducation du jeune prince:

> "Il serait mieux dans ce pays
> qu'à Rome, à mon avis,
> il y verrait des exploits chevaleresques (= *chevaleries*)
> et apprendrait les manières courtoises (= *cortoisies*).
> A présent il est prisonnier d'une tour
> il n'en sera jamais que plus fou." (voir K, vv. 443–48)

Car le motif de l'enfermement concerne aussi le processus didactique:

> A cause de l'animation qui était grande,
> afin que l'enfant ne se laisse pas distraire,
> ils (= les sages) font une tour dans un verger
> plus blanche qu'une fleur;
> les sept arts y étaient représentés.
> L'enfant y réside en permanence. (voir K, vv. 363–68)

L'enfant, tenu éloigné des principes de chevalerie et de courtoisie, connaît le même sort que la malmariée d'Inclusa. La dénonciation des abus conjugaux rejoint une sourde protestation contre une trop pesante discipline cléricale.

Inclusa semble appelé, par sa position stratégique, à produire les éléments d'une synthèse au sein de cet intense débat romanesque. Tout invite à y voir l'ébauche d'un lai d'amour.[9] Tout d'abord, il faut prendre acte de certaines similitudes de notre récit avec le lai de *Guigemar*. La tour où est enfermée la belle s'élève sur un rivage, comme celle décrite par Marie de France:

---

[8] Sapientes relate l'histoire d'un jeune prophète en butte à l'hostilité des sages de Rome. Ce scénario s'inspire sans doute des aventures de Merlin démasquant les conseillers d'Uther dans l'épisode de la tour de Vortigern, comme le montrait déjà Killis Campbell, "The source of the story *Sapientes* in *The Seven Sages of Rome*," *Modern Language Notes* 23 (1908), pp. 202–04 et Alexander D. Krappe, "Studies," *Archivum romanicum* 8 (1924), pp. 398ss; et 16 (1932), pp. 279ss. Comme Merlin, le héros de Sapientes, appelé Jessé dans K et Melin dans les versions en prose, est un enfant né sans père.

[9] Voir notre interprétation d'Inclusa sous la forme que lui donne le *Roman de Dolopathos* (Yasmina Foehr-Janssens, *Le Temps des fables: Le Roman des Sept Sages, ou l'autre voie du roman* (Paris: Champion, 1994), pp. 274–78).

> Près de la mer, il trouve un château
> entouré d'un mur récent.
> La tour en était de belle apparence,
> sans mentir, elle se dressait, haute, vers le ciel.
> [. . .] La tour était très imposante
> elle avait dix portes bien verrouillées
> d'une construction à toute épreuve.
> Le mari emportait les clés avec lui
> il ne se fiait en personne:
> sa femme y était enfermée,
> qui par sa beauté ressemblait à une fée.   (voir K, vv. 4253–56 et 4262–68)

La beauté de la dame est celle d'une fée. Dans K, un vers, trois fois répété (*Ki de biauté resambloit fee*, vv. 4268, 4412, 4498), le signale dans une formulation semblable au v. 704 de *Guigemar*, qui relate l'arrivée de la malmariée en Bretagne.

Enfin, lors de l'apparition trompeuse de la duchesse de Hongrie au banquet donné par le chevalier, l'attention du narrateur se porte sur la magnificence des atours de la dame. Par dessus tout, sa ceinture attire les regards:

> Elle avait une ceinture
> qui était belle sans mesure.   (voir K, vv. 4469–70).

Un soupçon nous vient, selon lequel cette ceinture pourrait être une allusion à l'intrigue de *Guigemar*. Cette impression se confirme si l'on songe que le thème de la reconnaissance d'une femme est au centre de chacune des deux scènes ainsi mises en regard. Guigemar est pris de vertige lorsqu'il voit apparaître son amie chez Mériaduc. Il hésite à la reconnaître (*Guigemar*, v. 773–80):

> "Est-ce là ma douce amie, fait-il, mon espérance, mon cœur, ma vie, ma belle dame qui m'a aimé? D'où vient-elle? Qui l'a amenée? Mais voilà de bien folles pensées! Je sais bien que ce n'est pas elle! Les femmes se ressemblent beaucoup, je me fais de vaines idées." (*Lais* de Marie de France, p. 75)

"Les femmes se ressemblent assez": tel est l'argument central d'Inclusa (*il se sont femmes assés ki s'entresamblent de biautés* K, vv. 4537–38). Le chevalier en joue pour tromper le duc de Hongrie.

La structure d'Inclusa semble donc s'approcher au plus près de celle d'un lai. On y trouve même un objet symbolique qui, comme souvent chez Marie de France, figure la communion secrète de ceux qui s'aiment. Ici un jonc creux envoyé par la belle à son amant prend le relais de la chanson d'amour de la première rencontre (K, vv. 4319–24). Dans ce motif revit peut-être aussi la scène du *Roman d'Enéas* qui voit la jeune Lavine lancer une flèche chargée d'un message d'amour en direction d'Enéas. L'ambiance courtoise du conte s'illustre également de l'apparition d'une merveille architecturale. La construction ingénieuse, qui transforme la tour de la malmariée en un piège pour le jaloux, fera sans doute songer à la tour de Jean dans le *Cligès* de Chrétien de Troyes. Mais ici tout bascule. L'habile maçon de Montbrison ne connaîtra pas le destin heureux du serf affranchi. Il ne sera pas, comme l'architecte de Constantinople, l'homme par lequel le mari dupé est contraint d'affronter la vérité, d'abandonner ses certitudes illusoires de bonheur. Au contraire, la mort l'attend une fois son oeuvre faite. Le bonheur des héros d'Inclusa se construit sur le meurtre du maçon, victime de leur volonté de secret:

Le chevalier commit une grande faute
en tuant le maçon,
mais il le fit pour garder le secret
car il voulait celer l'aventure.   (voir K, vv. 4371–74, cf. C, vv. 1639–42).

Ces quelques vers sont extrêmement intéressants du point de vue du dialogue intertextuel. Dans ce meurtre se scelle l'impossibilité de construire la remembrance du lai. En agissant "par couverture" (v. 4373), notre héros veut "celer l'aventure" ou, pour reprendre la formulation de C, empêcher que l'ouvrier *n'acontast l'aventure* (= qu'il ne raconte l'aventure).[10] L'expression du vers formule un projet poétique explicitement opposé à celui du genre littéraire rendu célèbre par Marie de France. En général, le pivot narratif du lai n'est autre que le moment de la mise à jour d'un secret. Cette transgression est à la racine de l'aventure dont le lai célèbre le souvenir. Mais le conte enchâssé dans les *Sept Sages* ne tire pas, quant à lui, sa vocation d'une oeuvre de mémoire. Nos récits font silence sur leur passé. Rien, dans leur diction, n'invite à méditer sur leur origine. La fable est là pour faire sens, elle s'oriente résolument vers son propre futur, sa capacité à produire du fruit par l'"entente" qu'elle suscite.

Il en va de même du jonc creux lancé par la dame à son ami. Aucun écrin ne viendra le recueillir pour en faire l'emblème d'une relation amoureuse vouée à la perte. Le jonc n'est pas une relique, il est signifiant et, comme tel, il fait effet:

Il saisit le jonc et le ramassa;
l'intérieur était vide: il pensa
que cela signifiait
qu'il devait chercher sans retard
comment il pourrait parler à la dame
et monter dans la tour.   (voir K, vv. 4325–30)

Le message est fonctionnel, entièrement tourné vers la réalisation du projet auquel il veut donner corps. On pourrait même y voir une allusion grivoise, en faire une lecture obscène, proche de l'esprit du fabliau.[11]

Il n'empêche que cette communication utilitaire entre les amants ne va pas sans quelque développement, malgré tout, d'une poétique du récit. Car c'est bien l'amour qui est à l'origine de la compréhension du message par le chevalier. De même que le songe amoureux initial est le catalyseur du récit en ce qu'il oblige celui qui le prend

---

[10] Le terme "aventure" apparaît fréquemment chez Marie de France pour désigner à la fois le noyau événementiel du lai et sa mise en récit, voir par ex. *Guigemar*, v. 24; *Frêne*, v. 515; *Yonec*, v. 555.

[11] On peut comprendre l'expression "*parler à aucun*" comme un euphémisme pour évoquer des relations sexuelles (cf. M.B. Speer, *Roman des Sept Sages*, note du vers 4329). On le voit, la lecture de nos récits est très délicate. Cependant une assimilation pure et simple de nos récits aux fabliaux me paraît difficile à admettre. Lorsqu'elles sont reprises sous forme de "contes à rire," les anecdotes contenues dans les *Sept Sages* connaissent d'amples remaniements. Les différences sont grandes entre le conte Vidua (histoire de la matrone d'Ephèse) et le fabliau connu sous le titre *Cele qui se fist foutre sur la fosse de son mari* (NRCF III, 20) ou entre Inclusa et le troisième récit enchâssé dans *Les trois dames qui troverent l'anel* (NRCF II, 11).

au sérieux à se dessaisir de ses certitudes pour partir en quête d'une image fantoma-
tique, de même l'interprétation du message est soumise à la relation entre les deux
êtres aimants. Elle repose sur un pari sur l'avenir, synonyme de l'audace de la
jeunesse. Dans un autre registre, mais de manière tout à fait parallèle, le jeune prince
trouvera son salut dans son amour pour la clergie ("il aimait la clergie de toute son
âme," voir K, v. 372) qui lui permet de tenir le pari difficile de son mutisme. On peut
montrer que le *Roman des Sept Sages* hérite des représentations courtoises de
l'amour pour mettre en scène l'aventure éducative du jeune prince.[12] Sans l'amour,
cette adhésion du coeur pourvoyeuse de liberté intérieure, l'enseignement des *Sept
Sages* n'est d'aucun effet.

En ce sens, il faut bien mesurer les enjeux du conflit entre le mari et le chevalier.
Leur rapport à la femme s'exerce en sens inverse. L'un s'acharne à libérer celle que
l'autre s'obstine à enfermer. Cette dichotomie se manifeste aussi autour du motif de
la reconnaissance de la femme. D'une part, le héros aventureux est à même de
découvrir la belle qu'il n'a jamais vue qu'en rêve. De l'autre le mari reste aveugle
lorsqu'il s'agit de s'assurer de l'identité de celle qu'il côtoie chaque jour. Le jaloux,
trop sûr de la clôture matérielle qu'il impose à sa femme, va chercher dans le réel les
preuves de l'identité de celle qu'il aime, au lieu de laisser parler son coeur.

Quel sort dérisoire que celui de cet homme, juste héritier du fanfaron de Plaute,
soumis au leurre d'une réalité trompeuse! Il en est réduit à étayer ses certitudes sur
une série de portes qui, en réalité, ne servent qu'à entraver son jugement. Il n'est sans
doute pas insignifiant que la plus ancienne version littéraire d'*Inclusa* connue en
Occident soit une pièce de théâtre. Le vieux thème de l'identité en crise est au centre
du *Miles gloriosus*. Ce ressort important du comique de théâtre antique et médiéval
donne également tout son sel au récit du XIIe s.

En ce sens, le personnage principal de l'intrigue est bien, dans la logique de la
tradition théâtrale, le mari dupé. La présentation du récit par le sage Berous en
témoigne:

> Je prie le Dieu véridique
> qu'il t'advienne la même chose
> qu'à celui qui accordait plus de foi
> à sa femme qu'à ce qu'il voyait.   (voir K, vv. 4183–86)

La croyance en ce que l'on voit s'oppose ironiquement à la confiance, relayée par le
discours de la femme, en la barrière des serrures. Car certaines évidences valent que
l'on s'y attache même si elles vont à l'encontre du bon sens.

Ainsi donc, malgré ses allures de lai, *Inclusa* ne présente pas l'apologie de la
fin'amor. Mais, en dénonçant les torts du jaloux, notre récit ne récuse pas pour autant
les valeurs de la courtoisie.[13] Bien plus, il semble ardemment engagé dans une

---

12 Voir Yasmina Foehr-Janssens, *Le Temps des fables*, p. 140.
13 En fin de compte, le traitement particulier que notre récit applique à la *fin'amor* invite à le
rapprocher de textes comme le *Castia Gilos* de Raimon Vidal de Besalù et le *Lai de l'épervier*.
Willem Noomen a consacré une étude à chacun de ces deux textes: "Le *Castia-gilos*: du
thème au texte," *Neophilologus* 71 (1987), pp. 58–371 et "*Le Lai de l'épervier*, une mise au
point," *Mélanges de linguistique, de littérature et de philologie médiévales offerts à J.R.
Smeets* (Leiden, 1982), pp. 207–25.

volonté de réforme de ce caractère malheureux. D'abord focalisée sur la personne du chevalier, la narration s'attache toujours plus fermement au sort du duc de Hongrie dont elle fait son pitoyable héros. Soumis à la fatalité de son péché, la victime va inexorablement vers sa mort, alors que tout le récit se structure comme une déploration sur son sort (cf. K, vv. 4575–76 et 4598), voire une exhortation à redresser son jugement et à sortir de l'impasse où il s'enferme chaque jour un peu plus. Le triple rappel de la beauté surnaturelle de la femme scande des épisodes dont le mari est l'agent principal:

> sa femme était enfermée à l'intérieur,
> qui par sa beauté ressemblait à une fée   (voir K, vv. 4267–68).
> Il avait appelé sa femme
> qui par sa beauté ressemblait à une fée   (id., vv. 4411–12).
> Le duc a regardé sa femme
> qui par sa beauté ressemblait à une fée   (id., vv. 4497–98).

La structure à double entente du *Roman des Sept Sages* donne consistance à cette disposition particulière. Au-delà du jaloux, c'est le père vindicatif de l'histoire cadre qui est visé. Si les remontrances du conte enchâssé échouent à ramener le personnage secondaire à la raison, elles auront leur effet sur l'issue heureuse du récit enchâssant. La technique formulaire de K travaille d'ailleurs à tisser des liens entre les deux niveaux de narration. Le roman se déroule, dans sa péripétie principale, celle du procès du prince, selon un rythme de sept jours. Les événements de cette semaine décisive s'organisent autour de la répétition de certains gestes qui prennent une dimension rituelle (lever de Vespasien, narration des sages, clémence accordée au fils, récit de la reine, colère du père, etc.). Or une scansion similaire apparaît dans Inclusa. Elle se répartit sur deux jours à partir du moment où les amants ont la possibilité de communiquer. La première préfiguration de la mésaventure du mari a lieu à propos de l'anneau échangé par les amants. Le rituel de la *fin'amor* est l'occasion d'une mise à l'épreuve du sens du mari. Affolé par la ressemblance de la bague qu'il aperçoit au doigt de son sénéchal avec celle de sa femme, le duc se précipite dans la tour. Mais l'amant a le temps de rapporter le bijou pendant que le pauvre mari ouvre et ferme soigneusement les fameuses dix portes. Une fois sa tranquillité retrouvée, le mari passe la nuit auprès de son épouse. Au matin, il se rend à l'église:

> Cette nuit-là, il coucha avec son épouse
> dans la chambre à l'intérieur de sa tour.
> Le mari se leva au matin:
> il va prier à Saint Martin   (voir K, vv. 4433–36).

La même scène se reproduit au soir du banquet donné par le chevalier. Au cours de la soirée, celui-ci fait paraître la femme en la présentant comme une fiancée arrivée de son pays. De nouveau, le mari veut vérifier que sa femme était bien dans sa tour. Il s'attarde une fois encore auprès d'elle:

> Cette nuit-là, il coucha avec son amie.
> La nuit suivante il ne l'aurait plus!
> [. . .] le duc se leva au matin
> pour entendre la messe a Saint Martin   (voir K, vv. 4541–42; 4549–50).

On aura remarqué l'importante variation qui se produit entre la première et la deuxième occurrence de cette scène. La femme qui était l'épouse de son mari devient son amie. L'enjeu d'amour se dévoile ici. On se souviendra, comme le propose l'éditrice, du roman de Chrétien de Troyes où Enide tente d'être et de rester à la fois la femme et l'amie d'Erec. Bien sûr cette notation n'a d'autre vocation que de souligner l'échec du mari. Sa femme n'est son amie que dans la mesure où il l'a d'ores et déjà perdue. Mais, une fois de plus, la description de la femme concerne le mari et non l'amant, confirmant que l'aventure est sienne. Le duc nous apparaît de plus en plus comme un Guigemar qui aurait échoué à reconnaître sa dame.

Mais la mention de Saint Martin a aussi son intérêt, car elle souligne la ressemblance entre le duc de Hongrie et Vespasien. Ce dernier se rend en effet régulièrement à l'église le matin. Par trois fois, le lieu saint est nommé: Saint Martin (vv. 1408, 2844, 4630). Les vers qui rapportent ces dévotions matinales sont pris dans le même moule métrique et syntaxique que ceux qui concernent le duc de Hongrie:

> Le roi se leva au matin
> pour entendre la messe à Saint Martin   (voir K, vv. 1407–08).

La reine le suit, comme faisait le chevalier dans Inclusa (K, vv. 1409–10 = vv. 4551–52 et vv. 4437–38):

> Et la reine tout aussitôt le suit,   Et le soldat de même le suit
> pleine de colère.   Rapidement.

Le moutier Saint Martin porte le même nom que le bourg, situé aux portes de Constantinople, où résident les sages pendant le procès. Peut-être faut-il donner tout son sens à la légende de Saint Martin, champion du dépouillement, figure de la déprise, antonyme de l'avare ou du jaloux. Grâce à cette rencontre forgée par la technique formulaire du roman, la peinture d'un amour impossible rejoint la quête d'une justice parfaite dans laquelle est engagé Vespasien.

La vocation du *Roman des Sept Sages* oblige à reconnaître aux enjeux amoureux du conte une portée plus large. Chacun des crimes fustigés dans les récits enchâssés, avarice, abus de pouvoir, cupidité, adultère, jalousie, idolâtrie appelle en fin de compte à une nouvelle entente du Décalogue. Une réflexion générale sur la condition humaine se dessine à travers le destin de ce mari jaloux qui vient couronner la série des dupes tracée par les sages et la reine. Le roi courroucé est sommé d'y entendre une leçon d'humanisme. Le roman appelle à la libération du prince, mais aussi de son père, voire même, pourquoi pas, de la femme sur qui pèse pourtant la plus dure des condamnations. Les figures féminines de nos textes, prisonnières des représentations contradictoires de la malmariée et de la reine perverse renvoient peut-être, tout simplement, entre Eve et Marie, entre duperie cynique et pureté sacrifiée, au caractère indécidable de la culpabilité humaine.

COURTLY DISCOURSE AND FOLKLORE IN *LA MANEKINE*

Carol J. Harvey

"Melodramatic, unrealistic, repetitive, lacking depth in human terms, the romance of *La Manekine* has little to recommend it."[1] This trenchant introductory sentence to an article by Jean-Guy Gouttebroze is hardly conducive to further study of the thirteenth-century romance written by Philippe de Rémi, sire de Beaumanoir. For many readers, *La Manekine* is an initiation romance, spanning the heroine's years from adolescence through to adulthood, marriage and an accepted place in society. For the author himself, speaking in the epilogue, the work is an *exemplum*, a moral tale whose heroine, Joïe, is a model of Christian piety and perseverance in the face of adversity:

> Se vous tentation avés
> Ou aucun grief en vous savés,
> Prendés garde a la Manequine,
> Qui en tant d'anuis fu si fine[2]
>
> [If you fall into temptation, or if you are troubled in any way, think about the Manekine, who faced her many problems with great equanimity.]

Beyond these superficial categorizations, *La Manekine* proves to be of interest to students of both courtly literature and folklore. For whereas the work initially appears to be a typical courtly romance written in octosyllabic rhyming couplets, it is well recognized that the narrative canvas is borrowed from the folktale of *The Girl Without Hands*. In his edition of *La Manekine*, published as long ago as 1884 but still useful today, H. Suchier first posits the folktale as the source of Philippe's romance.[3] For although many of its themes and motifs are of courtly inspiration, the darker elements of incest and self-mutilation, injustice and jealousy belong more to the

---

1 My translation of Jean-Guy Gouttebroze's words: "Mélodramatique, invraisemblable, répétitif, sans profondeur humaine, le roman de la *Manekine* a bien peu d'attraits," in "Structure narrative et structure sociale: notes sur la *Manekine*," *Senefiance* 26 (1989), p. 199.

2 *La Manekine*, edited by H. Suchier in *Oeuvres poétiques de Philippe de Rémi, sire de Beaumanoir*, 2 volumes (Paris, 1884), vol. 1, lines 8543–46; see also lines 8529–36. All further references to *La Manekine* in the present paper are taken from this edition and line numbers are given in parentheses following the quotation; translations into English are my own. *La Manekine* is also available in a modern French prose translation by Christiane Marchello-Nizia, with preface by Donatien Laurent (Moyen âge, Paris, Stock + Plus, 1980).

3 See Suchier's introduction to *La Manekine* (*Oeuvres poétiques*, vol. 1, pp. xxiii–xxv).

"innocent persecuted heroine" genre identified in folklore.[4] These apparently paradoxical areas of courtly discourse and folklore will be explored in the present
analysis.

Among the medieval versions of the folktale, of diverse genres, Suchier lists the
twelfth-century *Vita Offae Primi*, an epic adaptation entitled the *Chanson de Lion de
Bourges*, a dramatic interpretation included in the *Miracles de Notre Dame par
personnages* and a fifteenth-century prose adaptation by Jean Wauquelin. The folktale of *The Girl Without Hands* remains popular and widely distributed in both oral
and written traditions today, with versions recorded in French, Italian, English and
Russian folklore.[5] Its generic plot paradigm has recently been summarized as follows:

> Act I. The heroine has her hands cut off because she will not marry her father. Act II.
> The heroine escapes and is found by a king who marries her. Act III. After the birth of
> her child, the heroine is expelled when letters between herself and the king are changed.
> She wanders in the woods where her hands are magically restored and where she finds
> shelter for herself and her children. After searching for a long time, her husband finds
> her, is introduced to his children and they are reunited.[6]

Philippe de Rémi's thirteenth-century romance adheres remarkably closely to this
topological pattern, with relatively few changes to the space and sequencing of the
folktale:[7]

---

[4]   The genre is discussed in a recent article by Steven Swann Jones, "The Innocent Persecuted Heroine Genre: An Analysis of Its Structure and Themes," *Western Folklore* 52 (January 1993), pp. 13–41.

[5]   In addition to "The Girl Without Hands," in *The Complete Grimms Tales* (New York:
Pantheon Books, 1972, pp. 160–66), examples include an Italian version entitled "Olive,"
published by Italo Calvino in *Italian Folktales* (New York: Pantheon Books, 1980), pp.
255–61, and a Russian folktale entitled "The Armless Maiden," included in Aleksandr
Afanes'ev, *Russian Fairy Tales* (New York: Pantheon Books, 1983), pp. 294–99 (see Susan
Gordon, "The Powers of the Handless Maiden," in *Feminist Messages: Coding in Women's
Folk Culture*, edited by Joan Newlon Radner [Urbana and Chicago: University of Illinois
Press, 1993], p. 285, n. 2). In his preface to Hélène Bernier's *La Fille aux mains coupées:
conte-type 706* (Archives de folklore, 12, Québec: Les Presses de l'Université Laval, 1971),
Luc Lacourcière notes that French versions are known in four Canadian provinces (Prince
Edward Island, New Brunswick, Nova Scotia and Quebec) and two American states (Rhode
Island and Louisiana); the folktale is also known by two Amerindian tribes (the Micmacs of
Cape Breton Island and the Iroquois of New York). Recent literature includes an issue of the
journal *Western Folklore* devoted to the "Innocent Persecuted Heroine" folktale, including
"The Maiden Without Hands" (vol. 52, no. 1, January 1993). Also, in her popular book
Women Who Run With the Wolves: Myths and Stories of the Wild Woman Archetype (New
York: Ballantine Books, 1992), Clarissa Pinkola Estes devotes a chapter to "The Handless
Maiden" (pp. 387–455.)

[6]   Steven Swann Jones, art. cit., p. 19.

[7]   One notable change in the concluding events is the transposing of the reconciliation and
the episode of the reattaching of the hand. This has the effect of presenting a religious climax
to the romance, as Suchier notes, op. cit., p. lxvii. See also G. Huet, "Les sources de la
Manekine de Philippe de Beaumanoir," *Romania* 45 (1918–19), p. 94. For a discussion of the
religious elements in *La Manekine*, see my article "Philippe de Rémi's *Manekine*: Joïe and
Pain," in *Women, the Book and the Worldly* (Cambridge: D.S. Brewer, 1995), pp. 103–10.

Act I. In order to escape marriage with her father, the King of Hungary, Joïe resorts to cutting off her left hand. Condemned by him to be burnt alive for this act of defiance, she is saved by a compassionate seneschal, who casts her adrift in a boat without sails or rudder. Act II. Landing in Scotland, she refuses to divulge her identity and is known henceforth only as the 'Manekine' – the girl without hands. She marries the King of Scotland and, during his absence at a tournament in France, gives birth to their son. Act III, the letter announcing this happy event to the King is exchanged by the antagonistic Dowager Queen for one stating that Manekine has given birth to a monster. The King's reply that nothing should be done until he returns to Scotland is also substituted by the Queen Mother, this time for a letter saying that Manekine and her infant son should be burnt alive. Again, Manekine is saved by a compassionate seneschal and, arriving in Rome in the same boat without sails or rudder, she is rescued by a worthy old senator. After searching for his wife and son for seven years, the King of Scotland reaches Rome at Easter, at the same time as the now-repentant King of Hungary. All are finally reunited and reconciled, and miraculously, Joïe's hand, preserved intact in the belly of a sturgeon, is restored by the Pope. The King of Scotland is recognized as the heir to Hungary and, through Joïe, to Armenia, following which the royal couple settles in Scotland.

Although the proposed incestuous union is dictated by the folktale, Joïe is not the miller's daughter of Grimm's version of *The Handless Maiden* but a royal princess. As such, I have argued elsewhere, she is "first and foremost the quintessential courtly heroine of noble birth, the incarnation of both physical beauty and virtue."[8] In this regard, the *descriptio puellae* functions as an aesthetic marker, for the long and glowing portrait of Joïe includes all the standard attributes of the courtly heroine of both romance narratives and the late courtly lyric. The King of Scotland's amplified *laudatio* extends through some sixty lines (lines 1567–1629), vaunting her beauty and wisdom, virtue and nobility of character. Even when she is maimed and cast out and conceals her identity, her innate nobility is recognized by people of the highest and lowest estate, from the King of Scotland to the three fishermen who spot her drifting in the Tiber. As the Scottish provost says: "Je croi k'ele est de haut parage,/ Car ele est mout courtoise et sage" (lines 1259–60). Unknown she may be, but her very ability to play chess marks her as a courtly lady:

> Des eskès savoit ele tant,
> Que nus mater ne l'en peüst,
> Ja tant de ce jeu ne seüst.   (lines 1384–86)
>
> [She knew so much about chess that nobody could beat her at the game or knew more about it.]

In another significant departure from the folktale, in which the heroine has her hands cut off for refusing marriage, Joïe cuts off her own hand to escape the incest:

> "Mais roïne ne doi pas estre,
> Car je n'ai point de main senestre,
> Et rois ne doit pas penre fame
> Qui n'ait tous ses membres, par m'ame!"   (lines 795–98)
>
> [But I may not be a queen for I have no left hand; and, upon my soul, a king must not take as his wife a woman who does not have all her limbs.]

8   "Philippe de Rémi's *Manekine*: Joïe and Pain," p. 104.

Through this act of defiance, Joïe is portrayed as a young woman of considerable physical and moral courage. True, her persecution leads to the displacement common in folktales ("Father casts daughter forth when she will not marry him"),[9] doubled by the setting adrift motif, when in her boat without sails or rudder Joïe is buffetted by the waves, an innocent persecuted heroine "beset and battered by the dark impulses of the community".[10] Nonetheless, she escapes the stereotype of folklore. For example, the maiden of the Grimms' tale has been described as a "passive victim, saved by her own patient faith in God, and saved by God and other authoritative male figures."[11] While piety is certainly essential to Joïe's character in Philippe's *exemplum*, she is shown from the outset to be not without other resources.

In contrast to Joïe, who is a complex textual figure drawn from life as well as from lore, the Dowager Queen is a one-dimensional character who owes much to the unmotivated evil of folktales. Although initially she welcomes the unknown maiden brought to her court, subsequently her malevolence is such that it cannot be explained merely in terms of her function as guardian of cultural standards and Manekine's unsuitability as a royal bride. In descriptions of the old Queen, the discourse of courtliness is replaced by constant reference to her jealousy and hatred for Manekine: "Par envie a a li haïne" (line 2420). She is further demonized in occurrences throughout the text as "la male dame," an appellation often accompanied by the curse "Dix maldie son cors e s'ame!" (line 3156). More evidence of her demonization is seen in her evil actions, carried out in secret under cover of night, together with allegations that a monstrous child has been born to Manekine. This false accusation is all the more damning to Manekine because in the Middle Ages monstrous birth was thought to reveal the will of God and was often interpreted as punishment for past misdeeds.[12] The allegation lends credence to the misgivings voiced by the King of Scotland – but rapidly dismissed – that Manekine might have been maimed and cast adrift "par son mesfait":

[9] Motif s322.1.2 in Stith Thompson, *The Motif-Index of Folk Literature* (Bloomington: Indiana University Press, 1955–68).

[10] Carolyn Hares-Stryker, "Adrift on the Seven seas: The Mediaeval Topos of Exile at Sea," *Florilegium* 12 (1993), pp. 79–98. Although *La Manekine* is not included in the works analysed, the summary of the topos is particularly apposite for this work: "Often these stories present the bleakest view of human existence in their concentration on the lonely figure of the good and deserving person separated by water from the sins and vices of the community: jealousy, cruelty, treachery, infanticide, abandonment, and mindless victimization. Indeed, the motif is eminently suited for this dismal list of human weaknesses. The image of the boat adrift at once symbolizes the uniqueness and frailty of the hero/heroine. Separated from those around him/her, s/he is beset and battered by the dark impulses of the community". As for the water, it, too, is a doubly-resonant symbol, suggesting cleanliness and rebirth but also death and surrender to the unknown" (p. 83).

[11] John Radner, introduction to a presentation on "The Powers of the Handless Maiden," Annual Meeting of the American Folklore Society, Albuquerque, New Mexico, October 22, 1987. Quoted by Susan Gordon, "The Powers of the Handless Maiden," in *Feminist Messages: Coding in Women's Folk Culture*, p. 275.

[12] Marie-Hélène Huet's recent book on *Monstrous Imagination* (Cambridge, Mass.: Harvard University Press, 1993) offers a comprehensive analysis of the attitudes toward monstrous progeny.

Espoir qu'ele a la main colpee
Par son mesfait, est envoïe
Seule par mer sans compaignie.
Par son mesfet? Ce ne puet estre;
Ja le fist Dix de sa main destre.
Voir, a chou que je voi en li,
Chou c'on li fist ne desservi.   (lines 1550–56)

[Perhaps it was because of some bad deed she committed that she had her hand cut off and was set adrift alone upon the sea. Some bad deed? Impossible! God made her with his right hand. Indeed, from what I have seen of her, in no way did she deserve what happened to her.]

The old Queen's vindictiveness toward Manekine may also be indicative of her obsessive, exclusive love for her son, a love tainted with incestuous overtones.[13] Clearly, through various speakers and his own authorial discourse, Philippe presents a folktale character of uncompromising malevolence, the reversal of the values of the courtly world.

Although elements of both courtliness and folklore can be seen to contribute to the characters of *La Manekine*, the tone of the romance is predominantly courtly. No literary technique is more important to this colouring than the discourse of courtliness, and specifically the lengthy monologues in which the Kings of Hungary and Scotland and Joïe herself expound on the torments of love.[14] Constructed around the courtly conceit of love's sweet malady, they use a whole series of contradictions to explicate love's paradoxical effects of hope and despair, joy and sorrow, pleasure and pain, presence and absence, passion and indifference. To these descriptions of the general effects of love, Philippe adds the dilemma arising from the specific situation which Manekine and the King of Scotland must confront. On the surface, the love between these two young people may appear ideal. However, Manekine is well aware that the self-mutilation which freed her from one royal marriage is now an impediment to a match with the King of Scotland:

"Enne me souvient il et membre
"Que je colpai pour chou mon menbre
"Que roïne ne deüsse estre?"   (lines 1707–09)

["But have I forgotten that the very reason why I cut off my own hand was so that I could not be a queen?"]

---

[13] See for example Christiane Marchello-Nizia's discussion of the inverted Oedipus legend in her modern translation of *La Manekine*, pp. 267–71.

[14] In his article "Chanson de geste et roman: remarques sur deux adaptations littéraires du conte de 'La fille aux mains coupées'," Claude Roussel identifies the depiction of courtly life as one of the two main processes which give the romance its courtly colouring. The other process he notes is the incorporation in the narrative of lengthy monologues exposing the joys and pains of courtly love. "Ces deux éléments jouent indiscutablement le rôle d'une sorte de balisage littéraire du texte qui proclame aux yeux du public l'appartenance de *La Manekine* au registre du roman courtois." (*Essor et fortune de la chanson de geste dans l'Europe et l'Orient latin*, Actes du IXe Congrès international de la Société Rencesvals pour l'Étude des Épopées romanes, 2 volumes [Modena: Mucci, 1984], vol. 2, p. 569).

And the problem is further compounded by her refusal to divulge her identity. This is indeed the King of Scotland's preoccupation: expected to marry his equal in birth, rank and wealth, he has fallen in love with the maimed, impoverished Manekine, of unknown ancestry:

> ". . . Si en serai blasmés
> Et maintes fois fols rois clamés,
> Se je la preng."   (lines 1629–31)

> [And I shall be blamed for this and everybody will call me a foolish king if I take her for my wife.]

However much appearances may be against her, Joïe's innate nobility triumphs, leading to the celebration of the couple's marriage. Both characters are depicted by Philippe as exemplars of courtliness: Joïe's voice is unfailingly courtly, matched only by that of the King of Scotland, whose love for Manekine is resumed in his words "Saciés de voir, ma douce amie,/ Que vous estes mes cuers, ma vie" (lines 1907–08) ["Know truly, my sweet friend that you are my heart and my life itself"].

On the other hand, the King of Hungary's passion for Joïe gives rise to different considerations. Is it not ironic that his decidedly uncourtly aspirations to marry his own daughter should be couched in courtly terminology? Yet he is in fact portrayed in accordance with courtly theory as a helpless victim of Love. Striking him through the eyes, Love causes a wound to the heart which will never heal:

> Mais od lui em porte le dart
> D'amours, qui grant anui li fait.
> Car si soutilment li a trait
> Parmi les iex que dusc'al cuer
> Le feri; mais puis a nul fuer
> N'en pot trouver la garison,
> S'en eut mainte grant marison.   (lines 424–30)

> [But he takes with him Love's arrow, doing him great harm. For Love had struck him so cleverly through the eyes that it pierced his heart; never more could the King recover from such a wound, which caused him much distress.]

Similarly, his subsequent ethical dilemma is expressed in terms of a courtly debate between Love and Reason: Reason tells him that this passion for his daughter is unnatural and contrary to accepted custom, whereas Love insists that all he needs to do to end his suffering is accede to his barons' and prelates' wishes. The debate ends with Reason vanquished and the King surrendering to the powers of Love:

> Mais amours pas ne s'en parti,
> Ains est lie quant sens s'en fuit;
> C'ore est li rois en son estruit,
> Si le demaine a son voloir.   (lines 494–97)

> [But Love did not leave, instead it was glad when Reason fled; for now the King is in its power, and it can do as it wishes with him.]

That Philippe intended his romance for a courtly or aristocratic audience is indisputable. The initial catalyst for narrative events – the lack of a male heir to the kingdom of Hungary – establishes immediate complicity between the author and his audience, for the knights of even the smallest court would be familiar with the dynastic tensions created by such problems both in public life and in the personal domain. Subsequently, Joïe's drama is played out against that backdrop of kingdoms and courts, tournaments and festivities that characterize courtly romance.[15] Courtly scenes are crucial in the generation and elaboration of the narrative material incorporated into Philippe's version of the folktale and the techniques of both romance and lyric are mobilized to express the courtly ethic with its complex of ideas and sentiments. A case in point is the banquet held at Pentecost to celebrate the marriage of the King of Scotland with Manekine. The festivities are to be held outdoors, in a meadow beside the river. The scene may be said to constitute a lyric moment within the narrative text, for the lengthy vernal introduction typical of the courtly love-lyric provides the descriptive elements, including the topos linking love with the renewal of nature:

> Ce fu en la douce saison
> Que li roussignol ont raison
> De chanter pour le tans joli,
> Que li pre sont vert et flouri
> Et li vergié cargié de fruit;
> Que la bele rose est en bruit,
> Dont les dames font les capiaus,
> Dont li amant font leur aviaus;
> Que l'erbe vert est revenue,
> Qui par la froidure ert perdue.
> Cascuns oisiaus en son latin
> Cante doucement au matin
> Pour la saison que est novele.
> Toute riens adont se revele,
> Que la joie maintenir doivent.   (lines 2153–67)

[It was in that mild season when the fine weather makes the nightingales sing joyfully, when the meadows are green and full of flowers and the orchards laden with fruit. Then the lovely rose is in bloom for ladies to knot in their hair and for lovers to pledge their troth. The green grass, which dies off during the cold weather, springs anew. In the mornings, all the birds sing sweetly in their own tongues, rejoicing in the new season. Indeed, every creature is filled with rejoicing and sheer delight.]

The splendid apparel and precious jewels adorning the nobles and their ladies, the five hundred tables set out in the tents, the dishes of meat, poultry, game and fish and the flagons of wine, the music and dances: all these elements contribute to the courtly colouring of the text and further demonstrate Philippe's enthusiasm for the trappings of courtliness. Significantly, describing the guests at the feast, the narrator adds that "avoec aus vilains n'assamble" (line 2282). As for a courtly virtue such as

---

[15] Claude Roussel, loc. cit.: "Il n'est pas trace de guerre ou de combats dans *La Manekine*. La classe seigneuriale s'y caractérise seulement par le faste, la largesse, la courtoisie, l'attention prêtée à l'image que l'on doit donner de soi aux autres. Ainsi, le roi d'Écosse est en somme prisonnier des contraintes sociales et ne peut abréger, malgré son vif désir de regagner son royaume, la série de tournois dans laquelle il s'est engagé."

generosity – that largesse originally celebrated by the troubadours – it is shown in the magnificent gifts which the King and Queen offer their departing guests at the end of the three days:

> Li rois fist cascun departir
> Hanas d'or, de madre u d'argent,
> Selonc chou qu'estoient la gent.
> Tout ensement la Manequine,
> En qui toute bontés affine,
> Par le commandement le roy
> Donne as dames mout biau conroi
> Mainte chainture et maint anel
> Et maint fremail d'or bon et bel,
> Dount tousjours fu puis mout amee.   (lines 2350–59)

[The King gave each departing guest precious goblets of gold or silver, depending on their estate. Manekine, whose goodness was unmatched, did likewise: at the King's behest, she gave the ladies many a fine belt, girdle and ring and beautifully-wrought golden clasps, so that ever afterwards she was loved for her generosity.]

From Hungary to Scotland, France, Rome and Armenia, the social structures and codes of courtliness predominate. This is not to say that Philippe subscribes to the courtly code in its entirety. For instance, it would seem that he implicitly condemns vainglorious chivalry, for the King of Scotland, who disregards his pregnant wife's legitimate fears for her safety, preferring to court personal glory at tournaments in France, will spend fully seven years searching for her. Furthermore, as Claude Roussel has pointed out, however much he may wish to return home to Scotland when he is informed that his wife has given birth to a monster, he is in essence bound by courtly convention to complete the round of tournaments. From these examples, one might conclude that Philippe has certain reservations about the code of courtliness practised in the thirteenth century.

In fact, with this textual transformation of a folktale recounting an adventure that transgresses the boundaries of acceptable conduct, Philippe positions himself in the margins of conventional courtly literature. Reshaping the material of the folktale, superimposing the values of the courtly world but sublimating them to the higher moral authority of Christianity, he reconstructs *The Handless Maiden*. In this way, he creates a multi-layered romance of a rich immediacy and a lasting resonance.

La Manekine includes the courtly and the chivalric, the worlds of folklore and fantasy, secular and temporal concerns as well as those of a spiritual or transcendent nature. Nevertheless, the dialectic tensions that might spring from the fusion of divergent worlds and the interplay of contrasting values are quite skilfully balanced, so that the work has an inherent thematic unity. In fact, *La Manekine* opens a window on a textual world of remarkable originality. In this, the earlier of his two romances,[16] Philippe's narrative voice may not yet be refined but it is already distinc-

---

16 It is now generally agreed that both *La Manekine* and Philippe's second romance, *Jehan et Blonde* were composed between 1230 and 1240. For dating of the works and biographical

tive. Despite the admonitory tone appropriate to the narrative as an *exemplum*, this voice revels in courtliness; and despite the sophistication of the courtly code, this voice draws on the primitive yearnings of the folktale. Then, enshrined as narrator in his own text, he guides the reader with his comments on characters and events.

One cannot deny that in certain respects this romance is "unrealistic, melodramatic and repetitive." However, such miraculous episodes as the preservation and restoration of Joïe's hand serve to reinforce the author's stated intention of furnishing an *exemplum* in which, despite the evil ways of mankind, God's will is manifest. And through the repetitive pattern of its circular narrative structure, the romance records Joïe's long but ultimately successful quest for identity. The apparently disparate threads of courtly discourse and folklore are skilfully interwoven and incorporated as narrative material into the rich texture of this romance. Despite Philippe's concluding lines, offering his story as a Christian *exemplum*, he is clearly influenced by the lay cultures of his day.

information concerning the two Beaumanoirs, father Philippe de Rémi (man of letters) and son Philippe de Beaumanoir (man of law), see Jean Dufournet, "Introduction à la lecture de *Jehan et Blonde* de Philippe de Remy," in *Un roman à découvrir: Jehan et Blonde de Philippe de Remy (XIIIe siècle)*, ed. Jean Dufournet (Geneva: Slatkine, 1991), pp. 7–24; also, in the same collection of articles, Bernard Gicquel, "Jehan et Blonde en son temps" (pp. 85–99).

THE FIRST-PERSON NARRATOR IN MIDDLE DUTCH FABLIAUX*

Bart Besamusca

At the end of every year, the Dutch weekly *Vrij Nederland* asks dozens of literary critics to name the best books of the past twelve months. In the Christmas edition of 1994, several reviewers observed that the American author Nicholson Baker had written a remarkable book, entitled *The Fermata*. The title is a technical term in music designating a pause after a note or a short silence, but in Baker's book the "I," Arno Strine, who is writing his autobiography, uses it to indicate "a period of time of variable length during which I am alive and ambulatory and thinking and looking, while the rest of the world is stopped, or paused."[1] In other words, Strine is able to stop time. At unexpected moments and for an indefinite period of time, he has this power, and, being obsessed by sex, he uses it to create a kind of voyeur's paradise. When he is able to stop time, for example by pushing up his glasses in place or – rather inconveniently – by starting the washing machine in the basement, he likes among other things to temporarily undress women. It is obvious that the readers of *The Fermata* will consider Arno Strine a repugnant character, although Strine in his alleged autobiography tries to forestall that opinion by underlining that his conduct is indeed strange, but harmless. In his opinion, he does not abuse women and he will certainly not use his power for criminal activities. His story even has a happy ending: Strine accidentally passes on his power to a female colleague, who is pleased to be able to work harder, and starts an enduring relationship with her.

In all probability a similarity with the fabliaux will force itself upon medievalists who read Baker's novel, because the parallels are striking. Humour and sex are important ingredients of Baker's novel, whereas fabliaux are "contes à rire" that very often revolve around sex. Philippe Ménard is certainly right when he states: "Si l'on comparait les fabliaux les plus crus à des oeuvres modernes de même inspiration, on verrait vite que les textes médiévaux n'ont ni la brutalité ni la perversité des récits d'aujourd'hui."[2] But some episodes in Baker's novel would not be out of place in a fabliau. For example, at a certain moment Arno Strine spies on his former girlfriend when she is having sex with her new lover; she is on her knees, her head on a pillow. Strine feels hurt, because the couple's coital position once was Strine's and his girlfriend's favourite way. He triggers a pause, hauls the lover to the garage, stations himself in exactly the same position that the lover had been in, clips time

---

* I would like to thank Frank Brandsma and Erik Kooper for their comments on the first draft of this article.

[1] Nicholson Baker, *The Fermata* (New York: Random House, 1994), p. 3.
[2] Philippe Ménard, *Les fabliaux: Contes à rire du Moyen Age* (Paris: Presses Universitaires de France, 1983), p. 233.

back on, has some delightful moments, stops time again, restores everything to its original situation, and leaves the house. For obvious reasons, the confused new lover has lost his appetite. I am convinced that the average medieval fabliau writer would have envied Baker this scene.

Whereas in Baker's novel Arno Strine gives an account of the events, the fabliau stories are presented by an anonymous narrator. In the medieval texts there is usually no I-as-protagonist perspective, but a first-person narrator standing outside the story and intervening freely. He introduces the comic tales, gives a running commentary on the events, and tries to manipulate the audience's opinions. For authors of fabliaux the presence of an external omniscient first-person narrator is one of the ways to establish and maintain esthetic distance, with the effect that, to quote Norris Lacy, "subjects that are potentially sensitive or shocking become nothing more than ideal material for a *conte à rire*."[3] In this article I will analyze the role of the first-person narrator in some Middle Dutch fabliaux, the so-called *boerden*, with the intention of contributing a little to what Lacy has recently described as the necessary "assessment of the variety and vitality of fabliau narration."[4]

As is well-known, it is not easy to define the corpus of Old French fabliaux. The generally accepted, uncomplicated definition of a fabliau as a medieval funny story in verse[5] does not define a fixed number of texts. According to Joseph Bédier there are 147 fabliaux, Per Nykrog counts 160 stories, Philippe Ménard 130, and the editors of the *Nouveau Recueil Complet des Fabliaux* intend to publish 127 texts.[6] The Dutch state of affairs isn't any rosier.[7] A *boerde* has been characterized as a rather short medieval story in verse that describes a non-religious, often erotic event, and its direct consequences, generally accompanied by a not always serious moral.[8] Another, more recent definition reads as follows: a *boerde* is a short, comical Middle Dutch narrative, written in rhyming couplets or divided into stanzas.[9] But these definitions do not provide a fixed corpus either. For example, the most complete edition of the Middle Dutch fabliaux contains nineteen texts, but the editor readily admits that he included the lyrical text *Dmeisken metten sconen vlechten* (The girl with the beautiful tresses) solely because of the erotic nature of the poem.[10] That the

---

3 Norris J. Lacy, "Types of Esthetic Distance in the Fabliaux," in *The Humor of the Fabliaux: A Collection of Critical Essays*, ed. Thomas D. Cooke and Benjamin L. Honeycutt (Missouri: University of Missouri Press, 1974), p. 117.

4 Norris J. Lacy, *Reading Fabliaux* (New York and London: Garland, 1993), p. 100.

5 For example, see Per Nykrog, *Les fabliaux*, new edition, Publications romanes et françaises 123 (Geneva: Droz, 1973), p. 14; Ménard, *Les fabliaux*, p. 45; and Charles Muscatine, *The Old French Fabliaux* (New Haven and London: Yale University Press, 1986), p. 23.

6 Cf. Nykrog, *Les fabliaux*, p. 15; Ménard, *Les fabliaux*, p. 14; *NRCF* 1, pp. xv–xviii (Inventaire des fabliaux).

7 Cf. F.J. Lodder, "Een genre der boerden?" *Queeste* 2 (1995), pp. 54–71.

8 F.J. Lodder, "De moraal van de boerden," *De nieuwe taalgids* 75 (1982), p. 49.

9 Dini Hogenelst, "Sproken in de stad: horen, zien en zwijgen," in Herman Pleij a.o., *Op belofte van profijt: Stadsliteratuur en burgermoraal in de Nederlandse letterkunde van de middeleeuwen*, Nederlandse literatuur en cultuur in de middeleeuwen 4 (Amsterdam: Prometheus, 1991), p. 380, note 12.

10 *De Middelnederlandse boerden*, ed. C. Kruyskamp ('s-Gravenhage: Nijhoff, 1957), p. 3. See for the poem pp. 22–24.

text is indeed titillating the senses appears from a scribe's marginal note, stating: "Desen sproke mi doet alte sere verlanghen" ("This poem very much arouses my desire"; Kruyskamp, p. 24).

The Old French fabliaux that are known today far outnumber the extant Middle Dutch texts. Moreover, most of the *boerden* have come down to us in a single manuscript, which makes Jean Rychner's fascinating study of manuscript variants impossible for the Middle Dutch fabliaux.[11] One can add to this enumeration of differences that the *boerden* appear to have been written some time after the fabliaux: whereas the Old French genre flourished between 1200 and 1350, most Middle Dutch texts presumably date from the second half of the fourteenth century.[12]

The relations between the Middle Dutch stories and the Old French fabliaux are various. Translations seem exceptional; one of the rare translated Middle Dutch fabliaux is the *Vesscher van Parijs* (The fisherman of Paris), which is based on the *Pescheor de Pont seur Saine*.[13] In other cases a fabliau and a *boerde* can be characterized as variants, a fine example being the *Cnape van Dordrecht* (The young man of Dordrecht). It is the story of a gigolo offering his service to married women. At a certain moment he is caught in the act by a husband, the town's bailiff, who pays him for the job, provided that he will keep silent about it. One finds this motif in the Old French fabliau *Le foteor* as well.[14] There are, however, also Middle Dutch texts with no known Old French equivalent, which indicates that the tales are indigenous texts or based on lost Old French originals. That even an Old French author could make use of a Middle Dutch text can be deduced from the closing lines of the *Vescie a Prestre*: "Jakes de Baisiu, sans dotance, L'a de tieus en romanç rimee Por la trufe qu'il a amee" (Noomen, p. 1033).

Dutch scholars do not study Middle Dutch fabliaux intensively, although interest in the genre has been increasing of late. Fred Lodder, for example, has in recent years published articles about the corpus of Middle Dutch fabliaux, about the intended audience of some *boerden*, and about the sexual mentality in these texts.[15] Outside

---

[11] Cf. Jean Rychner, *Contribution à l'étude des fabliaux: variantes, remaniements, dégradations*, 2 vols., Université de Neuchatel, recueil de travaux publiés par la Faculté des Lettres 28 (Neuchatel and Geneva: Faculté des Lettres and Droz, 1960).

[12] Cf. Nykrog, *Les fabliaux*, pp. vii, 3; Ménard, *Les fabliaux*, p. 13; Muscatine, *The Old French Fabliaux*, p. 4; Omer Jodogne, *Le fabliau*, Typologie des sources du moyen âge occidental 13 (Turnhout: Brepols, 1975), p. 29; Kruyskamp, *De Middelnederlandse boerden*, p. 4.

[13] Cf. Willem Noomen, "Une réplique néerlandaise d'un fabliau français: *Le Pescheor de Pont seur Saine* et *Dits van den vesscher van Parijs*," in *Et c'est la fin pour quoy sommes ensemble: Hommage à Jean Dufournet*, vol. 3 (Paris: Champion, 1993), pp. 1029–44. I would like to thank Hans van Dijk for drawing my attention to Noomen's essay.

[14] Cf. Bart Besamusca and Erwin Mantingh, "Vanden cnape van Dordrecht," in *Klein kapitaal uit het handschrift-Van Hulthem*, ed. H. van Dijk et al., Middeleeuwse studies en bronnen 33 (Hilversum: Verloren, 1992), pp. 104–12.

[15] Lodder, "Een genre der boerden?"; Fred Lodder, "Corrupte baljuws en overspelige echtgenotes. Over het beoogde publiek van drie boerden," in Herman Pleij a.o., *Op belofte van profijt: Stadsliteratuur en burgermoraal in de Nederlandse letterkunde van de middeleeuwen*, Nederlandse literatuur en cultuur in de middeleeuwen 4 (Amsterdam: Prometheus, 1991), pp. 217–27, 393–98; Fred Lodder, " 'Ik vind het gewoon lekker'. Komische vers-

the Low Countries, the existence of the *boerden* is virtually unknown. It is significant that the texts are not mentioned in the valuable collection of essays on Middle
Dutch literature in its European context, edited by Erik Kooper and published in
1994.[16] For scholars who do not read Dutch, the sources of information are almost
exclusively restricted to Willem Noomen's already mentioned article about the *Vesscher van Parijs* and Erik Hertog's inspiring study of Chaucer's fabliaux.[17] Hertog
discusses two Middle Dutch texts: the *Bispel van ij Clerken*, a translation of Jean
Bodel's *Gombert et les deus Clers*, and *Heile van Beersele*, the funny story of the
Antwerp prostitute Heile, who has an appointment with three men the same evening
(Hertog, pp. 61–84, 106–18). Because the Middle Dutch fabliaux are almost unknown outside Belgium and the Netherlands, I consider it an additional advantage
that an article on the first-person narrator in these texts enables me to introduce some
of the *boerden*.

Concerning the narrator in Old French fabliaux, Erik Hertog has stated: "The
important point is that this narratorial voice never intrudes upon the narrative with a
specific identity of its own, but remains cool, detached, in control, and completely
congruent with, and submerged in the implied ethos the text sets out to transmit"
(Hertog, p. 188). This quote offers a point of departure for my discussion of the
Middle Dutch first-person narrator, starting with the untitled story about two knights
who are both in love with a beautiful and rich widow (Kruyskamp, pp. 84–95). In his
introduction the narrator complains of the importance of money in love affairs. His
story will demonstrate that this can only be compensated by cunning (lines 1–22).
The two knights are each other's opposites: one is noble, brave, generous and poor,
the other a coward, rich and miserly. To the narrator's annoyance (lines 71–87), the
widow prefers the stingy knight because of his wealth. When both men visit her, she
gives the rich knight a warm welcome and tries to get rid of the other. But the poor
knight doesn't leave and at night he resorts to a scheme. Whereas the rich knight has
been given a bed near the widow, the poor knight sleeps in the dogs' place. When the
miserly knight leaves the room, the noble knight throws his rival into such a confusion that he gets into the wrong bed. The widow, who has promised to visit the rich
man at night, does not notice that the knights have changed beds and makes love
with the noble man, who takes a ring from her finger and is very nice to her. To the
widow's surprise the outraged rich knight immediately leaves the next morning.
When she sees the poor knight wearing her ring she understands what has happened
and, appreciating the knight's cleverness, returns his affection. Then the narrator
wishes that God will raise generous people and bring shame on the misers. And, he
adds:

vertellingen over seksuele moraal," in J. Reynaert a.o., *Wat is wijsheid? Lekenethiek in de
Middelnederlandse letterkunde*, Nederlandse literatuur en cultuur in de middeleeuwen 9 (Amsterdam: Prometheus, 1994), pp. 246–58, 425–29.
16 *Medieval Dutch Literature in its European Context*, ed. Erik Kooper, Cambridge Studies in
Medieval Literature 21 (Cambridge: Cambridge University Press, 1994).
17 Erik Hertog, *Chaucer's Fabliaux as Analogues*, Mediaevalia Lovaniensia, Series I/Studia
XIX (Leuven: Leuven University Press, 1991).

> Mi wondert dat so menich katyf
> Hier so nodich is ende vrec,
> Bedi daer om valt hi in duuels drec
> Daer neder ende is der werelt scande. (lines 348–51)

> (I am surprised that so many a wretch on this earth is stingy, because for that reason he will fall in the devil's dung and will be the shame of the world.)

It is obvious that the first-person narrator's opinions are indeed congruent with the implied ethos of the text, but this Middle Dutch narrator is not detached.

In the *boerde* that I will discuss now, the narrator does not keep aloof either. The Middle Dutch fabliau, entitled *Vander vrouwen die boven haren man minde* (About the woman who loved another man more than she did her husband; Kruyskamp, pp. 115–18), resembles the first part of the fabliau of the *Tresces* (Noomen, p. 1030, Kruyskamp, p. 127). It is the story of a married woman who, unfortunately, cannot find an opportunity to sleep with her lover. Not knowing what else to do, they decide to use the conjugal bed; a cord tied to the wife's toe will lead her lover in the dark to her and not to her husband. But, of course, things go wrong: the lover embraces the husband, who grabs him, thinking he has caught a thief. Immediately the wife resorts to a trick. When her husband asks her to bring light, she extinguishes the fire. Pretending to be too frightened to search for fire outside the house, she offers to guard the thief. When her husband leaves, the lovers have sex, albeit hurriedly. Afterwards the woman brings a calf to her bedroom and deceives her husband, who, at his return, believes that he has mistaken the alleged thief for the beast.

The first-person narrator in this *boerde* is on the wife's side. He introduces his story as follows:

> Nadien dat ic gemercken can,
> Vrouwen die bouen haren man
> Minnen, si hebbens torens vele,
> Ochte si sijn vol van reinaerts spele. (lines 3–6)

> (As I know, women who love somebody other than their husband are much in distress unless they know Reynard's tricks.)

Because in medieval literature the fox is mainly used as an image of the evil deceiver, one is inclined to read the words "reinaerts spele" (Reynard's tricks) as a disapproval, but the story does not support this interpretation. Nowhere does the text condemn the clever wife who prevents the disclosure of her adultery. On the contrary, the narrator clearly takes great pleasure in the events, concluding his story with the remark that love and cunning belong together:

> Hier bi mach elc man nemen merc
> Dat minners moeten connen vele:
> Ochte si sijn vol van reynaerts spele,
> Ochte vernoy hebben si onder hen beiden,
> Eest dat comt dat si versceiden
> Ende reynardie hoert ter minnen,
> Dat mach men wel hier an bekinnen. (lines 128–34)

> (This story makes clear for everybody that lovers have to be capable of much: either they know Reynard's tricks or they grieve at living apart from one another. And cunning belongs to love, as can be deduced from the story.)

The two narratorial interventions just quoted demonstrate that the narrator is not neutral. Unmistakably, though not too emphatically, he tries to manipulate the audience's opinion in favour of the adulterous woman. As an interesting female character in a text probably written by a male author, the wife needs to be studied from a feminist perspective as set out in a book like E. Jane Burns' *Bodytalk*.[18]

So far I have discussed two *boerden* in which the first-person narrator appreciates a character's cunning. This is also true for the Middle Dutch fabliau *Vanden paep die sijn baeck ghestolen wert* (About the priest whose bacon was stolen; Kruyskamp, pp. 64–71). A rascal makes his confession to a priest, who of course disapproves of his conduct. The clever young man then remarks that he knows a place where two pieces of bacon are kept. He wants to steal one piece and offers the priest half of the bacon in exchange for absolution. At that moment the narrator intervenes, providing the following comment:

> Nu moechdi horen nijewe dinghen;
> Hoe die miede vanden knaep
> Sel verschalken desen paep,
> Dat wil ic v vertellen hier.   (lines 60–63)

> (Now you will hear something. I will tell you how this bribe shall outwit the priest.)

On the condition that it will be the young man's last crime the greedy priest agrees to the proposal. What he does not know, however, is that his own bacon is at stake. That night the young man goes out stealing and the next morning the priest's maidservant receives the promised quantity of bacon. When the priest discovers the deceit, he calls the thief to account. Hearing the young man's statement that he has already been granted absolution for his lapse, the priest realizes that he has been tricked. The narrator states:

> Ic woud mense alle dus verdoerde,
> Waer si quamen tenighen steden,
> Die om miede loesheit deden;
> Die menighe souts hem dan wel hoeden.   (lines 226–29)

> (I wish that all persons who are bribed were fooled; as a result many of them would abstain from it.)

This narrator is rather obtrusive, forcing his strong view on the listeners.

In the last three lines of the *boerde* about the bribed priest the author's name is mentioned:

> Dat heeft willem in zijn vermoeden
> Van hildegaersberch, dat weet ic wel,
> Die dichte dit ende nyemant el.   (lines 230–32)

18 For Burns' discussion of the Old French fabliaux, see her *Bodytalk: When Women Speak in Old French Literature*, New Cultural Studies (Philadelphia: University of Pennsylvania Press, 1993), pp. 27–70.

(This is what Willem of Hildegaersberch thinks, I am sure of that, who made this and nobody else.)

Willem was a well-known poet, who was born around 1350 and died in 1408 or 1409. As an itinerant author of short poems, he frequently visited the court in The Hague at the time of Albert of Bavaria, who ruled between 1358 and 1404, and that of his son Willem VI (who was in power between 1404 and 1417) to recite his texts. Although Willem made his appearance in towns as well, it is obvious that he was a typical court poet.[19]

Besides the *boerde* about the tricked priest, Willem has written another extant Middle Dutch fabliau, entitled *Vanden monick* (About the monk; Kruyskamp, pp. 72–79).[20] At the beginning of the text it is postulated that isolated human beings quickly fall from grace. And the first-person narrator adds:

> Ic en wilde minen biechtvader
> Sonderlinghe niet al betrouwen
> In enicheit mit schone vrouwen,
> Want die vyant is naradich.   (lines 22–25)

(I would not even completely trust my own confessor in the company of beautiful women, the devil being guileful.)

With these words the narrator concludes his introduction to the story of a pious preacher who hears a beautiful virgin's confession so often that they become lovers. When the girl turns out to be pregnant, people start gossiping and opportunity knocks for the devil. In the shape of a smart physician he offers to prove the desperate monk's innocence by temporarily removing his genitals. The devil's proposal need not surprise us, if we are to believe R. Howard Bloch, who states: "Detached sexual organs are an integral part of the representation of the body in the fabliaux and are more the rule than the exception."[21] Be that as it may, the monk accepts the devil's offer, and:

> Sonder smarte ofte pijn
> Dede hi hem quijt sijn voerghestel,
> Soe dattet slechts als ander vel
> Twisken sijn benen was ghebleuen.
> Die broeder taste daer bineuen,
> Hine vanter weder dat noch dit,
> Anders dan een weynich pit
> Daer hi sijn water mochte lozen.   (lines 124–31)

(he [the devil] painlessly took away his genitals, leaving nothing but ordinary skin. The brother groped around, finding nothing but a little hole to make water.)

---

19 For Willem van Hildegaersberch, see T. Meder, *Sprookspreker in Holland: Leven en werk van Willem van Hildegaersberch (ca 1400)*, Nederlandse literatuur en cultuur in de middeleeuwen 2 (Amsterdam: Prometheus, 1991).

20 Cf. also Gerrit Komrij, *De Nederlandse poëzie van de 12de tot en met de 16de eeuw in 1000 en enige bladzijden* (Amsterdam: Bert Bakker, 1994), pp. 292–302.

21 R. Howard Bloch, *The Scandal of the Fabliaux* (Chicago and London: University of Chicago Press, 1986), p. 63.

When the devil advises the monk to demonstrate his innocence in public, the brother lends him a ready ear. He delivers a fiery sermon, directed against liars, who have slandered him as well. At the moment he wants to prove his innocence by raising his habit, the devil rushes forward. Quick as lighting he replaces the monk's penis, very erect, the result being that the preacher is beaten up and banished.

It is striking that at the end of the story the narrator does not warn against lecherous preachers, but concludes with misogynist remarks that seem out of place. He alerts his listeners to the existence of willing women who undress easily and who quickly lie on their back with their legs in the air. He then adds a little extra:

> Mar stolpelinghe vallen si node;
> Dat doet si sijn van herten blode:
> Vellen si ontwee nose ofte mont,
> Therte en bleue niet ghesont;
> Quetsten si knye of ellenboghe,
> Soe en sijn si niet in goeden hoghe.
> Ende want si aldus sijn veruaert,
> Soe vallen si lieuer achterwaert,
> Al wortet hem een deel te suer,
> Dan si tlijf in dauontuer
> Setten of hoer zonde lede;
> Want vrouwen hebben altoes gheerne vrede.   (lines 223–34)

(But they do not like to fall forward, they are afraid of that: if they hurt their nose or mouth, it is bad for their heart. If they scrape their knee or elbow, they get sad. They fear this so much that they prefer falling backwards to risking their lives and limbs, although sometimes they find that hard to do, as women like to maintain peace and quiet.)

In all probability this comment is deliberately unclear. According to the Dutch scholar Theo Meder the narrator hints at nonstandard coital positions (Meder, pp. 381–82). The narrator seems to state that women prefer the so-called missionary position, supposedly because they fear hurting their nose, mouth, knee, and elbow. Actually there is another reason for their reluctance to fall forward. The narrator probably mocks the ecclesiastical ban on intercourse from behind (Arno Strine and his former girlfriend's favourite position, as can be recalled from the beginning of this article). This irregular coital position was thought to be both contraceptive and more pleasurable.[22] If this interpretation of the narrator's commentary is convincing, the narratorial voice in Willem's text can hardly be characterized as detached and cool.

Within the scope of this essay, my discussion of the first-person narrator in Middle Dutch fabliaux has not been exhaustive. Nevertheless I hope to have shown that these narrators are an interesting phenomenon. For clarity's sake, there are of course many modest narrators of Middle Dutch fabliaux who, hiding behind the story, do not openly try to influence the interpretation of the text. But in some other *boerden* the narrators are nearly as visible and self-conscious as their Old French

---

[22] Cf. James A. Brundage, "Let me count the ways: canonists and theologians contemplate coital positions," *Journal of Medieval History* 10 (1984), pp. 81–93.

colleagues studied recently by Norris Lacy (*Reading Fabliaux*, pp. 96–112). These Dutch first-person narrators are obtrusive manipulators. Just like their modest fellow craftsmen they have a story to tell, but due to their interventions they almost become the focus of their own narration.

THE DIABOLIC HERO IN MEDIEVAL FRENCH NARRATIVE: *TRUBERT* AND *WISTASSE LE MOINE*

Keith Busby

As long ago as 1904, Leo Jordan pointed out some fundamental similarities between *Trubert* and *Wistasse le Moine*, although his main interest was in the two texts as outlaw narratives and their relation to such traditions as that of Robin Hood.[1] Both texts date from roughly the middle of the thirteenth century, and both present a quickfire succession of unsavoury exploits concerning anarchic and, I will suggest, diabolic, heroes. Another feature they share which distinguishes them from outlaw tales is that their heroes are by and large downright bad. While it is true that the nemeses of Trubert and Wistasse are nobles, they are foolish, gullible, and impotent rather than unscrupulously wicked, as is the case with, say, the Sheriff of Nottingham. The curious ambiguity with which we respond to the outrages perpetrated by these diabolic heroes bears more than a passing resemblance to the combination of distaste and admiration provoked by that master deceiver, Renart. Such is the 'renardie' of Wistasse that Beate Schmolke-Hasselmann was led to consider him a "Fuchs in Menschengestalt."[2] Something similar is therefore true, *mutatis mutandis*, for Trubert, the very phonology of whose name is redolent of trickery.[3]

Although *Trubert* is a *unicum* in Old French narrative, an extended episodic *fabliau*, and although its manuscript transmission is both isolated and curious, it belongs fairly and squarely to the Old French intertext. The single manuscript of the poem, BN, fr. 2188, is a single-item codex, a relatively rare phenomenon for the second half of the thirteenth century, a period in which large anthology manuscripts, such as BN, fr. 1553, which contains the unique text of *Wistasse le Moine*, are the rule. So whereas *Wistasse* has a rich codicological context against which it can be

[1]   Leo Jordan, "Quellen und Komposition von *Eustache le Moine*, nebst Analyse des *Trubert* und Nachweis der Existenz mehrerer Robin Hood-Balladen im 13. Jahrhundert," *Archiv für das Studium der neueren Sprachen und Literaturen* 113 (1904), pp. 66–100.
[2]   Beate Schmolke-Hasselmann, "Füchse in Menschengestalt: die listigen Helden Wistasse le Moine und Fouke le Fitz Warin," in *Proceedings of the Third International Beast Epic, Fable and Fabliau Colloquium*, ed. Jan Goossens and Timothy Sodmann (Cologne/Vienna: Böhlau, 1981), pp. 356–79.
[3]   I am thinking, of course, of the general associations of the *tr*- sound in Indo-European, as well as specific words such as "trichier," "tromper," and "truffe." The name "Trubert" could best be rendered in English by "Trickbert."

read, *Trubert* offers a somewhat deceptive impression of isolation, which can only be dissipated by a careful intertextual reading.[4]

In one of the recent studies of *Trubert*, Luciano Rossi has rightly identified its parodic relationship to Chrétien's *Perceval*,[5] so I shall not dwell on that aspect here: the "nice" brought up by his widowed mother in the forest, the apostrophes of "mere" and "biaus fiz," the incapacity of both the Duke of Burgundy and of the Fisher King, and a good many other indications all suggest to Rossi the possibility that *Trubert* may be a kind of parodic *contrafactum*. I would add to Rossi's analysis the probability that Trubert's successful bartering at the beginning of the poem represents an illustration of the parable of the sower from the prologue to *Perceval*; Trubert's forceful approach to making love to the Duchess (186ff) is surely meant to recall Perceval's clumsy efforts to kiss the Tent Maiden; "Et si me feites a mengier" ("Make me something to eat") (919) reproduces *Perceval*, line 491: " 'A mengier,' fait il, 'me donez' " (" 'Give me something to eat,' he said"); and his mother's efforts to dissuade Trubert from joining the Duke's army (1519–24) have clear overtones of Perceval's sequestration in the forest. Rossi rightly points out that Trubert's red arms and the standard rhyme *vermeilles* : *merveilles* (1821–22) suggest the identity of the hero with the Perceval who donned his defeated opponent's accoutrements; a significant difference, however, is the fact that Trubert's behaviour resembles more closely that of the aggressor than that of Perceval.

In one sense, then, *Trubert* explores an alternative to the direction pursued by Chrétien: whereas Perceval acquires only the Red Knight's arms and goes on to learn positive knighthood from scratch, Trubert appropriates from the outset both the external and internal—in this case, evil—qualities of the aggressor. Both *Trubert* and *Wistasse le Moine* indicate by recurrent quasi-formulaic expressions that the hero is to be regarded as positively diabolic. In *Trubert*, line 786, for example, the narrator exclaims of Trubert: "Or oiez que pense de mal" ("Now hear how he thinks evil"), and the Duchess at line 1613: "Il set plus de mal que Judas" ("He knows more evil than Judas"); the squire who witnesses the newly-dubbed Trubert's first precarious outing on horseback is convinced he is "un deable enpanez" ("a winged devil") (1857) and a "deable" (1861). When he careens through the battle, "bien croient ce soit uns malfez" ("they think he is a demon") (1868). The duke says of Trubert: "il a bien ou cors l'anemi" ("he has the devil in him") (2344).[6] The devilishness of

---

[4] I refer to the following editions: Douin de Lavesne, *Trubert, fabliau du XIIIe siècle*, ed. Guy Raynaud de Lage (Paris/Geneva: Droz, 1974); *Wistasse le Moine, altfranzösische Abenteuerroman des XIII. Jahrhunderts*, ed. Wendelin Foerster and Johann Trost (Halle: Niemeyer, 1891).
[5] Luciano Rossi, "*Trubert*: il trionfo della scortesia e dell'ignoranza. Considerazioni sui *fabliaux* e sulla parodia medievale," *Studi francesi e portoghesi* 79 (1979), pp. 5–49, esp. pp. 30–42. The *Perceval* parody has also been noted by Jean-Charles Payen, "*Trubert* ou le triomphe de la marginalité," in *Exclus et systèmes d'exclusion dans la littérature et la civilisation médiévales* (Aix-en-Provence: CUER MA, 1978), pp. 121–33, and Massimo Bonafin, "La parodia e il briccone divino: modelli letterari e modelli antropologici del *Trubert* di Douin de Lavesne," *L'immagine riflessa* 5 (1982), pp. 237–72. Line references to *Perceval* are to my edition (Halle: Niemeyer, 1993).
[6] Payen suggests that Trubert's behaviour is amoral rather than immoral: "[il] déploie son

Wistasse is even more blatant in the light of the opening to the text, which describes his sojourn in Toledo, "Ou il ot apris nigremanche . . ./ . . ./ Ou parloit au malfé meïsme" ("Where he had learned necromancy . . . where he spoke to the devil himself") (7, 14):

> Quant Wistase ot assés apris,
> Au dyable congié a pris,
> Li dyables dist k'il vivroit
> Tant que mal fait assés aroit.   (33–36)

> (When Wistasse had learned enough, he took leave of the devil; the devil said he would live long enough to do much evil.)

His next act at Monferrant is called "dyablie" ("devilry") (42), and the narrator says of his deeds in the Abbey of St. Samer: "Illuec fist mainte dyablie/ Ains k'il issist de s'abbeïe" ("He there did much devilry before he left the abbey") (222–23). During the rest of the poem, the diabolic epithets accumulate rapidly and are too numerous to be listed here, although I would single out for mention the phrase ".I. dyable moigne adversier" ("a devilish adversarial monk") (561, 1571), where "adversier" (< *adversarius*) has the sense of "enemy of the human race," and thus "li anemis," the Devil.[7]

It is probably *Trubert*'s fundamental and auto-designated relationship to the *fabliau*, which sets the listener's horizon of expectation and takes a slight edge off the unremitting evil of the hero's deeds.[8] In other words, because we are expecting those kinds of situations and actions that characterize the *fabliau*, we respond as we would to other texts of the same genre. The sale of the multi-coloured goat for a *foutre* and five sous ("je la vos vandrai volentiers;/ un foutre et cinc sous de deniers" [155–56]) ("I'll willingly sell it to you for a fuck and five sous") is the same kind of transaction as the young man's trading the kite in Garin's *fabliau* of *La grue*: "Dame, por un foutre soit vostre" ("Lady, let it be yours for a fuck") (53).[9]

---

activité par delà le bien et le mal, dans un souci constant, à la fois ingénu et pervers, de semer la confusion universelle." Art. cit., p. 121.

[7]   Other instances are: "Qui mout sot de l'art au dyable" ("Who knew much of the Devil's art") (549), "Et cil a le dyable en la teste" ("And he has the Devil in his head") (569), "Li dyables, li anemis" ("The Devil, the enemy") (613), "Ainc ne fu si dyables moigne" ("There was never such a devil monk") (925), "del vif malfé" ("the living devil") (1062), "C'est un dyable moigne guerrier" ("He's a devil warrrior monk") (1317), "Puis fist il mainte dyablie" ("Then he did much devilry") (2250). Scholke-Hasselmann has also argued that such formulæ are characteristic of the *Roman de Renart*; see "Füchse in Menschengestalt," pp. 366–69. Anne-Dominique Kapferer, "Banditisme, roman, féodalité: le boulonnais d'Eustache le Moine," in *Economies et sociétés au moyen âge: mélanges offerts à Edouard Perroy* (Paris: Publications de la Sorbonne, 1973), pp. 22–37, p. 236, suggests that Wistasse concluded a "pacte avec le diable" during his stay in Toledo.

[8]   On the "piccola 'poetica'" of *Trubert*, see Rossi, art. cit., pp. 27–30, and on the poem as *fabliau*, see Guy Raynaud de Lage, "Trubert est-il un personnage de fabliau?" in *Mélanges d'histoire littéraire, de linguistique et de philologie romanes offerts à Charles Rostaing* (Liège: n.p., 1974), II, pp. 845–53.

[9]   Text as edited by Jean Rychner, *Contribution à l'étude des fabliaux: variantes, remaniements, dégradations* (Geneva: Droz, 1960), II, pp. 9–14.

Towards the end of the poem, the cross-dressed Trubert infiltrates the chamber of the Duke's maidens under the name of Coillebaude:

> "Coment avez vos non? fet Aude.
> – Dame, en m'apele Coillebaude."
> Quant Aude l'ot si en a ris
> et toutes les autres ausis.
> "Comment? comment? dites encor!
> – Par foi, je nel dirai plus or;
> je voi bien que vos me gabez!" (2403–09).

> ("What is your name?" said Aude. – "Lady, they call me Merryballs."
> When Aude heard this, she laughed, and all the others, too. "What? what?
> say it again! – In faith, I won't say it anymore; I see you are mocking me!")

He is quickly renamed "Florie" (2420) and shares a bed with the Duke's daughter, Roseite: "Si oil reseamblent de faucon,/ blanche la gorge et le menton,/ la bouche petite et riant" ("Her eyes were like those of a falcon, her breast and cheeks white, and her mouth small and smiling") (2441–43). The subsequent bout of euphemistic lovemaking lasts two weeks, at the end of which Roseite's complexion has become pale and wan (she is no longer herself and is thus "de-Florie" in more ways than one). When Trubert's member no longer responds to Roseite's ministrations, she laments its demise: "Certes je dout qu'il ne soit morz" ("I am surely afraid he is dead") (2554); fortunately, the beast in question has only fainted (2560–61) and is able to resume normal activity in short order. The episode ends with a parody of the Immaculate Conception as Roseite is said to have been visited by a white dove: "Mes sachiez bien, n'en doutez mie,/ dou saint Espir est raemplie!/ Trestoute est plaine d'angeloz!" ("Rest assured, don't doubt that she is full of the Holy Ghost! She is full of little angels!") (2599–601). Given Trubert's diabolic nature, they are, of course, more likely to be little devils.[10] Here, I would simply point to the similar and better-known euphemism in *De la demoiselle qui ne pouvait ouir parler de foutre* as a referent for the episode in *Trubert*.[11] The final episode (2741ff), in which the still transvestite Trubert places a purse between his legs to substitute for the female pudendum and deceives Golias into thinking that this is a particularly difficult defloration, is pure *fabliau*, as is the pulling of cords and bed-hopping that follow. One thinks in particular of the deception of the domineering lady in *De la dame escoilliee*, where bull's testicles are used in a mock "castration" in order to re-feminize her.[12]

After the opening Toledo sequence, *Wistasse le Moine* situates itself by means of a deferred exordium at the confluence of epic and *fabliau*[13] with the claim that

---

[10] There is a hint here of the story of *Robert le Diable* and its later transformations, such as *Rosemary's Baby*, although it is not elaborated. Payen, art. cit., pp. 127–28 sees here (and, of course, in the name Golias) more than a trace of the kind of irreverence typical of Goliardism.

[11] The texts of MSS *ABD* are printed in parallel by Rychner, II, pp. 12–35.

[12] The texts are presented most conveniently in the *Nouveau recueil complet des fabliaux*, ed. Nico van den Boogaard and Willem Noomen (Assen: van Gorcum, 1983–, 8 vols. to date), vol. 8, pp. 3–149.

[13] Kapferer, "Mépris, savoirs et tromperies dans le roman boulonnais d'*Eustache le Moine*

Wistasse was more skilled at deception than Maugis and Basin (from the epic *Maugis d'Aigremont*) or Travers, Barat and Haimet (from Jean Bodel's *fabliau*):

> D'Uistace le moigne dirai
> Qui mout sot plus que Amaugis,
> Ne que Basins, che m'est avis.
> Travers, ne Baras, ne Haimés
> Ne sorent onques tant d'abés. (294–99)

> (I will tell you of Wistasse le Moine, who knew more than Amaugis or Basin, I think. Neither Travers nor Barat nor Haimet ever knew as much trickery.)

Moreover, the narrator stresses his intention to amuse: "Je vous dirai encor anuit/ Tel chose qui vous fera rire" ("I'll tell you something tonight that will make you laugh") (280–81); we should not lose from sight, however, his earlier reference to the stories to come as "examples" (2), with its didactic associations. We can therefore assume his overall aim was the standard medieval one of both entertaining and instructing, *prodesse et delectare*. It is instructive to compare the cross-dressing episode in *Wistasse le Moine* with that from *Trubert* mentioned above, for despite an obvious affiliation with the *fabliau*, the crudity and brutality of the former nudge it perceptibly away from the usual type of comic tale. Wistasse meets a servant whose horse he wishes to mount. I quote at some length:

> Dist Witasces: "Lai moi monter,
> Et je te lairai bareter."
> "Mout volentiers," dist li sergant;
> "Sor cest bon palefroi amblant,
> Ma damoisele, or cha, montés!
> .iiij. deniers de moi arés
> Se vous me laissiés bareter."
> "Je t'aprendrai a culeter,"
> Dist Wistasces, "encor enqui,
> Ainc nus hom ne culeta si."
> Le pié li lieve le vallet,
> Et Wistasces lait corre .j. pet:
> "Ha! damoisele, vous peés."
> Dist Wistasces: "Ne vous doutés!
> Bials tres dous amis, ne vous poist,
> C'est ceste siele ki si croist." (1196–211)

> (Wistasse said: "Let me mount and I'll let you enjoy yourself." "Willingly," said the servant. "Here, mount this fair palfrey, damsel. I'll give you four deniers if you'll let me enjoy myself." "I'll teach you later today to do it from behind," said Wistasse, "no man ever did it like this." The servant lifted Wistasse's foot and Wistasse let fly a fart. "Ha! Damsel, you're farting." Said Wistasse: "No I'm not, fair sweet friend. Don't worry, it's just this saddle creaking.")

(XIIIe siècle)," in *Littérature et société au moyen âge: actes du colloque des 5 et 6 mai, 1978*, ed. Danielle Buschinger (Amiens: Univ. de Picardie, Centre d'Etudes Médiévales, 1978), pp. 333–51, p. 333, considers *Wistasse* to be "au carrefour du fabliau, de la geste locale et du roman."

This kind of callous vulgarity is very rare, even in a genre where the sexual act is openly described and is often the source of robust humour.[14]

The confusion of the sound of a creaking saddle with a fart is a kind of aural or phonological ambiguity – and one thinks of such texts as *Estula* – which is often the cause of incident in the *fabliaux*. In *Wistasse le Moine*, this is taken a stage further when Wistasse, disguised as a potter, climbs up a tree and deceives the count by pretending to be a nightingale; birdsong is both generated and interpreted as human language, causing the kind of deception around which the whole narrative of the poem revolves.

> Wistasces commenche a criër:
> "Ochi! ochi! ochi! ochi!"
> Et li quens Renaus respondi:
> "Je l'ocirai, par saint Richier!
> Se je le puis as mains ballier."
> "Fier! fier!" dist Wistasces li moigne.
> "Par foi!" dist li quens de Bouloigne,
> "Si ferai jou, je le ferai,
> Ja en cel liu ne le tenrai."
> Wistasces rest aseürés,
> Si se rest .ij. mos escriés:
> "Non l'ot! si ot! non l'ot! si ot!"
> Quant li quens de Bouloigne l'ot,
> "Certes si ot," che dist li quens;
> "Tolu m'as tous mes chevals buens."
> Wistasces s'escria: "Hui! hui!"
> "Tu dis bien," dist li quens, "c'ert hui
> Que je l'ocirai a mes mains
> Se je le puis tenir as mains."   (1145–63)

(Wistasse began to cry: "Kill, kill, kill, kill." And Count Renaut replied: "I'll kill him, by Saint Richier, if I can get my hands on him." "Strike, strike," said Wistasse the Monk. "In faith," said the Count of Boulogne, "I will strike, I'll strike him, even if I don't have him here yet." Wistasse relaxed and then shouted a couple of words: "He didn't have it! Yes, he did! He didn't have it! Yes, he did!" When the Count of Boulogne heard this, he said: "He certainly did. He stole all my good horses." Wistasse cried: "Today! Today!" "That's right," said the count, "it'll be today that I'll kill him with my hands, if I can catch him, that is.")

Yet the many gruesome deeds of Wistasse are not entirely redeemed by occasional flashes of *fabliau* humour: he cuts out the tongue of the boy guarding the monks' horses and sends him as messenger, simultaneously eloquent and mute, to the count (640–57), forces one of his own spies to commit suicide by hanging himself (698–724), puts out the eyes of two of the count's servants (725–39), etc., all without a trace of remorse. In *Trubert*, an innocent man is beaten up and hanged when mistaken for Trubert (1585–647); the hero severs a woman's genitals and sends them to the count, claiming they are the mouth and nose of King Golias (1919–82).

---

[14] Payen, art. cit, pp. 128–29, uses phrases such as "bestialité agressive," "comique grinçant," "excessivement corrosif," and "noirceur absolue" to describe Trubert's deeds.

Like the devils they are, both Trubert and Wistasse sow discord and anarchy wherever they go. In *Trubert*, one might point to the hero's wild charge through the ranks of the king's army mentioned above (1822–71) or the discord created between King Golias and the Duke which eventually leads to the brutal murder of the priest (2633–729). The anarchic scenes in the tavern and in the street at the beginning of *Wistasse le Moine* (41–159) are directly explained as the result of Wistasse's necromancy; the same is true of his deeds in the abbey of St. Samer (220–78). This discord and anarchy has been perceptively read with respect to *Trubert* by both Bonafin and Jean Batany as typifying Bakhtin's concept of Carnival; *Wistasse le Moine* could also usefully be seen in the same light.[15]

The satisfaction so evidently felt by both Trubert and Wistasse after the implementation of a successful ruse seems to stem as much from the pleasure in inflicting pain as from the delight in having deceived an adversary. There is something Renardian here and the fox's intertextual tracks are clearly visible, as Schmolke-Hasselmann pointed out in particular connection with *Wistasse le Moine*. In addition to the formulæ listed above, there is in *Trubert* a clear Renardian echo in the Duke's description of Trubert as "uns glouz [qui] ensi m'atorna/ par son art et par son engien" ("a rogue who set me up like this by his art and skill") (1176–77); line 1177 reverses the substantives from the opening line of Branch 1 of the *Roman de Renart* ("Perroz, qui s'engin et s'art" ["Perrot, who with his skill and art"]); the rhyme *Renart : art* is certainly a marker of the Old French animal epic; and the very use of the word *art* in a context such as this is evocative. The line "Et Trubert, qui mout set de gille" ("And Trubert, who knew much guile") (2338, 2764) also belongs to what begins to look like a set of expressions common to *Trubert, Wistasse* and the *Roman de Renart*; it also occurs verbatim (with the name changed, of course) in *Wistasse* (63, 1186, 1324).[16] Part of the pleasure in the conscious perpetration of evil for Trubert is in revealing himself after a successful deception, thereby increasing the frustration of the duke (for example, lines 827ff, 1314ff, 2124ff). And more diabolical still is his aside in response to the duke's assurance that they will henceforth be friends: "Et Trubert qui set toz les torz/ entre ses denz dit: 'Vos mentez;/ encore encui mout me harrez!' " ("And Trubert, who knew all wrongs, said between his teeth: 'You lie; you'll still hate me a good deal today' ") (1990–92). Likewise, after escaping from the count's men, Wistasse jumps on a stolen horse and gallops off, taunting the count by shouting: "Voisci le mogne, u il s'en va" ("See how the monk is going away") (891). The gratuitousness of much of the violence in *Wistasse le Moine* also underscores its fiendish nature. Wistasse can never leave the scene of one atrocity without committing another, should the possibility present itself. Having just deceived the count into believing he is a penitent and into giving him money, Wistasse steals all the horses and burns down the town:

> Li quens est el chastel entrés,
> Li cheval sont defors remés;

15 Bonafin, art. cit., and Jean Batany, "*Trubert*: progrès et bousculade des masques," in *Masques et déguisements dans la littérature médiévale*, ed. Marie-Louise Ollier (Montréal: Presses Universitaires de Montréal, 1988), pp. 25–34.
16 See Schmolke-Hasselmann, ibid.

> Wistasces tous les chevals prist,
> La vile aluma et esprist. (912–15)
>
> (The count entered the castle, leaving the horses outside; Wistasse took them
> all, set light to the town and burned it.)

Later, when in the service of King John, he destroys the palace he has been given in
London (at his request) for no apparent reason and has another one built in its stead,
much to the consternation of the king (2134–57).

This contempt for authority in any form is characteristic of the behaviour of both
Wistasse and Trubert, and may even be their prime motivation. Wistasse treats the
English King John with the same disdain as he does the Count of Boulogne, and with
the same scorn that had informed his doings in the abbey. As we have seen, he
mutilates a boy, blinds two servants, and then cuts the feet off four others. His
contempt and insolence do not discriminate between social classes, for anyone who
stands in his way or who can serve his ends is abused or butchered or both. Much the
same is true of Trubert, who heaps public and private humiliation on the Duke of
Burgundy on numerous occasions, deceives a king, and beats a horse dealer at his
own game. Not only does Trubert not discriminate between social classes, he also
has no compunction in crudely seducing the Duke's wife and daughter. Social
anarchy reigns supreme in both of these poems which more than hint at serious
contemporary social unrest.[17]

The events and characters of *Wistasse le Moine* are not, of course, entirely
fictitious, and represent a mimetic transformation of relations in the years
1200–1217 between Renaud de Dammartin, Count of Boulogne (1190–1214, †1227)
and his senechal turned enemy, Wistasse (c. 1170–†1217), son of Baudouin Busket.
It is possible to find historical sources for many episodes in the poem and to trace its
geography on a map of the Boulonnais and England in the early thirteenth century.[18]
Yet the very situation of a faithful seneschal deprived of his lands by an unscrupu-
lous lord is reminiscent of certain *chansons de geste* of the *cycle des barons révoltés*,
and like the Old French epic, *Wistasse le Moine* functions as a fictionalized commemoration of major historical events. However, unlike the *chanson de geste* and the
distant past of France, the events concerned are chronologically adjacent to the date
of the poem's composition and must have held considerable significance for contemporary audiences in the North East of France and England.[19] Post-Köhlerian readings
of much Old French narrative (*chanson de geste*, Arthurian romance, and the *Roman
de Renart* in particular) have stressed its political and social function and its mirroring of social tension between king and vassal.[20] To read the epic in this way requires
a chronological transposition from the Carolingian period to the twelfth and

---

17 See Payen, art. cit., p. 125, and Batany, art. cit., p. 26.
18 Kapferer, "Banditisme," passim.
19 Ibid., p. 231.
20 Karl-Heinz Bender, *König und Vassal: Untersuchungen zur Chanson de Geste des 12.
Jahrhunderts* (Heidelberg: Winter, 1967); Beate Schmolke-Hasselmann, *Der arthurische
Versroman von Chrestien bis Froissart: zur Geschichte einer Gattung* (Tübingen: Niemyer,
1980); Antonio Figueroa, *El 'Roman de Renart' documento crítico de la sociedad medieval*
(Santiago de Compostela: Univ. de Santiago de Compostela, 1982).

thirteenth centuries. As far as Arthurian romance is concerned, the leap is double, requiring both the transposition of chronology and the regeneration of historical meaning from the mythical *matière de Bretagne*. The very anthropomorphism of the *Roman de Renart* constitutes the text's own inherent invitation to view it as social allegory and commentary. Generally speaking, then, *Wistasse le Moine* has links to a large body of literature which tends to portray sympathetically the mid-rank of vassals to the detriment of the higher nobility and the institution of monarchy.

While it is an exaggeration to say that "tout le récit montre une forte sympathie pour le personnage et les aventures du moine-sénéchal devenu hors-la-loi, puis pirate, et une antipathie contre Renaud de Dammartin"[21] (and this precisely because of the diabolic presentation of Wistasse), it is true that the Count is always presented as a gullible, incompetent, and ill-tempered buffoon. A few examples will suffice. Although the Count seems to see through Wistasse's disguise as a monk in Clairmarais (" 'Par foi!' dist li quens de Bouloigne,/ 'Vous samblés Wistasce le moigne' " [" 'In faith,' said the Count of Boulogne, 'You look like Wistasse the Monk' "], 504–05), he allows himself to be persuaded that he is wrong (530–43). The occasions on which Wistasse disguises himself in order to deceive the Count are too numerous to list here, but it is interesting to note that the latter's incompetence is consistently underlined by long series of blustering expletives:

> "Vois," dist li quens, "por le cerviel,
> Por les boiaus, por la froissure!" (563–64)

> ("Truly," said the count, "by the brains, by the innards, by the pluck!")

> "Par les trumials bieu!" (604, 627)

> ("By God's hams!")

> "Vois," li quens dist, "por les trumiaus,
> Pour le ventre, por les boiaus
> De cel truant, de cel faus moigne
> Qui tant me fait honte et vergogne." (766–69)

> ("Truly," said the count, "by the hams, by the belly, by the innards of this crook, of this false monk who causes me such shame and grief.")

> "Vois," dist li quens, "por les boiaus,
> Por le ventre, por les trumiaus!
> Che fu ichil a la clikete
> Li moignes ki si nous abete." (1412–15)

> "Truly," said the count, "by the innards, by the belly, by the hams! This chatterbox was the monk who is tricking us thus.")

> "Vois," dist li quens, "por les trumials,
> Pour le ventre et por les boiaus,
> Por le gargate, pour les dens,
> Com cil cunchie toutes gens!
> Por les trumiaus bieu, n'en ira." (1630–34)

---

[21] *Li romans de Wistasse le Moine*, ed. Dennis Joseph Conlon (Chapel Hill: Univ. of North Carolina Press, 1972), p. 14.

"Truly," said the count, "by the hams, by the belly and by the innards, by the windpipe, by the teeth, how he tricks everybody! By God's hams, he won't get away.")

"Par les piés biu! trop me tient court;
Je li acorcherai sa vie,
Par les boiaus sainte Varie!"   (1811–13)[22]

("By God's feet! I've had enough of him; I'll skin his life out of him, by Holy Mary's innards!")

The Duke of Burgundy in *Trubert* also curses and swears vengeance in impotent rage, but in a somewhat more measured manner:

Tout en ist dou sens et enrage.
Dieu et tot son pooir en jure
que se jamés par aventure
puet trover Trubert ne avoir,
il le fera pendre ou ardoir.   (362–66)

(He left his senses and went wild. He swore to God and all his power that if he could ever by chance find or have Trubert, he would have him hanged or burned.)

". . . et se Deus me donoit encore
force et pooir de chavauchier,
jel feroie querre et gaitier
Tant que, s'il iert en terre entrez,
seroit il et pris et trouvez."   (1182–86)

(". . . and if God ever gives me the strength and force to ride again, I'll have him sought and watched until, if he comes onto my land, he'll be found and captured.")

Trubert's constantly deceiving the Duke demonstrates the superiority of native wit over inherited wealth, and the nature of some of the trickery is calculated to produce complete and utter humiliation of the nobility at the hands of the lower orders. Here is perhaps another sense in which *Trubert* is a *contrafactum* of *Perceval*: Chrétien's hero is an aristocrat with the upbringing of a *vilain* whereas Trubert is a *vilain* with the upbringing of a *vilain*. The kind of intellectual role reversal that characterizes *Trubert* is especially visible in the scenes where the hero, first disguised as a carpenter, ties the Duke to a tree and beats him senseless (735–867) and then, disguised as a doctor, pretends to cure him of the same wounds by daubing him in excrement and rubbing the "ointment" in (1060–448). In contrast with the general run of *fabliaux*, here it is the *courtois*, not the *vilain*, who is covered in excrement and humiliation.

The similarities between *Wistasse le Moine* and *Trubert*, in particular the struggle between the hero and a single nemesis from the ranks of the aristocracy, may suggest

---

[22] Cadoc, Senechal of Normandy, responds in the same manner after he and his men are trapped in a bog by Wistasse: " 'Vois!' dist Cadoc, 'por les trumiaus!/ Por le ventre! pour les boiaus!/ Por les dens biu! com sui honnis!' " (" 'Truly,' said Cadoc, 'by the hams! By the belly! By the innards! By God's teeth! How I've been disgraced!' ") (2050–52).

that the latter is a kind of further fictionalisation of the former. Unfortunately, the relative chronology of the two works does not permit any solid conclusions to be drawn in this regard, and it may simply be that they are both expressions of the same underlying hatred of the nobility in Northern France and England during the first half of the thirteenth century. In the one, this is articulated by another noble whose outlandish activities bring him into the orbit of the lower orders, and in the other, by means of a simple class conflict. In both poems, contemporary social instability is reflected by constantly shifting identities, usually achieved by disguise and the ensuing deception, and the continual redistribution of wealth in the form of money, horses, or possessions in general.

The multivalent interplay between the generation of historical and more purely intertextual meaning is exemplified in the episode from *Wistasse le Moine* in which Wistasse is captured by the Count of Boulogne (1606ff). If read in the context of the career of the historical Wistasse and his relations with the Count, it may be seen as referring either to a real or a potential event; if read against the background of Wistasse's 'renardie,' it looks like one of the many scenes from the *Roman de Renart* in which Renart is captured by Noble, only to escape and commit further abominations. I would argue that many episodes in both poems engender this kind of double signification, although it may be more evident in *Wistasse* than in *Trubert*.

The constant disguises of Trubert and Wistasse also recall that of another celebrated trickster of medieval literature, Tristan, the illicit nature of whose relationship with Iseut also requires him to become an expert in the art of deception.[23] Trubert becomes in turn a carpenter, a physician, a knight, and the winsome Coillebaude; Wistasse assumes the semblance of a monk, a shepherd, a pilgrim, a potter, a woman of easy virtue, a leper, a carpenter, a fishmonger, a pastrycook, and a *jongleur*. In particular, Wistasse disguised as a leper (1394ff) calls to mind the well-known episode from Béroul; his final act, as a *jongleur*, takes its cue from the two *Folies Tristan* and the *Tristan menestrel* from Gerbert de Montreuil's *Continuation de Perceval*, although its prime referent, as Schmolke-Hasselmann has shown, is Branch Ib of the *Roman de Renart*.[24] In addition to the *jongleur*'s claims to be an Englishman ("Englisseman de Canestuet,/ Ya, ya, coditouet") (2198–99), I would comment on two aspects of this scene. The first is that it contains a second list of Old French narratives (the first had contained, it will be recalled, a list of famous deceivers from the *chansons de geste* and one of Jean Bodel's *fabliaux*):

> "O je, d'Agoullant et d'Aimon;
> Je sai de Blanchandin la somme,
> Si sai de Flourenche de Romme.
> Il n'a el mont nule chançon
> Dont n'aie oï ou note ou son."   (2203–07)

("I know of Agolant and of Aimon, I know all about Blancandin, and I know

---

[23] The relationship between Tristan and Renart has been examined by Nancy F. Regalado, "Tristan and Renart: Two Tricksters," *L'Esprit Créateur* 16 (1976), pp. 30–38.
[24] Art. cit., pp. 369–72. On *Tristan menestrel*, see my "Der *Tristan Menestrel* des Gerbert de Montreuil und seine Stellung in der altfranzösischen Artustradition," *Vox Romanica* 42 (1983), pp. 144–56.

about Florence of Rome. There's no song in the world of which I have not
heard the melody or the words.")

It is difficult to know whether there is any particular significance to the choice of
texts mentioned here. All of them (*La chanson d'Aspremont, Renaud de Montauban,
Blancandin et l'Orgueilleuse d'amour,* and *Florence de Rome*) in one way or another
are concerned with the struggle against authority, although this could be said of most
chansons de geste and courtly romances. It is worth pointing out, however, that
Renaut de Montauban deals with the exploits of the rebel sons of Charlemagne's
vassal, Aimon de Dordonne, and that the second half of *Blancandin* relates a conflict
between Blancandin and his senechal, Subien. More notable, perhaps, is the name
given by Wistasse to the *jongleur* as whom he is disguised: "Sire, j'ai a non
Mauferas" ("Sir, my name is Mauferas") (2197). Like Wistasse le Moine, who has
done nothing but evil, the name of Mauferas the *jongleur* suggests the power of
poetry to bring about the ultimate deception by commingling and confusing truth and
fiction. And as Mauferas *does*, or perhaps *bears*, evil, so his brother Trubert is
resplendent (*bright*) with his own brand of trickery. Ultimately, Wistasse and Trubert
may be no more and no less than incarnations of the bearer of the most deceptive
light of all, *Luci-fer*, the Enemy, the Devil.